MW01006746

Commentary on Thomas Aquinas's *Treatise on Law*

Natural moral law stands at the center of Western ethics and jurisprudence and plays a leading role in interreligious dialogue. Although the greatest source of the classical natural law tradition is Thomas Aquinas's *Treatise on Law*, the *Treatise* is notoriously difficult, especially for nonspecialists. J. Budziszewski has made this formidable work luminous. This book – the first classically styled, line-by-line commentary on the *Treatise* in centuries – reaches out to philosophers, theologians, social scientists, students, and general readers alike. Budziszewski shows how the *Treatise* facilitates a dialogue between author and reader. Explaining and expanding upon the text in light of modern philosophical developments, he expounds this work of the great thinker not by diminishing his reasoning, but by amplifying it.

J. Budziszewski is a Professor of Government and Philosophy at the University of Texas, Austin. He also teaches courses in the religious studies department and in the law school, and he maintains a personal scholarly website, www.undergroundthomist.org. Dr. Budziszewski has published widely in both scholarly journals and magazines of broader readership. His books include *The Resurrection of Nature: Political Theory and the Human Character* (1986); *The Nearest Coast of Darkness: A Vindication of the Politics of Virtues* (1988); *True Tolerance: Liberalism and the Necessity of Judgment* (1992); *Written on the Heart: The Case for Natural Law* (1997), winner of a *Christianity Today* book award in 1998; *The Revenge of Conscience: Politics and the Fall of Man* (1999); *What We Can't Not Know: A Guide* (2003); *Evangelicals in the Public Square: Four Formative Voices* (2006); *Natural Law for Lawyers* (2006); *The Line Through the Heart: Natural Law as Fact, Theory, and Sign of Contradiction* (2009); and *On the Meaning of Sex* (2012).

Commentary on Thomas Aquinas's
Treatise on Law

J. BUDZISZEWSKI

Departments of Government and Philosophy
University of Texas at Austin

CAMBRIDGE
UNIVERSITY PRESS

CAMBRIDGE
UNIVERSITY PRESS

32 Avenue of the Americas, New York, NY 10013-2473, USA

Cambridge University Press is part of the University of Cambridge.

It furthers the University's mission by disseminating knowledge in the pursuit of education, learning, and research at the highest international levels of excellence.

www.cambridge.org
Information on this title: www.cambridge.org/9781107029392

© J. Budziszewski 2014

This publication is in copyright. Subject to statutory exception and to the provisions of relevant collective licensing agreements, no reproduction of any part may take place without the written permission of Cambridge University Press.

First published 2014

A catalog record for this publication is available from the British Library.

Library of Congress Cataloging in Publication data
Budziszewski, J., 1952– author.
Commentary on Thomas Aquinas's *Treatise on law* / J. Budziszewski.
pages cm
Includes bibliographical references and index.
ISBN 978-1-107-02939-2 (hardback)
1. Thomas, Aquinas, Saint, 1225?–1274. Summa theologica. Prima secundae. Quaestio 90–97. 2. Law – Philosophy. 3. Natural law. 4. Christianity and law. I. Thomas, Aquinas, Saint, 1225?–1274. Summa theologica. Prima secundae. Quaestio 90–97. English. II. Title.
K230.T54B83 2014
340'.1–dc23 2014030814

ISBN 978-1-107-02939-2 Hardback

Additional resources for this publication at http://UndergroundThomist.org

Cambridge University Press has no responsibility for the persistence or accuracy of URLs for external or third-party Internet websites referred to in this publication and does not guarantee that any content on such websites is, or will remain, accurate or appropriate.

To the Angelic Doctor
though unworthily

Analytical Table of Contents

Questions 90–97 are included here in full. Since this is an analytical table of contents, I have superimposed an outline format to show more clearly the place of each section in the whole. Sometimes St. Thomas phrases his section titles differently in his prologues than before the sections themselves; for clarity here, I have sometimes combined them. The various brief "Before Reading" sections are my own, distinct from the sections of commentary devoted to St. Thomas's various Prologues. Although the *Commentary* is self-contained, the *Companion to the Commentary*, an online book available via the Resources link at the *Commentary*'s catalogue webpage (http://UndergroundThomist.org), provides both additional commentary on brief selections from Questions 98–108 and additional discussion of various themes in each Prologue and Article, for readers who want to understand the *Treatise* in still greater depth. Topics covered in the *Companion* are listed immediately after this analytical table of contents.

Contents of the Online
Companion to the Commentary

II.   ADDITIONAL TOPICS EXPLORED

Acknowledgments

Although, like a hermit, I withdrew into a little cave to write this commentary, the effort has seemed almost communal, for my cleft in the rock has been filled with a dense cloud of friends, teachers, models, mentors, and ancestors, without whose encouragement, example, learning, and occasional chastisement, none of the work could have come to pass. From time to time one of them is mentioned in the footnotes. The others, including my gracious external reviewers, know who they are.

As I was working, the questions my students have asked over the years have tinkled and hummed continually in my ears, prodding me on. I am grateful for all of them, not only for those which they raised in perplexity, wonder, or delight, but also those which they blurted in dismay and consternation, for not only is Thomas Aquinas difficult, deep, and luminous, but he probes with needle-sharp instruments.

For material support for this project, I thankfully acknowledge my debt to the Earhart Foundation and the University of Texas at Austin.

Without my wife Sandra, fresh fountain of cool water, this work would have been utterly unthinkable.

Ante Studium
(*Before Study*)

Ineffable Creator, Who out of the treasures of Your wisdom appointed treble hierarchies of Angels and set them in admirable order high above the heavens; Who disposed the diverse portions of the universe in such elegant array; Who are the true Fountain of Light and Wisdom, and the all-exceeding Source: Be pleased to cast a beam of Your radiance upon the darkness of my mind, and dispel from me the double darkness of sin and ignorance in which I have been born.

You Who make eloquent the tongues of little children, instruct my tongue and pour upon my lips the grace of Your benediction. Grant me penetration to understand, capacity to retain, method and ease in learning, subtlety in interpretation, and copious grace of expression.

Order the beginning, direct the progress, and perfect the conclusion of my work, You Who are true God and Man, Who live and reign forever and ever. Amen.

Thomas Aquinas

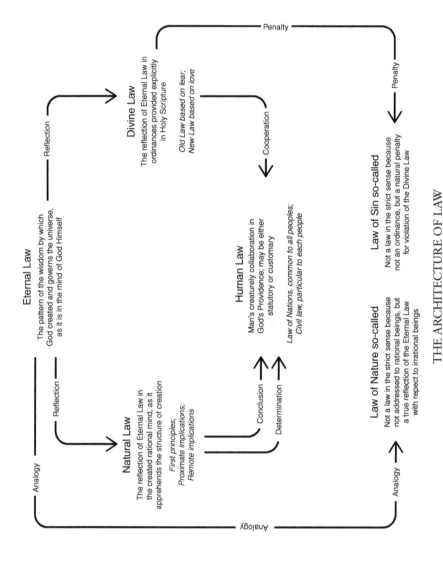

THE ARCHITECTURE OF LAW

Eternal Law
The pattern of the wisdom by which
God created and governs the universe,
as it is in the mind of God Himself

Divine Law
The reflection of Eternal Law in
ordinances provided explicitly
in Holy Scripture

*Old Law based on fear;
New Law based on love*

Natural Law
The reflection of Eternal Law in
the created rational mind, as it
apprehends the structure of creation

*First principles;
Proximate implications;
Remote implications*

Human Law
Man's creaturely collaboration in
God's Providence; may be either
statutory or customary

*Law of Nations, common to all peoples;
Civil law, particular to each people*

Law of Nature so-called
Not a law in the strict sense because
not addressed to rational beings, but
a true reflection of the Eternal Law
with repect to irrational beings

Law of Sin so-called
Not a law in the strict sense because
not an ordinance, but a natural penalty
for violation of the Divine Law

Reflection

Reflection

Analogy

Analogy

Analogy

Conclusion

Determination

Cooperation

Penalty

Penalty

xviii

Introduction

Who Is Thomas Aquinas?

By consent of learned opinion, St. Thomas of Aquino, "the Angelic Doctor," is one of the greatest philosophers and theologians of all time. A good many of those who know his work would say that the qualifying phrase "one of" gives him too little credit. Every cranny of reality is illuminated by his reflections, and his address is universal. Persuaded that Sacred Scripture and Apostolic Tradition are true and reasonable, he writes as a Christian, yet not a few atheists consult his writings assiduously; his works are too penetrating for anyone safely to ignore. For all these reasons, what we call Thomism is not just a dusty episode in the history of ideas, or a set of formulae written down in a book, but a living, unfolding tradition that continues to develop. As he challenges his critics, so he invites challenge in turn, asking for correction at any point where he turns out to be in error.

How mortifying it is to the contemporary intellect that so few in our day can read the work of this great mind. How surprising, for despite terrific resistance, our time is witnessing a modest renaissance of several of the themes about which he wrote so acutely, especially natural law. And how intolerable, for there is no need for such a doleful state of affairs to persist. The purpose of this book, a commentary on just one of St. Thomas's works, the *Treatise on Law* – itself but a part of his magnum opus, the *Summa Theologiae* – is to contribute in some small way to its amendment.

Born into an aristocratic family in 1225, St. Thomas died only forty-nine years later. He received his early education at the hands of Benedictine monks, and his parents expected him to become a Benedictine abbot. While still a boy, he was sent to the University of Naples, where he first came into contact with the Dominicans, an explosively popular mendicant preaching order, and received his first exposure to Aristotle, as well as to the philosopher's Jewish and Muslim commentators. In his late teens, he committed himself to become a Dominican friar. Anticipating that his family would interfere, the Dominicans sent the young man to Rome, planning that he would then go to Paris. En route, he was kidnapped by his brothers and returned to the family. For two years the family kept him behind locked doors, in hopes that he would lay down his vocation. At one point his brothers even tried to tempt him by sending a prostitute into his room; resisting the temptation, he drove her away and prayed for lifelong continence, a gift that was granted to him. Since all efforts to dissuade him from his vocation were unsuccessful, the family saved face by permitting him to escape, and he was lowered from his window in a basket to waiting Dominicans. Shortly thereafter he professed vows. He studied first in Paris, then under Albertus Magnus in Cologne. During his Cologne years he was ordained priest, and he later received his doctorate in theology from the University of Paris, where he had already become known for his writings and lectures on philosophy, theology, and Scripture. Traveling widely to teach and to preach, he produced a massive oeuvre of more than sixty major and minor works. These include three major theological summations (the *Summa Theologiae,* the *Summa Contra Gentiles,* and the *Commentary on the Sentences of Peter Lombard*); commentaries on various philosophers and books of the Bible; various other works on philosophical and theological topics; and a number of prayers, hymns, sermons, and popular works, for example the *Explanation of the Ten Commandments.*

Legends about St. Thomas abound. From the age of five, his teachers remarked that he was a boy of unusual piety who persistently asked, "What is God?" Often as he prayed, and more frequently toward the end of his life, he was in a state of contemplative ecstasy. Three of his Dominican brothers recorded that on one occasion, after he had completed a work on the Sacrament of the Eucharist and was praying before the altar, they heard a voice from the crucifix saying, "You have written well of me, Thomas. What would you have as reward?" St. Thomas replied, "Only you, Lord."

After another experience in prayer, St. Thomas suspended dictation to his friend, colleague, and confessor, Reginald of Piperno. When Reginald begged him to resume his work, St. Thomas replied that he could not do so, because such things had been revealed to him that everything he had written seemed straw by comparison. Not long afterward he received papal summons to attend the Second Council of Lyon, convened because of concern about the division of the Eastern and Western Church. On the way, he suffered an accident and collapsed. Taken to a nearby Cistercian monastery, he died, while composing, at the request of the monks, a commentary on the *Song of Songs*.

What Is Law?

Law is often viewed as a narrow and specialized topic, having to do only with the ordering of human society, and with only certain aspects of its ordering at that – especially control. Of course there is such a thing as human society, and it really is ordered by law. But to tear this order from its broader context is to make it unintelligible, because human law cannot pull itself up by its own efforts. It hangs like a chandelier from something higher.

In the view of St. Thomas, law is no less than the pattern for God's governance of everything he has made. This is not its *definition;* we will come to that in its proper place. But it is a true statement about what law does. Law begins in God's providential care for the universe, the pattern of which is eternal law. Man's finite participation in this providential care is human law. Linking the eternal and human orders are the two different reflections of eternal law that we humans can glimpse, one in the created intellect itself, the other in revelation. These two reflections are natural and Divine law, respectively. Created things that lie beneath us, like dogs and mushrooms, cannot catch these reflections. In one sense they too are under law, for God governs them no less than he governs us. But in a stricter sense they are not under law, because for them the mode of government is different. It has to be: They cannot recognize governance. There is no image of law in their minds, as there is in ours. Either, like the mushrooms, they do not have minds, or else, like the dogs, they do not have the sorts of minds that can participate in law. Of course dogs come much closer than mushrooms, for dogs recognize commands – sometimes even quite complex instructions. Yet not even the dog recognizes the command as *law.* He obeys for the sake of praise, or a treat, or the feeling of belonging to the group – not because he reflects that the command is an ordinance of reason, or that it serves the common good. This privilege belongs to us as *rational* creatures, and makes it true to say that although in one sense law is about the entire created universe, in another sense it pertains especially to man.

As St. Thomas conceives it, then, the topic of law, the topic of the *Treatise,* is immense. It should interest students and scholars in many different disciplines, as well as thinking people of all sorts. Astonishingly, St. Thomas manages to cover it in just nineteen sections.

How Does the Treatise on Law Fit into the Summa?

The title, *Treatise on Law,* is ours, not St. Thomas's. Though it is too late to do anything about it, in one way the term "treatise" is unfortunate, because it gives the impression of a free-standing and self-contained work. Though the *Treatise* is often read in that way, it was never meant to be. All of the limbs of the *Summa Theologiae* are interconnected, and the *Treatise on Law* is no exception.

The *Summa Theologiae* is divided into three main parts. Death interrupted St. Thomas's work before he could complete the Third Part, so an extra part, the Supplement, collects material on topics that he had intended to address. This additional material comes from one of his previous works, the *Commentary on the Sentences of Peter Lombard.* It was probably assembled by Reginald of Piperno, the friend mentioned previously.

Summa means "summation," and the *Summa Theologiae* is a summation of what can be known about God, man, and the relation between them. Each of the *Summa*'s main parts is organized into the topical sections we call treatises. The First Part inquires into God and his Creation, including the nature of man in general; the Second Part, into man more particularly; and the Third Part, into the work of Jesus Christ, as a mediator between man and God. The great movement of the whole work is from God, the creator, to man, God's creature, back to God, man's final end. Along the way we consider the things that may help or impede the return of man to God.

In turn, the Second Part is divided into the First Part of the Second Part, which considers morality in its broad principles, and the Second Part of the Second Part, which considers morality in more detail. These more detailed matters include the three theological virtues and four cardinal virtues, which pertain to everyone. They also include various acts that pertain not to everyone but only to some persons, because of the diversities of gifts and of states and ways of life, especially in the Church. Certain acts, for example, are incumbent upon priests but not lay people.

St. Thomas places the *Treatise on Law* in the First Part of the Second Part. He puts it *after* his treatises on man's ultimate purpose or end, on human acts in general, on passions, on "habits" or dispositions (which include virtues), and on vice and sin. All these things are preambles to law, and we will refer to them often. Equally important, however, is the fact that St. Thomas places the *Treatise on Law* before, not after, the *Treatise on Grace*. Just as law is not the first word about man, so it is not the last; justice is married to mercy. As the Psalmist declares, "Mercy and truth have met each other: justice and peace have kissed."[1]

For Whom Is this Commentary Written?

I am a scholar, and I mean this commentary to be worthy of the attention and use of scholars in a number of fields, especially law and jurisprudence, philosophy and theology of ethics, and philosophy and theology of politics. However, I am resolute that it should also be accessible to students, general readers, and other serious amateurs, and in this introduction they receive my first attention. Among a certain sort of scholar, one sometimes meets the prejudice that readable prose is a kind of slumming. The idea is that if ordinary people can grasp the meaning of what someone has written, then surely it can have nothing to offer to minds as erudite as theirs. St. Thomas himself would reprobate this attitude. Though his greatest work continues to challenge the most learned minds, he says on its opening page that he purposes to write "in such a way as may tend to the instruction of beginners."

St. Thomas explains that too often in other books, beginners are hampered by the multiplication of useless material, by repetition so frequent that it produces weariness and confusion, and by the fact that necessary topics are taught in the wrong order – not according to the nature of the subject, but according to the plan of the author's book or the opportunities it offers for digression. "Endeavoring to avoid these and other like faults," he says, he will try, by God's help, to present his explanations "as briefly and clearly as the matter itself may allow." This goal I have taken as my own, though a line-by-line commentary is inevitably longer than the work that it seeks to explicate.

My point about "beginners" should not be stretched too far. St. Thomas is not speaking of persons with no prior exposure to the doctrines he

---

[1] Psalm 84:11 (DRA), corresponding to Psalm 85:10 in more recent translations of the Bible. See the remark about translations at the end of this Introduction.

presents, but of students who have studied their philosophical preambles and are ready to move on to theology proper. Today, a good many of what he considers preambles are unfamiliar even to most philosophers. That is one of the reasons why a commentary is necessary. But the remedy is straightforward enough. As he goes along, the commentator must explain the preambles too.

A book of this sort can never move swiftly, but to keep it as brisk as may be, I omit much of the clutter that is rightly expected in specialist journals but not needed here. I cannot purge all the footnotes, but I keep them to an absolute minimum, mostly to give the sources of quotations. Digressions about how Professor X responded to what Professor Y said about Professor Z are cast into oblivion. For those who consider familiarity with such wrangles the very purpose of scholarship, I can only say that I disagree. Not that I don't have views about these debates. Those who are already familiar with them will no doubt try to guess the positions I would take. They may occasionally guess right. Yet the purpose of this book is not to discuss the discussions about what St. Thomas wrote, much less to discuss *those* discussions, but just to discuss what he wrote.

What Kind of Book Is the Treatise?

The literary genre in which the Treatise on Law is composed is the formal disputation – a form that contemporary readers tend to find chilly. Some of our feeling of chilliness arises from its structure; some from our ignorance of the reasons for this structure; and some from the fact the objections to which St. Thomas replies are not necessarily the ones we would have asked. Once these problems are addressed, most of the chill is dissipated.

How a Disputation Is Structured

A formal disputation is an extremely concise way of presenting and analyzing the state of a question that is under consideration. It puts all of the competing views in the clearest possible confrontation, so that one can pull up one's sleeves and solve the problem.

A disputation resembles a debate with a built-in review of the literature. The same format is always followed: First is the *ultrum*, the "whether," always in the form of a yes-or-no question, usually one to which the traditional answer is "Yes." In second place are the principal *objections* to a "Yes" answer, set forth in a list. These might also be called the difficulties. Third comes the *sed contra*, the "on the contrary" or "on the other hand," a statement of the traditional view. Fourth, the *respondeo*, or "I answer that," also called the *solutio*, or solution, expressing the author's own view. Finally the author makes use of the solution to reply to the objections, resolving each difficulty in turn.

The importance of the *ultrum* is often overlooked. In every field of learning, so much depends on asking the right question and framing it fittingly. If the wrong question is asked, the answer may be misleading; if the right question is asked, but framed in an unfittingly manner, one may never find the answer at all. So much time is needlessly lost, and so much ardor wasted, by failing to get the question right. Good teachers used to put their students through exercises in framing questions fittingly. Some still do. St. Thomas is a master of framing questions.

It may seem odd that St. Thomas states the objections before stating the view to which they object. But isn't that true to life? Aren't we all tempted to tell what is wrong with a proposition before we fully understand it? St. Thomas begins where people are already, even if they are confused. Only then does he present his own analysis, which he then uses to unravel whatever confusions he has found. If an objection is correct in some respect, he says so. If it is mistaken, he tells how. For purposes of a commentary like this one, it might be tempting to reorder each article so that the *respondeo* comes first and the objections afterward, each one followed by its reply. Many people do read them that way. Unfortunately, this is like skipping to the end of a mystery novel to find out whodunnit, then going back to the beginning; it misses the point. The objections are of the sort called naïve. Suppose the question on the table is "Whether Q." The objections aren't the kinds of things that might be said against St. Thomas's arguments for Q, by people who found these arguments wanting; they are the sorts of things that might be said against Q itself, by people who haven't yet grappled with his arguments.

Why St. Thomas Uses the Disputational Structure
St. Thomas has enormous respect for the authority of those who have thought about the questions before him. However, the authorities he consults are in disarray. One who believes that something is to be gained by consulting authority must first harmonize all the conflicting authorities – and that involves something more than just repeating what the authorities say.

The problem of conflicting authorities is endemic to all fields, but especially, perhaps, to law. In the sixth century A.D., the Byzantine Emperor

Justinian commissioned what we now call the *Corpus Juris Civilis*[2] in order to harmonize a sprawling mass of legal material that had accumulated over a period of a thousand years, including case law, enacted law, senatorial consults, judicial interpretations, and imperial decrees. Written under the supervision of Tribonius, the *Corpus* includes four parts: The *Codes,* a collection of imperial "constitutions" or legislation dating from the time of the Emperor Hadrian; the *Institutes,* a manual for students of law; the *Digest,* or *Pandects,* a collection of excerpts from Ulpian, Gaius, and thirty-seven other great Roman jurists; and the *Novels,* added later, a collection of "new" legislation. Ultimately, the *Corpus Juris Civilis* becomes one, but only one, of St. Thomas's sources.

As we approach St. Thomas's time, we find a similar legal disarray in Europe. The muddle is even worse, because not only have laws and precedents continued to multiply, but now they come from multiple sources, for imperial authority has declined, a variety of local authorities have interposed, and civil law is now paralleled by canon law. A century before St. Thomas wrote, the great thinker Gratian had undertaken a synthesis of canon law, harmonizing discordant materials including Scripture and Scriptural commentaries, the writings of the Fathers, the decisions of various Church councils and synods, and the letters and decretals of various popes.[3] Gratian adopted and developed a set of powerful tools for disentangling snarls, especially what is called *distinctio,* or distinction.

To illustrate how *distinctio* works, suppose veterinary science had fallen into disorder. A great deal of knowledge has been preserved, but in great confusion. One problem is that the great veterinarians of ancient times make a number of apparently conflicting statements about so-called dogs. A dog is a mammal, says one. A dog is a creature that barks, says another. A dog is a kind of wolf, says a third. A fourth says that men are dogs, or perhaps only that many men are dogs, although some hold that she was not actually a veterinarian but a controversialist in something called the war between the sexes. A fifth remarks merely that dogs are highly variable. Taking sides among these authorities, competing schools of thought have developed. Mammalists hold that all mammals are dogs, so cows are dogs. Barkists maintain that anything that barks

---

[2] *Corpus Juris Civilis,* meaning "body of civil law," is actually a modern name for the work, dating only to the sixteenth century.

[3] For discussion, see the Introduction, by Katherine Christensen, to Gratian, *The Treatise on Laws* [*Concordance of Discordant Canons*], trans. Augustine Thompson, *With the Ordinary Gloss,* trans. James Gordley (Washington, D.C.: Catholic University Press, 1993), p. 3.

is a dog, so that foxes and monkeys are dogs. Wolvists argue that only
wolves are dogs, so that white wolves, red wolves, and timber wolves are
dogs, but beagles and fox terriers are not. Masculinists claim that dogs
are a subdivision of male human beings. Rejectionists contend that the
ancient term "dog" is too vague to be of much use, and appears to have
been simply an informal synonym for "living thing." Much depends on
the resolution of this controversy, because an enormous mass of information has been accumulated about dogs, and it is crucial to know to
just what kind of creatures it refers. Finally, some genius realizes that
the various ancient authorities are not necessarily in disagreement. They
only appear to be, because they are answering different questions. Dogs
are related to mammals in the sense that mammal is the *genus* of dog (I
am the term in its Aristotelian-Thomistic rather than its Linnean sense).[4]
Dogs are related to barking in the sense that barking distinguishes the
species of dog from some of the *other* species in the genus mammal. Dogs
are related to wolves in the sense that the species wolf is the *ancestor* of
the species dog. Dogs are related to men by *analogy*, in that some men
are fierce, or promiscuous, like dogs. Finally, although all dogs share the
differentia of the species dog, in other respects dogs vary widely. The
puzzle about dogs has been dissolved by distinguishing among the senses
in which each authority is right. Not that an authority cannot be simply
wrong; that happens too. But one cannot discern whether an authority
is wrong unless one first investigates whether there is any sense in which
he is right.

What sets St. Thomas in the thirteenth century apart from Tribonius
in the sixth and Gratian in the twelfth is that he is trying to develop not
a mere synthesis of legal precedents, like a civil lawyer or canonist, but
something much more searching and difficult, a philosophy and theology
of law. For this reason his sources are even more diverse than theirs. To
the authorities on which Tribonius and Gratian relied, we must now add
figures like the pagan writer Aristotle, the Muslim writer Averroes, the
Jewish writer Maimonides, and the Christian writer Peter Lombard.

Yet by his time *distinctio* has become the hallmark of the Scholastic
method, and St. Thomas is a master of it. It enables him to solve all sorts
of riddles that had vexed previous thinkers, such as in what sense natural

---

[4] The Linnean system of classification, which we use today, is Aristotelian in spirit, but
employs finer distinctions. *Mammalia* is called not the genus but the "class" of dogs. Then
come their order, *carnivora*, their family, *canidae*, their *genus*, *canis*, their species, *canis
lupus*, and their subspecies, *canis lupus familiaris*.

law is and is not an expression of "what nature has taught all animals"; in what sense biblical law is and is not an expression of natural law; and the various senses in which different kinds of human law are "derived" from some higher law.

Common Difficulties in Reading the *Treatise on Law*

Although St. Thomas wrote *Treatise on Law* and the rest of the *Summa* to avoid the obstacles that other books set before readers, certain difficulties face the *Summa*'s readers too. I venture to say that if other books hamper readers because of their faults, the *Summa* detains them in large part because of its virtues. An obstacle that arises from merit is still an obstacle, so let us discuss some of these difficulties.

Perhaps the most common hindrances in reading the *Treatise on Law* are the supposed dryness and lack of warmth of St. Thomas's style, to which I alluded above; his view of intellectual authority; his view of faith and reason; his view of how to study reality; and his apparent failure to consider the objections that some people of our day find most cogent. It may be helpful to discuss each of these difficulties briefly before passing on to the *Treatise* itself.

St. Thomas's Supposed Dryness

Almost all first-time readers find St. Thomas's style forbidding. It is like climbing to the top of a great height, which is wonderful and exhilarating if you survive it. Some love the heights; others don't.

It may seem dry at the top of the mountain. Thomistic prose is clean, terse, minimalist. It epitomizes Mark Twain's rule, "eschew surplusage." It is like the Platonic ideal of concision, come to earth. This makes it essential that we read as precisely as St. Thomas writes, and take the time to unpack his succinct expressions. Take his very first characterization of the topic: "Law is a rule and measure of acts, whereby man is induced to act or is restrained from acting." Woe unto the reader who supposes that when he says "rule and measure," he is writing like a poet, echoing the same thought in two different ways. No. St. Thomas has nothing against poetry when poetry is called for. In fact, he is the author of a number of moving Latin hymns that have been sung for centuries. But even his poetry is precise, and the *Summa* is not the occasion for poetry. A rule is one sort of thing, a measure is another, and his point is that law is both.

Another aspect of the supposed aridity of St. Thomas's writing is its interconnectedness, the fact that each section of the *Summa* depends on each of the sections that precedes it. Those who overlook these connections sometimes think that the *Treatise on Law* crosses the border between terseness and insufficiency, that its arguments have missing pieces, that they jump over logical gaps. For example they complain that St. Thomas refers to the virtues without defining them, or that he merely assumes the reality of God without making a case for it. On the contrary, he carefully discusses all such things, but he does not discuss all of them *in this treatise*. One of the tasks of a commentator is to fill in the cross-references. Though St. Thomas provides many of the cross-references, he leaves some of them implicit. Surprisingly, the purpose of his reticence is not to make things harder for us, but to make them easier. As we saw earlier, he finds that readers are hampered by too much repetition. Let us not forget that his "beginners," being unspoiled by quick access to cheap books and searchable databases, have much better memories than we do. Not that we should despise cheap books and databases; but it would be good if we could keep our memories too.

Not only do the different treatises depend on each other, but so do the different sections within a given treatise. In Question 97, for example, St. Thomas's strong claim that custom has the authority of law builds on his much earlier definition of law in Question 90. By comparing Questions 90 and 97, we can see that their arguments are connected; custom has the authority of law *only because* it fulfills the definitional criteria of law as such. Does St. Thomas prompt us to compare these two sections? No. Like the author of a geometry textbook displaying his proof, he trusts that anyone who has reached step K will recall what was shown at step D.

Another thing that makes St. Thomas's prose seem arid to some readers is that it is so understated. To illustrate, let us consider his claim about custom a little further. If custom has the authority of law *only because* it fulfills the criteria of law, then it must have it *only to the extent* that it fulfills them. St. Thomas has explained in Question 96 that so-called unjust laws lack the authority of law just because they *fail* to fulfill these criteria; they are not true laws at all. But in that case, it follows that unjust customs would also lack the authority of law, and for just the same reason. Does he say this? No. He expects us to work it out. Again we are reminded of the authors of geometry textbooks, who sometimes say "I leave this theorem as an exercise for the reader." I rather like this about St. Thomas's writing. It is an invitation to further adventure. But one must learn to recognize the invitation.

St. Thomas's Supposed Lack of Warmth

Speaking of geometry, most people find mathematics not only arid but also cold. Mathematicians don't; although they certainly find it austere, they also find it heady, exhilarating, and above all, beautiful. It sets their pulses pounding, or, if not their pulses, something in the intellect that feels much the same. That raises an interesting question. Why don't the rest of us see what they see, feel what they feel, pound as they pound? Sometimes, perhaps, we do. Many of us can remember moments in our mathematical training when our minds leapt and our hearts caught, because suddenly it all came together and *had to be just that way*. The better we understood the math, the more often we experienced those moments; the more often we experienced them, the greater our desire to understand. So it is with St. Thomas. If we find his writing cold, we find it so in large part because it is difficult and austere. There is a warming cure for that: Study.

Another reason for finding St. Thomas's prose cold is that it is impersonal. Isn't law about human beings? Aren't humans personal creatures, subjectivities, beings with interior lives, lit from within by glowing meaning? Why, yes, but we should not suppose that St. Thomas is ignorant of these facts. In fact, his thought is one of the milestones in our understanding of what it is to be personal. The term "person," he says, "signifies what is most perfect in all nature – that is, a subsistent individual of a rational nature"[5] – a complete individual reality, existing in itself, different from all other somethings, made for rationality, the ultimate possessor under God of all it is and does.[6] A person is not just a piece or part of something, it is not just an instance or process of something, it is not just a clump of different somethings, nor is it merely a thing to be owned, a thing to be used, or a thing of any sort at all. It is not just a *what*, but a *who*. St. Thomas knows all this, and he also knows that personal knowledge – for example a loving husband's knowledge of his wife – is more perfect than abstract knowledge, because love unites the knower

---

[5] I, Q. 29, Art. 3.

[6] A person is the possessor of his properties in the sense that he is the one of whom they are predicated. If he has a sharp mind, we do not say that his intellect is intelligent but that he is; if he knowingly committed wrong, we do not say that his mind has guilt but that he does; if he habitually acts honestly, we do not compliment his will for honesty, we compliment him.

with the known, transforming the lover by accommodating him to the beloved.[7] These insights have transformed the Western world. But now wait a moment. Is it necessary for St. Thomas to gush about his own interior life to explain the principles that God provides for beings with interior lives? I suspect that he would consider it an impertinence. Worse yet, he would view it as a hindrance, as one of those things that "hampers" us from understanding. There is a time to speak personally, but there is also a time to speak impersonally, even about the reality of persons.

Still in the shadow of the Romantic movement in literature, we are accustomed to the idea that "creative people" must always be showing off their "passion." St. Thomas does not do that; not for him to write with the *sturm und drang* of a work like St. Augustine's *Confessions* (though he quotes from this beloved predecessor hundreds of times). Yet does this lack of "passion" make him cold? His prose ripples with the logic of argument, flows with the quickness of necessity, lures with the promise of insight, warms with the lamp of faith, and gleams with the lantern of reason.

So I find it, anyway, and I hope that others may come to find it so too. One may love other styles, yet come to love St. Thomas's too. His prose suits his purpose, like the perfectly calculated trajectory of a spacecraft en route to a light-years-distant rendezvous with Proxima Centauri.

St. Thomas's View of Intellectual Authority

Most contemporary readers find it difficult to swallow St. Thomas's view of intellectual authority – or at least what they take his view of it to be. Often my students are annoyed by the mere fact that he quotes so much from other thinkers. So little does our style of intellectual training cherish humility – and so thoroughly has it been drummed it into us that the so-called Argument from Authority is a fallacy – that we tend to confuse humility with fallacy. A popular bumper sticker commands, "Question authority!" There ought to be one that counsels, "Choose among authorities wisely."

The first point to be grasped is that not all consultation of authority is illegitimate – but some is. There is nothing wrong with asking a geologist about the chemical composition of limestone, since I can't possibly have

---

[7] See for example I-II, Q. 28, Art. 1, ad 3. "Knowledge is perfected by the thing known being united, through its likeness, to the knower. But the effect of love is that the thing itself which is loved, is, in a way, united to the lover, as stated above. Consequently the union caused by love is closer than that which is caused by knowledge."

first-hand knowledge of everything, and he knows more about limestone than I do. Careful use of authority serves the ends of reason, provided that one has reasonable assurance of the supposed authority's honesty, reliability, and qualifications, the question asked concerns his own field of expertise, one considers not just his answers but the reasons he gives for them, and, if authorities differ, one consults the other ones too.

This is exactly how St. Thomas does consult authority. He pays the debt of gratitude to pagan, Christian, Muslim, and Jew, especially Aristotle, whom he respectfully calls "the Philosopher," St. Paul, "the Apostle," each of the *iurisconsults* quoted in the *Digest,* "the Jurist," St. Augustine of Hippo, "the Theologian," Peter Lombard, "the Master," Averroes, "the Commentator," and Maimonides, "Rabbi Moses." It was no more than customary to consider the views of opponents, but St. Thomas transcends this common courtesy, taking his critics at their highest rather than their lowest points, sometimes even putting their objections more cogently than they did themselves.

Finally notice that not all *reference* to authority is *deference* to authority. Although humility requires that we consider what other respected thinkers have thought, it does not require that we accept their reasoning if we find something wrong with it. One must separate the wheat from the chaff, and this is exactly what St. Thomas tries to do. It is just that before discarding the chaff, we had better make sure it is really chaff.

St. Thomas's View of Faith and Reason

If anything an author does annoys modern readers more than quoting from thinkers of antiquity, it is quoting from the Bible. The notion that faith and reason are opposites has become a reflex with many of us. My graduate students are a good deal more thoroughly indoctrinated in the shibboleths of the academy than my undergraduates; only with the greatest difficulty am I able to get some of them to recognize that St. Thomas offers arguments at all. Like the citizens of Oceana, George Orwell's fictional dystopia, they have been conditioned in such a way as to find certain lines of reasoning impossible to recognize as lines of reasoning. Confronted with them, they can only say "fallacy of Argument from Authority," which is their way of saying "crimethink."

This conditioned response has a history. Early in the modern era, many thinkers began to mistrust faith, viewing it as "blind" and an enemy of reason. Their watchword was "reason alone." One of the difficulties of this stance is that reason cannot test its own reliability, any more than soapstone can test its own hardness. Any argument, accomplished by reasoning, that what reasoning accomplishes can be trusted, would be circular, because it would take for granted the very thing that it was trying to prove. Perhaps it is not surprising that the descendants of these thinkers began to mistrust reason itself, holding that the mind is locked in its own mazes, unable to penetrate external reality. "How can we know anything?" we complain. When it turns to someone like St. Thomas, the complaint becomes especially bitter: "Who is *he* to think he can know anything?"

St. Thomas certainly thinks it is *possible* for the mind to become locked in its own mazes. This is a permanent liability of our fallen state. Yet he takes an extraordinarily high view of the power of both reason and faith to illuminate reality, and he views them not as enemies, but as friends. He does not think they are the same thing. Although there may be rational grounds for trust in God, and rational grounds for believing that biblical revelation about God is authentic (and he thinks that there are), one must still take that step of believing. Suppose I am at the window of a burning building. Although I can hear the firemen calling to me from far below, I cannot see them because of all the smoke. They are telling me to jump. Though I may have every reason to believe that they will catch me in their net, I may not trust them enough to overcome my fear, and so, hesitating, I burn to death. Obviously, my reasons are not the same as trust; faith surpasses reason. Even so they are reasons *for* trust; though faith surpasses reason, it is not irrational.

Not only does reason come to the cleansing aid of faith, but also faith enables reason to reach farther, to ask better questions, to become in every way more fully what it is meant to be. In the first place, although trust in revelation may seem to demean reason, the truth of the matter is otherwise: It actually gives reason greater confidence, because from faith, we have additional reason to believe that rather than being a haphazard, undependable hodgepodge, which happened to come together in a blind process that did not have us in mind, human intelligence is a gift of the Divine Intelligence, given to us for knowledge. In the second place, revelation provides certainty – at least relative certainty, because God cannot err, although man can err in the interpretation of what God has disclosed. In the third place, revelation provides new data, illuminating reality more deeply than reason could have done on its own. Finally, revelation calls the mind's attention to a great many things that it *should* have been able to find out on its own, but might not have.

Everyday experiences makes the latter point clear, because so often we fail to notice things that ought to be perfectly obvious: "Have you seen

my glasses?" "Yes, you're holding them in your hand." Philosophy is like
that too. The facts of created reality may be right under our noses without our noticing. We may be nearly blind to them until their Creator says,
"Look here." Then we can see them for ourselves.

The co-dependence of faith and reason has been well expressed by
John Paul II: They are like the two wings of a bird. It needs both of them
to fly.[8]

St. Thomas's View of How to Study Reality

Moderns tend to view St. Thomas's approach to reality as naïve, unso-
phisticated, and obsolete, because it sets *things* before *knowledge*. He
approaches all kinds of *things* this way – material objects, volitions, qualities, whatever they may be – for no matter what we are studying, we
have to know something before we can investigate how we know it. But
in the modern era, we reverse this procedure. Before studying what there
is to know, we insist on a critique of our ability to know anything at all.

This shift, called the "epistemological turn," has had a variety of bad
results. First comes extreme skepticism, along with contempt for tradition and common sense. Of course even the skeptic has to assume that
something is true; otherwise he has no way to decide what to do and
how to live – the springs of action lose their springiness. In practice, then,
extreme skepticism turns into its opposite, extreme conventionalism. For
the supposed skeptic doesn't really reject prejudice; he unquestioningly
accepts every prejudice that has learned to put on skeptical airs.

Another way to say this is that someone who has made the epistemological turn has not really turned aside from the study of *things*. He
continues to practice it, but he does so ineptly, because he does not pay
attention to what he is doing. For a single potent example, consider the
effect of this carelessness on the abortion controversy. What kind of thing
is the unborn child? How often do we hear he is not an actual person,
but merely a "potential person"? This expression takes for granted that a
person is something one can turn into gradually. This is not so, for a subsistent being has the particular potentialities that it has only because of
what it is already. The child has the potentiality to develop into a mature
person precisely because he is an immature person. He isn't a stage of
development of a thing, but the very thing itself, persisting through all its
stages. I am a man; I was once a child. Yet it was I who was that child, as
it is I who am that man. What follows? That a thing that is not a person

[8] John Paul II, encyclical letter *Fides et Ratio* (1998), preface.

cannot become a person; the person either exists or he doesn't. What we misleadingly and dangerously call a "potential person" is *already* a person, a person with potential, potential for additional qualities that have not yet developed.

The father of the notion of putting the study of knowledge before the study of things known is Immanuel Kant, but its grandfather is René Descartes. The problem that bedeviled Descartes was how to know anything with certainty. Almost in despair of knowing anything for sure, at last he thought he had found a starting point. He could be certain of his existence, just because he was thinking about the problem. But this famous *cogito, ergo sum* is fallacious, for the certainty "I exist" does not follow from the bare premise "I think." One must also know for sure that thought requires a thinker. We derive this fact from experience. So we do know something already; we are beginning with *things* after all. Since we do this inevitably, wouldn't it be better to admit it? Rather than refusing to believe anything we are capable of doubting, wouldn't it make more sense to use the matters we are *less* in doubt about to test the ones we are *more* in doubt about? But to do that would be to return to the classical method that Descartes rejects.

From the failure of Descartes' experiment, subsequent thinkers should have drawn the lesson that putting the study of knowledge before the study of things known is a blind alley. Oddly, most of them drew a different lesson: That Descartes was right to put knowledge before *things*, and if he wasn't quite able to make this approach to inquiry work, we just need to try harder. That is like saying, saying, "Hitting the television monitor with the palm of my hand made the picture worse. Let me try hitting it with a hammer."

At first it seems modest and reasonable to proceed "critically," to scrutinize the instrument of knowledge before relying on the things that we supposedly know. How often we have been misled by things that seem obvious but turn out not to be true! A straight stick inserted halfway into water may look bent, but this is a mere illusion, produced by the diffraction of light. Shouldn't we guard against such errors? But there is something fishy about the illusion of the bent stick. Yes, it is really an illusion. But how did we find that out? How did we discover this weakness in our powers of knowing things? By knowing something: By finding out that the stick was straight after all.

How could we have thought that the instrument of knowledge could test itself before it had any actual knowledge to test itself against? "Test before you buy" is a good rule for reason to apply to other things, but not to itself; it isn't as though there were another sort of product on the shelf. First try to know something, *then* go ahead and criticize the power of knowing. You will find out the weaknesses of the reasoning power only in the act of using it. That is how St. Thomas proceeds.

Why Doesn't St. Thomas Take Up Our Own Objections?

St. Thomas takes objections seriously, and the ones he considers are the ones that he actually encountered. Some first-time readers are put off by the fact that these objections are not necessarily *our* objections, the sorts of concerns that some people of our day find cogent. In fact, some of the objections he considers seem downright odd. If he is considering objections people really raise, then why doesn't he consider more of the ones *we* raise?

Actually, sometimes the objections St. Thomas considers really are the ones we would raise, but we fail to recognize them because they are expressed in a philosophical vocabulary that provides greater precision than our everyday speech. Another reason for their seeming oddity is that we are insufficiently familiar with the issues and arguments with which he is dealing to think of the objections that we might think of if we did not have this limitation. If we were more well informed with, say, moderate realist metaphysics or Christian theology, then the objections St. Thomas considers might be our objections too.

But the complaint that St. Thomas is not responding to the objections of our own day may also take a more troubling form. To readers of our day, St. Thomas sometimes seems to be taking far too much for granted – even to be avoiding the most pressing points that might be raised against his views. Let us look into this protest.

From one point of view, the protest seems unfair. Quite often, the most noteworthy thing about the objections St. Thomas considers is not that they are so medieval, but that they are so contemporary. For example, law includes the natural law, and in our day, the most contentious part of natural law is the morality of sex. But the morality of sex was disputed in his day too. The Roman jurist, Ulpian, had written that the natural law is "what nature has taught all animals." But in that case, shouldn't we say that the restriction to a single mate is contrary to natural law, because among many animals one male is united with several females? Or that matrimony is against the natural law, because in other animals the male and female are united without it? Or that incest is compatible with the natural law, because animals of other species can be observed copulating with their mothers? The view of nature that lies behind these objections is startlingly similar to the one expressed in a contemporary lyric by the Bloodhound Gang, "You and me baby ain't nothin' but mammals, So let's do it like they do on the Discovery Channel."[9] St. Thomas takes up each of these objections in the Supplement, showing that they misunderstand the *sense* in which what is natural for human beings is like (and unlike) what is natural for subrational creatures.[10] So in this respect, St. Thomas is right up to date.

Yet from another point of view, he isn't. The objections St. Thomas takes up are conservative – conservative in the same odd sense that the Bloodhound Gang is conservative. After all, the rock band concedes that there is a natural standard for behavior; it merely misunderstands that standard. But what if there isn't any? What if there are no right and wrong at all? What if what we call "natural" is a kind of practical joke played on us by the universe? Philosopher Michael Ruse and biologist E.O. Wilson think so. "[E]thics as we understand it," they say, "is an illusion fobbed off on us by our genes to get us to co-operate (so that human genes survive) .... Furthermore the way our biology enforces its ends is by making us think that there is an objective higher code to which we are all subject."[11]

It is quite true that St. Thomas does not always engage *that* sort of objection. He takes for granted that the way we are made determines objective criteria for human flourishing, criteria that reflect a real good and evil, a real right and wrong. If any serious thinkers of his time disputed such views, he would take them on, but apparently none did; our own objections, far from being obvious and perennial – as we tend to think them – are odd and historically unusual. Of course, whether or not they are eccentric, his failure to address them is a real gap, a gap that this commentary must try to fill. I will try to address objections that St. Thomas did not encounter in the way he *might* have addressed them had anyone brought them up.

Should we fault St. Thomas for not anticipating all our own objections? For several reasons, I suggest that the answer is "No." One reason is that the possibilities of doubt are infinite; they can never be exhaustively

---

[9] From the Bloodhound Gang, "The Bad Touch," on the album *Hooray for Boobies* (Interscope Records, 2000).

[10] Supp., Q. 41, Art. 1, obj. 1; Q. 54, Art. 3, obj. 3; and 65, Art. 1, obj. 4. Throughout this commentary, references to the works of St. Thomas are understood to be to the *Summa Theologiae* except where otherwise indicated.

[11] Michael Ruse and E.O. Wilson, "The Evolution of Ethics," *New Scientist* 108:1478 (17 October 1985), pp. 51–52.

anticipated. New ways of hurling things into question can always be devised. Every defense against a doubt provides opportunities for new doubt; every new doubt provides new opportunities to elaborate truths. Of course there is such a thing as too much doubt, for we ought to accept what is true. But there is also such a thing as proper doubt, for we ought not accept what is false. The possibility of doubt is inherent in the longing to understand, and nothing less than complete and perfect knowledge can satisfy the mind. We do not possess such knowledge here on earth; it is reserved for the beatific vision. Until then, doubt will be with us. This is one of the reasons why the project that St. Thomas begins is never finished. It is also why it is so unreasonable to trust only what cannot be doubted, as Descartes proposed, because everything can be doubted. We should believe, not what we cannot doubt, but what we have the *best reasons to believe.*

The other reason for not faulting St. Thomas has to do with the peculiarity of some of the new objections that we raise. In one way they seem bold and radical, because we often talk like nihilists, who say that the difference between good and evil is merely an arbitrary social convention. In another way they don't, because we don't quite seem to mean it when we do. Suppose we met someone who did mean it, who was literally unable to recognize a difference between real good and real evil. If such a person could exist at all, he would be beyond the reach of moral reason. Even someone who sincerely calls the unjust "just" is still in the human conversation; he is still asking the question, "What is just?" But if asking means hopefully seeking the answer, then a true nihilist could no longer ask. He might utter the *words* "What is just?" – to manipulate the rest of us, perhaps, or just to try out the sound of them – but to him they would be only noises. If an objection is a phase in conversation, and if the sort of conversation we have in mind is a cooperative social practice aimed at knowledge, then the nihilist's "objection" is not really an objection. Trying to talk with him would have no more point than trying to talk with a monkey.

Are we really moral monkeys? I don't think so. We only strike the nihilist pose selectively, to put to shame rules that we no longer try to keep. When it suits us, we can be quite Puritanical: "Right and wrong are in the eye of the beholder, *and if you don't agree, you deserve severe punishment.*" The veneer is skeptical, but the core is rigid and punitive. The whole affair looks more like a fence around conduct that cannot bear close examination, than like a serious intellectual position.

How Is this Commentary Arranged?

This book is an amplified classical commentary – a commentary in the classical style, lacking none of its parts, but with extra parts added. Just as in classical commentary, the core of the book is line-by-line analysis of St. Thomas's text. Line-by-line analysis holds a venerable place in Western scholarship. In St. Thomas's own day, a line-by-line commentary on the *Sentences* of Peter Lombard was required of every candidate for the degree of Master of Theology. By itself, however, line-by-line analysis leaves something to be desired, so I have added sections of preparation, paraphrase, and online supplemental discussion, allowing these sections to vary in length according to need. The sequence of these sections will be explained a bit later. Although some who use this commentary will read it from front to back, I realize that many will dip only into particular sections. In such an interconnected work, this fact poses some difficulties. For this reason, I occasionally make the same point, in different ways, in more than one place (something St. Thomas does as well, despite his concern about repetition), and I also cross-reference his discussions of various topics (though selectively).

People write about St. Thomas for a variety of reasons. Some, like Yves Simon and Jacques Maritain, have adopted St. Thomas's insights as the seminal principle of their own investigations. Others, like John Haldane, have attempted to recast his thought into the idiom and question-set of contemporary analytical philosophy. Still others, like Alasdair MacIntyre, and in another way Russell Hittinger, have used St. Thomas to illuminate great moments in other traditions of inquiry. Then come writers of a more practical orientation, such as the "manualists" of a previous generation, who mined St. Thomas's work for rubrics that might be helpful to confessors. The purpose of this commentary is not quite like that of any of those works, because its chief goal is simply to explain what St. Thomas means. Even so, two different approaches to the task might have been adopted, other than the one I have chosen. For there are those who attempt analytical reconstruction, like Anthony Lisska, John Finnis, and on a grander scale Reginald Garrigou-Lagrange, and there are those who offer freer treatments of Thomistic themes and insights, like Ralph McInerny or Joseph Pieper. To each approach to the task there corresponds a particular literary form.

One of my earliest readers suggested that I "pick a fight" with the latter two forms, analytical reconstruction and freewheeling thematic discussion, to demonstrate the superiority of classical commentary. I certainly don't want to pick a fight, for I am indebted to those who use these other forms. Besides, it would be hypocritical to do so, for I have employed them myself. But it is no insult to the other two forms to point out that amplified classical commentary has certain sharp advantages. One is flexibility, for in principle, it can do most of what the other two forms do, and it can also do things that they can't. Another is objectivity, for it forces the author to sacrifice his own opinions in order to explicate St. Thomas's own text. If the author's opinions do intrude, they do so mainly in my supplementary *Companion to the Commentary*, and these are the icing, not the cake; the reader may ignore them if he wishes. Classical commentary enforces another kind of discipline too. How tempting it is to curry favor with readers, by reassuring them that today we know better than St. Thomas about this or that! Classical commentary makes it difficult to patronize an author in that way, because it forces us to make sure that we understand precisely what he is saying – just as if, and just because, it might be true. Of course it might not be true, at least not at every point, and it would be just as wrong to patronize readers as to patronize St. Thomas. But classical commentary allows him to speak, and the reader to listen, without static and background noise. It respects the reader by allowing him to decide for himself, freely and without manipulation, whether he agrees.

The version of the *Treatise on Law* employed in this commentary is the one incorporated in the well-known, very literal translation of the *Summa* by the Fathers of the English Dominican Province, which has been the gold standard for many years.[12] Hypertext versions are available in several locations online,[13] which makes the text not only readily accessible but also electronically searchable. Of course I in no way wish to disparage more recent translations, such as the translation of Alfred J. Freddoso, which I often recommend to my students.[14]

The *Treatise* contains nineteen main topics, called "questions," numbered 90 through 108. Each question is divided into "articles," or articulations, each of which poses a single *ultrum* or "whether." If it were possible

---

[12] *The Summa Theologica of St. Thomas Aquinas*, Second and Revised Edition, 1920, trans. by Fathers of the English Dominican Province, 2d rev. ed. (London: Burns, Oates, & Washbourne, 1912–1916). Public domain.

[13] Among others, New Advent, www.newadvent.org/summa, and Christian Classics Ethereal Library, www.ccel.org/a/aquinas/summa.

[14] See Alfred J. Freddoso, trans., *Treatise on Law: The Complete Text* (St. Augustine's Press, 2009), part of Freddoso's ongoing project to retranslate the entire *Summa*. The portions of his translation still underway and not yet published may be found at www.nd.edu/~afreddos/summa-translation/TOC.htm.

to treat all eighteen questions in a single volume, that would be ideal. That cannot be done. The next best is to present Questions 90–97, which provide an overview, in this book, along with selections from Questions 98–108, which focus on Divine law, online. Many scholarly treatments of the *Treatise* simply ignore Questions 98–108. In the aggressively secular milieu of contemporary scholarship, that is not surprising. However, anything that obscures the theological context of St. Thomas's great work will obscure the work itself, because St. Thomas views not only Divine law but also natural law in the context of the history of salvation. It was otherwise with the natural rights theories of the Enlightenment. They tried to bracket theology, on the assumption that the only way to talk about things like natural law, which we have in common, is to ignore everything that we don't have in common. Though initially this assumption seemed plausible, it turned out to be based on a fallacy, and one of the mysteries of modernity is why the fallacy was not obvious sooner. To ignore the history of salvation is not to be neutral about the history of salvation; rather it is to assume *a priori* that the history of salvation makes no difference to the understanding of anything else. A discussion among Protestants, Catholics, Jews, Muslims, and atheists, each of whom is invited to discuss his theological premises, may be difficult to conduct. But how is it easier to conduct than a discussion among all the same parties, each of whom is expected to impersonate the atheist?

For each question and article, the order of the commentary is the same: It is the order followed in classical commentaries, but, as I have suggested, with several parts added. At the front of each question, I place matters the reader should consider first: "Before Reading Question 90," "Before Reading Question 91," and so forth. At the opening of each article, I place the Dominican Fathers translation, called "Text," with my paraphrase, called "Paraphrase," in parallel columns. The Dominican Fathers translation is always italicized. Everything else is in ordinary font. Because the Dominican Fathers translation is usually very literal, and because parallel columns allow readers to decide for themselves just how freely or literally I am paraphrasing, I have the fortunate liberty to rephrase sometimes more freely, sometimes more literally, just as I think clarity requires. Sometimes the reader may compare my paraphrase with the Dominican Fathers translation and think, "How did he get that paraphrase from the words of the translation?" The answer is that I am not paraphrasing the translation, but paraphrasing the Latin itself. Every now and then I even disagree with the translators about the meaning of some point in the original language; sometimes I am even *more* literal.

Even so, the paraphrase is not an alternative translation and should by no means be mistaken for one. It is not even close to a translation. At the freest moments of the paraphrase, I change St. Thomas's verb tenses, add clarifications, insert transitions, remove phrases that seem redundant in English, and even reorder the sentences. In a translation, such liberties would be inexcusable. But to make the meaning of the prose transparent, they are indispensable. This may be a suitable place to insert my standard disclaimer. Where pronouns are concerned, I generally follow the traditional English convention – the one everyone followed, before politically motivated linguistic bullying became fashionable – according to which such terms as "he" and "him" are *already* "inclusive." Unless the context clearly indicates the masculine, they have always been used to refer to a person of either sex. Readers who choose differently may write differently; I ask only that they extend the same courtesy to me. In the meantime, since my language includes masculine, feminine, neuter, and inclusive pronouns, any rational being who feels excluded has only him-, her-, or itself to blame.

Interpolated between chunks of Text and Paraphrase are sections of line-by-line analysis. This analysis goes well beyond the paraphrase, but in doing so makes clear why the paraphrase is framed as it is. As I have mentioned, although the *Commentary* is self-contained, an online *Companion the Commentary* is also provided with this *Commentary*. In the *Companion*, readers will find supplemental discussions, flexible in length and style, keyed to the individual articles of the *Treatise on Law*, so that the themes each article discusses can be seen in even greater clarity and depth. One might say that the "Before Reading" sections prepare us to enter the forest; the paraphrase helps us walk among the trees; the line-by-line analysis helps study each tree closely; and the *Companion* help step back and consider the grove in its setting.

Because I also supply some cross-references, it may be helpful to explain how the sections of the great work to which the *Treatise on Law* belongs are cited. If the source is not already clear, the letters "S.T." are used to indicate the *Summa Theologiae* (or *Summa Theologica,* a form of the title that is also widely used). In this commentary, of course, the abbreviation is normally unnecessary. Next the part is indicated: "I" for the First Part, "I-II" for the First Part of the Second Part," "II-II" for the Second Part of the Second Part, "III" for the Third Part, or "Supp." for the Supplement. "Q.," followed by a numeral, identifies the Question; the numbering of questions begins anew in each part. "Art.," followed by a numeral, identifies the Article. Citations are further specified by the abbreviation "Obj.," with a numeral, for an objection, or the Latin preposition "ad," with a numeral, for a reply to an objection. If a citation specifies neither an objection, a reply to an objection, nor the *sed contra,* then it refers either to the whole article, or, if one is quoting from it, to the *respondeo.* For example, "S.T., I-II, Q. 94, Art. 4, ad 3," means "*Summa Theologiae,* First Part of the Second Part, Question 94, Article 4, Reply to Objection 3," but "S.T., I-II, Q. 94, Art 4," refers either to Article 4 in its entirety, or to the "I answer that" part of Article 4.

Several other systems of citation are also widely used. The First Part, or *Prima Pars,* is sometimes designated 1, 1a, or Ia; the First Part of the Second Part, or *Prima Secundae Partis,* is sometimes designated 1–2, 1a-2ae, or Ia-IIae; the Second Part of the Second Part, or *Secunda Secundae Partis,* is sometimes designated 2–2, 2a-2ae, or IIa-IIae; and the Third Part, or *Tertia Pars,* is sometimes designated 3, 3a, or IIIa. In an abbreviation like "1a-2ae," the "a" and "ae" are endings of the words *Prima* and *Secundae.* I should also mention that the body of an article is also sometimes called the *corpus,* abbreviated *cor.*

For the convenience of beginners, in quoting from works other than the *Summa,* such as the writings of Aristotle, whenever possible I use reliable editions that are in the public domain and are available on the Internet. Scholars, of course, will have their own favorite translations. When I provide quotations from the Bible, I most often use either the Douay-Rheims version (DRA), which is an English translation of the Latin Vulgate that St. Thomas used, and which is also employed by the Dominican Fathers; or the Revised Standard Version, Catholic Edition (RSV-CE), which is sometimes more clear and often more beautiful. Which translation I am using is always indicated in footnotes. When the chapter and verse divisions of the Douay-Rheims differ from those of more recent translations, I indicate this fact in footnotes too.

LAW ITSELF, IN GENERAL: QUESTIONS 90–92

Before Reading Question 90

St. Thomas views law as a rule and measure of distinctively human acts. As we see still more clearly later on, this makes it something *right* for humans to follow, something that "binds in conscience."[1] If we ask what conditions an enactment would have to satisfy in order to be such a thing, he replies that it must be an ordinance of reason, for the common good, made by those who have care for the community, and promulgated. To paraphrase, it must be something the mind can recognize as right, it must be good for community as such rather than just serving a special interest, it must be made by public authority rather than private individuals, and it must be made known – a secret or hopelessly obscure law is not a law at all.

Notice that this is a *fundamentally moral* approach to the definition of law. Against it stands something called legal positivism, the approach to law so dominant in contemporary law schools that law students may never hear of another. However, what positivists say is often misunderstood. Many positivists are perfectly happy to agree that law *ought* to be moral and just; that is not what they deny. So-called inclusive positivists even concede that at least in some legal systems, the question whether an enactment is moral plays a part in deciding whether it is a law in the first place, so that is not what they deny either. However, positivists insist

---

[1] The background is I-II, Q. 79, Art. 13, where St. Thomas remarks that "conscience is said to witness, to bind, or incite, and also to accuse, torment, or rebuke." In I-II, Q. 96, Art. 4, he will ask whether human law binds in conscience. The answer is that it does when it is just, because only then is it truly law, as defined here in Q. 90.

that even though such moral elements may sometimes be demanded, they are not logically necessary to the validity of law *as law*. *That* is what they deny.

To St. Thomas, the positivist enterprise would seem confused. For what does the positivist *mean* by the validity of law as law? Does he mean its authority? But authority is a *moral* concept – it means it is right that the precept be followed. If the positivist concedes this, then he has conceded St. Thomas's view. We may as well go on to the rest of St. Thomas's analysis – law is an ordinance of reason, for the common good, and so on.

But positivists don't think that authority *is* a moral concept. Some of them think that the term "authority" refers merely to the fact that law comes from a power people are accustomed to obey. Others think it refers simply to the fact that most of the time people do act as law tells them to. In the former case, we have Thomas Hobbes's and John Austin's definition of law as the command of the sovereign; in the latter case, H.L.A. Hart's definition of law as a system of conventional social rules.[2]

Neither definition works even on its own terms. The Hobbesian–Austinian definition leads to a circularity, because in order to know what law is we must consult the sovereign, but in order to know who the sovereign is, we must consult the law. Although the Hartian definition is not circular, it leads to an infinite regress. Law is something conventionally acknowledged to be a law. Acknowledged to be what? A law. But a law is what? Something conventionally acknowledged to be a law. And so on, ad infinitum.[3]

As viewed from St. Thomas's perspective, the circularity of the Hobbesian–Austinian definition and the infinite regress of the Hartian definition arise from two still deeper problems with legal positivism. The first: Generally speaking, people do not habitually obey edicts or conventions unless they do consider them right – or else they obey with resentment, because they *deny* the authority of these edicts. That is a moral issue. The second problem: Edicts and conventions are not self-interpreting. Generally speaking, even to figure out *what they mean* it is necessary to consider what is right. If we refuse to do so, we are literally

---

[2] See Thomas Hobbes, *Leviathan* (1651), John Austin, *The Province of Jurisprudence Determined* (1832), and H.L.A. Hart, *The Concept of Law* (Oxford: Oxford University Press, 1961, 1994). On the Continent, positivism is most often associated with Hans Kelsen, especially his work *Pure Theory of Law* (1934).

[3] My thinking concerning this double problem is in debt to conversations with my colleague, Robert C. Koons.

unable to obey, because we cannot figure out what is expected of us. That is a moral issue too.

I owe my favorite illustration of the latter point, that we must consider what is right even to know what the law means, to Professor Charles E. Rice. The 1932 *Restatement of Contracts* declares, "A promise which the promisor should reasonably expect to induce action or forbearance of a definite and substantial character on the part of the promisee and which does induce such action or forbearance is binding if injustice can be avoided only by enforcement of the promise."[4] Put more simply, if breaking a promise would cause injustice, then the promise is binding – but the *Restatement of Contracts* does not explain what "injustice" means. It expects readers to know that already. Now suppose language like this were contained in statutory law. In such a case, courts would be forced to work out some of the implications of the unwritten principles of justice, even if they were utterly deferential and their motive were merely to figure out what the statute meant by "injustice."

An Objector may say that in such a case the legislature has legislated badly. It should not have used undefined terms like "injustice" in the first place. It should have defined them. Go ahead, then; replace that word with a string of other words. What will result? Merely that the words in the string will also need definition. Suppose the Objector defines injustice as the violation of justice; then he must define justice. Suppose he defines justice, à la the *Corpus Juris Civilis* of Justinian, as "to live honestly, to hurt no one, to give everyone his due"; then he must define living honestly, hurting no one, and giving everyone his due. His difficulty is not vanishing; it is expanding, for although he can replace many undefined terms by defined terms, he cannot keep this up until nothing undefined is left. Unless he cheats, by allowing circularities, there will always be some rock-bottom undefined terms in terms of which all the rest of the terms are defined – and some of those undefined terms will inevitably have moral meaning. The moral of this story is that positive or man-made law points beyond itself; for the core of its meaning, it inevitably depends on morality.

The problem with defining authority in terms of a mere habit of obedience, then, is that both the willingness to obey and the ability to obey depend on recognized morality. If the positivist is trying to define morality out of the picture, then his enterprise is futile.

---

[4] *Restatement of Contracts* (American Law Institute, 1932), Section 90, "Promise Reasonably Inducing Definite and Substantial Action."

Suppose the positivist accepts these points. There is another move he might make, another way he might try to escape from the trap. He might become, so to speak, a hyper-positivist. That is, he might admit that authority is a moral concept, but say, "So what? Just as law is a system of conventional social rules, *so morality itself* is a system of conventional social rules – a custom, a convention, something we construct or invent." He would no longer say, like the old-fashioned sort of positivist, that law is independent of things, like morality, that we do not invent. Instead he would say that even if it does depend on morality, *we invent that too.* From law on down, it's constructs all the way!

Unfortunately for the hyper-positivist, this move would be equally futile, because it would miss morality's point. The whole idea of a moral law is that it binds us whether we like it or not. If it really were just a social convention – if we could make it up and change it to suit ourselves, so that we weren't bound unless we wanted to be – *then it wouldn't be morality.*

St. Thomas denies that the basic structure of morality is a construct. It is not rooted in human will and power. Rather it is rooted in nature, in the structure of creation, in the constitution of the human person – in something we cannot change by human will and power. In fact, as we will see, he holds that morality *stands in judgment* on human will and power. The good and the right are not things we invent, but things we discover. They are not constructs, but gifts. These gifts are the fount of the law.

St. Thomas's Prologue to Questions 90–92: Of the Essence of Law

TEXT	PARAPHRASE
[1] *We have now to consider the extrinsic principles of acts.* [2] *Now the extrinsic principle inclining to evil is the devil, of whose temptations we have spoken in the First Part, Q. 114. But the extrinsic principle moving to good is God,* [3] *Who both instructs us by means of His Law, and assists us by His Grace: wherefore in the first place we must speak of law; in the second place, of grace.*	Earlier in this *Summa,* we discussed the sources of acts, but we discussed only those sources that lie within us. Now we must turn to the sources that lie outside us. One such source is the devil, who prompts us to do evil. However, we have considered his temptations already. The other is God, who prompts us to do good, and who does so in two different ways. First, he prompts us through law, which *teaches* us to do good; this is the topic of the *Treatise on Law,* to which we are about to turn. Second, he does so through the gift of grace, which *strengthens* us to do good; this is the topic of the *Treatise on Grace,* which comes afterward.

[1]   In general, acts are the ways in which potentialities are brought into actuality. Here, St. Thomas is referring only to human acts, the ways in which the potentialities within human nature are brought into actuality. The principles of these acts are their beginnings, the sources from which they spring; *principium* is the word that Latin uses where Greek uses *arche* and English uses *beginning*. A good example is the first verse of the Gospel of John:

Greek   **En arche** en ho Logos, kai ho Logos en pros ton Theon, kai Theos en ho Logos

Latin (Vulgate)	**In principio** erat Verbum et Verbum erat apud Deum et Deus erat Verbum
English	**In the beginning** was the Word, and the Word was with God, and the Word was God.

St. Thomas says we now pass to the extrinsic principles of human acts, those that originate outside us, because he has already discussed their intrinsic principles, those that lie within us. As he has explained, their intrinsic principles are powers and habits. Powers, or capacities – means by which we act – have been discussed in I, Q. 77–83. Habits, or dispositions – tendencies that incline us to act in one way rather than another – have been discussed in I-II, Questions 49–77.

God is described as an extrinsic principle because He is distinct from us – he is not one of our own powers or habits. To say this is in no way to deny that we may experience his operations internally, for example when His grace pricks our conscience. For an analogy, we may think of how a signet ring impresses its form on the wax.

[2]   St. Thomas speaks of us being "moved" or "inclined" to evil rather than coerced to evil, because we have free will. He remarks earlier in the *Summa,* in I, Question 83, Art. 1, that without free will, "counsels, exhortations, commands, prohibitions, rewards, and punishments would be in vain." So the fact that our acts have extrinsic as well as intrinsic principles does not deprive us of personal responsibility.

We are moved to good by God. What is God? St. Thomas explains in I, Question 2, that if knowing what God is means knowing God's very essence, then we do not know what God is, for our intellects will not possess this knowledge until they are uplifted to the vision of God in heaven. As St. Paul wrote, "We see now through a glass in a dark manner; but then face to face. Now I know I part; but then I shall know even as I am known."[5] Yet even in this life we have a "general and confused" knowledge of God's existence. How so? Because the longing for perfect happiness that leaves nothing to be desired is implanted in us by nature; because everything to which our nature inclines us must exist, otherwise the desire would be pointless; and because it can be shown that such perfect happiness is not found in any created thing, but only in God. We can work out by reasoning many things *about* God, even though these fall short of knowing his essence: For example that he exists, that he is the first cause of all that is, that he is perfect in power, knowledge, and

[5] 1 Corinthians 13:12.

goodness, and that he is infinite, unchangeable, and eternal (I, Q. 2–26). Revelation takes us still further.

Although the topic of the devil is off the path of the *Treatise on Law*, a brief digression may not be amiss. There is, and can be, only one God, one uttermost good, one uttermost source of being. Satan is not another God – a negative God, so to speak – but only a created rational being, a fallen angel. St. Thomas observes that there is a fine gradation in created beings, from the lowest to the highest. If angels did not exist, then there would be an unexplained gap in this gradation. For this reason, he finds the biblical claims about angels to be reasonable not only from a theological but also from a philosophical point of view, for even though angels are infinitely short of God, these finite, non-bodily intellects occupy the rung between our finite, bodily intellects and God's infinite, non-bodily intellect. Now just as humans can sin through abuse of the gift of free will, so can angels, although, because angels are much greater, the consequences of their sins are much worse. The sin of the devil was desiring to be independent of God, desiring to have no happiness except that which he could provide to himself. From this desire arose an even more dangerous desire: "Since, then, what exists of itself is the cause of what exists of another, it follows from this furthermore that he sought to have dominion over others" (I., Question 63, Article 2.) The desire for dominion – a desire that we will also recognize in our own fallen selves, if we are honest – is what moves the devil to invent temptations.

[3] Law is an extrinsic principle of acts because it is promulgated by God, and in this sense comes from outside us. As we will see in Questions 91 and 93, however, in another sense it is inside us, for it finds an echo in our own created being; natural law is the "participation" of the rational creature in the eternal law. For this reason, obedience to God's law in no way diminishes human freedom. On the contrary, being made in his image,[6] we are most true to ourselves precisely when we are most true to him. This also shows that when Immanuel Kant distinguished between autonomy, or self-legislation, and heteronomy, or passive subjection to the law of another, he was posing a false alternative. To use an expression of John Paul II, the human sort of freedom is a third kind of thing, a "participated theonomy."[7]

---

[6] Genesis 1:27.
[7] John Paul II, encyclical letter *Veritatis Splendor* (6 August 1993), Sections 38–41.

Grace is the free gift of God – something God gives to us not because we have earned it, but *gratis* (I-II, Question 110, Art. 1). In this sense, even our nature is grace – as Russell Hittinger has reminded us, the "first grace" – because we did nothing to merit the gift of being.[8] However, the expression "grace" is normally used in a different sense, for those further gifts that assist nature and even raise it beyond its native powers. There are many kinds of supernatural grace, and the precise relationship between nature and grace is complex and subtle. But though nature is different from grace, it is made for and anticipates grace, as the dock is made for and anticipates the ship.

Here, of course, St. Thomas is distinguishing grace not from nature but from law. Like the distinction between nature and grace, the distinction between law and grace can be exaggerated so that it turns into a sheer contradiction. Our participation in the eternal law is itself an undeserved gift; our nature might have been so made that we were blindly pulled around by our impulses, yet we have been given a role in God's providence, something the subrational creatures cannot enjoy. But a further gift is the divine help that enables this participation to unfold. The need for extra help is charmingly conveyed by a parable in John Bunyan's *Pilgrim's Progress*.[9] A man attempts to sweep a parlor, but his efforts merely drive the dust into the air, and the room is as dirty as before. After a maid has sprinkled the dust with water, the man is able to sweep the dust into a pile and get rid of it. Law is like the broom; grace is like the sprinkling of water. Bunyan himself, committed to an un-Thomistic contradiction between law and grace, intended the parable to convey the point that the broom is useless. But the parable is better than Bunyan knew. What actually happens is that although the broom is useful and necessary, the sprinkling is also necessary so that the broom can achieve its end. So St. Thomas would view the matter.

[8] Russell Hittinger, *The First Grace: Recovering the Natural Law in a Post-Christian World* (Wilmington, DE: ISI Books, 2003), p. xi. Hittinger borrows the expression from a letter of retraction by the presbyter Lucidus, following the condemnation of certain doctrines at the Second Council of Arles in A.D. 473.

[9] John Bunyan, *The Pilgrim's Progress from This World to That Which Is to Come, in the Similitude of a Dream* (1678), Part 1, Section 2. The work is in the public domain and is available at many locations on the Internet, for example at www.ccel.org and www.bartleby.com.

[1] *Concerning law, we must consider: (1) Law itself in general; (2) its parts.* [2] *Concerning law in general three points offer themselves for our consideration: (1) Its essence; (2) The different kinds of law; (3) The effects of law.*	The *Treatise on Law* is in turn divided into two parts. The former part, Questions 90–92, considers law as such, and the latter part, Questions 93–108, considers each of the various kinds of law in depth. The former part is further divided into Question 90, which takes up the essence of law, Question 91, which presents a brief preface to the various kinds of law, and Question 92, which discusses the results that law brings about.

[1]   By the topic of law itself in general, St. Thomas means the general matters that serve as preliminaries to the discussion of law; by the parts of law he means its kinds. The various kinds of law are thus discussed twice: First, by way of orientation, in Question 91, under the rubric "law itself in general"; then, more fully, in Questions 93–108, under the rubric "its parts."

[2]   The essence of a thing is what defines it – *what it is.* In contemporary analytical philosophy, the essential qualities of a thing are often regarded as the properties it would have in all logically possible worlds. St. Thomas, however, is not thinking about logically possible worlds. What he means by the essential qualities of a thing are the properties it must have to be the kind of thing that it is, rather than some other kind of thing. Contemporary speech is uncomfortable with such ideas. We imagine that the essence of a thing is in the eye of the beholder. On the contrary, the essence of a thing is its underlying reality, the most fundamental thing about it, the thing about it *because of which* the other true things about it are also true.

The question St. Thomas proposes to discuss is the essence of law, but the idea may be clearer if we think of a more familiar essence, the essence of man. Man – the term includes both men and women – is our species. Rational animal is his definition, and expresses his essence. Animal is his genus, making him different from the angels, who are rational but not animal. Rationality is what distinguishes him from other species of animals, such as cats.

Animality and rationality are man's essential qualities, by contrast with, say, civilization and literacy. The latter are called "accidental" qualities, not in the sense that they come about by chance (after all, only a rational animal could *achieve* civilization and literacy), but in the sense that an uncivilized and illiterate man would yet be a man.[10] The definition of man as rational animal is not necessarily meant to exhaust his essential qualities, but only to say enough about them to get on with. No doubt, if Martians came into the picture, we would have to say more, if only to distinguish *that* kind of rational animal from *this* kind.

To say that the parts of law are the kinds of law is simple and clear. However, to prevent confusion later on we must add that St. Thomas distinguishes between several senses in which something can be called a part of something else. The *integral* parts of a principal thing (of a "something else") are the distinct elements that must concur for its perfection or completion. Thus, the roof is an integral part of a house. The *subjective* parts of a principal thing are its species or kinds. Thus, the species ox is a subjective part of the genus animal. The *potential* parts of a principal thing are various things connected with it, directed to certain secondary acts or matters, which do not have its whole power. Thus, filial piety, the reverence of children for their parents, is a potential part of the virtue of justice; it has something in common with justice because justice is giving to others what is due to them, but it does not have the full power of justice because it is impossible to give parents an equal return for what one owes them.[11] By the parts of law, then, St. Thomas means neither its integral nor its potential parts, but its subjective parts.

St. Thomas says that after a discussion of the essence of law culminating in its definition, and a brief distinction of its kinds, he will discuss its effects. The effects of law are the things that law does. For example, law commands, so in one sense a command may be called an effect of law. Law is also intended to accomplish certain results in the habits of the persons subject to it, so in another sense these habits may be called effects of the law.

---

[10] We might add that the characterization of man as a rational animal does not imply that the rational potentiality is always fully actualized, nor does it imply that those whose rational potentiality is not fully actualized are less than men. Children, persons with brain injuries, and even fools are full-fledged members of the human species and heirs to its dignity. Aristotle may seem to have disagreed, having famously remarked that "he who is unable to live in society, or who has no need because he is sufficient for himself, must be either a beast or a god" (Aristotle, *Politics,* trans. Benjamin Jowett, Book 1, Chapter 2.) However, Aristotle was referring to beings who *by nature* have no need for society. Persons in the categories I have mentioned certainly have need of it, but they are held back by immaturity, injury, or foolishness from fully enjoying its benefits.

[11] Strictly speaking, filial piety is a *quasi*-potential part of justice, but for present purposes the distinction between integral, subjective, and potential parts is sufficient. See II-II, Q. 80, Art. 1.

Under the first head there are four points of inquiry:	In order to understand the essence of law fully, Question 90 delves into four matters.
(1) Whether law is something pertaining to reason?	We ask in Article 1 whether something must appeal to reason to be true law; in Article 2,
(2) Concerning the end of law;	whether it must be directed to the common good to be true law; in Article 3, whether it
(3) Its cause;	must be enacted by legitimate public authority to be true law; and finally, in Article 4, whether
(4) The promulgation of law.	it must be made known to be true law.

By the cause of law, St. Thomas means what brings law into being. But if by a cause of a thing we mean whatever gives rise to it, whatever explains it, whatever is in any way its *reason why*, then there are four different senses in which the term "cause" may be used, and to give a rounded account of anything, we must identify all four.

St. Thomas borrows the fourfold classification of causes from Aristotle.[12] The pattern or functional organization of a thing is its *formal* cause, or *form*. The purpose for the sake of which it exists is its *final* cause, or *end*. The force, means, or agency by which it comes into being is its *efficient* cause, or *power*. The constituents or elements of which it is composed are its *material* cause, or *matter*. For example, the matter of the heart is muscle; its form is a functional arrangement of interlocking chambers; its power is embryogenesis; and its end is pumping blood. To head off confusions that might otherwise have arisen later on, let us add that for St. Thomas, the term "matter" has a broader meaning than it does in our own day. Matter is anything that can receive a form. The reason why muscle can serve as the matter of a heart is that it is able to take on the form of a heart. Different kinds of matter are in able to receive different forms, mostly because of the differences in the kinds of forms they have received already.

---

[12] Aristotle explains the matter as follows in *Metaphysics*, Book 5, Chapter 2: "'Cause' means (1) that from which, as immanent material, a thing comes into being, e.g. the bronze is the cause of the statue and the silver of the saucer, and so are the classes which include these. (2) The form or pattern, i.e. the definition of the essence, and the classes which include this (e.g. the ratio 2:1 and number in general are causes of the octave), and the parts included in the definition. (3) That from which the change or the resting from change first begins; e.g. the adviser is a cause of the action, and the father a cause of the child, and in general the maker a cause of the thing made and the change-producing of the changing. (4) The end, i.e. that for the sake of which a thing is; e.g. health is the cause of walking." I am using the translation of W.D. Ross, available online at ebooks.adelaide. edu.au/a/aristotle/metaphysics.

St. Thomas is proposing to give an account of the four causes not of the heart, but of the law. His first point of inquiry addresses its form, his second its end, his third its power, and his fourth its matter. In the strict sense of the term, the essence of law is expressed by its formal cause alone, discussed in Article 1. But St. Thomas brings in its other three causes, in Articles 2–4, because they are essentially connected with its formal cause.

Among the decisive events in modern thought has been rising skepticism, first, about whether the formal and final causes of natural things can be known, and second, whether human institutions such as marriage, family, civil society, and law can be said to be natural. Adding doubt to doubt, today many legal thinkers try to define law solely in terms of its material and efficient causes. As we go along, we will try to grasp why this way of thinking makes a difference, and why St. Thomas would reject it.

For further reflection on the preceding section of the *Treatise on Law,* the online *Companion to the Commentary,* accessible via the Resources link at the book's catalogue webpage, includes a discussion of the following topic:

THE ARCHITECTURE OF LAW

Question 90, Article 1:
Whether Law Is Something Pertaining to Reason?

TEXT	PARAPHRASE
Whether law is something pertaining to reason?	To be truly law, must a thing be reasonable? Must it relate in some essential way to reason?

The Latin word St. Thomas uses for "reason," *rationis,* is in the genitive case, so it would be equally correct for the English version of the question to ask whether law is something "of" reason. Law is of reason, or pertains to reason, if it is of the nature of reason, if it is reasonable in its very essence. Nothing unreasonable, and nothing related to reason in a merely accidental or contingent way, is truly the sort of thing law is.

[1] *Objection 1. It would seem that law is not something pertaining to reason.* [2] *For the Apostle says (Romans 7:23):* *"I see another law in my members," etc.* [3] *But nothing pertaining to reason is in the members; since the reason*	Objection 1. Apparently, to be truly law, a thing does *not* have to relate in some essential way to the power of reason. For reasoning is not a bodily activity, yet, as St. Paul says in his letter to the Romans, he sees a

does not make use of a bodily organ. Therefore law is not something pertaining to reason.

law of some kind in his bodily parts and appetites. If a law can be in something unrelated to reason, then law does not have to be reasonable to be what it is.

---

[1] To say that "law is something pertaining to reason" is to say that it pertains to the very essence of law to be reasonable rather than arbitrary, to address itself to the intellect rather than merely the will, to be something that the mind can recognize as right. The objections deny that this is essential to true law.

[2] Because St. Thomas could expect his readers to be familiar with the Bible, he often quotes only a few words to indicate the passage that he has in mind. The context of this passage is the seventh chapter of St. Paul's letter to the young church at Rome, in which he discusses the dislocation, which only Christ can cure, in the heart of fallen man. Offering himself as a paradigm case, St. Paul says in verses 22–23, "For I am delighted with the law of God, according to the inward man: But I see another law in my members, fighting against the law of my mind, and captivating me in the law of sin, that is in my members" (DRA). By his "members" he means the organs of his body along with the appetites that are "in" or associated with them. St. Paul is not arguing that all sins are sensual, because there are intellectual sins too. Nor is he arguing that the sensual appetites are bad in themselves, bad by nature, because everything God creates is good; taking the term "nature" in its proper sense, there is no such thing as an evil nature. Rather St. Paul's point is that these appetites are in a bad *condition,* for ever since the Fall, they have been disobedient to the mind. The whole matter of the Pauline "law of the members" is threshed out by St. Thomas at a later point in the *Treatise on Law.* Here, though, we are hearing the Objector's view.

[3] The Objector argues as follows. (1) St. Paul speaks of a law "in" the bodily organs. (2) This law has nothing in common with reason, because nothing pertaining to the mind is "in" the bodily organs. Therefore (3) law does not have to be reasonable to be law.

I note in passing that when the Objector says "nothing pertaining to reason is in the members," he is expressing a blunter view of the relation between mind and body than that of St. Thomas himself, who says in I-II, Q. 48, Art. 3: "Although the mind or reason makes no use of a bodily organ in its proper act, yet, since it needs certain sensitive powers for the execution of its act, the acts of which powers are hindered when the body is disturbed, it follows of necessity that any disturbance in the body hinders even the judgment of reason; as is clear in the case of drunkenness or sleep." St. Thomas understands perfectly well that the mind needs the body *in order* to reason, so that the body affects the mind, just as the mind affects the body. Even so, reasoning as such is not a bodily act.

The pairing of the opening sentence of the Objection, "It would seem that law is not something pertaining to reason," with its closing sentence, "Therefore law is not something pertaining to reason," seems tedious to us, but would not have seemed so to St. Thomas's contemporaries. Used in this way, it forms an instance of the rhetorical device called *inclusio,* also known as "envelope structure." *Inclusio* marks out the boundaries of a unit of argument by using similar language, or referring to similar ideas, at the beginning and end. Though it is often overlooked, the device is well-known in the ancient and medieval world, and is common to Greek and Latin literature, to both the Old and New Testaments of the Bible, and to English literature from the time of *Beowulf* if not earlier, not to mention the literature of other languages. Of course it would have been obvious that Objection 1 forms a unit even without its conspicuous *inclusio.* Sometimes, however, a reader who is unaware of this device will completely miss the thematic divisions in a unit of poetry or prose, for example, the way that the Lord's Prayer is illuminated by the envelope which is opened and closed by the phrase "in heaven." The literal words of the envelope are "Our Father which art in heaven, Hallowed be thy name. Thy kingdom come. Thy will be done on earth as it is in heaven." But the implied meaning of the clauses inside the envelope is "Our Father which art in heaven: Hallowed be thy Name on earth as it is in heaven. Thy Kingdom come on earth as it is in heaven. Thy Will be done on earth as it is in heaven."[13]

Besides *inclusio,* St. Thomas employs a variety of classical rhetorical devices in the *Summa.* One of the risks of the freer style of paraphrase I sometimes use is that, by rearranging phrases, it may obscure some of them. Partly for that reason, from time to time I call attention to important literary devices which might otherwise be overlooked. So far as I

---

[13] I draw this classical example from Richard G. Moulton, *The Literary Study of the Bible: An Account of the Leading Forms of Literature Represented in the Sacred Writings* (London: Isbister, 1896), pp. 69–70.

know, no one has made a comprehensive study of St. Thomas's rhetorical figures, but such effort would be richly repaid.[14]

| [1] *Objection 2. Further, in the reason there is nothing else but power, habit, and act.* [2] *But law is not the power itself of reason. In like manner, neither is it a habit of reason: because the habits of reason are the intellectual virtues of which we have spoken above (57).*[15] *Nor again is it an act of reason: because then law would cease, when the act of reason ceases, for instance, while we are asleep. Therefore law is nothing pertaining to reason.* | Objection 2. Moreover, if we seek to classify the things that relate essentially to reason, we find only capacities, dispositions, and instances of actual reasoning. Law is not the capacity to reason. Nor is it one of the dispositions connected with reasoning, which we have discussed already. Nor is it an act of reasoning, because in that case law would not exist while we are sleeping. Since law isn't any of these things, it must not be related essentially to reason. |

---

[1]   The powers of reason are its capacities, the habits of reason are the dispositions by which these powers are exercised, and the act of reason is its actuality, what it is or what it is doing when its sleeping potentialities are awakened. Now the act of reason is "in" reason, meaning that it pertains to reason. Because the act of reason springs from its powers and habits, these powers and habits may be said to be "in" reason or to pertain to reason too. What else is "in" reason? According to the Objector, nothing else; that's it.

[2]   The Objector argues that if nothing pertains to reason but its powers, habits, and acts, then in order to say that law pertains to reason, law must be either a power of reason, a habit of reason, or the very actuality of reason. Obviously, it is not a power of reason; this is so plain that no argument need be given. Neither is it one of the intellectual dispositions by which these powers are exercised, such as practical wisdom, also called prudence, because these have already been classified in I-II, Question 57, and law was not one of them. Finally, it is not the very actuality of reason – by contrast with the mere potentiality – because in that case, law would go to sleep when the mind goes to sleep, and obviously, this does not happen. Therefore, says the Objector, law is not one of the things that pertain to reason.

---

[14]   I gratefully acknowledge the stimulation of many conversations with my friends Arlen Nydam, a close student of Latin poetry, and William Dickson, who first called *inclusio* to my attention.

[15]   Like this one, most cross-references and references to other works are provided not by St. Thomas himself, but by the translators. In the rare instances in which a citation is erroneous, I correct it in a footnote.

[1] *Objection 3. Further, the law moves those who are subject to it to act aright.* [2] *But it belongs properly to the will to move to act, as is evident from what has been said above (9, 1). Therefore law pertains, not to the reason, but to the will;* [3] *according to the words of the Jurist (Lib. i, ff., De Const. Prin. leg. i):* "*Whatsoever pleaseth the sovereign, has force of law.*"	Objection 3. Still further, law prompts those who are subject to the law to act the right way. But as we saw earlier in the *Summa*, what prompts us to act is the will. Therefore, law is based on will, not on reason. The great jurist Ulpian says the same thing: "Whatever pleases the foremost man has the force of law."

[1]   Here the Objector anticipates something that St. Thomas himself will assert: That for those who are under the law, law functions as a rule of action. Its function is to command us, "Do this," so that we do it.

[2]   The Objector holds that commanding us to "Do this" pertains not to reason but the will. Therefore, law too must pertain not to reason but to will. He tries to call St. Thomas's own arguments to his aid, for as St. Thomas had said in I-II, Question 9, Art. 1, "the will moves the other powers of the soul to their acts, for we make use of the other powers when we will. For the end and perfection of every other power, is included under the object of the will as some particular good: and always the art or power to which the universal end belongs, moves to their acts the arts or powers to which belong the particular ends included in the universal end. Thus the leader of an army, who intends the common good – i.e. the order of the whole army – by his command moves one of the captains, who intends the order of one company."

As we will see, however, the Objector is taking these words out of context. Whenever St. Thomas uses the term "act," he is not thinking, as we do, of mere behavior – of something that I happen to do – but of *the actualization of a potentiality inherent in something*. One of the questions we always need to ask, then, is "inherent in what?" St. Thomas is preparing to explain that in this case, the "what" is reason.

[3]   This time the Objector calls to his aid the Roman *iurisconsult*, or legal authority, Ulpian, who seemed to say that law springs not from the reason of the *princeps* (literally, the first or foremost man, who in Rome was the emperor), but from his will – what "pleases" or is agreeable to him (*placuit*).[16]

---

[16] Ulpian's statement is quoted in *Digest*, Book 1, Title 4, Section 1. Compare his statement that the sovereign is exempt from the laws, discussed in Q. 96, Art. 5, Obj. 3 and ad 3.

Whatever one may think of this particular maxim – taking it in the Objector's sense, the English common law detested it, but as we see shortly, St. Thomas takes a very different view of it than the Objector does – the appeal to a traditionally accepted body of legal maxims is not a mere antiquarian quirk. Such maxims reflected a reservoir of the community's legal wisdom, hard-won by the convergence of many minds over centuries and tested in practice. In most cases, legal maxims were much more specific than the first principles of natural law, and they did not, like them, hold without exception. However, they were viewed as derivations from the first principles, and functioned as a basis for the derivation of further conclusions still.

Our own law too once depended on traditional juristic maxims to reach and justify legal decisions, such as *consuetudo est altera lex,* "custom is another law, *delegatus non potest delegare*, "a delegate cannot delegate," *nemo debet esse judex in propria causa*, "no one can be judge in his own cause," and *nemo tenetur ad impossibile*, "no one is required to do what is impossible." For centuries, such maxims shaped and nourished the minds of would-be advocates, judges, rulers, and legislators. Thus Sir John Fortescue recommends to the young English prince-in-exile, who prefers military exercises, that in but a year of study he could learn the elements "from which all the laws of the realm proceed" – especially those precepts "which those learned in the laws of England and mathematicians alike call maxims."[17] The waning of maxim jurisprudence in our own day probably reflects the rising disorder and contentiousness of legal thought in general.[18]

On the contrary, It belongs to the law to command and to forbid. But it belongs to reason to command, as stated above (17, 1). Therefore law is something pertaining to reason.	**On the other hand,** it has traditionally been held that commanding and forbidding are functions of law. But as we saw earlier, what commands is reason. From this it follows that law *must* be essentially reasonable to be law.

[17] John Fortescue, *In Praise of the Laws of England,* trans. S.B. Chrimes, rev. Shelley Lockwood, in Shelley Lockwood, ed., *Sir John Fortescue: On the Laws and Governance of England* (Cambridge: Cambridge University Press, 1997), pp. 14–15.
[18] For an intriguing discussion of the past, present, and possible future of maxim jurisprudence, see J. Stanley McQuade, "Ancient Legal Maxims and Modern Human Rights," 18 *Campbell Law Review* 75–120 (1996).

Having presented the objections, we now turn to a sympathetic restatement of the traditional view, the one the objections reject. Normally, when the *sed contra* or "on the other hand" cites someone, it cites a traditional authority. In this case that is not necessary, because the particular aspect of the traditional view that is here on display has already been discussed in I-II, Question 17, Article 1, "Whether command is an act of the reason or of the will?"

The tradition *agrees* with the Objector's claim that commanding and forbidding are functions of law, and St. Thomas returns to the point later, in Q. 92, Art. 2. But the tradition *disagrees* with the Objector's view that commanding and forbidding are functions of will alone, in isolation from reason. What St. Thomas had explained in Question 17 was that will functions only in partnership with reason, and reason functions only in partnership with will: "Command is an act of the reason presupposing, however, an act of the will. In proof of this, we must take note that, since the acts of the reason and of the will can be brought to bear on one another, in so far as the reason reasons about willing, and the will wills to reason, the result is that the act of the reason precedes the act of the will, and conversely." This means *the fact there is a command* requires an act of will, but *what the command directs* requires an act of reason.[19] This is true, by the way, not only when we are reasoning well, but even when we are reasoning badly, for example when we casually treat as good whatever the senses present as good, without investigation.

---

[1] *I answer that,* [2] *Law is a rule and measure of acts, whereby man is induced to act or is restrained from acting:* [3] *for "lex" [law] is derived from "ligare" [to bind], because it binds one to act.* [4] *Now the rule and measure of human acts is*

Here is my response. Law is both the governing ordinance and the measuring rod for distinctively human acts, because it makes us do the right thing in the right way. This is confirmed by the very origin of the Latin word for law, for it comes from an earlier word meaning "to bind," reflecting the fact that law binds us to act. As I made clear earlier, the governing ordinance and measuring rod of distinctively

---

[19] See also I-II, Q. 9, Art. 1, ad 3: "The will moves the intellect as to the exercise of its act; since even the true itself which is the perfection of the intellect, is included in the universal good, as a particular good. But as to the determination of the act, which the act derives from the object, the intellect moves the will; since the good itself is apprehended under a special aspect as contained in the universal true. It is therefore evident that the same is not mover and moved in the same respect." In other words, the will prompts the intellect to carry out the act, but the intellect prompts the will by presenting its object to it, so that it wills the very thing that it does.

the reason, which is the first principle of human acts, as is evident from what has been stated above (1, 1, ad 3); since it belongs to the reason to direct to the end, which is the first principle in all matters of action, according to the Philosopher (Phys. ii). [5] Now that which is the principle in any genus, is the rule and measure of that genus: for instance, unity in the genus of numbers, and the first movement in the genus of movements. Consequently it follows that law is something pertaining to reason.

human acts is the source from which they spring, the power of reason, because, as Aristotle teaches, the source from which all actions spring is the end that we seek, and reason is what directs us to this end.

To speak more generally, in any genus whatsoever, the governing principle and measuring rod for the things of that genus is whatever they spring from. For example, all numbers in the genus of numbers begin from unity, so unity is the governing ordinance and measuring rod of numbers; and all changes spring ultimately from the first cause of change, so the first cause of change is the governing ordinance and measuring rod of changes. We see from all this that law is essentially related to reason after all.

---

[1]   The fact that the "on the contrary" and the "I answer that" come to the same conclusion should not blur the difference between them. In the former, St. Thomas was restating the tradition; here he is presenting his own argument.

[2]   Wittgenstein once remarked that "The work of the philosopher consists in assembling reminders for a particular purpose."[20] Although Wittgenstein was no Thomist, with this point St. Thomas would agree. In his statement that law is a rule and measure of acts, St. Thomas is not dropping a formula upon us from on high, but reminding us of something we all know already. The discussion in Articles 1 through 4 unfolds this piece of knowledge one part at a time. Readers who wish to explore the "dialectical" character of this unfolding discussion may consult the online *Companion to the Commentary*. Here we consider its four phases one at a time, and Article 1 is the first.

To say that law is a *rule* of acts is to say that it tells us what to do; to say that it is a *measure* of acts is to say that it presents a standard with which our acts can be compared and by which they can be evaluated. But following a rule and measuring ourselves according to a standard are operations of reason. This is the point of St. Thomas's reference to *man*:

---

[20] Ludwig Wittgenstein, *Philosophical Investigations*, 3rd ed., trans. G.E.M. Anscombe (Oxford: Basil Blackwell, 1953, 1972), Section 127, p. 50.

He is not contrasting us with angels, who are also rational and bound by law, but with subrational animals. Animals are certainly subject to law in an analogical sense; the rational order of providence can be perceived in the design of their impulses. But they do not perceive that order; we do. *To them,* it is not law, but merely urge. In the strict sense, then, law – far from being a fetter – is a privilege of the rational mind.

Another way to think of the difference between rational and subrational animals is by analogy with dynamic physical systems. A subrational animal is extremely stable, not in the sense that it never changes, but in the sense that in most cases, its inbuilt impulses allow it to go only one way: It will fight, flee, mate, eat, whatever the dominant impulse of the moment requires. It is like a cart built for rolling downhill, which is very difficult to slow down, speed up, or steer. Though the cart has no pilot, it doesn't need one, because it will almost inevitably arrive just as far down the hill as it can go. In most cases that is fine, because as far down as possible is the right place to be. But the cart doesn't know what it is doing, so if the bottom of the hill is the wrong place to be, it will go there anyway.

By contrast, the rational creature is *unstable,* not in the sense that it cannot be controlled, but in the sense that it *requires* control. In fact it is designed to require it. Because its inbuilt impulses are pushing it in a dozen conflicting directions at once, it is very easy to direct; it is like an airplane that can go up, down, right, left, fast, or slow. Unlike the cart, however, it does need a pilot, a skilled and knowledgeable directive intelligence who knows what each control surface is for and can get the craft to a safe landing at its destination. Law is like the rules of flying, along with a map, on which the destination is marked. The map doesn't interfere with a journey by flight; it makes the journey possible.

[3] Modern etymologists believe that the Latin word *lex* is derived not from *ligare,* to bind, but from *legere,* to gather or read.[21] But the point is not whether St. Thomas got the etymology right. His faulty etymology functions not as a proof, but merely as an additional way of reminding us of something we already know. It is as though he had added, "We all understand law to be something that binds us. In fact, in Latin the very word for law comes from the notion of binding." As it turns out, that isn't really where it comes from, but what he thinks we all understand, we really do.

[21] Oxford English Dictionary, online version, entry for *law, n. 1.*

Interestingly, St. Thomas mentions the other hypothesis, that the word *lex* is derived from *legere,* in Article 4. We will comment on it when we come to it.

[4]   Here St. Thomas asserts what earlier in the paragraph he had only implied. Law is the rule and measure of *human* acts, and acts are properly called *human* only when they arise in the way that is distinctive to human nature. He had argued in I-II, Q. 1, that "man differs from irrational animals in this, that he is master of his actions." He is their master through a *deliberate will,* which means a will formed by rational deliberation with a view to some end perceived as good. The fact that deliberation begins by considering the end or purpose to be accomplished had been analyzed by Aristotle in *Physics,* Book 2, Chapter 9.

In passing, we should give some attention to the third objection in I-II, Q. 1, that "man does many things without deliberation, sometimes not even thinking of what he is doing; for instance when one moves one's foot or hand, or scratches one's beard, while intent on something else. Therefore man does not do everything for an end." St. Thomas replies to the objection, not that human beings never engage in such behaviors, but that they are not properly called "human acts," because they do not engage our distinctively human powers. Law is not a rule and measure of behaviors we perform without noticing, or of things we do while thinking of something else, but of acts that arise from a deliberate will.

[5]   The reasoning here is dependent on Aristotle, *Metaphysics,* Book 10 (Iota). It is a bit compressed because St. Thomas's "beginners" would have been familiar with that work already. Let us expand the argument a little. Obviously, the rule and measure for anything must be appropriate to the kind of thing it is. To be appropriate, it must be the *same sort* of thing, of the same genus, "homogeneous" with it. But not just any member of the genus is suitable to serve as the rule and measure for the others; we must identify the member of the genus from which the other members spring.

Numbers, for example, arise from the multiplication of unity. Therefore, the way to measure numbers is to consider how many unities are in them; two contains more multiples of unity than one, three more multiples of unity than two, and so on. "Movements," by which St. Thomas means changes,[22] arise as effects of logically prior causes. Therefore, the way to

---

[22]   We use the term movements for changes in *location,* which St. Thomas calls "local movements." But a change in, say, temperature, is also in his sense a kind of movement.

measure movements is to arrange them by their remoteness to the first cause of movement; the second effect in the chain is more remote than the first effect, the third effect is more remote than the second, and so on. Now in both of these examples, we are measuring things according to sequential order, but that is only one sort of order. The crucial point is that things are measured and set in order according to that from which they spring. From what then do distinctively human actions spring? From a deliberate will, a will formed by rational deliberation with a view to some end perceived as good. Therefore, the rule and measure appropriate to distinctively human actions – which we are calling law – must also address itself to reason, and also has reference to the good.

---

[1] *Reply to Objection 1.* *Since law is a kind of rule and measure, it may be in something in two ways. First, as in that which measures and rules: and since this is proper to reason, it follows that, in this way, law is in the reason alone. Secondly, as in that which is measured and ruled.* **[2]** *In this way, law is in all those things that are inclined to something by reason of some law: so that any inclination arising from a law, may be called a law, not essentially but by participation as it were.* **[3]** *And thus the inclination of the members to concupiscence is called "the law of the members."*

Reply to Objection 1. Law is a kind of governing ordinance and measuring rod, but in general, such a thing may be said to be "in" something in either of two ways. First, it may be said to be "in" the thing that does the measuring and governing. We may infer that in this sense, law is "in" reason, and not in anything else. Second, it may be said to be "in" the thing that is measured and governed. We may infer that in this sense, law is in everything over which law rules. So a disposition that arises from a law may itself be called a "law," not in the former sense (because it is not *essentially* law), but, so to speak, by participating or sharing in law's nature. It is in this latter sense that St. Paul calls the inclination of our sensual appetites to resist reason their *law*.

---

[1]   Since the Objector denies that law is "in" reason, and since St. Thomas holds that law is a kind of rule and measure, he investigates the senses in which a rule and measure can be said to be "in" something. First, it can be said to be "in" *the thing that is doing* the measuring and ruling, second, it can be said to be "in" *the thing that is done* according to that measure and rule.

For instance, when the ballerina is practicing dance, she is guided by her conception of the dance. This conception is "in" her mind or reason essentially, because that is where it is operating. But in another sense – by participation, so to speak – it is "in" the practiced habits of her body, because that is where it has its effect.

[2]   Now it is just the same with law as it is with the conception in the ballerina's mind. In its essence, law is "in" reason, and nowhere else. By participation, however, it may also be said to be "in" every inclination that is governed by law, in her case her trained habits of physical movement.

[3]   At first this concluding line seems to come out of nowhere. How does what has been said help us solve the puzzle of the "the law of the members"? Reason might be "in" the sensual desires, by participation, if they are obedient to reason – but isn't St. Paul's whole point that they *aren't* obedient to reason? This is one of the rare places in which, instead of building upon something that he has said earlier, St. Thomas anticipates something that he is not going to explain fully until later on, in Q. 91, Art. 6. What he says is that even though the disorder of our sensual appetites is *disobedient* to the rule of reason, nevertheless, in another sense it *arises* from the rule of reason. How could this be? The key is to recognize that something can arise from a rule in two different ways. In one sense, it arises from the rule only if it obeys the rule. In another sense, it arises from the rule if it is a penalty or consequence for disobedience, but one which arises from the nature of the rule itself. That is just what happens here. By habitually refusing to subordinate our desires to the rule of reason, we breed in them a habitual insubordination to the rule of reason. Eventually we cannot make them obey reason even when we want to, like a pilot who has lost control of his craft. Considered from a historical perspective, that is how original sin works; considered from the perspective of a single life, that is how actual sin works.

---

[1] *Reply to Objection 2. Just as, in external action, we may consider the work and the work done, for instance the work of building and the house built; so in the acts of reason, we may consider the act itself of reason, i.e. to understand and to reason, and something produced by this act.* [2] *With regard to the speculative reason, this is first of all the definition; secondly, the proposition; thirdly, the syllogism or argument.* [3] *And since also the practical reason makes use of a syllogism in respect of the work to be done, as stated above (13, 3;*

Reply to Objection 2. In external actions, we distinguish between the work itself and the result that the work accomplishes – for example, between the work of building, and the house that the work of building accomplishes. In just the same way, we may distinguish between the act of reason itself (understanding and reasoning) and the result that this act accomplishes. Taken in order, the results accomplished by theoretical reason are the definition, the proposition, and the syllogism or argument.

76, 1) and since as the Philosopher teaches (Ethic. vii, 3); hence we find in the practical reason something that holds the same position in regard to operations, as, in the speculative intellect, the proposition holds in regard to conclusions. [4] Such like universal propositions of the practical intellect that are directed to actions have the nature of law. [5] And these propositions are sometimes under our actual consideration, while sometimes they are retained in the reason by means of a habit.

But as we saw at a previous stage (and as taught by Aristotle), practical reasoning too uses syllogisms. It employs them to decide what is to be done, for the *decision* of a practical syllogism corresponds to the *conclusion* of a theoretical syllogism. The universal propositions with which practical syllogisms begin have the nature of law. They are not always in the mind as thoughts, but they are always in the mind as dispositional tendencies.

[1] This is very much like the distinction St. Thomas made in the reply to the previous objection. In our example of the ballerina, the work is practice, and the work done is the skill that this practice forms.

[2] The old-fashioned expression "speculative reason" makes most contemporary readers think of extravagant exercises of imagination, which we have come to call "speculations." That is not what St. Thomas has in mind, and today most translations use the expression "theoretical reason" instead. The Latin root *speculatio* and the Greek root *theoria* have essentially the same meaning: To view, to scrutinize, to consider.

Speculative or theoretical reasoning is reasoning directed simply to knowledge; by contrast, practical reasoning is reasoning directed toward choosing a course of action in the light of an end. St. Thomas is pointing out that just as in building a house (or practicing ballet), so too in speculative or theoretical reason, we may distinguish between the work itself and the thing that the work achieves. The exercise of building a house achieves a house; the exercise of practicing ballet achieves skill; the exercise of speculative or theoretical reason achieves definitions, propositions, and syllogisms.

[3] In the case of an ordinary syllogism, the premises and the conclusion are all propositions. For example, from the propositions "All men are mortal" and "Socrates is a man" follows the proposition "Socrates is mortal." In the case of what St. Thomas and Aristotle call a practical syllogism, however, the result is not a proposition, but a decision or judgment, followed by a choice (I-II, Q. 13, Art. 1, ad 2, and I-II, Q. 76, Art. 1). For example, from the proposition "Health is good," which supposes the appropriateness of pursuing it, and the proposition "Moderation in

eating promotes health," which tells how to accomplish it, a man with self-control arrives at the decision to practice moderation in eating, and he chooses to do so. Plainly, the *decision* to practice moderation because it is good is not the same as the *proposition* that it would be good to practice moderation; the former is an act of the will. However, this act of the will holds the same place in a practical syllogism that the concluding proposition holds in an ordinary syllogism.

[4] In the preceding example of a practical syllogism, the universal proposition, also called the major premise, was "Health is good." But the practical intellect makes use of many such universal propositions. Because these propositions are what the deliberate choice springs from, they are its rule and measure, and so they have the nature of law. This explains in what sense law pertains to reason even though nothing is "in" reason but powers, habits, and actions; the fact that nothing else is "in" reason is beside the point.

[5] Although St. Thomas has finished replying to the objection, he makes one more point to forestall a possible confusion. Although in a certain sense we always know the universal propositions he has just been speaking about, this does not mean that we are always thinking about them; they may also operate in the background, as *dispositions* of the mind, so that we deliberate *as though* we were thinking about them. For example, I may do something for the sake of health, even though at no point do I think to myself "Step one. Health is good, therefore …"

Sometimes the question arises whether St. Thomas's distinction between habitual and actualized knowledge is the same as the contemporary distinction between conscious and unconscious knowledge. I think it would be better to say that the contemporary distinction is an unsuccessful attempt to get at what the Thomistic distinction gets at more successfully. When we call knowledge "conscious," we seem to mean that it is under actual consideration. But when we call knowledge "unconscious," we do not seem to be able to make up our minds what we mean. It is as though we were trying to say that we are thinking about something, and at the same time that we are not thinking about it. When the inconsistency of this way of speaking is pointed out to us, we say "I am thinking of the thing in my unconscious mind, not my conscious mind. I don't have conscious access to what I am thinking unconsciously." But if I don't have access to my unconscious mind, then in what sense is it really "my mind?" St. Thomas might suggest, "Don't say that you are both thinking and yet not thinking about something, or thinking about it in what both is and yet is not your real mind. Rather say that you have *one* mind, but its operations are subtle and complex. Even when you are not actually thinking about something, you may actually think of it at any moment, and in the meantime, your mind may continue to be dispositionally influenced by it."

---

[1] *Reply to Objection 3. Reason has its power of moving from the will, as stated above (17, 1): for it is due to the fact that one wills the end, that the reason issues its commands as regards things ordained to the end.* [2] *But in order that the volition of what is commanded may have the nature of law, it needs to be in accord with some rule of reason.* [3] *And in this sense is to be understood the saying that the will of the sovereign has the force of law; otherwise the sovereign's will would savor of lawlessness rather than of law.*

Reply to Objection 3. Reason draws its ability to prompt us to action from the will. First reason sees what action the end in view requires, then, by means of the will, it commands it. But the former step is crucial, because for the underlying volition to be true law, it really must be directed by reason. For Ulpian's statement about the will or pleasure of the sovereign having the force of law to be true, it must be taken in this sense, not in the Objector's sense.

---

[1]   Remember the point made earlier: Reason and will function together, not in isolation. The function of reason is to identify the purpose that is to be pursued, which is always some good, and to work out what must be done to achieve it. The bodily senses present their own images of what is good, but reason need not accept these images at face value. It recognizes not just what seems good to appetite but also other kinds of goods; it takes account of circumstances; it ponders which goods are more important and which are less; and it distinguishes between what is really good and what merely seems to be good. The function of will, in turn, is to command what reason has indicated.

[2]   Without reason, will would not know what to will; but reason commands *through* will. Without will, reason would be unable to command.

[3]   The Objector took Ulpian's statement that "Whatsoever pleaseth the sovereign, has force of law," to mean that whatever the sovereign wills *even in isolation from reason* has force of law. Rather than saying that Ulpian's statement is wrong, St. Thomas says it is wrong *taken in that sense.* If taken in a different sense – which he considers its proper sense – it is perfectly reasonable: That whatever the sovereign wills *in accordance with reason* has the force of law.

For further reflection on the preceding section of the *Treatise on Law,* the online *Companion to the Commentary,* accessible via the Resources link at the book's catalogue webpage, includes a discussion of the following topic:

THE "DIALECTICAL" MOVEMENT OF QUESTION 90

Question 90, Article 2:
Whether the Law Is Always Something Directed to the Common Good?

TEXT	PARAPHRASE
Whether the law is always something directed to the common good?	To be truly law, must a thing have as its purpose the good of the whole community, rather than merely the good of particular individuals or groups? If it were directed merely to private purposes, would it fail to be true law?

The Latin expression St. Thomas uses here for the shared or common good is *bonum commune,* which can equally be translated "the good of the community." He is thinking of the community not merely as an aggregation of individuals who may be at odds with each other, but as a true partnership in a truly good life. To further develop the idea, however, we need to distinguish between two senses in which a good can be common.

In the weak sense of the term, a good is common merely when it is good for everyone, like pure water. Different people in the community may enjoy different amounts of goods that are common in this weak sense. In fact, if one person grabs more of a weakly common good, then other people have less. For example, I might divert part of the river away from your property and onto mine.

In the strong sense of the term, though, a good is common when one person's gain is *not* another's loss, so that our interests literally cannot diverge. For example, the goods of character are strongly common – I do not become less wise, or less just, or less courageous, just because my neighbor becomes more so. Another example of a strongly common good is the security of the community – if you and I are fellow citizens, and our country is invaded by a hostile power, then it is invaded for both of us. It is impossible for our country to be invaded for you but not for me.

Sometimes St. Thomas uses the expression "common good" in the strong sense, but sometimes only in the weak. One must pay close attention to keep from getting mixed up. Consider his discussion of distributive justice in II-II, Q. 61, Arts. 1–2. Distributive justice is the allocation of certain things to members of the community according to what is due to them. Now it is good for the community as a whole that its greatest benefactors attain the highest honors and offices; everyone is better off as a result. This shows us that distributive justice is a strongly common good. But St. Thomas also calls the honors and offices themselves "common goods." What kind then are they? Since some citizens receive a greater share of them than others, obviously they are not common in the strong sense; they are merely things that anyone may see as good. We see then that although distributive justice is a strongly common good, the things that it distributes are only weakly common goods.

More broadly, the aspect of justice that concerns the common good is called "general" justice. Special justice is doing good and avoiding evil in relation to my neighbor, with a view to what I owe him. But general justice is doing good and avoiding the opposite evils in relation to the community, or to God.[23]

Objection 1. It would seem that the law is not always directed to the common good as to its end. For it belongs to law to command and to forbid. But commands are directed to certain individual goods. Therefore the end of the law is not always the common good.	Objection 1. Apparently, in order to be truly law, a thing need not always have as its purpose the good of the whole community. We stated earlier, in Article 1, that commanding and forbidding are functions of law. But a command always has as its purpose a particular good of a particular individual. Since the purpose of law is particular and individual, it is not general and common.

---

[1]   St. Thomas does not mean that the law *only* commands and forbids; as he explains later, in Q. 92, Art. 2, its acts also include permitting and punishing. Commanding, forbidding, permitting, and punishing are *direct* acts of law. Doesn't it accomplish other purposes as well, such as directing, rewarding, and encouraging? Yes, but these purposes are achieved indirectly, mainly through commands and prohibitions, backed up by punishments for failure to comply. For example, the law directs traffic *through* forbidding excessive speed, and it rewards acts of valor *through* commanding that soldiers who have performed them be awarded medals.

It might seem that permitting is not so much an act of law as the omission of an act, because we take anything not explicitly forbidden to be permitted. However, certain kinds of permissions *must* be made explicit, because they provide individuals with ways to modify the legal obligations they would otherwise have. For example, the law encourages home ownership and construction *through* explicitly permitting homeowners to deduct mortgage interest from personal income taxes. By taking advantage of this permission, homeowners alter the amount of taxes they would otherwise be commanded to pay.

[23] II-II, Q. 79, Art. 1; compare II-II, Q. 58, Art. 6.

[2] Individual goods are goods of particular individuals. Sometimes the law issues commands like "No one may steal the property of any other person." This is quite different from a command like "No one may pollute the community water supply," because the other person is not the community as a whole, and his property, unlike the water supply, is an individual good, not a common good. From this, the Objector concludes that law does not always aim at the common good.

Objection 2. Further, the law directs man in his actions. But human actions are concerned with particular matters. Therefore the law is directed to some particular good.	Objection 2. Moreover, we saw in Article 1 that law is a rule and measure of human actions; it tells us what to do, and it presents a standard by which our acts can be evaluated. But every human action is carried out with a view to doing something in particular, to obtaining *this* good in *this* way for *this* person at *this* time. Since law directs human acts, and human acts are directed to particular rather than common goods, it follows that law is directed to particular rather than common goods.

Objection 2 is much like Objection 1, this time, however, viewed from the perspective of the persons who are under the law. Law regulates human actions, but very few human actions concern the common good as such. Mr. Romero is not taking out trash in general, but his own trash. Mr. and Mrs. Keller are not raising children in general, but little Luke and Ursula. Yet the public health authorities may take a legal interest if Mr. Romero's trash piles up, and the child welfare authorities may legally step in if Luke and Ursula appear at school covered with bruises. From cases like this, it seems to the Objector that law concerns itself with particular, not common goods.

---

[1] *Objection 3. Further, Isidore says (Etym. v, 3): "If the law is based on reason, whatever is based on reason will be a law."* [2] *But reason is the foundation not only of what is ordained to the common good, but also of that which is directed to private good. Therefore the law is not only directed to the good of all, but also to the private good of an individual.*	Objection 3. We may derive yet another argument against the thesis that true law is always directed to the common good from the scholar Isidore of Seville. Isidore says in his great compendium of classical learning, *Etymologies*,[24] that if law is grounded on reason, then everything reasonable is a law. But we follow reason not only when we are pursuing the good of all, but also when we are pursuing private good. Since acts directed solely to the private good are also grounded on reason, they too are truly law.

---

[24] In English, the title makes the work sound like a history of the origins of words. Although it contains a good deal of that, actually it is more an encyclopedia of the sources of human knowledge. Thus the title is sometimes given as *Origins*.

[1]   In Article 1, St. Thomas has already demonstrated that law, to be law, must be reasonable. Isidore turns this around: Whatever is reasonable is law (provided, he adds, that it is also in accord with religion, with knowledge, and with safety – conditions the Objector omits).

It may seem that St. Thomas could reply to Objection 3 simply by suggesting that Isidore's statement is fallacious, for at first it seems that Isidore has made the same mistake as someone who says, "If a cat is something with four paws, then everything with four paws will be a cat." A dog has four paws but is not a cat; in the same way, a theorem in geometry is based on reason but is not a law. St. Thomas must find a different response, however, because he considers Isidore's statement not fallacious, but merely elliptical. In context, he thinks, what Isidore means is something like, "If the term 'law' refers to a norm of conduct based on reason, then every norm of conduct based on reason will be a law."

[2]   According to the Objector, we do not deliberate in pursuing what is good for the community as a whole, but then strike out blindly when we are pursuing our own good. Rather we follow reason in both cases.

On the contrary, *Isidore says (Etym. v, 21) that "laws are enacted for no private profit, but for the common benefit of the citizens."*

On the other hand, in the same work Isidore *denies* that laws are made for the advantage of individual persons and groups, insisting instead that they are made for the good of all.

St. Thomas quotes this passage from Isidore more fully in Q. 95, Art. 3: "Law shall be virtuous, just, possible to nature, according to the custom of the country, suitable to place and time, necessary, useful; clearly expressed, lest by its obscurity it lead to misunderstanding; framed for no private benefit, but for the common good."[25]

[1] *I answer that,* As stated above (1), *the law belongs to that which is a principle of human acts, because it is their rule and measure.* [2] *Now as reason is a principle of human acts, so in reason itself there is something which is the principle in respect of all the rest: wherefore to this principle chiefly and mainly law*

Here is my response. As explained in Article 1, because law is the rule and measure of human acts, it must concern the source from which they spring. Just as human acts arise from reason, so at the bottom of reason lies something from which everything else in it arises. So it is this root of reason with which law must first and foremost be concerned.

[25] Isidore duplicates this passage in the *Etymologies,* including it in both Book 2 (*Rhetoric and Dialectic*), Chapter 10, and Book 5 (*Laws and Times*), Chapter 21.

must needs be referred. [3] Now the first principle in practical matters, which are the object of the practical reason, is the last end: [4] and the last end of human life is bliss or happiness, as stated above (2, 7; 3, 1). [5] Consequently the law must needs regard principally the relationship to happiness. [6] Moreover, since every part is ordained to the whole, as imperfect to perfect; [7] and since one man is a part of the perfect community, the law must needs regard properly the relationship to universal happiness. [8] Wherefore the Philosopher, in the above definition of legal matters mentions both happiness and the body politic: for he says (Ethic. v, 1) that we call those legal matters "just, which are adapted to produce and preserve happiness and its parts for the body politic": since the state is a perfect community, as he says in Polit. i, 1.

In what to do – the matters addressed by *practical* reason – this root of reason is the *ultimate goal* of human life. As explained earlier in this *Summa*, the ultimate goal of human life is complete happiness. So law must chiefly concern itself chiefly with the *order* that lies in such happiness.

One aspect of this order is that each proper part of something, being incomplete, can be properly understood only in its relation to the complete whole to which it belongs. This observation applies, among other things, to an individual man, viewed as a proper part of a complete community. So law necessarily addresses itself to *shared* happiness.

This is why, in defining the matters that pertain to law, Aristotle refers both happiness and the political community. For as he explains in his *Nicomachean Ethics*, Book 5, such legalities are called "just" when they produce and conserve happiness and its constituents among those who enjoy political fellowship. This is true because because, as he explains in his *Politics*, Book 1, the city is a complete community.

[1] Here St. Thomas alludes to his is claim in Art. 1, "that which is the principle in any genus, is the rule and measure of that genus." We have discussed the meaning of this statement previously.

[2] Practical reasoning is goal-oriented. The question that we ask ourselves when we deliberate, "What shall I do?", is more fully expressed "What shall I do to achieve the good that I intend?" This goal is the principle – the source – of the act.

[3] Particular goods may be pursued for the sake of still further goods. For example, we brush our teeth for the sake of health and sweet breath, and we seek sweet breath for the sake of avoiding offense to our friends. Is *every* good sought for the sake of something else, or is there some uttermost good which is sought for its own sake and for the sake of which everything else is pursued? If there is, then it is the uttermost spring of deliberation, the thing that imbues it with meaning. But if there were

not – if the chain of ends continued with no end – then our actions would
have no rational point. To the question, "Why are you doing that?" there
wouldn't be any final answer.

St. Thomas has taken up the question of the ultimate goal earlier in the
Summa, in the series of questions with which the First Part of the Second
Part begins, the *Treatise on Man's Last End*. Among the conclusions he
reaches there are the following: That we do act for an ultimate end; that
this fact about us essentially connected with our rational nature; that
there is only *one* ultimate end, not several; and that everything we will
is in some way directed to it. The qualification, "in some way," is important, because certain things short of the ultimate end are also worthy of
choice for their own sakes; however, they have this property *because of*
the ultimate end. I love my friend for his own sake, not just for the sake of
something else, but it is by virtue of the ultimate end *that he is* lovable for
his own sake. God has ordained that loving my friend for his own sake is
in fact ordered to God Himself.[26]

[4]   St. Thomas further concludes in the *Treatise on Man's Last End* that
the uttermost good at which everyone ultimately aims is happiness. We
may be tempted to say that although some seek happiness, others seek
something different. St. Thomas replies that although we all desire happiness, that complete happiness that leaves nothing further to be desired,
we disagree about where it is found, some thinking that it lies in wealth,
some that it lies in pleasures of the senses, and so on. Consequently, it is
these things that they seek. Against these confusions, he shows that the
complete happiness that leaves nothing further to be desired lies not in
any created thing, but in the beatific vision, the vision of God.

That the vision of God leaves nothing further to be desired does not
mean, by the way, that all of the desires that I had before, even for ungodly
things, even for things harmful to me, have been satisfied; rather it means
that in the perfect, piercing, all-illuminating light of the Supreme Good,
inappropriate desires are no longer possible. I cannot possibly want any
lower good in preference to it, and I can no longer be in doubt as to
which is which.

---

[26] For the distinction between being chosen *for the sake of* something else and being choice-
worthy *because of* something else in the context of St. Thomas's philosophy, see Robert
C. Koons, "Eros and Agape Revisited: Is Classical Eudaimonism Compatible with
Christian Love?", in Paul R. Dehart and Carson Holloway, eds., *Political Philosophy and
the Claims of Faith* (DeKalb, IL: Northern Illinois University Press, 2014).

[5]   If law is the rule and measure of human action, and human action is aimed ultimately at happiness, then law itself must be aimed ultimately at happiness. This does not mean that it must be aimed ultimately at *pleasure;* pleasure is merely one of those things that people tend to confuse with happiness. One way to see why fullness of pleasure is not the same as fullness of happiness is to ask, "Does pleasure leave nothing further to be desired?" But it does leave something to be desired. Pleasure can even become boring. I may have the greatest imaginable pleasure and yet ask, "Is this all there is?"

From the facts that law must be aimed at happiness, and that ultimate happiness lies in the beatific vision, it may at first seem as though St. Thomas thinks law must guide the community to the beatific vision. As we will see later, however, St. Thomas distinguishes between the role of the Church, which concerns itself with the supernatural aspects of our good, and the role of the state, which concerns itself only with the natural aspects of our good. The state should be amicable and helpful to the Church, but should not presume to take its place. In this context, when he speaks of our happiness he means our temporal happiness.

[6]   St. Thomas is emphasizing that an individual's life is bound up with his membership in the community. I am more than just a solitary atom; I am a part of a whole. The point is easy to misunderstand, because St. Thomas certainly does not believe the individual's identity is *exhausted* by his membership in the community. He explains elsewhere that the kind of unity that the commonwealth has is not a "unity of essence" or a "unity of matter," but only a "unity of order," amounting to no more than the fact that things stand in a shared relationship. "To be one in respect of order is not to be one unqualifiedly speaking," says St. Thomas, "since unity of order is the least of unities."[27]

Consequently, although I am a part of the community, I am not *only* a part. Human beings are persons, and persons, he holds, are "substances," something he never says about cities and countries. A person is not like a hand, which takes its entire identity from the body to which it belongs. He is a complete being, subsisting of himself, distinct from all else, the

---

[27] Thomas Aquinas, *Summa Contra Gentiles*, II, Chapter 58. See also IV, Chapter 35: "For things whose form is order ... are not natural things. The result is that their unity cannot be called a unity of nature." Thus, when we call certain forms of community "natural institutions," this is a statement about the conditions under which human nature flourishes; it does not mean that the communities themselves are "natures."

ultimate possessor of his properties in the sense that they are predicated of *him*, not of anything or anyone else.[28]

Even so, his membership in the community matters. It is not just something that affects him, but something about him. The fact that I *am* a part does not imply that I am *only* a part; but neither does the fact that I am *not only* a part imply that I am *not* a part.

[7]   Law could not concern itself *solely* with the welfare of the individual even if it tried to, because how the community fares is an aspect of how he fares. Neither his happiness, nor the happiness of the community, can be understood in isolation. A good way to think of the common good of the political community is the complete set of conditions, physical and social, that need to be satisfied *in order* for individuals to be able to pursue happiness effectively, both through their own actions and through the actions of smaller communities such as families, churches, and neighborhoods.

But wait: If the common good is the "universal happiness," as St. Thomas says it is, then why not think of it in a different way? Why not think of it the way utilitarians and cost–benefit analysts think of it, as an arithmetic sum of my happiness, your happiness, and everyone else's happiness? Isn't that what "universal happiness" would mean?

No, because society is not a mega-person. It is an association of persons, each of them distinct and irreducible. To the utilitarian and the cost–benefit analyst, persons seem to run together, like oil cans being emptied into a drum, gingerbread men placed too close on the cookie sheet, or lead soldiers melting down in the furnace. But this is absurd. To say "Your happiness is –3, mine is –3, and that other fellow's is +5, so the happiness of the aggregate is –1," makes about as much sense as saying "Iowa's temperature is 75°, Wisconsin's is 70°, and Minnesota's is 68°, so the temperature of the tri-state area is 213°."

[8]   As the reference to Aristotle suggests, the expression "perfect community" is a technical term, a term of art. By a perfect community, Aristotle did not mean a community that could not possibly be any better, and neither does St. Thomas. He is well aware that every real-life community is flawed and capable of improvement. When he calls the political community a perfect community, what he actually means is that it is a *complete* community (indeed, many translators prefer this expression) – one that

---

[28] See especially III., Q. 16, Art. 12, ad. 2.

possesses all of the physical and social elements essential to a partnership in life lived well.

In his *Treatise on Kingship,* Book 1, Chapter 2, Section 14, St. Thomas even uses the term "perfect" in a comparative sense, remarking that although the city is a perfect community, the province is a *more* perfect community, because it is still more richly endowed with these elements. Continuing this line of thought, some people suppose that a confederation composed of provinces (St. Thomas would say "empire") would be more perfect still, and that perhaps a world confederation would be the most perfect of all. But this would not be true unless a number of exacting conditions were satisfied. One shudders to think of a world confederation run by the tyrants who make up so much of the membership of the United Nations.

At any rate, the community St. Thomas has in mind is not a simple partnership in a life lived well, which would be a partnership among individuals. Rather it is a compound partnership, a partnership of partnerships. Individuals form families, individuals and families form other forms of association, and the association among all these associations makes up the community as a whole. The unity of the commonwealth, then, is much weaker than the unity of a living body, and rightly so. The term "body politic," in the Dominican Fathers translation, might seem to contradict this point. However, no such term is present in the Latin. The expressions St. Thomas actually used are *communione politica*, political communion or community, and *politica communicatione,* political sharing or fellowship. The closest he ever comes to the notion of a "body politic" is in II-II, Question 64, Article 2, where, in discussing capital punishment, he says "if the health of the whole body demands the excision of a member, through its being decayed or infectious to the other members, it will be both praiseworthy and advantageous to have it cut away. Now every individual person is compared to the whole community, as part to whole. Therefore if a man be dangerous and infectious to the community, on account of some sin, it is praiseworthy and advantageous that he be killed in order to safeguard the common good." Even in that passage, however, St. Thomas does not say that a commonwealth and a body are alike in every respect. They both have some kind of unity, and in both cases the disorder of a part affects the well-being of the whole. It does not follow that they have the same kind of unity, or that the parts are related to the whole in identical ways.

[1] *Now in every genus, that which belongs to it chiefly is the principle of the others, and the others belong to that genus in subordination to that thing: thus fire, which is chief among hot things, is the cause of heat in mixed bodies, and these are said to be hot in so far as they have a share of fire. [2] Consequently, since the law is chiefly ordained to the common good, any other precept in regard to some individual work, must needs be devoid of the nature of a law, save in so far as it regards the common good. Therefore every law is ordained to the common good.*

Now whatever is most characteristic or representative of a genus is the source from which the things in that genus arise. Fire, for example, is most characteristic or representative of the genus of hot things; it is fire from which the heat of composite bodies arises, and we call such bodies "hot" just to the degree that they are fiery. For the same reason, since the pursuit of the common good pertains especially to law, precepts about particular things have the character of law *only to the extent that they do* pursue the common good. So law is directed to the common good after all.

[1]   Most of these matters have already been discussed in connection with Article 1; we need comment only on St. Thomas's example. By "fire" he does not mean a particular exothermic oxidation reaction characterized by smoke and flames; he means something like primal heat, or perhaps radiant energy. It would be absurd to say that everything hot becomes hot because something is rapidly oxidizing, but it is not at all absurd to say that to become hot is to acquire primal heat. One need not subscribe to the outdated chemical theory that there are four elements of matter to see his point.

[2]   We saw in Article 1 the source from which human acts flow is reason, so law, which rules and measures them, must be reasonable. In the present Article we see that the still deeper source or principle underlying this act of reason is its final end, so law must be directed to the final end, which is the shared or common good.

[1] *Reply to Objection 1. A command denotes an application of a law to matters regulated by the law. [2] Now the order to the common good, at which the law aims, is applicable to particular ends. And in this way commands are given even concerning particular matters.*

Reply to Objection 1. The meaning of a *legal* command is an act that brings the law to bear on those matters that come under it. Now law is directed to the common good, but this includes setting particular goods in order *with a view* to the common good. When the law issues commands about particular things, this is what it is doing.

[1]   Laws themselves are always stated in universal terms: *Everyone* must observe the speed limit, *no one* may steal from *anyone* else, and *anyone* who fulfills the requirements and obtains a license may drive an automobile. St. Thomas is reminding us here that commands about particular matters are not contained in the law itself, but are reached by applying the law. The lawmakers decree that no one may steal from anyone else; the judge sentences John Smith for stealing from Mary Doe.

[2]   If the prohibition of theft in general is for the common good, then the application of the prohibition to John Smith and Mary Doe is also for the common good.

[1] *Reply to Objection 2.* *Actions are indeed concerned with particular matters: but those particular matters are referable to the common good,* [2] *not as to a common genus or species, but as to a common final cause, according as the common good is said to be the common end.*	Reply to Objection 2. The Objector is right to point out that every human action is carried out with a view to doing something in particular. Even so, all these particular actions are related to the common good. Although they have different *proximate* goals, so that it would be nonsense to classify them as the same *kind* of action, they do all share the common good as an *ultimate* criterion.

[1]   True, Mary Doe's property is not itself a common good. But the integrity of property as such is a strongly common good, because everyone gains from its protection. To uphold the integrity of property as such, the law must protect the property of Mary Doe. In this sense, the particular matter of prohibiting theft from Mary Doe is "referable to" – deemed right or wrong according to its relation to – the common good.

By the way, the converse is also true. Not only does the good of the community depend on good of the individuals within it, but also, as St. Thomas explains in II-II, Q. 47, Art. 10, ad 3, the good of the individual depends on the good of the community. This is true of communities of all sorts, from families to kingdoms. He gives two reasons for this conclusion. In the first place, the well-being of the individual is *influenced* by the well-being of the community. Whatever hurts it hurts him too. In the second place, he is *connected* with the community as one of members. This is not the whole of his identity, but it is part of it. The very meaning of his individual well-being is entangled with the well-being of the whole.

[2]   We have just seen that insofar as the individual is a member of his community, his acts are deemed right or wrong not just according to his own good but according to their relation to the common good. The question is why. Is it because all of these individual acts are acts of the same *kind* (the same genus or species)? Or is it because they all share the same *purpose* (the same final cause)? St. Thomas answers, "The latter." This is what the Objector had tried to deny.

But how could all individual actions have a common purpose? Does St. Thomas think that whenever anyone acts, he does so with the motive of advancing the common good (or at least not undermining it)? No, but motive is not the same thing as purpose. *Just insofar as he is a member of the community,* the citizen's acts are properly regarded from the view of the community's shared purpose, the flourishing of their partnership in a good life, because his own good and the good of the community are intertwined. This is what he rationally seeks, even if it is not what he actually seeks.

By contrast, the Objector is treating individual acts as though they *do* belong to a common genus or species. It may even seem that he is right, because earlier in the *Summa,* in I-II, Q. 1, Art. 3, St. Thomas had explained that human acts "take their species from their end." In other words, the purpose of the act determines what kind of act it is – and haven't we just seen that they share the end or purpose of the common good? But according to St. Thomas, what kind of an act an act is depends not on its shared ultimate purpose, but on its particular end or purpose. A grocer's particular end is to sell groceries; bus driver's particular end is to drive a bus. It would be absurd to suggest that the grocer is doing the same thing as the bus driver, just because both acts are "referable" to the common good.

Reply to Objection 3. Just as nothing stands firm with regard to the speculative reason except that which is traced back to the first indemonstrable principles, so nothing stands firm with regard to the practical reason, unless it be directed to the last end which is the common good: and whatever stands to reason in this sense, has the nature of a law.

Reply to Objection 3. When we are engaged in theoretical reasoning – reasoning about *what is the case* – the truth of a conclusion is not fully demonstrated until we have traced it all the way back, inference by inference, to starting points, or "first" principles, which cannot themselves be demonstrated. In just the same way, when we are engaged in practical reasoning – reasoning about *what is to be done* – the decision is not fully grounded until we have traced it all the way back, inference by inference, to the starting point, the ultimate goal, which is the common good. Isidore's statement that everything reasonable is a law is true *if taken in this sense.*

The point this reply makes is that the Objector has misinterpreted Isidore's statement about everything reasonable being a law. Isidore did not mean that any conclusion that we reach by reasoning is a law, even when we are reasoning about private goods. What he meant is that any precept that practical reason can trace back to its final purpose, the common good, is a law. Taken in this sense, Isidore's statement is quite right, but it does not justify the Objector's conclusion.

For further reflection on the preceding section of the *Treatise on Law*, the online *Companion to the Commentary*, accessible via the Resources link at the book's catalogue webpage, includes a discussion of the following topic:

WHAT IS THE COMMON GOOD, ANYWAY?

Question 90, Article 3:
Whether the Reason of any Man Is
Competent to Make Laws?

TEXT	PARAPHRASE
Whether the reason of any man is competent to make laws?	Granted that true law is a work of reason, may anyone perform such work? In order for the result to be true law, does anyone's reasoning suffice?

We are still delving into law's essence, discerning the requirements something must have to be true law rather than a fraud. At stake in Article 3 is the fact that these requirements include something more than private judgment: Granted that true law is a work of reason, will anyone's reasoning do?

Not only in the *Treatise on Law* but throughout the *Summa*, the *ultrum*, or "whether," is normally phrased in such a way that the traditional answer is "Yes." This is one of the few cases in which the traditional answer is "No." Had St. Thomas followed his custom, he might have phrased the *ultrum*. "Whether public authority is essential to a law?", which might have been paraphrased, "In order to be true law, must an enactment be made by public authority?"

| [1] *Objection 1. It would seem that the reason of any man is competent to make laws. For the Apostle says (Romans 2:14) that "when the Gentiles, who* | Objection 1. Apparently anyone's reasoning does suffice to make laws. We know this from a remark in the second chapter of St. Paul's letter to the Church in Rome, for he says that "when Gentiles, who do not have |

have not the law, do by nature	the law [of Moses] do by nature what the
those things that are of the law,	law requires, they are a law to themselves."[29]
... they are a law to themselves."	Because St. Paul says this of all Gentiles,
[2] Now he says this of all in	without exception, it follows that anyone
general. Therefore anyone can	can enact a law to govern himself, with
make a law for himself.	authority just like any other law.

[1]   The snippet quoted by the Objector should be read in context. In full, Romans 2:14–16 reads, "When Gentiles who have not the law do by nature what the law requires, they are a law to themselves, even though they do not have the law. They show that what the law requires is written on their hearts, while their conscience also bears witness and their conflicting thoughts accuse or perhaps excuse them on that day when, according to my gospel, God judges the secrets of men by Christ Jesus." This passage has profoundly influenced the natural law tradition.

St. Thomas argues in his *Commentary on the Letter to the Romans* that when St. Paul says "what the law requires is written on their hearts," he means that even Gentiles know God's basic moral requirements: "[N]o one can testify that an action is good or bad," he says, "unless he has knowledge of the Law. Hence, if conscience bears witness about good or evil, this is a clear sign that the work of the Law has been written in the man's heart. Another function is to accuse and defend. Here, too, knowledge of the Law is required."[30]

As we are about to see, however, the Objector draws a radically different conclusion from the passage than St. Thomas does.

[2]   The Objector seems to take the statement that the Gentiles are a law for themselves as though it meant that every human being can say, in the spirit of Louis XIV, "I am the law – the law is me." Put in the form of a syllogism, the Objector's argument runs like this:

(1) Anyone who is a law to himself is competent to make laws.
(2) But St. Paul says everyone is a law to himself.
(3) Therefore everyone is competent to make laws for himself.

The Objector is not claiming, by the way, that everyone is competent to make laws *for others*. What he claims is that each person is fully

---

[29] Substituting RSV-CE for DRA.

[30] Thomas Aquinas, *Lectures on the Letter to the Romans*, trans. Fabian Larcher, ed. Jeremy Holmes (Naples, Florida: Aquinas Center for Theological Renewal, Ave Maria University, 2008), Chapter 2, Lecture 3, Sections 219–220, available online at http://nvjournal.net/files/Aquinas_on_Romans.pdf. In the text, I give the more common title, *Commentary on the Letter to the Romans*.

competent to direct *himself* with no need for further direction from anyone else. In this sense he is a sort of anarchist.

[1] *Objection 2. Further, as the Philosopher says (Ethic. ii. 1), "the intention of the lawgiver is to lead men to virtue." [2] But every man can lead another to virtue. Therefore the reason of any man is competent to make laws.*	Objection 2. Moreover, as the great philosopher, Aristotle, says in the *Nicomachean Ethics,* those who make laws aim at steering the citizens to virtue. But anyone can steer someone to virtue. It follows that anyone's reason suffices to make laws.

[1]   There are no quotation marks in the Latin text, and the Objector
seems to be paraphrasing Aristotle rather than quoting him. However, he
accurately expresses his meaning, for as the philosopher had written in
the *Nicomachean Ethics,* "lawgivers make the citizens good by training
them in habits of right action – this is the aim of all legislation, and if it
fails to do this it is a failure; this is what distinguishes a good form of
constitution from a bad one."[31]

[2]   Anyone might prompt another to virtue by such means as persuad-
ing, advising, rebuking, reminding, and exhorting. The Objector seems to
be arguing something like this:

(1) The lawmaker's intention in making laws is to lead others to
    virtue.
(2) Anyone capable of acting on this intention is capable of
    making laws.
(3) But everyone is capable of acting on this intention.
(4) Therefore everyone is capable of making laws.

[1] *Objection 3. Further, just as the sovereign of a state governs the state, so every father of a family governs his household. [2] But the sovereign of a state can make laws for the state. Therefore every father of a family can make laws for his household.*	Objection 3. Yet another argument may be derived from the fact that just as the foremost man governs the commonwealth, so the father governs the family. Since the former governs the political community by making public laws, it follows that the latter can govern the familial community by making domestic laws.

[1]   Without argument, the Objector assumes that the governing means
exactly the same thing in the domestic and the political community.

[31] Aristotle, *Nichomachean Ethics,* Book 2, trans. H. Rackham, available online at http://
www.perseus.tufts.edu/hopper.

This assumption has found both defenders and critics in every period of history. Aristotle criticized the barbarians, who regarded a kingdom as merely a family writ large – with the subjects in the position of slaves. John Locke criticized royalists like Robert Filmer, who also regarded a kingdom as merely a family writ large – but with the subjects in the position of children. In our own time the assumption is widely held by radical feminists, who reverse the model by regarding a *family* as a kingdom, or a tyranny, writ *small* – the idea behind the phrase "sexual politics."

The Latin word here translated as "sovereign" is *princeps,* which means literally the first or foremost man. Under the republic, it referred to the first person of the Senate, but after the emperor Augustus, it came to mean the first person of the entire commonwealth, that is, the ruler. In English, the word *princeps* is often translated as "prince," but the Latin term does not necessarily refer to kingly rule; in fact, Augustus chose the title precisely to downplay his power, because in his day it had not yet acquired a royal ring. Considering the trajectory of the modern doctrine of sovereignty, the term "sovereign" is more unhelpful still.

Certainly a *princeps* may be the kind of ruler we call a king; in particular, God is a king. When we are speaking of human rulers, however, the idea of royalty does not necessarily apply, much less the idea of omnipotence. True, in *On Kingship,* St. Thomas does argue that kingship is the *best* form of government, and he argues at one point in the *Summa* that if we employ the figure of speech that calls everything good by the name of the best, then every good form of government may be called a kingdom or kingship.[32] From this is would seem to follow that any foremost man may be called a king. On the other hand, the kind of kingship St. Thomas has in mind for humans is *mixed* kingship, for it blends the good elements of the rule of one, the rule of a few, and the rule of many. We return to the question of the best form of government in Question 105, Article 1. For now, it is enough to say that St. Thomas is not necessarily as monarchical as our translation sometimes seems to imply.

[2] The tradition of thought to which St. Thomas belongs distinguishes commonwealths from households in a variety of ways. For example, although the household is a simple association in living well, the

---

[32] II-II, Q. 50, Art. 1, ad 2.

commonwealth is a compound association; although offices in the family are based on complementarity between the sexes, offices in the state are based (in the best case) on merit; and although parents rule their children by nature, public authorities rule over free citizens by consent.[33] However, the Objector has thrown a curve ball. Rather than addressing any of these contrasts, he calls attention to an apparent similarity: Both fathers and civil rulers govern by giving commands. Why shouldn't the father's commands be considered laws?

On the contrary, Isidore says *(Etym. v. 10): "A law is an ordinance of the people, whereby something is sanctioned by the Elders together with the Commonalty."*	On the other hand, as Isidore says in his *Etymologies,* a law is an enactment of the people, ratified by the great men together with the commoners.

Here the great encyclopedist, Isidore, gives the generic term "law" (*lex*) to what he considers the single best form of law; he is using the metonymy to pay homage, as one might call the single greatest mountain simply "the Mountain"; he does describe other ways of enacting legal measures, which we will distinguish later.[34] The *populi,* or people, are the whole people rather than a part; otherwise they would not be acting for the common good. This is why the great men and the plain folk must concur. In Rome, the *maiores,* or great men, would have been the aristocratic senate, and the *plebibus,* or plain folk, would have been the formal assemblies of the people; however democratic we fancy ourselves, some citizens take foremost place in every polity, with ordinary citizens making up the rest. *Sanxerunt,* which I have paraphrased "ratified," is a strong word, with a range of meanings including "firmly established," "unalterably fixed," "rendered inviolable," and even "sanctified," a word to which it is etymologically related. "Sanctioned," the word chosen in the Dominican Fathers translation, is another cognate, but a weaker one. The vigor of the original Latin word reminds us that the making of a law is a deeply serious act, not to be taken lightly.

---

[33] According to contemporary prejudice, only in modern times was it discovered that free persons should be ruled with their consent, not unwillingly, like slaves. This is a slander, or at least very ignorant, for the principle is ancient. See Q. 97, Art. 3, ad 3; Q. 105, Arts. 1–2.

[34] Isidore repeats this definition of law, *lex,* in two different places in his *Etymologies,* using almost identical language: Book 2 (*Rhetoric and Dialectic*), Chapter 10, and Book 5 (*Laws and Times*), Chapter 10. Compare Question 95, Article 4.

[1] *I answer that, A law, properly speaking, regards first and foremost the order to the common good.* [2] *Now to order anything to the common good, belongs either to the whole people, or to someone who is the vicegerent[35] of the whole people. And therefore the making of a law belongs either to the whole people or to a public personage who has care of the whole people: since in all other matters the directing of anything to the end concerns him to whom the end belongs.*

Here is my response. Using the term "law" in its proper sense, the first and chief concern of law is to set things in order so that they achieve the common good. Setting them in such order is the proper concern of either the whole people, or a public official who acts in their place. The same must be true of lawmaking. It follows that lawmaking is also the responsibility of either the people themselves, or someone to whom their care is entrusted – because the one responsible for directing things toward a purpose is *always* the same as the one to whom this purpose belongs.

[1]   St. Thomas says the common good is the concern of law *primo et principaliter,* literally "first and principal." It would be easy to think he is merely saying the same thing in two different ways, but these two words have different shades of meaning. He calls the common good the "first" concern because it is the first thing considered in making law. He calls it the "principal" concern not only because it is most important, but also because all else depends on it and proceeds from it.

[2]   Confusingly, St. Thomas places the most important premise, "in all other matters the directing of anything to the end concerns him to whom the end belongs," *after* the conclusion. Putting it in where a speaker of contemporary English would probably put it, the argument runs like this:

(1) What is the first and principal concern of law? Directing things toward their purpose, the common good.
(2) Who is responsible for directing things toward a purpose? The one to whom the purpose belongs.
(3) To whom does the purpose of the common good belong? To the whole people.
(4) Therefore, the people themselves, or someone acting in its place and on their behalf, is responsible for directing things toward the common good.
(5) From this it further follows that the people themselves, or someone acting in its place and on their behalf, is responsible for making law.

[35] Corrected from "viceregent." See the explanation in the commentary.

Ideally, St. Thomas thinks, the authorities who act for the people do so only with their consent. As he says in Q. 105, Art. 1, the best form of government is "partly democracy, i.e. government by the people, insofar as the rulers can be chosen from the people, and the people have the right to choose their rulers." A little later, in Q. 105, Art. 2., he speaks with approval of Marcus Tullius Cicero's definition of the commonwealth, "a nation is a body of men united together by consent to the law and by community of welfare." To put it another way, the best state of affairs is that in which the people have both the moral capacity and legal right to make their own laws – and also to choose their own rulers, since every community requires a source and focus of unity.[36] Such a people is called "free."

However, St. Thomas also concedes the possibility that through contempt for the common good, a people may lose the moral capacity to make laws. In such a case, they should also lose the legal right to make them. We see this in Q. 97, Art. 1, where he offers the following example from St. Augustine of an appropriate change in the laws:

> If the people have a sense of moderation and responsibility, and are most careful guardians of the common weal, it is right to enact a law allowing such a people to choose their own magistrates for the government of the commonwealth. But if, as time goes on, the same people become so corrupt as to sell their votes, and entrust the government to scoundrels and criminals; then the right of appointing their public officials is rightly forfeit to such a people, and the choice devolves to a few good men.

I have corrected the term used in the Dominican Fathers translation of St. Thomas's text, substituting the word "vicegerent" (from *gerentis vicem*, one who carries on in place of another) for "viceregent" (one who assists a regent). These two English words are often confused.

---

[1] *Reply to Objection 1. As stated above (A. 1 ad 1), a law is in a person not only as in one that rules, but also by participation as in one that is ruled.* [2] *In the latter way each one is a law to himself, in so far as he shares the direction that he receives from one who rules*	Reply to Objection 1. As I explained in Article 1, Reply to Objection 1, a law may be said to be "in" a person in either of two senses. In one sense, it is only "in" the person who rules through the law, but in the other, it is also "in" the person who is ruled by the law – in him by participation, so to speak, because he shares in the direction that the ruler imparts to his actions. It is the latter sense of the term that St. Paul had in mind in the verse the Objector has

---

[36] See St. Thomas's work *On Kingship, To the King of Cyprus*, Book 1, Chapter 3.

him. Hence the same text goes on: *"Who shows the work of the law written in their hearts."*

quoted. We see this from the very next verse, which the Objector does not mention: "They show that what the law requires is written on their hearts."[37]

---

[1]   In St. Thomas's view, the critical issue in the passage the Objector quotes from the Letter to the Romans is what St. Paul means by saying that even the Gentiles, thus all people, are "a law to themselves." Jumping to conclusions, the Objector seems to think the passage means that each person is the ultimate originator of the rules to be followed – that we make up for ourselves what is good and evil, right and wrong.[38] Needless to say, this is a common view in our own time too.

St. Thomas reasons more carefully. What St. Paul seems to be saying is that in some sense, the law is "in" the Gentiles already, even though they do not have the law of Moses. But as St. Thomas has already explained in Article 1, Reply to Objection 1, a law can be "in" something – in this case, in a person – in either of two senses.

[2]   The Objector thinks the law is "in" the Gentiles in the first sense: Each person is himself the originator of the norm to be followed. St. Thomas shows that this interpretation is impossible. Actually the law must be "in" the Gentiles in the second sense, because they receive the norm from someone else: It is "written on their hearts" by the Divine author of the conscience.

Certainly the law written on the heart is the foundation of human laws, as we will see later in the *Treatise*. But does this imply that everyone who has this foundation inscribed on his conscience is qualified to make human laws? In St. Thomas's view, certainly not. Nothing the Objector has said detracts from the conclusion St. Thomas has already reached, that laws for the whole community can be made only by public authority – that of either the community as a whole or their vicegerent.

---

[1] *Reply to Objection 2. A private person cannot lead another to virtue efficaciously: for he can only advise, and if his advice be not taken, it has no coercive power,* [2] *such as the law should have, in order to prove an efficacious inducement to virtue,*

Reply to Objection 2. True, in his private capacity anyone can steer someone to virtue, but in this way he cannot obtain sure results; all he can do is offer suggestions. If the person to whom he is speaking ignores his advice, he cannot make him follow

---

[37] Following the DRA's rendering of Romans 2:15a.

[38] As though the Tempter had been speaking the truth in Genesis 3:5, when he said to Eve, "your eyes will be opened, and you will be like God, knowing good and evil."

as the Philosopher says (Ethic. x. 9). [3] *But this coercive power is vested in the whole people or in some public personage, to whom it belongs to inflict penalties, as we shall state further on (Q. 92, A. 2 ad 3; II-II, Q. 64, A. 3). Wherefore the framing of laws belongs to him alone.*

it, for his counsel lacks the coercive power that Aristotle reminds us law requires. As I will explain later on in other contexts, this power to punish rests either to the whole people, or to a public authority who acts on their behalf. For this reason, the responsibility for making laws belongs solely to either the people themselves, or their representative.

[1]   A good illustration of St. Thomas's point is the family: "And as to those young people who are inclined to acts of virtue, by their good natural disposition, or by custom, or rather by the gift of God, paternal training suffices, which is by admonitions. But since some are found to be depraved, and prone to vice, and not easily amenable to words, it was necessary for such to be restrained from evil by force and fear[.]"[39]

[2]   Put another way, law, to be law, must be enforceable. Why? Isn't it enough to be a rule and measure of human actions? Certainly, but how could it be their rule and measure if it were *not* enforceable? Law is inseparable from the discipline of law. This is why St. Thomas after writing in Article 1 not just that "Law is a rule and measure of acts," he added "whereby man is induced to act or is restrained from acting." As he says later on, the discipline of law is a "kind of training, which compels through fear of punishment."[40]

[3]   The reasoning here is parallel to the reasoning in the *respondeo*. St. Thomas is *not* arguing that *because* only the people or their vicegerent can make laws, therefore only they or he can inflict penalties. That would beg the question, because the proposition that only they or he can make laws is what he is trying to prove. Rather, he is arguing that because only they or he may direct things to the common good, therefore only they or he can *either* make laws, *or* inflict penalties.

The translation is a bit misleading here, because the sentence, "Wherefore the framing of laws belongs to him alone," seems to refer only to the people's representative, "him." Has St. Thomas cut out the people from the picture? No, they are still there. *Eius*, the Latin word he uses, can mean either a person or a thing. What the concluding sentence really means, then, is more like "Wherefore the framing of laws

---

[39] I-II, Q. 95, Art. 1.
[40] Ibid.

belongs to *it or him* alone," which I have paraphrased "For this reason, the responsibility for making laws belongs solely to the people or their representative."

This is a good place to emphasize a point made in the Introduction: Even though I occasionally quibble with the translators about the Latin, the paraphrase is not an alternative translation; it serves a different function.

---

[1] *Reply to Objection 3. As one man is a part of the household, so a household is a part of the state:* [2] *and the state is a perfect community, according to Polit. i. 1.* [3] *And therefore, as the good of one man is not the last end, but is ordained to the common good; so too the good of one household is ordained to the good of a single state, which is a perfect community.* [4] *Consequently he that governs a family, can indeed make certain commands or ordinances, but not such as to have properly the force of law.*

Reply to Objection 3. Just as a man is but a single part of his household, so the household is but a single part of the commonwealth. Not until we reach the level of the commonwealth do we arrive at a *complete* community. It follows that just as a single man's well-being is rightly pursued only in relation to the well-being of his household, so the household's well-being is rightly pursued only in relation to the well-being of the community to which it belongs. From this it follows that although the head of the family can certainly give commands of a sort, they lack the full power of law.

---

[1]   St. Thomas is not declaring merely that one man is part of the household *and* one household is part of the commonwealth. His language suggests that he is making a stronger claim: That one man is part of the household *in the same manner* that the household is part of the commonwealth. So, just as the identity of the man is not exhausted by his membership in the household, so the identity of the household is not exhausted by its membership in the commonwealth.

[2]   Yet something can be said of the commonwealth that cannot be said of the individual or the household: It is a *perfect* community, not in the sense that it is without flaw or that it could not possibly be made any better, but in the sense that it contains within itself all of the physical and social requirements for the common good, everything necessary for partnership in a good life. This gives it a certain priority.

[3]   In an age like ours, in which many people deny that the family is a natural institution, the priority of the commonwealth can easily be

misunderstood. It does not mean that the law, in the name of the common good, may abolish families, subvert them, dishonor the principles of their well-being, or try to take their place. In fact, the common good *requires* caring for the good of families, and so, for example, parents have certain prerogatives that not even the law may disregard (a point to which we will return). St. Thomas's point is that even so, the common good requires caring for the good of *all* families, and the good of just one family is not the good of all.

[4] If the final purpose of human association really were the good of one's family, then, presumably, the head of the household could make binding laws for it. But the final purpose of human association – at least its final temporal purpose – is the good of the community as a whole. Consequently, it would not be fitting for the commands of the household head to be the last word. If one family is hurting other families, or if the parents of a family are abusing their children rather than caring for them, as the true good of the family requires, then the law may intervene.

For further reflection on the preceding section of the *Treatise on Law*, the online *Companion to the Commentary*, accessible via the Resources link at the book's catalogue webpage, includes a discussion of the following topic:

DO-IT-YOURSELF LAWMAKING

Question 90, Article 4:
Whether Promulgation Is Essential to a Law?

TEXT	PARAPHRASE
Whether promulgation is essential to a law?	To be truly law, must a thing be publicly made known?

If we were to rephrase the *ultrum* in the manner of modern debating tournaments, it might become "Resolved: There is no such thing as a secret law." Because laws are commonly promulgated by means of words, the word "promulgation" has the secondary meanings of announcement by voice and publication in writing. Both St. Thomas and his imaginary Objector play on these overtones of the word. However, the point of promulgation is simply to make something publicly known – to make it known to the public whom it is meant to govern.

[1] *Objection 1. It would seem that promulgation is not essential to a law. For the natural law above all has the character of law.* [2] *But the natural law needs no promulgation. Therefore it is not essential to a law that it be promulgated.*

Objection 1. Apparently, a law does not have to be publicly made known to be truly law. For nothing is more truly law than the natural law, and yet the natural law does not need public proclamation. From this it follows that promulgation is not one of the characteristics essential to law.

[1]   The reason why natural law "above all" has the character of law is that all human law is based on it. The sense in which human law is based on it – put another way, the manner in which human law is derived from it – will be taken up later in detail. For now, it is enough to make these two points: First, natural law possesses the essential qualities of law in an eminent degree (it is a rule and measure of human acts, reasonable, for the common good, and so forth). Second, to the degree that a human enactment violates the natural law, it deprives itself of these qualities and falls short of the character of law.

[2]   As we have already seen in Article 3, and as we will see in greater depth later, the general principles of the natural law are "written on the heart," inscribed on the conscience. Since they are already known, the Objector reasons that nothing needs to be done to *make* them known; they do not require public announcement.

[1] *Objection 2. Further, it belongs properly to a law to bind one to do or not to do something.* [2] *But the obligation of fulfilling a law touches not only those in whose presence it is promulgated, but also others. Therefore promulgation is not essential to a law.*

Objection 2. Moreover, anything that is truly called law obligates one to do or not do something. But the obligation to satisfy the law applies not only to those who are present *where* a public proclamation takes place, but to others too. Consequently, it is not a requirement of true law that it be publicly made known.

[1]   As we have already discussed in Articles 1 and 2.

[2]   The Objector reasons something like this: Suppose the popular assembly makes a law forbidding people to tap into the aqueducts for private use, because the aqueducts are the water supply for the whole city. Only those in the Forum hear the new law proclaimed, but everyone in the city is obligated to do as it says. Since even those who did not hear

the proclamation are bound by the law, plainly the law does not require promulgation to be true law.

[1] *Objection 3. Further, the binding force of a law extends even to the future, since "laws are binding in matters of the future," as the jurists say (Cod. 1, tit. De lege et constit. leg. vii).* [2] *But promulgation concerns those who are present. Therefore it is not essential to a law.*	Objection 3. Still further, an argument may be drawn from the fact that the obligations of law reach even future acts, for as the legal authorities whose opinions are collected in Justinian's *Codes* declare, "the necessity of law applies to future affairs." But the law is publicly proclaimed only to those who are present *when* the proclamation takes place. Therefore, law need not be publicly made known to be true law.

[1]   This objection is much like the previous one, except that it concerns when rather than where, separation in time rather than separation in space. Consider the generations that live after the enactment of the law about aqueducts. Even though it was proclaimed only once, and everyone who was alive at the time of its proclamation is now dead, yet so long as it is not repealed, the living must obey it too.

[2]   The Objector reasons that if the power to obligate continues into the future even though the act of proclaiming it does not continue into the future, then the power to obligate does not require proclamation. Consequently, law without proclamation is still true law.

On the contrary, *It is laid down in the Decretals, dist. 4, that "laws are established when they are promulgated."*	**On the other hand,** as Gratian declares in his authoritative *Concordance of Discordant Canons,* "laws are instituted when they are publicly declared."

St. Thomas is referring to the *Decretum Gratiani,* also known as the *Concordance of Discordant Canons,* Distinction 4, Chapter 3, Section 1. Decretals are papal decisions concerning points of discipline, communicated through letters. Until they were superseded by the codification of 1917,[41] they made up much of canon law. Various collections of decretals were used in the Middle Ages, Gratian's being the most renowned. However, the *Concordance of Discordant Canons* collects more than decretals, and it is more than a collection. It integrates and harmonizes a vast mass of legal material by the making of careful distinctions, a method that profoundly influenced the Scholastic movement.

---

[41] The present version of the *Codex Iuris Canonici* was adopted in 1983.

In the translation of Augustine Thompson, Gratian says "Ordinances are instituted when they are promulgated; they are confirmed when they have been approved by the usage of those who observe them."[42] Although here St. Thomas quotes only the former of these two clauses, he agrees with the latter clause too, as we will see in Question 97, Article 3, when he asks whether custom has the force of law.

[1] *I answer that, I As stated above (1), a law is imposed on others by way of a rule and measure.* [2] *Now a rule or measure is imposed by being applied to those who are to be ruled and measured by it. Wherefore, in order that a law obtain the binding force which is proper to a law, it must needs be applied to the men who have to be ruled by it.* [3] *Such application is made by its being notified to them by promulgation. Wherefore promulgation is necessary for the law to obtain its force.*	**Here is my response.** I have already stated in Article 1 the manner in which a law functions when it is laid upon others: It is a rule and measure of the distinctive acts of human beings. How then is it made a rule and measure of their acts? By being brought to bear on the persons themselves. We see from this that if law is to possess the obligatory power that all true law has, it must be applied to those whom law rules. This is done by making it known to them though public proclamation. For this reason, in order to have the vigor that true must have, it requires public proclamation.

[1]   When St. Thomas says a law is imposed on others by way of a rule and measure, he does not mean that it is imposed on others *by means* of a rule and measure – as though the rule and measure were a hammer, and the law were a nail. To think that way would be to conceive the law, and the rule and measure, as different things. In reality they are the *same* thing; a rule and measure of acts is simply what a law *is*. Hence, the only manner in which it *can* be brought to bear on someone is by ruling and measuring his acts.

[2]   In English, the former sentence seems almost tautological; actually it is merely elliptical. Law is a rule and measure of human *acts*, not a rule and measure of human persons. But the law reaches these acts only

---

[42] Gratian, *The Treatise on Laws*, [*Concordance of Discordant Canons*], trans. Augustine Thompson, *With the Ordinary Gloss*, trans. James Gordley (Washington, DC: Catholic University Press, 1993), p. 13.

through the persons who perform them. Therefore, in order for the law to regulate the acts, it must be brought to bear on the persons. How then is it brought to bear on these persons? That is what St. Thomas is about to answer.

[3] The law is brought to bear on them by no other means than making it known to them. Consequently, in order for law to be what it is, a rule and measure of human acts, law must be promulgated. The bottom line is that laws must be promulgated because their purpose is to direct the actions of citizens to the common good, and they can do so only if the citizens know what they are.

Among other things, this shows that secret decrees that criminalize certain actions of the citizens cannot qualify as true laws. Such decrees are not made for the purpose of directing the citizens, because they have no ability to do so; no one can obey a law he does not know. Why then are secret decrees issued? One reason is to keep the citizens in a state of fear, so that they can be manipulated for the convenience of the tyrants. The other is to provide a *pretense* of law for getting rid of those citizens who are insufficiently frightened.

Thus from the four preceding articles, the definition of law may be gathered; and it is nothing else than an ordinance of reason for the common good, made by him who has care of the community, and promulgated.	And so at last, summing up the conclusions of Articles 1–4, we arrive at the definition of law, which is just this: Law is something ordained by reason for the common good, made by public authority and publicly proclaimed.

We began, in Article 1, with a rough and ready, common sense definition of law as a rule and measure of human acts. Through the course of Articles 1–4, St. Thomas has been clarifying this definition and unfolding its implications – not casting it aside, but refining it. As a result, we now know that *in order* to be a rule and measure of human acts, a directive must have four properties: (1) It must be something reasonable, something the mind can recognize as right. (2) It must be directed not to private interests, but to the good of the whole community. (3) It must be made by not by private persons, but by public authority. (4) It must be made known publicly.

I have paraphrased the third condition, *ab eo qui curam communitatis habet,* as "made by public authority." A more literal rendering might be "made by whoever is responsible for the care of the community." The Latin *ab eo qui* need not refer to a "him," and besides, as St. Thomas has made clear in Article 3, the care of the community may belong either to someone acting on behalf of the whole people, or to the people themselves.

Taken together, the four conditions pertain to the essence of law. Any directive that satisfies all four of them is law. Any directive that fails to satisfy even one of them is an imposter rather than true law – something pretending to be a law, but that isn't one.

Reply to Objection 1. The natural law is promulgated by the very fact that God instilled it into man's mind so as to be known by him naturally.	Reply to Objection 1. The Objector has it backwards, for the natural law *is* publicly made known. God makes it publicly known it by inserting into man's mind, so that we know it by our very nature.

Our minds are so fashioned – we are endowed with such a nature – that deep down we all know the general principles of the natural law. God promulgated the natural law to us *just by* fashioning our minds in such a way, *just by* giving us such a nature that we know them. So it is incorrect to say that because we know them, they do not have to be promulgated. Instead we should say that we know them because they have been promulgated. We will take up the question of what these general principles include in Question 94.

Someone might think that just because we do know the principles of natural law, there is no need to enact human law. For a variety of reasons, though, human law is necessary too. One is that knowing something is not the same as doing it. Another is that although we have natural knowledge of the *general* principles of natural law, only the wise work out their remote implications. Yet another is that in some cases, a precept of the natural law might be satisfied in several different ways that would mutually interfere if some followed one way and some followed another; for the common good, then, human authority must make a choice among these ways. Each of these points is also taken up later on.

Reply to Objection 2. Those who are not present when a law is promulgated, are bound to observe the law, in so far as it is notified or can be notified to them by others, after it has been promulgated.	Reply to Objection 2. True, those not present when a law is publicly declared are still under obligation to fulfill it. But this is true only in as much as it reaches them – or *can* reach them – through someone else or by other means.

The town crier's shout, "It has been solemnly enacted that no one may drive a vehicle faster than thirty miles per hour in a residential neighborhood!" strikes only the ears of those present, and strikes them only during the few seconds of utterance. Yet although the cry itself is limited in space and time, its effects are extended by such means as memory, word of mouth, and written documents. For this reason, it is incorrect to think that the law has not been promulgated to those in remoter places and later times.

Reply to Objection 3. The promulgation that takes place now, extends to future time by reason of the durability of written characters, by which means it is continually promulgated. Hence Isidore says (Etym. v, 3; ii, 10) that "lex [law] is derived from legere [to read] because it is written."	Reply to Objection 3. Laws are publicly proclaimed not just *at* one moment, but *from* that moment, because they are written down. That is why Isidore says in the second book of his *Etymologies* that "the word *lex,* law, comes from the word *legere,* to read, because law is written."

By such means as written documents, laws are promulgated not only to those in the present but also to those in the future. The Isidore quotation raises an interesting question about so-called unwritten laws, such as customary and natural law. One might think St. Thomas would deny that such laws are truly promulgated. But the pivot of his argument is not that laws must be written literally, in ink on parchment. It is sufficient that there be some means of continuance, some kind of durable record, so that the act of promulgation continues into the future. Figuratively, laws may be "written" in the mind by way of conscience, "written" in habitual actions by way of custom, or "written" on the heart by way of conscience, as well as literally written on parchment by way of ink.

By the way, St. Thomas does not endorse Isidore's *theory* about the origin of the word *lex.* He couldn't, for as we know from Article 1, he holds a different theory – he thinks its origin is the word *ligare,* to bind.

What St. Thomas actually endorses is Isidore's *point*. The Angelic Doctor is simply telling us that whether Isidore was right about the origin of the word (as most modern linguists think), or wrong about the origin of the word (as St. Thomas himself thinks), at least Isidore was right to stress the connection between law and durable writing.

For further reflection on the preceding section of the *Treatise on Law*, the online *Companion to the Commentary*, accessible via the Resources link at the book's catalogue webpage, includes a discussion of the following topic:

SECRET LAWS, VAGUE LAWS, AND OTHER FAILURES OF PROMULGATION

Before Reading Question 91

In Question 91, St. Thomas considers the kinds, or varieties, of law. Although he does not continually remind us, we should bear in mind that for each of these to be a real species of the genus, "law," it must share in the essence of law, which he has just finished investigating in Question 90. For example, if there is such a thing as eternal law, it must be in some sense an ordinance of reason for the common good, made by public authority and publicly made known. The same must be true of natural law, human law, and Divine[1] law. If there is more than one kind of Divine law (as he argues that there is), then it must be true of each of them. The "law of sin" is a special case, as we will see, because it is not a law in this strict sense, but a *consequence* of something that is a law in this strict sense.

St. Thomas considers five kinds of law in turn: Eternal law, natural law, Divine law, human law, and the so-called law of sin. This should not be taken as an order of logical derivation, as though eternal law implied natural law, natural law implied Divine law, Divine law implied human law, and human law implied the so-called law of sin. It is merely the order

---

[1] There is no obvious reason why the Dominican Fathers translation should have capitalized the word "Divine," but not the words "eternal," "natural," or "human." None of them are capitalized in St. Thomas's Latin. If the translators' intention had been to dignify one kind of law over others, then the honor should have gone to eternal law, because it is highest in order of precedence. However, simply to forestall the confusion that might result if the translation capitalized "Divine" but the commentary did not, I have retained the capital D. I have also retained the capitals for the two types of Divine law, Old and New.

of discussion. Allowing for the fact that there are different *modes* of derivation or relationship, the order is actually like this:

- The original, primordial law is eternal law.
- Natural and Divine laws are reflections of eternal law, one in the created order and the other in Holy Scripture, as though these were two different kinds of mirror.
- Although Old Law and New Law are distinct kinds of Divine law, both reflect the same Divine intentions, each one adapted to the particular era of salvation history in which it was promulgated.
- Human law is derived from natural law in two different ways, called conclusion and determination, although they are not explored until later.
- In the strictest sense, human law is not "derived" from the Divine law, because the direction of the people to their supernatural end belongs to the Church, not the government. As we will see later on, however, human law is *related* to the Divine law and cooperates with it.
- The "law of sin" is not a law in the strict sense, but only in an analogical sense; it is "derived" from Divine law by way of penalty for violation. As a reminder, I normally enclose the phrase in quotation marks or precede it with the expression "so-called."

At this point readers may find it helpful to study the diagram of the architecture of law, which schematizes the various kinds of law and their relationships, found in black and white just before the Introduction to this *Commentary*, and in color at the beginning of the online *Companion the Commentary*. I have included one extra kind of "law" in the diagram to which St. Thomas does not give a name, but which I call the "law of nature so-called." Today, most people confuse it with the natural law, but surprisingly, the place where St. Thomas gives us the equipment to talk about it is his exploration of the eternal law, and I will take it up there. One might also ask where canon law belongs. In the *Treatise on Law*, St. Thomas does not explicitly discuss its relationship to the other kinds of law, but I think he would say that canon law is to Divine law as human law is to natural.

St. Thomas's Prologue to Question 91: Of the Various Kinds of Law

TEXT	PARAPHRASE
[1] *We must now consider the various kinds of law:* [2] *under which head there are six points of inquiry:*	We said in the Prologue to Questions 90–92 that we would begin the study of law by investigating several preliminary matters. The first of these has now been discussed: What law *is,* its essence. The second will be discussed later: What law *brings about,* its effects. Before that, we must embark on a brief consideration of the second: What kinds of law there are.
	A more complete investigation of these varieties must wait until Questions 93–108. Here we focus on the narrower question of whether each kind exists at all – whether it is real – six *whethers* in all.

[1]   The kinds of law are the species that belong to the genus of law.

[2]   Why just these six? Why not more? Why not less? Primarily because St. Thomas is continuing a conversation that has been going on for a long time. Tradition had already acknowledged such things as eternal law, natural law, Divine law, and human law, so it is fitting to ask whether tradition is right about the matter, and, if so, why. Similarly, tradition had already held that there are two varieties of Divine law – two "editions," one might say – the Old Law given to the Jewish people, and the New Law given to the Church – so it is fitting to ask whether that distinction is valid too. Finally, whether and in what sense the so-called law of sin is real law must be investigated, because this puzzling expression had been introduced by St. Paul.

Of the six questions, perhaps the strangest to our ears is "Whether there is a human law?" One is tempted to think that although the reality of eternal law, natural law, Divine law, and the "law of sin" might be called into question, the reality of human law is obvious. After all, human governments make law all the time, don't they? On closer consideration, the matter is not obvious at all. Human governments make things they *say* are laws, but are they? Since we humans do not create the world – since our minds take their cue from how things really are, rather than things taking their cue from our minds – what would it even *mean* for us to "make" laws? Considering that a rule and measure of human acts should be reliable, but our reasoning is uncertain and fallible, how *could* we make them? And in view of the fact that we have natural and Divine law already, why would we need them anyway?

[1] *(1) Whether there is an eternal law?*	Article 1: Is there such a thing as eternal law?
[2] *(2) Whether there is a natural law?*	Article 2: Is there such a thing as natural law?
[3] *(3) Whether there is a human law?*	Article 3: is there such a thing as human law?
[4] *(4) Whether there is a Divine law?*	Article 4: Is there such a thing as Divine law?
[5] *(5) Whether there is one Divine law, or several?*	Article 5: Granted that there is such a thing as Divine law, does it exist in only one variety, or in more than one?
[6] *(6) Whether there is a law of sin?*	
	Finally, Article 6: Is there such a thing as a "law of sin"?

[1]   Law is a rule and measure of human actions. Is there an *everlasting* rule and measure of human actions, as even the pagans suspected? Defying the tyrant, Creon, in order to obey the higher law of justice to her dead brother, Antigone declares,

Yes; for it was not Zeus that had published me that edict; not such are the laws set among men by the justice who dwells with the gods below; nor deemed I that thy decrees were of such force, that a mortal could override the unwritten and unfailing statutes of heaven. For their life is not of today or yesterday, but from all time, and no man knows when they were first put forth.[2]

It is astonishing that Antigone could have recognized unwritten and unfailing statutes of heaven. She did not get the idea from her pagan traditions, because the worship of the Olympians was not a legislative

---

[2] Sophocles, *Antigone*, trans. R.C. Jebb (public domain).

religion. Rather she seems to be expressing a primordial intuition of the transcendent cause of law. Was she right?

[2] Can it be said that a rule and measure of human actions is somehow reflected in the pattern of creation, in the nature of man himself? Were those thinkers right who spoke of nature as a "book" that could be "read" for the direction of life? This certainly contradicts the modern notion that nature is meaningless "stuff."

[3] Can the enactments of human authorities rise to the level of a rule and measure of human actions, despite the obvious differences between the Divine intellect and the human?

[4] Setting aside the question of whether God has imparted to us a rule and measure of human actions through the metaphorical book of nature, has He done so through the literal book of Holy Scripture, as tradition insists? Has He revealed a law to us in words?

[5] What is the relationship between the Divine law revealed in the Old Testament and the Divine law revealed in the New Testament? Are they different laws, or are they different records of the same law? If they are different, then in what sense are they different?

[6] What on earth could St. Paul have meant in referring to our sinful tendencies as a "law of sin"? Is there any sense in which impulses that it would be wrong to follow can be considered a law?

For further reflection on the preceding section of the *Treatise on Law*, the online *Companion to the Commentary*, accessible via the Resources link at the book's catalogue webpage, includes a discussion of the following topic:
ARE THESE THE ONLY KINDS OF LAW THERE ARE?

Question 91, Article 1:
Whether There Is an Eternal Law?

TEXT	PARAPHRASE
Whether there is an eternal law?	Is there such a thing as an eternal law?

This question should be taken in the simplest sense: Is any law eternal? Although later on we find out many things about the eternal law, for example, that it pertains to God and has to do with His providence, nothing of that sort is presupposed here. The Angelic Doctor is simply asking whether any law has the property of eternity.

Much earlier in the *Summa* (I, Question 10, Article 1), St. Thomas takes up the question of the definition of eternity, of what eternity is. There he emphasizes two points that lesser writers often fail to distinguish. The first is that whatever is eternal is *interminable* – it has neither beginning nor end. The second is that whatever is eternal *has no succession* – it is not an endless series of moments, one after the other, but simultaneously whole. So when St. Thomas asks here whether there is such a thing as an eternal law, he is asking whether there exists a *law* that is interminable and without succession, bearing in mind everything we have already learned about what is meant by law.

---

[1] *Objection 1. It would seem that there is no eternal law. Because every law is imposed on someone. [2] But there was not someone from eternity on whom a law could be imposed: since God alone was from eternity. Therefore no law is eternal.*	Objection 1. Apparently, there is no such thing as an eternal law. Law is not really law unless there is someone for it to govern, so eternal law is not really law unless there is eternally someone for it to govern. Since only God has existed eternally, who could that someone be? No one. So we see that no true law could be eternal.

---

[1]   As St. Thomas explained in Question 90, Article 4, "a rule or measure is imposed by being applied to those who are to be ruled and measured by it"; in order for the law to regulate human acts, it must be brought to bear on those who perform them. Therefore, the Objector reasons, unless there is someone on whom the law can be brought to bear, there is no law at all.

[2]   The Objector protests that we humans, to whom law could be applied, are not eternal, but came into being at a particular time.

---

[1] *Objection 2. Further, promulgation is essential to law. [2] But promulgation could not be from eternity: because there was no one to whom it could be promulgated from eternity. Therefore no law can be eternal.*	Objection 2. Moreover, law is not really law unless it is made known to someone, so eternal law is not really a law unless it is eternally made known to someone. Again, no such "someone" existed, and so again, we conclude that no true law could be eternal.

---

[1]   Just as there is no true law unless there is someone to whom it can be applied, so, the Objector reasons, there is no true law unless there is someone to whom it can be made known.

[2]   Just as the Objector argued in Objection 1 that those to whom the law could be applied are not eternal, so here he argues that those to whom the law could be promulgated are not eternal.

[1] *Objection 3. Further, a law implies order to an end.* [2] *But nothing ordained to an end is eternal: for the last end alone is eternal. Therefore no law is eternal.*

Objection 3. Still further, law concerns the direction of things toward a purpose. But only the final purpose itself is eternal; things that are *directed* to it, such as law, are not eternal. So there cannot be such a thing as an eternal law.

[1]   So far the Objector is merely pointing out that law has something to do with steering toward a final goal.

[2]   Here the Objector goes further, declaring *in what way* law has something to do with steering toward a final goal, *in what way* it "implies order to an end." His answer is that law is a *means* to the end. But this means is always transient; when it has accomplished what it is meant to accomplish, it passes away. Only the final end is eternal, not the means to the final end. For this reason, there is no such thing as an eternal law.

On the contrary, Augustine says *(De Lib. Arb. i, 6):* "*That Law which is the Supreme Reason cannot be understood to be otherwise than unchangeable and eternal.*"

On the other hand, in his dialogue *On Freedom of the Will,* St. Augustine speaks of a law which is the pinnacle of reason, its uttermost height, holding that it would be inconceivable for this law to be other than immutable and eternal. He, then, believed in an eternal law.

St. Thomas is quoting from St. Augustine's early dialogue with a bishop, Evodius, *On Free Choice of the Will.* Augustine's reference to the Supreme Reason in turn alludes to a remark in a work of the Roman statesman Marcus Tullius Cicero, *Laws,* 1.6.18, where Supreme Reason is described as a law, stamped on our nature, commanding what should be done and prohibiting the contrary. In a recent translation of the former work by Peter King, the relevant passage runs as follows.

AUGUSTINE: Then let us call a law *temporal* if, although it is just, it can justly be changed in the course of time. Do you agree?
EVODIUS: Fine.
AUGUSTINE: Well, consider the law referred to [by Cicero] as "supreme reason." It should always be obeyed; through it good people deserve a happy life and evil people an unhappy one; and finally through it temporal law is both rightly enacted and rightly changed. Any intelligent person can see that it is unchangeable and eternal. Can it ever be unjust that evil people are unhappy while good people are happy? Can it ever be unjust that an orderly and responsible society sets up governing officials for itself while a dissolute and worthless society lacks this privilege?
EVODIUS: I see that this law is eternal and unchangeable.

AUGUSTINE: I think you also see, along with this, that nothing in the temporal law is just and legitimate which human beings have not derived from the eternal law. If a given society justly conferred honors at one time but not at another, this shift in the temporal law, to be just, must derive from the eternal law whereby it is always just for a responsible society to confer honors and not for an irresponsible one. Is your view different?

EVODIUS: No, I agree.

AUGUSTINE: So to explain concisely as far as I can the notion of eternal law that is stamped on us: It is the law according to which it is just for all things to be completely in order. If you think otherwise, say so.[3]

Taken together, the statements by Cicero and St. Augustine maintain that the Supreme Reason is an everlasting and immutable rule and measure of human actions. It is known to us because it is implanted in human nature, and it serves as the standard by which just human laws are commended and unjust human laws condemned. All of this becomes relevant later in the *Treatise on Law;* we will discuss the "implanting" of eternal law in human nature under the rubric of natural law. At present, however, St. Thomas is only calling our attention to the fact that tradition (more adequately represented by St. Augustine than by Cicero himself) acknowledges that there is such a thing as an eternal law.

---

[1] *I answer that, As stated above (90, 1, ad 2; A3,4), a law is nothing else but a dictate of practical reason emanating from the ruler who governs a perfect community.* [2] *Now it is evident, granted that the world is ruled by Divine Providence, as was stated in the I, 22, A1,2, that the whole community of the universe is governed by Divine Reason.* [3] *Wherefore the very Idea of the government of things in God the Ruler of the universe, has the nature of a law.* [4] *And since the Divine Reason's conception of things is not subject to time but is eternal, according to Prov. 8:23, therefore it is that this kind of law must be called eternal.*

Here is my response. As I explained earlier, law is just a maxim of practical reason on the part of the ruler who governs a complete community. Now recall my explanation, still earlier in the *Summa,* that the world is ruled by Divine Providence. From this supposition it plainly follows that the whole community of the universe is governed by Divine Reason. The very Idea of the governing reason of things in God, considered as the ruler of the universe, has the character of law. Moreover, we must call this kind of law eternal, for as Proverbs 8:23 teaches us, Divine Reason is not caught up in time, but conceives things eternally.

---

[3] Peter King, trans., *Augustine: On the Free Choice of the Will, On Grace and Free Choice, and Other Writings* (Cambridge: Cambridge University Press, 2010), p. 13.

[1]   The definition of law given here is abbreviated. St. Thomas has not dropped the requirements that law serve the common good and be promulgated, but merely allowed them to remain tacit, because at the moment his attention lies elsewhere. Notice too that although he had stated earlier that law is made *either* by the people of a perfect (that is, complete) community, *or* by one who has care of them, he is not cheating to leave out the former possibility. Why not? Because we are not here considering the changing laws which human beings make and remake from time to time, but a law that is unchanging and immutable. Since, if an eternal law exists at all, it could not have its origin in a multitude of transient created beings, there is only one other possibility: It must have its origin in a *single* ruler who *eternally* governs them, *eternally* cares for their good. This raises a question: Who could this eternal ruler be?

[2]   The eternal ruler could only be God Himself; the Supreme Reason that even the pagan thinker Cicero acknowledged is the Reason of God. But St. Thomas is not asking us to take this on faith; he has already demonstrated the reality of Divine Providence earlier in the *Summa*.

There are really three issues here: Whether there is a God, whether He is responsible for the good in the world, and whether this good includes Providence. All three have been considered in the First Part. Discussion of this interesting theme may be found in the online *Companion on the Commentary*.

[3]   St. Thomas speaks not simply of the *governance* of created things by God, but of the *ratio* or "reason" of this governance. The translators render the term as "Idea," because it refers to something existing from eternity in the Divine Intellect. It is the *rational pattern* by which God, having created things and endowed them with natures, now directs each one toward the goods that are proper to it. Of course we finite creatures have ideas too. But the Ideas in the Divine Mind differ from the ideas in created minds like ours, because at best our ideas reflect created things, but God's Ideas are what created things themselves reflect.

The particular Idea of which we are speaking – the pattern in the Divine Intellect by which the Creator governs the universe – is properly called *law* because it has all four essential qualities of law. Preeminently, law is an ordinance of reason, but Divine Providence is one with Eternal Reason. Law is for the common good, but the good of His creatures is precisely what God's Providence concerns. Law is made by public authority, but God has authority over all of His Creation, for only from Him does anything exist or receive any good.

Of the four essential conditions of law, the only one St. Thomas has not yet addressed is that a law must be promulgated. However, he returns to this condition in the Reply to Objection 2.

[4]   The argument may be paraphrased like this: Each of the other three qualities of law arises from the primal quality of law, that it orders things according to reason. Now the ordering reason by which the Creator governs the universe is eternal, and it has the nature of law. Therefore, there is such a thing as an eternal law.

Like many of St. Thomas's scriptural references, the references to Proverbs 8:23 is a metonymy, a part representing a whole, for the entire chapter supports his point. Wisdom, an attribute of God, personified as a wise and magisterial woman, is calling out to "the sons of men." She is indeed the foundation of law, for as she proclaims in verses 15–16 (DRA), "By me kings reign, and lawgivers decree just things; by me princes rule, and the mighty decree justice." She is indeed eternal, for as she declares in verses 22–23, "The Lord possessed me in the beginning of his ways, before he made any thing from the beginning. I was set up from eternity, and of old before the earth was made." She is indeed the pattern of the Creator's governance of things, for as she exults in verses 27–30a, "When he prepared the heavens, I was present: when with a certain law and compass he enclosed the depths: When he established the sky above, and poised the fountains of waters: When he compassed the sea with its bounds, and set a law to the waters that they should not pass their limits: when he balanced the foundations of the earth: I was with him forming all things." The culmination of Wisdom lies in the Divine creation and governance of human beings, for as she says in verse 31, "my delights were to be with the children of men." But she concludes in verse 36 with a warning: "[H]e that shall sin against me, shall hurt his own soul. All that hate me love death."

---

[1] *Reply to Objection 1. Those things that are not in themselves, exist with God, inasmuch as they are foreknown and preordained by Him, according to Romans 4:17: "Who calls those things that are not, as those that are." [2] Accordingly the eternal concept of the Divine law [3] bears the character of an eternal law, in so far as*

Reply to Objection 1. In the fourth chapter of his letter to the Romans, St. Paul speaks of God as calling into being what does not exist. From this passage we see that God knows these things and sets them in order in advance. In that sense, they exist with Him, having no being but what they derive from Him. So it is that He eternally conceives the Divine law, which he sets in place over the things that he foreknows, so that it governs them.

it is ordained by God to the | Just by virtue of the fact that it does
government of things foreknown | govern them, this eternal conception of
by Him. | His is an eternal law.

---

[1]   Human minds are subject to change. For this reason, a human being might first think in a vague and general way about painting, or cooking, or teaching, only later deciding *what* to paint, *what* to cook, or *what* to teach. But the eternal mind of God is not subject to change. As we saw before, not only is it interminable, but it has no succession – rather than experiencing a succession of moments, it is simultaneously whole. Whatever Ideas there are in the mind of God, then, have been there, in their completeness, all along. God does not first conceive of governing created things, and then later conceive of the things He is going to create and govern; to conceive of the things and to conceive of their governance is all one.

To think of it another way, we have already seen that the governance of things preexists in the Divine Mind from eternity, even before there was anything to be governed. But this could not be unless the Ideas of the things themselves also preexisted in the Divine Mind from eternity, even before they were made.

[2]   St. Thomas has not yet discussed Divine law in the special sense of the law revealed in the Old and New Covenants. Here I believe he is using the term "Divine law" in a very general sense, meaning "God's law."

[3]   Surprisingly, St. Thomas does *not* say that a law can exist eternally even if there is no one to whom it eternally applies. What he says is that it is sufficient if the both the law and those to whom it applies preexist eternally as Ideas in the mind of God. Since they do, the objection is refuted.

---

[1] *Reply to Objection 2. Promulgation is made by word of mouth or in writing; and in both ways the eternal law is promulgated:* [2] *because both the Divine Word and the writing of the Book of Life are eternal.* [3] *But the promulgation cannot be from eternity on the part of the creature that hears or reads.*

Reply to Objection 2. Law may be made known by means of either spoken or written words. Contrary to the opinion of the Objector, the eternal law really is proclaimed eternally, and in fact, it is proclaimed not just in one of these ways but in both of them. It is eternally proclaimed in speech through the eternal Word of God, and it is eternally proclaimed in writing through the eternal Book of Life. We may concede that this eternal proclamation does not eternally *reach* the created beings who later hear or read it, but the important thing is that it is eternally *sent out* to them.

[1]   To refute the previous objection, that there is no true law until there is someone to whom it can be applied, it was sufficient to show that both the law and those to whom it applies preexist eternally in the mind of God; in other words, the pattern is complete. Why doesn't St. Thomas offer the same sort of response here? To refute the objection that there is no true law until there is someone to whom it is *promulgated,* why doesn't he simply say that both the law and the one to whom it is *promulgated* preexist eternally in the mind of God – that the *announcement* is complete? Because on the part of the being receiving the message, the announcement is *not* complete. Only a created being can receive a message. The Idea of a being, preexisting in God's mind, cannot receive a message; not even the Idea of a being *receiving a message,* preexisting in God's mind, can receive a message. Only the being himself can receive a message, and he cannot receive it until God has created him.

As we will see, St. Thomas concedes that the promulgation of the eternal law is not eternal "on the part of the creature." His position is that this does not prevent it from being a true law, for the promulgation of the eternal law is certainly eternal on the part of God. *What God does* to make the eternal law publicly known to His creatures is something He has done from eternity, even though it does not *become known* to His creatures until they have been created.

Intriguingly, St. Thomas says the eternal law is promulgated by actual words, both spoken and written. However, he is not referring to sounds made by the mouth, or for that matter to strings of alphabetic characters. Earlier in the *Summa,* he had explained that the expression "word" has three proper senses. The most fundamental sense is "the interior concept of the mind," because a vocal sound is not a word unless it signifies the interior concept of the mind. But of course the vocal sound that signifies this concept is also called a word, and so is the imagination of the vocal sound. At times, we also use the term "word" not for the word itself, but for that which the word means or brings about, as when we say "The word of the king is that such and such be done." However, this fourth meaning is figurative.[4]

[2]   The first half-line takes us into deep waters, but they are well worth swimming. The expression "Divine Word" refers to the Son of God. Why would the Son be called the Divine Word? Because, as we have just seen, in its primary meaning a word is something that proceeds from a mind's knowledge, and that is how the Son proceeds eternally from the Father. As

---

[4] I, Question 34, Article 1.

St. Paul had said, the Son of God is "the power of God and the wisdom of God" (1 Corinthians 1:24). In the same spirit, St. Thomas says "the Son of God proceeds naturally from the Father as Intellectual Word, in oneness of nature with the Father." What has this to do with the eternal law? The eternal law is the pattern of the eternal wisdom by which God governs the things He has created, a wisdom inseparable from the wisdom of creation itself. But the universe was created *through* the Son (III, Question 23, Article 3).

St. Thomas's description of the eternal law as a rational pattern pre-existing in the Divine Intellect may at first seem to suggest something impersonal and abstract. If we think of it that way, though, then we have missed the point, for nothing about God is impersonal and abstract. The reference to the Divine Word brings this missed point clangingly to the reader's attention, because it *personalizes* the creative power and wisdom of God. If we want to know what the eternal law is, we must look first and foremost to Christ, the Second Person of the Trinity – to *living* law, not law *Itself* but law *Himself* in person, disclosed implicitly in Creation and Providence, but explicitly in the Incarnation.

The expression "Book of Life" comes from a vision recorded in the last book of the Bible, where the seer declares, "And I saw the dead, great and small, standing in the presence of the throne, and the books were opened; and another book was opened, which is the book of life; and the dead were judged by those things which were written in the books, according to their works."[5] Expounding on the passage, St. Thomas observes that the book of life may refer either to the inscription of *those who are chosen* to eternal life or to the inscription of *things that lead us* to eternal life. The latter sense of the term may in turn refer either to *things to be done* or to *things already done* that are recalled to memory by the power of God. In all, this gives us three meanings.[6] He amplifies the third meaning in another passage, later in the *Summa*, where, after reminding us of St. Augustine's remark that the "books" are the redeemed persons who exemplify God's law, and Richard of St. Victor's remark that "Their hearts will be like the code of law," St. Thomas suggests that the book of life is each person's *conscience*.[7] All three of these complementary interpretations would seem to indicate manners in which the eternal law is disclosed to us.

---

[5] Revelations 20:12.
[6] I, 24, Article 1, ad 1.
[7] Supp., Question 87, Article 1.

[3] As mentioned previously, St. Thomas concedes *part* of the Objector's point – that although the promulgation of the eternal law is eternal with respect to God, it is not eternal with respect to the created rational being. Those *to whom* the eternal law is disclosed could not have become aware of this disclosure until they were created. But the act of disclosure itself – *that by which* God promulgates the eternal law to His creatures – is something He has been doing from eternity. For the eternal wisdom to be eternal law, that is enough.

---

[1] *Reply to Objection 3. The law implies order to the end actively, in so far as it directs certain things to the end; but not passively – that is to say, the law itself is not ordained to the end –* [2] *except accidentally, in a governor whose end is extrinsic to him, and to which end his law must needs be ordained.* [3] *But the end of the Divine government is God Himself, and His law is not distinct from Himself. Wherefore the eternal law is not ordained to another end.*

Reply to Objection 3. The Objector says vaguely that law concerns the direction of things toward a purpose, but which things? If he is speaking in the *active* sense – that is, if he means that law is the *director* – then yes, taken in that sense the statement is true. But if he is speaking in the *passive* sense – that is, if he means that *the law itself* is directed – then no, taken in that sense the statement is false. That is, law is not *in its essence* something directed – to put it another way, direction to something else is not part of the *meaning* of "law" – although law *can* be directed to something, in the special case that the ruler and lawmaker is subject to a purpose distinct from his own. Then, of course, he must direct the law to this purpose. But that is not how it is with God. He, His law, and the purpose of His governance are all one thing. So the eternal law is not ordained to a less-than-eternal purpose, different than God's. It partakes of His own eternity.

---

[1] Certainly law has to do with direction according to a purpose, but the statement law "implies order to an end" is equivocal. Should we think of law as something that sets other things in order so that they achieve their purpose? Or should we follow the Objector in thinking of law itself as the thing that must be set in order so that it achieves its purpose? St. Thomas holds that the former way is correct. The meaning of law is a thing that sets *other* things in order so that they attain their end.

[2] Things may have both essential and nonessential features. Their essential features are the ones they have because of the kind of things they are. Their nonessential features, called accidents, are the ones they merely happen to have. For example, the potentiality for red hair is not part of what it means to be a man. Even so, a man may happen to have red hair; such a man has red hair not essentially but "accidentally."

What St. Thomas is saying here, then, is that although it is not an essential property of law to be directed to an end, even so a law may happen to be directed to an end. When will this be the case? Whenever the lawmaker is subject to an end different than himself.

It is important to notice that this special case happens to apply to every human being and every human law. No human being can find his supreme fulfillment in himself (or for that matter in any created thing); only in God can it be found. Thus, every human lawmaker is subject to an end different than himself, and every human law – insofar as it is true law rather than a fraud – is ordained to that end.

Plainly, then, the "accident" of which we are speaking is a massive one. No doubt its magnitude is what misled the Objector so that he confused accident with essence. He assumed that what happens to be true of all *human* laws is true of all laws *as such*.

[3]   Although every human lawmaker is subject to an end different from himself, such is not the case with God. He is perfect, all-sufficient, lacking in nothing, simultaneously whole. He requires nothing beyond Himself for His fulfillment; He never has; He never will. The ultimate purpose for which He created and rules the universe is not something different from Him; it *is* Him, for everything exists for Him. Moreover the same is true of the law that expresses the pattern of this creation and governance. The eternal law is not something different from the eternal lawmaker, but it is the eternal lawmaker Himself, considered from a certain point of view.

For this reason, the Objector is mistaken to think that the law of which we are speaking is merely a transient means to an eternal end. Since it shares in the eternity of its end, it is entirely fitting to call it eternal law.

For further reflection on the preceding section of the *Treatise on Law*, the online *Companion to the Commentary*, accessible via the Resources link at the book's catalogue webpage, includes a discussion of the following topic:

Does the Eternal Lawmaker Really Exist?

Question 91, Article 2
Whether There Is in Us a Natural Law?

TEXT	PARAPHRASE
Whether there is in us a natural law?	Is there such a thing as a natural law, a law that is "in" us by nature?

The Prologue to Question 91 asked simply whether there is a natural law. Here the *ultrum* is stated in a slightly different way: Whether there is a natural law *in us*. The preposition "in" is slippery, because one thing can be in another thing in many different senses. Heat is in fire differently than light is in the eye. The soul is in the body differently than the heart is in the chest. Intelligence is in a plan differently than suspense is in a story. We do in fact speak of the natural law being in us, but the sense in which any law can be in us – and the sense in which it can be *naturally* in us – are yet to be analyzed.

[1] *Objection 1. It would seem that there is no natural law in us.* [2] *Because man is governed sufficiently by the eternal law: for Augustine says (De Lib. Arb. i) that "the eternal law is that by which it is right that all things should be most orderly."* [3] *But nature does not abound in superfluities as neither does she fail in necessaries. Therefore no law is natural to man.*	Objection 1. Apparently, there is no such thing as a law that is in man by nature. As St. Augustine remarks in his dialogue *On Freedom of the Will*, the eternal law is the law "according to which it is just for all things to be completely in order."[8] From this it is plain that we are already adequately governed by the eternal law. But in that case, it would be superfluous to have a natural law too, and just as our nature is not deficient in anything necessary to us, neither does it overflow with things that are superfluous. It follows, then, that no law is natural to man.

[1]   The Objector's expression "in us" – which St. Thomas accepts – reminds us that by a natural law, we mean one that is somehow implanted in us, impressed upon us, built into us. Further discussion of the sense in which it is implanted may be found in the online *Companion to the Commentary*.

[2]   St. Thomas and the Objectors often clash over what St. Augustine means. Here he points out that the Objector is taking St. Augustine's remark out of context, for what Augustine actually says is "So to explain concisely as far as I can the notion of eternal law *that is stamped on us*: It is the law according to which it is just for all things to be completely in order." Since St. Augustine considers the eternal law to be "stamped on us," that is, on our nature, plainly he does believe in a natural law.[9] The Objector does not really deny that St. Augustine believes this. As we are about to see, for him the important thing is that St. Augustine

---

[8]   Peter King, trans., *Augustine: On the Free Choice of the Will, On Grace and Free Choice, and Other Writings* (Cambridge: Cambridge University Press, 2010), p. 13.

[9]   King, *ibid.*, emphasis added.

characterized eternal law as *sufficient* to set all things in order. Therefore, he thinks, why is any additional, natural law *needed*?

[3] Aristotle had famously held that God and nature make nothing in vain.[10] The maxim may at first seem redundant, because nature itself is a work of God. Perhaps a clearer way to put it is that God makes nothing in vain *either* in the order of nature *or* in the order of grace, and this is the sense in which St. Thomas takes it. For him, the maxim "nature makes nothing in vain" is a paraphrase of the principle that God makes nothing in vain in the order of nature.

It may at first seem that this principle is logically empty, a tautology. Certainly it would be, if it meant only something like "Organized wholes found in nature do, in fact, display organization." However, what it maintains is that naturally organized wholes display *purposeful* organization, to such a degree that nothing in them is superfluous to their ends. Taken in this way it is far from tautologous.

How far does this principle extend? Are we speaking only of the natures of biological organisms such as plants, animals, and men? Or are we speaking of nature as a whole? St. Thomas applies the principle to nature as a whole. Biological organisms provide more convenient examples, because it is relatively easy to distinguish their various powers and organs and to identify their purposes (something notoriously difficult in other cases, as we see in Aristotle's errors concerning the heavens). The purposes of the human sexual powers are procreation of young and the unity of their parents; the purpose of the heart is to pump blood. However, St. Thomas is convinced that all creation displays purposeful organization, not just biological organisms. This does not mean that we can meaningfully ask, "What is the purpose of that gust of wind just now?" or "What is the purpose of this pebble?" But St. Thomas would regard it as an eminently scientific procedure to ask what is the purpose of naturally recurring structures, such as suns. Such a view is easy to satirize; God, say some satirists, made foxes for the pleasure of English

---

[10] Aristotle, *On the Heavens*, Book 1, Chapter 4. St. Thomas explains, "But God makes nothing in vain, because, since He is a being that acts through understanding, He acts for a purpose. Likewise nature makes nothing in vain, because it acts as moved by God as by a first mover, just as an arrow is not moved in vain, inasmuch as it is shot by the bowman at some definite thing. What remains, therefore, is that nothing in nature is in vain." Thomas Aquinas, *Exposition of Aristotle's Treatise on the Heavens*, Book 1, Lecture 8, trans. Fabian R. Larcher and Pierre H. Conway (Columbus: College of St. Mary of the Springs, 1964). Available online at dhspriory.org/thomas/DeCoelo.htm. Compare *Politics*, Book 1, Chapter 2.

aristocrats in hunting them. That idea would of course be absurd. But would it be so absurd to analyze rigorously the roles played by foxes in the ecosystems to which they belong?

Considering St. Thomas's Christian faith, it is hardly astonishing that the *Summa* frequently invokes the principle that God and nature make nothing superfluous, nothing in vain. Much more surprising is that St. Thomas puts the premise in the mouths of his Objectors at least as often as he makes use of it himself. For example, one Objector claims that would be superfluous to suppose that God exists, because all natural things can be explained by natural causes and all voluntary things by human will or reason. Another holds that it would be superfluous for God to work in every agent, because His work in each single agent is sufficient. Yet another argues that it would be superfluous for human beings to be guarded by angels, because they are already guarded by God. And then there is the one who says it would be superfluous for the virtue of hope to reside in the will, because the virtue of charity already perfects the will.[11] Considering all of these appeals to the Nothing Superfluous Principle, the argument of the present Objector, who claims that natural law would be superfluous because eternal law already sets everything in order, comes almost as a thing to be expected.

These examples suggest that although St. Thomas fully accepts the principle that God and nature make nothing in vain, he is more struck by the misuse of the principle than by its use, and in each of these objections, including the present one, he thinks it is being abused. Today's Objectors go much farther. Our tendency is to scoff not at the abuses of the principle, but at the principle itself. How often do we hear that nature *does* overflow in superfluities? Examples of superfluities popular in the previous generation include the appendix and the tonsils. Those two are not so often mentioned in the present generation, as word has spread that they have functions after all. Among other things, the appendix may preserve useful symbiotic bacteria, and the tonsils may play a role in the immune system. But our time has come up with its own chief example: so-called "junk DNA," nucleic acid sequences that do not code for proteins, which are presented as superfluous on the assumption that coding for proteins is the only thing DNA is for.

Some of those who criticize the Nothing Superfluous Principle are motivated by the desire to score points in favor of all-powerful natural

---

[11] Respectively, I, Question 2, Article 3, Obj. 2; I, Question 105, Article 5, Obj. 1; I, Question 113, Article 1, Obj. 2; and II-II, Question 18, Article 1, Obj. 2.

selection, and against an all-powerful God. The argument runs, "Nature is filled with useless things; therefore it is absurd to think that God created and governs it by His wisdom." This is a singularly silly line of reasoning, for even an atheist who stakes everything on natural selection should expect useless things to disappear, just because their preservation would confer no advantage to the organism. To be loaded down with useless things imposes costs. Confronted with things the purposes of which are unknown, then, neither theists nor atheists should leap to the conclusion they haven't any. A more promising research strategy would be to *try to discover* their purposes. For example, numerous functions have already been discovered for so-called junk DNA; its dismissal as junk turns out to have been embarrassingly premature.[12]

We see then that the point of inescapable disagreement between theists and atheists is not whether nature overflows in useless things, but whether the fact that it *doesn't* overflow in useless things implies a directing intelligence. For further discussion of this point, see the remarks about Article 1 in the *Companion to the Commentary.*

---

[1] *Objection 2. Further, by the law man is directed, in his acts, to the end, as stated above (90, 2).* [2] *But the directing of human acts to their end is not a function of nature, as is the case in irrational creatures, which act for an end solely by their natural appetite; whereas man acts for an end by his reason and will. Therefore no law is natural to man.*

Objection 2. Moreover, as we have seen in Question 90, Article 2, law directs human actions to their purpose. But we are not like the unreasoning animals, which are directed toward purposes simply by their natural appetites. On the contrary, we are directed toward purposes by our reason and will. So again we conclude that no law is in us by nature.

---

[1]   The Objector alludes to St. Thomas's argument earlier in the *Treatise* that law is directed to the common good.

[2]   The Objector begins from two premises. First, he equates "nature" with the subrational urges we sometimes call "instincts." This is the same

---

[12] Jonathan Wells, *The Myth of Junk DNA* (Seattle, WA: Discovery Institute Press, 2011). Wells is a proponent of the contemporary theory of Intelligent Design, but his examples are taken from the work of conventional biologists, the overwhelming majority of whom are proponents of unguided natural selection. Intelligent Design thinkers reason that given the laws of physics as they are known to us, certain forms of organization that we observe would be unbelievably unlikely to arise apart from an intelligent cause. St. Thomas's approach is more like saying that without an intelligent cause, there could be no laws of physics in the first place. Although these two modes of argument are different, they may – contrary to the opinion of some Thomists – be viewed as complementary.

way people speak when they say of a person who acts without thinking, "he is acting naturally." Second, the Objector agrees with St. Thomas that law is not just a blind impulse or tendency, but an ordinance of reason, followed by rational deliberation. Consequently, it seems to the Objector that a creature is subject either to nature but not law, like wolves or worms, or to law but not nature, like human beings. In neither case is there such a thing as natural law; the very expression, "natural law," is inconsistent, like "odd evens," "future yesterdays," or "irrational reasoning."

---

[1] *Objection 3. Further, the more a man is free, the less is he under the law.* [2] *But man is freer than all the animals, on account of his free-will, with which he is endowed above all other animals.* [3] *Since therefore other animals are not subject to a natural law, neither is man subject to a natural law.*	Objection 3. Still further, subjection to law is the opposite of freedom; the more free a man is, the less he is subject to law. Now man is the freest of all animals, because he is the only one with free will. Yet they are not subject to a natural law; therefore, he couldn't be either.

---

[1] This is a startlingly modern objection. History presents to us two nearly opposite meanings of freedom. Among the classical thinkers (bearing in mind that not all ancient thinkers were classical), the term referred not to the absence of governance, but to a certain kind of governance, whether over a multitude of people, a single man, or an aspect of a man. Thus, in the political sense, the people of a republic were called "free" because they collectively ruled themselves (rather than being under the thumb of a tyrant). In the domestic sense, a freeman was called "free" because he ruled himself (rather than being ruled by a master). In the moral sense, a virtuous man was called "free" because he was ruled by the principle that most fully expressed his nature, this being his reason (rather than being at the mercy of his desires). And in the religious sense, a Christian was called "free" because he served the Author of his being, in whose image he was made, apart from whom he could not truly be himself, for to be alienated from the one in whose image I am made is to be alienated from my own being.

By degrees, the meaning of the term changed. So long as they do not think too deeply about the matter, modern people tend to regard freedom not as freedom from the wrong kind of rule, but as *freedom from rule.* In the political sense, this would make the people of a republic freer than the people of a tyranny only if they happened to make fewer rules for themselves than a tyrant would. In fact, the only true freedom would be anarchy, which has no rules at all, although freedom in this sense turns out to be inconvenient. In the domestic sense, a freeman would be freer than a slave not because he ruled himself, but only because he was more nearly able to do as he pleased – if, in fact, he was more nearly able. In the moral sense, a virtuous man would be freer than a vicious one only if his reason happened to put less constraint on his will than his base desires did. The only true freedom would be following whatever impulse one happened to have at the moment. However one might dress this up by calling it "autonomy," as though we were gods, the condition is less superhuman than subhuman. In the religious sense, a person would be free only if he served nothing and no one. Since in this view of things, God looks like a tyrant, some suppose that the only free spirit is the atheist. Carrying the line of reasoning still further, some take the view that not even the atheist is truly free, if he serves the cause of atheism. The culmination of the idea is that no one is truly free unless he does what he does merely because he does it; unless he has no particular reason for doing anything at all; unless his choices are meaningless. In this sense, freedom is not so much inconvenient as futile, and human existence is absurd. Which is just what such people conclude.

Plainly, the Objector understands freedom more in the way that most unreflective modern people do, than in the way that classical thinkers did.

[2]   In keeping with the Objector's view of freedom as such, he views free will not as something that enables a being to conform itself to reasonable rule, but as something that sets it free from all rule.

[3]   Including both its tacit and explicit premises, the argument runs like this:

1. The other animals are irrational; but law has to do with rationality; therefore the other animals are not subject to a natural law.
2. Alone having free will, man is the freest of all animals; but the measure of freedom is *not* being subject to law; therefore man, being freest, could certainly not be *more* subject to a natural law than the other animals are.
3. Since the other animals are not subject to natural law, and man is no *more* subject to law than they are, neither could man be subject to natural law.

The Objector's argument is posed in terms of natural law. Notice, though, that if he is right about the meaning of freedom, then his argument also applies to all law. It would follow that man is not subject to any kind of law, whether natural, eternal, human, or divine.

On the contrary, A gloss on Rm. 2:14: "*When the Gentiles, who have not the law, do by nature those things that are of the law,*" comments as follows: "*Although they have no written law, yet they have the natural law, whereby each one knows, and is conscious of, what is good and what is evil.*"	**On the other hand,** a commentary on St. Paul's remark in Romans 2:14, that even gentiles who do not have the law do by nature the things required by the law, declares that "Even though no law has been given them via writing, yet a law has been given them via nature, so that each one both knows and is aware of what is good and what is evil."

Intriguingly, this *sed contra* or "On the contrary" can be read in two ways. St. Thomas may be saying, "*According to St. Paul* in Romans 2:14, even the gentiles have the natural law, as a traditional commentary points out." But he may be saying something a bit different: "*According to a traditional commentary* on Romans 2:14, even the gentiles have the natural law." If we follow the former interpretation, St. Thomas is giving St. Paul himself as the traditional authority for the view that there is a natural law. If we follow the latter, St. Thomas is giving the commentator as the traditional authority, allowing for the possibility that the commentator may have been mistaken about what St. Paul meant.

A possible reason for the passage's ambiguity may be found in St. Thomas's *Commentary on the Letter to the Romans,* where he poses a puzzle about the meaning of the Pauline text. "But the expression, *by nature,* causes some difficulty," he says, "for it seems to favor the Pelagians, who taught that man could observe all the precepts of the Law by his own natural powers." He offers two possible solutions.

Hence [the first solution], *by nature* should mean nature reformed by grace. For he [St. Paul] is speaking of Gentiles converted to the faith, who began to obey the moral precepts of the Law by the help of Christ's grace. Or [the second solution,] *by nature* can mean by the natural law showing them what *should* be done, as in Psalm 4:6: *There are many who say, 'Who shows us good things!' The light of thy countenance, O Lord, is signed upon us,* i.e., the light of natural reason, in which is God's image. All this does not rule out the need of grace to move the affections any more than the knowledge of sin through the Law (Rom 3:20) exempts from the need of grace to move the affections.[13]

---

[13] Thomas Aquinas, *Lectures on the Letter to the Romans,* trans. Fabian Larcher, ed. Jeremy Holmes (Naples, FL: Aquinas Center for Theological Renewal, Ave Maria University, 2008), Chapter 2, Lecture 3, Section 216, available online at http://nvjournal.net/files/Aquinas_on_Romans.pdf, emphasis added to the word "should." In the text, I give the more common title, *Commentary on the Letter to the Romans.*

If the former of these two solutions is correct, then St. Paul is not really saying that *all* gentiles do "by nature" the things contained in the law; he is speaking only of gentile converts to Christianity, who have experienced the reforming influence of God's grace. But if the latter solution is correct, then although St. Paul *is* speaking of all gentiles, he is not saying that they actually do what the law requires; he is saying only that they know that they should. Taken in a certain way, both interpretations may be correct: St. Paul may be saying that although only gentile converts *follow* the law, even unredeemed gentiles *know* the law.[14]

Whatever St. Thomas's view of St. Paul's remarks in Romans 2, he finds a much clearer testimony to the natural law in other passages of Scripture, especially the passage in Psalm 4, above, about the light of God's countenance signed upon us. In the *Summa*, he cites this passage five times, always in the *respondeo*, the presentation of his own view.[15] Although the Romans 2 passage comes up just as frequently, he never brings it up in the *respondeo*, preferring to leave it to the *sed contra* (where it appears twice) or the objections (where it appears three times).[16]

---

[1] *I answer that, As stated above (90, 1, ad 1), law, being a rule and measure, can be in a person in two ways: in one way, as in him that rules and measures; in another way, as in that which is ruled and measured, since a thing is ruled and measured, in so far as it partakes of the rule or measure.* [2] *Wherefore, since all things subject to Divine providence are*

Here is my response. In the previous Question, I explained that law is a yardstick and measuring rod of human acts, and I also explained that such a rule and measure can be "in" a thing (in this case, in a person) in either of two ways. First, it may be said to be "in" the thing that does the measuring and ruling. Second, it may be said to be "in" the thing that is being measured and ruled, because only to the degree that it *has a share* in what is ruling and measuring it is it actually ruled and measured.

---

[14] Concerning the subsequent verse, 2:15, where St. Paul writes that the consciences of the gentiles bear witness, and their conflicting thoughts accuse or perhaps excuse them, St. Thomas explains, "[N]o one can testify that an action is good or bad unless he has knowledge of the Law. Hence, if conscience bears witness about good or evil, this is a clear sign that the work of the Law has been written in the man's heart. Another function is to accuse and defend. Here, too, knowledge of the Law is required." Ibid., Section 219.

[15] I, Question 79, Article 4; I, Question 84, Article 5; I, Question 93, Article 4; I-II, Question 19, Article 4; and I-II, Question 91, Article 2. Especially pertinent are second and third of these references.

[16] I-II, Question 90, Article 3, Obj. 1; I-II, Question 91, Article 2, *sed contra*; I-II, Question 94, Article 6, Obj. 1; I-II, Question 100, Article 1, *sed contra*; and I-II, Question 109, Article 4, Obj. 1.

ruled and measured by the eternal law, as was stated above (1); it is evident that all things partake somewhat of the eternal law, in so far as, namely, from its being imprinted on them, they derive their respective inclinations to their proper acts and ends. [3] Now among all others, the rational creature is subject to Divine providence in the most excellent way, in so far as it partakes of a share of providence, by being provident both for itself and for others. [4] Wherefore it has a share of the Eternal Reason, whereby it has a natural inclination to its proper act and end: and this participation of the eternal law in the rational creature is called the natural law. [5] Hence the Psalmist after saying (Psalm 4:6): "Offer up the sacrifice of justice," as though someone asked what the works of justice are, adds: "Many say, Who showeth us good things?" in answer to which question he says: "The light of Thy countenance, O Lord, is signed upon us": thus implying that the light of natural reason, whereby we discern what is good and what is evil, which is the function of the natural law, is nothing else than an imprint on us of the Divine light. [6] It is therefore evident that the natural law is nothing else than the rational creature's participation of the eternal law.

Of these two senses, the one that concerns us presently is the latter. Still earlier in this *Summa*, I explained that all things in subjection to divine providence are ruled and measured by the eternal law. From this and the previous point, it follows that all things have some share in the eternal law. They share in it just to the degree that it is imprinted on them, so that each kind of thing derives from it the natural inclinations, or dispositional tendencies, toward the acts and purposes that pertain to them particularly.

Of all creatures, *rational* creatures are subject to divine providence in the best and most distinguished way. They share in God's providence for all things through caring for themselves and for others. In this way they partake of Eternal Reason, for that is what gives them their dispositional tendencies to their due acts and purposes. This sharing of rational creatures in the eternal law is the natural law.

This is why, in Psalm 4, in the Old Testament, when the inspired poet urges that God be offered just sacrifices, he says what he does. As though people were asking *what* sacrifices are just, *what* offerings to God are good and bad, he remarks, "Many say, Who shows us good things?" His answer to the question is "The light of Your countenance, O Lord, is signed upon us" – the light of God's face is impressed upon us like a signet. In other words, the light of natural reason which enables us to distinguish good offerings from evil – the very work which is characteristic of the natural law – is nothing other than an impression of the Divine light upon us. And this is the very same conclusion we reached by rational demonstration: Natural law is nothing else but the mode in which rational creatures share in eternal law.

[1] *We are ruled and measured* in the sense that we receive our nature from the Creator, rather than giving our inclinations to our proper ends to ourselves. *We ourselves rule and measure* in the sense that we participate in His Providence, caring in turn for the persons and the matters entrusted to us.

[2] The critical point is that one of the ways in which the eternal law becomes effective is that our nature has been fashioned as a reflection of it; natural law is an imprint of the eternal law, just as St. Augustine had suggested.

The English translation renders two Latin words by a single English word, "proper." However, these two Latin words have slightly different meanings. Here we find the first instance, in the phrase *in proprios actus et fines,* here rendered "their proper acts and ends." In this case the translation is correct, for the word *proprios* really does mean "proper." What is proper to a thing is what pertains to it but does not pertain to other things, as when we say that pumping blood is proper to the heart, but taking in oxygen is proper to the lungs.

[3] One might protest that subrational creatures also provide for themselves and others. The robin builds a nest; the antelope flees from the lion; the pheasant lures the fox from its hatchlings; the lioness joins with others in the hunt. Yes, but St. Thomas has not yet finished with his explanation. These creatures act toward their purposes in a lower fashion than we do. They do not *consider* their ends, or ask what they mean, or take thought for the future. Nor do they have true culture, for although they seek means to their ends, they do so in rigid ways. A raccoon may pass on to its young the discovery that dumpsters contain good things to eat, but the raccoon does not invent agriculture; nor does it seek or pass on knowledge for its own sake, knowledge valued simply because it is true. Rationality is not a matter of the score a creature achieves on an intelligence test. One could imagine a creature that achieved a higher score than humans do, yet still lacked rationality. The point is not that there *couldn't* be another rational animal. On earth, however, we don't know of any.

[4] Unlike the subrational creatures, we humans pursue our ends by deliberation and seek to know their meaning. We seek not mates, but spouses. We try not only to obtain what we need, but also to understand what we need. Rather than pursuing our ends formulaically, we invent arts and build civilizations. All creatures are governed by God's eternal

reason, but we are governed by it in a different way than other species are, for among all the animals, we alone have minds that can contemplate the principles of our own order, reflect on the pattern of our natural inclinations, and recognize and conform to the natural law. We must, of course, choose to do these things, for although the subrational creatures have no choice but to follow their instincts, we can turn away from the truth. There is no such thing as a wicked lion; there is certainly such a thing as a wicked man.

We come now to the second place where the English translation renders a Latin word as "proper." However, the word *debitum,* in the phrase *ad debitum actum et finem,* here rendered "its proper act and end," actually means not what is proper, but what is due or owing – a debt. *Proprios,* a descriptive term, signifies function or proper work. By contrast, *debitum* is a legal term, signifying obligation, something that ought to be paid or given. Thus, by the subtlest shading of phraseology – a mere shift from the "proper" to the "due" – St. Thomas hints at one of the ways in which nature is connected with law. What things are naturally for is connected with how we ought to employ them. The respiratory powers are for breathing, not for sniffing glue; the sexual powers are for bringing about new life and uniting the parents, not for wantonness. These are not just the purposes these things are made for; they are also what is right.

[5]   So far, although the argument has been theological simply in the sense that it concerned God, even so it has proceeded by reason alone, without help from Revelation. Now there is a turn; to supplement his argument, St. Thomas appeals to his favorite among the numerous Scriptural passages that might be cited in support of natural law. The *reason* why we alone among the animals can contemplate our own principles of order, why we alone can recognize and follow the natural law, is that we alone are given true minds, capable of being lit by the light of the mind of God. According to St. Thomas, it is precisely this illumination that the psalmist has in mind when he speaks of the light of God's face.

Of course the expression "light" does not refer to physical light. Yet in St. Thomas's view, it is much more than metaphor, for the analogy between physical and intellectual light is precise. Just as things become visible to our eyes only to the degree that they are illuminated by the physical light of the sun, so things become intelligible to our minds only to the degree that they are illuminated by the intellectual light of Divine reason. To be sure, in this life we cannot perceive God in Himself, any more than our unaided eyes can gaze directly at the sun. Yet the problem is not that the light is too dim for our eyes, but that it is too bright. Even so, just as the sun's light makes it possible for other things to be seen, so the Divine light makes it possible for other things to be understood.

[6] From all the foregoing, it follows that natural law is the distinctive way in which rational creatures share in eternal law – a mode quite different from the one in which subrational creatures share in it. Their way of sharing in eternal law is passive; ours is active. Their way does not rise to the level of law; ours, being rational, does. They cannot recognize it *as* law. We can, and we do.

Reply to Objection 1. This argument would hold, if the natural law were something different from the eternal law: whereas it is nothing but a participation thereof, as stated above.	**Reply to Objection 1.** This objection would be valid if natural law were something *different* from eternal law. But that is not what it is. As we saw previously, natural law is how the rational creature *shares* in eternal law.

The Objector's fundamental mistake lies in thinking that there are two entirely distinct laws, one eternal and one natural. Actually, what we call the natural law is the manner in which we experience the eternal law, via our created rational nature. Could God have dispensed with the natural law? Certainly. He could have governed us as He governs irrational creatures. But this does not make natural law superfluous, because it is *better* to govern us by means of natural law – by drawing our minds up into the very pattern of His Providence.

In the Third Part, Question 65, Article 4, St. Thomas distinguishes between two ways in which a thing may be necessary. Some things are necessary in the sense that without them, the end cannot be attained at all; others in the sense that even though the end can be attained without them, it cannot be attained in such a fitting way. The natural law is not necessary in the first way, but it is necessary in the second. So it is not superfluous.

---

[1] *Reply to Objection 2. Every act of reason and will in us is based on that which is according to nature, as stated above (10, 1):* [2] *for every act of reasoning is based on principles that are known naturally, and every act of appetite in respect of the means is derived from the natural appetite*	**Reply to Objection 2.** The Objector is right to say that we are directed toward the purposes that are proper for us by our reason and will. But on what are our reason and will based? On our nature. How so? In the first place, every act of reasoning is based on principles that are naturally known. In the second place, every appetite is directed toward

in respect of the last end. [3]
*Accordingly the first direction of
our acts to their end must needs
be in virtue of the natural law.*

obtaining some end, and every such end
is a means to our ultimate end, which
we naturally desire.

---

[1] Remember that in the Objector's view, the natural and the rational were opposites; animals act naturally, but humans act rationally. St. Thomas shows that this view is superficial and wrong. Animal nature is irrational, *but human nature is rational.* To put it another way, the natural and the rational are opposites for beings of their nature, but not for beings of our nature. Yes, we share certain inclinations with the animals, but to us they are not brute instincts. They *make sense* to us – they are something we reason about.

[2] The deep structure of the human intellect is itself natural. We know *by nature* such principles as "good is to be done and pursued, and evil is to be avoided," and we are endowed *by nature* with the ability to recognize what is good.

[3] So, although for a beast it is natural to pursue what seems good to it, heedless of greater considerations, for us it is natural to pursue what reason recognizes as *really* good for us, in light of the ultimate purpose. The natural law indicates what this requires.

Notice the precision of the reply to Objection 2. St. Thomas maintains that every act of reason and will in us is based on something that is according to nature. But he does *not* maintain that everything we build upon this base is according to nature, nor does that conclusion follow.

---

[1] *Reply to Objection 3. Even irrational animals partake in their own way of the Eternal Reason, just as the rational creature does.* [2] *But because the rational creature partakes thereof in an intellectual and rational manner, therefore the participation of the eternal law in the rational creature is properly called a law, since a law is something pertaining to reason, as stated above (90, 1).* [3] *Irrational creatures, however, do not partake thereof in a rational manner, wherefore there is no participation of the eternal law in them, except by way of similitude.*

Reply to Objection 3. Both rational and irrational creatures partake of the eternal reason, each in its own way. Only the rational creature participates in the eternal reason *by means of its intellect, by reasoning.* Since law is essentially related to reason, the rational creature's mode of participation in eternal law may itself be called law. Although the irrational creatures' mode of participation in eternal law is *something like* a law, even so it is not truly a law, because it does not partake of reason.

[1]   In St. Thomas's view, Objection 3 hinges on a misunderstanding of *what it means* to say that man is subject to a natural law, but irrational animals are not. To clear up this misunderstanding, he must first clarify the difference between us and the beasts. The difference is *not* that we are drawn into God's eternally reasonable governance of the universe, and they are not. Both partake of Eternal Reason, but we partake of it in a distinctive way.

[2]   Eternal Reason governs us *by way of* our own reason. For just this reason, the way in which it governs us has the character of a law, since law is addressed to minds; it is something the mind can recognize as right.

[3]   Eternal Reason governs the beasts not by way of their understanding, but without it, since they have no understanding. Because it is not addressed to their minds, the way in which it governs them may resemble true law, but it is not true law.

We see, then, that the Objector has things exactly backwards. Man is not the only creature who is exempt from natural law, but the only creature who is governed by it. Only rational beings can enjoy such an exalted mode of governance, and in this privilege lies their freedom.

For further reflection on the preceding section of the *Treatise on Law*, the online *Companion to the Commentary*, accessible via the Resources link at the book's catalogue webpage, includes a discussion of the following topic:

IF THE NATURAL LAW IS REALLY NATURAL, WHY BRING GOD INTO IT?

Question 91, Article 3
Whether There Is a Human Law?

TEXT	PARAPHRASE
Whether there is a human law?	Is there such a thing as human law? Can a human enactment ever be true law?

St. Thomas does not suppose that we are ignorant of the fact that there are such things as governments, and that these governments enact things they say are laws. What he is asking is whether these enactments are what they appear to be.

[1] *It would seem that there is not a human law.* [2] *For the natural law is a participation of the eternal law,*	Objection 1. Apparently, "human law" is not really law at all. We already have the eternal law, which

as stated above (2). Now through the eternal law "all things are most orderly," as Augustine states (De Lib. Arb. i, 6). [3] Therefore the natural law suffices for the ordering of all human affairs. Consequently there is no need for a human law.

orders everything perfectly, and we already have the natural law, through which we partake of the eternal law. There is nothing left for so-called human law to do, and if it has nothing to do, it must not be true law.

[1]   Not all so-called laws are true laws; in Question 90, Article 4, for example, we saw that so-called secret laws are frauds. The Objector makes a more radical claim: That *all* so-called human laws are frauds, not just certain categories of them.

[2]   Obviously, the Objector has been reading Question 91, Article 2. Consequently, even though the eternal law governs perfectly, he concedes the need for natural law too, because natural law is the means by which rational beings share in eternal law's governance.

[3]   The tacit principle, which we have seen before, is that God and nature make nothing in vain, which we have seen in Article 2.

[1] *Objection 2. Further, a law bears the character of a measure, as stated above (90, 1). [2] But human reason is not a measure of things, but vice versa, as stated in Metaph. x, text. 5. [3] Therefore no law can emanate from human reason.*

Objection 2. Moreover, we have already seen that besides being a governing ordinance, law is also a measuring rod – a standard used to test acts, to see whether they measure up. But as Aristotle points out, our human mental concepts don't test reality to see whether it measures up. It is the other way around: Reality tests our mental concepts to see whether *they* measure up. So nothing produced by human reason can be a true measure of acts, a "law."

[1]   Here we are merely reminded that law is a rule and measure of distinctively human acts, the common-sense definition of law that St. Thomas dialectically elaborated in the four articles of Question 90.

[2]   Suppose the dog in the middle of my room is a Schnauzer, but I think it is a poodle. We do not say that the Schnauzer is inaccurate because it fails to correspond with my thought of a poodle; we say that my thought is inaccurate because it fails to correspond with the reality of the Schnauzer. Knowledge bows to reality, not reality to the mind, except for the mind of the Creator Himself. This fundamental principle of sanity is brought to mind by Aristotle at several points in his *Metaphysics*, especially where he remarks that "while knowledge might be thought to

be the measure, and the knowable the thing measured, the fact [is that] knowledge is measured by the knowable."[17]

[3] Without making the point explicit, the Objector expects us to remember the finding of Question 90 that law is an ordinance of reason, so that whatever does not emanate from reason is not true law.

[1] **Objection 3.** *Further, a measure should be most certain, as stated in Metaph. x, text. 3.* [2] *But the dictates of human reason in matters of conduct are uncertain, according to Wis. 9:14: "The thoughts of mortal men are fearful, and our counsels uncertain."* [3] *Therefore no law can emanate from human reason.*	Objection 3. Still further, Aristotle reminds us that a measuring rod must be completely reliable. Is human reason completely reliable? Revelation reminds us that quite the opposite is true. Our thoughts are shaky and hesitant, and our plans are dubious. Then could a true law be framed by *human* reason? Obviously not.

[1] The Objector is overstating Aristotle's point. Aristotle offers his comment in the context of quantitative measurement, where we do seek the most exact measure possible, one that is unitary and indivisible. But not all measurement is quantitative. In the other cases, says Aristotle, "we imitate this sort of measure."[18]

[2] Another translation renders the verse, "For the reasoning of mortals is worthless, and our designs are likely to fail."[19] Although St. Thomas makes the point from Revelation, what Revelation does here (and throughout the Old Testament "wisdom" books) is purify and sanctify our common sense.

[3] Again, the tacit premise is that to be true law, an ordinance must be reasonable.

---

[17] Aristotle, *Metaphysics*, Book 10, Chapter 6, trans W.D. Ross (public domain). Compare what Aristotle says in Chapter 1: "Knowledge, also, and perception, we call the measure of things ... because we come to know something by them – while as a matter of fact they are measured rather than measure other things." He adds that because of knowledge and perception, "Protagoras says 'man is the measure of all things' .... [But] such thinkers are saying nothing ... while they appear to be saying something remarkable." while they appear to be saying something remarkable." (Note that the "text." numbers in the English translation do not always correspond to the "chapter" numbers in Ross.)

[18] Aristotle, *Metaphysics*, Book 10, Chapter 1.

[19] Wisdom 9:14 (RSV-CE).

On the contrary, Augustine *(De Lib. Arb. i, 6) distinguishes two kinds of law, the one eternal, the other temporal, which he calls human.*	**On the other hand,** St. Augustine claims in *On Freedom of the Will* that there *is* such a thing as human law, the temporal counterpart of eternal law.

This passage was quoted and discussed in the commentary on Question 91, Article 1. There the reason for citing it was to suggest the traditional case for the reality of eternal law; here the reason for citing it is to suggest the traditional case for the reality of human law.

[1] *I answer that,* As stated above *(90, 1, ad 2), a law is a dictate of the practical reason. Now it is to be observed that the same procedure takes place in the practical and in the speculative reason: for each proceeds from principles to conclusions, as stated above (De Lib. Arb. i, 6).* [2] *Accordingly we conclude that just as, in the speculative reason, from naturally known indemonstrable principles, we draw the conclusions of the various sciences, the knowledge of which is not imparted to us by nature, but acquired by the efforts of reason, so too it is from the precepts of the natural law, as from general and indemonstrable principles, that the human reason needs to proceed to the more particular determination of certain matters.* [3] *These particular determinations, devised by human reason, are called human laws, provided the other essential conditions of law be observed, as stated above (90, A2,3,4).* [4] *Wherefore Tully says in his Rhetoric (De Invent. Rhet. ii) that "justice has its source in nature; thence certain things came into custom by reason of their utility; afterwards these things which emanated from nature and were approved by custom, were sanctioned by fear and reverence for the law."*

Here is my response. I have already thoroughly explained that a law is a command of practical reason. Let me offer a comparison between the way reasoning works in theoretical reason, where we are trying to understand how things stand in reality, and how it works in practical reason, where we are trying to determine what to do. Both kinds of reasoning have starting points, and both work from these starting points to conclusions. In the former case, the conclusions are detailed findings of each field of knowledge, and in the latter case, they are detailed dispositions concerning what to do about *this* or *that*. Now where do the starting points come from? In both cases, the uttermost starting points are axioms that cannot be proven, but that we use to prove other things – and that do not have to be proven, because we know them naturally. In practical reasoning, these indemonstrable, naturally known starting points are precepts of the natural law, and the detailed dispositions of affairs that we reach from them are human laws – assuming, of course, that we have not run afoul of any of the other conditions for law.

What I have just explained is what Marcus Tullius Cicero had in mind when he wrote in his *Rhetoric* that justice comes forth from nature. Certain practices became widely shared because they were found to be of good purpose. Having their origin in nature, they were approved by custom, and were afterward upheld by awe and reverence for law.

[1]   The conclusion of a sequence of theoretical reasoning is *propositional*. All men are mortal, and Socrates is a man. Conclusion: Socrates is mortal. The conclusion of a sequence of practical reasoning is *volitional*. I must protect my children from imminent danger, and that big angry dog is an imminent danger. Conclusion: *Not* "I must protect them from the dog," but *I act to protect them from the dog*. If the conclusion were put into words, it would be more like "Here goes!"

[2]   St. Thomas's explanation that knowledge proceeds from indemonstrable principles is often misunderstood. He is not saying that all of the material of reasoning comes from indemonstrable first principles and that none of it comes from experience. On the contrary, he holds that all human knowledge whatsoever comes from experience, even the knowledge of the indemonstrable first principles. What he means then is that the knowledge of indemonstrable principles is in a certain sense contained in all other knowledge. Just by grasping that my cat, Chesterton, *is,* that he has being, I grasp something about being; and so, from experience, my mind recognizes not only particular truths like "Chesterton is a cat," but also universal truths like "nothing can both be and not be in the same sense at the same time." Particular truths can be demonstrated; I can examine Chesterton to see whether he is, in fact, a cat. By contrast, universal truths *cannot* be demonstrated; I cannot examine everything to see whether it can simultaneously be and not be. But I don't have to; it would not normally occur to me to try. One of the miracles of the created human mind is that the experience of *even a single thing* is sufficient for it to grasp not just that *this* thing cannot both be and not be, but that *nothing* can both be and not be – that the principle of contradiction is necessarily true of all things whatsoever.[20]

For rational minds, the knowledge of such universal truths is quietly present in all knowledge of particulars. If I didn't know that a thing cannot both be and not be, I wouldn't even know what it means for Chesterton to be a cat, for in that case Chesterton might be a cat and yet *not* be a cat, which makes no sense. If I didn't know that there is such a thing as good and that I seek it, I would have neither motive nor direction for my action. I would not even understand the notion of "action."

By the way, the terms "precept" and "principle" are not synonyms. A principle is a source or starting point, a seed or root from which

---

[20]   This knowledge is not prior to experience, for to have it, I must have experienced *something*. Yet in a certain sense it transcends experience, for it tells me something about even those things which I haven't experienced yet.

something grows, and a precept is a rule that must be followed. But of course precepts and principles are related. When St. Thomas remarks that the precepts of the natural law function as general and indemonstrable principles, he means that the most basic rules serve as the sources or starting points from which more detailed rules flow.

[3] First-time readers sometimes object that legislators don't reason like philosophers; they don't start from first principles and work out theorems. Of course they don't, but that is not what St. Thomas means. The starting points of practical reason are *logically* prior, in the sense that conclusions presuppose them. But they are not necessarily *temporally* prior. It is the same in ordinary life. My practical conclusion, "Cross the street," presupposes a great many more fundamental considerations: That it would be good to get to the other side, that it would be bad to be hit by a car, that cross-traffic has been stopped by the red light, and so forth. But of course I do not set out in the way that a geometry textbook does, thinking, "Now let me see. Good is to be done and pursued, and evil is to be avoided. And so ..."

One small difficulty: If not corrected, the term "determinations," used in the English translation, might cause confusion later on, because here St. Thomas seems to say all human law comes from these "determinations," but later on, in Question 95, Article 2, he explains that human law comes about in two different ways, "determinations" and "conclusions." Does he contradict himself? No, because although the Latin term he uses later is *determinationes,* which really does mean "determinations," here he is using a broader term, *disponenda,* which means merely "dispositions" or "arrangements." "Dispositions" is the term used in my paraphrase.

[4] The quotation is from Marcus Tullius Cicero, *On Rhetorical Invention,* Book 2, Chapter 53. Cicero is not confusing the just with the expedient, nor is he endorsing what today is called "utilitarianism." He is saying that the first principles of justice are known to us by nature, that just social practices are further articulated in view of what experience shows helpful to human well-being, and that these practices are solemnized by law.

---

[1] *Reply to Objection 1. The human reason cannot have a full participation of the dictate of the Divine*

Reply to Objection 1. True, human reason does not *fully* share in the judgments of Divine Reason. Yet, in its own incomplete way, it really does partake of them. Allow me to return to

Reason, but according to its own mode, and imperfectly. [2] *Consequently, as on the part of the speculative reason, by a natural participation of Divine Wisdom, there is in us the knowledge of certain general principles, but not proper knowledge of each single truth, such as that contained in the Divine Wisdom; so too, on the part of the practical reason, man has a natural participation of the eternal law, according to certain general principles, but not as regards the particular determinations of individual cases,* [3] *which are, however, contained in the eternal law.* [4] *Hence the need for human reason to proceed further to sanction them by law.*

my previous comparison. The manner in which our theoretical reasoning shares in Eternal Wisdom is that we are naturally endowed with the ability to recognize the truth of the indemonstrable, universal principles that ground all reasoning about how things stand in reality. But are we also naturally endowed with the knowledge of particular realities – the knowledge that about the object I am studying, *this* fact and *that* fact are true? Of course not. In much the same way, our practical reasoning shares in God's Wisdom in that we are naturally endowed with the ability to recognize the truth of the indemonstrable, universal principles that ground all reasoning about what to do. But, like our theoretical reasoning, it has a limitation, for we are not naturally endowed with particular dispositions of affairs – the conclusions that in the case before me, *this* and *that* should be done (even though, in a certain sense, these conclusions are "contained" in the starting points). So, eternal law (in which we share) and natural law (the mode in which we share in it) are not enough by themselves. Human reason must go further. It must actually decide what to do, and uphold the resulting arrangements by law.

[1] One being can participate in the intelligence of another being in various ways and in various degrees. The puppet, for example, partakes of the intelligence of the puppeteer, not in the sense that it has any mind of its own, but just insofar as it is governed by *his* mind. The loyal and well-trained sheepdog participates in the intelligence of the shepherd in a more excellent way, because the sheepdog does have a mind and can recognize commands. Yet the sheepdog does not understand why sheep should be herded; the idea of a "reason why" does not even occur to it. Indeed, a beloved herding dog may even try to "herd" all of the members of its human family into a single room; I have even seen a border collie "herd" all of the stones in the yard into a single pile. Herding is just something it does. Far higher up on the scale is the way that a soldier participates in the intelligence of the commander of the army. Like the commander, he has not just a mind, but a rational mind. Though he too is under command, he understands that the commands he is given are connected with the overarching purpose of the war. One may even hope that

he can distinguish between legitimate commands, such as "direct your fire on the attacking enemy helicopter," and illegitimate commands, such as "bayonet the abdomens of the captured pregnant women."

In different modes and degrees, created things also partake of the Divine Reason. The way in which a mollusc participates in God's directive intelligence does not require the mollusc itself to reason. Far more exalted is the way in which a rational being participates in it, for his thoughts may imitate God's thoughts. Even so, the distance between the created mind and the Mind of the Creator is infinitely great, so this participation is incomplete. Only God fully knows the Mind of God.

[2]   This point has already been explained in the *respondeo*. The Latin term here translated "determinations" is not *determinationes*, but *directiones*, which refers to "arrangements."

[3]   God's directive wisdom specifies not only that good should be done in general, but also what is to be done to fulfill the good in each particular case. Our minds naturally know the general principles, but they don't naturally know in detail what to do about them. We have to work these things out, through careful deliberation. Shall I do *this*, or shall I do *that?*

[4]   Insofar as we humans are reasoning not just about our personal affairs, but about the common good, the well-being of the community as a whole, detailed dispositions about what to do must be reached not by private individuals but by public authority, and made solemn and binding by law.

---

[1] *Reply to Objection 2. Human reason is not, of itself, the rule of things:* [2] *but the principles impressed on it by nature, are general rules and measures of all things relating to human conduct,* [3] *whereof the natural reason is the rule and measure, although it is not the measure of things that are from nature.*

Reply to Objection 2. True, human reason is not the governing ordinance and measuring rod of reality. We do not say that reality is false when it does not match the conceptions in our minds; rather we say that our conceptions are false when they do not match reality. Yet the matter is somewhat different when we are considering not *what is,* but *what we should do.* The conceptions in our minds really can govern our actions, and really can tell us whether our actions measure up. They are able to do so, not in themselves, but insofar as they arise from the general principles of practical reason of which we have been speaking. These are naturally impressed into our intellects; we do not make them up.

[1]   The relation between a created being's mind and the universe is the opposite of the relation between the Creator's Mind and the universe. The ideas in God's Mind *cause* created reality, but our minds *respond to* created reality. In this sense, things establish the governing ordinance of the human mind; our minds do not establish the governing ordinance of things.

[2]   At this point, one might expect St. Thomas to say that although *in general* our minds do not rule things, they do rule our actions. His view of the matter is considerably more subtle. The directive principles of our actions are in our minds, yes. But we do not *invent* them in our minds; we *discover* them in our minds. They are naturally implanted in our minds, imprinted on it by the Creator of the mind.

[3]   *Only in the sense just described* can human reason be the governing ordinance and measuring rod of anything. Even then, it is the governing ordinance and measuring rod of our actions alone, not of other things, such as whether the sun shall shine and the birds shall sing.

---

[1] *Reply to Objection 3. The practical reason is concerned with practical matters, which are singular and contingent: but not with necessary things, with which the speculative reason is concerned.* [2] *Wherefore human laws cannot have that inerrancy that belongs to the demonstrated conclusions of sciences.* [3] *Nor is it necessary for every measure to be altogether unerring and certain, but according as it is possible in its own particular genus.*

Reply to Objection 3. True, human practical reason is not an utterly reliable measuring rod. However, it is enough for a measuring rod to be *as reliable as possible,* taking into account the kinds of matters that we are dealing with. Complete freedom from error is possible when we are reasoning about necessary truths, because they have no exceptions. However, complete freedom from error is not possible when we are reasoning about practical matters, because, even though the universal principles of practical reason have no exceptions, we are confronted with endless variation when we try to apply them. Now the mere fact that human enactments inevitably contain imperfections does not make them intrinsically unreasonable. So human law is law after all.

---

[1]   Theoretical reason deals with necessary things, things that cannot be other than they are. For example, two things equal to a third thing cannot be other than equal to each other. The principle that expresses this fact is a necessary truth, and it holds of all things universally. Deliberation, however, deals with things that *can* be other than they are. That is why we have to deliberate about them. Yes, of course, there are certain unfailingly true practical principles that give us our fundamental reasons for doing

things – they get deliberation going and the guide it along the path. For instance, I should always honor my parents. Yet these principles must be applied, and application is something different than deducing theorems from necessary truths. What does honoring my parents require of me? Which acts count as honoring them? May I honor them while beating them? Obviously not. Must I do whatever they ask of me? That is a much more difficult question, the answer to which depends on innumerable circumstances such as what they have asked of me, whether it is a good or an evil thing, whether it is compatible with my other duties, whether it would hurt them, whether I can do it, and so on. There is no way to know in advance how all these circumstances will turn out. The rule of honoring parents must be applied; I may not cheat or hedge. But correctly applying it requires much more than a rule.

[2] St. Thomas's point is not that because life is complicated, we will inevitably make mistakes. He is saying something altogether different. Even if we *don't* make mistakes, rules about matters of detail can never be stated in such a way that they have no exceptions. "You should always have regard for the safety of other motorists" – that holds true universally. "You should never go faster than twenty-five miles per hour in a residential neighborhood" – that is stated in universal form, but it certainly does not hold universally. What if someone in the car behind me is shooting at me with a gun? What if my neighbor has had an accident, and I must get him to the hospital before he bleeds to death? What if my child was kidnapped by a stranger, and I am chasing him? As we will see later in the *Treatise*, one of the great questions in the study of law is how to correct the deficiency that all human laws possess just because rules that are not universally valid must be formulated as though they were.[21]

[3] As Aristotle had remarked, "Our discussion will be adequate if it has as much clearness as the subject-matter admits of, for precision is not to be sought for alike in all discussions, any more than in all the products of the crafts .... for it is the mark of an educated man to look for precision in each class of things just so far as the nature of the subject admits; it is evidently equally foolish to accept probable reasoning from a mathematician and to demand from a rhetorician scientific proofs."[22]

---

[21] Question 96, Article 6, and Question 77, Art 4.
[22] Aristotle, *Nicomachean Ethics*, trans. W.D. Ross, Book 1, Chapter 3 (public domain). Compare Book 1, Chapter 7: "And we must also remember what has been said before, and not look for precision in all things alike, but in each class of things such precision as accords with the subject-matter, and so much as is appropriate to the inquiry."

For further reflection on the preceding section of the *Treatise on Law*, the online *Companion to the Commentary*, accessible via the Resources link at the book's catalogue webpage, includes a discussion of the following topic:

WHY NOT BASE HUMAN LAW ON A SOCIAL CONTRACT?

Question 91, Article 4
Whether There Was Any Need for a Divine Law?

TEXT	PARAPHRASE
Whether there was any need for a Divine law?	Is Divine law a distinct kind of law that provides something the other kinds don't?

In the Prologue to Question 91, St. Thomas indicated that the *ultrum* for Article 4 would be whether there *is* a Divine law. But doesn't Revelation say there is? Yes, and St. Thomas has no intention of second-guessing Revelation; he is asking something different. Even conceding the authenticity of Revelation, one might still wonder whether the Divine law of which it speaks is a distinct *kind* of law, alongside the eternal, natural, and human laws – or merely a rehashing or recapitulation of one of the other kinds of law. For just this reason, the question of whether there is a Divine law boils down to whether a Divine law was *needed* – whether it provides anything that the other kinds don't.

[1] *Objection 1. It would seem that there was no need for a Divine law. Because, as stated above (2), the natural law is a participation in us of the eternal law. But the eternal law is a Divine law, as stated above (1).* [2] *Therefore there was no need for a Divine law in addition to the natural law, and human laws derived therefrom.*	Objection 1. Apparently, what Revelation calls Divine law is superfluous. Considering its Divine origin, the eternal law is already, so to speak, a Divine law. True, there must be some way for us to participate in the eternal law, but we have that in the natural law. True, more detailed dispositions of affairs need to be derived from the natural law, but we have those in the human law. Since nothing is left for a supposed Divine law to do, it is not a distinct *kind* of law at all.

[1]   In its special sense, the expression "Divine law" actually refers to the law – or what seems to be a law (that is what is in question) – contained in Revelation, in the Old and New Testaments of the Bible. But the Objector is taking the expression "Divine law" in a much broader sense, as though it meant "any law the authority of which is rooted in God."

Many first-time readers (some second- and third-time readers too) make the same mistake. But the authority of all true law is rooted in God, so if the term is used in that sense, all law would count as Divine. The eternal law would count as Divine because it is in the mind of God, the natural law would count as Divine at one remove because it is our participation in eternal law, and the human law would count as Divine at two removes because it is a more detailed articulation of natural law as applied to local circumstances.

[2] The Objector has fallen into something of a rut. In Article 2, Objection 1, he said that there was no need for a natural law because man is governed sufficiently by the eternal law; in Article 3, Objection 1, he said that there was no need for a human law because man is governed sufficiently by the eternal law *through* the natural law; now he says there is no need for a *Divine* law because man is governed sufficiently by the eternal law through the natural law.

[1] *Objection 2. Further, it is written (Sirach 15:14) that "God left man in the hand of his own counsel."* [2] *Now counsel is an act of reason, as stated above (14, 1).* [3] *Therefore man was left to the direction of his reason. But a dictate of human reason is a human law as stated above (3). Therefore there is no need for man to be governed also by a Divine law.*	Objection 2. Moreover, Scripture teaches that "God left man in the hand of his own counsel." What this means is that God allows man to reason out for himself what to do. This is done through human law, so any so-called Divine Law would be superfluous.

[1]   St. Thomas cites Sirach 15:14 no less than seven times in the *Summa*.[23] Two of the citations occur in *sed contras,* restatements of the traditional view, one of them affirming free will, the other defending it against the view that we act by necessity. Another citation occurs in a reply to an objection, arguing that because the first man had free will, he could have resisted temptation. Interestingly, the other four citations occur in objections. In one way or another, these four Objectors keep missing what St. Thomas views as the Sirach verse's point – they deny that everything is subject to Divine providence, deny the need for a Divine law, deny the need to coercively restrain wrongdoers, and deny that any man must ever obey another. It would seem that St. Thomas is not only taken by Sirach's teaching, but also concerned to make sure that we get it right.

[23] I, Question 22, Article 2, Obj. 4; I, Question 83, Article 1, sed contra; I-II, Question 10, Article 4, sed contra; I-II, Question 91, Article 4, Obj. 2; II-II, Question 65, Article 3, Obj. 2; II-II, Question 104, Article 1, Obj. 1; and II-II, Question 165, Article 1, ad 2.

[2] In I, Question 14, Article 1, St. Thomas remarks that "man has different kinds of knowledge, according to the different objects of His knowledge. He has 'intelligence' as regards the knowledge of principles; he has 'science' as regards knowledge of conclusions; he has 'wisdom,' according as he knows the highest cause; he has 'counsel' or 'prudence,' according as he knows what is to be done." Counsel, then, means the conclusions of *practical* reasoning.

[3] At first the Objector seems to be arguing that since God allows man to reason out for himself what to do, *no* law but human law is needed. That would be radical indeed. But in that case, one would have expected this objection to turn up much earlier, in Article 1. It doesn't. Probably, then, the Objector concedes the need for eternal and natural law, and is merely arguing that human reason does not need any help from *yet another* kind of law to work out more detailed conclusions.

[1] *Objection 3. Further, human nature is more self-sufficing than irrational creatures.* [2] *But irrational creatures have no Divine law besides the natural inclination impressed on them.* [3] *Much less, therefore, should the rational creature have a Divine law in addition to the natural law.*	Objection 3. Still further, human beings are by nature more fully equipped to direct themselves than such creatures as plants and animals are. We have the help of reason and the guidance of natural law; they have neither. Considering that even they can get by without a Divine law, surely we can. There is simply no need for such a thing.

[1] What the Objector means is that humans are better equipped than lower creatures are for the practical needs of life. He does not mean they are better equipped in *all* respects. Wolves, for example, have fur, so they are better equipped to stay warm; they have fangs and claws, so they are better equipped to defend themselves; and they have four legs, so they are better equipped to run swiftly. Yet even in these respects, we are not altogether deficient. We can find ways to stay warm, to defend ourselves, and move swiftly. Moreover we have something that wolves do not have at all: The power of rationality.

[2] The Objector is not claiming that their natural inclinations are the only *law* the irrational creatures possess, because law is an ordinance of reason. He is saying that their natural inclinations are the only *guide* they possess. Animals are not subject to Divine law, and they don't need it. No crow was ever told not to steal, no cat not to kill mice, nor was any shark ever commanded to honor its father and mother.

[3]   The argument runs like this:

1. If creatures less well equipped to direct themselves than we are can get along without a Divine law, then certainly we can get along without it.
2. But such creatures *can* get along without it.
3. Therefore so can we.

On the contrary, David prayed God to set His law before him, saying (Psalm 118:33):[24] *"Set before me for a law the way of Thy justifications, O Lord."*	**On the other hand,** we see the Old Testament hero, David, imploring God in prayer to teach him His decrees. If the Divine law were unnecessary, why would David beg for it?

In the course of answering one question, the *sed contra* may seem to raise another. In some sense David already knew the Divine law, for Torah had already been revealed. Why then would he ask God to instruct him in it? Because to "know" the law may be taken in two ways. As we read in the prophet Jeremiah, "I will make a new covenant with the house of Israel, and with the house of Juda: Not according to the covenant which I made with their fathers, in the day that I took them by the hand to bring them out of the land of Egypt .... I will give my law in their bowels, and I will write it in their heart: and I will be their God, and they shall be my people."[25]

In one way, to know the law is merely to have intellectual knowledge of it, to have it inscribed in the memory. David had that already. In another sense, to know the law is to have the power to fulfill it, to have it inscribed on the heart. In that sense, David did not yet have it, but begged for it.

---

[1] *I answer that, Besides the natural and the human law it was necessary for the directing of human conduct to have a Divine law. And this for four reasons. First, because it is by law that man is directed how to perform his proper acts in view of his last end.* [2] *And indeed if man were ordained to no other end than that which is*	**Here is my response.** To complete the guidance of human life – to complete man's engagement with the eternal law – Divine law is needed because it accomplishes four things that natural and human law cannot do by themselves. The first has to do with the fact that man was created for *two* ends: Not just the happiness of this life, but the happiness of the life to

---

[24] Contemporary translations number the psalm as 119.
[25] Jeremiah 31:31–33 (returning to DRA).

proportionate to his natural faculty, there would be no need for man to have any further direction of the part of his reason, besides the natural law and human law which is derived from it. [3] But since man is ordained to an end of eternal happiness which is inproportionate to man's natural faculty, as stated above (5,5), therefore it was necessary that, besides the natural and the human law, man should be directed to his end by a law given by God.

come. We are naturally equipped to direct ourselves to temporal happiness, because our power of reasoning suffices both to grasp the natural law and to derive from it human laws. But our power of reason is utterly inadequate to steer us toward eternal happiness, beatitude, which exceeds all our natural experience. In order for us to reach that second, higher end, we need God to tell us directly what to do, through Revelation. His revealed commands are Divine law.

[1]   In Article 2, we saw that even in a limited and natural sense, our happiness requires friendship with God. St. Thomas is about to make an even greater claim: That we were made for a yet higher end that *transcends* our natural experience, one that exceeds what our natural powers can achieve or imagine. For the happiness of the life to come is not simply a longer-lasting version of the happiness of this life, but an infinitely higher happiness, the complete joy of *union* with God, of knowing Him as we are known.

[2]   At first it seems puzzling that two different things, one lower and one higher, could both be called "ends" or goals. One is tempted to say that the lower thing is not our end at all, but only a stage on the way to our end. This is not correct. In St. Thomas's view, temporal happiness is a real end in the sense that it is desirable in itself, not just as a means to something else. But it cannot be our final end, because for that it would have to be completely satisfying, leaving nothing further to be desired. Eternal happiness, or beatitude, has both of these properties.[26] It is the "sweetness" of "the ultimate and most complete participation in his goodness," which lies in "the vision of His essence, so that we live together in His company, as His friends."[27]

Even if we do have two ends, why do we need two laws? Couldn't the same law direct us to *both* our natural and our supernatural ends,

---

[26]   See also the commentary on Question 90, Article 2.

[27]   *Ultima autem et completissima participatio suae bonitatis consistit in visione essentiae ipsius, secundum quam ei convivimus socialiter, quasi amici, cum in ea suavitate beatitudo consistat. Commentary on the Sentences of Peter Lombard,* III, Dist. 19, Question 1, Article 5, Qc. 1.

to both temporal and eternal happiness? This question may be taken in several ways.

1. Do natural and Divine laws agree with each other? Yes. It would not be possible for them to contradict each other, for they have the same author, God, whose perfect Wisdom cannot contradict itself.
2. Do natural and Divine laws overlap? Yes. Many of the precepts of Divine law are included in natural law too, for example, the prohibition of murder, and many of the precepts of Divine law promote temporal happiness, such as the advice in the book of Proverbs, "Go to the ant, O sluggard; consider her ways, and be wise."[28]
3. Could God then have guided us without natural law, employing only Divine law to direct us to both our natural and supernatural ends? No. This question supposes that we might have been just as we are, naturally endowed with a power to deliberate, yet without knowing any of its first principles. The supposition is inconsistent. Divine law presupposes natural law.
4. Could He have guided us without *Divine* law, employing only *natural* law to guide us to both our natural and supernatural ends? No. This time the question supposes that we might have been able to use our natural powers to grasp things that are beyond natural experience. Again the supposition is inconsistent. Natural law is exceeded by Divine law.

It follows that to direct true human beings to both their natural and supernatural end requires both natural and Divine law. We can think of this in terms of a ship: Not only does it need to be preserved in good condition, which requires the knowledge the ship's carpenter has, but it also needs to be guided to its destination, which requires the knowledge the pilot has.[29]

One more thing: Although human law does not concern itself with man's supernatural end *per se*, it does not follow that supernatural matters have no bearing whatever on his natural end. Several of St. Thomas's remarks later on in the *Treatise* shed light on what human law *does* and *does not* do concerning God. What he says in Question 99, Article 2, is much like what he says here: "[J]ust as the principal intention of human law is to create friendship between man and man; so the chief intention of the Divine law is to establish man in friendship with God." But in

[28] Proverbs 6:6 (RSV-CE).
[29] St. Thomas develops this analogy in *On Kingship*, esp. Chapter 15, Sections 102–107.

Article 3, he goes further: "Hence human laws have not concerned them-selves with the institution of anything relating to Divine worship except as affecting the common good of mankind: and for this reason they have devised many institutions relating to Divine matters, according as it seemed expedient for the formation of human morals, as may be seen in the rites of the Gentiles." In our day an analogy might be found in the fact that although human law sets aside a day of Thanksgiving to acknowl-edge Divine blessing and protection, it does not set forth instructions about baptism, holy communion, or the worship of God as the Trinity. To put it another way, the public expression of gratitude to God encourages good moral character on earth, but it does not carry us to heaven.

[3]   How do we know that man *is* ordained to a supernatural end? From Revelation, of course, but not only from Revelation. This is the conclu-sion of a long and complex, but brilliantly illuminating philosophical argument, most of which is contained in the *Treatise on Man's Last End,* which is placed right at the beginning of the same major subdivision of the *Summa* that contains the *Treatise on Law.* Here we may only touch on a few high points. Everything we do is for the sake of an end. The end we seek is final and perfect happiness that leaves nothing else to be desired. Since we desire such happiness, and since God and nature do nothing in vain (a point we have discussed before), it is impossible that such happiness be impossible. After knocking down a series of other hypotheses – that final and perfect happiness lies in wealth, fame, power, pleasure, and so on – St. Thomas concludes that it lies not in any created good whatsoever, so it must lie in union with God. Now man cannot be united with God through his body or his senses, so he must be united to God through his mind (though he remarks that the body and senses do receive a certain completing "overflow," I-II.3.3). But since the mind could not be satisfied by anything less than seeing God as He is, so it beholds Him. Final and perfect happiness consists in nothing else that this vision of God in His essence.

But how do we know that the attainment of this end lies beyond our natural powers? The gist of the answer is given in I, Question 12, Article 4. It begins with the observation that our natural knowledge begins from sense experience. This being the case, our natural knowledge cannot go further than what we can learn from sensible things. Now although God is the cause of such things, He is infinitely greater than all of them taken together. Therefore, even if we knew everything that could be known from them, we would still fall short of knowing *Him.* It follows that the

vision of God cannot be attained by our natural powers, but requires
supernatural grace.

[1] *Secondly, because, on account of the uncertainty of human judgment, especially on contingent and particular matters, different people form different judgments on human acts; whence also different and contrary laws result.* [2] *In order, therefore, that man may know without any doubt what he ought to do and what he ought to avoid, it was necessary for man to be directed in his proper acts by a law given by God, for it is certain that such a law cannot err.*	The second thing Divine law provides is practical certainty. A moment ago, we said that human reason suffices to direct man to temporal happiness. In one respect, that is an overstatement. It is one thing for human reason to grasp the general principles of natural law; it is quite another for it to apply them to matters of detail, where the fallibility of human judgment is all too evident. The further we descend into details, the more likely it is that different people will reach different judgments about what to do and not do. Worse yet, the same is true of lawmakers; consequently, the laws are filled with confusion and contradiction. Divine law replaces the fallibility of human judgment with the certainty of instructions given directly by God.

[1]   St. Thomas puts this uncertainty in historical context in remarks
he offers later in the *Summa* about the condition of human beings after
the Fall, but before the coming of Christ: "[A]s time went on sin gained
a greater hold on man, so much so that it clouded man's reason, the consequence being that the precepts of the natural law were insufficient to
make man live aright, and it became necessary to have a written code of
fixed laws, and together with these certain sacraments of faith."[30]

His remarks in this Article about the uncertainly of human judgment
are easy to misunderstand. Perhaps because our culture has been so
deeply influenced by moral skepticism, many first-time readers leap to
the conclusion that he thinks people reach different judgments about *general principles:* One person judges stealing to be right, and another judges
it to be wrong. This interpretation fails; although St. Thomas considers
our reason fallible, he does not consider it that fallible. Notice that in the
remark about the clouding of man's reason, quoted previously, he does
not say man stopped *knowing* the precepts of natural law; he says only
that the precepts became insufficient to make him live right. But *could*
he have stopped knowing them? No, for as he maintains later on in the
Treatise,[31] "there are certain things which the natural reason of every

---

[30] III, Question 61, Article 3.
[31] Question 100, Article 1.

man, of its own accord and at once, judges to be done or not to be done: e.g. 'Honor thy father and thy mother,' and 'Thou shalt not kill, Thou shalt not steal': and these belong to the law of nature absolutely."

All this leaves us with a certain puzzle. Just what is it that we are uncertain about? Could we wiggle out of the difficulty by saying that St. Thomas is not speaking of how we recognize rules, but about how we apply them? On this hypothesis, everyone does know deep down that stealing is wrong, but they give different answers when asked whether *this act* is theft. Unfortunately, this interpretation falls short too, because in this case Divine law would have been provided as a corrective to applying rules incorrectly, but it is not.

The solution is that St. Thomas is speaking neither of general rules, nor of their application to particular acts, but of the intermediate rules that stand between these two poles. For there are three issues: Whether stealing *in general* is wrong, which *categories* of acts count as stealing, and whether *this particular* act is stealing. Divine law does not rectify uncertainty about the first point, because we are not really uncertain; though we may need reminders, we all really know that stealing is wrong. Nor does it rectify uncertainty about the third point, because the number of particular acts is infinite; to set them all down in writing would be impossible. The sort of uncertainty that it rectifies concerns the second. This sort of thing is stealing, and that sort of thing is stealing, but these other four kinds are not. For example, The Divine law given to the Hebrew people instructs that you may eat grapes in your neighbor's vineyard, so long as you do not carry any of them out with you, and that you may pluck ears of his standing grain and eat the kernels, but if you reap them with a sickle, you are going too far.[32]

Such ordinances gave full weight to both the wrong of theft and the need of the poor to have something to eat. They also provided data points to which later ethical thinkers could fit their curves: Is taking what belongs to another what stealing is? Not quite. Is taking what *rightly* belongs to another what stealing is? Not quite. Is taking what rightly belongs to another *against his will* what stealing is? Not quite. Is taking what rightly belongs to another against his *reasonable* will what stealing is? Yes, that's it. To refuse to allow a poor man to pluck a few grapes would be unreasonable.

[2]   By this means human laws are substantially protected from error. Then is St. Thomas suggesting that *all* differences in human laws are due

---

[32] Deuteronomy 23:24–25.

to error? No. If one commonwealth punishes petty theft with imprisonment, and another makes the thief pay a fine, it does not necessarily follow that one of these laws is a bad one, for general principles may sometimes be applied in different ways. This brings us to a related question: Does St. Thomas think every nation must follow precisely the same civil laws as those given in Divine law to the Hebrews? We will have much more to say about this later. Briefly, though, the answer is once again "No." The Divine law contains a mixture of different types of material; its underlying moral principles are valid everywhere, but the details of its application to the Hebrews are not.

---

[1] *Thirdly, because man can make laws in those matters of which he is competent to judge. But man is not competent to judge of interior movements, that are hidden, but only of exterior acts which appear:* [2] *and yet for the perfection of virtue it is necessary for man to conduct himself aright in both kinds of acts. Consequently human law could not sufficiently curb and direct interior acts; and it was necessary for this purpose that a Divine law should supervene.*

The third reason we need Divine law has to do with the fact that not all of the acts required for complete virtue are outwardly detectable – some are interior movements of the heart, like wishes, intentions, beliefs, and desires. Human law cannot directly command or forbid such acts, because no one who tried to enforce such a command or prohibition would be able to tell who was in compliance and who was not. For the complete direction and discipline of human life, Divine law is necessary, because it is free from this limitation. The enforcer is not a human authority, but God Himself.

---

[1]   How can human law command or prohibit what is undetectable? The authorities would have no way to know whether or not you were in compliance. It makes sense for human law to forbid me from getting into a drunken brawl, because the brawl can be seen, but not to command me to have a love of sobriety, because love cannot be seen. It makes sense for it to command me to pay child support, because child support can be seen, but not to command me to take an interest in how my children are doing, because interest cannot be seen. Notice too that interior movements of the heart include movements of the intellect. Thus it makes sense for human law to forbid me from committing an act of murder, because murder can be seen, but not to command me to hold a belief in the sacredness of human life, because belief cannot be seen. St. Thomas is not suggesting that human authority is unable to judge which kinds ought to be performed. The problem is that it cannot tell *whether* they are being performed. The distinction is subtle. I do not have a "right" to

believe or love or take an interest in whatever I please; nevertheless the law cannot forbid me from having the beliefs or loves or interests that I shouldn't.[33]

One might object that it would be an injustice for the law *not* to look into interior acts. In Anglo-American common law, for example, one of the elements in the legal definition of murder is that the killer must have *intended* to kill; the principle is *actus non facit reum nisi mens sit rea,* which means "the act does not make guilty unless the mind is also guilty."[34] Even though the intention to kill is hidden and cannot be seen, can't juries infer its presence from other circumstances? Yes. Notice, however, that in such a case the authorities are not trying to detect an interior act *directly*; rather they are inferring its presence *from* "exterior acts which appear."

It turns out that St. Thomas agrees. Not only does he permit such inferences, he requires them. Approvingly, he writes, "what a man does in ignorance, he does accidentally. Hence according to both human and Divine law, certain things are judged in respect of ignorance to be punishable or pardonable," but "according to jurists, if a man pursue a lawful occupation and take due care, the result being that a person loses his life, he is not guilty of that person's death: whereas if he be occupied with something unlawful, or even with something lawful, but without due care, he does not escape being guilty of murder, if his action results in someone's death." Conclusions about ignorance and due care require inferences *from* visible outward acts *about* invisible inward acts. What does his stricture about the inability of human law to detect an interior act mean, then? Apparently it concerns the very different case in which the inward act is *not* accompanied by a visible outward act: "For human law does not punish the man who wishes to slay, and slays not: whereas the Divine law does, according to Matthew 5:22: 'Whosoever is angry with his brother, shall be in danger of the judgment.'"[35]

[2]   Having covetous wishes is just as vicious, just as contrary to virtue, as carrying them out. Yet so long as they are not carried out, the human law must ignore them; the ticklish experiment of peering into souls, even

---

[33] Not until much later do we take up the question of whether we have rights of other sorts or in other senses. See esp. Question 94, Before Reading, and Question 96, Article 4.
[34] Shamefully, in contemporary criminal regulatory law, the element of *mens rea*, guilty mind, is often violated. A person may be convicted of a regulatory offense even if it is conceded that he had no intention of doing wrong.
[35] 8I-II, Question 100, Article 9; II-II, Question 64, Article 8; I-II, ibid. Concerning intention, see also I-II, Question 7, Article 4; I-II, Question 19; and I-II, Question 20, Article 5.

with the circumstantial evidence of outward acts, is not to be too often repeated. The Divine legislator, who sees directly into hearts, has no need of experiments, no necessity to make inferences, risky or otherwise; hence the Divine law can stride confidently into regions where the human law should not, commanding "Thou shalt not covet."

Yet this limitation of merely human law is easily misunderstood. True, it would be foolish and pointless to enact a law requiring those who nourish covetousness to pay a fine. In a certain sense such a law would be impossible; one could go through the motions of enacting it, but the resulting so-called law would be a dead letter. But would it be so foolish to enact a law requiring teachers in public schools to warn their young charges against covetousness? That would be a different kettle of fish. The law would not be forbidding something undetectable, but commanding something detectable; covetousness cannot be seen, but teacherly warnings can be. So we must not say that law may not *take an interest* in the interior movements of the heart, only that it may not command or prohibit them *per se*. As we will see later, St. Thomas does think the law should take an interest in them. He thinks the law should cherish the virtues as a hen her chicks.

[1] *Fourthly, because, as Augustine says (De Lib. Arb. i,5,6), human law cannot punish or forbid all evil deeds: since while aiming at doing away with all evils, it would do away with many good things, and would hinder the advance of the common good, which is necessary for human intercourse. [2] In order, therefore, that no evil might remain unforbidden and unpunished, it was necessary for the Divine law to supervene, whereby all sins are forbidden.*	The fourth and final reason Divine law is needed is that even in the case of exterior acts that *can* be seen, it is infeasible to inflict human penalties and prohibitions on every single kind of wicked deed. The attempt to suppress every single evil by human authority would end up crushing a great many goods. So although such sweeping laws might be intended to improve the moral condition of the community, they would actually cause it to deteriorate. We see then that human law cannot forbid every sin. But Divine law can and does.

[1]   If the cardinal error of the Puritan understanding of government was to confuse the functions of Divine and human law, then we see here how far St. Thomas is from being a Puritan. All sin is dreadfully harmful to us, but that does not make all of it the business of the government. Do we reach this conclusion by suspending judgment about goods and evils? On the contrary, we reach it by judging them more intelligently – by

soberly asking which evils the blunt instrument of human law *can* do something about.

The principle that an overambitious war on evil can also damage good is not pagan; Christ himself taught it in the parable of the "tares" or weeds.[36] If wheat and weeds are matted together, an ill-advised yank on one may uproot the other too. Chide the nobility for pursuing glory, and they grow slothful.[37] Punish the merchants for being greedy, and they grow indolent. Forbid the craftsmen from boasting of their skill, and they let their standards slip. Flaunting, greed, and boasting are bad, but he who criminalizes them will pay a mighty price. Men must be not only directed in their actions, but also transformed in their motives, and human law cannot do this for them. Divine law is different because it is coupled with God's grace. Indeed, as St. Thomas argues in Question 106, Article 1, the very essence of the New Law is God's grace.

Puritans ask, "If human law cannot repress every evil, then what good is it?" In the passage that St. Thomas cites, St. Augustine gives the answer: "For it seems to you that the law that is enacted to govern states tolerates and leaves unpunished many things, which are nevertheless redressed by divine providence (and rightly so). Yet it does not follow that just because the law does not accomplish everything, we should disapprove of what it *does* accomplish."[38] We return to this topic in Question 96, Article 2.

[2]   Divine law is enforced by God, not by the government. The penalty of human law is the loss of temporal goods – liberty if I am imprisoned, comfort if I am scourged, wealth if I am made to pay a fine. The penalty of Divine law is that by destroying love within us, we separate ourselves from God, "in whom alone man can have the life and happiness for which he was created and for which he longs."[39] If human law tries to forbid every evil, it ends up destroying many goods. No such consequence follows from the fact that the Divine law forbids every sin.

[36] Matthew 13:24–43.

[37] I am thinking of St. Augustine's argument in *The City of God*, Book 5, Chapters 12–21, that in the time of the Republic, the Roman nobility performed acts of conspicuous benefit to the commonwealth only for the sake of glory, that is, the opinion of others who thought well of them.

[38] Peter King, trans., *Augustine: On the Free Choice of the Will, On Grace and Free Choice, and Other Writings* (Cambridge: Cambridge University Press, 2010), p. 11. St. Augustine is summarizing, clarifying, and approving some remarks of his friend, Evodius.

[39] *Catechism of the Catholic Church*, Section 1057.

And these four causes are touched upon in Ps. 18:8 [19:7],[40] *where it is said: "The law of the Lord is unspotted,"* i.e. allowing no foulness of sin; *"converting souls,"* because it directs not only exterior, but also interior acts; *"the testimony of the Lord is faithful,"* because of the certainty of what is true and right; *"giving wisdom to little ones,"* by directing man to an end supernatural and Divine.*	The same four final causes or purposes of Divine law are briefly mentioned in a verse of the Psalms, "The law of the Lord is unspotted, converting souls: The testimony of the Lord is faithful, giving wisdom to little ones." Its *unspottedness* refers to its fourth purpose, forbidding all sins; its *conversion of souls* refers to its third purpose, setting in order even the hidden movements of the heart; its *faithfulness* refers to its second purpose, providing practical certainty; and its *giving of wisdom to little ones* to its first purpose, directing us to our ultimate supernatural goal, which natural reason alone cannot understand.

The verse of the Psalms that St. Thomas is citing makes use of the Hebrew poetic device of parallelism, for the second half of the sentence duplicates the structure and echoes the thought of the first. By taking the verse apart into four pieces, St. Thomas obscures the parallelism; however, as though to do homage to the lost Hebrew trope, he substitutes a Latin trope, *chiasmus*, or reversal – for the first purpose in the *respondeo* corresponds to the fourth purpose in the verse, the second to the third, the third to the second, and the fourth to the first. Reversal is out of fashion today, perhaps because one needs a good memory to enjoy it. To St. Thomas's original readers, who had far better memory training, its cadence and anticadence would have been elegantly simple, like unrolling a carpet and then rolling it up. The reversal has the further merit of keeping the reader from thinking that the order in which St. Thomas discusses the four purposes corresponds to their order of importance.

This particular Psalm is especially well chosen for St. Thomas's purposes in Question 91. The first three articles of the Question show how God's Providence is reflected in nature, while the last three articles show how it is reflected in Revelation. As we see in the following translation, the two halves of the Psalm have exactly the same dual purpose[41]:

The heavens are telling the glory of God; and the firmament proclaims his handiwork. Day to day pours forth speech, and night to night declares knowledge. There is no speech, nor are there words; their voice is not heard; yet their voice

---

[40] The English translation gives the number of the Psalm as 118:8, but this is a typo for 18:8. Adding to the confusion, most modern translations of the Bible list the verse as 19:7.

[41] Psalm 19 (RSV-CE), verse divisions suppressed.

goes out through all the earth, and their words to the end of the world. In them he has set a tent for the sun, which comes forth like a bridegroom leaving his chamber, and like a strong man runs its course with joy. Its rising is from the end of the heavens, and its circuit to the end of them; and there is nothing hid from its heat.

The law of the Lord is perfect, reviving the soul; the testimony of the Lord is sure, making wise the simple; the precepts of the Lord are right, rejoicing the heart; the commandment of the Lord is pure, enlightening the eyes; the fear of the Lord is clean, enduring for ever; the ordinances of the Lord are true, and righteous altogether. More to be desired are they than gold, even much fine gold; sweeter also than honey and drippings of the honeycomb. Moreover by them is thy servant warned; in keeping them there is great reward. But who can discern his errors? Clear thou me from hidden faults. Keep back thy servant also from presumptuous sins; let them not have dominion over me! Then I shall be blameless, and innocent of great transgression. Let the words of my mouth and the meditation of my heart be acceptable in thy sight, O Lord, my rock and my redeemer.

---

[1] *Reply to Objection 1. By the natural law the eternal law is participated proportionately to the capacity of human nature.* [2] *But to his supernatural end man needs to be directed in a yet higher way. Hence the additional law given by God, whereby man shares more perfectly in the eternal law.*

Reply to Objection 1. True, we already share in eternal law through the natural law. But this mode of sharing in eternal law is incomplete, because it is limited by our natural powers; it can direct us only to our natural end, not to our supernatural end. To complete our participation in eternal law, we need additional instruction, which God provides through Divine law.

---

[1] The Objector points out that through natural law, man already shares in the eternal law. What he overlooks is that every created being shares in the eternal law only in the mode that its nature makes possible. Although the rational mode in which humans share in it is far nobler than the irrational mode in which flatworms share in it, there remains an infinite gap between our minds and God's.

[2] Our finite minds are certainly capable of working out that we *have* a supernatural end. They can even work out in a limited sense *what it is* – that it must lie in union with God, however inconceivable that is to our finite minds. As we saw previously, these conclusions can be drawn just from natural experience – from our longing for happiness, the insufficiency of created things to satisfy us, the fact that nature makes nothing in vain, and so on. The problem is that natural reason cannot *direct* us to union with God, because none of our natural powers can achieve it. God would have to lift us beyond ourselves, so to speak, and only He can tell

us how to hold onto the rope – what we must to do to cooperate with supernatural grace.

[1] *Reply to Objection 2. Counsel is a kind of inquiry: hence it must proceed from some principles.* [2] *Nor is it enough for it to proceed from principles imparted by nature, which are the precepts of the natural law, for the reasons given above:* [3] *but there is need for certain additional principles, namely, the precepts of the Divine law.*	Reply to Objection 2. What does it really mean that man is left in the hand of his counsel? That he must look into the goal, inquire into what he must do, yes, but how does that work? All seeking needs starting points, something to get it going and guide it in the right direction. As we have seen, the starting points for looking into our natural goal are implicit in our nature and contained in the commands of natural law. But natural law cannot provide the additional starting points needed for looking into our *supernatural* goal. For these, we need Divine law.

[1] The term "counsel" refers to conclusions of practical reasoning, as we have seen previously. But we cannot reach conclusions without premises; we cannot get anywhere without starting somewhere.

[2] An inclination to seek those things we recognize as good and shun those things we recognize as evil is part of our natural equipment. Stated as a principle of practical reason, it can be expressed "good is that which all things seek after," and as a precept of law, "Good is to be done and pursued, and evil avoided" (Question 94, Article 2). If our minds didn't already know this, deliberation about what to do could never get started. It would never occur to us that there is something to deliberate about; we would not even grasp what deliberation is. The other starting points of practical reason are implanted in us in the same way; we are designed with a view to seeking certain goods, in certain ways, in a certain order.

[3] Our natural inclinations get us started on the pursuit of temporal happiness, direct us for instance to make friends, to form families, and to pursue truth. That is fine so far as it goes, but it does not go far enough, because our natural inclinations are insufficient to tell us how to reach our supernatural good.

Reply to Objection 3. Irrational creatures are not ordained to an end higher than that which is proportionate to their natural	Reply to Objection 3. The Objector argues that since we are better equipped than irrational beings to direct ourselves, and *they* get by without Divine law, surely we don't need Divine law. But direction is always direction to some end. True, we are better equipped than irrational beings to direct ourselves

powers: consequently the comparison fails.	to our *natural* end. But this is where the analogy breaks down, because irrational creatures have *only* a natural end. We don't.

A plant is driven by automatic processes to take in nutrition, grow, and propagate; that is its natural end. An animal is prompted by instinct and sense perception to pursue its necessities and to procreate; that is its natural end. A man is guided by reason to seek not only the ease of the senses, but the fulfillment of the rational soul, to live well as reason understands living well, which includes seeking the truth and living in communities patterned by it; that is *his* natural end. Is this the conclusion of the story? For plants, animals, and other irrational beings (viruses, procaryotes, what have you), yes. For us, it is not. The Objector is not mistaken about our excellent equipment; he is quite right about it. Granted reasonably favorable circumstances, if we do not attain temporal happiness, we have only ourselves to blame. Yet there is something more to be said, isn't there? All that satisfaction is strangely unsatisfying, and we find ourselves asking, "Is this all there is?" With our well-equipped minds, we can find out a great many truths, even the truth that we were made by an all-good and all-powerful Creator. Yet in its way, that knowledge is the most unsatisfying of all – for it is one thing to know *of* God, but quite another to *know God*. For knowing *of* God, our natural powers are enough. For *knowing God*, they fall infinitely short. All this is a hint that we were made not only for a natural end, like the irrational beings, but for a supernatural end that transcends all our powers. So what that *they* have no need of Divine law? What has that to do with *us*?

For further reflection on the preceding section of the *Treatise on Law*, the online *Companion to the Commentary*, accessible via the Resources link at the book's catalogue webpage, includes a discussion of the following topic:

THE RELATION BETWEEN NATURAL AND DIVINE LAW

Question 91, Article 5:
Whether There Is but One Divine Law?

TEXT	PARAPHRASE
Whether there is but one Divine law?	Are the laws of the Old and New Testament different kinds of law, or merely repetitions of the same law?

St. Thomas is not floating the notion of several Divine laws as a mere abstract possibility. Had that been his intention, he would have followed Article 2 with an article asking "Whether there is but one natural law?" and Article 3 with an article asking "Whether there is but one human law?" Rather the *ultrum* is posed against the background of the tradition that there *is* more than one Divine law – the law of the Old Testament, called the Old Law, given to the chosen nation, the Jews: and the law of the New Testament, called the New Law, given to the Church. One might hold that these are not literally two laws, but two promulgations of one law. Is this the case? Or are they somehow different?

[1] *Objection 1. It would seem that there is but one Divine law. Because, where there is one king in one kingdom there is but one law.* [2] *Now the whole of mankind is compared to God as to one king, according to Ps. 46:8: "God is the King of all the earth." Therefore there is but one Divine law.*	Objection 1. Apparently, the answer to the query is "No." Even in earthly government, we see that a single kingdom has a single king and a single law. Psalm 46 suggests that the entire human race is one kingdom, and God its one king. It follows that the Divine law is its one law.

[1]   St. Thomas emphasizes the need for unity of rule in his practical work, *On Kingship*: "[S]everal persons could by no means preserve the stability of the community if they totally disagreed. For union is necessary among them if they are to rule at all: several men, for instance, could not pull a ship in one direction unless joined together in some fashion. Now several are said to be united according as they come closer to being one. So one man rules better than several who come near being one."[42]

[2]   The English translation, "the whole of mankind is compared to God as to one king," is misleading because it seems to suggest that mankind is being compared with God. I prefer Freddoso's rendering of the line, "the whole human race is related to God as to a single king."[43]

Notice how the analogy works. We do not *project* what we see in earthly kingship onto God; He is the one true King, from whom all earthly kings take their name.

[42] Thomas Aquinas, *De Regno: On Kingship, To the King of Cyprus*, trans. Gerald B. Phelan and I. Th. Eschmann, O.P., re-edited by Joseph Kenny, O.P. (public domain); available online at www.dhspriory.org/thomas.

[43] Thomas Aquinas, *Treatise on Law: The Complete Text*, Alfred J. Freddoso, trans. (South Bend, IN: St. Augustine's Press, 2009), p. 15.

[1] **Objection 2.** *Further, every law is directed to the end which the lawgiver intends for those for whom he makes the law.* [2] *But God intends one and the same thing for all men; since according to 1 Tim. 2:4: "He will have all men to be saved, and to come to the knowledge of the truth." Therefore there is but one Divine law.*

Objection 2. Moreover, different kinds of laws are distinguished according to the purposes intended by the legislator in making them. But as we see in St. Paul's first letter to Timothy, God's purpose does not vary; he intends the same thing, salvation, for everyone. Since all of God's law has the same intended purpose, it is all the same law.

[1]   As we know from Question 90, Article 2, this end is their common good.

[2]   The biblical idiom of *salvation* refers to deliverance or safety; to be saved is to be rescued or redeemed from some great peril or danger. The Bible speaks of being saved or delivered from slavery or captivity, enemies, violence, extinction, trouble, temptation, unrighteousness, guilt, punishment, and death, both physical or spiritual.[44] In the passage St. Thomas cites, St. Paul is thinking of rescue from spiritual death and futility, so that instead of eternal exile, one may enjoy eternal life in His presence.

[1] **Objection 3.** *Further, the Divine law seems to be more akin to the eternal law, which is one, than the natural law, according as the Revelation of grace is of a higher order than natural knowledge.* [2] *Therefore much more is the Divine law but one.*

Objection 3. Still further, although Divine law and natural law both come from eternal law, the former is closer to eternal law than the latter. For consider how much higher the revealed knowledge of grace is than the knowledge imparted by nature! So if even natural law is one, how much greater the reason to think that Divine law is one.

[1]   The knowledge in the mind of God Himself is more exalted than the knowledge human beings can attain through Revelation, which in turn is more exalted than the knowledge they can attain through their created powers of reasoning. For this reason, the Objector suggests that eternal law is a closer neighbor to Divine law than to natural law.

[2]   With the tacit premises restored, the argument works like this:

[44] Exodus 6:6, Jeremiah 30:10, Psalm 18:3, 2 Samuel 22:3, 2 Kings 14:27, Psalms 37:39, Proverbs 2:16, Isaiah 45:8, Psalm 51:14, Joshua 22:31, Psalm 68:20, and James 5:20.

1. God is in the highest degree one.[45]
2. Since God is not composed of different things,[46] God is one with His knowledge; so His knowledge is one.
3. Since eternal law lies in His knowledge, eternal law is one.
4. Now the more a law is like eternal law, the greater the reason we have to think it too is one.
5. Since Divine law is even more like eternal law than natural law is, there is even greater reason to think Divine law is one than to think natural law is one.
6. Yet even natural law is one. So Divine law *must* be one.

---

[1] *On the contrary, The Apostle says, (Hebrews 7:12): "The priesthood being translated, it is necessary that a translation also be made of the law." [2] But the priesthood is twofold, as stated in the same passage, viz. the levitical priesthood, and the priesthood of Christ. Therefore the Divine law is twofold, namely the Old Law and the New Law.*	On the other hand, St. Paul teaches in his letter to the Hebrews that "when there is a change in the priesthood, there is necessarily a change in the [Divine] law as well."[47] But as he teaches a little later in the same letter, there *has* been a change in the priesthood: Although the Hebrew people were served by the levitical priesthood, the Church is served by the priesthood of Christ. Since there were two priesthoods, old and new, there must be two Divine laws, Old Law and New Law.

---

[1]   The reason why a change in the priesthood necessitates a change in Divine law is that Divine law contains the *rules* for priesthood, and the reason why Divine law contains the rules for priesthood is that the priest is a *mediator* between man and God.

[2]   Christ, who is both truly man and truly God, is the true and perfect mediator between man and God. The priests of the levitical priesthood – the priesthood ordained in the book of Leviticus – offered gifts and sacrifices for sins, but these actions merely symbolized and foreshadowed Christ's gift and sacrifice of Himself. The meaning of the change in the priesthood is that when Christ, the reality that the levitical priesthood symbolized and foreshadowed, finally came, the symbol and shadow was retired.

The meaning of Christ's sacrifice may be obscure to those who are not of St. Thomas's faith. Brutally condensing, it may be explained as follows.

---

[45]   St. Thomas has established this in I, Question 11, Articles 2 and 3.
[46]   I, Question 3, Article 7.
[47]   Hebrews 7:12 (RSV-CE).

To be acceptable to God, we need to put to death the sinful and selfish things we have made of ourselves. This is the price of our rebellion; we truly owe it, but just because we are so sinful and selfish, we are unable to pay it. In lovingly offering Himself for our sins, Christ offered on our behalf the perfect sacrifice that we cannot. If we are united with Him – as we are in the Church, the Body of which He is the Head – then we are united with His sacrifice too. Thus, through His death, we can die to our sins, and through His resurrection, we can experience new life, the kind He intends for us. In this connection, St. Thomas quotes St. Augustine's work *On the Trinity*, Book 4, Chapter 14: "There are four things to be noted in every sacrifice – to wit, to whom it is offered, by whom it is offered, what is offered, and for whom it is offered – that the same one true Mediator reconciling us with God through the peace-sacrifice might continue to be one with Him *to* whom He offered it, might be one with them *for* whom He offered it, and might Himself be the offerer and what He offered."[48]

[1] *I answer that, As stated in the I, 30, 3, distinction is the cause of number.* [2] *Now things may be distinguished in two ways. First, as those things that are altogether specifically different, e.g. a horse and an ox. Secondly, as perfect and imperfect in the same species, e.g. a boy and a man: and in this way the Divine law is divided into Old and New.* [3] *Hence the Apostle (Galatians 3:24–25) compares the state of man under the Old Law to that of a child* [4] *"under a pedagogue"; but the state under the New Law, to that of a full grown man, who is "no longer under a pedagogue."*	**Here is my response.** I explained much earlier in the *Summa* that how many things of a given kind there are depends on the differences or distinctions among them. There are two ways to make distinctions. One way is to indicate that one species, such as *horse,* is different from another species, such as *ox.* The other way is to indicate that an incompletely developed member of a species, such as *boy,* is different from a fully developed member of the same species, such as *man.* There really are two Divine laws, but the difference between them is of the latter kind, not the former; they are not different species, but incomplete and complete members of the same species. St. Paul has the same idea. That is why his letter to the Galatians says that people under the Old Law were like children being led to school by their custodian, but that people under the New Law are like adults who no longer need a custodian because they have already arrived.

---

[48] III, Question 48, Article 3, "Whether Christ's Passion operated by way of sacrifice?"

[1]   The idea sounds very difficult, but it is really very simple. If there is no distinction to be made, we speak of one thing; if there is one distinction to be made, we speak of two things; and so on.

[2]   To say that the Old Law was imperfect does not mean that there was a flaw in it, so that God could have done better. The Old Law was perfectly adapted to an as-yet imperfect people.

[3]   St. Thomas speaks of the state of man in general. Initially the chosen nation was like the gentiles; through centuries of Divine instruction, it became gradually more mature.

[4]   In English, the word "pedagogue" means a teacher. But the Greek word that it comes from, *paidagogos,* literally "boy-leader," refers to a custodian – a servant who accompanies the children at all times, makes them behave and mind their manners, and sees to it that at the right time, they get safely to the real teacher, who instructs them in his home. St. Paul explains in Galatians 3:23–26 that the Old Law – the law of Moses – acted as the custodian who escorted the people of Israel to the teacher, Christ. When he says that the people under the New Law no longer need a custodian, he is not saying that they no longer need a *teacher*; rather they no longer need to be *led* to the teacher, because they are already in His presence.

---

[1] *Now the perfection and imperfection of these two laws is to be taken in connection with the three conditions pertaining to law, as stated above.* [2] *For, in the first place, it belongs to law to be directed to the common good as to its end, as stated above (90, 2). This good may be twofold. It may be a sensible and earthly good; and to this, man was directly ordained by the Old Law: wherefore, at the very outset of the law, the people were invited to the earthly kingdom of the Chananaeans (Exodus 3:8,17).* [3] *Again it may be an intelligible and heavenly good: and to this, man is ordained by the New Law.* [4] *Wherefore, at the very*

The completeness of the New Law, and the incompleteness of the Old, can be seen in three ways. First, as we saw in Question 90, every true law's purpose is to guide us to the common good. But the expression "common good" may be taken in two senses, one lower and one higher. It may refer to a good of the earthly life, something experienced by the senses – or it may refer to a good of the heavenly life, something experienced by the mind. The Old Law set the Hebrew people on the path to the former sort of good; from the moment the Old Law was first promulgated to them, God invited them into the earthly kingdom which had previously been held by the Canaanites. But the New Law set the people on the path to the latter sort of good; from the moment he first began

beginning of His preaching, Christ invited men to the kingdom of heaven, saying (Matthew 4:17): "Do penance, for the kingdom of heaven is at hand." [5] Hence Augustine says (Contra Faust. iv) that "promises of temporal goods are contained in the Old Testament, for which reason it is called old; but the promise of eternal life belongs to the New Testament."	to preach, Christ invited men into His heavenly kingdom, telling them to turn away from their sins and be converted, because the kingdom of heaven is near and easily reached. St. Augustine gives the same explanation in his book *Against Faustus.* He remarks that the Old Testament is called *old* because its promises have been surpassed by the New; the former promised only the goods of this life, but the latter promises life eternal.

[1] The translation "three conditions pertaining to law" gives the impression that St. Thomas is speaking of the elements in the definition of law – the conditions that must be satisfied for a law to be authentic. But there are *four* such conditions, not one, so why the discrepancy? The solution to the riddle is that there is no discrepancy. The Latin, *tria quae,* does not mean "three conditions" for law, but "three things" about law. Only one of the "three things" St. Thomas mentions is taken from the four elements in law's definition.

[2] St. Thomas is probably thinking of the words spoken by God after giving the Old Law to the people, which read in part,

If you obey the commandments of the Lord your God which I command you this day, by loving the Lord your God, by walking in his ways, and by keeping his commandments and his statutes and his ordinances, then you shall live and multiply, and the Lord your God will bless you in the land which you are entering to take possession of it. But if your heart turns away, and you will not hear, but are drawn away to worship other gods and serve them, I declare to you this day, that you shall perish; you shall not live long in the land which you are going over the Jordan to enter and possess. I call heaven and earth to witness against you this day, that I have set before you life and death, blessing and curse; therefore choose life, that you and your descendants may live[.][49]

[3] The intelligible and heavenly good to which St. Thomas is referring is epitomized by the words of Christ, "Blessed are the pure in heart, for they shall see God," and of St. Paul, "For now we see in a mirror dimly, but then face to face. Now I know in part; then I shall understand fully, even as I have been fully understood."[50]

---

[49] Deuteronomy 30:15–20, quoting 16–19.
[50] Matthew 5:8, 1 Corinthians 13:12 (RSV-CE).

[4] For "do penance," some translations of the verse have "repent." The two meanings are inseparable; to repent is to turn sorrowfully from sin, and to do penance is to show the sorrow of repentance by performing an act that symbolizes this repentance and assists in the mending of the heart.

[5] The expressions "eternal life" and "kingdom of heaven" refer to the superabundant life that the blessed experience in union with God. Although it culminates in heaven, St. Thomas holds that Christ's followers have a foretaste of it in the life of faith. As he remarks about Hebrews 11:1, "faith is said to be the 'substance of things to be hoped for,' for the reason that in us the first beginning of things to be hoped for is brought about by the assent of faith, which contains virtually [*virtute,* in potentiality] all things to be hoped for."[51]

[1] *Secondly, it belongs to the law to direct human acts according to the order of righteousness (4):* [2] *wherein also the New Law surpasses the Old Law, since it directs our internal acts,* [3] *according to Mt. 5:20: "Unless your justice abound more than that of the Scribes and Pharisees, you shall not enter into the kingdom of heaven."* [4] *Hence the saying that "the Old Law restrains the hand, but the New Law controls the mind" (Sentent. iii, D. xl).*	As we saw in the previous article, another feature of the way law guides us is that it changes *how* we act, uplifting and purifying our motives so that we are not only externally but internally upright – so that we become thoroughly just, wholly virtuous people. In this respect, the New Law goes much farther than the Old, because it instructs us not only in outward acts, but also in the inward movements of the heart. This is what Christ meant when He taught His followers that they could not share in His heavenly kingdom unless their justice surpassed even the justice of the experts in the Law of Moses and the members of the rigorist sect called the Pharisees. As Peter Lombard put it in his *Sentences,* "The Old Law regulates the hand, the New the rational soul."

[1] The term *iustitiae,* translated "righteousness," refers to the wholly just and lawful, to the complete rightness or integrity which is pleasing to God. "According to the order of righteousness" means "in accordance with righteousness."

[2] Although at many points the Old Law seems to direct interior acts – for example, forbidding the interior act of covetousness and commanding the interior act of love – St. Thomas thinks that on closer consideration, the Old Law turns out to have been commanding the exterior acts of

[51] II-II, Question 4, Article 1, emphasis added.

these virtues, not the virtue themselves. More about his view of this matter later – both defending and qualifying the claim.

[3]   The Scribes were a professional class, not just copyists, but legal experts who applied themselves to the detailed requirements of the Old Law. The Pharisees were a rigorist sect that believed in both the written and the oral Law and emphasized strict observance. Christ was not demanding an even more punctilious external observance than theirs, but a transformation of the heart: "Woe to you, scribes and Pharisees, hypocrites! for you tithe mint and dill and cummin, and have neglected the weightier matters of the law, justice and mercy and faith; these you ought to have done, without neglecting the others. You blind guides, straining out a gnat and swallowing a camel!"[52]

[4]   The Dominican Fathers translation uses two different English words, "restrains" and "controls," for the single Latin verb, *cohibet,* which has both of these meanings. I have used the single English word "regulates," which can also be taken both ways.

[1] *Thirdly, it belongs to the law to induce men to observe its commandments.* [2] *This the Old Law did by the fear of punishment: but the New Law, by love, which is poured into our hearts by the grace of Christ, bestowed in the New Law, but foreshadowed in the Old.* [3] *Hence Augustine says (Contra Adimant. Manich. discip. xvii) that "there is little difference between the Law and the Gospel – fear [timor] and love [amor]."*[53]	Finally, the law persuades people to *carry out* what it commands. The Old Law persuaded by fear of punishment; the New Law persuades by love. This love is infused into our hearts by Christ, as an undeserved gift. Although the Old Law looked forward to it, expressing its anticipation by way of symbols, the New Law actually confers it. In his book *Against Adimantus, a Disciple of Manichaeus,* St. Augustine expresses the difference in a pun: "There is only a small difference between the [Old] Law and the [New Law of the] Gospel – the difference between *timorous* and *amorous.*"

[1]   This recalls the rough and ready definition of law from Question 90, Article 1, which St. Thomas then unpacks into four conditions: "Law is a rule and measure of acts, whereby man is induced to act or is restrained from acting."

[52] Matthew 23:23–24 (RSV-CE).
[53] I have re-edited the interpolations. The Dominican Fathers translation renders the passage, "there is little difference between the Law and the Gospel – fear and love," inserting the parenthetical note, "The 'little difference' refers to the Latin words 'timor' and 'amor'–'fear' and 'love.'"

[2]   In a certain type of symbolism, something that comes earlier, usually called the *type,* foreshadows or prefigures something higher that comes later, usually called the *antitype.* The Old Testament contains numerous prophesies about the coming of the Messiah (translated "Christ"), but Christian tradition holds that many things even in the non-prophetic parts of the Old Testament anticipate the New. For instance, the sanctuary of the ancient Jewish Temple is a *type* or foreshadowing of heaven, the Old Testament sacrifice of animals is a *type* or foreshadowing of the sacrifice of Christ, and the mysterious priest of God, Melchizedek, who ministers to Abraham centuries before the institution of the levitical priesthood, is a *type* or foreshadowing of Christ Himself. St. Thomas holds that this typological relationship holds between the Old Law as a whole, and the New Law as a whole.

[3]   By "Law," St. Augustine means the Old Law, and by "Gospel" he means the New Law. Readers of some traditions may object to the fact that St. Thomas describes the Gospel in terms of *law,* but apparently Christ had no hesitation in doing so: At the Passover meal he shared with his disciples before His death, He announced, "A new commandment I give to you, that you love one another; even as I have loved you, that you also love one another."[54] To someone who objects, "That is grace, not law," St. Thomas would reply that it is the law that describes the very life of grace: For although grace is offered freely, there is no way to receive it except by cooperating with it, by letting it pass into us, and this is done by loving one another in the way we are loved by Christ.

   Here and elsewhere in Question 91, St. Thomas almost gives the impression that the Old Law had nothing to say about love. He is perfectly aware that it did, but we must remember that in Question 91 he is giving only a quick preview of topics he will discuss in greater detail later on. In Question 108, he takes up the objection that the New and Old Laws cannot be distinguished with reference to fear and love, because even the Old Law included such precepts as "Thou shalt love thy neighbor" and "Thou shalt love the Lord thy God."[55] Though St. Thomas concedes the importance of these precepts to the Old Law, he insists nonetheless that between Old and New Law there is a radical shift in orientation. In the Old Law, even the precepts of love were backed up by fear of penalties, penalties that were tangible and belonged to this life;

---

[54] John 13:34 (RSV-CE).
[55] Question 108, Article 1, Obj. 2 and ad 2. The internal references are to Leviticus 19:18 and Deuteronomy 6:5.

although people were commanded to perform the *exterior acts* of love, few people would have been performing them *because of the interior virtue* of love. By contrast, in the New Law, the motive for performing the acts of love is love itself. To be sure, the New Law promises rewards, but even these rewards are objects of love: For what does it mean to enjoy eternal life? Simply to be united with God, who *is* love, and who is loved for His own sake.

St. Thomas adds that even so, some people mentioned in the Old Testament were moved by love, "and in this respect they belonged to the New Law." In the same way, some people mentioned in the New Testament were unmoved by love, and these people had to be moved by fear of punishment and by promises of things in this life. Quoting St. Paul in Romans 5:5, he concludes, "But although the Old Law contained precepts of [love], nevertheless it did not confer the Holy Ghost by Whom '[love] … is spread abroad in our hearts.'"

Reply to Objection 1. As the father of a family issues different commands to the children and to the adults, so also the one King, God, in His one kingdom, gave one law to men, while they were yet imperfect, and another more perfect law, when, by the preceding law, they had been led to a greater capacity for Divine things.	Reply to Objection 1. From the fact that there is a single realm and a single ruler, it does not follow that there must be a single law. Do we say "One family, one father, one directive"? No, for the father directs the children of the household in one way, the adults in another. In the same way, we should not say "One kingdom, one king, one law," for the one King, God, in His one kingdom, mankind, gave one law to men when they were spiritually immature, in order to prepare them by this means for another more, complete law, when they were ready to take it in.

St. Thomas is careful to describe household regulations as commands or injunctions rather than as laws in the strict sense. As he explained in Question 90, Article 3, "he that governs a family can indeed make certain commands or ordinances, but not such as to have properly the force of law."

[1] *Reply to Objection 2. The salvation of man could not be achieved otherwise than through Christ, according to Acts 4:12: "There is no other name … given to men, whereby we must be saved."* [2] *Consequently the law that brings all to salvation could not be given until after the coming of Christ. But before His*	Reply to Objection 2. The Objector is right to say that God's unchanging purpose in all law is to lead men to salvation, but salvation is brought about only through Christ. Obviously, the New Law, which leads people to Christ, could not be promulgated

coming it was necessary to give to the people, of whom Christ was to be born, a law containing certain rudiments of righteousness unto salvation, in order to prepare them to receive Him.

until Christ came. Even so, the Old Law was not useless; it *prepared* them to receive Christ by providing their first beginnings in the consummate integrity of salvation.

[1] St. Thomas does not disagree with the Objector's view that all Divine law must be one in purpose; he only points out that to achieve this one purpose, people in different spiritual conditions must be governed in somewhat different ways.

To say that men can be saved by no other "name" than Christ is to say that men can be saved only through appeal to the One who is truly called the Messiah or Christ. The reason no other means but these suffice is that Christ took the burden of human sin and guilt upon Himself to accomplish what we could not accomplish for ourselves.

[2] In Latin, the term *rudimenta,* rudiments, refers to the beginnings or first attempts at something. Holding back from adultery and murder, loving one's neighbor, limiting revenge to "an eye for an eye and a tooth for a tooth" – such things were beginnings, but the New Law goes much further. Not only adultery and murder, but also lustful fantasy and murderous anger are forbidden. Revenge is not just limited, but banned. Men are commanded to love not only neighbors, but even enemies.[56]

The meaning of "receiving" Christ is epitomized by St. Paul's statement that "I have been crucified with Christ; it is no longer I who live, but Christ who lives in me; and the life I now live in the flesh I live by faith in the Son of God, who loved me and gave himself for me."[57]

[1] *Reply to Objection 3. The natural law directs man by way of certain general precepts, common to both the perfect and the imperfect: wherefore it is one and the same for all.* [2] *But the Divine law directs man also in certain particular matters, to which the perfect and imperfect do not stand in the same relation. Hence the necessity for the Divine law to be twofold, as already explained.*

Reply to Objection 3. The reason there is only one natural law is that the general rules by which it steers us are the same for everyone, both mature and immature. But the Divine law includes not only general rules, but also instructions about certain details of conduct that are *not* the same for everyone; the mature and immature must be directed differently, and so they need two different laws.

---

[56] Old Law: Exodus 20:13–14 (cf. Deuteronomy 5:17–18), Exodus 21:23–24, Leviticus 19:18. New Law: Matthew 5:21–22, 27–28, 43–45.
[57] Galatians 2:20 (RSV-CE).

[1] The natural law directs the spiritually immature and the spiritually mature by the same rules. People in both conditions should pay honor to their parents; people in both conditions should abstain from stealing; and so on.

[2] Perhaps the most conspicuous example of a difference between how the Old Law directs the spiritually immature and how the New Law directs the spiritually mature lies in the ordinances for matrimony. The Old Law explicitly allowed men to divorce their wives, "because of the hardness of their hearts"; as St. Thomas suggests, if they had not been allowed to divorce them, they would have killed them. But the New Law makes matrimony indissoluble.[58]

For further reflection on the preceding section of the *Treatise on Law*, the online *Companion to the Commentary*, accessible via the Resources link at the book's catalogue webpage, includes a discussion of the following topic:

REVELATION – SAYS WHO?

Question 91, Article 6:
Whether There Is a Law in the *Fomes* of Sin?

TEXT	PARAPHRASE
Whether there is a law in the fomes of sin?	Is the so-called law of sin – our tendency to burst into flames of sin, as though we contained kindling-wood – really a law?

What St. Thomas says in this article should be compared with what he says about Question 90, Article 1, Objection 1, which anticipates it. The Latin term *fomes* refers to tinder, or kindling-wood. It is a metaphor for the tendency we suffer, in our unredeemed condition, for the carnal appetites – this means all of our subrational impulses, not only the "concupiscible" impulses such as hunger and sexual desire, but also the "irascible" impulses such as anger – to resist the guidance of the mind, so that a single spark of temptation makes them burst into flames. St. Paul says that by themselves – that is, apart from the experience of the grace of Christ in the New Law – the commandments of the Old Law merely

---

[58] The Old Law on divorce: Deuteronomy 24:1–4. The New Law on divorce: Matthew 5:31–32, 19:3–12. St. Thomas on the danger of wife-murder: S.T., Supp., 67, Article 6; *Summa Contra Gentiles*, III, Chapter 123.

stir up the tendency even more, "in order that sin might be shown to be sin."[59] In a famously unnerving passage, he assumes the perspective of a person under the Old Law in order to describe the result.

> We know that the [Divine] law is spiritual; but I am carnal, sold under sin. I do not understand my own actions. For I do not do what I want, but I do the very thing I hate. Now if I do what I do not want, I agree that the law is good. So then it is no longer I that do it, but sin which dwells within me. For I know that nothing good dwells within me, that is, in my flesh. I can will what is right, but I cannot do it. For I do not do the good I want, but the evil I do not want is what I do. Now if I do what I do not want, it is no longer I that do it, but sin which dwells within me. So I find it to be a law that when I want to do right, evil lies close at hand. For I delight in the law of God, in my inmost self, but I see in my members[60] another law at war with the law of my mind and making me captive to the *law of sin* which dwells in my members. Wretched man that I am! Who will deliver me from this body of death? Thanks be to God through Jesus Christ our Lord! So then, I of myself serve the law of God with my mind, but with my flesh I serve the *law of sin.*[61]

St. Thomas, then, is asking whether St. Paul's expression "law of sin" refers to a true law, or merely uses the word "law" in some other sense.

---

[1] *Objection 1. It would seem that there is no law of the "fomes" of sin. For Isidore says (Etym. v) that the "law is based on reason." [2] But the "fomes" of sin is not based on reason, but deviates from it. Therefore the "fomes" has not the nature of a law.*

Objection 1. Apparently, our "kindling" or "ignitability," our susceptibility to flare up into sin at the least spark, is not a true law. Isidore reminds us that law is a directive of reason, but the kindling is resistant to reason's guidance. Whatever its true character may be, we may be sure that it isn't a law.

---

[1] St. Thomas agrees that a law is an ordinance of reason, which seems to put him in a spot. The Objector has employed this quotation from Isidore previously, in Question 90, Article 2, Objection 3.

[2] Had human nature remained in its unfallen condition, it would be like fertile soil in which a garden can be planted and tended. In its fallen condition, the soil is overwatered and overfertilized, filled with wild growths that smother the flowering plants of reason. Our unnaturally hypertrophied passions and desires tempt us to think that by giving into them, we will be happy, but actually just the opposite is true. The weeds are not a garden, but a jungle.

[59] Quoting from Romans 7:13 (RSV-CE); cf. Romans 5–12.
[60] "Members" means "limbs" – our bodily parts, and, by extension, their appetites.
[61] Romans 7:14–25, emphasis added.

[1] *Objection 2. Further, every law is binding, so that those who do not obey it are called transgressors.* [2] *But man is not called a transgressor, from not following the instigations of the "fomes"; but rather from his following them. Therefore the "fomes" has not the nature of a law.*

Objection 2. Moreover, law is something we ought to obey; lawbreakers are people who don't. In the case of our "kindling," it is the other way around. We don't become lawbreakers by *not* bursting into flames, but by bursting into them. This proves that the kindling isn't a true law.

[1]   "Binding" is a very literal translation. The Objector is saying that we ought to obey, not just that we will be punished if we do not. Our consciences are bound with cords of duty.

[2]   The Objector is not speaking of what a man is called, but of what he is. He is *established* or *rendered* a transgressor – more idiomatically, he *becomes* one – by giving in to his overheated impulses, not by refusing them. How can they be a law, if following them puts him in the wrong?

[1] *Objection 3. Further, the law is ordained to the common good, as stated above (90, 2).* [2] *But the "fomes" inclines us, not to the common, but to our own private good. Therefore the "fomes" has not the nature of a law.*

Objection 3. Still further, we saw back in Question 90 that law directs us to the *shared* good. By contrast, our "kindling" makes us shoot up in flames of selfishness. This is yet another reason why the it cannot be truly a law.

[1]   The eternal law is ordained to the common good of all creatures, but in different ways, by means of subordinate laws. Each kind of creature is directed by its natural inclinations to the common good of the species, each human to the common good of humanity, each member of the community to the common good of the community – all this for the good of the whole creation.

[2]   What the Objector means is that a person whose appetites are too easily ignited will tend to take for himself what is rightly due to others; he is not thinking of the common good, but of his own good. We might add that such a person does not achieve his own good either, because we are social creatures who cannot truly thrive by selfishly "looking out for number one."

On the contrary, The Apostle says (Romans 7:23): "I see another law in my members, fighting against the law of my mind."

On the other hand, St. Paul *does* call our susceptibility to sin a law. He says in his letter to the Romans that he perceives in his body a law not only different from the Divine law that instructs his mind, but also hostile to it.

Whether there is "another law in our members" is not just a question of biblical interpretation, but a question about the nature of man, as illuminated by the history of salvation. A pagan philosopher would consider natural law from one perspective alone. By contrast, St. Thomas thinks it must be viewed in a triple light: From the perspectives of Creation, the Fall, and Redemption. If we did not know that there is something *wrong* with our present condition, we might imagine that our inflamed desires and passions are natural, like a man who has been sick since birth, has never known health, has never known anyone who was healthy, and so takes his pain and fever for granted. Even if we did know there was something wrong with us, if we did not know of the healing grace of Christ, then we might be tempted to despair.

To understand St. Thomas's thoughts on these matters, one must avoid three misunderstandings about St. Paul's. In the first place, St. Paul is not saying that the body God created is evil in itself, but only that it is in an evil condition; we have not lost our original nature and acquired an evil nature, but retained our original nature and fallen sick. Second, by emphasizing the body, St. Paul is not denying that there is such a thing as mental sin; the problem is that even though the mind of person under the Old Law has been instructed, he cannot make his ardor and appetite *obey* his instructed mind. Third, St. Paul is not suggesting that our insubordinate ardor and appetite are irresistible; however, the Fall has so intensified them that they are much more difficult to resist, and no one does a good job.

---

[1] *I answer that, As stated above (2; 90, 1, ad 1), the law, as to its essence, resides in him that rules and measures; but, by way of participation, in that which is ruled and measured; so that every inclination or ordination which may be found in things subject to the law, is called a law by participation, as stated above (2; 90, 1, ad 1).* [2] *Now those who are subject to a law may receive a twofold inclination from the lawgiver. First, in so far as he directly inclines his subjects to something; sometimes indeed*

Here is my response. Several times before, I have had occasion to observe that law, as a rule and measure of distinctively human acts, can be "in" someone in more than one way. Once more, then: In its primary or essential sense, it is "in" the legislator, because he is the one doing the ruling and measuring. But in another sense we can say that it is "in" those who are under the law – in those who are being ruled and measured – just because they share in it. For these reasons, it ought to be clear that any sort of tendency or order that the law imparts to people can also be called a law, a "law by participation." But law may impart such a tendency to people in either of two ways, one way direct, the other indirect. In

different subjects to different acts; in this way we may say that there is a military law and a mercantile law. [3] *Secondly, indirectly; thus by the very fact that a lawgiver deprives a subject of some dignity, the latter passes into another order, so as to be under another law, as it were: thus if a soldier be turned out of the army, he becomes a subject of rural or of mercantile legislation.*	the first way, the legislator simply directs people to act in a certain way. Different classifications of people, such as soldiers and merchants, may even be directed to act in different ways. But the indirect way to impart a tendency is to impart it through penalty: The legislator deprives someone of an honor and status so that he is no longer on his old footing – he comes, so to speak, under another law. For example, if a soldier is expelled from the army, henceforth he is no longer under military law, but under rural or mercantile law.

[1]   The general idea has been thoroughly explained in two previous articles. Here we need only call attention to a small complication. "As to its essence," eternal law is in the mind of God alone. Through the inclinations that the eternal law imparts to them, however, both man and irrational creatures participate in the eternal law; so, as St. Thomas explains, we can say that the eternal law is in both of them – not of course "as to its essence," but "by way of participation." But there is an important difference, because to man God has imparted *rational* inclinations, while to the other animals God has imparted only *irrational* inclinations. We don't experience even our so-called animal appetites in the same way that other animals experience theirs, because in us they communicate with reason, and in the animals they don't.

Why is this difference important? Because law in the strict sense is an ordinance of reason. Since only man participates in the eternal law *by means* of his reason, his participation in the eternal law, his law by way of participation, *is* law in the strict sense. Since the other animals participate in the eternal law only by means of irrational impulses, their participation in the eternal law, their law by way of participation, is law only in an analogical sense. Their mode of participation is indirect and passive; ours is direct and active. For this reason, using the English convention of "scare quotes" or warning quotes, we might say that man has a natural law, but the other animals have only a natural "law." St. Thomas, of course, does not use scare quotes, but he has his own ways of warning us when he is speaking in an extended, qualified, or analogical sense, as we see below when he says "as it were," "I might say that," "after a fashion," and "yet only in so far as a law may be said to be in such things."

[2]   As the author of the natural law, God directly inclines us to act in certain ways by how he *makes* us; as the author of the Divine law, He directly inclines us to act in certain ways by how he *commands* us. Only the latter way, command, is available to a human legislator. To say that the legislator "directs," by the way, is not necessarily to say that his directions are completely effective, for one may receive a directive and yet ignore or disobey it.

One is tempted to paraphrase St. Thomas's term "subjects" as "citizens," but although the same person may be both a citizen and a subject, the terms have different meanings. By calling him a subject, we are pointing out that he is subject to the law. By calling him a citizen, we are pointing out that he is a member of the community.

[3]   The example is a little confusing because today, in our neglect of customary law, we view military, rural, and mercantile law as the same kind of thing: The legislator issues certain commands to soldiers, other commands to country people, and still other commands to merchants. Aren't they all commands, and don't they all come from the same legislator? So in what sense has the soldier passed under another law, and in what sense has he done so through being deprived of a dignity?

For us, then, perhaps a different analogy might convey St. Thomas's point more clearly, and I beg his pardon for offering it. The prince of a certain rough country allows only honest and law-abiding persons to reside in the homeland. Incorrigibles lose this privilege, and are exiled to the colonies. As they are being loaded onto the colony boat, the prince says to them, "Since you will not obey my law, the best I can do for you is leave you to yourselves. You think you know what you desire. I will teach it to you even better, for you shall have it. Henceforth you shall live by the law of your own contumacy. After five years, we will see how well you have learned." Now is "the law of your own contumacy" the prince's law? In the direct sense, no, for he has not commanded them, "Be contumacious," and the law of the homeland is that they should *not* be contumacious. But in the indirect sense, yes, for it is by his command that they are deprived of the privilege of the homeland, and pass, so to speak, under a different law.

---

[1] *Accordingly under the Divine Lawgiver various creatures have various natural inclinations, so that what is, as it were, a law for one, is against the law for*

Just as the human legislator imparts different regulations to people of different social stations, so God, the Divine Legislator, imparts different tendencies to creatures of different

another: thus I might say that fierceness is, in a way, the law of a dog, but against the law of a sheep or another meek animal. [2] *And so the law of man, which, by the Divine ordinance, is allotted to him, according to his proper natural condition, is that he should act in accordance with reason:*[3] *and this law was so effective in the primitive state, that nothing either beside or against reason could take man unawares.* [4] *But when man turned his back on God, he fell under the influence of his sensual impulses: in fact this happens to each one individually, the more he deviates from the path of reason,* [5] *so that, after a fashion, he is likened to the beasts that are led by the impulse of sensuality, according to Ps. 48:13:*[62] *"Man, when he was in honor, did not understand: he hath been compared to senseless beasts, and made like to them."*

natures. The law for one creature contradicts the law for another – "law" not in the strict sense but in an analogical sense. Speaking this way, I might say that the law of the dog is to be fierce, but the law of gentle animals like sheep is not to be fierce.

The law of man – dealt out to him by God, in keeping with *his* natural condition – is neither "Be fierce" nor "Be gentle," but "Be reasonable." In his first state, before the Fall, this law of reason was so effective that no impulse different from reason, or contrary to reason, could catch him by surprise. How different it was after man turned away from God, and became prey to sensual attack! This is true not only of the history of the human race as a whole, but of the history of each man in particular. The more he turns away from reason, the more – in a qualified sense – he resembles the beasts, who are carried away by their sensuous urges. This is what the inspired poet of the Psalms meant when he wrote that man, unable to abide in honor, became like the beasts.

---

[1] Fierceness and gentleness are laws for the dog and the sheep in the sense that these respective inclinations are imparted to them by the Divine Lawgiver. The distancing expression "I might say that," *ut si dicam,* reminds us that they are laws for them only in an analogous sense, because their mode of participation in the eternal law is irrational.

[2] For man, natural law and reason are not different things; his law is to be guided by reason, which includes paying attention to his sensual appetites in an intelligent rather than an unintelligent way, keeping in mind what they are for, and in what way and to what degree it is fitting to respond to them. Here St. Thomas does not use a hedging expression like "I might say that," because man's law really is an ordinance of reason, and so really is a law.

---

[62] The English translation incorrectly cites the verse as 48:21. The DRA numbers it 48:12; more recent translations follow a different numbering system, giving the number as 49:12.

[3]   To people of my generation, conditioned by motion pictures and penny dreadfuls, the word "primitive" conjures up images of witch doctors and big drums. To many of my students, it conjures up something more like the *National Geographic* vista of indigenous peoples uncorrupted by the West. Neither of these pictures is what St. Thomas has in mind. He is speaking of the *first* state, the state of innocence in which man was created, before the catastrophe of the Fall.

[4]   The line speaks of both *man* and *each* man, of what happened to the human race as a whole when it turned away from God, and what happens to each member of the race when he duplicates that betrayal by his own. To members of some traditions it may seem strange to identify deviation from reason with deviation from God. St. Thomas would reply that it is *unreasonable* not to follow God, our greatest good, the very Truth – and *ungodly* not to follow reason, a privilege given to no other animal but man.

[5]   The man who behaves unreasonably – the sullen man, the envious man, the lustful man, the glutton – has become like an animal in one respect, because animals do not behave reasonably. This is deeply important, and it is the main theme of the passage. Yet St. Thomas qualifies the theme with the phrase "after a fashion," *ut sic quodammodo.* Why? Because not even such a man has become like an animal in all respects; he still has a rational mind. The animal does not have to shut off his mind to be ruled by sensuality. The human must try to do just that – and he doesn't succeed even then, because, unlike the animal, he is giving himself all sorts of reasons for acting like one. Paradoxically, he thinks it is *reasonable* to surrender his reason to his senses. Perhaps he is saying, "This is the life," but an animal cannot form conceptions like the good life. Or perhaps he is saying "I can't help it," but an animal cannot consider whether it can help it.

---

[1] *So, then, this very inclination of sensuality which is called the "fomes," in other animals has simply the nature of a law (yet only in so far as a law may be said to be in such things), by reason of a direct inclination.* [2] *But in man, it has not the nature of law in this way, rather is it a deviation from the law of reason.* [3] *But*

So we see that the sensual tendency we have been speaking of, "kindling" or "ignitability," is a law for the animals (loosely speaking), and also a law for us. But there is a difference, because for them the tendency is imparted directly, for us indirectly. To put the matter another way, they are susceptible to sensuality because the Divine legislator made them that way, but we are

since, by the just sentence of God, man is destitute of original justice, and his reason bereft of its vigor, [4] *this impulse of sensuality, whereby he is led, in so far as it is a penalty following from the Divine law depriving man of his proper dignity, has the nature of a law.*	susceptible to it as a deserved penalty – something called a law in an extended sense, because it is a justly deserved punishment for *disobedience* to law. We have been deprived of the complete and spontaneous integrity that we enjoyed when we were created; we incline toward sensuality because our reason has forfeited its original vigor.

[1]   God created the animals to be guided by sensuality. It is their law "by way of participation" in eternal law. Even it is not law in the strict sense, but only analogous to law, because the animals do not participate by means of their reason.

[2]   Though God gave us sensual impulses, He created us to be guided by reason. Our sensual impulses should not be our masters, but our servants and assistants. Anger, for example, should not tell me what to do. Instead it should be transmuted into zeal, so that it can serve under close discipline in the palace-guard of love: "a man is said to be zealous on behalf of his friend, when he makes a point of repelling whatever may be said or done against the friend's good. In this way, too, a man is said to be zealous on God's behalf, when he endeavors, to the best of his means, to repel whatever is contrary to the honor or will of God[.]"[63]

[3]   "Original justice" is a theological term for the inward harmony that our first parents possessed, so that their sensuous impulses submitted to the guidance of reason, and their reason to the guidance of God. When their minds turned away from God, their sensuous impulses turned away from reason.

Imagine that the master of a house goes away and puts the steward in charge. Instead of managing the house, the steward hands it over to the servants, who run riot. After they rough up the steward, he commands them to go back to their posts, but they are no longer inclined to follow his orders. When the master discovers what the steward has done, he says "This is your punishment: That for now, the state of affairs you have brought into being will continue."

[4]   The sin of the first human beings transgressed Divine law because it willfully violated a direct Divine command. What kind of Divine law was this command? If we associate the Old Law with the Law of Moses,

[63] I-II, Question 28, Article 4.

then it was neither Old or New Law, but, so to speak, generic Divine law. However, a case can be made for considering it Old Law, because it commands an outward rather than an inward act ("of the tree of the knowledge of good and evil you shall not eat"), and induces obedience not by the sheer grace of love but by warning of a tangible penalty in this life ("for in the day that you eat of it you shall die").[64] One may object that to say this is to understand the tree too literally, that its meaning is really allegorical. St. Thomas would consider this a false alternative, for he has written earlier in the *Summa,*

> The tree of life is a material tree, and so called because its fruit was endowed with a life-preserving power as above stated. Yet it had a spiritual signification; as the rock in the desert was of a material nature, and yet signified Christ. In like manner the tree of the knowledge of good and evil was a material tree, so called in view of future events; because, after eating of it, man was to learn, by experience of the consequent punishment, the difference between the good of obedience and the evil of rebellion. It may also be said to signify spiritually the free-will as some say.[65]

Through this primordial sin of pride, our first parents denied their dependence on God, imagining that they could "be like God, knowing good and evil" apart from His illumination of their minds. In some way the temptation appealed to sensuality as well, because the fruit of the tree was to be desired not only "to make one wise," but also because it was "good for food" and "a delight to the eyes."[66] The weakness of reason's power over the sensuous appetites resulted directly from the offense: By cutting ourselves we bleed, by refusing to eat we starve, by abusing our reason and submitting to sensuality we enfeeble reason's government of the senses. Though we have not lost our rational nature, we live up to it so poorly that we have lost most of the glory and honor of it. Taken in this sense – not as an instruction, but as a penalty, as a way of teaching us "the hard way" – our inclination to sensuality is a law, just as we say "Thieves are sent to prison; that's the law."

---

[1] *Reply to Objection 1. This argument considers the "fomes" in itself, as an incentive to evil. It is not thus that it has the*

Reply to Objection 1. Two things can be said about our "ignitability": First, it inclines us to evil; second, it is a penalty for disobedience to God. The Objector is thinking of it in the first way, and in that way it is certainly not a

---

[64] Genesis 2:17 (RSV-CE).
[65] I, Question 102, Article 1, ad 4.
[66] Genesis 3:4–6 (RSV-CE).

nature of a law, as stated above, [2] but according as it results from the justice of the Divine law: it is as though we were to say that the law allows a nobleman to be condemned to hard labor for some misdeed.

law, for doing evil is contrary to reason. But in the second way, it is a law, and we speak in this way about human law too. Suppose a nobleman has been sentenced to hard labor. "It is the law," we say. What? Is there a law that says "Noblemen should perform hard labor"? Certainly not. But the nobleman has violated some *other* law, and hard labor is the assigned penalty for violation.

[1]   The Objector reasons like this: The *fomes* tempts us to sin; whatever tempts us to sin is unreasonable; nothing unreasonable can be a law; therefore sensual "ignitability" cannot be a law. St. Thomas says, "Yes, but when we call the *fomes* a law, we are using the term "law" in a different sense."

[2]   The condemnation of the nobleman to hard labor partakes of law not by way of command, but by way of penalty. So it is with the condemnation of the human race to the riotous insubordination of its sensual appetites.

[1] *Reply to Objection 2. This argument considers law in the light of a rule or measure: for it is in this sense that those who deviate from the law become transgressors. [2] But the "fomes" is not a law in this respect, but by a kind of participation, as stated above.*

Reply to Objection 2. Again the Objector is thinking about our "ignitability" simply as an inclination to evil. This time his protest is that in that way, it is not a law, for doing evil is not a *rule and measure of human acts*. In itself, no. But it *shares* in the rule, simply because it is a penalty for violating the rule. When we call it a law, we are speaking in that second, indirect sense.

[1]   In calling law binding, the Objector reminds us that law is a rule and measure of acts. His protest is that the *fomes* is neither of these things: It is neither a governing ordinance for our acts, nor a standard to see whether they measure up.

[2]   The insubordination of our sensual appetite to our reason is not the rule and measure of our acts, but a penalty for violating the rule and measure. It participates in the law in the sense that it is the penalty ordained for violating the law.

[1] *Reply to Objection 3. This argument considers the "fomes" as to its proper*

Reply to Objection 3. The Objector is thinking of our "ignitability" in its strict sense – as sensuality gone wild, burning out

inclination, and not as to its origin. [2] And yet if the inclination of sensuality be considered as it is in other animals, thus it is ordained to the common good, namely, to the preservation of nature in the species or in the individual. [3] And this is in man also, in so far as sensuality is subject to reason. But it is called "fomes" in so far as it strays from the order of reason.

of control. Certainly he is right that this bonfire does not promote the common good. But after all, disordered sensual appetite originates in sensual appetite, and if he considered this root of the matter, he might see that he is missing something. In the other animals, sensual appetite *does* promote the common good, because it preserves both the individual animal and the species. Even in man, who was made to follow reason, sensual appetite promotes the common good *just to the degree* that it obeys reason; we speak of "ignitability" only to the degree that it doesn't.

[1]   As he often does, St. Thomas concedes the Objector's point, but says he is missing a more important point. Considering the *fomes* in itself, yes, it inclines us to selfishness. But considering its origin, we find that like every evil, it is the perversion of something that is good in itself.

One suspects that in pointing this out, St. Thomas is trying to head off the heresy that holds that the body and its appetites are intrinsically evil. God likes human nature. Not only did He invent it, but He even took it upon Himself for our salvation. The problem lies not in our nature, which is good, but in its condition after the Fall, which is very far from good. The paradox of fallenness is that we are not simply bad, but created good and broken; not a sheer ugliness, but a sullied beauty. If we had not been set on such a height in the first place, we could not have fallen so far. The irrational creatures are beneath the possibility of both virtue and sin.

[2]   The "something good" that excessive susceptibility to sensuous impulses perverts is the sensuous impulses themselves. Consider first their good purpose in irrational creatures. If birds did not eat when they were hungry, they would starve. If deer did not go into rut, there would soon be no more deer.

[3]   Human desires and passions serve the common good too, provided that they are taken up into reason. The problem is that they so rarely are. So often anger serves revenge instead of justice, eros incites lust instead of love, and the urge to great deeds spurs envy instead of emulation. According to St. Thomas, this is not what we were made for.

What then were we made for? What are we? According to St. Thomas, no other creature must govern sensual impulses by means of reason; the task is unique to man, for though we have one foot in each of two realms, we are not proper citizens of either of them. Having bodies, we have something in common with beasts; having intellects, we have something in common with angels. Yet we are neither of these things. Our bodies are not beasts' bodies, for our bodies are made what they are by rational souls. Our intellects are not angelic intellects, for our intellects know what they know by bodily senses.[67] What a high charge is given to us – that reason should rule the bodily ardors and appetites, rationalize them, transfigure them! Yet how poorly do we live up to our charge, the government of our reason still crippled by its ancient rebellion against its Maker. Without the grace of the New Law we would be lost indeed, for in the words of St. Paul, just after the passage on the "law of sin," "the creation was subjected to futility, not of its own will but by the will of him who subjected it in hope; ... we ourselves, who have the first fruits of the Spirit, groan inwardly as we wait for adoption as sons, the redemption of our bodies."[68]

For further reflection on the preceding section of the *Treatise on Law*, the online *Companion to the Commentary*, accessible via the Resources link at the book's catalogue webpage, includes a discussion of the following topic:

THE ARCHITECTURE OF LAW, REVISITED

---

[67] See esp. I, Question 76.
[68] Romans 8:20,23b (RSV-CE).

Before Reading Question 92

We are about to enter a territory in the *Treatise on Law* in which many readers find the questions so preposterous that they can hardly bring themselves to read the answers. In the first place, St. Thomas suggests that in a certain sense, law both can and should make men good. Among our contemporaries, his view that law *can* make them good tends to be dismissed as quixotic because we humans are incorrigible, and his view that it *should* do so tends to be dismissed as bigoted because "law must not enforce morality."

In the second place, he suggests that law's operations – its *only* operations – are to command, prohibit, permit, and punish. Many readers today would view this as absurdly limited, on grounds that law has innumerable additional functions such as honoring, taxing, recognizing, subsidizing, facilitating, promoting, and "setting national goals."

But there are at least four good reasons to keep reading. The questions do not mean exactly what we think; the answers are not exactly what we expect; many of our objections have been anticipated and answered; and our own quick answers turn out to be less transparently obvious than we suppose.

St. Thomas's Prologue to Question 92:
Of the Effects of Law

TEXT	PARAPHRASE
We must now consider the effects of law; under which head there are two points of inquiry:	Continuing the program we sketched out earlier, we must now investigate what law *does*. Two separate matters must be investigated.

Having investigated the essence of law in Question 90, and determined how many kinds of law there are in Question 91, one more general task remains before examining each kind of law in detail. The overarching goal of Question 92 is to investigate law's effects. However, because the *ultrum* is always posed in the form of a yes-or-no question, St. Thomas does not ask "What are law's effects?" but rather "Are law's effects as they have been traditionally described?" This requires two *ultra*, not one, because law's effects have traditionally been described in two different ways. As we will see, these two descriptions complement each other, because each takes "effect" in a different sense.

(1) Whether an effect of law is to make men good?	Does law bring about the result of making men good (as Aristotle claims)?

This question takes law's "effect" in the sense of what it brings about. Since St. Thomas has made so much of the fact that every true law aims at the common good, it is a little surprising that the question is not "Whether an effect of law is the common good?" It may seem that the focus of his attention has changed from the effect of law on the community as a

137

whole to its effect on the individual members. Not so, for as we will see, he views these two matters as connected: The virtue of the individual members is one of the most important elements of the common good itself.

For the sake of completeness, my paraphrase inserts a reference to Aristotle, St. Thomas's source for this first description of the effects of law, whom St. Thomas mentions later.

(2) Whether the effects of law are to command, to forbid, to permit, and to punish, as the Jurist states?	Are the operations of law to command, forbid, permit, and punish (as the jurist Modestinus claims)?

This time the question takes law's "effect" in the sense of its operation. For an analogy: A running man snatches a woman's purse; seeing it happen, a nearby policeman is moved to perform his function. What is the effect of the policeman's resolve? In the operative sense, the effect is that he tackles the man; in the sense of result, the effect is that the man is prevented from getting away with his crime.

The jurist whom St. Thomas has in mind is Modestinus, a student of Ulpian, who is quoted in the *Digest,* a part of the *Corpus Juris Civilis,* as saying that "The force of a law is this: To command, to prohibit, to permit, or to punish."[1]

For further reflection on the preceding section of the *Treatise on Law,* the online *Companion to the Commentary,* accessible via the Resources link at the book's catalogue webpage, includes a discussion of the following topic:

THE ELEMENTAL OPERATIONS OF LAW

Question 92, Article 1:
Whether an Effect of Law Is to Make Men Good?

TEXT	PARAPHRASE
Whether an effect of law is to make men good?	Does law tend to make men good?

[1] Alan Watson, ed., *The Digest of Justinian,* rev. ed., Vol. 1 (Philadelphia: University of Pennsylvania Press, 1998), p. 12. The translator of the passage I am quoting (Book 1, Title 3, Section 1) is D.N. MacCormick.

Although St. Thomas answers "Yes," he does not suppose that law makes men good unfailingly, completely, unproblematically, or without further qualification – as we will see.

---

[1] *Objection 1. It seems that it is not an effect of law to make men good. For men are good through virtue, since virtue, as stated in Ethic. ii, 6 is "that which makes its subject good."* [2] *But virtue is in man from God alone, because He it is Who "works it in us without us," as we stated above (55, 4) in giving the definition of virtue. Therefore the law does not make men good.*

Objection 1. Apparently, law does not make men good; virtue does. This point is so fundamental that Aristotle makes it the very basis of his definition of virtue: Virtue is the quality that "makes its possessor good." Expanding on the idea, another traditional definition reminds us that virtue is brought about in us by God, and that He brings it about without our help – without the help, then, of human law. We conclude that law makes man good neither in itself (because virtue does that), nor by making us virtuous (because God does that).

---

[1] The sense in which virtue "makes" man good is that his goodness *simply is* his virtue. Virtue is what makes the difference between a good man and a bad one; if he is virtuous he is good, if he is not virtuous he is not good. This relationship holds not just for moral good but for all kinds of good; it holds not just for the moral virtues but for every kind of excellence; and it holds not just for man but for all things whatsoever. What makes a racehorse a good racehorse? Swiftness; so swiftness is the virtue – the proper excellence – of the racehorse.

[2] In I-II, Question 55, Article 4, St. Thomas had explained and approved a traditional definition which called virtue "a good quality of the mind, by which we live righteously, of which no one can make bad use, which God works in us, without us." It may seem, by the way, that a person *can* "make bad use" of virtue. For example, doesn't the bank robber make bad use of the virtue of courage, to suppress his fear of being caught? No, because according to the classical understanding, courage is more than the mere ability to repress fear. A courageous man represses fear for the right reasons; a bank robber represses it for the wrong ones. If we need a term for the quality that a fearless robber has, we might call him, *brave*, but not courageous.[2]

---

[2] See also later in this Commentary, concerning Q. 95, Art. 1.

[1] **Objection 2.** *Further, Law does not profit a man unless he obeys it.* [2] *But the very fact that a man obeys a law is due to his being good. Therefore in man goodness is presupposed to the law. Therefore the law does not make men good.*

Objection 2. Moreover, the enactment of a law does a man no good by itself. He must obey it. But he obeys it only if he is already good; the law that commands him takes his goodness for granted. So the claim that law makes men good turns out to be false.

[1]   Today many think of law as something that keeps us from pursuing our good. By contrast, the Objector is willing to believe that obedience to law provides a man some kind of good. What he denies is that it *makes* the man good.

[2]   The Objector is expressing a paradox: One tries to get men to obey the law in order to make them good; but unless they were already good, they wouldn't obey the law.

[1] **Objection 3.** *Further, Law is ordained to the common good, as stated above (90, 2). But some behave well in things regarding the community, who behave ill in things regarding themselves.* [2] *Therefore it is not the business of the law to make men good.*

Objection 3. Still further, we have seen that law is directed to the common good. But some men do the things the common good requires, and yet fail to do the things their private good requires. Consequently, law does not extend to making men good.

[1]   The Objector reflects that men who follow the law may still regulate their personal affairs badly. So, even if law succeeded in making men good with respect to the community's shared concerns, it would not succeed in making them good with respect to their private concerns.

[2]   St Thomas's language, *non ... ad legem pertinet quod faciat homines bonos,* could mean that law does not *pertain* to making men good, but the primary meaning of the Latin root *pertineo* is to stretch out, reach, or extend, and this captures the Objector's meaning more adequately. His point is that even if the effects of the law extend to making men good with respect to the community's well-being, they do not extend to making them good with respect to their individual well-being. So, he concludes, the unqualified statement that law "makes men good" is unjustified.

Objection 4. Further, some laws are tyrannical, as the Philosopher says (Polit. iii, 6). But a tyrant does not intend the good of his subjects, but considers only his own profit. Therefore law does not make men good.	**Objection 4.** Besides, as Aristotle reminds us, some regimes are tyrannies, and the laws of tyrannies serve the good of the rulers, not the good of the people. The general proposition, "law makes men good," cannot be supported.

Aristotle had classified the various kinds of regime according to two criteria: The size and composition of the ruling group, and whether the rulers aim at the common good or merely at their own. Concerning the first criterion, St. Thomas remarks elsewhere that the composition of the ruling group is fundamental, and its size is merely incidental.[3] Rule by the One for the common good is monarchy, the individual government of a good man; rule by the One for his own good is tyranny, the selfish individual government of a bad one. Rule by the Few for the common good is aristocracy, the class government of the well-bred; rule by the Few for their own good is oligarchy, the selfish class government of the merely rich. Rule by the Many for the common good is polity, the government in which rich and poor share power, balanced by the middle class; rule by the Many for their own good is democracy, the selfish class government of the poor alone. The three bad forms of government, tyranny, oligarchy, and democracy, are perversions of the three true or good ones, monarchy, aristocracy, and polity. St. Thomas modifies Aristotle's analysis in certain interesting ways that we take up in Question 105, but they do not concern what he is saying here.

On the contrary, The Philosopher says (Ethic. ii, 1) that the "intention of every lawgiver is to make good citizens."	**On the other hand,** the same great thinker to whom appeal was made in Objection 4 claims that without exception, legislators *do* intend to make the citizens good.

Aristotle goes on to say, "this is the wish of every legislator, and those who do not effect it miss their mark, and it is in this that a good constitution [a good form of government] differs from a bad one."[4]

---

[3] See his commentary on Aristotle's *Politics*, Book 3, Lecture 6.
[4] Aristotle, *Nicomachean Ethics*, trans. W.D. Ross, Book 2, Chapter 1 (public domain).

[1] *I answer that, as stated above (90, 1, ad 2; A3,4), a law is nothing else than a dictate of reason in the ruler by whom his subjects are governed.* [2] *Now the virtue of any subordinate thing consists in its being well subordinated to that by which it is regulated:* [3] *thus we see that the virtue of the irascible and concupiscible faculties consists in their being obedient to reason; and accordingly "the virtue of every subject consists in his being well subjected to his ruler," as the Philosopher says (Polit. i).* [4] *But every law aims at being obeyed by those who are subject to it. Consequently it is evident that the proper effect of law is to lead its subjects to their proper virtue:* [5] *and since virtue is "that which makes its subject good," it follows that the proper effect of law is to make those to whom it is given, good, either simply or in some particular respect.* [6] *For if the intention of the lawgiver is fixed on true good, which is the common good regulated according to Divine justice, it follows that the effect of the law is to make men good simply.* [7] *If, however, the intention of the lawgiver is fixed on that which is not simply good, but useful or pleasurable to himself, or in opposition to Divine justice; then the law does not make men good simply, but in respect to that particular government.* [8] *In this way good is found even in things that are bad of themselves: thus a man is called a good robber, because he works in a way that is adapted to his end.*

Here is my response. Remember that law is just a maxim of reason followed by the presiding person, the one by whom the subjects are governed. Now virtue also has to do with the subjection of certain things to others. In every case, the virtue of a subordinate thing lies in its complete obedience to the thing that governs it. Consider, for example, the powers of the soul called "concupiscible" and "irascible," which attract us to various kinds of goods of sense. Their virtue lies in complete obedience to the direction of reason.

But the point we are making applies to persons, too. This is what Aristotle meant when he said that "the virtue of every subject consists in his being well subjected to his ruler." But isn't this what law aims at – the obedience of the subjects? So we see that the result characteristic of law is just this: To bring those it governs to their own particular virtue. And since virtue is the quality that makes those who have it good, it follows that the result characteristic of law is to make those to whom it is given good.

Now it may make them either *simply* good, or good merely with respect to some criterion. Consider two cases. In the first case the legislator intends the true good, which is the common good guided by Divine justice. Then the law makes men simply good. In the second case his intention tends toward what he finds personally useful or delightful instead of to the common good – or toward what resists or violates Divine justice instead of agreeing with it. Even then, although obviously his "law" does not make men simply good, it does make them *good for that kind of regime.* For even things that are evil in themselves may be good with respect to *some* criterion; for example, an evil *man* may be a good *robber,* just because he carries out his robberies in a way that leads to success.

[1]   As in Question 91, Article 1, the definition of law given here is abbreviated. Certain elements are omitted, just because at the moment they are not needed. However, they are tacitly assumed.

The term used for the ruler is *praesidente*, literally, the one who presides. We return to the idea of "presiding" in Question 105, Article 1.

[2]   Because St. Thomas's own example is difficult, some simpler examples may help. The virtue of a thing – its characteristic excellence – is its ability to perform its proper work well. Now the proper work of the fingers is to grasp; they can do this well only by cooperating with the thumb; so their virtue lies in their cooperation. The proper work of the sheepdog is to herd the sheep; it can do this well only by obeying the shepherd; so its virtue lies in its obedience. The proper work of the lungs is to take in oxygen; they can do this well only by responding to the diaphragm; so their virtue lies in their responsiveness.

One might object that being well-subordinated is not the *only* virtue of something that is subordinated. For example, another virtue of the fingers is that they aren't slippery, another virtue of the sheepdog is that he is faster than the sheep, and another virtue of the lungs is that they have sufficient capacity. True, but the fact that the fingers aren't slippery *enables* them to cooperate with the thumb, the fact that the sheepdog is faster than the sheep *enables* him to obey the shepherd, and the fact that the lungs have sufficient capacity *enables* them to respond to the diaphragm. The excellence of their subordination to a well-tuned regulator, and their ability to perform their proper work well, are one and the same thing.

[3]   (1) A dog lies down affectionately at a girl's feet, expecting his belly to be rubbed. (2) Anticipating the pleasures of taste, the girl takes a sip from her cup of hot chocolate. (3) Dismayed that the chocolate is hotter than she expected, she sets it down on the table for later. (4) A young man unknown to the dog enters the room, greets the girl, and asks her for a kiss. (5) Protecting the girl, the dog growls at the young man. (6) Irate over the dog's interference, he locks it in another room. (7) Returning, he accidentally knocks the hot chocolate into the girl's lap, and she angrily orders him to leave.

Now concupiscibility is the power to be stirred up to pursue what the senses find delectable, and avoid what they find harmful; irascibility, in turn, is the power to be aroused to resist what hinders the delectable, or threatens it with harm.[5] So what moves the dog in (1), the girl

---

[5]   I-II, Q. 23, Art. 1.

in (2). and the young man in (4) is the concupiscible power, and what moves the dog in (5), the young man in (6), and the girl in (3) an (7) is the irascible power. St. Thomas's point here is simply that for humans, the two powers are well disposed when they are guided by reason, and badly disposed when they aren't, so that in obedience to reason lies their virtue.

Later on I paraphrase the names of the conscupiscible and irascible powers in various ways, especially as "appetite" and "ardor," respectively.

[4] To obey the law is to be well-subordinated to the regulating agency, which is precisely what brings the citizens to their "proper" virtue, that is, to the excellence that is appropriate to them. But shouldn't we possess *every* excellence? Of course not, because excellence concerns proper work. A teacher does not require the excellence in fighting fires appropriate to a fireman, and a fireman does not require the excellence in judging appropriate to a judge, any more than a human being requires the excellence in swimming appropriate to a fish.

[5] Being well-subordinated to the law may not make the citizens good in *every* respect. It will make them good citizens – that is, good with respect to that particular form of government – but whether being good citizens makes them good men remains to be seen.

[6] In this case (and in this case alone), being good citizens *does* contribute to making them good men.

[7] In this case being good citizens does *not* contribute to making them good men.

[8] In conceding that even a bad man may be good according to *some* criterion, we are not sinking into relativism, for we are not necessarily approving of the criterion. To say that a man is a good robber is not the same as to say that it is good to be a robber.

---

[1] *Reply to Objection 1. Virtue is twofold, as explained above (63, 2, 3), viz. acquired and infused.* [2] *Now the fact of being accustomed to an action contributes to both, but in different ways; for it causes the acquired virtue; while it disposes to infused virtue, and preserves and fosters it when it already exists.*

Reply to Objection 1. I explained earlier in the *Summa* that some virtues are acquired by the human action of practicing the acts of virtue, others infused by the Divine action of grace. The more one is used to exercising the acts of virtue, the more readily an *acquired* virtue is formed, because the habit of exercise is what causes it. And the more one is used to Divine action, the more readily an infused virtue is formed, but this time in a different way – for although the

[3] *And since law is given for the purpose of directing human acts; as far as human acts conduce to virtue, so far does law make men good.* [4] *Wherefore the Philosopher says in the second book of the Politics (Ethic. ii) that "lawgivers make men good by habituating them to good works."*

habit of submission to Divine action does not *cause* infused virtue, it prepares us to receive it, preserves it when it already exists, and promotes its development.

Since the purpose of law is to direct human acts, law makes men good to the same degree that human acts contribute to making them good – no more, no less. This is why Aristotle remarks in his *Nicomachean Ethics*[6] that legislators make men good by getting them in the habit of performing good actions.

[1] Acquired virtues come about by human discipline, infused virtues come about by the action of God. However, these two kinds of virtue are not locked away in separate compartments. In fact, their relationships are complex. The three theological virtues, which are faith, hope, and charity or love, are *wholly* infused; but even the four cardinal virtues, which are temperance, justice, fortitude, and practical wisdom, or prudence, may have certain infused elements. The general rule is that to the degree that a virtue directs us to our natural good, it can be acquired by discipline, but to the degree that it directs us to our supernatural good, it has to be infused. Thus, we must distinguish between acquired and infused temperance, acquired and infused fortitude, and so forth. Making matters still more complex, not even the infused virtues are infused without our willing cooperation (as St. Thomas is about to explain), and not even the acquired virtues can abide in us without some help from grace. Another way to put the latter point is that to reach our natural end, we need divine assistance to *support* what our nature can do, but to reach our supernatural end, we require divine assistance not only to support but also to *supplement* what our nature can do so that it transcends its intrinsic limits.[7]

[2] Even human effort needs God's assistance[8]; yet the cause of the acquired virtues is the effort of man. Even infused virtue requires the human vessel to be willing to receive it; yet the cause of the infused virtues is the action of God. (For that matter, the ability and readiness of the human vessel to submit is a gift of Divine grace too.)

---

[6] St. Thomas slips, referring to Aristotle's *Politics*, but he means his *Nicomachean Ethics*.

[7] I-II, Q. 61, Art. 2, and Q. 62, Arts. 1, 3.

[8] Man "is directed to his connatural end, by means of his natural principles, *albeit not without Divine assistance*." I-II, Q. 62, Art. 1, emphasis added.

[3]   Just to this extent, no more and no less, law makes them good; thus it cannot impart the infused virtues.

[4]   To put this quotation in context (but using a different translation), Aristotle explains that "the things we have to learn before we can do them, we learn by doing them, e.g. men become builders by building and lyre-players by playing the lyre; so too we become just by doing just acts, temperate by doing temperate acts, brave by doing brave acts. This is confirmed by what happens in states; legislators make the citizens good by forming habits in them."[9] Through being made to act justly, for example, citizens become habituated to acting justly, and justice is simply the full and rational development of such a habit. In another work, St. Thomas summarizes, "Like actions produce like habits."[10]

It would be naïve to think that law succeeds completely in habituating men to good works, nor is that what St. Thomas means. But it would be equally naïve to think that law can contribute nothing to this goal. Later on, in the section on human law, he returns to the question of how law makes men good: Does it repress *every* vice? Does it command *every* act of virtue?

Reply to Objection 2. It is not always through perfect goodness of virtue that one obeys the law, but sometimes it is through fear of punishment, and sometimes from the mere dictates of reason, which is a beginning of virtue, as stated above (63, 1).	Reply to Objection 2. True, a completely good person would obey the law just because of his virtue, but those who are not completely good obey for other reasons. Sometimes they obey because they are afraid of being punished, sometimes just because of the principles that are instilled into man's reason. These principles are not virtue, but they provide the initial impulse toward it.

Earlier, in I-II, Question 63, Article 1, St. Thomas called these first principles the seeds of virtue (in the winsome rendering of the translators, its "nurseries"). Although he does not call fear of punishment a seed of virtue, even the fear of punishment might get an imperfect person into the habit of doing the right things.

[9] Aristotle, *Nicomachean Ethics*, Book 2, Chapter 1, trans. W.D. Ross (public domain). St. Thomas mistakenly refers to Book 2 of Aristotle's *Politics*.
[10] Thomas Aquinas, *Commentary on Aristotle's Nicomachean Ethics*, Book 2, Lecture 1, trans. C.J. Litzinger, O.P., rev. ed. (Notre Dame, IN: Dumb Ox Books, 1993), p. 86.

[1] *Reply to Objection 3. The goodness of any part is considered in comparison with the whole; hence Augustine says (Confess. iii) that "unseemly is the part that harmonizes not with the whole."* [2] *Since then every man is a part of the state, it is impossible that a man be good, unless he be well proportionate to the common good: nor can the whole be well consistent unless its parts be proportionate to it.* [3] *Consequently the common good of the state cannot flourish, unless the citizens be virtuous, at least those whose business it is to govern. But it is enough for the good of the community, that the other citizens be so far virtuous that they obey the commands of their rulers.* [4] *Hence the Philosopher says (Polit. ii, 2) that "the virtue of a sovereign is the same as that of a good man, but the virtue of any common citizen is not the same as that of a good man."*

Reply to Objection 3. To judge the goodness of a single element of a composite, we must view it in relation to the whole. Augustine expresses the same thought when he remarks, "For every part is defective that is not in harmony with the whole."[11] So, since every man is a part of the civic body, no man can be good unless he is in harmony with the *common* good, and the civic community cannot stand firmly unless its parts are well-ordered to it. For this reason, the common good of the civic community cannot abide vigorously unless the citizens are virtuous. At least those citizens whose place it is to rule must be virtuous, though it suffices for the good of the community that the other citizens be virtuous enough to obey their injunctions. This is why Aristotle comments that although the meaning of virtue is the same for the *foremost* citizen and the good man, it is not the same for *any* citizen and the good man.

[1] The context of St. Augustine's remark is his argument in *Confessions*, Book 3, Chapter 8, that customs confirmed by the community should not be violated by lawless whim.

[2] As discussed previously, although each person is a part of the commonwealth, he is not *only* a part; the commonwealth possesses only "unity of order," much weaker than the kind of unity that a person possesses. A person is a subsistent being; a commonwealth is merely an ordered collection. I emphasize this point because it is so often overlooked; interpreters commonly attribute to St. Thomas a view that is the opposite of what he actually believes.

[3] One can think of the community flourishing or not flourishing, but it seems odd to think of the common good flourishing or not flourishing.

---

[11] St. Augustine of Hippo, *Confessions*, trans. F.J. Sheed (Indianapolis, IN: Hackett, 1993), Book 3, Chapter 8, quoting from p. 43.

What St. Thomas actually says is that it is impossible for the common good of the community to "hold itself well," *bene se habeat,* unless the citizens are virtuous. This means that it cannot well continue, cannot persist, cannot abide – that it cannot easily go on in its goodness. St. Thomas is calling our attention to the fragility of any commonwealth in which the citizens lack virtue.

But *which* citizens must have virtue? All, but to different degrees. For the commonwealth to abide, the legislators must be very good indeed, otherwise they will not make good laws. The rest of the citizens need only be good enough to follow the laws made for them (which in turn help maintain their own virtue). St. Thomas is not here considering the case of republics, commonwealths in which, as he later puts it, the people are "free, and able to make their own laws"?[12] It would seem that in this case, *all* of the citizens must be very good indeed, which is perhaps why there are not many republics.

[4]   Not counting republics, where every citizen shares in making laws, to be a good legislator one must be a completely good man, but to be a good citizen one need not be a completely good man.

The term translated "sovereign" is *principis*, which literally means "foremost man."

---

[1] *Reply to Objection 4. A tyrannical law, through not being according to reason, is not a law, absolutely speaking, but rather a perversion of law;* [2] *and yet in so far as it is something in the nature of a law, it aims at the citizens' being good.* [3] *For all it has in the nature of a law consists in its being an ordinance made by a superior to his subjects, and aims at being obeyed by them, which is to make them good, not simply, but with respect to that particular government.*

Reply to Objection 4. Bearing in mind that true law is an ordinance of reason, a tyrannical "law" is not a true law but a twisting of law, simply because it is *not* an ordinance of reason. Yet just to the degree that it has *something* in common with true law, even a tyrannical "law" seeks to make the citizens good *in some respect.* What then does it have in common with true law? Just this (and nothing else): It is a command, framed by the presiding person and issued to those subject to him, with the purpose of being obeyed. Obeying it does not make them good *men,* though it certainly makes them good *subjects of his tyranny.*

---

[1]   We saw in Question 90, Article 2, that to be a true law, an enactment must serve the common good. So-called tyrannical laws, then, are

---

[12] Q. 97, Art. 3.

not true laws because they serve the selfish good of the tyrant. As we will see later on, in Question 96, Article 4, they cannot even generate an obligation to obey.

[2]   A so-called tyrannical law does not aim at the *common* good or at the citizen's *moral* good, but it does aim at making him good for something. Good for what? St. Thomas is about to explain.

[3]   Even tyrants want their so-called laws to be obeyed, and just so far as they are obeyed, they make the citizens good for – well, for the continuation of tyranny. This is a dreadful parody of how true laws make men good – as we should expect, because tyrannies are dreadful parodies of true government.

If imaginary personages can be said to feel anything, the Objector must feel as though he has been sucker-punched. He was probably expecting St. Thomas to respond, "Oh, I agree that tyrannical laws don't make men good, but tyrannical laws aren't true laws; they don't count." Instead St. Thomas responds, "The proposition reaches further than you think; it illuminates not only the noble but the sordid. Even tyrannical laws, which are more akin to acts of violence than to true laws, make men good *for something* – even if only for slavery."

For further reflection on the preceding section of the *Treatise on Law*, the online *Companion to the Commentary*, accessible via the Resources link at the book's catalogue webpage, includes a discussion of the following topic:

MAKING MEN GOOD

Question 92, Article 2:
Whether the Acts of Law Are Suitably Assigned?

TEXT	PARAPHRASE
Whether the acts of law are suitably assigned?	Is the traditional view correct in designating command, prohibition, permission and punishment as the acts of law?

In the Prologue to Question 92, the *ultrum* was posed in terms of law's "effects" (*effectibus*). Here it is posed in terms of law's "acts" (*actus*). An act of law is that in which the law is actualized or completed – that *by which it achieves* its effect.

Much like St. Thomas's Objectors, contemporary readers would probably list the acts of law differently than the tradition did, but they would also regard the question as pedantic. In St. Thomas's view, it is not at all pedantic; people list law's acts differently because they view law itself differently. That is why this article belongs to the first division of the *Treatise on Law*, "law itself in general."

[1] *Objection 1. It would seem that the acts of law are not suitably assigned as consisting in "command," "prohibition," "permission" and "punishment."* [2] *For "every law is a general precept," as the jurist states.* [3] *But command and precept are the same. Therefore the other three are superfluous.*	Objection 1. Apparently, the traditional view lists more acts of law than there really are. Command and precept are the same thing, so Ulpian's remark that "Every law is a general precept" may be paraphrased "Every law is a general command." But if this is true, then we need not include prohibition, permission, and punishment as acts of law; command is law's only act.

[1]   For the four acts of law, St. Thomas's Objector is thinking again of Modestinus's statement, quoted in the Prologue to Question 92, that "The force of a law is this: To command, to prohibit, to permit, or to punish."

[2]   For law as a general precept, the Objector is quoting another Roman legal authority, Papinian: "A statute (*lex*) is a command of general application, a resolution on the part of learned men, a restraint of offenses committed either voluntarily or in ignorance, a general covenant on the part of the state."[13] The esteem in which Papinian was held in Roman times is illustrated by the following passage in the Law of Citations, issued in the time of Theodosius: "We confirm all the writings of Papinian, Paul, Gaius, Ulpian and Modestinus, so that the same authority shall attend Gaius as attends Paul, Ulpian and the rest ... But when conflicting opinions are tendered, the greater number of authors shall prevail, or, if the numbers are equal, the group in which Papinian (a man of outstanding ability) is prominent shall have precedence: As he defeats a single opponent, so he yields to two."[14]

---

[13] *The Digest of Justinian*, trans. Charles Henry Monro (Cambridge: Cambridge University Press, 1904), Book 1, Title 3, Section 1, p. 19.
[14] The Law of Citations, *Codex Theodosianus*, Book 1, Chapter 4, Section 3, as translated by Alan K. Bowman and Greg Woolf, *Literacy and Power in the Ancient World* (Cambridge: Cambridge University Press, 1997), p. 173.

[3]   The nub of the objection is that although all laws are precepts, only
the act of command is accomplished by precept. The other three acts of
law should have been left off the list.

Objection 2. Further, the effect of a law is to induce its subjects to be good, as stated above (Article 1). But counsel aims at a higher good than a command does. Therefore it belongs to law to counsel rather than to command.	Objection 2. Moreover, as we have just seen in Article 1, the effect of law is to make men good. But the legislator may move man to good not only by command, but also by counsel, and of these two, counsel aims at a higher good – a more complete and comprehensive one. Therefore we should strike command from the list and add counsel.

The Objector's argument here is highly elliptical. Filling in the tacit
parts, it seems to go like this:

1.   By law, the legislator moves men to good.
2.   But the legislator may move man to good not only by command,
     but also by counsel.
3.   Should we then keep command on the list, and add counsel?
4.   No, for that would make the list redundant. Command aims at a
     lower good that is a mere element in, or precursor to, the more com-
     plete and comprehensive good at which counsel aims. Therefore,
     counsel subsumes or encompasses command; it presupposes what
     the command aims at, and goes yet further.
5.   This being so, rather than keeping command on the list and adding
     counsel, we should *substitute* counsel for command.

Objection 3. Further, just as punishment stirs a man to good deeds, so does reward. Therefore if to punish is reckoned an effect of law, so also is to reward.	Objection 3. Still further, the rationale for considering punishment seems to be that it moves man to do good. But reward has that effect too. Therefore, to consider punishment but *not* reward as an act of law is arbitrary; we should include either both, or neither.

The Objector is reasoning analogically. If punishment is an act of law,
then whatever has the same effect as punishment must also be an act
of law.

---

[1] *Objection 4. Further, the intention of a lawgiver is to make men good, as stated above (Article 1). But he that obeys the law, merely through fear of being punished, is not good:*	Objection 4. Besides, punishment should not be considered an act of law at all. Those who make the laws aim at making men good, but the fear of punishment has no

[2] *because "although a good deed may be done through servile fear, i.e. fear of punishment, it is not done well," as Augustine says (Contra duas Epist. Pelag. ii). Therefore punishment is not a proper effect of law.*

such effect. For good men not only do the right deeds, but do them well, or in the right way – and as Augustine points out in *Against Two Letters of the Pelagians,* to do something through slavish fear is not to do it well. For this reason, punishment should be struck from the list of acts of law.

[1]   This time the Objector is attempting to draw a further conclusion from the finding of Article 1: If law makes men good, then each of the acts of law should make men good. But although the fear of punishment makes men obey, it does not make them truly good; to be truly good they would have to obey for the sheer love of good. So fear of punishment is not an act of law.

[2]   St. Augustine is making the point that the crowning perfection of virtue depends on the grace of God (a point with which St. Thomas fully agrees): "For good begins then to be longed for when it has begun to grow sweet. But when good is done by the fear of penalty, not by the love of righteousness, good is not yet well done. Nor is that done in the heart which seems to be done in the act when a man would rather not do it if he could evade it with impunity. Therefore the 'blessing of sweetness' is God's grace, by which is caused in us that what He prescribes to us delights us, and we desire it – that is, we love it[.]"[15]

On the contrary, Isidore says (Etym. v, 19): "Every law either permits something, as: 'A brave man may demand his reward'": or forbids something, as: "No man may ask a consecrated virgin in marriage": or punishes, as: "Let him that commits a murder be put to death."

On the other hand, Isidore supports the traditional view of the acts of law. As he writes in his encyclopedia, *Etymologies,* "every law either allows something, as 'a strong man may seek reward,' or it forbids, as 'no one is allowed to seek marriage with a sacred virgin,' or it prescribes punishment, as 'Whoever has committed murder shall suffer capital punishment.'"[16]

[15] St. Augustine of Hippo, *Against Two Letters of the Pelagians,* trans. Peter Holmes and Robert Ernest Wallis, rev. Benjamin B. Warfield, Book 2, Chapter 21 (public domain, available online at www.newadvent.org/fathers). The internal reference to the "blessing of sweetness" is from Psalm 20:4 (DRA), numbered Psalm 21:3 in most contemporary translations.
[16] *The Etymologies of Isidore of Seville,* trans. Stephen A. Barney, W.J. Lewis, J.A. Beach, and Oliver Berghof (Cambridge: Cambridge University Press, 2006), Book 5, Chapter 19, p. 119.

The paraphrase suffices for the commentary. Had it been quoted in its entirety, the Isidorean quotation could also have been used to support Objection 3, for the great encyclopedist adds, "Indeed, human life is regulated by the *reward or* punishment of law."[17]

[1] *I answer that, Just as an assertion is a dictate of reason asserting something, so is a law a dictate of reason, commanding something.* [2] *Now it is proper to reason to lead from one thing to another. Wherefore just as, in demonstrative sciences, the reason leads us from certain principles to assent to the conclusion, so it induces us by some means to assent to the precept of the law.*	Here is my response. Both assertions and laws are declarations of reason; the difference is that an assertion states that something is true, but a law commands that something be done. Now just as in fields of learning that depend on proofs, so in law, reason does not arrive at its declarations all at once; starting from certain principles, law leads up to them step by step, so that we are able to agree to its precepts.

[1]   That the dictate of law always *commands* something was exactly the point that the Objector was making when he quoted Papinian in Objection 1. Thus far St. Thomas agrees, but he adds that it is a dictate *of reason,* that is, practical reason, concerned with directing us toward good.

[2]   The Latin word *scientia,* like the German word *Wissenschaft,* encompasses all disciplined fields of knowledge, not just the physical sciences. St. Thomas's point is that just as we must have reasons to assent to a conclusion in history, chemistry, or poetics, so we must have reasons to assent to a law. We need not suppose that the chain of inference is spelled out as clearly or as explicitly in legislation as in the sciences. Even so, one must begin somewhere in order to end somewhere. As St. Thomas has stated previously, the starting points of the sciences, even if tacit, are the first principles of theoretical reason; the starting points of legislation, even if tacit, are the first principles of practical reason.

To say this is in no way to slight empirical observation; neither the scholar nor the legislator will get far along the path of inference without detailed knowledge of particular facts. Strictly speaking, however, these particulars are not starting points, for in order to know what to make of an observation, one must know something else first. No one will correlate cause A with effect B unless he already knows the principle that every effect has a cause; no one will correlate act P with end Q unless he already knows the principle that every human act is done with a view to some end.

---

[1] *Now the precepts of law are concerned with human acts, in which the law directs, as stated above (90, A1,2; 91, 4). Again there are three kinds of human acts: for, as stated above (Question 18, Article 8), some acts are good generically, viz. acts of virtue; and in respect of these the act of the law is a precept or command, for "the law commands all acts of virtue" (Ethic. v, 1). Some acts are evil generically, viz. acts of vice, and in respect of these the law forbids. Some acts are generically indifferent, and in respect of these the law permits;* [2] *and all acts that are either not distinctly good or not distinctly bad may be called indifferent.* [3] *And it is the fear of punishment that law makes use of in order to ensure obedience: in which respect punishment is an effect of law.*

To view these precepts clearly we must remember what they are about: Law directs human acts. As I explained earlier in the *Summa*, the goodness or badness of human acts depends not only on what kind of acts they are, but also partly on circumstances. Some acts, taken as a class, are always good – such are acts of virtue. Others, taken as a class, are always evil – such are acts of vice. Still others, taken as a class, are indifferent – they are neither always good nor always bad, or at any rate neither good enough nor bad enough to belong in either of the other two classes.

Law, then, commands or prescribes generically good acts, prohibits generically bad acts, and permits generically indifferent acts. Consequently, command, prohibition, and permission must be reckoned as acts of law. Punishment must be added to the list too, because the fear of punishment is what the commands and prohibitions of law use to induce people to obey.

---

[1] So far the meaning is transparent. Law sets human acts in order with a view to the common good. Consequently it commands acts that are always good, forbids acts that are always evil, and permits acts that cannot be assigned to either of these classes. Later on, in Question 96, Articles 2 and 3, St. Thomas qualifies the broad statements that law commands acts of virtue and forbids acts of vice. It concerns itself with acts of virtue only to the degree that they affect the common good; it concerns itself with acts of vice only to the degree that prohibition does more good than harm.

[2] The Latin clause *qui sunt vel parum boni vel parum mali* has been variously translated – "that are either not distinctly good or not distinctly bad" (Dominican Fathers), "which are either slightly good or slightly bad" (Dewan), "that have either just a little goodness or just a little badness"

(Freddoso)[18] All such renderings miss something, because, literally, St. Thomas is referring not to acts that are *a little* good or bad, but to acts that are *insufficiently* (*parum*) good or bad.

This raises the question: Insufficiently good or bad for what? The answer can only be: Insufficiently good or bad to be commanded or prohibited by law. Between the lines lies the insight that not all goods and bads are worth law's attention. But why should this be true? Presumably because regulation itself imposes a certain burden, so that too much regulation injures the common good. What then is the test – how much is not too much? A law should be enacted only if the particular good that it brings about is greater than the generic burden of loading down the citizens with yet another law. This unexpected thought, rather contrary to our stereotypes about medieval thinkers, is not developed in the present passage, but is thoroughly characteristic of the way St. Thomas balances goods and harms in other places, especially Question 96, Articles 2 and 4, and Question 97, Article 2.

[3] But the hope of reward also motivates obedience, so why isn't reward also an effect of law? St. Thomas answers this question below, in his Reply to Objection 3.

Reply to Objection 1. Just as to cease from evil is a kind of good, so a prohibition is a kind of precept: and accordingly, taking precept in a wide sense, every law is a kind of precept.	Reply to Objection 1. Viewing a precept as an instruction to do something good, the Objector thinks only commands can be described as such instructions. But to desist from evil is to do a kind of good. If, then, any instruction to do something good is a precept, then prohibitions, which instruct citizens to desist from evil, are precepts too. Continuing this line of reasoning, we soon discover that not just commands, but all laws, are precepts in the broad sense.

Though St. Thomas assures us that just as prohibitions turn out to be precepts, so do permissions and punishments, he doesn't show how; he leaves us to work it out for ourselves. What he has in mind is probably something like this:

---

[18] The first translation is of course that of the Fathers of the Dominican Province; the second that of Lawrence Dewan, *Wisdom, Law, and Virtue: Essays in Thomistic Ethics* (New York: Fordham University Press, 2007), p. 383; and the third that of Alfred J. Freddoso, *Treatise on Law: The Complete Text* (South Bend, IN: St. Augustine's Press, 2009), p. 23.

1. Every law is a precept in the sense that it instructs something good.
2. A command fits the definition directly, because it instructs citizens to perform good deeds. But each of the other three acts of law fits the definition indirectly:
3. A prohibition fits, because it instructs citizens to desist from a bad deed, and desisting from a bad deed is a kind of good deed.
4. A permission fits, because it instructs each citizen to follow his own prudent judgment about which acts are good, and following one's own prudent judgment about what is good is a kind of good deed.
5. A punishment fits, because it instructs the citizens, "to avoid the law's penalty, do as the law requires." Though fear of penalty is not a completely good motive, doing as the law requires is a kind of good deed.

Reply to Objection 2. To advise is not a proper act of law, but may be within the competency even of a private person, who cannot make a law. Wherefore too the Apostle, after giving a certain counsel (1 Corinthians 7:12) says: "I speak, not the Lord." Consequently it is not reckoned as an effect of law.

Reply to Objection 2. True, a legislator may advise, but advising is not a distinctively legislative thing to do; private persons can do the same thing. St. Paul makes the same distinction between his legislative and non-legislative acts in his first letter to the Church in the city of Corinth, where, after giving certain advice, he emphasizes that it is coming from him, not from the Lord; it expresses his judgment, not God's law. So although a legislator may give counsel, counsel is not a distinctively legislative act.

We saw in Question 90 that law is an ordinance of reason, for the common good, made by public authority, and promulgated or made known. Even a private person may make known to the community at large a judgment of reason for the common good, but the decisive element that his counsel lacks is public authority; it is not a law. St. Thomas's point is not that the law *cannot advise,* but that advising is not something that pertains to law uniquely, like issuing public commands, prohibitions, and permissions that have public authority.

At first this seems a little arbitrary. Couldn't one say that although counsel as such is not an act of law, counsel *that has public authority* is an act of law? I think St. Thomas would reply that counsel as such does not have "authority," even if it is given and taken by public persons. It may be an act of legislative deliberation that *leads up* to the enactment of a law, but it is not *itself* a law until it has taken on the ligaments of command, prohibition, or permission.

Reply to Objection 3. To reward may also pertain to anyone: but to punish pertains to none but the framer of the law, by whose authority the pain is inflicted. Wherefore to reward is not reckoned an effect of law, but only to punish.	**Reply to Objection 3.** Just as there is nothing distinctively legislative about giving someone counsel, so there is nothing distinctively legislative about giving someone a reward; even a private person can do that. By contrast, punishments can be assigned only by those to whom belongs the authority to make laws. At this point the analogy between reward and punishment fails; punishment is an act of law, but reward is not.

Our first impulse on reading this reply is to think that St. Thomas has made a mistake: Isn't public authority *equally* unnecessary for punishment and for reward? Just as I reward a good student with a glowing letter of recommendation, don't I punish a bad one by refusing one? The answer is "No": To reason like that is to confuse two different senses of punishment. Certainly I can withhold from my student a benefit that I might otherwise have chosen to give him. That is a punishment in a sense. But the punishments lawgivers assign for violation of the law go beyond anything that I may do as a private person, for the law can deprive persons of benefits of life, liberty, or property that would otherwise be due to them simply by virtue of being humans and citizens. Whether to recommend a student is up to me, but I may not execute him, put him in jail, or make him pay a fine.

But if the criterion of being a distinctive act of law is that the kind of act in question exceeds my ability to perform as a private person, then aren't there also rewards that exceed my ability to confer as a private person? I can reward a student with a glowing recommendation, but I cannot confer upon a soldier the medal of honor. So if punishments that exceed my ability to impose are acts of law, why aren't rewards that exceed my ability to confer also acts of law? Perhaps St. Thomas would reply that when public authority confers an honor upon the soldier, it is not doing something *different* than command, prohibition, or permission; rather it is *commanding* all citizens to hold him in honor, and commands, in turn, are made effective by punishment. So the parallel between reward and punishment does not hold.

| *Reply to Objection 4.* From becoming accustomed to avoid evil and fulfill what is good, through fear of punishment, one is sometimes led on to do so likewise, with delight and of one's own accord. Accordingly, law, even by punishing, leads men on to being good. | **Reply to Objection 4.** The Objector is right to remind us that law is aimed at making men good. He is also right to point out that a man who obeys only to escape punishment is far from wholly good. Even so, just through becoming habituated to good acts, a man sometimes comes to do them from different motives: At first just through fear and by compulsion, but over time with joy and by his own will. So even punishment contributes to making men good. |

St. Thomas had made much the same point in reply to Article 1, Objection 2: Though a man who obeys the law through fear alone is not yet virtuous, he may be on the way to virtue through the school of hard knocks.

For further reflection on the preceding section of the *Treatise on Law*, the online *Companion to the Commentary*, accessible via the Resources link at the book's catalogue webpage, includes a discussion of the following topic:

IS THERE ANYTHING LAW MAY NOT COMMAND?

THE PARTS OF LAW: QUESTIONS 93–108

Before Reading Question 93

Eternal law is the foundation and origin of all law, its *sine qua non*. In view of this fact, it is curious that so many readers try to make sense of the other kinds of law without it. Let us consider what happens, then, if eternal law does not exist.

If eternal law does not exist, then neither does natural law. In fact, properly speaking, we have no nature at all. What! Aren't we a certain way, and not another? Aren't we humans, and not snakes or insects? Yes, but if there is no eternal law, then the way we are no longer expresses a meaningful and purposeful pattern; it is merely a transitory phase in a haphazard, aimless process that could have gone otherwise, and presumably is still going on – a process that, since there is no mind behind it, does not even rise to the level of idiocy. "I will praise you, for I am fearfully and wonderfully made," says the psalmist.[1] But if there is no eternal law, then we are not "made" at all, and there is no reason for fear and wonder. Instead we should view matters as the convicted wife-murderer George Delury does. He admits that after dosing his wife with lethal drugs and suffocating her with a plastic bag, he suffered for months from an "almost physical" sense of guilt. But he told himself that this feeling was "irrational"; it was not "an awareness of having done something ethically wrong," but merely "the dissonance of a primate over the violation of a fundamental instinct," the "instinctive block against killing our own kind."[2]

---

[1] Psalm 139:14 (KJV).
[2] George E. DeLury, *But What If She Wants to Die? A Husband's Diary* (Secaucus, NJ: Birch Lane Press/Carol Publishing Group, 1997), pp. 178–179.

If Delury's premise is true, then so is his conclusion; the only puzzle is why he should have thought that there is such a thing as ethical wrong at all. Conscience itself would be just another of those primate things, another clot of instincts and dissonances. So what if we have conscience? We might have developed differently and had different instincts and dissonances, like mantis females, which devour their mates. In the future, perhaps we will. If we find our instincts inconvenient, there is no reason to follow them; if our dissonances bother us, we can always take pills or have surgery to settle them down. Perhaps some day we will even find a way to reprogram ourselves so that we have only those instincts we wish to have – though this is a strange prospect, because the only reasons for deciding which instincts to program into ourselves would be the instinctual likes and dislikes that we happened to have already. Reprogramming would be just one more arbitrary stage in a process that ended in the thermodynamic death rattle of the universe, an eons-long lurch from one void to another.

If there is no eternal law, and consequently no natural law, then neither is there human law. In fact, properly speaking, there is no government. What! Aren't there powerful groups of men who rule us? Don't they enact edicts that they call laws? Yes, but true laws and governments require more than naked power; they need authority. The difference between authority and naked power is just this, that authority depends on a standard that human will and power did not invent. If those who rule us may make and remake the standard to suit their own naked will (or the naked will of their constituents), then authority no more exists than pixie-dust. There is only power, the power of those who make the standard against the weakness of those who suffer it. The Jew has no more grounds to protest the Nazi, the unborn child to protest the abortionist, the victim to protest the rapist, than the fly to protest the spider that nets and poisons him. The fly strives against the spider, certainly, but the spider is stronger, and has its way. There is no law that the stronger should have their way, nor is there a law that they should not, for there is neither law nor *should*. Having their way is simply what the strong do. Without eternal law, *should* is but a mystification, a projection of human power into realms beyond man.

But isn't that just what *should* is? For suppose there is an eternal law; so what? How does it help to push the source of authority back onto God? We may say all we like that authority depends on a standard that does not depend on man's will and power; but then why should we not say that authority depends on a standard that does not depend on God's will and power? This objection misconceives what is meant by eternal law. It is not something *under* God, as though He were beyond good and evil, arbitrarily defining what should count as good. What, then? Is it *higher* than God? Is it the highest thing, so that He is under it, just as we are under it? Not that either. He is all that can be meant by *highest* – the highest being, the highest wisdom, the highest good. But if so then He is neither above nor below the highest law – He is identical with it.

What, God identical with an abstract set of legal formulae, of dos and don'ts? Not at all. We saw at the very beginning of our inquiry that law is an ordinance of reason. If eternal law is the highest reason, then it is not enough for it to reflect reason; it must *be* Reason. It must be personal, as God is personal; it must be the very wisdom of His mind. God's law then is His own wisdom, viewed from the perspective of His governance of creation. It is *living* law. That is much more than a set of dos and don'ts, although, of course, it implies them.

But this reply provokes quite a different objection. If God is good and His law governs creation, then why *does* the spider net and poison the fly? Why does God permit such things? Is He such a poor governor as that? We have already considered one way to answer this protest: God's goodness does not require that He eliminate every evil. What it requires is that evil not have the last word. From any evil God permits, He must bring forth some great good. Those interested in exploring this response further may turn to the discussion of Question 91, Article 1, in the online *Companion to the Commentary*.

But suppose one is not satisfied by the response. Being unsatisfied with it is different than finding it logically flawed. If we are honest with ourselves, we will find that we are sometimes disturbed even by arguments that are logically impeccable. We may have every logical reason to concede that God *must* be good, and therefore *must* prevent evil from having the last word. Yet we are distressed by the delay of God's justice, and our distress tempts us to wonder whether there is something wrong with all those logical reasons.

What then shall we say? That since we are distressed by the delay of God's justice, therefore there is no eternal law? The very possibility of such distress testifies to the reality of the eternal law. Eternal law alone makes the meaning of justice intelligible; without it, we could not be distressed by its delay. To deny the standard of justice because some things violate it is like denying the reality of drink because we thirst. It would be more sensible to say that *because* we are able to thirst, there must be such a thing as drink – and *because* we are able to experience the agony of injustice, there must be a standard of justice.

In the meantime, God knows of our distress. Among the works of St. Thomas is a commentary on Job, which is a poetic meditation on the evils suffered by the just. God chides Job only lightly for his bitter complaints, but reprimands three friends of Job sternly for minimizing Job's suffering and blaming it on Job himself. In the end, although much about Job's suffering remains mysterious, he is comforted by the hope of redemption and by the visit of God Himself.[3] We must never forget that according to St. Thomas Aquinas, redemption is a real possibility, and God has visited man; all his explanations of other things are in service to these facts.

---

[3] By the hope of redemption, in Job 19:23–27; by the visit of God, in the concluding chapters.

St. Thomas's Prologue to Questions 93–108:
Of the Eternal Law

TEXT	PARAPHRASE
[1] *We must now consider each law by itself; and (1) The eternal law; (2) The natural law; (3) The human law; (4) The old law; (5) The new law, which is the law of the Gospel.* [2] *Of the sixth law which is the law of the "fomes," suffice what we have said when treating of original sin.*	Up to this point we have considered the different kinds of law just enough to grasp the nature of law in general, but now we are ready to look into each kind in itself. With one omission, these are the same kinds we have considered before: Eternal law, natural law, human law, and the two kinds of Divine law, Old and New (New Law being the law of the Gospel). The one omission is the so-called law of the "kindling" – our "ignitability" – about which we said everything necessary when we discussed original sin.

[1] Although St. Thomas raises many new issues in Question 93, he also revisits several of the issues he discussed in Question 91, Article 1. The difference is that there he explained eternal law just enough to distinguish the kinds of law, whereas here he plunges more deeply into its mysteries.

[2] By "what we have said," St. Thomas is thinking partly, perhaps, of the discussion of the "law of sin," in Question 92, Article 6, but even more of the discussion of original sin proper, in I-II, Questions 82–83. For additional discussion, see the online *Companion to the Commentary.*

We remember from Question 92, Article 6, that the *fomes* or "kindling" is our tendency to burst into flames of desire and passion at the least little spark. When he says that his previous discussion of the *fomes* must suffice, he does not mean that he will not mention it again, for it comes up again in just a little while (Article 3, Objection 1). He simply means that there is no need to devote an entire Question to the topic.

Concerning the first there are six points of inquiry:	Six queries present themselves for investigation. We ask in Article 1 whether the eternal law is correctly described as a supreme Idea in the mind of God; in Article 2, whether all men know this law; in Article 3, whether it is the basis for every other kind of law; in Article 4, whether it governs necessary and eternal things; in Article 5, whether it governs contingent things that exist in nature; and finally, in Article 6, whether it governs all human affairs.
(1) What is the eternal law?	
(2) Whether it is known to all?	
(3) Whether every law is derived from it?	
(4) Whether necessary things are subject to the eternal law?	
(5) Whether natural contingencies are subject to the eternal law?	
(6) Whether all human things are subject to it?	

My paraphrase of the text reflects the fact that St. Thomas expresses the six *ultra* in more detailed form later than he expresses them here. We will comment on these differences as we go along, but it is helpful to see them all at once, as an overview.

For further reflection on the preceding section of the *Treatise on Law*, the online *Companion to the Commentary*, accessible via the Resources link at the book's catalogue webpage, includes a discussion of the following topic:

ETERNAL LAW, ORIGINAL JUSTICE, AND ORIGINAL SIN

Question 93, Article 1:
Whether the Eternal Law Is a Sovereign Type [Ratio] Existing in God?

TEXT	PARAPHRASE
Whether the eternal law is a sovereign type [Ratio] existing in God?	Granted the reality of the eternal law, is it correct to view it as a supreme Idea in the mind of God?

It may seem that St. Thomas has already covered this ground in Question 91, Article 1. Not so. There he asked whether there is such a thing as an eternal law, considering objections that arise from the nature of law as such. His replies to those objections *assumed* the eternal law to be what it is proposed to be here – a *ratio summa,* a supreme Idea, the pinnacle of reason in the mind of God, the rational pattern or template of His governance of all things. However, in Question 91 St. Thomas did not go on to consider possible objections to this view of it. Here, he does.

[1] *Objection 1. It would seem that the eternal law is not a sovereign type existing in God. For there is only one eternal law.* [2] *But there are many types of things in the Divine mind; for Augustine says (Qq. lxxxiii, qu. 46) that God "made each thing according to its type." Therefore the eternal law does not seem to be a type existing in the Divine mind.*	Objection 1. Apparently, the eternal law is something other than a supreme Idea or template in God, because there is only one eternal law, but God's mind contains numerous thoughts or Ideas. This is clear from St. Augustine's remark in *Eighty-Three Different Questions,* Question 46, "On the Ideas," where he declares that God made each thing according to its own Idea or template. So whatever the eternal law is, it could not be a single supreme Idea in God's mind.

[1] There is one eternal law because there is one eternal legislator, God, and it because it directs all creatures to a single end, the supreme good. The Objector is not suggesting that it entails (via the natural law) but a single *precept,* but that issue is not taken up until Question 94, Article 2.

[2] Genesis describes God as creating each sort of thing – the plants (1:11–12), the creatures of sea and air (1:21), and the beasts of the earth (1:25) "according to their kinds." In the passage from which the quotation is taken, Augustine does not mention Genesis, but asks who would dare to deny that each of these things that have their own natures is made by God and lives by Him, held fast and governed by His laws. He goes on to say that it would be absurd to think man is created according to the same Idea as the horse; therefore, each individual thing is created according to its own Idea.

We are reminded, yet again, of how deeply St. Thomas is indebted to St. Augustine. He does not proceed the same way as the Augustinians who immediately preceded him, who did not have the benefit of Aristotle; but he certainly considers himself an Augustinian.

[1] *Objection 2. Further, it is essential to a law that it be promulgated by word, as stated above (90, 4).* [2] *But Word is a Personal name in God, as stated in the I, 34, 1:* [3] *whereas type refers to the Essence. Therefore the eternal law is not the same as a Divine type.*	Objection 2. Moreover, we saw earlier that law is not law unless it is promulgated or made known – in fact, promulgated by word. But as we saw earlier still, "Word" is a personal name for the second person of the Trinity, the Son. Now a personal name in God is one thing, but an Idea in God is another, because it has to do with God's very essence. So it is impossible for the eternal law to be a Divine Idea.

[1] St. Thomas had written that promulgation is accomplished *et verbo et scripto,* by word or by writing; the Objector takes this as equivalent to "by spoken or written word."

[2] What St. Thomas means by "a Personal name in God" is a name for one of the three Divine Persons. The Second Person of the Trinity, the Son, is named the "Word" in the Prologue to the Gospel of John: "In the beginning was the Word, and the Word was with God, and the Word was God."[4]

[3] The Objector reasons like this:

1. God is three in Person, but one in essence.
2. "Word" is a name for just one of the Divine Persons, the Son.
3. But a Divine Idea pertains to the very essence of God, which all three Persons share.
4. Something that refers to only one of the Divine Persons must be different from something that pertains to all three of them.
5. Therefore, the Word cannot be an Idea.
6. But a law is something promulgated by the Word.
7. Therefore the eternal law cannot be an Idea either.

[1] *Objection 3. Further, Augustine says (De Vera Relig. xxx): "We see a law above our minds, which is called truth." But the law which is above our minds is the eternal law. Therefore truth is the eternal law.* [2] *But the idea of truth is not the same as the idea of a type. Therefore the eternal law is not the same as the sovereign type.*	Objection 3. Still further, the eternal law is the law above our minds. But in *On True Religion*, St. Augustine says the law above our minds is Truth. Therefore the eternal law is Truth. It follows that the eternal law could be a supreme Idea only if *Truth* and *Idea* had the same meaning. But they do not, so the eternal law is *not* a supreme Idea.

[4] John 1:1 (DRA).

[1]   In the passage from which the Objector is quoting, St. Augustine argues that we judge the qualities of changeable things by fixed and absolute standards: For example we judge the squareness of a tabletop or square-cut gem by the fixed and absolute standard of squareness. "This standard of all the arts is absolutely unchangeable," he says, "but the human mind, which is given the power to see the standard, can suffer the mutability of error. Clearly, then, the standard which is called Truth is higher than our minds."[5]

[2]   The Objector does not explain what Truth is. Instead he contents himself with asserting that *Truth* and *Idea* "are not the same idea": *Sed non est eadem ratio veritatis et rationis.*

On the contrary, *Augustine says (De Lib. Arb. i, 6) that "the eternal law is the sovereign type, to which we must always conform."*	**On the other hand,** St. Augustine himself *affirms* the hypothesis under consideration – that the eternal law, which we must always obey, is the supreme Idea, the pinnacle of reason.

The portion of dialogue from which this quotation is taken was presented at greater length in the commentary on Question 91, Article 1. The translation consulted there renders the passage, "Well, consider the law referred to [by Cicero] as 'supreme reason.' It should always be obeyed ..."

[1] *I answer that, Just as in every artificer there pre-exists a type of the things that are made by his art, so too in every governor there must pre-exist the type of the order of those things that are to be done by those who are subject to his government.* [2] *And just as the type of the things yet to be made by an art is called the art or exemplar of the products of that art, so too the type in him who governs the acts of his subjects, bears the character of a law, provided the other conditions be present which we have mentioned above (90).*	**Here is my response.** Every master of a craft carries in his mind ahead of time an Idea of the things that his craft is to make. In the same way, every ruler carries in his mind ahead of time an Idea of the order that his governance is to bring about in the actions of those whom he rules. Just as the Idea of the things craftsmanship brings forth is called their art or their model, so the Idea of the order that governance brings about is rightly called a law (so long as all the other elements of law are present too).

[5] Augustine, *Of True Religion,* Chapter 30, in J.H.S. Burleigh, trans., *Augustine: Earlier Writings* (Philadelphia: Westminster Press, 1953), p. 253, capitalizing "Truth."

[3] *Now God, by His wisdom, is the Creator of all things in relation to which He stands as the artificer to the products of his art, as stated in the I, 14, 8. Moreover He governs all the acts and movements that are to be found in each single creature, as was also stated in the I, 103, 5. [4] Wherefore as the type of the Divine Wisdom, inasmuch as by It all things are created, has the character of art, exemplar or idea; so the type of Divine Wisdom, as moving all things to their due end, bears the character of law. [5] Accordingly the eternal law is nothing else than the type of Divine Wisdom, as directing all actions and movements.*

Now all this applies to God as well. In the first place, He creates everything by His wisdom, and in this respect, His relationship to created things is like the relationship of the master craftsman to the products of his craft. Even more: Not only does He create each thing, He also governs all its acts and changes. Now because it creates everything, the rational pattern or Idea of God's wisdom has the nature of art, exemplar, or ideas; and because it directs everything to its purpose, it also has the nature of law. And so, to the question with which we began – "Is it correct to think of the eternal law as the Idea of God's wisdom, which governs all the actions and changes of created things?" – the answer is "Yes."

[1] As St. Thomas makes explicit in Article 3, by an artificer he means a master craftsman, not a mere journeyman or apprentice. In building, for example, he is not thinking of a carpenter's helper, who merely pounds a nail where he is told, but of the master builder, the architect, the person who directs the building of the house and understands everything to be done. Just as the architect holds in his mind a template of the order to be achieved in the house, so the governor of a commonwealth holds in his mind a template of the order to be achieved in the commonwealth.

The analogy is worth exploring further. The idea in the architect's mind includes not only an understanding of the house to be built, but also an understanding of what each subordinate craftsman must do to build it. In the same way, the idea in the governor's mind includes not only an understanding of political order, but also an understanding of how each citizen must behave to achieve it. But we must not push the analogy too far, because although the house is composed of inanimate objects such as wooden boards and slabs of concrete, the commonwealth is made up of free and rational beings, the citizens themselves. To put it another way, in the case of the house, the materials and the subordinate craftsmen are distinct, but in the case of the commonwealth, they are the same thing. St. Thomas is well aware of these differences, and his analogies should be used only for the purposes he intends.

By the way, the obvious resemblance of St. Thomas's and St. Augustine's view of the ideas to Plato's view of the ideas should not be overstated either. Plato seemed to view the Ideas as independently existing necessary beings. For St. Thomas and St. Augustine, the only necessary being is God Himself, and the Ideas are in His mind. God was not under any necessity to clothe each of His Ideas with created existence. In fact, the number of Divine Ideas in His mind is infinitely greater than the number of things that He has created. Had He so willed, He could even have created a different universe than the one He did.

Readers may notice that I have taken the liberty of stripping away certain redundancies from the paraphrase to make certain parallel constructions read more clearly.

[2] The rational plan in the craftsman's mind, which pre-exists, underlies, and gives unity to the products of his art can itself be called his art. In a similar way, the rational plan that preexists, underlies, and gives unity to particular laws may itself be called a law. We express a similar idea when we call a country's constitution its "higher law."

[3] St. Thomas is pointing out that in a certain way, the Creator-to-creature relationship and the craftsman-to-product relationship are alike. In both cases, the pattern in the mind comes first, and the thing made according to this pattern comes second. However, he is not suggesting that the Creator-to-creature relationship and the craftsman-to-product relationship are alike in *all* ways. God creates things and their properties from nothing, but the craftsman only reworks and conjoins existing things, making use of the forms and properties that they already have.[6] This difference has further consequences, as we will see in the Reply to Objection 3.

As mentioned previously, St. Thomas uses the term "movement" to refer not only to changes in spatial position, but also to all kinds of changes.

[4] The same Idea in God's mind may be regarded in either of two ways, as an exemplar or as a law, depending on whether we are considering it from the perspective of its role in Creation or its role in Providence.

[5] Recalling what we said about constitutions a few lines previously, perhaps it would not be too great a stretch to call the eternal law the Divine Constitution of the universe.

[6] I, Q. 45, Art. 5.

[1] *Reply to Objection 1. Augustine is speaking in that passage of the ideal types which regard the proper nature of each single thing; and consequently in them there is a certain distinction and plurality, according to their different relations to things, as stated in the I, 15, 2.* [2] *But law is said to direct human acts by ordaining them to the common good, as stated above (90, 2). And things, which are in themselves different, may be considered as one, according as they are ordained to one common thing. Wherefore the eternal law is one since it is the type of this order.*

Reply to Objection 1. In the passage quoted, St. Augustine is speaking of the template Ideas of *particular things* in the mind of God, and yes, just as God created many things, so He has many such Ideas. Remember, though, that law directs human acts to the common good. Even though these acts differ from one another, they may be viewed as making up a single whole, just insofar as they are set in order toward a single goal. So, the multiplicity of Ideas in God's mind should not prevent us from speaking of the eternal law as one, because it is the Idea of this one order.

[1]   St. Thomas explained in I, Question 15, Article 2, that if God created and intended the order of the universe (as He did), then the Idea of this order must have been present in His mind. But just as a builder must have the idea of walls, floors, and so on to have the idea of a house, so God must have had the idea of each thing He created to have the Idea of their order.

[2]   The kind of unity that things possess by being virtue of being directed to a common goal is called the "unity of order." A good example is the unity among the soldiers in an army. Viewed from the bottom up, it is a multiplicity of many different persons, but viewed from the top down, it is a single army, because each of these many persons is directed to a single purpose. Just as the general must have an understanding of the unity of order among the soldiers, so God has in His mind the Idea of the unity of order among all His creatures. This Idea is the eternal law.

[1] *Reply to Objection 2. With regard to any sort of word, two points may be considered: viz. the word itself, and that which is expressed by the word. For the spoken word is something uttered by the mouth of man, and expresses that which is signified by the human word. The same applies to the human mental word, which is nothing else that something conceived by the mind, by which man expresses his thoughts mentally.*

Reply to Objection 2. No matter what kind of word we are considering, we must distinguish between the word itself and what the word expresses. This is true of the human spoken word, which is produced by the mouth and used to give outward expression to what the word means; and it is also true of the human mental word, which is conceived by the mind and used to give mental or inward expression to a man's thoughts.

[2] *So then in God the Word conceived by the intellect of the Father is the name of a Person: but all things that are in the Father's knowledge, whether they refer to the Essence or to the Persons, or to the works of God, are expressed by this Word, as Augustine declares (De Trin. xv, 14).* [3] *And among other things expressed by this Word, the eternal law itself is expressed thereby. Nor does it follow that the eternal law is a Personal name in God: yet it is appropriated to the Son, on account of the kinship between type and word.*

A Word is conceived by the mind of God the Father too, and this Word is the name of a Person, God the Son. But, as St. Augustine explains, this Word expresses everything the Father knows – whether about the Divine essence, the Divine Persons, or the Divine works – and among all other things, it expresses the Idea of the eternal law.

By themselves, these facts do not make the eternal law a name for one of the Divine Persons. However, the eternal law is attributed in a special way to the Second Person, who is named the Word simply because of the relationship between Word and Idea.

---

[1]   A mental word is the conception in the mind that *signifies* what the mind is thinking of. St. Augustine says it is "born of our knowledge" and describes it as "that word ... of ours which has neither sound nor thought of sound, but is of that thing in seeing which we speak inwardly."[7]

[2]   According to St. Thomas, the proper name of a person stands for what distinguishes that person from all other persons. The three Persons of the Trinity cannot be distinguished according to their essence, because they are not three gods but one God – one in Substance though diverse in Person, one *What* with three *Whos*. Instead, their names distinguish them according to their relations.[8]

The Second Person of the Trinity has three such names, each signifying a different relationship. He is called *Son* because He is begotten by the Father, meaning that He originates from the Father, not at a point in time, but from all eternity. He is called *Word* because He emanates from the Father's intellect. And He is called *Image* because He is alike with the Father in being.[9]

---

[7] St. Augustine of Hippo, *On the Trinity*, trans. Arthur West Haddan, Book 15, Chapter 14, Section 24 (available at www.newadvent.org/fathers; public domain).

[8] Respectively, I, Q. 33, Art. 2, and I, Q. 28. Although the number of Persons in God cannot be ascertained or proven by reason, St. Thomas says that it can be "declared" or explained "by things which are more known to us." I, Q. 32, Art. 1; I, Q. 39, Art. 7.

[9] Respectively, I, Q. 33, Art. 3; I, 34, Art. 3; and I, Q. 35, Arts. 1–2.

In the passage that St. Thomas mentions, St. Augustine says "Accordingly, as though uttering Himself, the Father begot the Word equal to Himself in all things; for He would not have uttered Himself wholly and perfectly, if there were in His Word anything more or less than in Himself.... The Father then, and the Son know mutually [they know, in each other, all of the same things]; but the one by begetting, the other by being born."[10]

[3] To "appropriate" a property to one of the Divine Persons means to associate it with that Person especially, even though recognizing that because they are one in being, the property actually belongs to all three. The reason we do this is that it helps our weak minds: Since in this life, the human intellect is led to acknowledge the reality of God by way of reflection on the things He has created, it must think of Him in a manner derived from created things.[11]

Here, St. Thomas is arguing that the eternal law is "appropriated" to the Son especially, because of the kinship between Word on the one hand, and Idea or supreme Reason on the other, is suggested by the name applied to Christ in the Prologue to the Gospel of John: *Logos*. This Greek term, which the Vulgate translates as *Verbum*, can mean either Word or Reason.

The concept of the Divine *Logos,* of the rational pattern undergirding all reality, was well known to pre-Christian philosophers. However, as Joseph Cardinal Ratzinger (later Pope Benedict XVI) has written, "By deciding in favor of the God of the philosophers and logically declaring this God to be the God who speaks to man and to whom one can pray, the Christian faith gave a completely new significance to this God of the philosophers .... [T]his God who has been understood as pure Being or pure thought, circling round for ever closed in upon itself without reaching over to man and his little world ... now appeared to the eye of faith as the God of men, Who is not only thought of all thoughts, the eternal mathematics of the universe, but also *agape,* the power of creative love."[12]

---

[10] St. Augustine of Hippo, *On the Trinity,* trans. Arthur West Haddan, Book 15, Chapter 14, Section 24 (available at www.newadvent.org/fathers; public domain).

[11] I, Q. 38, Art. 8.

[12] Ibid., p. 99.

[1] *Reply to Objection 3. The types of the Divine intellect do not stand in the same relation to things, as the types of the human intellect. For the human intellect is measured by things, so that a human concept is not true by reason of itself, but by reason of its being consonant with things, since "an opinion is true or false according as it answers to the reality." [2] But the Divine intellect is the measure of things: since each thing has so far truth in it, as it represents the Divine intellect, as was stated in the I, 16, 1. Consequently the Divine intellect is true in itself; and its type is truth itself.*	Reply to Objection 3. The Ideas in God's mind do not have the same relationship to things that the ideas in a human mind have. In the case of a human being, things are the measure of the intellect. That is, human concepts are not true in themselves; they are true only to the degree that they conform to how things are in reality. But in the case of God, the intellect is the measure of things. That is, God's intellect really is true in itself; things are true only to the degree that they conform to His mind. From this we see what the Objector is missing: For the Idea of this intellect is Truth itself.

[1]   If I think dogs are cats, I am simply mistaken, because dogs are not cats. My concept of dogs is not the test of what dogs are in reality; rather, what dogs are in reality is the test of my concept of dogs.

The statement the English translation renders as "an opinion is true or false according as it answers to the reality," is more literally rendered as "an opinion is true or false according to whether the thing is or is not." This seems to be quick way of putting what Aristotle said more wordily in *Metaphysics,* Book 4, Chapter 7: "To say of what is that it is not, or of what is not that it is, is false, while to say of what is that it is, and of what is not that it is not, is true."[13] St. Thomas expresses the idea even more strikingly in his oft-repeated remark that "truth is the equation of intellect with thing."[14]

[2]   Here St. Thomas reminds us that intellect can be equated with things in two different ways. In the case of man, things come first; the ideas in his mind must adjust themselves to how things are. But in the case of the Creator, intellect comes first; the Ideas in His mind are the rational pattern by which he *made* them what they are. To put the matter differently, we are at the receiving end; seeing that dogs are different from cats,

[13]   Aristotle, *Metaphysics,* trans. W.D. Ross, public domain.
[14]   See for example I, Q. 16, Art. 2, Obj. 1 and *corpus*; I, Q. 21, Art. 2; *On Truth,* Q. 1, Art. 3.

we conceive two different ideas of them. But God is at the giving end; because He conceived two different Ideas for them, dogs are different from cats.

For this reason, although man's mind is measured by truth, Truth is identical with God's mind. We see then why St. Augustine spoke as he did: Truth is a law *above* the mind of man. But it is not *above* the mind of God, for it simply is the pattern of His mind: The supreme Reason, the Idea, the sovereign type.

For further reflection on the preceding section of the *Treatise on Law*, the online *Companion to the Commentary*, accessible via the Resources link at the book's catalogue webpage, includes a discussion of the following topic:

GOD AS ORIGINATOR OF REALITY; TRUTH AS CORRESPONDENCE WITH REALITY

Question 93, Article 2:
Whether the Eternal Law Is Known to All?

TEXT	PARAPHRASE
Whether the eternal law is known to all?	*Does every human being know the eternal law?*

We had a foretaste of this issue in Question 91, Article 1, Objection 2, where the Objector argued that there couldn't be an eternal law because there was no one to whom it could be promulgated, or made known, from eternity.

| [1] *Objection 1. It would seem that the eternal law is not known to all. Because, as the Apostle says (1 Corinthians 2:11), "the things that are of God no man knoweth, but the Spirit of God." [2] But the eternal law is a type existing in the Divine mind. Therefore it is unknown to all save God alone.* | Objection 1. Apparently, *no* human beings know the eternal law. In his letter to the Church in Corinth, St. Paul declares that no one but God's Spirit knows the things in God. Yet the eternal law is a thing in God – an Idea in God's mind – so it follows that no one but God's Spirit knows the eternal law. |

[1]   The things that are of God are the things in God's mind. St. Paul's argument is that just as a man's thoughts are known only by the man's spirit, so the thoughts of God are known only by God's Spirit. Therefore, they are not known by men.

[2] The premise – that eternal law is an archetype, or template, in the Divine mind – was established in Article 1.

[1] *Objection 2. Further, as Augustine says (De Lib. Arb. i, 6) "the eternal law is that by which it is right that all things should be most orderly." [2] But all do not know how all things are most orderly. Therefore all do not know the eternal law.*	Objection 2. Moreover, the eternal law is what puts everything in perfect order, as Augustine remarks. But do we all grasp how everything is put in perfect order? Obviously not. It follows that we do not all know the eternal law.

[1] This quotation is an old friend; we met it back in Question 91, Article 2. The explanation given there is sufficient for our purposes here as well.

[2] Consider all the things that seem *not* in perfect order, such as misfortune and death. Even if God fully knows what He is doing – a point the Objector does not deny, and which St. Thomas has demonstrated in I, Question 103 – the fact remains that *we* do not know what He is doing (at least we do not *fully* know, though on this point the Objector hedges). The reasoning of the Objector is that if eternal law is the law by which God puts things into order, and we do not understand this order, then it implausible to suggest that we know the eternal law.

[1] *Objection 3. Further, Augustine says (De Vera Relig. xxxi) that "the eternal law is not subject to the judgment of man." [2] But according to Ethic. i, "any man can judge well of what he knows." Therefore the eternal law is not known to us.*	Objection 3. Still further, Aristotle reminds us in his *Nicomachean Ethics* that every man is a good judge of what he knows. It follows that anyone who knows the eternal law can judge it. But as Augustine points out, no one can judge the eternal law. Therefore, no one knows it either.

[1] The Objector is quoting selectively, for in the same chapter of *On True Religion*, St. Augustine writes "Pure souls *may rightly know* the eternal law but may not judge it."[15] More about this below.

[2] In context, Aristotle's comment reads, "Now each man judges well the things he knows, and of these he is a good judge. And so the man

---

[15] Augustine, *Of True Religion*, Chapter 31, in J.H.S. Burleigh, ed., *Augustine: Earlier Writings* (Philadelphia: Westminster Press, 1953), p. 255, emphasis added.

who has been educated in a subject is a good judge of that subject, and the man who has received an all-round education is a good judge in general."[16] The Objector's point is that no conceivable experience and education could raise our finite minds to the understanding of eternal law.

On the contrary, *Augustine says (De Lib. Arb. i, 6) that "knowledge of the eternal law is imprinted on us."*	**On the other hand,** St. Augustine says we *do* know the eternal law, for the knowledge of it is stamped on us.

This is the *other half* of the statement quoted partially in Objection 2. In full, the statement reads "So to explain concisely as far as I can the notion of eternal law that is stamped on us: It is the law according to which it is just for all things to be completely in order."[17] The Objector suppresses the part about the knowledge of eternal law being stamped on us, and the *sed contra* reinstates it.

We need not think the Objector is being dishonest, for the *ultrum* is not whether St. Augustine *believed* that the eternal law is known to all, but whether the eternal law *really is* known to all. Nor need we think that the *sed contra* squelches the Objector, for it does nothing but remind us that the Objector and the tradition disagree. Which one is right – the Objector or the tradition – is not taken up until the *respondeo*, to which we now turn.

[1] *I answer that, A thing may be known in two ways: first, in itself; secondly, in its effect, wherein some likeness of that thing is found: thus someone not seeing the sun in its substance, may know it by its rays.* [2] *So then no one can know the eternal law, as it is in itself, except the blessed who see God in His Essence.* [3] *But every rational creature knows it in its reflection, greater or less. For every knowledge of truth is a kind of reflection and participation of the eternal law,*	**Here is my response.** The question "Do we know P?" is equivocal, for there are two different senses in which a thing can be known, and it is possible to know it in one way without knowing it in the other. In the first place a thing can be known *directly*, that is, in itself; in the second, it can be known *indirectly*, that is, through its effects, because these effects provide a certain semblance to it. So it is that a man who does not "see" the sun's essence may nevertheless "know" it by means of its rays. In the same way, no one on earth knows the eternal law in itself (although the blessed in heaven do, because they see God's very essence). Yet every created being endowed

[16] Aristotle, *Nicomachean Ethics*, trans. W.D. Ross (public domain), Book 1, Chapter 3.
[17] Peter King, trans., *Augustine: On the Free Choice of the Will, On Grace and Free Choice, and Other Writings* (Cambridge: Cambridge University Press, 2010), p. 13.

[4] *which is the unchangeable truth, as Augustine says (De Vera Relig. xxxi).* [5] *Now all men know the truth to a certain extent, at least as to the common principles of the natural law:* [6] *and as to the others, they partake of the knowledge of truth, some more, some less; and in this respect are more or less cognizant of the eternal law.*

with a rational nature knows the eternal law to some degree, greater or less, through its reflection. I say this because *all* knowledge of truth is a reflection of and a sharing in the eternal law, which, as St. Augustine affirms, is the Truth that does not change.

Consequently, all men know something of the truth – if nothing more, at least the shared principles of the natural law. Beyond this, they participate in the truth to different degrees, some more and some less. In just this sense, they know the eternal law itself to different degrees, some more and some less.

[1] In an intriguing play on words, St. Thomas distinguishes between "seeing" the sun's essence and "knowing" its light. But he is not just having fun; behind this play on words is a serious point. One of his characteristic themes is that just as we can see things only because they are lit by the light of the senses, which streams, especially, from the sun, St. Thomas holds that we can know things only because they are illuminated by the light of the mind, which streams from God.[18]

To highlight the parallel between seeing the sun in itself and seeing God in Himself, my paraphrase substitutes the term "essence" for the term "substance." St. Thomas comments earlier in the *Summa* that the term "substance" can refer to either an essence, or to a subject – to that which underlies its changing properties.[19] When he speaks of seeing the substance of the sun, he seems to be using the term in both senses.

[18] "[T]he intellectual power of the creature is called an intelligible light, as it were, derived from the first light, whether this be understood of the natural power, or of some perfection superadded of grace or of glory." I, Q. 12, Art. 2. "For the intellectual light itself which is in us, is nothing else than a participated likeness of the uncreated light, in which are contained the eternal types. Whence it is written (Psalm 4:6–7), 'Many say: Who showeth us good things?' which question the Psalmist answers, 'The light of Thy countenance, O Lord, is signed upon us,' as though he were to say: By the seal of the Divine light in us, all things are made known to us." I, Q. 84, Art. 5. "Hence we must say that for the knowledge of any truth whatsoever man needs Divine help, that the intellect may be moved by God to its act. But he does not need a new light added to his natural light, in order to know the truth in all things, but only in some that surpass his natural knowledge. And yet at times God miraculously instructs some by His grace in things that can be known by natural reason, even as He sometimes brings about miraculously what nature can do." I-II, Q. 109, Art. 2.
[19] As he puts it, something that "underlies the accidents," using the term "accident" to refer to nonessential properties. I, Q. 29, Art. 2.

[2]   In other words, *in this life* we cannot see God as He is, although those in heaven do, and this vision is their supreme joy. St. Thomas has argued earlier that "Final and perfect happiness can consist in nothing else than the vision of the Divine Essence."[20] St. Paul exclaims of this vision, "Now I know in part; then I shall understand fully, even as I have been fully understood."[21]

[3]   The famous definition of the natural law as the "participation of the eternal law in the rational creature" was propounded and explained in Question 91, Article 2.

[4]   In the passage cited, St. Augustine writes "We must not have any doubt that the unchangeable substance which is above the rational mind, is God. The primal life and primal essence is where the primal wisdom is. This is unchangeable truth, which is the law of all the arts and the art of the omnipotent artificer."[22]

[5]   What St. Thomas claims here is that the foundational principles or starting points of natural law are not only right for everyone, but also known to everyone, a point which we consider more closely in Question 94, Article 4. He calls these the *principia communia* – the common, shared, general, or universal principles.

[6]   The "others" appear to be those who know more than the common principles – those who to a greater or lesser degree grasp some of their remote implications.

Reply to Objection 1. We cannot know the things that are of God, as they are in themselves; but they are made known to us in their effects, according to Rm. 1:20: "The invisible things of God ... are clearly seen, being understood by the things that are made."	**Reply to Objection 1.** If the Objector denies that we can know the things that pertain to God as they are in themselves, he is correct. But if he denies that they we can know them through their effects, he is mistaken. As St. Paul declares in his letter to the Church at Rome, God's invisible attributes have been seen clearly ever since the creation of the cosmos; they have been grasped through His workmanship.

In full, the verse reads "For the invisible things of Him, from the creation of the world, are clearly seen, being understood by the things that

---

[20] I, Q. 3, Art. 8.
[21] 1 Corinthians 13:9–12 (RSV-CE).
[22] Augustine, *Of True Religion*, ibid., p. 254.

are made; His eternal power also, and divinity: so that they are inexcusable."[23] The passage from which it is taken is very much worth further comment. One might have expected St. Paul to complain that although the pagans should have known about God, they don't. His charge is more serious: At a certain level they do know about God, but tell themselves that they don't. In their wickedness they "hold back" or "hold down" the truth (1:18), denying due honor to the Creator and giving it instead to the things that He created. Their sin is "inexcusable" (1:20) because they do this in defiance of evidence that is clear *even to them*.

Commenting on this passage, St. Augustine asks,

How did those philosophers know God? From the things which He had made. Question the beautiful earth; question the beautiful sea; question the beautiful air, diffused and spread abroad; question the beautiful heavens; question the arrangement of the constellations; question the sun brightening the day by its effulgence; question the moon, tempering by its splendor the darkness of the ensuing night; question the living creatures that move about in the water, those that remain on land, and those that flit through the air, their souls hidden but their bodies in view, visible things which are to be ruled and invisible spirits[24] doing the ruling; question all these things and all will answer: 'Behold and see! We are beautiful.' Their beauty is their acknowledgment. Who made these beautiful transitory things unless it be the unchanging Beauty?[25]

[1] *Reply to Objection 2. Although each one knows the eternal law according to his own capacity, in the way explained above, yet none can comprehend it:* [2] *for it cannot be made perfectly known by its effects. Therefore it does not follow that anyone who knows the eternal law in the way aforesaid, knows also the whole order of things, whereby they are most orderly.*	**Reply to Objection 2.** The Objector confuses knowledge with full comprehension. Everyone *knows* the eternal law, each according to his ability; just as I have explained. But we are not to imagine that anyone comprehends it in its totality, because it is always greater than the effects that it produces. Our claim, then, is not that a person who knows the eternal law through its effects grasps the whole order of things, the perfect order of which St. Augustine spoke.

[23] Romans 1:20 (DRA), capitalizing "Him" and "His."

[24] The "spirits" are those of the creatures themselves; for example, a bird's visible body is directed by the bird's invisible spirit.

[25] St. Augustine of Hippo, Sermon 241.2, from *The Writings of Saint Augustine*, Volume 38, trans. Mary Sarah Muldowney, R.S.M. (New York: Fathers of the Church, Inc., 1947), p. 256.

[1]   As St. Thomas explains earlier in the *Summa*, to comprehend something is to know it perfectly – to know it so far as it is capable of being
known.[26]

[2]   The reason the eternal law cannot be comprehended by its effects
is that effects are *always* inferior to their causes; there is always more to
them than what they bring about.[27] This principle, which is true of all
causes whatsoever, is preeminently true of God, who infinitely exceeds all
His works. As St. Thomas remarks elsewhere, "God is not a part of, but
far above, the whole universe, possessing within Himself the entire perfection of the universe in a more eminent way."[28]

---

[1] *Reply to Objection 3. To judge
a thing may be understood in two
ways. First, as when a cognitive
power judges of its proper object,
according to Job 12:11: "Doth
not the ear discern words, and the
palate of him that eateth, the taste?"
It is to this kind of judgment that
the Philosopher alludes when he
says that "anyone can judge well
of what he knows," by judging,
namely, whether what is put
forward is true. [2] In another way
we speak of a superior judging of a
subordinate by a kind of practical
judgment, as to whether he should
be such and such or not. And thus
none can judge of the eternal law.*

Reply to Objection 3. The Objector
is confusing different senses of the
same word, for two things may be
meant by "judging." In one sense, a
person judges when he applies one
of his intellectual powers to make
an assessment of something within
the scope of that power. A good
illustration is found in the book of
Job, where Job asks "Isn't the ear
for judging words, as the palate is
for judging tastes?" This is the kind
of judging that Aristotle has in mind
when he says everyone is a good judge
of what he knows – in other words,
that anyone can assess whether or not
something declared to him about his
own area of knowledge is true.

---

[1]   St. Thomas says Aristotle's statement that "anyone can judge well
of what he knows" is to be taken in the sense that the intellect can make
accurate assessments only of the sorts of things that lie within its capacity;

---

[26] I, Q. 12, Art. 7.
[27] "An effect is inferior to its cause," II-II, Q. 23, Art. 3, ad 3. Compare I, Q. 19, Art. 5, *sed
contra* (quoting St. Augustine), "Every efficient cause is greater than the thing effected";
I-II, Q. 66, Art. 1, "a cause is always more excellent than its effect"; I-II, Q. 112, Art. 1,
"the cause must always be more powerful than its effect"; II-II, Q. 34, Art. 2, ad 2, "a
cause is greater than its effect."
[28] I, Q. 61, Art. 3. ad 2.

this is the first meaning of judgment, and it means judging *what is the case* about these things.

Apart from its context, the quotation from Job may be puzzling. Zophar has been criticizing Job for daring to complain to God about the bad things that have been happening to him. Angrily, Job replies to Zophar, "I have understanding as well as you; I am not inferior to you." In the quoted sentence, he sarcastically announces that he is perfectly capable of judging the words that Zophar says against him. So this is an example of judgment in the first sense.

[2] Judgment in the second sense is assessing *what should be done*. Our knowledge is sufficient for us to assess things in the light of the eternal law, but it is not sufficient to assess what the eternal law should be. St. Augustine carefully explains the point in the passage from *On True Religion* which the Objector is so determined to misunderstand:

> [I]t is most truly said, "we must all appear before the judgment throne of Christ" (2 Cor. 5:10).... Accordingly, the law is that according to which he judges all things and concerning which no man can judge. In the case of temporal laws, men have instituted them and judge by them, and when they have been instituted and confirmed no judge may judge them but must judge according to them. He who draws up temporal laws, if he is a good and wise man, takes eternal life into account, and that no soul may judge. He determines what is to be commanded and forbidden according to the immutable rules of eternal life. Pure souls may rightly know the eternal law but may not judge it. The difference is that, for knowing, it is enough to see that a thing is *so* and *not so*. For judging, it is necessary in addition to see that a thing *can* be thus or not thus: as when we say it *ought* to be thus, or to have been thus, or to be thus in the future, as workmen do with their works.[29]

So we certainly have the sort of knowledge that is needed to judge "by" the eternal law, even though we do not have the sort of knowledge that would be needed to judge the eternal law as such.

For further reflection on the preceding section of the *Treatise on Law*, the online *Companion to the Commentary*, accessible via the Resources link at the book's catalogue webpage, includes a discussion of the following topic:

How the Finite Intellect Knows What It Knows

---

[29] Augustine, *On True Religion*, ibid., pp. 254–255.

Question 93, Article 3:
Whether Every Law Is Derived from the Eternal Law?

TEXT	PARAPHRASE
Whether every law is derived from the eternal law?	Is every law based on the eternal law?

It is tempting to paraphrase "every law" as "every law to which human
beings are subject," because Objection 1 concerns the so-called law of
sin which afflicts humans, while Objections 2 and 3 concern laws made
by human governors. However, the argument St. Thomas presents in the
respondeo is entirely general. Though, for obvious reasons, the discussion
focuses on beings of our kind, the scope of the *ultrum* includes whatever
laws may apply to other rational creatures as well, whether purely intellectual (the angels) or embodied (such as Martians, should there happen
to be any).

| [1] *Objection 1. It would seem that not every law is derived from the eternal law. For there is a law of the "fomes," as stated above (91, 6), [2] which is not derived from that Divine law which is the eternal law, since thereunto pertains the "prudence of the flesh," of which the Apostle says (Romans 8:7), that "it cannot be subject to the law of God." Therefore not every law is derived from the eternal law.* | Objection 1. Apparently, there is a kind of law that is not based on the eternal law: The law of sin, associated with our tendency to shoot up in flames like kindling, which we have discussed previously. St. Paul calls this law "the wisdom of the flesh" which "is not subject to the law of God, neither can it be."[30] |

[1]   St. Thomas has already gone over the topic of the *fomes* or "kindling" in detail – both directly, in the first article of Question 90 and the
sixth article of Question 91, and, indirectly, in Questions 82–83, earlier
in the *Summa*, where he took up original sin. Though he does not mind
cross-referencing, he does not often repeat himself. Moreover, he has dismissed the matter in the Prologue to Question 93. One would hardly
have expected him to allow the Objector to drag it in yet again, yet he
does. What then could be the reason? One surmises that there must have
been a great deal of confusion about the "law of sin" in his day, just as

---

[30] Romans 8:7 (DRA); for "the wisdom [*phronema*] of the flesh," some translations have
"the carnal mind."

there is in ours. Sometimes, when people are either very muddled or very worried, they need to hear something many times before it sinks in.

[2] In the verse just before the one quoted, St. Paul starkly contrasts "the wisdom of the flesh" with "the wisdom of the spirit," declaring that the former brings death, but the latter life and peace.[31] By "the spirit" he means the spirit of God; by "the flesh" he means not the body *per se,* a creation of God which is good in itself, but the body in its present condition. As he declares in another letter, the body in itself is "for the Lord, and the Lord for the body."[32] After the Fall, though, its desires and appetites so violently rebel against reason that it seems to have an outlook of its own, opposed to the outlook of our minds. This outlook is what St. Paul calls the prudence of the flesh.

The insubordination of bodily desires to reason does not imply that all sin is bodily. According to St. Thomas, the very sin by which this dreadful condition came to infect us was not a bodily sin, but the sin of pride: it lay in man's "coveting some spiritual good above his measure," since he desired to "be like God, knowing good and evil." St. Paul is so far from thinking all sin bodily that he says that although a man who commits fornication sins against his own body, "Every other sin which a man commits is outside the body."[33] In the same vein, John of Damascus writes, "Do not despise matter, for it is not despicable. Nothing is that which God has made. This is the Manichean heresy. That alone is despicable which does not come from God, but is our own invention, the spontaneous choice of will to disregard the natural law – that is to say, sin."[34]

In speaking of "that Divine law which is the eternal law," the Objector is using the term "Divine law" in an atypical sense. Normally it refers to the reflection of eternal law in Revelation. Here, however, it refers to the eternal law itself, Divine in the sense of being inseparable from God.[35]

---

[31] Romans 8:6 (DRA). "Flesh" translates *sarkos.* For "the wisdom [*phronema*] of the spirit," some translations have "the mind of the spirit."
[32] 1 Corinthians 6:13 (RSV-CE). "Body" translates not *sarkos* but *soma.*
[33] II-II, Q. 163, Art. 1; Genesis 3:5 (RSV-CE; DRA has "Gods"); 1 Corinthians 6:18 (RSV-CE).
[34] John of Damascus, *Apologia Against Those Who Decry Holy Images,* available at www.fordham.edu/halsall/basis/johndamascus-images.html (Medieval Sourcebook).
[35] See also Q. 95, Art. 3, and Q. 97, Art. 3, Obj. 1.

[1] *Objection 2. Further, nothing unjust can be derived from the eternal law, because, as stated above (2, Objection 2), "the eternal law is that, according to which it is right that all things should be most orderly." [2] But some laws are unjust, according to Is. 10:1: "Woe to them that make wicked laws." Therefore not every law is derived from the eternal law.*

Objection 2. Moreover, as we have just been discussing in Article 2, eternal law puts everything in perfect order. This being the case, nothing unjust can be based on it. Yet some laws *are* unjust, as the prophet Isaiah declares when he inveighs against those who make them. *These* laws are not based on the eternal law; so not all laws are based on the eternal law.

[1]   We have seen this quotation from St. Augustine's *On Freedom of the Will* not only in Question 93, Article 2, Objection 2, but earlier still, in Question 91, Article 2.

[2]   The Objector is not quoting Isaiah because apart from Scripture we would not know that some laws are unjust, but because Isaiah expresses God's condemnation of unjust laws with such pungent authority. More fully, the prophet writes, "Woe to those who decree iniquitous decrees, and the writers who keep writing oppression, to turn aside the needy from justice and to rob the poor of my people of their right, that widows may be their spoil, and that they may make the fatherless their prey! What will you do on the day of punishment, in the storm which will come from afar? To whom will you flee for help, and where will you leave your wealth?"[36]

If the eternal law be that which requires all things to be most orderly, the Objector argues, then surely those laws by which rulers make widows their spoil and orphans their prey are not derived from it; therefore not all laws are derived from it.

[1] *Objection 3. Further, Augustine says (De Lib. Arb. i, 5) that "the law which is framed for ruling the people, rightly permits many things which are punished by Divine providence." [2] But the type of Divine providence is the eternal law, as stated above (1). Therefore not even every good law is derived from the eternal law.*

Objection 3. Still further, Augustine reminds us that human law permits many things that God's Providence punishes – moreover that it is *right* to do so. But eternal law is the rational pattern of this Providence; therefore, to say that human law rightly permits what Providence punishes is to say that it rightly permits what eternal law punishes. Now if human law rightly permits something that eternal law punishes, then surely it could not be based on the eternal law. Hence, not even all good laws are based on the eternal law.

---

[36] Isaiah 10:1–3 (RSV-CE).

[1]   The Objector must think he has St. Thomas over a barrel, for up to this point, the Angelic Doctor agrees: As he has written in Question 91, Article 4, "human law cannot punish or forbid all evil deeds: since while aiming at doing away with all evils, it would do away with many good things, and would hinder the advance of the common good, which is necessary for human intercourse. In order, therefore, that no evil might remain unforbidden and unpunished, it was necessary for the Divine law to supervene, whereby all sins are forbidden." St. Thomas will have still more to say about this topic in Question 96, Article 2.

[2]   Objection 2 held that *bad* laws are not based on the eternal law; Objection 3 carries the ball further by saying that *not even all good* laws are based on the eternal law. The Objector quotes only part of St. Augustine's statement, perhaps expecting the reader to remember the rest. For us, who have weaker memories, this is unfortunate, because the idea that a law may be good even though it permits something the eternal law forbids is even clearer from the second portion of the statement, which the Objector does not quote. As St. Augustine approvingly remarks to his friend Evodius, "For it seems to you that the law that is enacted to govern states tolerates and leaves unpunished many things, which are nevertheless redressed by Divine providence (and rightly so)." He continues, "Yet it does not follow that just because the law does not accomplish everything, we should disapprove of what it does accomplish."[37]

---

[1]   *On the contrary,* Divine Wisdom says (Proverbs 8:15): "By Me kings reign, and lawgivers decree just things." [2] *But the type of Divine Wisdom is the eternal law, as stated above (1). Therefore all laws proceed from the eternal law.*

On the other hand, soliloquizing in the book of Proverbs, Divine Wisdom declares, "By me kings reign, and rulers decree what is just."[38] But as we have already explained, the rational pattern of Divine Wisdom is the eternal law. From this it follows that *by the eternal law* kings reign and rulers decree what is just; so all laws do come from the eternal law.

---

[1]   As we saw in Question 91, Article 1, where the same passage was quoted, the Wisdom of God is figuratively represented as a wise woman crying out at the city gates to anyone who will listen and turn from his

[37] Peter King, trans., *Augustine: On the Free Choice of the Will, On Grace and Free Choice, and Other Writings* (Cambridge: Cambridge University Press, 2010), p. 11.
[38] Proverbs 8:15 (RSV-CE).

foolish ways. It is through her that princes rule and the mighty command justice.

[2]   Had he chosen, St. Thomas could have fortified this part of the *sed contra* with another quotation from Wisdom's soliloquy, for she declares, "The Lord possessed me in the beginning of his ways, before he made any thing from the beginning.... When he prepared the heavens, I was present: when with a certain law and compass he enclosed the depths."[39]

---

[1] *I answer that,* As stated above *(90, A1,2), the law denotes a kind of plan directing acts towards an end.* [2] *Now wherever there are movers ordained to one another, the power of the second mover must needs be derived from the power of the first mover; since the second mover does not move except in so far as it is moved by the first.* [3] *Wherefore we observe the same in all those who govern, so that the plan of government is derived by secondary governors from the governor in chief; thus the plan of what is to be done in a state flows from the king's command to his inferior administrators: and again in things of art the plan of whatever is to be done by art flows from the chief craftsman to the undercraftsmen, who work with their hands.* [4] *Since then the eternal law is the plan of government in the Chief Governor, all the plans of government in the inferior governors must be derived from the eternal law. But these plans of inferior governors are all other laws besides the eternal law.* [5] *Therefore all laws, in so far as they partake of right reason, are derived from the eternal law. Hence Augustine says (De Lib. Arb. i, 6) that "in temporal law there is nothing just and lawful, but what man has drawn from the eternal law."*

Here is my response. As we have seen, law is a kind of Idea or plan directing acts toward a purpose. Now in every case of coordinated action among causes that bring about change, the power of the secondary causes can come only from the power of the initiating cause – for the latter is what sets the former into motion. This is just what we see in governing, for subordinate governors derive the plan of governing only from the supreme governor. So it is that the king issues his directions for the administration of the commonwealth to the functionaries below him. Similarly, the architect or master craftsman tells the subordinate craftsmen what to do. And so, because the eternal law is the Supreme Governor's plan of government, all policies of government employed by those who govern under him must be derived from His eternal law.

Now what is meant by these policies of government? What is meant is all the other laws, to the extent that they share in rightly ordered reason. And so just to the degree that they do share in it, all laws are derived from the eternal law. This fact leads Augustine to the further conclusion that even those laws that change in the course of time contain nothing just and *truly* lawful except what men have derived from the unchanging eternal law.

---

[39] Proverbs 8:22,27 (DRA).

[1]   The word here rendered "plan" is a form of the same Latin word, *ratio*, which the Dominican Fathers translation renders elsewhere as "idea," "type," or "reason."

[2]   Again, the term "movement" refers to any sort of change, so a "mover" is a cause of change.

[3]   God, the supreme Governor, does not make the eternal law in the sense of bringing it into being at a point in time, because it is one with Himself. It is the rational and everlasting pattern of His care for those creatures He has freely willed to bring into being. If He so willed, He could exercise His care for us directly, with no need to bring our own intellects into it. Instead, He raises us to the dignity of sharing in this care: Parents exercising providence for their children, friends for their friends, governors for their commonwealths. Human legislators, then, make law not in the sense that the meaning, standard, or plan of care originates with them, but in the sense that they receive this plan from Him and in turn apply it to matters that lie within their responsibility.

The same is true of the relation between God, the Creator, and the "undercraftsmen," whether human or angelic, who craft beautiful or useful things. They are not subordinate *creators,* for only God can create. Rather they build and shape things from what God has already created, imitating and evoking in these perishable works the Beauty that never perishes.[40]

[4]   St. Thomas's wording in the second sentence is infelicitous; taken literally it would imply that the natural and Divine laws are plans of inferior governors, which is not his view, since, as he has made clear, they reflect the eternal law directly. He seems to mean, "Of such a kind are all the plans of inferior governors, the plans by which they make their own laws, distinct from but dependent on the eternal law."

[5]   In the passage from which St. Augustine's remark is taken, he defines temporal law as law which, "although it is just, can justly be changed in the course of time." Plainly, some human laws, like the prohibition of murder, *cannot* justly be changed in the course of time. Yet others can be, and these are the ones that St. Augustine has in mind. His example is that it is fitting that the people of a responsible society be able to choose their own public officials; yet if, in the course of time, the same people become corrupt, then it is fitting that they should lose this privilege. St. Augustine

[40]   I, Q. 45, Art. 5: "to create can be the action of God alone."

remarks, "this shift in the temporal law, to be just, must derive from the eternal law whereby it is always just for a responsible society to confer honors and not for an irresponsible one."[41]

So it turns out that by quoting from St. Augustine, St. Thomas is not merely confirming his conclusion, but also giving it a surprising twist that deepens it. Some just laws, because they reflect principles of eternal law the application of which does not depend on circumstances, cannot be changed at all. Other just laws, because they reflect principles of eternal law the application of which *does* depend on circumstances, can be changed if the circumstances change; but even the justice of the change itself is derived from the eternal law. Not only the properly permanent parts of law, but even the properly changeable parts of law, depend on eternal law.

Reply to Objection 1. The "fomes" has the nature of law in man, in so far as it is a punishment resulting from Divine justice; and in this respect it is evident that it is derived from the eternal law. But in so far as it denotes a proneness to sin, it is contrary to the Divine law, and has not the nature of law, as stated above (91, 6).	Reply to Objection 1. The "kindling" is a law just in the sense that it is a punishment for the *violation* of law, that is, of Divine justice. Considered as a punishment, yes, it is based on the eternal law. Considered as a tendency to sin, however, it is contrary to God's law, and is not truly a law. We have already explained all of this.

The tacit premises are that Divine justice is the same thing as Divine law, and Divine law is in turn a reflection of eternal law, so whatever is contrary to Divine law is contrary to eternal law. These points should be clear from Question 91, Articles 4 and 5.

[1] *Reply to Objection 2. Human law has the nature of law in so far as it partakes of right reason; and it is clear that, in this respect, it is derived from the eternal law.* [2] *But in so far as it deviates from reason, it is called an unjust law, and has the nature, not of law but of violence.* [3] *Nevertheless even an unjust law, in so far as it retains some appearance of law, through being framed by one who is in power, is derived from the eternal law; since all power is from the Lord God, according to Rm. 13:1.*	Reply to Objection 2. What human legislators enact is truly law only to the degree that it conforms to rightly ordered reason, and in this, we see that it is derived from eternal law. But to the degree that their enactments withdraw from reason, they are called "unjust laws" – and in fact they are not truly laws at all but acts of violence. Even so, an "unjust law" depends on the eternal law just to the degree that it *resembles* a law through being made by someone in power, for as St. Paul declares in his letter to the Church at Rome, all power is from our Lord, Who is God.

[41] Peter King, trans., *Augustine: On the Free Choice of the Will, On Grace and Free Choice, and Other Writings* (Cambridge: Cambridge University Press, 2010), p. 13.

[1] That an enactment has the nature of true law only to the degree that it is reasonable has been fully explained in Question 90, Article 1. The concept of "right reason," which I have paraphrased "rightly ordered reason," has been deeply important in the history of thought. Right reason is more than proficiency in drawing conclusions from premises. It indicates that healthy condition of mind, that moral common sense, without which human beings have difficulty framing reasonable premises in the first place.

[2] Later on, in Question 96, Article 4, St. Thomas will call on St. Augustine to support this statement, quoting his remark that an unjust law "seems to be no law at all."

[3] The verse to which St. Thomas alludes is "Let every person be subject to the governing authorities. For there is no authority except from God, and those that exist have been instituted by God." The tradition to which he adheres does not take St. Paul's command to require unquestioning obedience, however, for with equal authority, on an occasion when the local authorities unjustly commanded the Apostles to stop preaching about the risen Christ, St. Peter responded, "We must obey God rather than men."[42] The *Companion to the Commentary* offers further reflections on how these imperatives are to be reconciled.

---

[1] *Reply to Objection 3. Human law is said to permit certain things, not as approving them, but as being unable to direct them.* [2] *And many things are directed by the Divine law, which human law is unable to direct, because more things are subject to a higher than to a lower cause.* [3] *Hence the very fact that human law does not meddle with matters it cannot direct, comes under the ordination of the eternal law. It would be different, were human law to sanction what the eternal law condemns.* [4] *Consequently it does not follow that human law is not derived from the eternal law, but that it is not on a perfect equality with it.*

Reply to Objection 3. Human law permits some things without approving them, simply because it is powerless to control them. But many things that exceed its reach are directed by Divine law, for a greater number of things fall under the control of a superior cause than of a subordinate cause. We see then that the very fact that human law does not interfere with matters it cannot direct comes from eternal law's arrangements – although if any human law *did* approve what eternal law condemns, then of course this would not be the case. Logically, then, we should not say that laws that permit wrongs they are unable to control are *not based* on the eternal law, but that they cannot attain the *perfect reach* of eternal law.

---

[42] Romans 13:1, Acts 5:29 (RSV-CE).

[1]   The difference between toleration and approval is often overlooked in our day too. Some assume that because an act is legal, it must be right. Others assume that whenever an act is wrong, it ought to be illegal. St. Thomas points out that sometimes human law permits an act merely because it cannot control it, at least not without doing more harm than good.

[2]   A higher cause is a cause that gives rise to other causes, which are called lower causes. St. Thomas argues in I, Question 65, Article 3, that "the higher the cause, the more numerous the objects to which its causation extends …. the underlying principle in things is always more universal than that which informs and restricts it."[43]

[3]   One may err about acts that the law permits in two opposite ways. The first is to think that to tolerate is always to approve. The second is to think that to tolerate is *never* to approve – to suppose that law may tolerate anything whatsoever without blame. Although the Reply to Objection 3 warns mainly against the former error, here St. Thomas makes clear that he does not want us to fall into the latter error either. For example, he would have no patience with those who say they are not pro-abortion but only "pro-choice." For the law to permit abortion is to authorize the private use of lethal violence, thus abdicating from the most fundamental condition of the common good, the protection of human life.

[4]   And so the fact that human law cannot regulate everything that eternal law regulates does not imply that it is not derived from eternal law. Some wrongs are simply beyond its control. The most obvious case, and the one that St. Thomas has in mind here, is that it *literally cannot* control them. As we have seen, however, he also acknowledges another possibility, that their control would lie beyond its authority. For example, even though it is wrong to neglect the baptism of children, whether to have them baptized lies in the hands of the parents.[44]

For further reflection on the preceding section of the *Treatise on Law*, the online *Companion to the Commentary*, accessible via the Resources link at the book's catalogue webpage, includes a discussion of the following topic:

Law and the "Appearance Of Law"

---

[43]   I, Q. 65, Art. 3.
[44]   II-II, Q. 10, Art. 12; see the commentary on Question 92, Article 2.

Question 93, Article 4:
Whether Necessary and Eternal Things Are Subject
to the Eternal Law?

TEXT	PARAPHRASE
Whether necessary and eternal things are subject to the eternal law?	Whether the eternal law regulates things that exist eternally and necessarily?

At stake in this Article is the sovereignty of God, the comprehensiveness of the Divine governance, first asserted much earlier, in I, Question 105, Article 3. Someone might argue that God is not truly sovereign, because eternal and necessary things seem to escape the reach of His eternal law. St. Thomas certainly wants to defend the sovereignty of God, but his answer is not quite what one might expect, because it turns out that one must rethink what God's sovereignty means. This is one of the rare cases in which his response to the *ultrum* is not "Yes." Instead he answers, "Yes and no, depending."

To clear up the wording of the *ultrum:* The "things" about which St. Thomas is asking include not only beings, but also properties, relationships, states of affairs, and so on – anything that may be necessary, eternal, or both. The meaning of the *eternal* is that which is both interminable (having no beginning or end) and simultaneously whole (rather than being divided into successive moments).[45] The meaning of *necessity* is that which must be, that which cannot be other than it is. Although there are various kinds of necessity, all the distinctions in its meaning grow from this root, though sometimes a thing is necessary in more than one sense.

Two kinds of necessity are called "intrinsic" (also called "natural" or "absolute"), meaning that the cause of necessity lies in the thing itself. The first, "material" necessity, results from the matter of which something is composed, the other, "formal" necessity, results from its form, its essential pattern. The other kinds of necessity are "extrinsic," meaning that the cause of necessity lies in something else. One kind of extrinsic necessity exists with respect to the agent; also called "necessity of coercion," it means that someone is compelled to do something so that he cannot do otherwise. The other two kinds of extrinsic necessity are

---

[45] I, Q. 10, Art. 1.

classified as "necessity of end," which in English is often called "usefulness" or "need." In the first case of necessity of end, a thing is called necessary or fitting because without it, an end cannot be attained as well (swift conveyance, for example, is necessary or fitting for a journey). In the other case, necessity of end *per se,* a thing is called necessary because without it, the end cannot be attained at all (food, for example, is necessary for life).[46] Additional discussion, with examples, may be found in the online *Companion to the Commentary.*

Objection 1. It would seem that necessary and eternal things are subject to the eternal law. For whatever is reasonable is subject to reason. But the Divine will is reasonable, for it is just. Therefore it is subject to (the Divine) reason. But the eternal law is the Divine reason. Therefore God's will is subject to the eternal law. But God's will is eternal. Therefore eternal and necessary things are subject to the eternal law.	Objection 1. Apparently, the eternal law does regulate necessary and eternal matters. For consider: Everything reasonable is regulated by reason, and, being just, the Divine will is reasonable. From this we draw the conclusion that the Divine will is regulated by reason. But the *Divine* reason and the eternal law are the same thing. This shows that the eternal law regulates the Divine will, and therefore regulates eternal and necessary matters.

Even freely paraphrased, the Objector's argument is highly elliptical. With all the tacit steps filled in, it runs something like this:

1. Whatever is just, is reasonable; the Divine will is just; therefore the Divine will is reasonable.
2. Whatever is reasonable is regulated by reason; therefore the Divine will is regulated by reason.
3. Whatever is regulated by reason must be regulated by the supreme reason; but the supreme reason is the Divine reason; therefore the Divine will is regulated by the Divine reason.
4. But the Divine reason is the same as the eternal law; therefore the Divine will is regulated by the eternal law.
5. But the Divine will is eternal; therefore (at least some) eternal things are regulated by the eternal law.

---

[46] I, Q. 82, Art. 1; III, Q. 1, Art. 2. Thomas Aquinas relies on Aristotle, *Metaphysics*, Book 5, Chapter 5, but knits the different meanings together more logically.

[1] *Objection 2. Further, whatever is subject to the King, is subject to the King's law.* [2] *Now the Son, according to 1 Cor. 15:28,24, "shall be subject ... to God and the Father ... when He shall have delivered up the Kingdom to Him." Therefore the Son, Who is eternal, is subject to the eternal law.*

Objection 2. Moreover, everything under the rule of a king is under the rule of his law, and we may apply this point to the supreme King, God. St. Paul writes to the Church in Corinth that in the end, when the Son delivers the Kingdom to God the Father, the Son will be under the rule of the Father. It follows that the Son will be under the rule of the Father's eternal law. But the Son is eternal, so it further follows that the eternal law regulates things that are themselves eternal.

[1] For by contrast with a tyrant, a true king rules by law, not by arbitrary decrees.

[2] Although the Objector is faithful to St. Paul's meaning, he rearranges and blends the parts of the two verses from which he is quoting. In the Douay-Rheims translation of the Vulgate, verse 24 runs, "Afterwards [comes] the end, when he [the Son] shall have delivered up the kingdom to God and the Father, when he shall have brought to nought all principality, and power, and virtue," and verse 28 runs, "And when all things shall be subdued unto him, then the Son also himself shall be subject unto him that put all things under him, that God may be all in all."

It may seem strange to speak of the Son bringing "virtue" (*virtutem*) to nothing, but here the word is used, not in the sense of moral virtue, but in the Latin sense of strength or vigor, now rare in English. St. Thomas is thinking of St. Paul's exclamation that Christ has been set "above all principality, and power, and virtue, and dominion, and every name that is named, not only in this world, but also in that which is to come"[47] – in other words, above every subordinate agency of ruling whatsoever, whether human or angelic, whether obedient to God or rebellious.

Taking these agencies to be angelic, various writers prior to St. Thomas had theorized the existence of nine ranks or "choirs" of angelic beings,

---

[47] Ephesians 1:21 (DRA); compare Romans 8:38, Ephesians 3:10 and 6:12, and Colossians 1:16 and 2:15.

partly on the basis of various Scriptural hints, partly on the basis of other considerations.[48]

[1] *Objection 3. Further, the eternal law is Divine providence as a type. But many necessary things are subject to Divine providence: [2] for instance, the stability of incorporeal substances and of the heavenly bodies. Therefore even necessary things are subject to the eternal law.*	Objection 3. Still further, the eternal law is the same thing as the rational pattern of Divine Providence. But Divine Providence regulates many necessary matters, such as the incorruptibility of non-bodily substances and of astronomical objects. It follows that even necessary matters are regulated by eternal law.

[1] Notice from the Objector's examples, which follow, that he is speaking of necessity in created things, not in the uncreated essence of God. This turns out to be decisive to St. Thomas's response.

[2] The natural philosophers of St. Thomas's time thought that celestial bodies such as stars are incorruptible. Contrary to the contemporary prejudice about ancient science, however, they did not reach this conclusion by deduction from first principles in defiance of observation. Rather, they *observed* that the celestial bodies do not seem to decay, and then worked out the principles that such a state of affairs would require. Thus, St. Thomas argues that the matter of each celestial body would have to be in potentiality to only a single form, the form that it in fact possesses.[49] In other words, the reason celestial bodies do not decay is that they cannot decay; for unless God intervenes, *everything* decays that is capable of decay. Our second law of thermodynamics comes to much the same thing: Every isolated system tends toward its greatest possible entropy, or disorder.

On the other hand, the conclusion that incorporeal intellects are also incorruptible *was* worked out by means of deduction from first principles.

[48] The Scriptural hints include Romans 8:38, Ephesians 3:10 and 6:12, and Colossians 1:16 and 2:15, as well as the passage quoted in the text. In *The Celestial Hierarchy*, Pseudo-Dionysius the Areopagite lists the angelic choirs in three triads, as Seraphim, Cherubim, and Thrones; Dominions, Virtues, and Powers; and Principalities, Archangels, and Angels properly so-called. In *Homilies on the Gospels*, Homily 24, Gregory the Great lists them in almost the same order, but with the Virtues and Principalities interchanged. These triads are the treble hierarchies of Angels mentioned in St. Thomas's prayer *Ante Studium*, set at the beginning of this commentary. St. Thomas compares the arguments of Gregory and Pseudo-Dionysus in I, Q. 108, Article 6, finding both of their respective theories plausible.

[49] I, Question 66, Article 2.

Scripture, of course, testifies to the reality of the incorporeal intellects that we call angels, and St. Thomas regards this as real data. He does not think philosophy can prove that they must exist, but it can certainly show that their existence is reasonable, for the completion of God's good purpose in creation would seem to have required creation to include them; they close the gap in the order of being between God and corporeal creatures. To be sure, He could have created the universe without creating angels, for there is nothing logically absurd in the proposition that angels do not exist (see the discussion of absolute possibility below). However, *if* He chose to create the universe with corporeal creatures (as He obviously has), then it would have been unfitting for Him not to create angels too, and whatever He does, He does in the most fitting way.[50] Now we come to the point in question, for granted the existence of such creatures, they would have to be free from decay: They would not have any matter, and decay comes about only by matter's loss of form.[51]

To all this, the Objector adds only one point: Since angels and celestial bodies are necessarily free from decay, and since they are directed by eternal law, it must be that necessary things are directed by eternal law.

A final point in passing. Just above we discussed the *fittingness* of closing the gap in the order of being between God and corporeal creatures. Fittingness is a kind of aesthetic principle, and someone might object that science has no room for aesthetic principles. But aesthetic considerations figure largely in our own science too. All other things being equal, scientists prefer theories that are beautiful. In much the same way, St. Thomas insists that our explanations of things recognize the beauty of God's works.

---

[1] ***On the contrary,*** *Things that are necessary cannot be otherwise, and consequently need no restraining.* [2] *But laws are imposed on men, in order to restrain them from evil, as explained above (92, 2). Therefore necessary things are not subject to the eternal law.*	**On the other hand,** As we saw in our previous discussion of the acts of law, the purpose of human laws is to restrain men from evil. This is a special case of the principle that the purpose of law in general is to restrain whatever needs to be restrained. But necessary things do not need to be restrained, because they cannot be other than they are. Therefore, necessary things are not directed by the eternal law.

---

[50] In Article 1, St. Thomas speaks of God creating angels for the sake of the "perfection" of the universe, but he uses the term is used in the sense of its completeness, rather than in the sense that no better universe could have been created. Concerning this point, see the online *Companion to the Commentary*.

[51] I., Q. 50, Arts. 1, 2, and 5.

[1]   The Objector flew to one extreme, holding that all necessary matters come under the regulation of eternal law – but the *sed contra* flies to the other extreme, holding that *no* necessary matters come under the regulation of eternal law. For if they cannot be other than they are, then from what could they need to be restrained, and how could they be?

[2]   Even granted St. Thomas's discussion of the acts of law, in Question 92, Article 2, it is not altogether clear why the *sed contra* draws the conclusion that laws are imposed on men for the *sole* purpose of restraining them from committing evils. Evidently the *sed contra* views not only prohibition and punishment, but even command and permission, as having an exclusively negative purpose, a view that St. Thomas himself does not seem to hold. But of course, the *sed contra* need not correspond to his own thinking.

---

[1] *I answer that, As stated above (1), the eternal law is the type of the Divine government. Consequently whatever is subject to the Divine government, is subject to the eternal law: while if anything is not subject to the Divine government, neither is it subject to the eternal law.* [2] *The application of this distinction may be gathered by looking around us. For those things are subject to human government, which can be done by man; but what pertains to the nature of man is not subject to human government; for instance, that he should have a soul, hands, or feet.* [3] *Accordingly all that is in things created by God, whether it be contingent or necessary, is subject to the eternal law: while things pertaining to the Divine Nature or Essence are not subject to the eternal law, but are the eternal law itself.*

Here is my response. As we have seen, the eternal law is the rational pattern, the Divine Idea, for God's governance of the universe. Therefore, anything regulated by God's government is regulated by eternal law, and anything not regulated by God's government – if there is such a thing – is not regulated by eternal law. We can see the same distinction in our own affairs, for the things man is able to make come under human government, but his nature – for example that he has a soul, hands, and feet – does not come under human government. With the Divine government it is just the same, for eternal law regulates everything pertaining to what God has created, whether contingent or necessary. But what pertains to His nature or essence is not regulated by the eternal law; it *is* the eternal law.

---

[1]   St. Thomas speaks hypothetically; he does not say that there is anything not subject to the Divine government.

[2]   Many people speak glibly of "changing human nature." But man's nature is the unchanging essence that underlies all changes in his

nonessential attributes, such as whether he is hurried or sedate, has red hair or blond, lives in a house or a tent, or writes letters or only text messages. To suggest a change in human nature itself is to misunderstand what is meant by the term "human nature." Suppose self-styled transhumanists got their wish; suppose that by dint of nanotechnology, biotechnology, and God knows what else, they succeeded in erasing some of man's essential attributes and putting others in their place.[52] The correct way to describe such an event would not be "Man's nature has changed," but "Man's nature has ceased to exist." In the strict sense, the artifacts that resulted from this change would have no "natures" at all.

[3] The brilliance of the *respondeo* is that it upholds the sovereignty of God without giving in to the view that to be sovereign is to regulate everything. Yes, there are some necessary and eternal matters that God's eternal law does not regulate. Yet what matters are these? Just those matters pertaining to His own nature or essence. It would be mistaken, then, to say that they *escape* His eternal law, because they simply *are* His eternal law, viewed, so to speak, from another angle.

To grasp the argument we must keep in mind that ruling is a dyadic relationship: P can rule Q, but P cannot rule P. But wait a moment! *Can't* P rule P? In the case of human beings, don't we speak of such things as "self-mastery" and "self-control"? Don't we even consider them virtues? We do, but these expressions are not to be taken literally. When we say that a man exercises self-control, what we mean is that his power of reason regulates his sensitive appetites, the desires and emotions, so the relation is dyadic after all. But aren't these sensitive appetites just as much *his,* as the power to reason is *his*? Then why do we call it *self*-control for reason to rule the sensitive appetites, but not for the sensitive appetites to rule reason? Because unless reason is in command, he is not well-ordered; he cannot flourish; his life does not fulfill the pattern that his rational essence demands. Just for this reason, even though both his reason and his sensitive appetites are truly his, he is more strongly identified with his reason.

---

[52] Such aspirations are no longer limited to the readers and writers of science fiction: See, for example, Mihail C. Roco and William Sims Bainbridge, eds., *Converging Technologies for Improving Human Performance: Nanotechnology, Biotechnology, Information Technology and Cognitive Science* (National Science Foundation and U.S. Department of Commerce, June 2002; Dordrecht, The Netherlands, Kluwer Academic Publishers, 2003), available on the Internet at http://www.wtec.org/ConvergingTechnologies/Report/NBIC_report.pdf

St. Thomas's move in the discussion of sovereignty should be compared with his move in the discussion of omnipotence earlier in the *Summa*. Just as he seeks to uphold the Divine sovereignty, so he seeks to uphold the Divine omnipotence. But just as God's sovereignty does not mean that His eternal law regulates everything, so His omnipotence does not mean that He can do all things whatsoever. For example, He cannot make the past not to have been, or a man to be a donkey. Omnipotence means that God can do anything *absolutely possible* – anything that does not involve a predicate that is incompatible with its subject. However, the notion of a past that has not been is simply nonsense, because if it is past then it *has* been. Equally absurd is the notion of a man who is a donkey, because if he is a donkey then he is *not* a man.[53]

[1] *Reply to Objection 1. We may speak of God's will in two ways. First, as to the will itself: and thus, since God's will is His very Essence, it is subject neither to the Divine government, nor to the eternal law, but is the same thing as the eternal law.* [2] *Secondly, we may speak of God's will, as to the things themselves that God wills about creatures; which things are subject to the eternal law, in so far as they are planned by Divine Wisdom.* [3] *In reference to these things God's will is said to be reasonable [rationalis]: though regarded in itself it should rather be called their type [ratio].*	Reply to Objection 1. We may speak of God's will in two ways – considering either what it is in itself, or what it wills about the things He creates. In itself, God's will is identical with His essence. So we should not say that it is ruled by Divine governance or regulated by eternal law, but that it *is* the eternal law. With the things God creates, matters stand differently. The eternal law regulates them, just because the Divine Wisdom conceives them. We commonly say that God's will concerning these things is reasonable. Viewing it in itself, though, it would be better to call it their very Reason.

[1]   St. Thomas is not saying that God's will *rather than God's reason* is His very essence. On the contrary, His will is His very essence, which is the same thing as the eternal law, *which is, as we have seen before, His reason*. All these things that different to us are one in Him.

[2]   The second point follows from St. Thomas's previous demonstration that the eternal law is the rational pattern of his creation and governance of the universe.

[53] I, Q. 25, Arts. 4–5.

[3]   To speak again about the movement in the passage from God's will to God's reason: Though St. Thomas's view of God is sometimes called "intellectualist" rather than "voluntarist," this terminology is a little unfortunate because it gives the false impression that instead of putting God's will above His reason, St. Thomas puts His reason above His will. Certainly St. Thomas doesn't put God's will above His reason, but neither does he put His reason above His will. To think that way is be to suppose that God's will might *oppose* His reason and need to be held in check. That sort of thing happens all too often in us, but it cannot happen in God, because in Him, will and reason are not distinct from each other. They are the same Divine Essence, viewed in two different ways, as the north and south elevations of a house are different ways of viewing the same house.[54]

[1] *Reply to Objection 2. God the Son was not made by God, but was naturally born of God.* [2] *Consequently He is not subject to Divine providence or to the eternal law: but rather is Himself the eternal law by a kind of appropriation, as Augustine explains (De Vera Relig. xxxi).* [3] *But He is said to be subject to the Father by reason of His human nature, in respect of which also the Father is said to be greater than He.*	Reply to Objection 2. The Son of God was not *made* by God, but by nature *begotten* by God. Rather than being *ruled* by Divine Providence or eternal law, He *is* the eternal law (not in the sense that this is more true of Him than of the Father or the Spirit, but by a kind of "appropriation," as St. Augustine makes clear). Then how can He be said to be subject to the Father? Not because of His Divine nature, but because of His human nature. It is for the same reason that the Father is said to be greater than the Son.

[1]   St. Thomas is not speaking of Christ's having been physically born as a man, but of His having been begotten of the Father. The former was an event in time, but the latter is a *relation* that subsists in the one Divine nature eternally.

[2]   We have discussed "appropriation" in Article 1. Here St. Thomas is probably alluding to the passage in *On True Religion* where, shortly after quoting John 5:22, "The Father judges no one, but has given all judgment to the Son," St. Augustine says "*the law* is that according to which he

---

[54]   I, Q. 3, Art. 7, and I, Q. 28, Art. 3. See also I-II, Q. 97, Art. 3, "All law proceeds from the reason and will of the lawgiver; the Divine and natural laws from the reasonable will of God; the human law from the will of man, regulated by reason."

judges all things and concerning which no man can judge." The context makes clear that the law to which he refers is the eternal law.[55]

[3]   St. Thomas's point is premised on the article of Christian faith that holds the incarnate Son of God to be a single Person in whom two natures are united – not God rather than Man, not Man rather than God, not some third thing half-God and half-Man, but at the same time both fully God and fully Man. St. Thomas explains that with respect to His Divine nature he is equal to the Father, but with respect to His human nature He is subject to Him.

The third objection we grant, because it deals with those necessary things that are created.	We concede the third objection, because it concerns *created* necessity, which we too hold to be governed by eternal law.

The Objector had mentioned only celestial bodies and incorporeal angels. St. Thomas points out that these are created beings. Yes, they are free from the possibility of decay, and yes, they possess this incorruptibility by necessity. But they owe this very necessity to the way they were made – celestial bodies cannot decay because they were *created* in potentiality to only one kind of matter, and the angelic intellects cannot decay because they were *created* with no matter at all. Since the necessity of their incorruptibility depends on the rational plan of creation, it is governed by that plan. But this plan *is* the eternal law, so St. Thomas agrees that they are governed by eternal law. Had Objection 3 claimed that matters pertaining to the uncreated essence of *God Himself* are governed by eternal law, he would have to disagree, but that is not what the Objection said.

[1] *Reply to the Argument for the Contrary:* [2] *As the Philosopher says (Metaph. v., text. 6), some necessary things have a cause of their necessity: and thus they derive from something else the fact that they cannot be otherwise.* [3] *And this is in itself a most effective restraint; for whatever is restrained, is said to be restrained in so far as it cannot do otherwise than it is allowed to.*	Reply to the Argument to the Contrary. As Aristotle explains in the fifth book of his *Metaphysics,* not all necessity is intrinsic. On the contrary, some necessary matters are *caused* to be necessary; the very fact that they cannot be other than they are is brought about by something else. Concerning this sort of necessary thing, it is not correct to say there is no need for restraint, because the external cause of its necessity *is* itself a kind of restraint – and a most effective one, for a restraint is simply that which makes it impossible for a thing to do other than what it is allowed to do.

[55] Augustine, *Of True Religion,* Chapter 31, in J.H.S. Burleigh, trans., *Augustine: Earlier Writings* (Philadelphia: Westminster Press, 1953), p. 254, emphasis added.

[1] I have changed the heading, for although the Dominican Fathers translation confusingly labels this response "Reply to Objection 4," St. Thomas is actually replying to the *sed contra*; there is no Objection 4. In most cases the *sed contra* is not far from his own view. In this case, it needs a bit of correction.

[2] Aristotle writes, "Now some things owe their necessity to something other than themselves; others do not, but are themselves the source of necessity in other things."[56]

[3] The *sed contra* took a view diametrically opposed to the Objector, protesting "Since necessary things cannot be other than they are, how could they need to be restrained?" St. Thomas answers, "But why *can't* they be other than they are?" In the case of necessity in created things, the answer is that they are subjected to necessity by the nature with which God endowed them – the Reason or purpose implanted in them by the Divine craftsmanship. To put this another way, the only reason they do not need to be restrained *subsequent* to the act of creation is that they were restrained *by* the act of creation – and the rational pattern of this act is the eternal law.

For further reflection on the preceding section of the *Treatise on Law*, the online *Companion to the Commentary*, accessible via the Resources link at the book's catalogue webpage, includes a discussion of the following topic:

COULD GOD HAVE CREATED A DIFFERENT NATURE?

Question 93, Article 5:
Whether Natural Contingents Are Subject to the Eternal Law?

TEXT	PARAPHRASE
Whether natural contingents are subject to the eternal law?	Does the eternal law regulate created things that might have been other than they are?

St. Thomas explains that the term "nature" is used in a manifold variety of ways. In its most general sense, it simply refers to a *being* – any being whatsoever, such as a rock.

More particularly, however, it is used for a *substance* – a subject of which properties are predicated, rather than just one of the proper parts

---

[56] Aristotle, *Metaphysics*, Book 5, Chapter 5 (trans. W.D. Ross, public domain).

or properties of a subject. In this sense, an olive tree is a substance, but green and foliage are not substances.

Still more particularly, the term is used for the *essence* of such a thing, as expressed by its definition; better yet, we use the term for that element in the definition which makes the thing different from other things in its genus, and so gives it its *form*. In this sense, the nature of man is rational animal; but in comparison with other animals, his nature is rationality, which is ordered to truth as its end.

Finally, we use the term for the *intrinsic principle* of such a thing, its seed of change or development, whether material or formal. For example, the nature of an oak is to germinate from an acorn, whereupon it thrusts down roots and thrusts up trunk, branches, leaves, and nutty fruit.[57]

In the present Article, the focus of St. Thomas's discussion lies in the final sense. But there is a little twist: Although rational creatures have natures too, for purposes of the present Article he is speaking only of irrational creatures. He returns to rational creatures in Article 6.

[1] **Objection 1.** *It would seem that natural contingents are not subject to the eternal law.* [2] *Because promulgation is essential to law, as stated above (90, 4).* [3] *But a law cannot be promulgated except to rational creatures, to whom it is possible to make an announcement.* [4] *Therefore none but rational creatures are subject to the eternal law; and consequently natural contingents are not.*	Objection 1. Apparently, the suggestion that eternal law rules natural contingents is false. We have understood ever since Question 90, Article 4, that in order to be a true law, something must be promulgated or announced. But one can announce something only to rational created beings. This being the case, only they can be ruled by eternal law. Natural contingents are beyond its reach.

[1]   In the *ultrum,* I paraphrased "natural" as "created," but here I have let the word stand, because the Objector turns out to use the term "natural" in a different sense, restricting attention to subrational natures.

[2]   Law cannot serve as a rule and measure of distinctively human acts unless it is known, and it cannot be known unless it is promulgated or announced.

---

[57] See I, Q. 29, Art. 1; I, Q. 115, Art. 2; and I-II, Q. 10, Art. 1. St. Thomas draws especially from Aristotle, *Metaphysics*, Book 5, and also refers to Boethius, *On the Person and the Two Natures Against Eutyches and Nestorius.*

[3] As we have seen earlier, in the strictest sense only rational creatures are ruled by law, because only they can grasp the law as an ordinance of reason.

[4] Much as in Question 91, Article 2, Objection 2, the Objector is viewing the rational and the natural as opposites. Though St. Thomas teaches that rational creatures have natures too, in this Article he allows the usage. The point is that since the eternal law cannot be *promulgated* to contingent beings that lack rationality, it cannot not rule them either.

---

[1] *Objection 2. Further, "Whatever obeys reason partakes somewhat of reason," as stated in Ethic. i.* [2] *But the eternal law, is the supreme type, as stated above (1).* [3] *Since then natural contingents do not partake of reason in any way, but are altogether void of reason, it seems that they are not subject to the eternal law.*	Objection 2. As we have already seen, the eternal law is the supreme reason. Now as Aristotle explains, in the *Ethics,* Book 1, Chapter 13, whatever listens to reason and obeys it may be said in a sense to share in reason. But natural contingents do not share in reason even in this way; they have no part in it at all. Therefore we must conclude that they are not ruled by eternal law.

---

[1] The Objector is probably thinking of Aristotle's statement, "[T]he irrational element also appears to be two-fold. For the vegetative element in no way shares in a rational principle, but the appetitive and in general the desiring element in a sense shares in it, in so far as it listens to and obeys it.... And if this element also must be said to have a rational principle, that which has a rational principle ... will be twofold, one subdivision having it in the strict sense and in itself, and the other having a tendency to obey as one does one's father."[58]

In his commentary on the work, St. Thomas explains, "But reason here does not play the role of a mere theorist like the reason of a mathematician, for the irrational part of the soul does not partake in any way of reason understood in this sense."[59] Rather it partakes of reason insofar as it *follows the guidance* of reason.

[2] The phrase rendered "supreme type" in the Dominican Fathers translation is *ratio summa,* complete or perfect Reason, the understanding

---

[58] Aristotle, *Nicomachean Ethics,* Book 1, Chapter 13, trans. W.D. Ross (public domain).
[59] Thomas Aquinas, *Commentary on Aristotle's Nicomachean Ethics,* Book 1, Lecture 20, trans. C.J. Litzinger, O.P., rev. ed. (Notre Dame, IN: Dumb Ox Books, 1993), p. 80.

of all things in the mind of God, viewed from the perspective of His governance.

[3]   As in Objection 1, the Objector is viewing the rational and the natural as opposites. The idea is that since the eternal law cannot be *understood* by contingent beings that lack reason, it cannot rule them either.

[1] ***Objection 3.** Further, the eternal law is most efficient.* [2] *But in natural contingents defects occur.* [3] *Therefore they are not subject to the eternal law.*	**Objection 3.** Still further, the eternal law superlatively brings about what it intends. Yet sometimes natural contingents fall short of what they ought to be. If eternal law governed natural contingents, this would be impossible; therefore, it must not rule them.

[1]   Something is said to be efficient if it operates as an efficient cause – that is, if it brings something about or maintains something in being. A carpenter, for example, is efficient because he constructs or preserves assemblies made of wood; God is efficient because He creates and governs the universe. He is *most* efficient in at least three senses, for He causes *all* things, He the *first* cause of all things, and His causality does not fail. The third sense is the one the Objector has in mind.

[2]   Limbs may grow crookedly. Crops may die from lack of water. Tomatoes may succumb to blight.

[3]   If something goes wrong in the development of a thing's nature, the Objector reasons, then how could God's eternal law have been in charge?

On the contrary, *It is written (Proverbs 8:29): "When He compassed the sea with its bounds, and set a law to the waters, that they should not pass their limits."*	**On the other hand,** Proverbs 8:29 implies that eternal law *does* govern natural contingents, for it speaks of God enacting a boundary for the sea, so that its expanse is confined by His decree.

The sea is certainly a natural contingent, a created thing that might have been other than it is. Moreover, it is an irrational creature, a thing without understanding. So the significance of the statement of Lady Wisdom, quoted here, is that eternal law does govern natural contingents, even those that lack minds capable of comprehending what the eternal law demands of them.

[1] *I answer that,* We must speak otherwise of the law of man, than of the eternal law which is the law of God. For the law of man extends only to rational creatures subject to man. [2] The reason of this is because law directs the actions of those that are subject to the government of someone: wherefore, properly speaking, none imposes a law on his own actions. [3] Now whatever is done regarding the use of irrational things subject to man, is done by the act of man himself moving those things, for these irrational creatures do not move themselves, but are moved by others, as stated above (1, 2). [4] Consequently man cannot impose laws on irrational beings, however much they may be subject to him. [5] But he can impose laws on rational beings subject to him, in so far as by his command or pronouncement of any kind, he imprints on their minds a rule which is a principle of action.

Here is my response. We must not think that human law is exactly like the eternal law of God, because the former governs only those rational creatures who are under human authority. For *every* law regulates only those under the legislator's authority, and only rational creatures come under a human legislator's authority. (By the way, this is why no one can really make a law for himself – for how could anyone be *under* his own authority?)

Certainly, man *uses* those irrational things that are under his control, but the only way he can do so is to impose external constraint on them. That is how irrational things are, for they don't give rise to their own movements, like a rational creature thinking "This is what I will do." Rather they are acted upon by others. Just for this reason, no man can give true laws to irrational things – that is, he cannot give them inward reasons for doing things.

With rational beings, it is different. When the legislator issues anything in the nature of a decree or instruction to rational beings who are under his authority, he presses into their minds a rule by which they subsequently they direct themselves.

[1]   The wording here implies two exceptions to the scope of human law: It does not extend to irrational creatures, and it does not even extend to rational creatures who are not subject to the legislator.

Probably no one would challenge the latter exception; no one supposes that the Chinese are subject to the laws of Germany. But many would challenge the former exception. Doesn't the law of man extend to irrational but animate creatures, like dogs and horses? Don't they respond to commands? In a sense, yes, but not in the fullest sense, because not all commands are appeals to the *reason* of the one under command. When the shepherd commands the sheepdog to return a straying sheep to the herd, the dog knows what to do and can do it excellently. Yet however eager the dog may be to obey, and however it may enjoy keeping the sheep together, it does not understand why any of this is being done. What is it all about? What is the point? The command is an ordinance of reason only from the shepherd's point of view, not the dog's.

[2]   The transition here is obscure, and the example is a little surprising. In what way is the point made here the reason for the point made just before?

St. Thomas is reminding us that governing is a dyadic relationship; one party governs, the other is governed. True, we sometimes speak as though a person could rule himself, but such language is figurative. To say that Franklin possesses the quality of self-mastery is to say that his reason regulates his desires and emotions. The relation is still dyadic: P does not regulate P, but Q regulates R.

The point that governing is dyadic reminds us that the one who is governed must really be under the authority of the one who governs – otherwise there is no governing. It is in this sense that the previous point has been explained.

[3]   The claim that irrational creatures do not move themselves, but are moved by others, may at first seem strange. Doesn't a cat move itself to chase the mouse? What St. Thomas means is that such creatures lack the power of free will guided by reason. His point is more clearly stated in I-II, Q. 1, Art. 2, where he says,

> … those things that are possessed of reason, move themselves to an end; because they have dominion over their actions through their free-will, which is the "faculty of will and reason." But those things that lack reason tend to an end, by natural inclination, as being moved by another and not by themselves; since they do not know the nature of an end as such, and consequently cannot ordain anything to an end, but can be ordained to an end only by another.

So, yes, the cat is moved to chase the mouse, but it is pushed into the chase by blind impulse. We too have natural inclinations, but for us these act not blindly, but through reason and under its control. The cat never asks, "What is the purpose of chasing mice? Could I achieve it in some other way?" Not so with man. Jean-Jacques Rousseau, though an atrociously poor guide to human nature, puts the point splendidly:

> One chooses or refuses by instinct, and the other by an act of liberty. This means that the animal cannot deviate from the rule which is prescribed for it, even when it would be advantageous to do so, and that man can deviate from the rule, often to his own prejudice. That is why a pigeon would die of hunger next to a bowl

filled with the best meats, and a cat on piles of fruit or grain, although both of them could nourish themselves very well on the food they reject, if they were of a mind to try it.[60]

[4] Within the limits of their natures, the soil and the wheat are subject to man, for the soil furrows if he plows it, and the seed sprouts if he sows it. We can take advantage of the preexisting properties of things; we can even take advantage of the principles of action intrinsic to DNA to make hybrids. But we cannot decree what intrinsic principles of action DNA shall have – for example, it is not up to us that it replicates.

It might seem that although man cannot imprint inward dispositions on minerals or plants, he can imprint inward dispositions on irrational animals. Consider the sheepdog again; the shepherd can train it to herd sheep. So isn't the statement "man cannot impose laws on irrational beings" too sharp?

Although it is true that the shepherd can train the dog to herd sheep, when he does so he is only taking advantage of inward dispositions that suitable breeds have already. One can train a border collie to herd sheep, but one cannot train a cat to do so. The ultimate, foundational principles of action of these creatures are still beyond us.

[5] "Drive only on the right side of the street," decrees the legislator. There may be nothing special about the right as contrasted with the left, but we see that the law prevents collisions, and so (one hopes) we obey. Such a law compels through fear of punishment, yes. Even so, it is an ordinance of reason; it directs citizens not just from the outside, as when cowboys herd cattle into a stockade, but from inside, by giving them a *reason* to obey.

Legislation is not the only way that one person may implant a principle of action into the mind of another. If you and I take counsel and you convince me by sound reasoning to follow your plan, then you have implanted a principle of action in my mind. The reasoning of the legislator has the added element of authority. For anyone may see by means of reason that we ought to drive not on both sides of the road, but only on one – but on which side shall we drive on? The legislator has the authority to say, "This one."

---

[60] Jean-Jacques Rousseau, *Discourse on the Origin of Inequality Among Men*, trans. Ian Johnston (2006, 2012; available at http://records.viu.ca/~johnstoi/rousseau/seconddiscourse.htm.

[1] *Now just as man, by such
pronouncement, impresses a kind
of inward principle of action on
the man that is subject to him,
so God imprints on the whole of
nature the principles of its proper
actions.* [2] *And so, in this way,
God is said to command the whole
of nature, according to Ps. 148:6:
"He hath made a decree, and it
shall not pass away." And thus
all actions and movements of the
whole of nature are subject to
the eternal law.* [3] *Consequently
irrational creatures are subject
to the eternal law, through being
moved by Divine providence;
but not, as rational creatures are,
through understanding the Divine
commandment.*

Just as a human legislator implants
principles of action in the *minds* of
other men by means of *announcement*,
so God implants principles of action
in the *natures* of contingent things
by means of *creation*. It is in just this
way – not in the way human legislators
use – that God is said to give dictates
to everything in nature, as when the
psalmist writes, "He established them
for ever and ever; he fixed their bounds
which cannot be passed."[61] So we see
that even the irrational things God
has created are ruled by His eternal
law. They are ruled not through
understanding His commandment,
like rational creatures, but through
the promptings of His foreknowing
government.

[1] It is said that Friedrich Nietzsche once challenged God, "I too can create a man." God replied to Nietzsche, "Go ahead and try." Nietzsche took a fistful of dust and began to mold it. God said, "Disqualified. Get your own dust."

[2] The emphasis should lie on the word "this." It is in *this* way that God is said to command the whole of nature, not in the way that the human legislator commands. In both cases, Divine and human commands, an inward impetus to action is implanted. But the mind of the human legislator can impart an inward impetus only by instructing other minds as to what is to be done, whereas God can impart an inward impetus even to things that have no minds.

[3] God does not enlighten the mind of the sea as to what it should do, for it has no mind to be enlightened. Rather His law directs it inwardly, by making it what it is, by giving it the properties that it has.

[61] Psalm 148:6 (RSV).

[1] *Reply to Objection 1. The impression of an inward active principle is to natural things, what the promulgation of law is to men:* [2] *because law, by being promulgated, imprints on man a directive principle of human actions, as stated above.*

Reply to Objection 1. God imprints upon the nature of each created thing a principle of action. Rulers promulgate laws. These two things, so different in other respects, have something in common nonetheless, because the promulgation of law imprints inward direction on distinctively human actions.

[1]   In the fullest sense of law, only that which is imparted to rational creatures is law, because law is an ordinance of reason. But the way God's Providence directs irrational creatures may be called a law in an analogous sense, for the reason about to be given.

[2]   Even though the eternal law does not implant an inward principle in the *mind* of the irrational creature, it does implant an inward principle *in* the irrational creature. This is sufficient to justify the analogy.

[1] *Reply to Objection 2. Irrational creatures neither partake of nor are obedient to human reason: whereas they do partake of the Divine Reason by obeying it; because the power of Divine Reason extends over more things than human reason does.* [2] *And as the members of the human body are moved at the command of reason, and yet do not partake of reason, since they have no apprehension subordinate to reason; so too irrational creatures are moved by God, without, on that account, being rational.*

Reply to Objection 2. The ruling intellect of God reigns over more things than human reason does. Irrational created things do not share in the understanding or obey the dictates of human minds; yet in a certain sense they do share in the rational plan of God, just by obeying it. Something of this sort is familiar to us from the operations of our own bodies, for even though our limbs and parts do not literally share in or grasp things by reason, yet they are put into action by reason. In just the same way, even those creatures that lack rationality in themselves are put into action by the rational direction of God.

[1]   The Objector says irrational creatures are not subject to eternal law because they do not partake of God's reason in any way. In response, St. Thomas asks us to distinguish among being subject to someone's reason, sharing in his reason, and responding inwardly to his reason.

When the mind of the human potter conceives a pot and accordingly he uses his hands to shape the clay, he is subjecting the clay to his reason. Now the clay does not share in his reason, because it does not understand what he is doing to it, and it does not respond inwardly to his reason, because he pushes it into shape with his hands. If it were rationally subject to him, he might impress an inward principle upon it by commanding, "Clay, take the form of a pot." But since it is irrational, he cannot.

Compare how the Divine potter works, for example, when he creates the stars. He too subjects them to His reason, and they too have no understanding of what He is doing to them. But now comes the difference, because He *can* make them respond inwardly to His reason. Such is His omnipotence that it is He who gives them their nature in the first place. Just in this sense – just by being what He causes them to be, which is their obedience – they share in His rational plan.

[2]   Here the Angelic Doctor is heading off a possible misunderstanding. Someone might think that whatever follows God's rational direction is by that very fact rational. This in turn might lead him to conclude that anything that is *not* rational must *not* follow God's rational plan – so Objection 3 would seem valid. But the premise is mistaken. Would we say that whatever follows *our* rational direction is *ipso facto* rational? Certainly not; consider the fingers. Why then should we say that whatever follows God's rational direction is *ipso facto* rational?

---

[1] *Reply to Objection 3. Although the defects which occur in natural things are outside the order of particular causes, they are not outside the order of universal causes,* [2] *especially of the First Cause, i.e. God, from Whose providence nothing can escape, as stated in the First Part (22, 2).* [3] *And since the eternal law is the type of Divine providence, as stated above (1), hence the defects of natural things are subject to the eternal law.*

Reply to Objection 3. A defect that arises in a natural thing is certainly inconsistent with that thing's own principle of action, its particular cause. Yet the manner in which the defect arises does not at all contradict the universal principles of action, the universal causes that *bring about* the particular causes. This is especially true of the First Cause of everything, God, whose Providence governs all things without exception. Now the eternal law is nothing but the rational pattern of this Providence. From this we see that eternal law governs not only the natures of created things, but even the defects that arise in them.

---

[1] Suppose a bug chews on the fruit of a tomato plant so that it is blighted. The blighting of the fruit is obviously contrary to the nature of the tomato plant, to the particular cause of its activity. But is it contrary to the arrangement that God has imparted to the ensemble of *all* natural things, whether tomato plants or bugs? Not in the least. The bugs are part of His plan too.

[2] St. Thomas's argument in I, Question 22, Article 2 may be put as follows. Although every finite agent tries to arrange things so that they work toward his end, his efforts to do so may be impeded by other things that are beyond his control. God too directs things toward His end, but with Him it is different, because His causality extends to everything whatsoever. Nothing is beyond His control. It follows that nothing can frustrate His purposes, and from this it further follows that if defects occur in natural things, in some way even they must be directed toward His end. Some purpose is served, for example, by His having made a bug which chews on tomato plants. We have discussed this theme previously, in Question 91, Article 1.

[3] The rational pattern of God's direction of things toward His end – of which we were just speaking – is the eternal law. So to say that even the defects of natural things are within His control is the same as to say that they are subject to His eternal law, and the objection is defeated.

For further reflection on the preceding section of the *Treatise on Law*, the online *Companion to the Commentary*, accessible via the Resources link at the book's catalogue webpage, includes a discussion of the following topic:

Two Ways of Imposing Order

Question 93, Article 6:
Whether All Human Affairs Are Subject to the Eternal Law?

TEXT	PARAPHRASE
Whether all human affairs are subject to the eternal law?	Does the eternal law regulate all that pertains to human beings?

Each of Articles 4, 5, and 6 asks whether matters of a certain kind are regulated by eternal law. Article 4 poses the question about eternal matters and matters that cannot be other than they are; Article 5 poses it about irrational created beings that *could* be other than they are; and Article 6 poses it about the affairs of human beings, who are created *rational* beings who could be other than they are. Together, then, these three articles take in everything except angels (the other created rational beings who could be other than they are), whom St. Thomas has discussed thoroughly in I, Q. 50–64, sometimes called the *Treatise on the Angels,* and with whom the *Treatise on Law* is not concerned.

The Objector hurls Molotov cocktails of quotation. St. Thomas adroitly defuses them, by examining the quoted texts with greater care.

[1] **Objection 1.** *It would seem that not all human affairs are subject to the eternal law. For the Apostle says (Galatians 5:18): "If you are led by the spirit you are not under the law." [2] But the righteous who are the sons of God by adoption, are led by the spirit of God, according to Rm. 8:14: "Whosoever are led by the spirit of God, they are the sons of God." Therefore not all men are under the eternal law.*	Objection 1. Apparently, the reply to the *ultrum* should be "No." As we learn in St. Paul's letter to the Galatians, the righteous whom God adopts are led by the Holy Spirit. As we learn further from his letter to the Romans, those who are led by the Holy Spirit are not under the law. From these two premises, it follows that at least some men – the righteous whom God adopts – are not under the law. But if at least some men are not under the law, then not all human affairs are subject to the law.

[1]   The Objector seems to take not being "under the law" to mean not being under the law *in any sense,* so that those who are not under the law need not obey it. This protest has a decidedly contemporary feel; students of certain denominational backgrounds sometimes say to me, "God's moral law doesn't apply to me, because I am free in Christ." In context, St. Paul's remark reads as follows:

For the flesh lusts against the spirit: and the spirit against the flesh; for these are contrary one to another: so that you do not the things that you would. But if you are led by the spirit, you are not under the law. Now the works of the flesh are manifest, which are fornication, uncleanness, immodesty, luxury, idolatry, witchcrafts, enmities, contentions, emulations, wraths, quarrels, dissensions, sects, envies, murders, drunkenness, revellings, and such like. Of the which I foretell you, as I have foretold to you, that they who do such things shall not obtain the kingdom of God. But the fruit of the Spirit is, charity, joy, peace, patience, benignity, goodness, longanimity, mildness, faith, modesty, continency, chastity. Against such there is no law.[62]

[2]   Again the objection feels contemporary. A young man who wrote to me viewed the liberty of those whom St. Paul calls "sons of God" and

---

[62] Galatians 5:17–23 (DRA), changing "lusteth" to "lusts."

heirs to His kingdom like this: "My parents had a rule about spilling milk: Don't! But in my house I can spill the milk if I want to." He reasoned that just as the parental rule against spilling milk no longer bound him, so God's law no longer bound him. He did concede that just as he might avoid spilling the milk just to avoid having to clean it up, so he might follow God's law "as if" it were binding, just to avoid other undesired consequences.

[1] *Objection 2. Further, the Apostle says (Romans 8:7): "The prudence [Vulg.: 'wisdom'] of the flesh is an enemy to God: for it is not subject to the law of God."* [2] *But many are those in whom the prudence of the flesh dominates. Therefore all men are not subject to the eternal law which is the law of God.*	Objection 2. Moreover, St. Paul gives us another reason to deny the *ultrum* in his remark to the Romans that after the Fall, the desires and appetites of the body set themselves against God and refuse to submit to His law. Many are dominated by this carnal outlook, this false "wisdom of the flesh." Obviously, then, they are not ruled by God, and so not by His eternal law.

[1]   We have discussed the "prudence of the flesh" in Q. 93, Art. 3, Obj. 1 and ad 1. The expression refers to the tendency of the fallen desires and appetites to run riot rather than following the guidance of true wisdom, or reason.

[2]   The Objector argues that if men were really ruled by the eternal law, then they would not obey their fallen desires appetites; yet they do. Students often voice a similar objection to natural law: There couldn't be a natural law, because if there were, wouldn't people always obey it?

[1] *Objection 3. Further, Augustine says (De Lib. Arb. i, 6) that "the eternal law is that by which the wicked deserve misery, the good, a life of blessedness."* [2] *But those who are already blessed, and those who are already lost, are not in the state of merit. Therefore they are not under the eternal law.*	Objection 3. Still further, St. Augustine explains that the eternal law is the basis of final desert – the reason why the wicked deserve misery, and the good, happiness. But it makes no sense to say that the lost and the blessed, who have *already* received what they deserve, *still* deserve it; they have passed out of range of all deserving. But in this case, they are no longer under the eternal law. So the *ultrum* is refuted.

[1]   We deserve something when it is just that it should be given to us. Augustine's point is that if there were no standard of justice, we could not

say that anyone deserved anything. Desert is real because there is such a standard, the eternal law.

According to Thomas Aquinas, strictly speaking no one deserves anything for his acts unless they are done for love of God. By our own power we are not able to do this, but because of His own goodness, God offers the grace that makes it possible to love Him in return. Moreover, He treats many acts that were not done for love as though they were; this is why, even when good works are done without love, those who perform them do receive some good in return. Merit in the former, strict sense is called *condign*; merit in the latter, "as if" sense is called *congruous*.[63]

[2]   The Objector views merit as a *present* claim to receive a *future* reward or punishment. It seems to him that the blessed in heaven, and the lost in hell, can no longer be said to merit their rewards or punishments, because they are receiving them already.

On the contrary, *Augustine says (De Civ. Dei xix, 12): "Nothing evades the laws of the most high Creator and Governor, for by Him the peace of the universe is administered."*	**On the other hand,** as Augustine says in *The City of God,* "Nothing can withdraw from the laws through which the supreme Creator and Ruler administers the peace of the universe."

I am rendering *subtrahitur* as "withdraws" rather than "evades," but of course if nothing can withdraw from the eternal law, then nothing evades it either. The point is that all creatures are ruled by it, including human beings.

[1] *I answer that, There are two ways in which a thing is subject to the eternal law, as explained above (5): first, by partaking of the eternal law by way of knowledge; secondly, by way of action and passion, i.e. by partaking of the eternal law by way of an inward motive principle: and in this second way, irrational creatures are subject to the eternal law, as stated above (5).* [2] *But since the rational nature, together with that which it has in common with all creatures, has something proper to itself*	**Here is my response.** We saw in Article 5 that things may be ruled by eternal law in either of two different ways, for they may share in it either through knowledge, or through principles of change and development imprinted on their natures. Eternal law rules irrational beings only in the second way, but it rules rational beings in both ways.

[63] Supp., Q. 14, Art. 4.

inasmuch as it is rational, consequently it is subject to the eternal law in both ways; because while each rational creature has some knowledge of the eternal law, as stated above (2), [3] it also has a natural inclination to that which is in harmony with the eternal law; [4] for "we are naturally adapted to [be] the recipients of virtue" (Ethic. ii, 1).	In the former way it rules them because they know something of the eternal law, as discussed in Article 2. In the latter way it rules them because they naturally inclined toward it. In particular, as Aristotle explains in the *Ethics,* we are naturally prepared to acquire virtue.

[1]   Created things may be ruled by eternal law in either of two ways. One is through understanding what is expected of them, so that they knowingly conform their behavior to it. The other way is through an interior impetus, so that in the first place they are impelled to follow it (that is, they are subject in action) and in the second place they receive its effects (that is, they are subject in passion).

St. Thomas does not actually say "inward motive principle," but simply "motive principle," *principii motivi.* However, the adjective "inward" in the Dominican Fathers translation is entirely justified, and he used it in the previous article when he wrote that "the impression of an inward active principle [*activi principii intrinseci*] is to natural things, what the promulgation of law is to men." I take up certain subtleties in the concept of an inward motive principle in the online *Companion to the Commentary.*

[2]   Here is a way to think of the matter. Purposes exist in one way in things, and in another way in minds, and in yet another way in the mind of God.[64] In birds and barnacles, purposes exist only in the first way. They strive and burgeon, imitating in the organic realm the limitless life of God, but they do not know this about themselves. In human beings, purposes exist in *both* the first and second ways, for we too are so made as to seek things like nutrition, shelter, offspring, but we also know this about ourselves, which introduces a new principle of order and changes everything. We *knowingly* make plans to do such things as plant crops,

---

[64] In *The First Grace: Rediscovering the Natural Law in a Post-Christian World* (Wilmington, DE: ISI Books, 2007), p. 9, Russell Hittinger aptly calls these "the three foci" of natural law. It derives its specific character *as law* from its residence in the mind of God; but our own minds recognize it from its residence in nature (including our own nature). The point had previously been developed by Yves R. Simon, in *The Tradition of Natural Law: A Philosopher's Reflections,* ed. Vukan Kuic (New York: Fordham University Press, 1992, orig. 1965), p. 129.

erect buildings, raise up a posterity for ourselves; moreover we seek knowledge *in itself,* especially the knowledge of God. In Him, purposes exist in yet another way, because His eternal law is the first cause of all this purposeful order in creation.

[3] The term "natural inclination" refers to what is necessary for the fulfillment of this rational nature, which in view of the Fall may often be quite different from what it would like to do.

[4] St. Thomas is thinking of Aristotle's statement that "Neither by nature, then, nor contrary to nature do the virtues arise in us; rather we are adapted by nature to receive them, and are made perfect by habit."[65] In his commentary on the work, St. Thomas explains, "We do have a natural aptitude to acquire them inasmuch as the appetitive potency is naturally adapted to obey reason. But we are perfected in these virtues by use, for when we act repeatedly according to reason, a modification is impressed in the appetite by the power of reason. This impression is nothing else but moral virtue."[66]

Irrational creatures like plants and animals do not need virtue in order to fulfill their natural inclinations; we do. Virtue must be laboriously acquired, since we are not born with it. Even so, we are naturally drawn to acquire it, in the sense that without it, we are thwarted and diminished; our lives used up in smoke and spume, at best enjoying only caricatures of friendship, love, and wisdom. Irrational creatures do not have these things either, but there is a difference: They do not feel the lack. The only mode of flourishing possible to a *rational* creature is bound up with the exercise of virtue.

---

[1] *Both ways, however, are imperfect, and to a certain extent destroyed, in the wicked; because in them the natural inclination to virtue is corrupted by vicious habits, and, moreover, the natural knowledge of good is darkened by passions and habits of sin.* [2] *But in the good both ways are found more perfect: because in them, besides the natural knowledge of good,*	In those who are evil, neither of these modes is completely carried out – in fact, both are to some degree corrupted. For their natural knowledge of good is made dark and obscure by sinful passions and habits, and their natural inclination to virtue is twisted by acquired inclinations to vice. But in those who are good, it is just the opposite – both modes are carried out

---

[65] Aristotle, *Nicomachean Ethics*, Book 2, Chapter 1, trans. W.D. Ross (public domain).
[66] Thomas Aquinas, *Commentary on Aristotle's Nicomachean Ethics*, Book 2, Lecture 1, trans. C.J. Litzinger, O.P., rev. ed. (Notre Dame, IN: Dumb Ox Books, 1993), p. 85.

there is the added knowledge of faith and wisdom; [3] *and again, besides the natural inclination to good, there is the added motive of grace and virtue.*	more fully. For their natural knowledge of good is supplemented by the knowledge of faith and wisdom, and their natural inclination to it is supplemented by the stirring of grace and virtue.

[1] The term "habit" can refer to any kind of disposition or inclination. In this case St. Thomas is thinking of bad dispositions, which, like good ones, are built up by exercise: *Habitum vitiosum*, vicious or faulty habits, and *habitus peccatorum*, sinful habits. When he says both modes of rule by eternal law are to some extent destroyed in the wicked, he may be thinking of St. Paul's chilling description of pagan life. Although the pagans knew God, they did not acknowledge Him; consequently, "they became futile in their thinking and their senseless minds were darkened." Having dropped their minds' anchors in futility, they lost their bodies to futility as well, for the mind and the body are connected: God "gave them up in the lusts of their hearts to impurity, to the dishonoring of their bodies among themselves."[67]

[2] Wisdom and faith strengthen the rule of eternal law by adding to the *knowledge* of good. The former is knowledge of the first and highest causes of all things, those that explain everything else. The latter, which is imparted by Divine grace, is also is directed to the First Truth, but it refers to those things to which the mind assents because they are revealed by God.[68]

[3] Virtue and grace strengthen the rule of eternal law by supplementing *the inward inclination* to good. Virtue is the disposition to perform those acts that are good in themselves and that make us good; some virtues may be acquired by the exercise of our natural powers, others must be infused by grace, and all are assisted by grace. Grace, in turn, is the undeserved gift of God, which among other things instills into us the spiritual dispositions that move us to the supernatural good which transcends all that can be achieved by our natural powers.[69]

---

[67] Romans 1:21,24 (RSV-CE).
[68] I-II, Q. 57, Art. 2; II-II, Q. 1, Art. 1.
[69] I-II, Q. 55, Arts. 1, 3, 4; Q. 110, Arts. 2–3.

[1] *Accordingly, the good are perfectly subject to the eternal law, as always acting according to it: whereas the wicked are subject to the eternal law, imperfectly as to their actions, indeed, since both their knowledge of good, and their inclination thereto, are imperfect;* [2] *but this imperfection on the part of action is supplied on the part of passion, in so far as they suffer what the eternal law decrees concerning them, according as they fail to act in harmony with that law.* [3] *Hence Augustine says (De Lib. Arb. i, 15): "I esteem that the righteous act according to the eternal law"; and (De Catech. Rud. xviii): "Out of the just misery of the souls which deserted Him, God knew how to furnish the inferior parts of His creation with most suitable laws."*[70]

So, good people are ruled fully by eternal law in the sense that they always act as it directs. Regarding bad people, though, we must make a distinction. What they *do* is not fully ruled by eternal law, because both their knowledge of good and their inclination to good are defective, just as we have been explaining. But what *happens* to them makes up the gap, because they certainly suffer the penalties that eternal law decrees about violations.

The same distinction between the two senses of being ruled by eternal law was familiar to St. Augustine. For in *On Freedom of the Will*, he says that the righteous *follow* the eternal law – and in *On Catechizing the Uninstructed* he says that God knew how to make suitable laws for souls who desert Him, that is, who *violate* the eternal law.

[1]　Subjection "as to their actions" is the mode of subjection to eternal law that Objection 2 threw in St. Thomas's face. The Objector reasoned that since the wicked are not obedient to eternal law, they must not be ruled by it. St. Thomas concedes that they are not obedient to it, but points out that this is only one of the two senses of being ruled by it.

[2]　In some contexts, the word "feeling" or "emotion" can substitute for the term "passion," but the meaning of the latter term is much broader. Etymologically, it is related to the word "passive," for a passion is not something we cause to happen, but something that happens to us because of someone or something else. This is why the sufferings of Christ are called His Passion. Here, of course, St. Thomas is speaking of the passion of *punishment*, for punishment too is not something done, but something suffered.

According to St. Thomas, one might be said to experience a passion in several different senses. In one sense, I merely receive something, for

[70] Correcting the quotation marks in the English translation.

example a feeling. In another sense, I receive one thing but lose something else, as when my appetite drives me toward one thing and away from another. The latter sense includes two cases, because I may be either fleeing from something evil toward something good, or fleeing from something good toward something evil. (I-II, Q. 22, Art. 1; I-II, Q. 25, Art. 4.)

Consider, for example, a case discussed in Talmud that is introduced with the remark, "A man once conceived a passion for a certain woman, and his heart was consumed by his burning desire." The passion was brought about him by the woman's beauty. Though it drove him toward her, it drove him away from sexual purity, and also from life, because he was wasting away.[71] The protestation of this sort of passion is the mainstay of the variety of seducer who says he will die if he has no relief; as Elvis Presley once crooned in days of old, "tomorrow will be too late."[72]

[3]   The point of this pair of quotations is to show that the righteous follow the eternal law, but that those who desert God suffer its penalties for violation. Each is subject to eternal law, but each in a different sense.

The first quotation, from *On Free Choice of the Will*, is actually a paraphrase. The speaker is not St. Augustine himself, but Evodius (though St. Augustine immediately agrees with him), and he refers not to the righteous but to the blessed (though they are righteous too): *Nam beatos illos ob amorem ipsorum aeternorum sub aeterna lege agere existimo*, roughly "I reckon that the blessed follow the eternal law for the love of things eternal."

---

[1] *Reply to Objection 1. This saying of the Apostle may be understood in two ways. First, so that a man is said to be under the law, through being pinned down thereby, against his will, as by a load. Hence, on the same passage a gloss says that "he is under the law, who refrains from evil deeds, through fear of punishment threatened by the law, and not from love of virtue."*

Reply to Objection 1. There are two valid ways to interpret St. Paul's comment that those who are led by the Spirit are not under the law. First, he may be thinking of being "under" the law as we would think of being "under" a heavy burden, so that being under the law means being unwillingly weighed down. One of the commentators has this sense in mind when he writes that a man is "under" the law if he holds back from

---

[71] Babylonian Talmud, Tractate Sanhedrin, Folio 75a.
[72] Elvis Presley, "It's Now or Never," words and music by Aaron Schroeder and Wally Gold, *Elvis' Golden Records Volume 3* (RCA Victor, 1963).

[2] *In this way the spiritual man is not under the law, because he fulfill the law willingly, through charity which is poured into his heart by the Holy Ghost. [3] Secondly, it can be understood as meaning that the works of a man, who is led by the Holy Ghost, are the works of the Holy Ghost rather than his own. [4] Therefore, since the Holy Ghost is not under the law, as neither is the Son, as stated above (4, ad 2); it follows that such works, in so far as they are of the Holy Ghost, are not under the law. [5] The Apostle witnesses to this when he says (2 Corinthians 3:17): "Where the Spirit of the Lord is, there is liberty."*

wrongdoing only through fear of punishment rather than love of virtue. Someone who is led by the Spirit is certainly not under the law in this sense, for through the love the Spirit pours into his heart, he does what the law commands not unwillingly, but willingly.

St. Paul may also mean that when a man is led by the Holy Spirit, his works are not his, but the Holy Spirit's. But of course God's works are not *under* the law, as though God and His law were two different things; He *is* His law. In Article 4, we explained this point with reference to the Second Person of the Trinity, the Son, and it is equally true in reference to the Third Person of the Trinity, the Holy Spirit. St. Paul testifies to this truth when he writes in his second letter to the Corinthians, "Where the Spirit of the Lord is, there is freedom."

[1]   The Objector assumes that when St. Paul speaks of being "under the law," he means simply being ruled by it. Actually, St. Paul seems to be thinking chiefly of being ruled by it unwillingly, through fear rather than love, so that obedience is burdensome.

[2]   The will of the man who is led by the Holy Spirit is transformed by the infusion of Divine love. He is certainly ruled by the law; here St. Thomas might have quoted St. Paul's question to the Church in Rome, "What then? Are we to sin because we are not under law but under grace? By no means!"[73] But what the man formerly did unwillingly, he now does willingly. So this is one of the possible meanings of St. Paul's statement about not being "under the law."

[3]   Insofar as the transformation of the man's will is the work of the Holy Spirit, the acts to which his transformed will leads him can also be attributed to the Holy Spirit.

[73] Romans 6:15 (RSV-CE).

[4] God is not *under* His law as though it were something separate from and higher than Himself; He is *identical* with it, just as He is identical with His love, wisdom, power, and so on. In Article 2, St. Thomas made this point with regard to the Second Person of the Trinity, the Son, but it applies equally to the Third Person of the Trinity, the Holy Spirit. Since the Holy Spirit is not *under* the law, a man wholly led by Holy Spirit is not *under* it either. He is free, not in the sense that he does not follow it, but in the sense that when he does follow it, he is following the impulse of his own heart – of a will that is united with God. So this is the other possible meaning of St. Paul's statement about not being "under the law."

[5] The fact that the Holy Spirit is not *under* the law, as though it were an authority separate from and higher than Himself, is confirmed by what St. Paul writes in his second letter to the Church at Corinth. The eternal law is *His* law – His own eternal Wisdom, considered as governing the universe. Whatever He does, then, He does not under external constraint, but by His own nature; He is free.

---

[1] *Reply to Objection 2. The prudence of the flesh cannot be subject to the law of God as regards action; since it inclines to actions contrary to the Divine law: yet it is subject to the law of God, as regards passion; since it deserves to suffer punishment according to the law of Divine justice.* [2] *Nevertheless in no man does the prudence of the flesh dominate so far as to destroy the whole good of his nature: and consequently there remains in man the inclination to act in accordance with the eternal law. For we have seen above (85, 2) that sin does not destroy entirely the good of nature.*

Reply to Objection 2. Let us distinguish between being ruled by God's law with respect to what we do, and being ruled by it with respect to what we suffer – between being subject in our actions, and being subject in the consequences of our actions. What St. Paul calls the "wisdom of the flesh" is insubordinate to God's law in the first way, because it pushes us into violation. Even so, it is ruled by His law in the second way, since it cannot escape the just punishment that His law decrees for such violation.

Concerning the first point, let us not misunderstand. No one is so completely dominated by the outlook of the flesh that the natural inclination to follow the eternal law is entirely destroyed. This natural good remains in him, even though obstructed from fulfillment. The inability of sin to completely destroy the natural good has been thoroughly explained in I-II, Question 85, Article 2.

---

[1]   Our fallen appetites have, so to speak, a mind of their own, contrary to the Mind of God. It would be absurd to say that they are ruled by eternal law in the sense of obedience, because they are not obedient; this is the grain of truth in the Objector's position. What he overlooks is that in another sense, they are utterly ruled by eternal law. Their very obstinacy dooms them to futility, bitterness, and frustration.

[2]   Although sin has obstructed the fulfillment of man's nature, not even sin can pull it up by the root. For additional discussion of this deeply interesting point, see the online *Companion to the Commentary.*

---

[1] *Reply to Objection 3. A thing is maintained in the end and moved towards the end by one and the same cause: thus gravity which makes a heavy body rest in the lower place is also the cause of its being moved thither.* [2] *We therefore reply that as it is according to the eternal law that some deserve happiness, others unhappiness, so is it by the eternal law that some are maintained in a happy state, others in an unhappy state.* [3] *Accordingly both the blessed and the damned are under the eternal law.*	Reply to Objection 3. The Objector speaks as though deserving something and receiving it could be separated from each other. Not so. The very same cause is always at work when a thing moves toward what it tends to and when it stays there. Gravity, for example, both causes a heavy body to seek the lowest place and causes it to rest there. The same principle applies here. Thus, we answer the Objector that the very same eternal law that causes us to deserve final happiness or unhappiness also causes us to rest in it. So the blessed in heaven, and the damned in hell, are under the eternal law after all.

---

[1]   Gravity makes a boulder roll down the mountainside, and gravity makes it rest when it reaches the bottom. This illustrates a general principle: The influence that brings things to their final state is the same one that keeps them there.

[2]   The Objector had argued that if one is already receiving something, then he can no longer be said to deserve it. St. Thomas points out that this is absurd; just like water running downhill and pooling at the bottom, the cause that moves him toward his end and the cause that keeps him there are one and the same. He deserved eternal separation from God for violating eternal law, and he receives eternal separation from God for the same reason.

[3]   The blessed sought God, but the damned rejected Him; the former obeyed the eternal law, but the latter rebelled against it. Yet both

experience the consequences that eternal law decrees, and so both are under the law.

For further reflection on the preceding section of the *Treatise on Law*, the online *Companion to the Commentary*, accessible via the Resources link at the book's catalogue webpage, includes a discussion of the following topics:

THE "INWARD MOTIVE PRINCIPLE"

THE INDESTRUCTIBILITY OF THE GOOD OF NATURE

Before Reading Question 94

St. Thomas's thinking epitomizes the classical natural law tradition. But exactly what does this statement mean – what distinguishes classical natural law philosophy from other philosophies that speak of natural law, for example, the early modern natural rights thinkers?

The term "classical" is often misunderstood. Is classical music called classical because it is the oldest kind of music? No, for music was unthinkably ancient before classical music was developed. Is it so named because it is the best kind of music? No, for people may disagree about which music is best and yet agree about which music is classical. Because it is obsolete? No, for a classical tradition can remain vibrantly alive, continuing to develop and give birth to new work. The proper meaning of the term "classical" is none of these. Rather it signifies, "Here is the body of work that sets the standard for all subsequent achievement." This holds for classical traditions in all fields, not just music. A classical tradition of thought might not pose all the important questions, might not answer all those that they do pose, and might not give the right answers, but it sets the standard for *what sort of things count* as good questions and good answers. So even if one rejects a classical tradition, one is most unwise to ignore it.

Classical natural law theories share a conviction that the most basic truths of right and wrong – I do not say all the details – are not only right for everyone, but at some level also known to everyone, by the ordinary exercise of reason. They are an heirloom of the family of man. Of course, to say that they are at some level known to everyone is not to say that they are consciously admitted by everyone, and there's the rub. Any moral theory that fails to take account of excuses, rationalizations, and self-deceptions will badly misunderstand the human condition. Even so, the classical thinkers are convinced that natural law is real, not just that it seems real to them. They believe that to mature minds, the thing itself is obvious, even though the theories about it may not be obvious to most people at all.

Classical natural law theories call natural law *law* because it has the same qualities as all law, qualities that, taken together, generate real obligation. They call natural law *natural* because it is embedded in the pattern of our being, a pattern that is not blind or mechanical, but imbued with rational meaning.

Although even most nonclassical theories of natural law agree about the content of the moral basics – about honoring parents, not stealing, not murdering, and so forth – the various kinds of natural law thinkers explore the roots and branches of this content in different ways. Classical theories are "thick" theories, in the sense that their manner of exploration weaves together at least four different kinds of consideration.

The first of these considerations is the deep structure of the deliberating human mind, as distinguished from patterns of thought that take root in the mind merely through the way we are taught. Apart from this deep structure, no teaching could take root anyway; seeds require soil in which to germinate. We might call this deep structure "deep conscience"; in keeping with his predecessors, St. Thomas uses the technical term *synderesis*. As we will see, he views the foundations of the deliberative mind as analogous to the foundations of the reflective mind – in other words, the deep structure of reasoning about what to do is analogous to the deep structure of reasoning about how things are. It is also crucial to understand that these first principles are not just "regulative hypotheses," à la Immanuel Kant, or ways of thinking that we cannot escape, à la Friedrich Nietzsche, but actually true. The mind is designed to put us in touch with reality.

Second is our design, our teleology – that is, the deep structure of the faculties and inclinations *subordinate* to mind, for we are not bodiless intellects like the angels, but rational animals. Only a being with a rational mind can be subject to true law. Yet although for the angelic nature, natural law is *nothing but* the laws of the mind, for us things stand differently. St. Thomas never forgets that our kind of animality is rational, but neither does he forget that our kind of rationality is animal.

Third is recognition of the system of natural consequences. Of course, some consequences of our actions are not natural, but merely adventitious; for example, a dog may bite me just because I look like the man who gave him a beating the other day. But other results of our actions are connected with the kinds of beings that we are. Habitual drunkards develop liver trouble. Habitual adulterers lose the faculty for marriage. Liars find that they must tell more lies to cover up the ones they have already told, and eventually start lying to themselves. To call attention to the natural consequences of our acts is not "consequentialism"; a consequentialist is someone who thinks that if you can prevent all the bad results from happening, the act becomes all right. By contrast, classical natural law thinkers view the system of natural consequences as an index to the system of natural purposes and meanings. Besides, though efforts to dodge natural consequences may meet with a certain limited success, they inevitably have bad consequences of their own. Simply because the birth control pill so effectively prevents conception, it changed attitudes and thereby ushered in an era of out-of-wedlock pregnancies.

Fourth is the recognition that the source and authority of all these structures and patterns is God. From His uncreated goodness all of their own meaning and goodness takes its origin. Insofar as these matters are contemplated in the light of Revelation, we have Divine law. But insofar as they are contemplated in the cooperating light of natural reason, we have natural law. I speak of "cooperation" because according to the classical tradition, faith and reason are not antagonists, but allies. Divine law and natural law proceed from the same Creator, and they reflect His mind in complementary ways. Just because of this complementarity, it should not be surprising that Revelation confirms all four of the considerations we have been discussing.[1] For example, St. Paul alludes to the first consideration in Romans 2:14-15, which speaks of a law written on the heart, and to much the same effect, Psalm 4:7 (which St. Thomas prefers) has the inspired poet saying that the light of God's face is imprinted upon us.

These four considerations may be viewed as four testimonies to moral reality, embedded in the structure of our nature. Placing the last one first, we have the witness of designedness as such; the witness of deep conscience, which is the design of our practical intellect; the witness of the rest of our design; and the witness of natural consequences, which is caused

---

[1] See J. Budziszewski, "Isaiah, David, and Paul on the Natural Law," in *What We Can't Not Know: A Guide*, rev. ed. (San Francisco: Ignatius Press, 2011).

by our design. I use the term "design" advisedly, not to suggest that we are mechanisms, but that we are fearfully and wonderfully made.

By contrast with classical, "thick" theories of natural law, nonclassical theories are "thin." They fail to weave all four of these considerations together, either because they reject some of them, or because they emphasize some at the expense of the others. The history of these thin theories has been complex and paradoxical. Often, considerations that have been pushed out the front door creep back in through the back door. For instance, a thinker who denies the idea of *synderesis* may go on speaking in ways that make no sense apart from it.

The American founding is an intriguing mixed case, because although the fashioners of the new republic drew from and admired some of the thinkers of the classical natural law tradition, even so the Enlightenment varieties of natural law theory best known to them had been substantially thinned and flattened. The Enlightenment thinkers said they believed in natural law, but they ripped out most of its theoretical equipment, then scrambled to plug the gaping holes that resulted. For example, to take the place of natural teleology, they proposed a thoroughly unnatural state of nature and a thoroughly unhistorical social contract. Although such ideas inspired revolutions, they came over time to seem more and more implausible. Eventually, the very idea of natural law was dismissed by great swaths of the intellectual class – with incalculable harm to the good institutions based upon it.

Although, as with every Question, the commentary on Question 94 is self-contained, it raises numerous themes worthy of deeper investigation, which I take up at greater than usual length in the online *Companion to the Commentary.*

St. Thomas's Prologue to Question 94:
Of the Natural Law

TEXT	PARAPHRASE
[1] *We must now consider the natural law; concerning which there are six points of inquiry:*	The next kind of law to be investigated in detail is the natural law. This part of our study requires six queries. We
[2] *(1) What is the natural law?*	ask in Article 1 about the *essence* of
[3] *(2) What are the precepts of the natural law?*	natural law, what it *is*; in Article 2, what precepts or commands it includes; in Article 3, whether it commands us to
[4] *(3) Whether all acts of virtue are prescribed by the natural law?*	perform every virtuous act; in Article 4, whether it is the same in each person; in
[5] *(4) Whether the natural law is the same in all?*	Article 5, whether in any way or in any sense it can be changed; and in Article
[6] *(5) Whether it is changeable?*	6, whether man's knowledge of it can be blotted out.
[7] *(6) Whether it can be abolished from the heart of man?*	

[1]   The natural law has already been touched on in Question 91, but only enough to show that it really is one of the kinds of law. The six articles of Question 94 develop its character more fully.

[2]   At first this question may seem superfluous, for in Question 91, Article 2, St. Thomas has defined the natural law as the "participation of the eternal law in the rational creature." He has no intention of plowing that ground again; this time he is asking the narrower question of what sort of thing this participation is in us. In particular, is it some kind of "habit," some deep-seated disposition to act in a particular way?

[3]   If we listed not only most general precepts of the natural law, but also the detailed precepts that flow from them, the list might have no end. As we are soon to see, however, St. Thomas offers not so much a list, but an approach to the generation of a list; he shows us the *root* precepts from which all the others flow. The closest he comes to providing a conventional enumeration is in Question 100, Article 1, where he asks whether all of the moral precepts of the Old Law are included in the natural law. (He concludes that they are.)

[4]   Since virtues are in a sense "in" us, just as the natural law is in a sense "in" us, we need to investigate their relation. Notice that St. Thomas is not asking whether the natural law commands us to *acquire every virtue* – for example, to be prudent, just, and so forth – but whether it commands us to *perform every act* of that virtue – every prudent deed, every just deed, and so forth.

[5]   Could different persons be subject to different natural laws? Could it ever make sense for someone to say that a particular natural law is "right for you, but wrong for me"? What if someone were to say, "Your conscience may tell you 'Never murder, but mine doesn't tell me that"?

[6]   In the sense that relativists would take this question – the sense in which it was taken by the "someone" just above – the answer is no. But if the idea of a "change" in the natural law is properly analyzed, it turns out that the answer is much more subtle.

[7]   The question is not whether, say, murder could ever cease to be wrong, but whether anyone could be utterly devoid of the *knowledge* that murder is wrong.

For further reflection on the preceding section of the *Treatise on Law,* the online *Companion to the Commentary*, accessible via the Resources link at the book's catalogue webpage, includes a discussion of the following topics:

THE ORGANIZATION OF QUESTION 94
NATURAL LAW AND NATURAL RIGHTS

Question 94, Article 1:
Whether the Natural Law Is a Habit?

TEXT	PARAPHRASE
Whether the natural law is a habit?	Is the natural law a *habitus,* a "habit" or disposition of the soul, to act in a certain way? Is it just *something we tend to do,* rather than a rule and measure for what we do?

The Latin word *habitus* has a wider range than the English word "habit." One difference is that we use the English term especially for acquired dispositions to bodily movements that we perform without thinking about them, like shuffling our feet when we walk, or muttering when we are performing mental calculations. The Latin term, though, can be used not only for acquired but also for natural dispositions, not only dispositions to bodily movements but also dispositions to "movements" of the soul, not only movements to what we do without thinking but also movements of thought.

---

[1] *Objection 1. It would seem that the natural law is a habit. Because, as the Philosopher says (Ethic. ii, 5), "there are three things in the soul: power, habit, and passion."* [2] *But the natural law is not one of the soul's powers: nor is it one of the passions; as we may see by going through them one by one. Therefore the natural law is a habit.*

Objection 1. Apparently, the natural law really is a "habit." For if it is not a habit, then it must be either a power or a passion, because as Aristotle points out, habit, power and passion are the only kinds of things that the soul contains. Obviously, it is not a power. If we run down the list of the soul's passions, which can be worked out by analysis, we can see that it is not a passion either. By elimination, it must be a habit.

---

[1] What are these three principles of action, and in what sense are they "in" the soul? The *powers* of the soul are its natural capacities, for instance, that it is able to reason; these are "in" the soul in the sense that they pertain to its essence. Its *passions* are the various ways in which it can respond passively to an external agent; these are "in" it in the sense that they can be received or lost. Certain passions involve receiving something without losing anything, as when we receive feeling or understanding – these are "in" the soul essentially. Others involve receiving one thing but losing another, as when we receive sorrow but lose tranquillity – these are "in" it only indirectly, by way of its union with the body. Finally, the *habits* of the soul are the ways in which it is disposed either to *be* a certain way (for example, by having the habit of cheerfulness), or to *do* something in a certain way (for example, by having the habit of honesty). The Objector has in mind the latter sense. Habits are "in" the soul in the sense that they are its own, although, in a secondary sense, they are "in" the body through which the soul acts.[2]

---

[2] I, Q. 77, Art. 6; I-II, Q. 22, Art. 1; I-II, Q. 50, Art. 1. The term "habit" can also be used in other ways that do not concern us here; I-II, Q. 49, Arts. 1–2.

[2]   The Objector asserts that natural law is neither a property of the soul (a power), nor a response of the soul to an external agent (a passion). Therefore, it must be a disposition of the soul to act in a certain way (a habit).

Objection 2. Further, Basil [Damascene, De Fide Orth. iv, 22 says that the conscience or "synderesis is the law of our mind"; which can only apply to the natural law. But the "synderesis" is a habit, as was shown in the I, 79, 12. Therefore the natural law is a habit.	Objection 2. Moreover, as St. Basil of Caesarea writes in his homily *On Faith,* conscience, in the sense of synderesis, "is the law of our mind." The term *synderesis* must refer to natural law. But as we showed earlier, *synderesis* is a habit; so, assuming Basil is right, natural law must be a habit.

Synderesis, which St. Thomas has discussed much earlier in the *Summa,*[3] is one of the several different things contemporary people mean by "conscience," but which St. Thomas carefully distinguishes. It is the natural disposition or "habit" by which the mind understands the first principles of practical reason, the necessary starting points of all deliberation about what to do. *Conscientia* is the act of judgment that applies it. Although the distinction between *synderesis* and *conscientia* was already widely accepted in St. Thomas's day, no consensus about how it should be drawn had yet been reached. For this reason, the terminology had not yet stabilized either, for some thinkers used the term *synderesis* for what others called *conscientia,* and vice versa. This is probably why the Objector uses both terms; when he says "*conscientia* or *synderesis,*" he means "*conscientia* in the sense of *synderesis,*" following St. Thomas's analysis of the two things earlier in the *Summa.* There were, by the way, several distinguished Basils, but the Basil to whom the Objector refers is the one who was bishop of Caesarea.

Much has been made of the distinction between St. Thomas's and Plato's hypotheses about what is going on when we recognize first principles. Where St. Thomas speaks of *synderesis* or deep conscience, Plato speaks of *anamnesis* or remembering.[4] The former thinker holds that we are exercising a natural tendency built into the mind; the latter maintains that we are literally remembering something that we learned before we were born. Plato's hypothesis has two great weaknesses. Not only does it require us to believe that the soul existed before the present life, but

[3] I, Q. 79, Art. 12.
[4] See his dialogue *Meno.*

it also leaves obscure how the soul learned in that life what it remembers in this one. For these reasons, St. Thomas's hypothesis seems rationally superior. Yet even though listening to deep conscience is not a literal remembering, it is often very much *like* remembering. So even though *anamnesis* is an incorrect theory, it has a certain value as a metaphor, just because it reminds us of the texture of the experience.

This suffices to understand the Objection, but the whole matter of conscience is so important that we return to it in several places. See Question 96, Article 4, in this *Commentary,* and see the discussion of the present Article in the online *Companion to the Commentary.*

[1] *Objection 3. Further, the natural law abides in man always, as will be shown further on (6).* [2] *But man's reason, which the law regards, does not always think about the natural law. Therefore the natural law is not an act, but a habit.*	Objection 3. Still further, if we ask whether natural law falls into the category of an act or a habit of acting, it is certainly not an act. For consider two facts about it: First, it persists in us; second, that which thinks about it is our reason. Now if it were an act, then since it does persist in us, reason would be thinking about it all the time. Plainly, this is not the case, so it must be not an act, but a habit of acting.

[1] The Objector – who, as St. Thomas's alter ego, knows what St. Thomas is going to say later – alludes to St. Thomas's subsequent argument that it is impossible for the general principles of the natural law to be blotted out from the heart of man.

[2] I always *know* the first principles of practical reason; if I did not always know that good is to be done and evil avoided, how could I have any reason for action whatsoever? But that is far from saying that I am always revolving these first principles in my mind, as though I were to begin every deliberation by thinking, "Let's see, good is to be done and evil avoided. And so ..."

[1] *On the contrary, Augustine says (De Bono Conjug. xxi) that "a habit is that whereby something is done when necessary."* [2] *But such is not the natural law: since it is in infants and in the damned who cannot act by it. Therefore the natural law is not a habit.*	On the other hand, as St. Augustine suggests in *On the Good of Marriage,* "a habit is that by which we do a certain act whenever we need to." But this is not true of the natural law, since even though it is in infants and in the damned, they cannot act by it. So if Augustine's definition of "habit" is correct, natural law cannot be a habit.

[1]   Sometimes, when put into words, even a matter of common sense sounds rather odd, and that is the case here. The reasoning is quite simple, however, and works like this: How am I able to walk? By means of a habit – in this case, an acquired one – of walking. Generalizing, a habit is that which enables us to do something. Which enables us to do it when? Whenever we need to.

[2]   The reasoning continues like this: If a habit enables us to do something when we need to, then we can always act by it (even if we do not always do so). Yet if we can always act by natural law, then it is not in infants and the damned, because they *cannot* act by it – children because they have not yet reached the age of reason, the damned because their will is irremediably corrupt. Yet it has traditionally been held that the natural law *is* in some way in both infants and the damned. So natural law is not a habit.

---

[1] *I answer that, A thing may be called a habit in two ways. First, properly and essentially: and thus the natural law is not a habit. For it has been stated above (90, 1, ad 2) that the natural law is something appointed by reason, just as a proposition is a work of reason.* [2] *Now that which a man does is not the same as that whereby he does it: for he makes a becoming speech by the habit of grammar. Since then a habit is that by which we act, a law cannot be a habit properly and essentially.*

Here is my response. We must distinguish two different senses in which something may be called a habit. Taking the term "habit" in the strict sense, natural law is not a habit. The reason for this conclusion is that natural law, like a proposition, is something determined by reason. Now the habit by which we act is not the same as the act itself – for example, the grammatical habit by which we speak is not the same as a grammatical utterance. So if natural law is an *act* of reason, it cannot strictly be called a habit.

---

[1]   The critical point is that to say that the natural law is appointed by reason is to say that it is an *act* of reason – something in which rationality is *actualized*.

[2]   If natural law is an *act* of reason, then it cannot be the same as the habit by which the act is carried out. So natural law is not a habit in the strict sense.

[1] *Secondly, the term habit may be applied to that which we hold by a habit: thus faith may mean that which we hold by faith. And accordingly, since the precepts of the natural law are sometimes considered by reason actually, while sometimes they are in the reason only habitually, in this way the natural law may be called a habit.* [2] *Thus, in speculative matters, the indemonstrable principles are not the habit itself whereby we hold those principles, but are the principles the habit of which we possess.*

But in another, weaker sense, something which is not strictly a habit may be called a habit just because we possess or hold onto it habitually. An example of this weaker sense of the term may be found in theology, for the term "faith" may be applied either to the habit of faith itself, or to the things that we habitually believe. Now this distinction applies to the precepts of the natural law too. Even though we are not always thinking about them, we are always able to do so – even though they are not always "in" reason actually, they persist "in" reason habitually. By the way, the same distinction holds in theoretical reason, for though its indemonstrable principles are not themselves a habit, we do habitually possess them.

[1]   Notwithstanding what we have said above, can natural law be called a habit in a loose sense? The answer is "Yes." In the strict sense, the term "habit" refers only to the disposition that enables us to do something; but in a loose sense, it refers to the "something" that the habit enables us to do. Examples: *Walking* is a habit only in the loose sense, but the disposition we employ *in order* to walk is a habit in the strict sense. The *content* of faith is a habit only in the loose sense, but *faith itself* is a habit in the strong sense. The *actual precepts* of the natural law are a habit only in the loose sense, but *synderesis,* the disposition of the practical intellect by which we understand them, is a habit in the strict sense.

[2]   The word "thus" is used here merely to introduce a parallel, rather than a conclusion. Just as we distinguish the indemonstrable starting points of *practical* reason from the disposition that enables us to grasp them, so we must distinguish the indemonstrable starting points of *theoretical* reason from the disposition that enables us to grasp them.

Reply to Objection 1. The Philosopher proposes there to discover the genus of virtue; and since it is evident that virtue is a principle of action, he mentions only those things

Reply to Objection 1. Aristotle is right, but the Objector has misunderstood Aristotle. That thinker is trying to determine what kind of thing virtue is, and he begins by observing that it is a principle of action. So he is not listing *all* of the things in the

which are principles of human acts, viz. powers, habits and passions. But there are other things in the soul besides these three: there are acts; thus "to will" is in the one that wills; again, things known are in the knower; moreover its own natural properties are in the soul, such as immortality and the like.

soul, but only the things in the soul that are principles of action. Though powers, habits, and passions exhaust the soul's principles of action, they certainly do not exhaust the things "in" the soul. Acts, for example, are in the soul – the act of willing is in the willer, the act of knowing is in the knower. Moreover, the soul's own natural properties, such as immortality, are in the soul. So it is not true that everything in the soul must be either a power, a habit, or a passion; nor does it follow that natural law must be one of these three things.

The paraphrase almost entirely satisfies the purposes of the commentary. Only one point is a bit puzzling. St. Thomas mentions the soul's natural properties as examples of things *other than* its powers, habits, and passions; yet at an earlier point in the *Summa* he defined the soul's powers *as* its natural properties.[5] The solution to the puzzle is that there he was thinking of those powers of the soul that are principles of action (such as reason), but here he is thinking of those powers of the soul that are not principles of action (such as immortality).

Reply to Objection 2. "Synderesis" is said to be the law of our mind, because it is a habit containing the precepts of the natural law, which are the first principles of human actions.

Reply to Objection 2. The reason Basil calls *synderesis* the law of our mind is that it is the habit *by which we know* the commands of the natural law, which are the starting points of what we humans do. This is not the same as saying that the commands *themselves* are a habit.

The key to this passage is found in Question 90, Article 1, which shows that law is above all an ordinance of reason. The inbuilt tendency by which reason is able to declare these ordinances is *synderesis*, and the ordinances that it thereby declares are the precepts of natural law.

Reply to Objection 3. This argument proves that the natural law is held habitually; and this is granted.

Reply to Objection 3. The Objector's argument does not show that the natural law *is* a habit, as he thinks. Rather it shows that we know the natural law *by means of* a habit, and this is true.

5 I, Q. 77, Art. 1, ad 5; I-II, Q. 110, Art. 4, ad 3.

The Objector had pointed out that although the natural law is always "in" us, we are not always thinking about it. From this, he drew the conclusion that natural law is not an act, but a habit. St. Thomas says this conclusion is *almost* correct. What the Objector should have concluded is that although the natural law itself is not a habit, it persists in the mind *by means* of a habit – just as explained in the *respondeo*.

[1] *To the argument advanced in the contrary sense we reply that sometimes a man is unable to make use of that which is in him habitually, on account of some impediment: thus, on account of sleep, a man is unable to use the habit of science. [2] In like manner, through the deficiency of his age, a child cannot use the habit of understanding of principles, or the natural law, which is in him habitually.*	Reply to the Argument to the Contrary. From the fact that a man has a habit, it does not follow that he is always able to exercise the habit, for sometimes an obstacle intervenes. For example, the mind of a sleeping man *has* the deep dispositional structure that normally enables him to consider the dependence of conclusions on premises, but because he is asleep, he cannot use it. In the same way, the mind of a child *has* the deep dispositional structure that will one day enable him to grasp first principles – or even the natural law – but because he has not yet reached the age of reason, he cannot yet actually grasp them.

[1]   The argument advanced in the contrary sense is the *sed contra*. In most cases, the *sed contra* not only opposes the gist of the objections, but also prepares the way for St. Thomas's own view. Here, though – as in Question 93, Article 4 – it needs a bit of tweaking. St. Thomas reads St. Augustine's statement that "a habit is that whereby something is done when necessary," not in the sense that "a habit is that whereby, whenever something needs to be done, *it is done without fail* (the sense in which the *sed contra* took it), but in the sense that "a habit is that whereby necessary things are done *when they are* done." True, some impediment may prevent a necessary thing from being done. Even so, he explains, *when it is* done, then the habit is what we exercise to do it.

[2]   The point St. Thomas is making could easily be misunderstood, for even the child *implicitly* responds to the first principles. Obviously the child seeks what seems good to him and avoids what seems evil to him, for otherwise he could have no motive for doing anything whatsoever. So isn't he "using" the first principle that good is to be done and evil avoided? No, because in the strictest sense, to "act" is to fully actualize these first principles. They cannot be *fully* actualized in the child because

they are principles of reason, and the child does not choose reflectively or with sound understanding. Because of the immaturity of his intellect, he often ends up pursuing things that seem good but are not really good, and avoiding things that seem evil but are not really evil. But don't adults do that too? Certainly, but when they do, they are to blame. By contrast, the child cannot help it.

In children, we hope, this condition is temporary. In the damned, it is permanent. For although they too desire to possess good and avoid evil, their minds and wills are frozen in the attitudes by which they chose to live on earth. Utterly set on those lower things that they insist on regarding as the highest things, they obstinately spurn even God Himself.

For further reflection on the preceding section of the *Treatise on Law*, the online *Companion to the Commentary*, accessible via the Resources link at the book's catalogue webpage, includes a discussion of the following topic:

CONSCIENCE, CONSCIENCE, AND CONSCIENCE

Question 94, Article 2:
Whether the Natural Law Contains Several Precepts, or Only One?

TEXT	PARAPHRASE
Whether the natural law contains several precepts, or only one?	Does the natural law contain a number of different commands, or a single master command from which everything we ought to do follows?

It is easy to misunderstand what this Article is driving at. No doubt natural law requires many different things at many different times. The question is whether at bottom, all these things are applications of a single overarching rule. The Objector thinks that they are.

[1] *Objection 1. It would seem that the natural law contains, not several precepts, but one only. For law is a kind of precept, as stated above (92, 2).* [2] *If therefore there were many precepts of the natural law, it would follow that there are also many natural laws.*	**Objection 1.** Apparently, the natural law contains only one general precept from which all more detailed conclusions flow. For as asserted in Question 92, Article 2, "every law belongs to the genus of precept." So if the natural law contained more than one general and fundamental precept, there would be more than one natural law – more than one true morality.

[1]   The Dominican Fathers translation slightly obscures the point of the Objection. In Question 92, Article 2, St. Thomas said was that every law is a *general* precept (*lex enim omnis praeceptum commune est*). The Objector paraphrases by saying that all law belongs to the *genus* of precept (*lex enim continetur in genere praecepti*). Having read their Aristotle – or at least having read Question 90, Article 1 – the "beginners" of St. Thomas's day would remember that all of the elements of the same genus share the same root, which serves as their governing ordinance and measuring rod. So the Objector reasons that the diverse requirements of the natural law are merely different applications of a single general command.

In our own day, an example of this view is the doctrine called Act Utilitarianism. In the Act Utilitarian view, the only real moral rule is "Do whatever brings about the greatest possible pleasure for society." The view has egregious consequences. It implies that so-called secondary precepts, such as "Never murder," have no real authority, because they do not infallibly maximize aggregate pleasure.

[2]   The Objector is worrying, "If there were more than one ultimate precept, then how could they harmonize? How could morality have unity? Wouldn't it be a chaos?" In fact, chaos is just what some contemporary people think morality is. They believe that "dirty hands" are inevitable – that to fulfill one moral precept, one must often violate another – a view that both the Objector and St. Thomas oppose.

---

[1] *Objection 2. Further, the natural law is consequent to human nature.* [2] *But human nature, as a whole, is one; though, as to its parts, it is manifold.* [3] *Therefore, either there is but one precept of the law of nature, on account of the unity of nature as a whole; or there are many, by reason of the number of parts of human nature.* [4] *The result would be that even things relating to the inclination of the concupiscible faculty belong to the natural law.*

Objection 2. Moreover, the natural law is what it is because human nature is what it is. Now human nature has many parts; yet it also has a fundamental unity. Consequently, there are two possibilities. Perhaps, because of the unity of human nature as a whole, everything we ought to do flows from a single general precept; or perhaps, because of the diversity of human nature's parts, the various things we ought to do flow from different general precepts. The problem with the latter hypothesis is that if it is true, then natural law would command us to follow even our base desires, which cannot be the case. Consequently, the former hypothesis must be true. But in that case, natural law contains not several precepts, but only one.

[1]   The Objector means that in some sense natural law results from human nature; the nature God has given us is the cause, and the natural law that binds us is its effect. To be sure, some things could never be lawful for any created nature. It could never be lawful to oppose good or hate God, for instance. Yet many duties might be different if our nature were different.[6] Suppose, for instance, the Creator had fashioned us to procreate by dividing, like amoebas, instead of by sexual union. Then there would not be a duty of fidelity to spouses, because there would not be any spouses.

[2]   By the "parts" of human nature, the Objector has in mind such things as concupiscibility, the power to be stirred up to pursue what our senses find delectable and avoid what they find harmful, and irascibility, the power to be aroused to resist what threatens or hinders the delectable.[7]

[3]   The underlying issue is whether these "parts" of human nature are what are called integral parts, as walls and roof are parts of a house, or what are called potential parts, abilities that deal with certain secondary matters but lack the power of the whole. If they are potential parts, then a human being possesses substantial unity; he is a single subsistent thing with a single nature. In this case the law of nature has unity too. If they are integral parts, as some thinkers have regarded them, then a human being does not possess substantial unity. He is not a single thing with a single nature; each of his parts has its own "nature." In this case each of them has its own law of nature.

[4]   The phrase, "The result would be ...," should be read, "But this cannot be the case, because its result would be ..." Why is the result intolerable? Because if each part of us has its own "law of nature," then even greed and lust are a natural law. True, while the law of nature *of the concupisible faculty* would command the seduction of every woman and the eating of every pie, the law of nature *of the rational faculty* would command restraint. But this would do no good, for since the human being would lack substantial unity, neither of these so-called laws would have a greater claim on his obedience. Strictly speaking, it would not even be possible to speak of "his obedience," since each of his parts might lay claim to being "him."

---

[6] This is merely a manner of speaking, since our nature defines us. If our nature were different, then it would not be "our" nature, but the nature of a different sort of being, albeit, perhaps, one that resembled us.

[7] I-II, Q. 23, Art. 1.

Finding this conclusion intolerable, the Objector holds that the parts of human nature must, after all, form a unity. He takes for granted – this is the weak part of his argument – that to do so, they must all be under the regulation of a single master precept.

---

[1] *Objection 3. Further, law is something pertaining to reason, as stated above (90, 1).* [2] *Now reason is but one in man. Therefore there is only one precept of the natural law.*	Objection 3. Still further, all law is the work of reason, as we saw in Question 90, Article 1. But human reason possesses unity; so the natural law must possess unity. It follows that all its particular precepts must flow from one general precept.

---

[1]   Law is *essentially* an ordinance of reason; unless something is reasonable, it is not really law.

[2]   Although reason understands many things, that which understands them is only one thing; although it exercises many subordinate powers, such as memory, the principal power that employs them is only one power. From this the Objector concludes that it must be ruled by a single precept.

---

[1] *On the contrary, The precepts of the natural law in man stand in relation to practical matters, as the first principles to matters of demonstration.* [2] *But there are several first indemonstrable principles. Therefore there are also several precepts of the natural law.*	On the other hand, the way we reason about what to do is analogous to the way we reason about what is true. But in reasoning about what is true, we ultimately depend not on a single indemonstrable first principle, but on several. This being the case, there must be more than one foundational precept of the natural law too.

---

[1]   St. Thomas often emphasizes the close resemblance between practical reasoning (about what is to be done) and theoretical reasoning (about what is the case). He repeats the point made here in the *sed contra* almost word for word in the *respondeo*.

[2]   The shortcoming of the *sed contra* is that although it provides a reason for thinking that natural law includes more than one precept, it does not show how to square this multiplicity with the unity of human nature. As we are about to see, St. Thomas agrees with the Objector that in a certain sense, every moral duty flows from a single first precept. However, he does *not* agree with him that all we need to do is apply this first precept

without troubling about secondary precepts. In the first place, unless we view the first precept through the spectacles of how we are made, we cannot make sense of it at all. In the second place, these spectacles turn out to have more than one lens, for human nature has three aspects or dimensions. The upshot is that natural law includes not just one, but a number of self-evident, exceptionless precepts – and yet that all of these reflect and take their unity from a single yet deeper precept.

[1] *I answer that, As stated above (91, 3), the precepts of the natural law are to the practical reason, what the first principles of demonstrations are to the speculative reason; because both are self-evident principles.* [2] *Now a thing is said to be self-evident in two ways: first, in itself; secondly, in relation to us. Any proposition is said to be self-evident in itself, if its predicate is contained in the notion of the subject: although, to one who knows not the definition of the subject, it happens that such a proposition is not self-evident.* [3] *For instance, this proposition, "Man is a rational being," is, in its very nature, self-evident, since who says "man," says "a rational being": and yet to one who knows not what a man is, this proposition is not self-evident.* [4] *Hence it is that, as Boethius says (De Hebdom.), certain axioms or propositions are universally self-evident to all; and such are those propositions whose terms are known to all, as, "Every whole is greater than its part," and,*

Here is my response. The precepts of natural law are the first principles of reasoning about what to do. Now as we have already seen, the way we reason about what to do is analogous to the way we reason about what is true, for in both cases, we depend on certain principles that are known in themselves, or self-evident. But there are two different senses in which a proposition may be called self-evident. Paradoxically, even though it may be evident in itself, it may not be evident to us. For a proposition is self-evident when its predicate belongs to the idea of its subject – when what is said about it is implicit in its definition, in the idea of what it *is*. Yet to anyone who does not know this definition – who fails to grasp what it *is* – the proposition will not be known in itself. For example, the proposition "Man is rational" is self-evident because the subject, "man," *means* something rational – to speak of man *just is* to speak of something rational. Yet the proposition would not be known in itself to someone who did not know what a man is.

For example, Boethius, in his treatise *On the Hebdomads,*[8] says that certain "dignities," certain especially noble propositions,[9] are self-evident to

---

[8] The topic of *On the Hebdomads* is why all substances are good just by virtue of having being. This is obviously relevant to St. Thomas's point, just a bit further on, that humans share the good of being with all substances whatsoever.

[9] Latin, *dignitates vel propositiones.*

"Things equal to one and the same are equal to one another." [5] *But some propositions are self-evident only to the wise, who understand the meaning of the terms of such propositions:* [6] *thus to one who understands that an angel is not a body, it is self-evident that an angel is not circumscriptively in a place: but this is not evident to the unlearned, for they cannot grasp it.*

everyone. These are the propositions whose terms *are* understood by everyone, such as "Every whole is greater than its part" and "Things that are equal to the same thing are equal to each other." But not all self-evident propositions are like this, because some are known in themselves only to those who have enough learning to grasp the meanings of the terms. For instance, to anyone who understands that an angel is not a body, it is self-evident that an angel does not have a specific location, but this is not clear to the uninstructed, who cannot take firm hold of the idea.

[1]   One cannot help but be struck by how often St. Thomas calls our attention to the analogy between theoretical and practical reason. He is not asserting, as careless readers suppose, that reasoning proceeds entirely from self-evident principles with no need for new observations. Nor is he saying that we somehow know self-evident principles without any experience. Rather, it is *in and through* experience that the self-evident principles make their self-evidence manifest to us, and *by means* of these principles that we are able to make sense of what we observe. For example, whenever we perceive that the door is open, we necessarily perceive that the door is not closed – and the mind takes in not only the fact, but also the necessity itself. The reason St. Thomas gives so much emphasis to self-evidence is that if the foundational precepts of the natural law were not known, then they could not be said to have been promulgated, so they would not be true law.

[2]   When St. Thomas speaks of the definition of a man, he is not speaking of its nominal or verbal definition (of the words we associate with it), but of its real definition (of what it truly is). The influence of so-called nominalism has made this distinction difficult for many readers of our day to grasp. Just because we can call a thing whatever we wish, we suppose that the thing can actually be whatever we wish. The error is tempting: Something that is not the same being as man can be called "man," something that is not the same quality as virtue can be called "virtue," something that is not the same relationship as marriage can be called "marriage," and so it goes. But the mere change of words does not erase the differences.

[3]   Because rationality pertains to man's essence – because to be a man *is* to be rational – the proposition "man is a rational being" is true in itself. To someone who knows what a man is, it will also be *known* in itself, but to someone who does know what a man is, it will not.

The distinction between what is evident in itself and what is evident to us is tremendously important, yet rarely grasped in our day. We suppose that if something is really self-evident, it must be known to everyone, and conversely that if something is not known to everyone, it cannot be self-evident. This is utterly false.

[4]   Just as to be a man *is* to be rational, so to be a part *is* to be less than the whole, and to be equal to the same thing *is* to be equal to each other. Consequently, anyone who understands the terms necessarily understands the relations among them, and sees that these propositions are true.

[5]   In the strictest sense, St. Thomas uses the term "wisdom," *sapientia,* for the gift of the Holy Spirit that enables a person to make sound judgments about the Highest Cause, which is God.[10] However, the context suggests that in this case "the wise" may take in not only the supernaturally inspired, but also those who have attained human wisdom, for human wisdom is sufficient to grasp the sorts of proposition that Boethius has in mind.

[6]   Only bodies have physical locations. It makes no more sense to say that an immaterial thing like an angel is "inside this box" or "on the other side of that wall" than to say that a thought is. Yet even though this proposition is true in itself, it is not obvious to those whose minds have not been cultivated. To say this is not "elitist"; St. Thomas expresses no judgment about which minds are capable of being cultivated and which are not.

---

[1] *Now a certain order is to be found in those things that are apprehended universally. For that which, before aught else, falls under apprehension, is "being," the notion of which is included in all things whatsoever a man apprehends.* [2] *Wherefore the first indemonstrable principle is that*	Now a certain ordered sequence may be observed whenever the mind takes hold of anything, for we grasp *being* before we grasp anything else – whatever else we may know about a thing, we know that it *is*. This is the reason for the most fundamental indemonstrable principle, that the same *proposition* cannot be both *affirmed and denied* at the

[10] II-II, Q. 45, Art. 1.

"the same thing cannot be affirmed and denied at the same time," which is based on the notion of "being" and "not-being": and on this principle all others are based, as is stated in Metaph. iv, text. 9. [3] Now as "being" is the first thing that falls under the apprehension simply, so "good" is the first thing that falls under the apprehension of the practical reason, which is directed to action: since every agent acts for an end under the aspect of good. [4] Consequently the first principle of practical reason is one founded on the notion of good, viz. that "good is that which all things seek after." [5] Hence this is the first precept of law, that "good is to be done and pursued, and evil is to be avoided." [6] All other precepts of the natural law are based upon this: so that whatever the practical reason naturally apprehends as man's good (or evil) belongs to the precepts of the natural law as something to be done or avoided.

same time, which finds its basis in the fact that the same *thing* cannot both *be and not be* at the same time. As Aristotle points out in *Metaphysics*, Book 4, Chapter 4, every other principle of theoretical reason flows from this one.

But just as *being* is the first thing that we grasp simply, so *good* is the first thing we grasp by means of practical reason, which governs action. Why is this? Because whenever an agent acts for the sake of an end, he considers the end good. We see, then, that the most fundamental principle of practical reason rests on the fundamental idea of good as what all things seek after – and for this reason, the most fundamental *precept of law* is that good is to be done and pursued, and evil avoided. Although this is not the only precept of natural law, all the other precepts stand upon it as their foundation. Hence, whenever practical reason grasps naturally that something is good, natural law commands that it be done, and whenever practical reason grasps naturally that something is evil, natural law commands that it be avoided.

[1]   We must be careful not to misunderstand what St. Thomas means in saying that we grasp being "before" we grasp anything else. Being is first in the order of *what is* – something must be a being in order to be anything else. But it is certainly not first in the order of *discovery* – we do not first think, "Ah, this is a being," only afterwards considering what kind of being it is. Rather, in considering what kind of being it is, we realize that we have been tacitly recognizing it to be a being all along. One might say that it is first in the order of *inescapable tacit presuppositions*.

[2]   The latter principle makes the same point as the former principle, but in a form adapted to demonstration – to working out the conclusions of given premises.

[3]   Good is the object of practical reason in the same way that being is the object of theoretical reason. We cannot look into anything without grasping that it *is;* and we cannot deliberate about the means to any end whatsoever without grasping that it is *good.* Whenever we think about anything, we presuppose being, and whenever we deliberate about anything, we presuppose good.

[4]   This principle is stated in the first sentence of the *Nicomachean Ethics,* where Aristotle remarks, "Every art and every inquiry, and similarly every action and pursuit, is thought to aim at some good; and for this reason the good has rightly been declared to be that at which all things aim."[11] St. Thomas alludes to the proposition often, and considers it self-evident, for to say "good" is to say "desirable"; the desirable is what the good *is.*[12] As always, however, the fact that the proposition is evident in itself does not necessarily make it evident *to us.* Subjectivists, for example, confuse the desirable with what they happen to desire – not the same thing at all.

The sorts of "things" that seek or desire good are beings with substantial unity, with natures. They desire it, not necessarily in the psychological sense, which requires a mind, but in the ontological sense. For example, though an acorn is oriented toward becoming an oak, its orientation is certainly not reflected in the thought, "Gosh, I wish I were an oak." In his commentary on the *Nicomachean Ethics,* St. Thomas explains as follows:

The saying "...what all desire" is to be understood not only of those who knowingly seek good but also of beings lacking knowledge. These things by a natural desire tend to good, not as knowing the good, but because they are moved to it by something cognitive, that is, under the direction of the divine intellect in the way an arrow speeds towards a target by the aim of the archer. This very tendency to good is the desiring of good. Hence, he says, all beings desire good insofar as they tend to good. But there is not one good to which all tend; this will be explained later. Therefore [Aristotle] does not single out here a particular good but rather discusses good in general. However, because nothing is good except insofar as it is a likeness and participation of the highest good, the highest good itself is in some way desired in every particular good. Thus it can be said that the true good is what all desire.[13]

[11] Aristotle, *Nicomachean Ethics,* Book 1, Chapter 1, trans. W.D. Ross (public domain).
[12] I, Q. 5, Art. 4, ad 1; I-II, Q. 29, Art. 5. See also St. Thomas's response to misuses of the principle: I, Q. 6, Art. 1, Obj. 2 and ad 2; I-II, Q. 34, Art. 2, Obj. 3 and ad 3.
[13] Thomas Aquinas, *Commentary on Aristotle's Nicomachean Ethics,* Book 1, Lecture 1, trans. C.J. Litzinger, O.P., rev. ed. (Notre Dame, IN: Dumb Ox Books, 1993), p. 4.

As in the case of the acorn, for a being with a nature to seek its particular good is to aim at what perfects, fulfills, or completes it – what it is made for, what it is ordered to, what fully actualizes its potentiality. Not even an addict who craves heroin seeks destruction *as such;* he seeks some lesser good that he mistakes for his greatest good but that really destroys it. So often, when people say they are seeking fulfillment, what they mean is merely "I am trying to get what I desire." They assume that this will be fulfilling, even when what they desire is destructive of their nature.

[5] The analogy between theoretical and practical reason is now complete.

1a. The ontological form of the first principle of theoretical reason is that nothing can both be and not be at the same time;

1b. The propositional form of the same principle is that nothing can be both affirmed and denied at the same time;

2a. The ontological form of the first principle of practical reason is that good is that which all things seek after; and

2b. The preceptive form of the same principle (which is the first precept of natural law) is that good is to be done and pursued, and evil is to be avoided.

Just as statement (1b) expresses statement (1a) in a form adapted to demonstration, so statement (2b) expresses statement (2a) in a form adapted to deliberation.

[6] Because all of the precepts of the natural law are based on statement (2b), in a certain sense the natural law *does* include only one utterly fundamental precept, as St. Thomas explicitly concedes in the reply to Objection 1. But as we are about to see, this is not the end of the story.

---

[1] *Since, however, good has the nature of an end, and evil, the nature of a contrary, hence it is that all those things to which man has a natural inclination, are naturally apprehended by reason as being good, and consequently as objects of pursuit, and their contraries as evil, and objects of avoidance.*
[2] *Wherefore according to the order of natural inclinations, is the order of the precepts of the natural law. Because in man there*

But what does it mean for practical reason to grasp *naturally* that something is good or evil? Good corresponds to the idea of an end, and evil to the idea of something contrary to an end. But the ends we are speaking of are our *natural* ends. Man's reason grasps naturally that all of the things *to which he has a natural inclination* are good and to be pursued by effort, and that their contraries are evil and to be avoided. We see from this that the precepts of the natural law stand in the same order as the natural inclinations.

is first of all an inclination to good
in accordance with the nature
which he has in common with
all substances: inasmuch as every
substance seeks the preservation
of its own being, according to
its nature: and by reason of this
inclination, whatever is a means
of preserving human life, and of
warding off its obstacles, belongs
to the natural law. [3] *Secondly,*
there is in man an inclination to
things that pertain to him more
specially, according to that nature
which he has in common with
other animals: and in virtue of this
inclination, those things are said to
belong to the natural law, "which
nature has taught to all animals"
[*Pandect. Just. I, tit. i*], such as
sexual intercourse, education of
offspring and so forth. [4] *Thirdly,*
there is in man an inclination to
good, according to the nature of
his reason, which nature is proper
to him: thus man has a natural
inclination to know the truth about
God, and to live in society: and
in this respect, whatever pertains
to this inclination belongs to the
natural law; for instance, to shun
ignorance, to avoid offending those
among whom one has to live, and
other such things regarding the
above inclination.

What then is this order? The first of man's
natural inclinations pertains to what he
naturally has in common with all beings
that have substantial unity – for all such
beings, all "substances," seek to preserve
their being in the particular manner
that is natural to them. For this reason,
natural law commands whatever is a
means to the preservation of human life,
and whatever opposes its dissolution.

Man's second natural inclination pertains
to him not because of what he has
in common with all beings that have
substantial unity, but just because of
what he naturally has in common with
other animals. This is the inclination
that Ulpian had in mind in the remark
quoted at the beginning of the *Digest,*
to the effect that natural law includes
those things "which nature has taught
all animals," for example, the union of
male and female and the education of the
young.

Finally, man possesses an inclination to
what is good for him, not because of
the nature he shares with all substances
whatsoever, and not because of the
nature he shares just with other animals,
but because of the *rational* nature that
is his alone. For this reason, natural
law commands whatever pertains to
distinctively human rationality, such as
avoiding ignorance, forbearing from
offense to his neighbors, and other things
of this sort.

---

[1]   St. Thomas is speaking of *natural* inclinations – not of what we
happen to crave, but of what we are designed to pursue, what the unfolding of our inbuilt potentialities requires. When all goes well, our natural
inclinations and our cravings correspond, yet the match can certainly fail.
Those who suffer physical or psychological disorders may subjectively
long for things that are bad for them; so may the immature; so may those
who are habituated to vice. Just as a ball may roll *up* instead of down
an inclined plane if some other force is acting on it, so a person may not

desire what he is naturally inclined to desire, but this in no way shows that he is naturally inclined not to desire it.

In our day it will inevitably be objected that by grounding natural laws on natural inclinations, St. Thomas is committing the so-called naturalistic fallacy – deriving an evaluative conclusion from a descriptive premise, an "ought" from an "is." But this is a shibboleth; there is no such fallacy. Certainly there are invalid ways of deriving an *ought* from an *is,* just as there are invalid ways of deriving an *is* from an *is,* or an *ought* from an *ought.* But not all ways of doing so are fallacious. If the purpose of eyes is to see (descriptive), then eyes that see well are good eyes, and eyes that see poorly are poor ones (evaluative). Given their purpose, is this not what it means for eyes to be "good"?

OPHTHALMOLOGIST: "You are more nearsighted than the last time I examined you."
YOU: "Would new eyeglasses clear up my vision?"
OPHTHALMOLOGIST: "Yes, completely. I could make them for you easily."
YOU: "Then I guess I ought to have you make them."
OPHTHALMOLOGIST (PUZZLED): "Why?"
Wouldn't you look for a new ophthalmologist?

To analyze this little parable: There is a difference between predicative and attributive adjectives. The adjective "red" is predicative; it means the same thing no matter what kind of thing we are talking about. By contrast, the adjective "fast" is attributive; what it means depends on what kind of thing we are talking about. Now the evaluative adjective "good" is attributive, its meaning depending on the function of the thing. The thing is the eye; its function is to see; so a good eye is one that sees well.[14] Since good is to be done and pursued, I should pursue what enables my eyes to see well.

[2]   It goes without saying that the fact that the natural inclinations have a "first, second, third" contradicts any theory that denies that fundamental goods can be ordered. However, we will not be able to understand in just what way the inclinations are ordered unless we understand each

---

[14] See Peter Geach, "Good and Evil," *Analysis* 17 (1956), 32–42. Christian Smith helpfully adds concerning the so-called naturalistic fallacy, "the descriptive observation is first made that is and ought belong to different orders, from which is then derived the normative injunction that we should keep them separate. But if we really cannot get an ought from an is, where did that injunction come from?" Christian Smith, *What Is a Person? Rethinking Humanity, Social Life and the Moral Good from the Person Up* (Chicago: University of Chicago Press, 2010), p. 387.

inclination in itself, so let us look more closely into the first natural inclination, the inclination to the preservation of our being.

St. Thomas's use of the singular – *an inclination* to the preservation of being – can be confusing, because St. Thomas is speaking of *all* those propensities that direct a thing to preserve its being. In animals, for example, the tendency to avoid extreme heat or cold, to hunger when in need of food, to eat when hungry, to flee from danger – these and many other tendencies are all part of the same "inclination" to preservation. But in plants, the inclination to preservation includes different tendencies, such as bending toward sunlight and sending out roots toward moisture.

The same examples show that what is needed for the preservation of one kind of being differs from what is needed for the preservation of another. Moreover, preservation of its *being* means not the preservation of its bare existence, but the preservation of the *mode* of life that the *fullfillment* of its nature requires – a mode of life that is shaped by *all* of its natural inclinations, not just the first inclination, but the others too. So, even though it is true that to live well, one must live, it does not follow that to live, one may degrade himself. To put this differently, the fact that the inclination to preservation comes first in order does *not* imply the precept, "Stay alive at any cost *even if doing so distorts your human nature* – lie, cheat, steal, do whatever it takes"!

We see too how mistaken it is to say, as Thomas Hobbes did, that the preservation of my nature means nothing but the preservation of my biological life[15] – or to conclude, as many others do, that although natural law commands me to preserve my life, moral law limits the means I may use. On the contrary, the natural law of the preservation of my being and the moral law of the preservation of my life are one and the same thing: To live, yes, but to live humanely, not at the expense of my humanity. Under some circumstances, the preservation of my humanity may even require that I sacrifice my life. Who but the most unnatural parent would not risk death to save his child?

[3] Just as the "inclination," singular, which we share with all beings with substantial unity, is not a single disposition, but the entire family

---

[15] According to Hobbes, "'The right of Nature,' which writers commonly call *jus naturale*, is the liberty each man hath to use his own power as he will himself for *the preservation of his own nature, that is to say, of his own life*; and consequently of doing *anything* which in his own judgment and reason he shall conceive to be the aptest means thereunto." Thomas Hobbes, Leviathan, Part 1, Chapter 14, emphasis added.

of all those natural dispositions directed to preservation, so the "inclination," singular, which we share with all animals, is not a single disposition, but the entire family of all those natural dispositions directed to the dimension of life that we have in common with the beasts. Plants, such as vegetables, trees, and mosses, exist beneath the animal level; they share with animals the inclination to preservation, but not the more particular animal dispositions such as those pertaining to motility, sensation, and the joining of the sexes for procreation and the raising of the young.

By the way, what St. Thomas actually says, following the Roman *iurisconsult* Ulpian, is not "sexual intercourse," as in the Dominican Fathers translation, but "the union of male and female," *coniunctio maris et feminae*,[16] the joining of the man and woman *by means* of sexual intercourse. We saw above that preservation is not to be understood as the preservation of bare existence at any cost, but as the preservation of the mode of being appropriate to the nature in question. In just the same way, the union of male and female is not to be understood as "doing like they do on the Discovery Channel,"[17] but as the mode of sexual joining appropriate to the nature in question. For subrational animals, the appropriate mode is rutting whenever moved by an urge. For humans, the appropriate mode is quite different. Their union joins only the two bodies, but ours also joins the two patterns of embodied life – that is, the two souls.

Why does St. Thomas single out sexual union for mention, among all these other animal things such as motility and sensation? Probably because sexual union lights up the step up from the first natural inclination to the second. All beings with substantial unity seek to preserve their being, but animals go one step further – they aim not only at individual preservation but also at the preservation of their kind. They turn the wheel of the generations, and so, in our own way, do we. The sexual inclination does not require each person to practice the sexual act. It does require all those who practice it to honor and uphold its procreative and unitive ends – which is just why it has traditionally and sweetly been called the *marital* act, for every human child needs a mother and father who love not only the child but also each other.

This is also a good place to reflect that although not everyone is called to *biological* motherhood and fatherhood within marriage, everyone is called to motherhood and fatherhood. Thus St. Paul writes to the Christians in Corinth, who are not his biological offspring, "I do not

---

[16] Ulpian's remark may be found in the *Digests*, Book 1, Title 1, Section 3.
[17] See the Introduction, footnote 8.

write this to make you ashamed, but to admonish you as my beloved children. For though you have countless guides in Christ, you do not have many fathers. For I became your father in Christ Jesus through the gospel." Full discussion would take St. Thomas beyond the realm of nature, into the realm of grace, so he does not embark on it here.[18]

[4]   Considering that we are rational beings, it is not surprising that third in order come all the inclinations pertaining to reason in itself. Plants and animals don't have these inclinations; they are a rational privilege. Animal appetites are self-organizing, in the sense that the order among them that is right for an animal emerges through appetite itself. But the order among the appetites that is right for us emerges only with the help of reason.

But we are considering only our own particular mode of rationality. If there are rational animals on Mars, we are not considering them. Nor are we considering rational beings that are not animals, such as God and angels. The topic is *properly human* rationality.

This completes our roster of natural inclination: first, those pertaining to preservation; second, those pertaining to animal life; and third, those pertaining to rationality. Yet even though we share the first and second inclinations with subrational creatures, we do not follow them in the way they do, but in a specifically rational way. Plants seek their ends automatically, without even knowing what these ends are. Animals "know" their ends in a sense, but not in the reflective sense; they do not grasp the *concept* of an end.[19] We know them, pursue them, and *know that they are ends* – we know them not just as felt impulses, but as meanings, as rational purposes, as reasons for doing what we do. St. Thomas had addressed the point in an earlier work, the *Commentary on the Sentences of Peter Lombard,* in which he explained as follows:

[I]n those things which participate in knowledge, the principles of acting are knowledge and appetite. Wherefore, it is necessary that in the cognitive power there be a natural concept, and in the appetitive power a natural inclination, by which the operation that befits the genus or the species may be rendered suitable to the end. But since man, among all the other animals, knows the notion of the end, and the proportion of his deed to the end, therefore, the natural concept

[18] See 1 Corinthians 4:14–15 (RSV); II-II, Q. 102, Art. 1; II-II, Q. 152, entire.
[19] In the same way, although the animal can distinguish friend from enemy, it cannot grasp the universal concepts "friend" and "enemy." The faculty that serves animals in place of true rationality is called the estimative power. I, Q. 78, Art. 4, ad 4; I-II, Q. 6, Art. 2; Supp., Q. 92, Art. 2. See also the next quotation in the text.

endowed upon him, by which he may be directed to working fittingly is called the natural law; in the other animals, it is called a natural estimation. For the beasts are impelled by the force of nature to working those acts that are fitting, rather than regulated as if acting by their own judgment. Therefore, the natural law is nothing other than a conception naturally endowed upon man by which he may be directed to acting in a fitting manner in his own actions, whether they befit him from the nature of the genus, such as to generate, to eat, and such; or from the nature of the species, as to reason and the like.[20]

Rationality changes everything. We seek not bare life, but a human life, which is a considered life. We seek not the bare union of male and female, but marriage – the sole mode of union suffused with the *meaning* of union, with the awareness of mutual self-gift between beings who can mutually make, and thoughtfully care for, new life. We not only follow our inclinations, but wonder about them and inquire into them, just as we wonder about all things. Until we find their meaning – until we are accord with their meaning through and through – with their real meaning, not just one that comes to hand – we cannot be at rest. For us, that is what it *is* to follow our inclinations, because what we *are* is rational.

Rationality, then, is much more than being clever, or knowing many things. One could even imagine an animal that was cleverer than we are, knew far more than we do, and could do many more things than we can – yet that was not rational.

The first branch of the family of tendencies that belong to rationality includes everything pertaining to seeking the truth, especially the most important truth, the truth about God. As the purpose of eyes is to see, so the purpose of the mind is to deliberate and to attain knowledge. Unexpectedly, though, St. Thomas indicates that the family of tendencies that belong to rationality has a second branch too: Everything pertaining to "living in society," for example, avoiding unnecessary offense. Why doesn't he group the inclination to live in society with the inclinations we share with animals? After all, many animals are also naturally social. But just because we are rational, human society is a radically different kind of thing than the "society" of cows. For us, to be social is to belong not just to an association for finding food or avoiding predators, important as those things are, but to a partnership in pursuit of the truth. Seeking and knowing the truth is not a private endeavor; it is not the kind of thing

[20] Thomas Aquinas, *Commentary on the Sentences of Peter Lombard*, IV, Dist. 33, Q. 1, Art. 1, trans. Kevin Keiser, "Rhonheimer, Part III: Virtue Ethics," available at http:// novantiqua.com/2011/01/18/rhonheimer-virtue-ethics, posted January 18, 2011.

that can be done apart from community. This fact has profound implications for the ordering of human society.

The fact that we are rational beings does not mean that we will never abuse our rational powers. But when we have bad reasons, even then we have reasons; when we obstinately choose to rationalize the unreasonable, even then we engage in reasoning. Such is our paradoxical dignity, even in the way that we sin. We are but little lower than the angels, some of whom fell, as did we.

Reply to Objection 1. All these precepts of the law of nature have the character of one natural law, inasmuch as they flow from one first precept.	**Reply to Objection 1.** The various precepts of the natural law really do form a unity because of their dependence on a single first precept – but not in the sense that the Objector has in mind.

St. Thomas agrees with the Objector that everything the natural law bids us to do must flow from a single first precept. However, the Objector fails to grasp *how* everything flows from it, because he confuses the application of a precept with the derivation of a secondary precept. Authoritative secondary precepts *do* flow from the first precept, some of them even exceptionless, as it is. But we must view the first precept through the lenses of our natural inclinations; thus it is *not* the case that we reach our duties by applying the first precept directly – as though just from the fact that good is to be done, I could know what, in particular, I should do.

Much the same is true of Divine law, which also has a first precept. St. Paul says, "Owe no one anything, except to love one another; for he who loves his neighbor has fulfilled the law. The commandments, 'You shall not commit adultery, You shall not kill, You shall not steal, You shall not covet,' and any other commandment, are summed up in this sentence, 'You shall love your neighbor as yourself'" (Romans 13:8–9, RSV-CE). St. Paul's statement that he who loves his neighbor has fulfilled the law leads some to the mistaken conclusion that the rest of those commandments are unnecessary – that if only I do it lovingly, for example, I *may* commit adultery. On the contrary, the commandment of love and the particular commandments are interdependent. We learn from the commandment of love the *point* of the particular commandments and the spirit in which they should be practiced; but we learn from the particular commandments what genuine love actually requires. Adultery is of such a nature that it cannot be committed lovingly; love is of such a nature that it loathes the very thought of adultery.

---

[1] *Reply to Objection 2. All the inclinations of any parts whatsoever of human nature, e.g. of the concupiscible and irascible parts, in so far as they are ruled by reason, belong to the natural law, and are reduced to one first precept, as stated above:* [2] *so that the precepts of the natural law are many in themselves, but are based on one common foundation.*

Reply to Objection 2. The natural law really does bid us follow the inclinations of each part of our nature. However, it bids us follow them *only as each part is directed by and taken up into reason.* In this way they manifest their unity with a single shared originating precept, reason, for as we have discussed, each of them grows from a single root.

---

[1]   The Objector was concerned about whether the "parts" of human nature are potential parts or integral parts. We see now that the "parts" of human nature are nothing but the *powers* of the soul, for example, the power to be attracted to delectable goods (concupiscibility) and the power to be aroused to their defense (irascibility). Such powers are potential parts, for although they can be distinguished, they are not truly separate things. Rather they are aspects of a single thing, the soul, the underlying unity of which is shown by their relation to the soul's master power, which is reason. Like magnets, each of these powers is polarized toward certain ends, although by itself this polarization is not enough; they still need reason's guidance.

The Latin term *reducuntur,* translated here as "reduced," can also be rendered "led back." The natural inclinations are "led back" to reason in two senses: Intellectually, they are *traced* back to reason when we come to see how they depend on it; morally, they are *brought* back to reason when they are cured of the mutinous attitude that they suffer as a result of the Fall (a cure that requires the help of grace). Like a child being led back to school, our subordinate faculties must be conducted to reason, instructed by reason, suffused with reason, supercharged by reason, and set free under its direction.

This fact also sheds a new light on the ordering of the natural inclinations. Even though the lower inclinations are not rational in their essence, they are rational "by participation" through accepting reason's rule.[21]

---

[21] I-II, Q. 60, Art. 1.

The inclination to preservation is listed first, because the experience of every other good presupposes it; but in another sense the inclination to rationality comes first, because the pursuit of every other good is directed by it.

[2] Although the Objector grasped that the precepts of natural law are many in themselves, he did not grasp their underlying unity. There are two errors to be avoided, and one truth. We should not say that our nature has a single taproot, good, and stop there; nor should we say that it has three independent roots: preservation, animality, and rationality. Rather we should say that the singe taproot, good, is braided from three strands: The good of preservation in the light of reason, the good of animal life in the light of reason, and the good of reason itself.

Reply to Objection 3.	Reply to Objection 3. The Objector is not
Although reason is one in	wrong to point out the unity of practical
itself, yet it directs all things	reason, because it does rest on one
regarding man; so that	first precept. Yet this one thing governs
whatever can be ruled by	everything that can be brought to follow it,
reason, is contained under the	in particular, our various parts. Unity in the
law of reason.	former sense is perfectly compatible with
	diversity in the latter.

To live "like an animal" isn't really to live like an animal, but only to live as a human badly: For although we too have animal powers, we do not, we cannot, experience our animal powers as animals do – nor would it be good for us if we could. For us, the notion of a "raw feel" is a dissipated fantasy, because every impulse is mediated by mind. Ideally, the mind acquires wisdom; ideally, the lower powers acquire discipline. Then, rather than champing at the bit, they are taken into partnership with reason. Like salt dissolved in water, they remain themselves, and yet they are drawn out of themselves – held in solution by a flood of rational meaning.

For further reflection on the preceding section of the *Treatise on Law*, the online *Companion to the Commentary*, accessible via the Resources link at the book's catalogue webpage, includes a discussion of the following topics:

THE NATURAL INCLINATIONS

Question 94, Article 3:
Whether All Acts of Virtue Are Prescribed by the
Natural Law?

TEXT	PARAPHRASE
Whether all acts of virtue are prescribed by the natural law?	Does the natural law command the performance of each particular virtuous act?

The question is whether the natural law includes a distinct precept for each distinct act of virtue: for each act of fidelity, each act of fortitude, each act of temperance, and so on. It would seem that it should, but the Objector proposes persuasive reasons to think that this could not be the case.

[1] *Objection 1. It would seem that not all acts of virtue are prescribed by the natural law. Because, as stated above (90, 2) it is essential to a law that it be ordained to the common good.* [2] *But some acts of virtue are ordained to the private good of the individual, as is evident especially in regards to acts of temperance. Therefore not all acts of virtue are the subject of natural law.*	Objection 1. Apparently, natural law does not command the performance of each particular virtuous act. The reason is that natural law is a species of law, and as we saw earlier, law is not directed to the good of particular persons but to the good of the community as a whole. But some virtuous acts *are* directed to the good of particular persons – a point that is especially obvious in the exercise of the virtue of temperance. Plainly, then, not every virtuous act is a concern of the natural law.

[1] An individual may take counsel with himself about what his own good requires, but the ordinances of public authority concern only what the good of all requires.

[2] If Dmitri intemperately forms a habit of getting drunk, he will injure his health. But the Objector reasons that although this hurts Dmitri, it does not necessarily hurt the community.

Objection 2. Further, every sin is opposed to some virtuous act. If therefore all acts of virtue are prescribed by the natural law, it seems to follow that all sins are against nature: whereas this applies to certain special sins.	Objection 2. Moreover, every act of sin is opposed to some act of virtue. Now if every act of virtue is commanded by natural law, then it seems that every sin must be forbidden by it. In this case, every sin would be against nature. But we call only certain sins unnatural, not all of them.

The Objector might have cited St. Thomas's own words earlier in the *Summa,* where he says, "human virtue, which makes a man good, and his work good, is in accord with man's nature, for as much as it accords with his reason: while vice is contrary to man's nature, in so far as it is contrary to the order of reason."[22] In most contexts the term "sin," *peccatum,* and the term "vice," *vitium,* are interchangeable; they refer to the same acts, though from different angles of view.

Objection 3. Further, those things which are according to nature are common to all. But acts of virtue are not common to all: since a thing is virtuous in one, and vicious in another. Therefore not all acts of virtue are prescribed by the natural law.	Objection 3. Still further, since human nature is the same for everyone, the acts that are required by natural law must also be the same for everyone. But what counts as a virtuous act is *not* the same for everyone, for sometimes an act that would be virtuous for one person would be vicious – contrary to virtue – for another person. It follows that natural law does not command every virtuous act.

Offering instruction in mathematics is virtuous for someone trained in mathematics, but vicious for someone ignorant of the subject. Dashing into the burning building is virtuous for a member of the firefighting crew, but vicious for a bystander who needs to stay out of the way. Enjoying the marital act with Peggy is virtuous for her husband, but vicious for the fellow next door. How then can the natural law give a general command, "Teach mathematics," "Dash into the burning building," or "Sleep with Peggy"?

On the contrary, Damascene says (De Fide Orth. iii, 4) that "virtues are natural." Therefore virtuous acts also are a subject of the natural law.	On the other hand, as John of Damascus remarks in *On the Orthodox Faith,* Book 3, "virtues are natural." Since virtues are natural qualities, it follows that the acts of virtue belong to the natural law.

More fully, John of Damascus writes, "For the virtues are natural qualities, and are implanted in all by nature and in equal measure, even if we do not all in equal measure employ our natural energies. By the transgression we were driven from the natural to the unnatural. But the Lord led us back from the unnatural into the natural. For this is what is the meaning of *in our image, after our likeness.* And the discipline and trouble of this life were not designed as a means for our attaining virtue which was

[22] I-II, Q. 71, Art. 2.

foreign to our nature, but to enable us to cast aside the evil that was foreign and contrary to our nature: just as on laboriously removing from steel the rust which is not natural to it but acquired through neglect, we reveal the natural brightness of the steel."[23]

[1] *I answer that, We may speak of virtuous acts in two ways: first, under the aspect of virtuous; secondly, as such and such acts considered in their proper species.* [2] *If then we speak of acts of virtue, considered as virtuous, thus all virtuous acts belong to the natural law.* [3] *For it has been stated (2) that to the natural law belongs everything to which a man is inclined according to his nature. Now each thing is inclined naturally to an operation that is suitable to it according to its form: thus fire is inclined to give heat. Wherefore, since the rational soul is the proper form of man, there is in every man a natural inclination to act according to reason: and this is to act according to virtue. Consequently, considered thus, all acts of virtue are prescribed by the natural law: since each one's reason naturally dictates to him to act virtuously.* [4] *But if we speak of virtuous acts, considered in themselves, i.e. in their proper species, thus not all virtuous acts are prescribed by the natural law: for many things are done virtuously, to which nature does not incline at first; but which, through the inquiry of reason, have been found by men to be conducive to well-living.*

Here is my response. When we speak of virtuous acts, we may have either of two things in mind. Taken in the first sense, the phrase "virtuous acts" means simply acts that are virtuous, without regard to their particularities. Now whenever an act is virtuous, it is commanded by natural law. Why? Just because, as we have already shown, everything to which we are naturally inclined is commanded by natural law. For consider: What a thing is naturally inclined to do is determined by its form; for example, the formal properties of fire incline fire to give heat. But the form of *man* is the rational soul. So the natural inclination of each man is to act reasonably – and to act reasonably is to act virtuously. Viewed just insofar as they are virtuous, then, all acts of virtue are commanded by natural law, just because each person's reason tells him that it is fitting to act virtuously.

Taken in the second sense, however, the phrase "virtuous acts" refers to virtuous acts of particular kinds. Now the foundational principles of natural law do *not* include commands to perform *every* kind of virtuous act. For there are many acts to which the first precepts do not immediately incline us, but which have shown helpful to good life by rational inquiry.

---

[23] John of Damascus, *Exposition of the Orthodox Faith*, trans. E. W. Watson and L. Pullan, Book 3, Chapter 14 (public domain, available at www.newadvent.org/fathers). The internal reference is to Genesis 1:26.

[1]   St. Thomas means that when we ask whether the natural law commands us to perform every virtuous act, we may be asking whether the
natural law includes the command, "Perform every virtuous act," or we
may be asking whether it includes commands to perform specific virtuous
acts such as teaching mathematics, rushing into burning buildings, and
enjoying the marital act with Peggy.

The *species* of the act is *what kind of act it is*. What kind of act the
act is *formally and essentially* is determined by its end, by the will's
intention; this includes both what the aims at doing and what it aims at
bringing about by doing so. In turn, what kind of act the act is *materially* is determined by its object, by that on which the action is brought to
bear. Consider, for instance, a lie. In the fullest sense, falsehood requires
three things at once: that one wills to say what is false (formal falsehood), that he intends by so doing to deceive (effective falsehood), and
that what he says is false (material falsehood). But for the act to have
the specific nature of a lie, it is not necessary that what he says is false; if
he says something true, thinking it to be false and intending to deceive,
he is lying.[24]

[2]   St. Thomas is claiming that the natural law commands us, "Do
whatever is virtuous."

[3]   Now St. Thomas explains *why* natural law commands us "Do
whatever is virtuous." The argument has five steps: (1) Natural law commands everything to which we are naturally inclined; (2) we are naturally
inclined to act in the way that is suitable to our form; (3) since our form
is the rational soul, to act in the way that is suitable to our form is to act
reasonably; (4) but to act reasonably is to act virtuously; (5) so the natural law commands us to act virtuously.

It may seem that since acting in the way that is suitable to our form
means acting according to reason, we could have skipped Article 2's
analysis of the inclination we share with all "substances" and the
inclination we share just with other animals, jumping straight to the
inclination to rationality. But this is mistaken, because to be reasonable
is to pursue *something* in a reasonable manner, and virtue lies in the
details.

So if we are asked *what it is* that we are to pursue in a reasonable manner, the answer lies in a threefold good: the aspect of natural good that

[24] I-II, Q. 18, Arts. 6–7; II-II, Q. 110, Art. 1.

we share with all substances, which is preservation; all those aspects of natural good that we share with other animals, for example, those things pertaining to the union of the sexes and the education of the young; and finally the aspect of natural good that we do not share with them, the one which pertains to our rationality.

And if we are asked *what it means* to pursue this threefold good reasonably, the answer is to pursue it neither automatically, like plants, nor unreflectively, like animals, but with understanding of our ends. At all three levels, such understanding is utterly transformative: Understanding the preservative end, we alone seek not just to endure, but to abide meaningfully in the truth. Understanding the procreative and unitive ends, we alone seek not only to placate the sexual urge but also to marry, and not only to pacify the blind impulse to nest but also to work and plan in love and hope for posterity. Understanding our rational ends, we alone look into things not just to get what we want, nor even just because of catlike curiosity, but because of awe and wonder; and we seek companions not only in the quest for truth, but in its enjoyment.

[4] The expression "to which nature does not incline at first" refers to the order of the precepts. Just as in Article 2, when we were investigating the order of the inclinations, the words are to be taken logically, not chronologically. So when St. Thomas says "many things are done virtuously, to which nature does not incline at first," he means that there are many acts of virtue that the natural law does not *proximately* impel us; the first precepts alone do not inform us that these acts are virtuous. Before the invention of mathematics, for example, nobody could have known that for some people it is virtuous to teach mathematics.

Even so, the natural law *ultimately* impels us to such acts. In the first place, as soon as the inquiry of reason shows that they are helpful to living well, the precept "Do whatever is virtuous" kicks in. But something else happens too, for as St. Thomas explains elsewhere in the *Summa*, things to which nature does not incline "at first" can become "connatural," or "second nature," through habituation and custom. In this way, so to speak, they fill in the blanks that the generalities of nature leave undetermined. The result is that we acquire new inclinations to certain things, and we come to find pleasure in things in which we did not find pleasure before.

Things can become second nature in a variety of ways. For example, the lover becomes connatural with the beloved: Our nature adapts itself to whatever, or whoever, we love. This is how a loving wife and husband know each other's thoughts; they understand each other connaturally.[25]

Reply to Objection 1. Temperance is about the natural concupiscences of food, drink and sexual matters, which are indeed ordained to the natural common good, just as other matters of law are ordained to the moral common good.

Reply to Objection 1. The virtue of temperance regulates the natural desires related to food, drink, and sex. But just as other provisions of law are directed to the moral common good, these too are naturally good for everyone. So it is incorrect to say that they concern only private and not common good.

How do temperance and intemperance concern the *common* good? Earlier we considered Dmitri, who has formed a habit of getting drunk. But drunkenness doesn't hurt just Dmitri. In the first place, *anyone* who forms such a habit injures his health, not just Dmitri. In the second place, Dmitri's drunkenness injures *other people* by impairing his ability to fulfill his obligations to them. In the third place, if he becomes so sick that he is unable to care for himself, then he makes himself a burden to them.

Another fitting example is intemperance in sex. Those who say that their personal sexual habits "don't hurt anyone" must have very little imagination. At the beginning of the sexual revolution most physicians had to worry about only two or three sexually transmitted diseases; now it is more like two or three dozen. In fact, broken bodies and infertility are the least of the trouble. Consider, for example, broken childhoods. What is it like for your family to break up because dad has found someone new, then to break up again because mom has? What is it like to be passed from stepparent to stepparent to stepparent? What is it like to grow up knowing that you would have had a sister, but she was aborted? More and more of us are finding out.

---

[1] *Reply to Objection 2. By human nature we may mean either that which is proper to man–and in this sense all sins, as being against reason, are also against nature, as Damascene states (De Fide Orth. ii, 30):*

Reply to Objection 2. When we speak of human nature, we may have in mind either the aspects of nature that belong specifically to man, or the aspects of nature that man shares with other animals. If the term is taken in the former sense, then as John of Damascus points

---

[25] See especially I-II, Q. 32, Art. 2, ad 3, Art. 3, ad 3, and Art. 8, ad 3. For further discussion, see J. Budziszewski, *The Line Through the Heart: Natural Law as Fact, Theory, and Sign of Contradiction* (Wilmington, DE: ISI Books, 2009), Chapter 4, "The Natural, the Connatural, and the Unnatural."

| [2] *or we may mean that nature which is common to man and other animals; and in this sense, certain special sins are said to be against nature; thus contrary to sexual intercourse, which is natural to all animals, is unisexual lust, which has received the special name of the unnatural crime.* | out, all sins are unnatural, because all sins are against reason. But if our nature is taken in the latter sense, then only certain kinds of sins are said to be unnatural. It is in this sense that sexual conjunction of persons of the same sex has been designated as unnatural vice, for the animal aspect of our nature directs males to seek union with females, and females to seek union with males. |

[1]   "Bear in mind, too," says John of Damascus, "that virtue is a gift from God implanted in our nature, and that He Himself is the source and cause of all good, and without His co-operation and help we cannot will or do any good thing.... While then we abide in the natural state we abide in virtue, but when we deviate from the natural state, that is from virtue, we come into an unnatural state and dwell in wickedness. Repentance is the returning from the unnatural into the natural state, from the devil to God, through discipline and effort."[26]

[2]   To say that the union of male and female is natural to all animals is not to say that animals never behave inappropriately, as when one male animal attempts to mount another. Rather it means that the creational design provides a standard for considering the behavior unfitting. In such a case, what nature provides to draw males and females together has misfired. The fact that the creature may become habituated to such behavior leaves this judgment untouched; St. Thomas has much to say about how not only things that are good for us but also things that are bad for us can become "second nature."[27]

It is easy to see how misfires can happen among subrational animals. During breeding season, the territorial defense response of the male stickleback fish is triggered by the sight of red, because competing male sticklebacks have red bellies. But the male stickleback attacks anything red, not just other fish, because it is incapable of understanding its ends. Among human beings, the etiology of misfires is much more complex because we have rational souls. Even though we are capable of grasping our ends, we may misunderstand them, sometimes willfully.

---

[26] John of Damascus, ibid., Book 2, Chapter 30.
[27] Budziszewski, ibid.

Reply to Objection 3. This argument considers acts in themselves. For it is owing to the various conditions of men, that certain acts are virtuous for some, as being proportionate and becoming to them, while they are vicious for others, as being out of proportion to them.	**Reply to Objection 3.** The Objector is quite right to say that *particular* virtuous acts may be virtuous for some and yet vicious for others, because whether a particular act is virtuous depends on conditions that may be fulfilled for some men but not others. So the natural law certainly does not command such acts of everyone.

Because acts like teaching mathematics, dashing into the burning building, and enjoying the marital act with Peggy are virtuous for certain persons but not for others, the natural law certainly does not command everyone to do them. So far, the Objector is right. The point that he misses is that the precept "Do whatever is virtuous" belongs to the natural law even so; it *does* demand such acts *of those for whom they are virtuous.* Thus the math teacher should teach his subject, the firefighter should help put out the fire, and the husband of Peggy should make love to his wife.[28]

For further reflection on the preceding section of the *Treatise on Law*, the online *Companion to the Commentary*, accessible via the Resources link at the book's catalogue webpage, includes a discussion of the following topics:

JUST BE REASONABLE?
SO-CALLED VIRTUE ETHICS

Question 94, Article 4:
Whether the Natural Law Is the Same in All Men?

TEXT	PARAPHRASE
Whether the natural law is the same in all men?	Does natural law give the same commands to everyone?

This time the *ultrum* folds two questions into one: Whether the natural law is the same for all with respect to rectitude, and whether it is the same for all with respect to knowledge. To ask whether it is the same as to rectitude is to ask whether the same commands are *right* for everyone:

---

[28] St. Thomas discusses how such circumstances affect the species of the act especially in I-II, Q. 7, Arts. 1,3; Q. 18, Art. 5, ad 4; and Q. 18, Art. 10.

Could it ever make sense for someone to say, for example, "Honoring parents is right for you, but wrong for me," or "For you natural law requires being faithful to your wife, but for me it requires adultery"? To ask whether it is the same for all as to knowledge is to ask whether the same commands are *known* to everyone: Even if, say, murder and adultery are wrong both of us, could it ever be possible that I know this, but you don't?

By now we will not be surprised that the solution to the puzzle requires a distinction. Neither will be surprised that error lies in two opposite directions.

1. Those who think that *nothing* concerning right or wrong is the same for everyone are mistaken. The same applies to those who think that nothing *meaningful* is the same for everyone, that nothing is universal but what is tautologically vague, for that comes to much the same thing.

2. But those who think that *every detail* concerning right and wrong is the same for everyone – they have erred too.

---

[1] *Objection 1. It would seem that the natural law is not the same in all. [2] For it is stated in the Decretals (Dist. i) that "the natural law is that which is contained in the Law and the Gospel." [3] But this is not common to all men; because, as it is written (Romans 10:16), "all do not obey the gospel." Therefore the natural law is not the same in all men.*

Objection 1. Apparently, the natural law is not one thing, the same for everyone. We see this from Gratian's comment in the *Concordance of Discordant Canons* that "Natural law is what is contained in the Law and the Gospel." Plainly, the Law and the Gospel are not common to all men, because, as St. Paul remarks, "they have not all obeyed the gospel." So the natural law is not one for all either.

---

[1]   Literally, the Objector says natural law *non est una apud omnes,* "is not one among all."

[2]   Gratian writes as follows in his *Decretals* or *Concordance of Discordant Canons,* citing Isidore's *Etymologies,* Book 5, Chapter 2:

The human race is ruled by two things, namely, natural law and usages. Natural law is what is contained in the Law and the Gospel. By it, each person is commanded to do to others what he wants done to himself and prohibited from inflicting on others what he does not want done to himself. So Christ said in the

Gospel: "Whatever you want men to do to you, do so to them. This indeed is the Law and the Prophets."[29]

Note well that Isidore and Gratian are not saying that Divine law *is the same as* the natural law, but only that it *contains what is in* the natural law – that is, all of its moral precepts. As the natural law commands the Golden Rule, for example, so does the Gospel.

[3]   St. Paul is speaking of the *spiritual* precepts of the Gospel. Here is the context of his statement:

For, "every one who calls upon the name of the Lord will be saved." But how are men to call upon him in whom they have not believed? And how are they to believe in him of whom they have never heard? And how are they to hear without a preacher? And how can men preach unless they are sent? As it is written, "How beautiful are the feet of those who preach good news!" But they have not all obeyed the gospel; for Isaiah says, "Lord, who has believed what he has heard from us?"[30]

The Objector reasons like this:

1. Natural and Divine law include all the same things. (As we saw above, this is not what Isidore and Gratian said, and in the Reply St. Thomas argues that it is not true.)
2. Therefore natural law contains all the spiritual precepts of Divine law. (Isidore and Gratian had actually suggested that Divine law contains all the moral precepts of natural law, which is not at all the same thing.)
3. Since natural law contains all the spiritual precepts of Divine law, and the New Divine law is the same as the Gospel, natural law contains all the spiritual precepts of the Gospel.
4. Now if natural law really is the same in all men, then all men will obey its precepts.
5. But not all men do obey the spiritual precepts of the Gospel.
6. Therefore natural law is not the same in all men.

---

[29] Gratian, *The Treatise on Laws* [*Concordance of Discordant Canons*], trans. Augustine Thompson, *With the Ordinary Gloss*, trans. James Gordley (Washington, DC: Catholic University Press, 1993), p. 3.

[30] Romans 10:13–16 (RSV-CE).

[1] **Objection 2.** Further, "Things which are according to the law are said to be just," as stated in *Ethic. v.* [2] *But it is stated in the same book that nothing is so universally just as not to be subject to change in regard to some men. Therefore even the natural law is not the same in all men.*	**Objection 2.** Moreover, consider what Aristotle says in the fifth book of his *Ethics.* First he explains that "all lawful acts are in a sense just acts." Then, just a little later, he says of what is naturally just, "yet all of it is changeable." Assuming that Aristotle is right, it follows that not even the natural law is the same for all.

[1]   Aristotle distinguishes several different senses of the term "just." In the least demanding sense, justice is equated to legality; so long as a person's actions conform to enacted or customary norms, we call them "just." Justice in this sense is sometimes called "the legal just." The words the Dominican Fathers translation places inside quotation marks are a paraphrase of Aristotle's statement that "The just, then, is the lawful and the fair, the unjust the unlawful and the unfair.[31]

[2]   Again the Objector is paraphrasing. What Aristotle actually says is that *some think* justice is changeable. In a famously obscure passage (which St. Thomas later clarifies), Aristotle at first seems to deny what "some think" but then to affirm it "in a sense":

Now some think that all justice is [legal and conventional rather than natural], because that which is by nature is unchangeable and has everywhere the same force (as fire burns both here and in Persia), while they see change in the things recognized as just. This, however, is not true in this unqualified way, but is true in a sense; or rather, with the gods it is perhaps not true at all, while with us there is something that is just even by nature, yet all of it is changeable; but still some is by nature, some not by nature. It is evident which sort of thing, among things capable of being otherwise, is by nature, and which is not but is legal and conventional, assuming that both are equally changeable.[32]

The Objector's point is that if everything in the natural law changes among us, then it is not the same among us.

Objection 3. Further, as stated above (2, 3), to the natural law belongs everything to which a man is inclined according to his nature.	**Objection 3.** Still further, remember what has been said in the previous two Articles: Natural law extends to everything to which a man is inclined

[31] Aristotle, *Nicomachean Ethics*, Book 5, Chapter 1, trans. W.D. Ross (public domain).
[32] Aristotle, *Nicomachean Ethics*, Book 5, Chapter 7, trans. W.D. Ross (public domain).

Now different men are naturally inclined to different things; some to the desire of pleasures, others to the desire of honors, and other men to other things. Therefore there is not one natural law for all.

by his very nature. Yet different men are naturally inclined to different things – some to the lust of concupiscence, some to the longing for honors, still others to other things. So the natural law must vary among them too.

This third Objection finds is the most popular in our own day. It amounts to saying that there is no universal human nature, there are no universal human inclinations, and there is no universal natural law. Each of us has his own nature, different from all the rest. Given my nature, it is natural for me to do P but avoid Q, so for me, this is the law. Given your nature, it is natural for you to do Q but avoid P, so for you, that is the law.

Notice that the Objector is using the expression "natural inclinations" in a very different sense than St. Thomas uses it. For St. Thomas, a natural inclination is what I am *made* to seek, what the well-being of a creature like me *requires* me to seek. By contrast, for the Objector, a natural inclination is whatever I do, in fact, seek; the very fact that I desire it makes it "natural." Needless to say, such a view of nature makes it impossible for natural law to condemn anything that I ever want to do.

On the contrary, Isidore says (*Etym. v,* 4): "The natural law is common to all nations."

On the other hand, Isidore speaks for the tradition when he says in his *Etymologies* that "natural law is common to all nations."

The expression that Isidore actually uses is *ius naturale,* "natural right," rather than *lex naturalis,* "natural law." As the use of this quotation in the *sed contra* suggests, however, the tradition treats these two expressions as interchangeable, for whatever is naturally right is commanded by natural law, and whatever natural law commands is naturally right.[33] Here is what Isidore writes:

What natural law is [*Quid sit ius naturale*]. 1. Law is either natural, or civil, or of nations. Natural law (*ius naturale*) is common to all nations, and, because it exists everywhere by the instinct of nature [*instinctu naturae*], it is not upheld by any regulation. Such is the union of a man and woman, the children's inheritance and

---

[33] The reason for the equivalence is that the just, which is the same as the *ius,* is "a kind of equality" whereby "things are adjusted when they are made equal." This equality is what is "due," and "a thing is a matter of precept, in so far as it is something due." II-II, Q. 57, Art. 1; I-II, Q. 61, Art. 3; II-II, Q. 44, Art. 1.

education, the common possession of everything, a single freedom for all, and the right to acquire whatever is taken from the sky, the earth, and the sea. 2. Also the return of something which was entrusted and of money which was deposited, and the repulsion of violence by force. Now this, or whatever is similar to it, is never unjust, but is held to be natural and fair.[34]

Certain oddities of this passage – the ownership of all things in common, and universal freedom in the sense of an absence of human authority – are taken up in Article 5, so we will not deal with them here. It may be helpful to explain, though, that the Latin term *instinctu* does not have the mechanistic overtones of its English cognate, "instinct."

---

[1] *I answer that, As stated above (2, 3), to the natural law belong those things to which a man is inclined naturally: and among these it is proper to man to be inclined to act according to reason.* [2] *Now the process of reason is from the common to the proper, as stated in Phys. i.* [3] *The speculative reason, however, is differently situated in this matter, from the practical reason. For, since the speculative reason is busied chiefly with the necessary things, which cannot be otherwise than they are, its proper conclusions, like the universal principles, contain the truth without fail.* [4] *The practical reason, on the other hand, is busied with contingent matters, about which human actions are concerned: and consequently, although there is necessity in the general principles, the more we descend to matters of detail, the more frequently we encounter defects.* [5] *Accordingly then in speculative matters truth is the same in all men, both as to principles and as to conclusions: although the truth is not known to all as regards the*

Here is my response. As the Objector reminds us, the previous two Articles have shown that the natural law extends to everything to which man has a natural inclination. Remember, though, that man's special natural inclination is to follow reason. The way reason works (as explained in Aristotle's *Physics*) is to apply universal truths to particular situations. But at this point, the analogy between theoretical and practical reason breaks down. In what way? Theoretical reason concerns itself principally with necessary truths – with things that cannot be other than they are. Neither its universal principles, nor the conclusions that follow from them, have any exceptions. By contrast, practical reason concerns itself with the contingencies of human acts. For this reason, even though its universal principles are necessarily true, the more we look into the particulars on which these principles are brought to bear, the more often we run into exceptions. So, then, in theoretical matters, both the universal principles and their particular conclusions are *true* for all, though only the principles, not their conclusions, are

---

[34] *The Etymologies of Isidore of Seville*, trans. Stephen A. Barney, W.J. Lewis, J.A. Beach, and Oliver Berghof (Cambridge: Cambridge University Press, 2006), Book 5, Chapter 4, p. 117.

conclusions, but only as regards the principles which are called common notions. [6] *But in matters of action, truth or practical rectitude is not the same for all, as to matters of detail, but only as to the general principles: and where there is the same rectitude in matters of detail, it is not equally known to all.*

known to all. But in practical matters, even though the universal principles are also true or right for everyone, their particular conclusions are *not* necessarily true or right for everyone. Indeed, even in cases in which they *are* true or right for everyone, they are not necessarily *known* by everyone.

[1]   For the other animals, the natural and the rational are two different things. But our nature itself is rational; for us, the natural includes not just what we share with the other animals, but also what is ours alone. In us, moreover, even the aspects of nature that we do share with animals are recast by rationality.

[2]   To work from the common to the proper means to work from the universal to the singular. Both theoretical and practical reason work this way. A few examples make this clear. Theoretical: A whole is greater than any of its parts; a single angle of a triangle is a part of the sum of its angles; therefore the sum of the angles of a triangle is greater than any single angle. Practical: All gratuitously dangerous acts are wrong; such and such an act is gratuitously dangerous; therefore I will not do such and such an act. (The conclusion of the theoretical syllogism, by the way, is a proposition, something to be affirmed, but the conclusion of the practical syllogism is a decision, something to be done.)

[3]   The properties of triangles cannot be other than they are. Whether the sum of the angles equals two right angles in the Euclidean plane is not changed by such contingencies as whether we are working out the theorem in the morning or afternoon.

[4]   Unlike, say, the properties of triangles, the properties of acts can be other than they are. For example, though it is always wrong to expose myself needlessly to danger, it is impossible to enumerate all of the contingencies that might expose me to danger, or that might make exposing myself to it needless. As a result, the more details we incorporate into the description of such and such an act, the more likely the proposition like "Such and such an act is safe and permissible" will encounter exceptions. Perhaps it is usually safe to cross a street less than ten yards in width, at the intersection, when no approaching vehicle is closer than fifty yards away – but I may not be able to see very well, vehicles may be

approaching more swiftly than expected, I may be assisting someone who walks slowly, and so on. Perhaps I should not usually run into moving traffic, but my child might have wandered into the street, someone may be chasing me with a gun, a runaway truck may have careened onto the sidewalk, and so forth.

[5] Consider again the theoretical syllogism about triangles offered above. The major premise, that a whole is greater than any of its parts, is true for everyone, and the conclusion, that the sum of the angles of a triangle is greater than any single angle, is also true for everyone. But although everyone knows the major premise, some people may be confused about the conclusion.

[6] Consider again the practical syllogism about needlessly dangerous acts offered above. In practical reason, truth and rightness have the same meaning. The major premise of the syllogism, that all needlessly dangerous acts are wrong, is true or right for everyone. But the conclusion, that I will not do such and such an act (such as crossing this street at this time), is *neither* true or right *nor* known for everyone: In the first place, crossing the street may not always be needlessly dangerous, and in the second place, even if it is, not everyone may be aware of its needlessness or danger.

[1] *It is therefore evident that, as regards the general principles whether of speculative or of practical reason, truth or rectitude is the same for all, and is equally known by all.* [2] *As to the proper conclusions of the speculative reason, the truth is the same for all, but is not equally known to all: thus it is true for all that the three angles of a triangle are together equal to two right angles, although it is not known to all.* [3] *But as to the proper conclusions of the practical reason, neither is the truth or rectitude the same for all, nor, where it is the same, is it equally known by all.* [4] *Thus it is right and true for all to act according to reason: and from this principle it follows as a proper conclusion, that goods entrusted*

These things, then, are clear:

1. In both theoretical and practical reason, the universal principles are both true or right for everyone, and equally known by everyone.

2. In theoretical reason, the conclusions that follow from these universal principles are true for everyone but *not* equally known by everyone. For example, the fact that the sum of the three angles of a triangle is equal to two right angles is true for all, but not known to all.

3. In practical reason, the conclusions that follow from these universal principles are neither always true or right for everyone, *nor* equally known by everyone, even when they *are* true or right for everyone. For example, it is right and true for everyone to follow reason; and it follows as a conclusion

to another should be restored to their owner. Now this is true for the majority of cases: but it may happen in a particular case that it would be injurious, and therefore unreasonable, to restore goods held in trust; for instance, if they are claimed for the purpose of fighting against one's country. [5] And this principle will be found to fail the more, according as we descend further into detail, e.g. if one were to say that goods held in trust should be restored with such and such a guarantee, or in such and such a way; because the greater the number of conditions added, the greater the number of ways in which the principle may fail, so that it be not right to restore or not to restore.

from this principle that goods held in trust for someone should be given back to him when they are claimed. But even though in most cases reason directs restoring such goods, there may arise a few cases in which doing so would be pernicious, and therefore unreasonable – for instance, if he wants them in order to make war against his homeland.

The more we descend into particulars, the more often we find such exceptions. Suppose, for example, that we specify the rule about goods held in trust by saying that the goods should be restored only with a certain precaution, or only in a certain way. The more such conditions we tack on, the more ways the rule can go wrong, so that neither answer, "Restore" or "Don't restore," holds in every case.

[1] With the common principles of reason – its shared starting points – it makes no difference whether we are speaking of theoretical or practical reason. These principles never fail to be true, and never fail to be known.

[2] With the particular conclusions of reason – its diverse ending points – whether we are speaking of theoretical or practical reason *does* make a difference. To consider theoretical reason first: Although the conclusions are true for all, they are not known to all. St. Thomas uses the same example about triangles that I used above.

[3] Now we consider practical reason. Like the conclusions of theoretical reason, *some* of the conclusions of practical reason are true or right for all; although St. Thomas makes this point only by implication, is it quite important. For example, it follows from the wrong of harming my neighbor that I should not steal from him, and this conclusion holds true without exception. However, unlike the conclusions of theoretical reason, *not all* of the conclusions of practical reason are true or right for all in every case, as we saw above. Moreover, even in those cases in which a practical conclusion *is* true or right for all in every case, it may well be that not everyone knows it.

[4]   The return of entrusted property as an example of natural law might have been suggested to St. Thomas by the fact that Isidore includes it as an example in his *Etymologies*, Book 5, Chapter 4, as we saw above: "Also the return of something which was entrusted and of money which was deposited." St. Thomas points out that although this good principle usually holds, it does have exceptions.

[5]   The reason for this inference has already been explained.

---

[1] *Consequently we must say that the natural law, as to general principles, is the same for all, both as to rectitude and as to knowledge.* [2] *But as to certain matters of detail, which are conclusions, as it were, of those general principles, it is the same for all in the majority of cases, both as to rectitude and as to knowledge; and yet in some few cases it may fail, both as to rectitude, by reason of certain obstacles (just as natures subject to generation and corruption fail in some few cases on account of some obstacle), and as to knowledge, since in some the reason is perverted by passion, or evil habit, or an evil disposition of nature;* [3] *thus formerly, theft, although it is expressly contrary to the natural law, was not considered wrong among the Germans, as Julius Caesar relates (De Bello Gall. vi).*

For these reasons, we must say that the first universal starting points of natural law are both right for all and known to all. But in certain points of detail – in the conclusions of these universal principles, so to speak – the matter stands a bit differently.

Even in such conclusions, it is *usually* both right for all and known to all. Yet occasionally such conclusions may fall short of being *right* for all because of some obstacle or hindrance. (Hindrances of various sorts may cause natural beings subject to generation and decay to fall short in other ways, too.)

Moreover, occasionally such conclusions may fall short of being *known* to all because the reason of some people is depraved by passion, bad custom, or bad natural disposition. For example, as Julius Caesar reports in his *Commentaries on the Gallic Wars*, there was a time when the Germans did not count [their] banditry as unjust, even though banditry emphatically violates the natural law.

---

[1]   What St. Thomas actually says is "with respect to the *first* common principles (*quantum ad prima principia communia*). By "common," he signifies that they are the same for everyone – and as we have now learned, they are the same for everyone in two different ways: Not only are they right for all, but they are also known to all. By "first," he signifies that we begin with them – but he seems to be using the expression "first" in a relative rather than absolute sense. If he had in mind only the absolutely first

principles, such as "good as to be done," then he would not equate the "first" with the "common," for as we saw above, even some conclusions of the absolutely first principles hold universally. By "first" principles, then, he seems to mean the principles we normally begin with – the sorts of principles found in the Decalogue – rather than the still deeper ones on which the very possibility of deliberation depends.

[2] The phrase *seu ex mala consuetudine,* "or by evil habit," is better rendered "or by evil custom." A custom is not an individual habit, but a habit shared widely in a given society.

The phrase *seu ex mala habitudine naturae,* "or an evil disposition of nature," is more difficult. St. Thomas writes earlier in the *Summa* that something can be said to be natural to a person in either of two senses: It may pertain to his species nature, the human form that makes him *what* he is, or it may pertain to his individual nature, the particular body that makes him *who* he is.[35] The *normative* sense of the term "natural" is species nature, not individual nature. Otherwise, there really would be a different natural law for every person, something St. Thomas is at pains to deny.[36]

There is no such thing as an evil species nature: Everything that has substantial unity, everything with a species nature, is good in its way; one might say that to have a nature *is* to express a certain form of goodness. This point is not only sound metaphysics, but also sound theology, because God cannot create evil. The book of Genesis describes Him as considering each thing that He has created and calling it very good.[37] On the other hand, even a good thing can exist in either a good or bad condition. A person with an evil nature, or an evil disposition of nature, is not

---

[35] I-II, Question 63, Article 1.
[36] Cicero had written much the same thing in *On Duties:* "We must realize also that we are invested by Nature with two characters, as it were: One of these is universal, arising from the fact of our being all alike endowed with reason and with that superiority which lifts us above the brute. From this all morality and propriety are derived, and upon it depends the rational method of ascertaining our duty. The other character is the one that is assigned to individuals in particular. In the matter of physical endowment there are great differences; some, we see, excel in speed for the race, others in strength for wrestling; so in point of personal appearance, some have stateliness, others comeliness. Diversities of character are greater still." Marcus Tullius Cicero, *De Officiis,* trans. Walter Miller (Cambridge, MA: Harvard University Press, 1913), Book 1, Section 107 (public domain).
[37] Genesis 1:31.

a person with a different species nature, but a person in whom human species nature is in bad condition.

This is very important to understand. If I have a disease, I do not have a "different health" than other people, but my health has fallen into some sort of disorder; it deviates from the standard common to me and all others. In the same way, if I have an evil disposition of nature, I do not have a "different virtue" than other people, but I have a twist of individual temperament, an innate bodily condition, that makes me unusually susceptible to the temptations of some vice. For example, I might have been born with a genetic abnormality that makes me excessively susceptible to violent anger, to inappropriate sexual desires, or to the abuse of intoxicating substances.

Differences in individual temperament may suit people to different walks of life – this one would make a better soldier, this one a better craftsman, this one a better teacher. But the cardinal consideration in what is *right* is not individual temperament, but shared human nature. Unreasonable violent anger is contrary to natural law even if my temperament makes me susceptible to it, just because I remain a human being; neither the soldier, the craftsman, or the teacher should commit acts of brutality, dishonesty, or lust. So a bad disposition of nature is a misfortune, but not an excuse. If I suffer such a disposition, I will have to work harder than others to control myself, just as if I have a weak sense of balance, I will have to work harder than others to walk.

St. Thomas is not making the obvious point that persons under the influence of passions, bad customs, or bad dispositions of nature are more likely to act badly (though that is true). Rather he is making the more intriguing point that persons under such influences are more likely to *think* badly, to suffer a perversion of reasoning itself. Although no human mind can fail to grasp the shared starting points of practical reason, distorted thinking can certainly prevent someone from grasping some of the particular conclusions that follow from them. He may therefore judge good what is really bad, or bad what is really good.

[3]   The Dominican Fathers translation is dreadfully misleading here, and misinterpretations of the passage have given rise to endless confusion. The passage has nothing to do with theft in general. *Latrocinium*, the word here translated "theft," actually means banditry, or plundering. It is a form of robbery, or taking by force, which St. Thomas distinguishes from theft, or taking by stealth, as did Roman law. The ancient Germans knew very well that banditry in general is wrong, for they

punished it severely. The problem is they cut an exception for themselves, *for they did not seem to recognize the raiding of other tribes as banditry.* This fascinating issue deserves much more discussion than it can be given here, but I take it up at full length in the online *Companion to the Commentary.*

---

[1] *Reply to Objection 1. The meaning of the sentence quoted is not that whatever is contained in the Law and the Gospel belongs to the natural law, since they contain many things that are above nature;* [2] *but that whatever belongs to the natural law is fully contained in them.* [3] *Wherefore Gratian, after saying that "the natural law is what is contained in the Law and the Gospel," adds at once, by way of example, "by which everyone is commanded to do to others as he would be done by."*	Reply to Objection 1. When Gratian says natural law is what is contained in the Law and the Gospel, he could not mean that everything in the Law and Gospel belongs to natural law, because many of the things in them are beyond nature. Rather he means that the Law and Gospel fully convey everything in natural law. That is why he immediately provides the example that each person is commanded to treat others as he would want to be treated himself.

---

[1]   Many of the teachings of the Law and Gospel pertain not to what God gives us in our very nature, but to what He gives us by His grace, which is *supra naturam,* beyond nature, supernatural.

[2]   The Law and Gospel confirm everything in the natural law, though not always explicitly. Consider for example Exodus 20:2: "I am the Lord your God, who brought you out of the land of Egypt, out of the house of bondage." Does this passage explicitly declare the natural law principle of gratitude – that the conferring of great benefits brings about great obligations? No, but it presupposes it; otherwise its position as a prologue to the Decalogue has no point. The Decalogue itself, not in its bare bones, but taken together with what it presupposes, implies, and suggests, is an excellent summary of the natural law.

[3]   Notice that St. Thomas does not treat the Golden Rule as an all-sufficient statement of natural law, but as an example of its precepts. It might be asked why it does belong to the natural law to do unto others as I would be done by. Many reasons might be offered. One is that law is a rule and measure of actions, and to the things of the same kind – human beings – reason requires applying the same rule and measure: If I love myself, then, I must also love you. Another is that man is a social being;

in other words, we are of such a nature that no life is good to us unless its good can be shared with others.

Without in any way shoving these natural reasons aside, Revelation adds to them. I ought to love both myself and my neighbor because God commands it. He commands it because my neighbor and I are both made in His image, which reflects the mutual love of the three Divine Persons: the Father, Son, and Holy Spirit.

Reply to Objection 2. The saying of the Philosopher is to be understood of things that are naturally just, not as general principles, but as conclusions drawn from them, having rectitude in the majority of cases, but failing in a few.	Reply to Objection 2. Aristotle's remark that every matter of natural justice is changeable does not refer to the common principles of natural justice. Rather it should be taken to refer to the conclusions that follow from these principles, which are usually right, though in a few cases they fall short.

In other words, Aristotle is not saying that even the common principles of natural law can change and become untrue, but that the detailed propositions that follow from them can change and become untrue, because of the flux of circumstances to which they are applied. We saw why this is so in considering the rule about restoring property held in trust. Although St. Thomas's is not the only possible interpretation of Aristotle's words, it has the enormous merit of making sense of them, as well as saving Aristotle from seeming to express a relativism that he surely did not intend.[38]

[1] *Reply to Objection 3. As, in man, reason rules and commands the other powers, so all the natural inclinations belonging to the other powers must needs be directed according to reason.* [2] *Wherefore it is universally right for all men, that all their inclinations should be directed according to reason*	Reply to Objection 3. Just as man's reason exercises lordship over his other powers and commands them, so it is fitting that it direct the natural inclinations pertaining to these powers. It follows that the rational guidance of the inclinations is right not just for some men, but for all of them in common, without exception.

---

[38] See also St. Thomas's discussion of the passage in his *Commentary on Aristotle's Nicomachean Ethics*, Book 5, Lecture 12.

[1] *Dominatur* is such a strong word that although the Dominican Fathers rendering, "rules," is perfectly correct, it seems weak by comparison. The Latin term expresses the idea of being lord over something, of having dominion over it.

[2] The reduplication in the English, *universally* right for *all* men, reflects a reduplication in the Latin, *omnes communiter rectum*, "right for *all* in *common*." Evidently St. Thomas wants to be very sure we get the point.

For further reflection on the preceding section of the *Treatise on Law*, the online *Companion to the Commentary*, accessible via the Resources link at the book's catalogue webpage, includes a discussion of the following topics:

THE PROBLEM OF COMMON GROUND

ARE NATURAL RIGHTS MORE "EVIDENT" THAN NATURAL DUTIES?

THE CASE OF THE GERMAN TRIBES: IS IT POSSIBLE NOT TO KNOW THAT THEFT IS WRONG?

Question 94, Article 5:
Whether the Natural Law Can Be Changed?

TEXT	PARAPHRASE
Whether the natural law can be changed?	Is any sort of alteration possible in natural law? Can anything that was not originally part of it come to belong to it, or can anything that was originally part of it cease to belong to it?

What could be clearer than the opposition between the doctrines of natural law and of relativism? Relativists say that everything is changeable, that everything is up for grabs; the theory of natural law says that nothing is changeable, that morality is absolute. Or does it? If a new human law is enacted, commanding me to drive only on the right side of the road, then a genuinely new moral duty has come into being. True, this new duty has a foundation in previously existing duty – we were always obligated to do what the common good requires. Even so, something new seems to have been joined onto natural law. That isn't what relativism means by everything being changeable – but it is a change, isn't it? Obviously the matter needs further investigation.

[1] *Objection 1. It would seem that the natural law can be changed. Because in Sirach 17:9, "He gave them instructions, and the law of life,"* [2] *the gloss says: "He wished the law of the letter to be written, in order to correct the law of nature." But that which is corrected is changed. Therefore the natural law can be changed.*

Objection 1. Apparently, natural law can indeed be changed. The Book of Sirach teaches that God gave human beings discipline and the law of life, and a well-known collection of commentaries, the *Ordinary Gloss*, explains that He did so in order to amend the natural law. To amend it is to alter it; so alteration is possible.

[1] The Book of Sirach teaches that "God created man of the earth, and made him after his own image .... he gave them counsel, and a tongue, and eyes, and ears, and a heart to devise: and he filled them with the knowledge of understanding .... Moreover he gave them instructions, and the law of life for an inheritance."[39] In the Vulgate, the word translated as "instructions" is *disciplinam,* discipline or training.

[2] As we saw above, according to the *Glossa Ordinaria,* or Ordinary Gloss, "the law of life" is the written Divine law. This raises the question: If human beings had the natural law already, then why was a written Divine law necessary? The traditional commentator argues that it was necessary because the natural law needed *correctionem* – correction, amendment, improvement. This gives the Objector the wedge he needs.

[1] *Objection 2. Further, the slaying of the innocent, adultery, and theft are against the natural law.* [2] *But we find these things changed by God: as when God commanded Abraham to slay his innocent son (Genesis 22:2);* [3] *and when he ordered the Jews to borrow and purloin the vessels of the Egyptians (Exodus 12:35);* [4] *and when He commanded Osee [Hosea] to take to himself "a wife of fornications" (Hosea 1:2). Therefore the natural law can be changed.*

Objection 2. Moreover, the natural law forbids killing the innocent, as well as adultery and stealing. Yet we find in Scripture that God changed all three of these natural law precepts, for in Genesis 22, He commanded Abraham to kill his innocent son; in Exodus 12, he commanded the Jews to ask the Egyptians for certain objects and steal them; and in Hosea 12, he commanded Hosea to marry a whore. It follows that natural law can be changed.

[39] Sirach 17:1,5,9 (DRA), in modern translations corresponding approximately to Sirach 17:1,3,6,11. Sirach, also known as Ecclesiasticus (not to be confused with Ecclesiastes), is one of the Wisdom books of the Old Testament; it is not included in the Protestant version of the Bible.

[1]   Such deeds are against Divine law too: All three are prohibited in the Decalogue, both in Exodus 20:13–15 and Deuteronomy 5:17–19.

[2]   The story is contained in Genesis 22:1–18. God, who has promised Abraham to make a great nation of his descendants, tests Abraham in his old age by commanding him to offer his only son, Isaac, as a sacrifice. The Old Testament expresses God's abhorrence for the sacrifice of innocent children, as practiced by the surrounding pagan nations, in numerous vehement, terrifying oracles,[40] and we learn at the end of this story that it was never God's intention that Isaac actually be killed; once the fact of Abraham's obedience is ascertained, an angel intervenes to stay Abraham's hand. Thus the point of the story is not the rightness of child sacrifice, but the trial of Abraham's faith in God's promise to provide him with the promised descendants. Since God Himself provides an alternative sacrifice for Abraham to make (a ram caught by its horns in the briar bushes), the story is also taken as foreshadowing the sacrifice of the Son of God.

However, nothing in the story puts in question the legitimacy of God's having given such a commandment to Abraham in the first place. So far as Abraham knows, gods simply do at times command the sacrifice of children, as in our day the god Convenience does. The true God does not desire such things, but Abraham doesn't know this, for it has not yet been revealed. The Objector's claim is simply that if God did desire their sacrifice, He could, being God, command it, and in this case natural law would be changed.

[3]   The incident, in Exodus 12:35–36, recalls God's earlier promise to Moses, in Exodus 3, that when the terrified Egyptians at last released their Hebrew slaves, "I will give this people favor in the sight of the Egyptians; and when you go, you shall not go empty, but each woman shall ask of her neighbor, and of her who sojourns in her house, jewelry [or vessels, or implements] of silver and of gold, and clothing, and you shall put

---

[40] Psalm 106:34–41 (RSV-CE): "[B]ut they mingled with the nations and learned to do as they did. They served their idols, which became a snare to them. They sacrificed their sons and their daughters to the demons; they poured out innocent blood, the blood of their sons and daughters, whom they sacrificed to the idols of Canaan; and the land was polluted with blood. Thus they became unclean by their acts, and played the harlot in their doings. Then the anger of the Lord was kindled against his people, and he abhorred his heritage; he gave them into the hand of the nations, so that those who hated them ruled over them." See also Leviticus 18:21 and 20:2–5; Deuteronomy 12:30–31; 2 Kings 3:27, 16:2–3, 17:29–31, and 23:10: 2 Chronicles 28:1–3; Isaiah 57:4–5; Jeremiah 7:30–34, 19:4–7, and 32:33–35; and Ezekiel 16:20–21, 20:31, and 23:37–39.

them on your sons and on your daughters; thus you shall despoil the Egyptians."[41] The spoiling of the Egyptians might be viewed as a kind of restitution for their enslavement of the Israelites.

Interestingly, the phrase "spoiling the Egyptians" has come to be used figuratively for making holy use of the logical methods of the pagan philosophers, as St. Thomas does.[42] It is a much more accurate figure of speech than "baptizing Aristotle," since the Angelic Doctor knows full well that Aristotle is ignorant of the Gospel. But the Objector is not concerned with any of that. He is merely arguing that if God could command the erstwhile Hebrew slaves to despoil their former masters, then the natural law's prohibition of theft can be altered.

[4]   The Old Testament, which is the Jewish Bible, often calls God Israel's husband, but at a number of points it also calls His chosen nation a prostitute for "whoring" after the false gods of the surrounding nations. Sometimes, the prophets were instructed to act out their prophecies rather than putting them into mere words. So when, at God's command, Hosea marries first a harlot, and later an adulteress, these are stages in a vividly acted-out allegory about God's coming judgment of His people:

When the LORD first spoke through Hosea, the LORD said to Hosea, "Go, take to yourself a wife of harlotry and have children of harlotry, for the land commits great harlotry by forsaking the LORD." So he went and took Gomer the daughter of Diblaim, and she conceived and bore him a son. And the LORD said to him, "Call his name Jezreel [Hebrew, "God will sow"]; for yet a little while, and I will punish the house of Jehu for the blood of Jezreel, and I will put an end to the kingdom of the house of Israel."
       * * *
And the LORD said to me, "Go again, love a woman who is beloved of a paramour and is an adulteress; even as the LORD loves the people of Israel, though they turn to other gods and love cakes of raisins." So I bought her for fifteen shekels of silver and a homer and a lethech of barley. And I said to her, "You must dwell as mine for many days; you shall not play the harlot, or belong to another man; so will I also be to you." For the children of Israel shall dwell many days

---

[41]   3:21–22 (RSV-CE).

[42]   The expression "sharpening one's knives in the tents of the Philistines" is used in the same figurative sense, and for similar reasons. Under Philistine oppression, the Hebrew people were not allowed to learn ironwork: "Now there was no smith to be found throughout all the land of Israel; for the Philistines said, "Lest the Hebrews make themselves swords or spears"; but every one of the Israelites went down to the Philistines to sharpen his plowshare, his mattock, his axe, or his sickle; and the charge was a pim for the plowshares and for the mattocks, and a third of a shekel for sharpening the axes and for setting the goads. So on the day of the battle there was neither sword nor spear found in the hand of any of the people with Saul and Jonathan; but Saul and Jonathan his son had them." 1 Samuel 13:19–22 (RSV-CE).

without king or prince, without sacrifice or pillar, without ephod or teraphim. Afterward the children of Israel shall return and seek the LORD their God, and David their king; and they shall come in fear to the LORD and to his goodness in the latter days.[43]

This time the Objector is stretching a point, for he seems to regard marrying an adulteress as equivalent to committing adultery.

[1] *Objection 3. Further, Isidore says (Etym. 5:4)* [2] *that "the possession of all things in common,* [3] *and universal freedom, are matters of natural law."* [4] *But these things are seen to be changed by human laws. Therefore it seems that the natural law is subject to change.*	Objection 3. Still further, we find in Isidore's *Etymologies* that natural law includes common ownership of everything, and the same liberty for all. Yet human laws changes natural law in both of these respects. Apparently, then, natural law *is* changeable.

[1] Isidore says natural right "is common to all nations, and, because it exists everywhere by the instinct of nature, it is not upheld by any regulation." His examples include "the union of a man and woman, the children's inheritance and education, the common possession of everything, a single freedom for all, and the right to acquire whatever is taken from the sky, the earth, and the sea."[44]

[2] By the common possession of everything, Isidore means that when human beings first appeared on earth, nothing was mine or yours; everything could be used by everyone. Surely, the Objector reasons, their condition was not unnatural.

[3] By a single freedom for all, Isidore means that when human beings were first created, not only was there no private ownership of property, but there was no servitude of human beings; each person governed himself. If this was the condition in which we were created, the Objector asks, then how could it be anything but natural?

The term "freedom" is here used in its ancient meaning of self-government. A republic is free in that the people make their own laws, a freeman is free in that nobody owns him, and a virtuous man is free in that he is not jerked around by his passions. In St. Thomas's time, the term "freedom" was rarely if ever used in its common contemporary sense

---

[43] Hosea 1:2–4, 3:1–5 (RSV-CE).

[44] *The Etymologies of Isidore of Seville*, trans. Stephen A. Barney, W.J. Lewis, J.A. Beach, and Oliver Berghof (Cambridge: Cambridge University Press, 2006), Book 5, Chapter 4, p. 117.

of being able to do anything one wishes. That was regarded not as self-government, but as the absence of government, which, in the end, means the rule of the biggest bully.[45]

[4]   Though in the beginning, nothing was yours or mine, things *came to be* yours and mine, and this must be all right, because it is wrong to steal what belongs to another. Though in the beginning, no one served anyone else, some *came* to serve others, and this too seems all right. If something can become right that was not right before, then hasn't the natural law been changed?

On the contrary, It is said in the Decretals (Dist. v): "The natural law dates from the creation of the rational creature. It does not vary according to time, but remains unchangeable."	On the other hand, as Gratian writes in the *Concordance of Discordant Canons,* natural law has been in being as long as rational creatures have been in being. It does not change over time, but abides immutably.

In context, Gratian says, "Now, let us return to the difference between natural law and other laws. Natural law receives first place among all others because of its age and dignity. For it began with the appearance of rational creatures and does not change over time, but remains immutable."[46] We see shortly that although in a certain sense St. Thomas accepts this statement, he thinks it requires qualification.

[1] *I answer that, A change in the natural law may be understood in two ways. First, by way of addition.* [2] *In this sense nothing hinders the natural law from being changed: since many things for the benefit of human life have been added over and above the natural law, both by the Divine law and by human laws.*	Here is my response. A change in natural law may be taken in either of two senses. The first way is that something is *added into* it. Nothing prevents natural law from changing this way. Indeed, many things helpful to human life *have* been superadded to our natural obligations, some by Divine law, some by human.

[45] The meaning of liberty which predominates today was certainly not unknown to the ancients: For example, Florentinus is quoted in Justinian's *Digest* as defining liberty as "one's natural power of doing what one pleases, save insofar as it is ruled out either by coercion or by law." However, the recognition of natural law tempers even this definition. Alan Watson, ed., *The Digest of Justinian,* rev. ed., Vol. 1 (Philadelphia: University of Pennsylvania Press, 1998), p. 15. The translator of the passage I am quoting (Book 1, Title 5, Section 4) is D.N. MacCormick.

[46] Gratian, *The Treatise on Laws* [*Concordance of Discordant Canons*], trans. Augustine Thompson, *With the Ordinary Gloss,* trans. James Gordley (Washington, DC: Catholic University Press, 1993), pp. 15–16.

[1]   In speaking of "addition" to natural law, St. Thomas does not mean that natural law can acquire *new first principles,* but that, precisely because of its first principles, new precepts can also become right. One way this happens is through human authority; for example, if the legislature enacts, "Drive only on the right side of the road," the new law is genuinely binding, even though it had not previously been wrong to drive on the left. Another way it happens is through Divine authority; for example, if God commands, "Only on the evidence of two witnesses, or of three witnesses, shall a charge be sustained," then the new command too is also truly binding, even though it had not previously been wrong to convict with on the testimony of one witness alone.[47]

[2]   By the way, genuinely new obligations can arise not only by new Divine and human laws, but in other ways too. For example, it may become right for me to loan you money – something I had no previous obligation to do – just because I have promised you that I would, and it may become right to imprison William – something it was not previously right to do – just because he has committed a punishable offense. Why then doesn't St. Thomas include instances like these as additions to natural law? Perhaps because although they generate new *duties,* they do not establish new *precepts;* the new duties arise by strict application of preexisting precepts.

---

[1] *Secondly, a change in the natural law may be understood by way of subtraction, so that what previously was according to the natural law, ceases to be so. In this sense, the natural law is altogether unchangeable in its first principles:* [2] *but in its secondary principles, which, as we have said (4), are certain detailed proximate conclusions drawn from the first principles, the natural law is not changed so that what it prescribes be not right in most cases.* [3] *But it may be changed in some particular cases of rare occurrence, through some special causes hindering the observance of such precepts, as stated above (4).*

The second way is that something is *taken away* from natural law: It no longer commands something that it commanded at first. Here we must make a distinction. Its first starting points are utterly immutable. However, the matter stands differently with some of the conclusions that lie in their near neighborhood. Even so, natural law does not change in such a way as to withdraw such detailed precepts from being true or right in *most* cases. Yet in a few, rare cases, special reasons can impede their observance in some detail.

---

[47] Deuteronomy 19:15 (RSV-CE).

[1]　Change by subtraction does not mean that the natural law can *lose* any of its first principles, any more than change by addition means that it can *gain* new first principles.

[2]　Just as in the case of change by addition, so also in the case of subtraction, we are speaking only of precepts that depend on the first principles. These secondary precepts are more detailed than first principles in that they specify a greater number of circumstances: "Do P *when Q, R, and S.*" They are proximate to first principles not in the sense that they follow immediately from them, but in the sense that they come after a short chain of inference, rather than a long one with many links.

[3]　St. Thomas is not thinking of precepts such as "Do not steal," but of more finely honed precepts such as "Upon demand, return property that has been entrusted to you." Stealing – properly understood – is always wrong. Refusing to return property held in trust is *almost* always wrong. But as we have already seen in Article 4, certain impediments may hinder the observance of the latter precept. Perhaps I have entrusted my hunting rifle with you while away on a trip. On my return, I appear at your door in a drunken, murderous rage, swaying and shouting, "Hurry up and give me my rifle. Get it right now, do you hear me? I'm going to blow that bastard's head off." Is this a time for you to give me my rifle, no questions asked? Obviously not.

Even though the more detailed precepts of the natural law have exceptions, St. Thomas is quite clear that the circumstances that give rise to these exceptions can be analyzed, so that "the inquiry of counsel" can come to an end. Otherwise, we would never be able to reach firm conclusions about what to do. The argument is presented in an Article about "whether the process of counsel is indefinite." He concedes that nothing prevents counsel from being infinite "potentially," in the sense that no matter the number of different questions of conduct about which one has taken counsel, one can always take counsel about another. But he insists that counsel is infinite "actually," in the sense that about any given question of conduct, we can always know definitely both of the two things we need to know. First, we can know definitely how to deliberate about it – the end to be pursued, the principles to be applied, and the circumstances are to be considered. Second, and as a result of this reasoning, we can work out definitely what to do – not our entire future course of action, but what to do right now.[48]

---

[48] I-II, Q. 14, Art. 6. For the distinction between potential and actual infinity, see also I, Q. 7, Arts. 3–4.

[1] *Reply to Objection 1. The written law is said to be given for the correction of the natural law, either because it supplies what was wanting to the natural law;* [2] *or because the natural law was perverted in the hearts of some men, as to certain matters, so that they esteemed those things good which are naturally evil; which perversion stood in need of correction.*

Reply to Objection 1. Where the commentator says that God gave written Divine law to *correct* natural law, he may mean either of two things. One possibility is that written law is needed to fill up the gaps in the natural law. The other is that in the hearts of certain people, and about certain things, natural law has been so strongly corrupted that they view certain evils as good; this deviation needs to be straightened out.

[1]   Natural law tells us to have regard for our neighbor's safety, but it doesn't tell us how to make the roads safe. One person may say "Perhaps everyone might drive on the right"; another may say "Perhaps everyone might drive on the left"; and a third may say "Perhaps all the roads could be one-way." Each of these answers may be equally reasonable, equally concordant with natural law, but no answer can be put into effect without an exercise of authority. Human law fills in the gap.

Similarly, natural law told the Hebrews not to punish accused persons without well-grounded confidence in their guilt, but it didn't tell what kind of evidence should be required. One person says "One witness should be enough, if he is trustworthy"; another says "It would be safer to have more than one"; and a third may say "Circumstantial evidence might be sufficient." Each of these answers might be reasonable, equally concordant with natural law, but fairness to accused persons requires a single standard of evidence in every case. This time Divine law filled in the gap.

[2]   For an instance of such perversion, see the discussion of the Germans in Article 4; for further exploration of this intriguing theme, see the online *Companion to the Commentary.*

[1] *Reply to Objection 2. All men alike, both guilty and innocent, die the death of nature: which death of nature is inflicted by the power of God on account of original sin, according to 1 Kgs. 2:6: "The*

Reply to Objection 2. All persons die a natural death, the guilty and innocent alike. Natural death was introduced by God's power because of original sin, for as Hannah comments in her prayer to God, recorded in 1 Samuel 2:6,[49] "The

[49] The designations of some of the Old Testament books vary; what St. Thomas calls 1 Kings 2:6 is what modern translations call 1 Samuel 2:6.

Lord killeth and maketh alive."
Consequently, by the command of
God, death can be inflicted on any
man, guilty or innocent, without
any injustice whatever. [2] *In like*
manner adultery is intercourse
with another's wife; who is allotted
to him by the law emanating from
God. Consequently intercourse
with any woman, by the command
of God, is neither adultery nor
fornication. [3] *The same applies*
to theft, which is the taking of
another's property. For whatever
is taken by the command of God,
to Whom all things belong, is
not taken against the will of its
owner, whereas it is in this that
theft consists. [4] *Nor is it only*
in human things, that whatever is
commanded by God is right; but
also in natural things, whatever
is done by God, is, in some way,
natural, as stated in the I, 105, 6,
ad 1.

Lord kills and makes alive." So, without
any injustice, God's command can inflict
death upon anyone, whether guilty or
innocent. Similarly, adultery is lying
with the wife of another man, meaning
the wife assigned to him by the law
God has handed down. But if the law
saying whose wife is whose comes from
God, then to approach a woman by the
mandate of God is neither adultery nor
fornication. The same reasoning applies
to stealing, which involves taking
what belongs to someone else without
permission. Ultimately, everything
belongs to God, so to take something
by His command is *not* taking what
is His without permission, and so it
is not theft. As I explained earlier, the
point just made – that whatever God
commands is due or right – holds true
not just of human beings, but of nature
in general: Since God is the Author of
Nature, whatever He does is in some
way natural.

---

[1]   We belong to God by right, and He may do with us according to His good will. He is under no requirement to give us endless life on earth, or take our lives only in old age. He did, originally, give us immunity from death, but our present susceptibility to bodily death is just, for even apart from actual deeds of sin, the entire human race is under sentence of judgment because of its primordial rebellion against Him. Insofar as this just penalty brings us to repentance, it is also an act of mercy. For his supporting passage, St. Thomas chooses the grateful prayer of the formerly barren woman Hannah, who had implored God to grant her a child:

There is none holy like the LORD, there is none besides thee; there is no rock like our God .... The barren has borne seven, but she who has many children is forlorn. The LORD kills and brings to life; he brings down to Sheol and raises up .... He raises up the poor from the dust; he lifts the needy from the ash heap, to make them sit with princes and inherit a seat of honor.[50]

---

[50] 1 Samuel 2:2,5b,6,8a (RSV-CE).

At issue is God's command to Abraham to slay Isaac, something that would certainly have been wrong for Abraham to do on his own authority. The question of *how Abraham could know* that God had commanded him to do it is interesting, and tends to preoccupy modern readers, but it is presently irrelevant. St. Thomas is concerned only to point out that any command that *is* known to be God's is right; God is not commanding Abraham to commit murder, because all life is under God's lordship and judgment.

Even so, it seems that in St. Thomas's view, commands of the sort given to Abraham are not God's ordinary mode of governance; He normally governs by law. Scripture represents God calling Abraham precisely in order to form a people who *could* eventually receive His law. If Abraham had to be called in order for that time to come to fruition, then obviously the time had not come yet. St. Thomas returns to the question of Abraham's obedience in Question 100, Article 8.

[2]   Interestingly, St. Thomas's reply goes beyond even what the Objector had in mind. Apart from God's authoritative arrangements, both in how He made us (the basis of natural law) and what He has told us (the basis of Divine law), marriage would not even exist. But by the same authority by which He gives someone to this spouse, He can give that person to another spouse – and the union is licit just because it is done by His authority. Again, we must remember that this is not God's ordinary mode of governance.

[3]   Theft is taking another's property against his reasonable will, but ultimately, all things belong to God; so to take it by His command is not theft. "For every beast of the forest is mine, the cattle on a thousand hills. I know all the birds of the air, and all that moves in the field is mine. If I were hungry, I would not tell you; for the world and all that is in it is mine."[51]

[4]   When St. Thomas says "but also in natural things," *sed etiam in rebus naturalibus,* he does not mean to imply that human beings are not natural; we have a nature too, or there could be no natural law. His point is that the proposition holds true not just for human nature, but for the other natures as well. The fact that God can make exceptions to the law for human nature without destroying its integrity is just a special case of a larger truth.

---

[51] Psalm 50:10–12 (RSV-CE).

What then is this larger truth? As he argues in the First Part, Question 105, the order of nature is the order that God Himself ordains for the things that He created. God Himself is not subject to that order; on the contrary, it is subject to Him. Thus, He could have created a different order of things, and He can act outside this order of things, without in any way acting contrary to Himself as the ultimate origin of that order. For example, one of the secondary causes that God has ordained is tides, but if, as part of the same plan by which He created tides, He chooses on some occasion to interfere with them, He has not acted "unnaturally," because His ruling wisdom is the source and standard of what is natural.

The statement that whatever God commands is right could easily be misunderstood. It does not mean that God can command anything whatsoever and thereby make it right. He cannot command things that are intrinsically evil, because He is Himself the Supreme Good, and He cannot deny Himself. St. Thomas discusses this further in Question 100, Article 8, taken up in the online *Companion to the Commentary*.

---

[1] *Reply to Objection 3. A thing is said to belong to the natural law in two ways. First, because nature inclines thereto: e.g. that one should not do harm to another.* [2] *Secondly, because nature did not bring in the contrary: thus we might say that for man to be naked is of the natural law, because nature did not give him clothes, but art invented them.* [3] *In this sense, "the possession of all things in common and universal freedom" are said to be of the natural law, because, to wit, the distinction of possessions and slavery were not brought in by nature, but devised by human reason for the benefit of human life. Accordingly the law of nature was not changed in this respect, except by addition.*

Reply to Objection 3. The statement that something belongs to natural law may be taken in two senses, only one of which is normative. First, it might mean that a natural inclination *indicates* it: This is the sense in which not harming others belongs to natural law. Second, it may merely mean that nature *does not forbid* it: This is the sense in which we might say that nakedness belongs to natural law. After all, nature did not provide clothing – it was devised by human craft. In just the same sense, common ownership of everything, and one freedom for all, belong to natural law. For nature itself did not make one thing yours and another mine; nor did nature make one person a servant and another a master. These institutions were invented by men for the advantage of human life. So did these institutions change the natural law? Yes, but only by addition.

---

[1]   The Objector, remember, has claimed on Isidore's authority that universal freedom and common ownership belong to the natural law; yet today it is acknowledged to be right that freedom is *not* universal and things are *not* universally owned in common. Has natural law then changed? In one way yes, but in another way no.

Something can belong to the natural law in either of two senses. One is that the fulfillment of our nature *requires* that thing. It is this sense in which the "natural" is normative, but it is not the sense in which Isidore is speaking. Isidore does not think universal freedom or common ownership of all things is necessary to the fulfillment of human nature.

[2]   The other sense in which something can belong to the natural law is that matters stood that way when human beings first came onto the scene, before human ingenuity had come up with anything else. Nakedness is natural in this sense, because clothing had to be invented. Nudists mistakenly conclude that for this reason, clothing is wrong. But the nudists have erred, for although nakedness is natural in the primitive sense, it is not natural in the normative sense; it is not a requirement for living in a way suitable to our nature. We do need protection from the elements, such as boots and jackets. We draw both convenience and innocent delight from distinctions of rank, sex, and personal taste, such as a policeman's cap, a woman's pretty skirt, and our friend's bright Hawaiian shirt. At least under the circumstance of the Fall, we also need provisions for modesty.

[3]   St. Thomas explains elsewhere that individual ownership of property has three advantages. First, each person takes better care of his own property than of what belongs to everyone at once. Second, it is easier to pinpoint responsibility if each person is charged with caring for particular things. Third, when goods are divided so that each person has something of his own, there are fewer quarrels. So even though some may have more or better property, the institution of private ownership makes everyone better off than if everything were owned in common.[52] Since St. Thomas's time, other advantages of private property have also been discovered, such as the fact that a collective economy – which is of necessity a planned economy – cannot allocate resources to their most efficient uses, as a market does spontaneously.

[52] II-II, Q. 66, Arts. 1–2.

Slavery – St. Thomas's second example of an innovation helpful to human life – is more problematic. Who could possibly think that slavery makes everyone better off? What on earth could St. Thomas have in mind? The answer is that St. Thomas is not thinking of chattel slavery as practiced in the antebellum American South, but of something like what we call penal servitude. In his sense, whenever we compel prisoners convicted of crimes to perform labor, we are subjecting them to slavery. Although this brief remark suffices for present purposes, readers who wish to explore the matter further may consult the online *Companion to the Commentary.*

For further reflection on the preceding section of the *Treatise on Law,* the online *Companion to the Commentary,* accessible via the Resources link at the book's catalogue webpage, includes a discussion of the following topics:

INVENTIONS, INNOVATIONS, AND NATURE
THE PROBLEM OF SLAVERY

Question 94, Article 6:
Whether the Law of Nature Can Be Abolished from the Heart of Man?

TEXT	PARAPHRASE
Whether the law of nature can be abolished from the heart of man?	Can human beings entirely lack knowledge of the natural law, so that the orientation of their wills toward it is utterly destroyed?

This inquiry is framed with a view to St. Augustine's remark, paraphrased in the *sed contra,* that theft is punished by God's law and the law written in men's hearts (*lex tua, Domine, et lex scripta in cordibus hominum*), which sin itself cannot abolish (*quam ne ipsa quidem delet iniquitas*). What sort of thing is the heart? St. Thomas describes it in many ways. It can be sad or joyful, frozen or melted, pure or soiled; it can love God or fail to love Him. It is the place where our secret thoughts and intentions are hidden, and though we may try without success to rub out the letters, it is imprinted with God's law. But what *is* it? In short, the heart is the will. We are moved toward what seems good to us by two kinds of longing, one arising from the senses, the other from the mind. Sensitive appetite has traditionally been called "the flesh," while intellectual appetite, which is the same as the will, has traditionally been called "the heart."

Curiously, love songs tend to confuse the heart with the flesh, so that the refrain "I love you with all my heart" means not "My whole mind delights in you, and my will is committed to you," but merely "You excite my feelings to the highest possible degree." According to St. Thomas, our fulfillment requires these two kinds of appetite to be completely in agreement, fixed not just on what seems good, but on what really is:

> Accordingly just as it is better that man should both will good and do it in his external act; so also does it belong to the perfection of moral good, that man should be moved unto good, not only in respect of his will, but also in respect of his sensitive appetite; according to Psalm 83:3: 'My heart and my flesh have rejoiced in the living God': where by 'heart' we are to understand the intellectual appetite, and by 'flesh' the sensitive appetite.[53]

The *ultrum* – whether the law of nature can be abolished from the heart of man – is meant not only individually but also collectively. We are asking not only whether it can be abolished from the heart of a single man or woman, but also whether it can be abolished from the hearts of a nation, a generation, or the whole human race.

Contemporary readers would probably add one more to the list of Objections, perhaps something like this: "It would seem that the natural law can be abolished from the heart of man. For clinical psychology has found certain persons, called sociopaths or psychopaths, to be utterly devoid of remorse when they do wrong. Therefore the law of nature can be blotted out." This protest requires extended treatment, but because this is not one of St. Thomas's original list of objections, I take it up not here but in the online *Companion to the Commentary*.

---

[1] *Objection 1. It would seem that the natural law can be abolished from the heart of man. Because on Rm. 2:14, "When the Gentiles who have not the law," etc.* [2] *a gloss says that "the law of righteousness, which sin had blotted out, is graven on the heart of man when he is restored by grace." But the law of righteousness is the law of nature. Therefore the law of nature can be blotted out.*

Objection 1. Apparently, human beings can altogether lose their fundamental orientation toward natural law. In his letter to the Romans, St. Paul writes that a law is written even on the heart of the Gentiles, but as the commentator explains, St. Paul is speaking of the law of righteousness. Having been obliterated by sin, it is re-inscribed on the inner man through the renewal that comes from grace. But the law of righteousness is the same thing as the law of nature, so it follows that the law of nature can be obliterated.

---

[53] I-II, Q. 24, Art. 3; see also I, Q. 83, Art. 3.

[1]   In this verse and the next, St. Paul argues that when Gentiles, who have not been given the law of Moses, do by nature what it requires, they show that what it contains is written on their hearts.

[2]   In his *Commentary on the Letter to the Romans*, St. Thomas considers two possible interpretations of St. Paul's statement that the law is written on the hearts of the gentiles. According to one, he is speaking only of redeemed gentiles, who both know the law and do it. According to the other, he is speaking of unredeemed gentiles too, but he means only that they know the natural law, not that they do it.[54] The Objector does not distinguish these possibilities. He merely argues that if the law of righteousness can be obliterated, then the natural law can be obliterated, because they are the same thing.

[1] **Objection 2.** *Further, the law of grace is more efficacious than the law of nature.* [2] *But the law of grace is blotted out by sin. Much more therefore can the law of nature be blotted out.*	Objection 2. Moreover, the law of grace is more powerful than the law of nature. Yet sin wipes out the law of grace. If sin can destroy what is more powerful, then surely it can destroy what is less powerful. It follows that the law of nature can be wiped out.

[1]   St. Thomas holds that grace is the most effective remedy for the avoidance of sin; and that by grace, anyone who does evil may be moved to repent. Only by grace can concupiscence be repressed; only by grace can fallen man obey the Divine commandments; only by grace can the breach between God and man be repaired. Grace alone makes it possible to acquire faith, hope, and love, and grace alone makes it possible for sins against them to be avoided.[55] None of these things can be said of the law of nature.

[2]   Sin destroys the very source of the order that keeps man's will obedient to God. The virtues infused by grace can be destroyed by even a single sin against charity, which is their root.[56] The Objector reasons that if even the law of grace can be obliterated by sin, then certainly the natural law can be.

[54] See the Commentary on Question 91, Article 2.
[55] Respectively, see Supp., Q. 13, Art. 2; III, Q. 86, Art. 1; Supp., Q. 42, Art. 3, *sed contra*; I-II, Q. 109, Art. 4; I-II, Q. 87, Art. 3; I-II, Q. 62, Art. 1; I-II, Q. 63, Art. 2, ad 2.
[56] I-II, Q. 71, Art. 4, and Q. 87, Art. 3.

Objection 3. Further, that which is established by law is made just. But many things are enacted by men, which are contrary to the law of nature. Therefore the law of nature can be abolished from the heart of man.	Objection 3. Still further, whatever the law enacts is by that act made just. But many human enactments are contrary to natural law. It follows that natural law can be wiped out of the heart.

The Objector does not mean that unjust statutes turn wickedness into good (we see later that St. Thomas does not take him in this sense – and since the Objector is his alter-ego, he ought to know). The sense in which they abolish the law of nature from the heart of man is that the wicked deeds they command or permit are *conventionally considered* just.

[1] *On the contrary, Augustine says (Confess. ii): "Thy law is written in the hearts of men, which iniquity itself effaces not."* [2] *But the law which is written in men's hearts is the natural law. Therefore the natural law cannot be blotted out.*	On the other hand, St. Augustine writes in his *Confessions* that not even sin can erase the law written in men's hearts. Since he is speaking of the natural law, it follows that the answer to the *ultrum* is "No." Natural law cannot be abolished.

[1]   The quotation is taken from St. Augustine's lengthy reflection on the paradox that in his adolescence, he delighted in stealing pears, even though – *and just because* – God's law was written in his heart. He wanted to thumb his nose at that law, to vaunt his own will over it.

Theft is punished by Your law, O Lord, and by the law written in men's hearts, which iniquity itself cannot blot out. For what thief will suffer a thief? Even a rich thief will not suffer him who is driven to it by want. Yet had I a desire to commit robbery, and did so, compelled neither by hunger, nor poverty, but through a distaste for well-doing, and a lustiness of iniquity. For I pilfered that of which I had already sufficient, and much better. Nor did I desire to enjoy what I pilfered, but the theft and sin itself.[57]

[2]   For purposes of the *sed contra*, St. Thomas emphasizes the indelible inscription on St. Augustine's heart, rather than the delight St. Augustine he took in thumbing his nose at it. Objectors who use the delight as evidence against the inscription miss the point of St. Augustine's psychological analysis; had there been no law, there would have been no thrill in

[57] Augustine of Hipp, *Confessions*, Book 2, Chapter 4, trans. J.G. Pilkington, ed. Philip Schaff, rev. and ed. by Kevin Knight. Available at www.newadvent.org/fathers/110102. htm.

violating it. That thrill – not hunger, poverty, or pleasure in the flavor of pears – was his one and only motive.

[1] *I answer that, As stated above (4,5), there belong to the natural law, first, certain most general precepts, that are known to all; and secondly, certain secondary and more detailed precepts, which are, as it were, conclusions following closely from first principles.* [2] *As to those general principles, the natural law, in the abstract, can nowise be blotted out from men's hearts.* [3] *But it is blotted out in the case of a particular action, in so far as reason is hindered from applying the general principle to a particular point of practice, on account of concupiscence or some other passion, as stated above (77, 2).* [4] *But as to the other, i.e. the secondary precepts, the natural law can be blotted out from the human heart, either by evil persuasions,* [5] *just as in speculative matters errors occur in respect of necessary conclusions;* [6] *or by vicious customs and corrupt habits, as among some men, theft, and even unnatural vices, as the Apostle states (Rm. i), were not esteemed sinful.*

Here is my response. Before all else, the natural law contains the most universal precepts, which are known to everyone. Closely following are certain secondary precepts, which are more detailed.

Precepts of the former kind cannot in any way be erased from men's hearts – that is, not as universal rules. As I have explained earlier in the *Summa*, however, they can be nullified in practice, just to the degree that concupiscence or another passion holds reason back from correctly applying the universal rules to particular things.

Precepts of the latter kind, which we may call secondary precepts, *can* be erased from men's hearts. Sometimes this happens because of bad opinions. This is much like the way theoretical reason makes mistakes about necessary conclusions. Sometimes, too, it happens because of depraved customs and corrupt habits. This is why some men have failed to regard acts of banditry – or even unnatural vices, as St. Paul explains – as transgressions.

[1] As in Article 4, general precepts are precepts that hold without exception in either rectitude or knowledge – they are not only right in every case, but also known to every person. Since here he also calls them first principles or starting points, many readers mistakenly think that by the most general precepts, St. Thomas means "the firstest" first principles, the axioms, so to speak. In that case, then by secondary precepts, he would mean everything proved from the axioms, that is, all the theorems. The problem with that interpretation is that some of the theorems of natural law, such as "Do not steal," also hold universally.

For that reason, it makes better sense to take the expression "general principles" as referring not only to the axioms, but also to their most universal corollaries: To *all* precepts that hold without exception. Thus, when he calls the general precepts "first principles," he means not that they are absolutely first, but only that they are relatively first – first with respect to the secondary precepts derived from them, which are the everyday moral rules.

This view of St. Thomas's reference to general precepts harmonizes with his statement in Question 100, Article 1, that "there are certain things which the natural reason of every man, of its own accord and at once, judges to be done or not to be done: e.g. 'Honor thy father and thy mother,' and 'Thou shalt not kill, Thou shalt not steal': and these belong to the law of nature absolutely." For although a precept like the prohibition of murder does hold without exception and does serve as a basis for further reasoning, it is not an *absolutely* first principle; behind it lies the prohibition of harm in general, and behind even that, the precept to do good and avoid evil.[58]

[2]   The English translation, "in the abstract," is correct but a little misleading. What St. Thomas actually says is *in universali,* which may be rendered "considered as universals" or "as universal rules." His point is to distinguish whether reason knows the precepts themselves from whether it applies them correctly. As we are about to see, one can certainly misapply them. He holds here, though, that it is literally impossible for a reasonable person not to have a habitual grasp of the fact that they are true and right in themselves.

[3]   Passion hinders reason from applying universal rules to particular things in three ways, which St. Thomas lists in I-II, Question 77, Article 2. One is distraction; my mind may be so absorbed with passion that there is no room left for rational consideration. Another is opposition; though I know that a certain thing is wrong in general, I may be so strongly attracted to it that my imagination leads my judgment astray. The third is bodily change; I may be so worked up by passion that I become unable to reason correctly, as though insane – just as in other bodily conditions, such as drunkenness and sleep, I lose the power of reasoning altogether.

When passion hinders a person from applying a principle he knows to be true to a particular case, he isn't really basing his reasoning on that principle, but on a different principle, a false one suggested by his passion. For example, reason may tell him the true principle that fornication

---

[58] For now I am skirting the knotty question of whether *all* harm to others is to be avoided, to which I return in Question 95, Article 2.

is wrong, yet at the same time, passion may tell him the false principle that pleasure must be pursued. What happens? That depends on which kind of person we are talking about. *Temperate* people do not have this problem; they habitually reason from the general principles suggested by reason. *Intemperate* people know the general principles suggested by reason, but habitually allow passion to shove them out of the way, so they reason from general principles suggested by passion. Then come *continent* people; the term is used in various senses, but St. Thomas uses it for people who are self-controlled, but not self-mastered. Although they are habitually torn between the general principles suggested by reason and by passion, in the end, the principles suggested by reason tend to prevail. *Incontinent* persons are also habitually torn, but in their case, the principles suggested by passion tend to prevail.[59]

[4] As we saw above, it is literally impossible to have a sane adult mind and yet not to understand the universal precepts. Everyone knows, for example, the negative form of the Golden Rule – that he should not do to someone else what he would not wish done to him – even if he is not thinking of the principle at every moment. But it *is* possible to have a sane adult mind and yet fail to understand some of the secondary precepts. I may know that I should not do to someone else what I would not wish done to me, but what if I have perverse ideas about what I would wish done to me? I may know that adultery is always wrong, but what if I entertain eccentric and self-serving ideas about what counts as adultery?

[5] Mistakes in deriving necessary conclusions from first principles can happen in theoretical reasoning too. One might grasp the axioms of plane geometry, and yet think a false theorem true or a true theorem false. One might grasp the propositional form of the principles of identity, non-contradiction, and excluded middle, and yet be quite poor at logic.

[6] As explained in Article 4, St. Thomas distinguishes between robbery and theft. The word here incorrectly translated as "theft" is *latrocinia*, referring to banditries, which are not acts of theft but acts of a particular kind of robbery. He is thinking again of the ancient Germans, who knew that banditry in general was wrong but failed to recognize banditry against other tribes as wrong. So this first example is not nearly as sweeping as it seems.

---

[59] St. Thomas presents a sketch of the idea in I-II, Q. 77, Art. 2, ad 4, and a more complete discussion in *De Malo* ("On Evil"). Q. 3, Art. 9, ad 7, as well as in Book 7, Lecture 4 of his commentary on Aristotle's *Nicomachean Ethics*.

The example of unnatural vice comes from Romans 1:18–32 – a complex passage, the argument of which may be analyzed and paraphrased as follows. From the beginning, the eternal power and deity of God have been recognized from the evidence of Creation. The pagans who refused Him honor have no excuse, since they are not genuinely ignorant of His reality, but suppress what they know. In view of this fact, God surrendered them to the natural consequences of their obstinacy, allowing it to take its course. Their imaginations became futile, and their hearts were darkened. Having exchanged the supreme truth about God for a lie, they lost their grasp on other aspects of truth as well. Instead of adoring the Creator, they worshipped things He had made. Their understanding of what He had made became increasingly distorted, so that they regarded as good what is really evil. Although it is not their only vice, the most startling manifestation of their downward slide was the fact that women and men alike exchanged natural intercourse for unnatural, each joining sexually with those of the same sex, suffering further natural consequences for doing so.[60]

Reply to Objection 1. Sin blots out the law of nature in particular cases, not universally, except perchance in regard to the secondary precepts of the natural law, in the way stated above.	Reply to Objection 1. Sin does nullify the correct application of natural law to particulars. But it does not erase the [orientation of the heart toward] the general rules – unless, perhaps, we are speaking of the secondary precepts, as I have explained.

Someone might object that to say sin blots out the law of nature "in particular cases" is to suppose that a person could hold two contrary opinions at the same time: A true universal proposition, and a false particular judgment – which is impossible. St. Thomas responds in Question 77 that if we are speaking of those items of knowledge or belief that a person holds "actually" – the ones he is actually thinking about – then no, he cannot entertain contraries at the same time. But it is quite possible for him to know a universal principle *habitually* at the same time that he maintains a contrary particular judgment *actually*. He is only thinking about one of them.[61]

---

[60] For St. Thomas's discussion of the passage, see *Lectures on the Letter to the Romans*, trans. Fabian Larcher, ed. Jeremy Holmes (Naples, FL: Aquinas Center for Theological Renewal, Ave Maria University, 2008), Chapter 1, Lecture 6, Sections 109–168, available at http://nvjournal.net/files/Aquinas_on_Romans.pdf.

[61] I-II, Q. 77, Art. 2, ad 3.

Reply to Objection 2. Although grace is more efficacious than nature, yet nature is more essential to man, and therefore more enduring.	Reply to Objection 2. Even though grace is more powerful than nature, nature is more permanent because it pertains more to man's essence.

Since we did not make ourselves, in a certain sense even our nature is a gift of grace. Even so, there is a difference between the grace that gratuitously brought humans into being and the grace that may be gratuitously added to their being. Our nature is what we *are*. In this sense, nature is more essential to man. Moreover, that which is added to something can simply be removed from it, but what it *is* can be taken away only by destroying it. In this sense, nature is also more enduring.

Reply to Objection 3. This argument is true of the secondary precepts of the natural law, against which some legislators have framed certain enactments which are unjust.	Reply to Objection 3. The Objector's reasoning is sound, if taken in reference to the secondary precepts of natural law. Opposing them, some legislators do enact crooked statutes.

St. Thomas's point is that not even wicked rulers enact statutes that violate the universal precepts, commanding, for example, "Rob anyone, whenever you wish," or "Shed any innocent blood at any time." Rather they violate the secondary precepts; they authorize *particular* wicked acts. "Neighboring tribes may be raided whenever the chieftain commands." "You shall put Jews to death in gas chambers, but leave non-Jews alone." or "At your own convenience, you may employ lethal violence against unborn human lives." Such so-called laws are *iniqua:* slanted, uneven, in the broad sense unjust. For the reasons explained in Question 90, however, they are not true laws, but frauds, because they are incapable of serving as rules and measures of our acts, or of binding us in conscience.

For further reflection on the preceding section of the *Treatise on Law*, the online *Companion to the Commentary*, accessible via the Resources link at the book's catalogue webpage, includes a discussion of the following topics:

Do Even Sociopaths and Psychopaths Know the Natural Law?

Is Every Apparent Case of Moral Ignorance a Real One?

Before Reading Question 95

Those with a practical cast of mind may be tempted to begin reading the *Treatise on Law* here, in the section on human law. To these I say: Resist. The *Treatise* needs to be studied in the context of the rest of the *Summa,* and the discussion of human law in the context of the rest of the *Treatise on Law.*

Suppose we do try to read these three *quaestiones* by themselves. What will happen? We will approach them with our own preconceived views of law, which for most of us means the views we absorb from the surrounding culture.

One reason why this is a bad idea is that we will miss the opportunity for St. Thomas's help in seeing what might be wrong with these preconceived views. When his discussion of human law mentions God, for instance, we will raise all sorts of objections that he doesn't answer – because he has answered them earlier.

The other is that, since St. Thomas does not share our preconceived views, we will have difficulty grasping what he says at all. In fact, we may even find it hard to understand why he asks the questions he does. To consider but a single example, suppose we hold the common view that law and justice are nothing but what our rulers – or the majority – or the smart people – say it is. If this view is true, then nothing they ordain could ever be unjust, and it will be very hard to see why St. Thomas should even ask how we should respond when they do enact what is unjust.

St. Thomas's Prologue to Question 95:
Of Human Law

TEXT	PARAPHRASE
[1] *We must now consider human law; and (1) this law considered in itself;* [2] *(2) its power;* [3] *(3) its mutability.*	The investigation of human law will occupy us for some time, because it involves three broad inquiries, each of which contains a number of smaller inquiries. Question 95 looks into the essence of human law – what kind of law it is. Question 96 asks how far it reaches. Finally, Question 97 considers how it changes.
[4] *Under the first head there are four points of inquiry: (1) Its utility.* [5] *(2) Its origin.* [6] *(3) Its quality.* [7] *(4) Its division.*	Concerning the essence of human law, Question 95 raises four distinct subquestions. Article 1 concerns what human law is good for; Article 2, the foundation from which it springs; Article 3, the qualities it needs; and Article 4, the varieties it contains.

[1]   The *Treatise on Law* began in Question 90 by inquiring into the essence of law: What is it in general? Each time St. Thomas takes up another kind of law, he takes up the question of essence in more detail: What is *that kind* of law?

[2]   The term translated as "power," *potestate*, is usually given as "power," "ability," "capacity," or "force." It is a little unusual to describe *potestate* as "reach," but as we see when we come to the six *ultra* or queries of Question 96, the scope, or reach, of human law is just what St. Thomas is asking about. For example, he wants to know whether it may suppress every vice, whether it must be followed even if unjust, and whether one must follow it to the letter.

[3]   Eternal law is altogether unchangeable. Concerning the other kinds of law, however, the question of change has already presented some surprises. The underlying purpose of Divine law cannot change, but God has promulgated two editions of it, each for a different phase in the history of the plan of salvation. The foundations of natural law cannot change, but new secondary precepts may acquire the force of natural law on the basis of the general precepts, and occasionally a secondary precept meets an "obstacle." We may well surmise that the question of change in human law will present surprises too.

[4]   This is one of those cases in which the most literal translation is the most misleading, because when English readers see the word "utility," they think of the doctrine called Utilitarianism, and St. Thomas is as far from being a Utilitarian as it is possible to be. To ask about the *utilitate* of human law is simply to ask why we need it, what service it performs for us, how we are better off having it than doing without – in short, what it is good for.

[5]   It may seem that the origin of human laws is obvious: Human lawmakers make them. Yes, of course, but this is not what St. Thomas means when he asks about their origin. He is asking from what deeper well human lawmakers are drawing water – on what deeper considerations their commands depend in order to be laws, rather than mere episodes in the history of coercion.

[6]   Speaking for the tradition, Isidore enumerates nine qualities that all laws should have, nine rules of thumb that good lawmakers try to follow. But is this tradition correct? Are all nine really needed? Have any been left out? And what happened to the four criteria enumerated in Question 90?

[7]   Anyone can list different kinds of human law, but a good classification is a difficult achievement. For example, Roman discussions of human law distinguished between civil law and law of nations, but from a certain point of view it may seem that law of nations belongs not to human but to natural law. What varieties does human law really contain, and how do they really differ?

For further reflection on the preceding section of the *Treatise on Law*, the online *Companion to the Commentary*, accessible via the Resources link at the book's catalogue webpage, includes a discussion of the following topic:

ARE WE CO-LEGISLATORS WITH GOD?

Question 95, Article 1:
Whether It Was Useful for Laws to Be Framed by Men?

TEXT	PARAPHRASE
Whether it was useful for laws to be framed by men?	What good are human laws? Do we really need them?

The first objection amounts to suggesting that no human government is needed, at least if we understand government as something that has authority to use force; the second and third objections concede the necessity of human government, but instead of the rule of laws, they promote the rule of men.

| [1] *Objection 1. It would seem that it was not useful for laws to be framed by men. Because the purpose of every law is that man be made good thereby, as stated above (92, 1).* [2] *But men are more to be induced to be good willingly by means of admonitions, than against their will, by means of laws. Therefore there was no need to frame laws.* | Objection 1. Apparently, human laws serve no purpose. As we have already seen, the only purpose in framing any law is to make men virtuous. But to make men virtuous, one must cooperate with the will rather than fight it. Hence, though something may be accomplished by gentle words of correction, one can hardly expect success by means of laws. |

[1]   The Objector refers only to the positive purpose of law: Not the restraint of vice, but the encouragement of virtue.

[2]   Virtue has to do with how we habitually make choices. The Objector argues that because it is a disposition *of* the will, it would be difficult to make people virtuous *against* their wills.

In place of laws, the Objector proposes substituting mere admonitions. Presumably there would still have to be an admonishing agency, though it would not be a true government because it could not coerce. This is somewhat different from the proposal of today's anarchists, who propose in place of laws not admonitions, but spontaneous order, and who propose it not for the sake of virtue, but for the sake of what they consider freedom. The anarchistic proposal is discussed briefly in the online *Companion to the Commentary.*

| [1] *Objection 2. Further, As the Philosopher says (Ethic. v, 4), "men have recourse to a judge as to animate justice." [2] But animate justice is better than inanimate justice, which contained in laws. Therefore it would have been better for the execution of justice to be entrusted to the decision of judges, than to frame laws in addition.* | Objection 2. Moreover, laws are dead justice. Aristotle points out that for *living* justice, people turn to judges. Since living justice is better than dead justice, we would have been better off if no laws had been given out at all, and justice had been administered by judges alone. |

[1]   A judge, who is an embodied living mind rather than an inert rule, can consider the circumstances of the case at hand. Aristotle writes,

[W]hen people dispute, they take refuge in the judge; and to go to the judge is to go to justice; for the nature of the judge is to be a sort of animate justice; and they seek the judge as an intermediate, and in some states they call judges mediators, on the assumption that if they get what is intermediate they will get what is just.[1]

St. Thomas remarks in his commentary on the *Nicomachean Ethics* that for a judge to be living justice is for his soul to be "entirely possessed by justice."[2]

[2]   Even if there are laws, there must be living justice, because someone must be found to establish the facts of the case and to declare how the law applies to them – a point to which St. Thomas later returns. The point in dispute is whether there can be living justice without laws. Biblically informed readers may wonder why the Objector doesn't supplement Aristotle with the authority of Scripture. After the Israelites have crossed over into the Promised Land, and after Moses and Joshua have died, for a time the Hebrew people are ruled solely by judges. Moreover, when they ask that the system of judges be converted into a kingship, God chastises them on grounds that He Himself is their king.[3] However, this Scriptural example is beside the point. The question on the table is whether to be ruled by judges *instead of having laws*, rather than whether to be ruled by judges instead of by other sorts of rulers; it not about the best form of government, but about the relationship between government

---

[1]   Aristotle, *Nicomachean Ethics*, Book 5, Chapter 4, trans. W.D. Ross (public domain).
[2]   Thomas Aquinas, *Commentary on Aristotle's Nicomachean Ethics*, Book 5, Lecture 6, trans. C.J. Litzinger, O.P., rev. ed. (Notre Dame, IN: Dumb Ox Books, 1993), p. 302.
[3]   1 Samuel 8. We return to this incident in I-II, Q. 105, Art. 1.

and laws. Even during the period of the Judges, the Israelites were subject to the Old Law, the Law of Moses. St. Thomas turns to the question of the best form of government later on, in Question 105.

[1] **Objection 3.** *Further, every law is framed for the direction of human actions, as is evident from what has been stated above (90, A1,2). [2] But since human actions are about singulars, which are infinite in number, matter pertaining to the direction of human actions cannot be taken into sufficient consideration except by a wise man, who looks into each one of them. [3] Therefore it would have been better for human acts to be directed by the judgment of wise men, than by the framing of laws. Therefore there was no need of human laws.*	**Objection 3.** Still further, the purpose of all law is to regulate human acts – something we established much earlier. But there is no such thing as an act in general, for every act is a particular act, having to do with particular things. Since these particularities are beyond counting, no law can possibly lay down the right thing to do in every case. The better way to regulate human acts is not even to try, to put matters in the hands of wise men, who consider each case as it comes up.

[1] St. Thomas had written in Question 90, Article 1, "Law is a rule and measure of acts, whereby man is induced to act or is restrained from acting."

[2] As we saw in Question 94, Article 4, all but the most general precepts of natural law have exceptions. The more we try to account for the exceptions by writing conditions into our human laws, the more exceptions they will have. Although there are an infinite number of possible circumstances, there cannot be an infinite number of laws. Consequently, the Objector reasons, we must give up the futile attempt to govern human actions by laws, and rely instead on the case-by-case judgments of wise men.

[3] With an adequate supply of men wise enough for case-by-case judgment, the Objector reasons that human laws would be unnecessary.

[1] **On the contrary,** *Isidore says (Etym. v, 20): "Laws were made that in fear thereof human audacity might be held in check, that innocence might be safeguarded in the midst of wickedness, and that the dread of punishment might prevent the wicked from doing harm."* [2] *But these things are most necessary to mankind. Therefore it was necessary that human laws should be made.*	**On the other hand,** Isidore holds that laws were made so that the insolent might be restrained by fear, the innocent guarded from the reprobate, and the irreverent curbed by dread of punishment from doing harm. Human laws are needed because these purposes are of supreme importance to human life.

[1] Interestingly, Isidore refers to the negative purpose of law: Not the encouragement of virtue, but the restraint of vice. This reverses the emphasis of Objection 1.

[2] Isidore's remark is telling, but all it really shows is that human actions need to be regulated. It does not show why "these things" could not have been accomplished by admonitions or judges, rather than by laws.

---

[1] *I answer that, As stated above (63, 1; 94, 3), man has a natural aptitude for virtue; but the perfection of virtue must be acquired by man by means of some kind of training.* [2] *Thus we observe that man is helped by industry in his necessities, for instance, in food and clothing. Certain beginnings of these he has from nature, viz. his reason and his hands; but he has not the full complement, as other animals have, to whom nature has given sufficiency of clothing and food.* [3] *Now it is difficult to see how man could suffice for himself in the matter of this training: since the perfection of virtue consists chiefly in withdrawing man from undue pleasures, to which above all man is inclined, and especially the young, who are more capable of being trained. Consequently a man needs to receive this training from another, whereby to arrive at the perfection of virtue.* [4] *And as to those young people who are inclined to acts of virtue, by their good natural disposition, or by custom, or rather by the gift of God, paternal training suffices, which is by admonitions.* [5] *But since some are found to be depraved, and prone to vice, and not easily amenable to words, it was necessary for such to be restrained from evil by force and fear, in order that, at least, they might desist from evil-doing, and leave others in peace, and that they themselves, by being habituated*

Here is my response. We have already seen that man has a natural aptitude for virtue, but this aptitude lies fallow until cultivated by discipline. It is much the same with necessities such as food and clothing: Though nature provides a beginning by providing us with minds and hands, it does not provide all that is needed, as it does with other animals. We have to work for it.

Self-discipline hardly suffices, because the main requirement for the full development of virtue is holding men back from inappropriate pleasures, which they seek above all else. It is especially important to restrain the young, with whom discipline is more effective. So to become completely virtuous, a man cannot give this sort of training to himself; he must receive it from someone else.

Now some young men are predisposed to virtue by good natural temperament, by good social customs, or, still better, by the gift of God. For them, a father's training is sufficient, and such training does operate by gentle warnings. We find, however, that other young men are impudent and reckless, predisposed to vice. Since they are not easily turned by mere words, they must be curbed by force and dread. If they are consistently trained in this way, they may at least cease from doing evil and let others live in peace. Perhaps, in time, they will even come to act willingly in the way they at first acted only through fear – and so come to practice virtue.

in this way, might be brought to do willingly what hitherto they did from fear, and thus become virtuous.[6] Now this kind of training, which compels through fear of punishment, is the discipline of laws. Therefore in order that man might have peace and virtue, it was necessary for laws to be framed: [7] for, as the Philosopher says (Polit. i, 2), "as man is the most noble of animals if he be perfect in virtue, so is he the lowest of all, if he be severed from law and righteousness"; because man can use his reason to devise means of satisfying his lusts and evil passions, which other animals are unable to do.

But this kind of discipline, which compels through dread of punishment, is the very kind that laws apply. We find, then, that laws had to be enacted, not only that man might have peace, but even so that he might have virtue. That most esteemed of all philosophers, Aristotle, draws a corollary when he remarks that although man is the best of animals when perfectly virtuous, he is the worst of them when divorced from law and justice. For with his mind, which other animals lack, he ponders ways to glut his lusts and furies.

---

[1]　St. Thomas explains in Question 63, Article 1, that virtue is natural to man, but in an "inchoate" way – that is, only in the sense that we have a readiness to develop it. This readiness consists in the facts that the will has a natural appetite to seek good in the way reason judges best, and that certain starting points for deliberation are naturally instilled in our minds. But nature does not endow us with fully formed virtue; the outline that nature provides us must be filled out by discipline.

[2]　Here St. Thomas draws an analogy between how nature has equipped us for virtue, and how it has equipped us for physical nourishment and protection from the elements. In both cases, our equipment is real but incomplete.

[3]　If the development of virtue requires discipline, then could self-discipline be enough? No, because the young find it difficult to understand that not everything pleasant is good; they could hardly be expected to hold *themselves* back from inappropriate pleasures.

　　Although the "inclination" to pursue undue pleasure is with us from birth, it is not a natural inclination in the sense of Question 94, Article 2, because it is harmful to creatures of our kind, not good for them; our sensual appetites are made to be ruled by reason. The Fall has disordered us in such a way that our sensual appetites demand to rule themselves, and even many grown-ups find it hard to see why they shouldn't.

[4] Of course fathers use coercion as well as admonition: When children misbehave, they may apply corporal punishment such as spanking, or force them to sit in the corner of the room to calm down and consider their offenses. However, St. Thomas is not thinking of children; he is thinking of young men. In the first place, though not yet fully trained, they are too big for their fathers to coerce (with mothers, they reach this point even sooner). In the second place, unlike small children, they roam freely through the city, so they are not always under the parental eye.

For discussion of individual differences in natural disposition, see the commentary on Question 94, Article 4.

[5] St. Thomas is probably reflecting on Aristotle's remarks at the very end of the *Nicomachean Ethics*. Paternal admonitions have advantages that law can never match, Aristotle writes, because "the children start with a natural affection and disposition to obey" and because a father can treat each child in just the way that the child's own temperament requires. On the other hand, law has a unique advantage too, because "the paternal command indeed has not the required force or compulsive power." As St. Thomas explains elsewhere, the law is more powerful by way of fear, but the paternal command is more powerful by way of love.[4]

[6] Unlike either Objection 1, which mentioned only the positive purposes of law, or the *sed contra*, which mentioned only its negative purposes, St. Thomas emphasizes both the restraint of evil and the encouragement of good – peace and virtue.

One must proceed carefully: Many readers take St. Thomas's statement as though he were giving a definition of law: That which compels through fear of punishment. He is certainly defining something, but he is defining the *discipline* of law, not law as such. As we saw in Question 90, and have been reminded in Objection 3, law is a rule and measure of distinctively human acts; therefore it must be an ordinance of reason, for the common good, made by public authority and promulgated. Punishment is merely the discipline by which it is enforced.

[7] More fully, Aristotle writes, "For man, when perfected, is the best of animals, but, when separated from law and justice, he is the worst of all;

---

[4] Aristotle, *Nicomachean Ethics*, Book 10, Chapter 9, trans. W.D. Ross (public domain); Thomas Aquinas, *Commentary on the Nicomachean Ethics*, Book 10, Lecture 15.

since armed injustice is the more dangerous, and he is equipped at birth with arms, meant to be used by intelligence and virtue, which he may use for the worst ends. Wherefore, if he have not virtue, he is the most unholy and the most savage of animals, and the most full of lust and gluttony. But justice is the bond of men in states, for the administration of justice, which is the determination of what is just, is the principle of order in political society."[5]

St. Thomas takes Aristotle to mean that in a certain sense virtue and prudence themselves may be used as weapons for evil purposes. Taken in this way, however, the term "virtue" refers not to true but to crippled virtue, and the term "prudence" refers not to true but to deformed prudence. Recall the discussion of the fearless robber in the commentary on Question 92, Article 1; certainly his crimes are aided by his bravery. As St. Thomas remarks, wicked men also "cleverly plan various frauds, and, by abstaining from food and drink, become capable of enduring hunger and thirst so as to persevere longer in wickedness."[6] But bravery, slyness, and endurance fall short of full courage, prudence, and temperance, because although the wicked man represses his fear, trains his intelligence, and disciplines his appetites, he does all this for the wrong reasons.

[1] *Reply to Objection 1. Men who are well disposed are led willingly to virtue by being admonished better than by coercion:* [2] *but men who are evilly disposed are not led to virtue unless they are compelled.*	Reply to Objection 1. Men of good disposition are more easily led to virtue by gentle warnings than by pressure; but men of evil disposition can be brought to virtue only if coerced.

[1]   St. Thomas concedes that the method of admonition proposed by the Objector works for *some* men. In fact, for those already predisposed to develop in the right way, the shame of reproof provides a stronger and more reliable motive to mend their ways than the fear of punishment.

[2]   Unfortunately, some men are not all men. Even if all fathers were perfect, some sons would need to be coerced; admonitions alone would not move them.

---

5   Aristotle, *Politics*, Book 1, Chapter 2, trans. W.D. Ross (public domain).
6   Thomas Aquinas, *Commentary on Aristotle's Politics*, Book 1, Chapter [Lecture] 1, trans. Richard J. Regan (Indianapolis, IN: Hackett, 2007), p. 19.

[1] *Reply to Objection 2. As the Philosopher says (Rhet. i, 1), "it is better that all things be regulated by law, than left to be decided by judges":* [2] *and this for three reasons. First, because it is easier to find a few wise men competent to frame right laws, than to find the many who would be necessary to judge aright of each single case.* [3] *Secondly, because those who make laws consider long beforehand what laws to make; whereas judgment on each single case has to be pronounced as soon as it arises: and it is easier for man to see what is right, by taking many instances into consideration, than by considering one solitary fact.* [4] *Thirdly, because lawgivers judge in the abstract and of future events; whereas those who sit in judgment of things present, towards which they are affected by love, hatred, or some kind of cupidity; wherefore their judgment is perverted.*

[5] *Since then the animated justice of the judge is not found in every man, and since it can be deflected, therefore it was necessary, whenever possible, for the law to determine how to judge, and for very few matters to be left to the decision of men.*

Reply to Objection 2. The Objector tries to support his complaint by appealing to the authority of Aristotle, but as the same philosopher explains in another work, matters are better ordered by laws than by judges. Aristotle gives three reasons. First, it is easier to find a few wise men to make good laws than the huge number of wise men who would be needed to hear every particular case and render the right judgment. Second, legislators may take as much time as they need to make these general rules, taking into consideration whatever varieties of circumstance they think likely to arise, but judges must judge each case right away, considering only the facts it presents. Finally, because judges must give decisions about the particular matters brought before them, their judgments are easily warped by love, hate, or one of various kinds of greed. Legislative judgments are less susceptible to such distortion, because they concern not present and particular matters, but prospective and general matters.

So because the living justice of a judge is not often found among men, and because judicial decisions can so easily be swayed, we must settle as many things as possible by law, committing the smallest possible number to the discretion of judges.

[1]   The three reasons St. Thomas offers for why acts are better regulated by laws than by judges almost exactly follows the three reasons offered by Aristotle, with only a few small exceptions discussed below.

[2]   Of course, even if good laws are enacted ahead of time, judges will still be need to adjudicate the cases that arise under them. The point is that far fewer judges will be needed to do so than if there were no laws at all.

[3]   The second disadvantage of leaving everything to judges is that because legislators are making rules for cases that have not yet arisen, they can take their time; judges cannot.

Oddly, the clause, "and it is easier for man to see what is right, by taking many instances into consideration, than by considering one solitary fact," anticipates the next disadvantage to be considered; it is not about having to render judgment quickly, but about having to render it about particulars. At first it does not seem to belong here. Perhaps, however, St. Thomas is trying to suggest that the third disadvantage *compounds* the second one. *Just because* judges must consider one instance at a time rather than many instances at one, they need more time for sound judgment, and yet they have less. Aristotle does not make this interesting point.

[4]   When a legislator is making general rules to cover all sorts of possible future contingencies, it may be difficult for him to anticipate how they might affect his friends, enemies, and vested interests. But when the judge's enemy has been accused of a crime, when his friend has brought suit against someone, or when a legal complaint has been made about an enterprise in which the judge holds a share of the stock, there can be no doubt. So no matter how difficult it is for legislators to resist the perversion of judgment, for judges it is harder still.

[5]   The preceding consideration would not apply if all judges embodied the living perfection of the requisite virtue of justice – but not many do.

[1] *Reply to Objection 3. Certain individual facts which cannot be covered by the law "have necessarily to be committed to judges," as the Philosopher says in the same passage:* [2] *for instance, "concerning something that has happened or not happened,"* *and the like.*	Reply to Objection 3. As Aristotle concedes in the same passage of the *Rhetoric* quoted above, singular facts that the law does not cover are necessarily committed to judges – facts such as whether something has or has not been done, and that sort of thing.

[1]   To illustrate such individual facts, Aristotle mentions "whether something has happened or has not happened, will be or will not be, [or] is or is not."[7] In speaking of facts which cannot be comprehended (*comprehendi*) by the law, St. Thomas might also be thinking of circumstances

---

[7]   Aristotle, *Rhetoric*, Book 1, Chapter 1, trans. W. Rhys Roberts (public domain).

the lawmakers did not anticipate, so that application of the letter of the law produces a result contrary to what they would have intended. This raises the problem of *equitable* judgment, to which St. Thomas returns in Question 96, Article 5.

[2] St. Thomas and Aristotle picture the process the same way: Legislators enact the law, judges come afterward. Judges determine both the facts of the case (what happened?) and how the law applies to these facts (what does it tell us to do about what happened?). Our own jurisprudence separates the latter two roles, assigning the determination of the facts to temporary citizen judges (whom we call not judges but "jurors"), and the determination of how the law applies to the facts to permanent professional judges (whom we do call "judges").

In some legal systems, judges themselves make a subordinate kind of law, because from a multitude of decisions that apply the law to the facts of different cases, they accumulate precedents, and from these precedents, they generalize precepts. This is not necessarily wrong. If we follow St. Thomas, however, the ultimate purpose of such precepts should be to elucidate what the legislators have enacted, not to displace it. If judicial precepts do displace it, then the judges have acted unjustly, because they have usurped an authority that belongs to someone else.

For further reflection on the preceding section of the *Treatise on Law*, the online *Companion to the Commentary*, accessible via the Resources link at the book's catalogue webpage, includes a discussion of the following topic:

THE FUTILITY OF ANARCHISM

Question 95, Article 2:
Whether Every Human Law Is Derived from the Natural Law?

TEXT	PARAPHRASE
Whether every human law is derived from the natural law?	Must every human law be rooted in the natural law, or can a human law rest on human enactment alone?

"Theft of property worth up to P shall be punishable by Q, and of property worth more than P by R." If we say the statute is rooted in natural law because natural law prohibits theft, then where in nature do those details about P, Q, and R come from? Or if we say that the laws of marriage are rooted in the natural institution of marriage, then where in nature do we find rules about licenses, waiting periods, and filing a signed certificate with the registrar? Since various legal systems arrange such matters in various ways, it is easy to see how someone might view human law as resting on nothing but the sheer fact of having been enacted. But since deeper considerations lie in the background, it is equally easy to see how someone might view human enactment as mere recognition of what natural law has already decreed. How should we think of such matters?

In solving the puzzle, St. Thomas forces us to ask, not just whether every human law is rooted in the natural law, but whether every human law is rooted *in the same way* and *in every respect* in the natural law.

[1] *Objection 1. It would seem that not every human law is derived from the natural law. For the Philosopher says (Ethic. v, 7) that "the legal just is that which originally was a matter of indifference." But those things which arise from the natural law are not matters of indifference.* [2] *Therefore the enactments of human laws are not derived from the natural law.*	Objection 1. Apparently, human laws do not have to be rooted in the natural law. In the *Nicomachean Ethics*, Aristotle explains that conventional or "legal" justice includes things that, before the intervention of human authority, might as well be done one way as another. But in matters that do arise from natural law, it does matter which way they are done. This shows that not all of the arrangements of human law are rooted in natural law.

[1]   Aristotle defines conventional or "legal" justice as "that which is originally indifferent, but when it has been laid down is not indifferent"[8] – in other words, that which does not have to be a particular way *until the matter is settled by formal enactment,* after which it does have to be a particular way. His illustrations of legal justice are how much must be paid to ransom a prisoner (since the ransom might have been set at a different amount), what animals must be offered in a sacrifice (since different animals might have been required), and whether such and such a military hero is to be commemorated with a public sacrifice (since he might have been honored differently or not at all).

To say that these arrangements are "indifferent" prior to enactment does not mean that any possible way of settling them would have been equally prudent or fitting, but merely that no one way of settling them was obligatory. But isn't it always obligatory to do the *one best* thing?

[8]   Aristotle, *Nicomachean Ethics*, trans. W.D. Ross, Book 5, Chapter 7 (public domain).

Not always, for although there are better and worse things, there isn't always a one best thing. For example, it would be foolish for lawmakers to enact that high-speed vehicles may drive on either lane of the highway, but it isn't obviously better to have them drive in the right lane than in the left.

[2] What the Objector really says is that the enactments of human laws are not *all* derived (*non omnia derivantur*) from natural law. Logically, this makes better sense; he is not saying that *no* human laws are derived from it. His point is that since matters of conventional or "legal" justice could just as well be arranged differently than they are, they must not be grounded in nature.

[1] *Objection 2. Further, positive law is contrasted with natural law, as stated by Isidore (Etym. v, 4) and the Philosopher (Ethic. v, 7).* [2] *But those things which flow as conclusions from the general principles of the natural law belong to the natural law, as stated above (94, 4). Therefore that which is established by human law does not belong to the natural law.*	Objection 2. Moreover, as Isidore and Aristotle remind us, positive and natural laws are different things. But we saw earlier that conclusions derived from the general principles of natural law belong to natural, not human law. It follows that things that originate in human legal procedures do *not* belong to natural law.

[1] In the sense employed here, positive law is law that has been *posited,* given legal force just through being enacted. A positive law makes an act right or wrong that would otherwise have been indifferent, like what to do when the signal light turns yellow. Although such a law can be posited either by human enactment or Divine revelation, the Objector is speaking only of human enactment, distinguishing it from what we know to be right by nature. The same distinction is implicit in Isidore's trifold classification of natural law, civil law, and law of nations, and in Aristotle's distinction between natural and legal justice.

In the history of jurisprudence, a good deal of trouble might have been avoided if only so-called legal positivists had paid attention to St. Thomas's analysis of positive law, especially in Question 95, Articles 1–3, and in Question 96, Article 1.

[2] The Objector's argument runs like this.

  1. Natural law is composed of (a) the general principles of natural law and (b) the conclusions derived from them.

2. But positive human law is neither (a) nor (b); it comes from nothing but formal human enactment.
3. Therefore positive human law is not a part of natural law.

[1] *Objection 3. Further, the law of nature is the same for all; since the Philosopher says (Ethic. v, 7) that "the natural just is that which is equally valid everywhere." [2] If therefore human laws were derived from the natural law, it would follow that they too are the same for all: which is clearly false.*	Objection 3. Still further, the same natural laws are right for everyone. Though in slightly different words, Aristotle makes essentially the same point when he remarks that the same natural justice is right everywhere. Therefore, if human laws really were rooted in natural law, they too would have to be the same for everyone – but they aren't.

[1]   Aristotle adds, "and does not exist by people's thinking this or that." As St. Thomas explains elsewhere, "in practical matters there are some principles naturally known as it were, indemonstrable principles and truths related to them, as evil is to be avoided, no one is to be unjustly injured, theft must not be committed and so on."[9]

[2] In one place the laws require that the ceremony of marriage be performed before an official of the state, in another place merely that the marriage be registered with the state, in yet another place neither. In one place they recognize only physical property, in another place intellectual property too. Criminals might be executed, scourged, enslaved, imprisoned, exiled, made to pay damages, publicly disgraced, injured in proportion to the injuries they inflicted, or deprived of other privileges, all depending on the laws of the country.[10] With so many variations, the Objector wonders, how could it be that all human law arises from the unvarying natural law?

[9] Aristotle, *Nicomachean Ethics*, ibid.; Thomas Aquinas, *Commentary on Aristotle's Nicomachean Ethics*, Book 5, Lecture 12, trans. C.J. Litzinger, O.P., rev. ed. (Notre Dame, IN: Dumb Ox Books, 1993), p. 325.
[10] The first eight of these correspond to Marcus Tullius Cicero's list of the punishments recognized by Roman law, as cited by St. Augustine in *City of God Against the Pagans*, Book 21, Chapter 11. St. Thomas discusses the passage in II-II, Question 108, Article 3.

[1] ***Objection* 4.** *Further, it is possible to give a reason for things which are derived from the natural law.* [2] *But "it is not possible to give the reason for all the legal enactments of the lawgivers," as the jurist says [Pandect. Justin. lib. i, ff, tit. iii, v; De Leg. et Senat.]. Therefore not all human laws are derived from the natural law.*

Objection 4. Besides, whenever something is rooted in natural law, we can give a reason for it. But as the venerable legal authority Julianus has said, it is not possible to give a reason for everything established by great men. If follows that not everything instituted by human law is rooted in natural law.

[1] The reason is given by stating the principle from which they are derived, and the rule of inference for each step in the derivation.

[2] What Julianus actually says in this quotation from the *Digest* is not "lawgivers," but "great men" (*maioribus*), which in this context probably refers to ancestors, great men of the past.[11] Reasons for their enactments cannot always be given because in many cases they reflect judgments about particular matters rather than conclusions from general premises.

On the contrary, *Tully says (Rhet. ii): "Things which emanated from nature and were approved by custom, were sanctioned by fear and reverence for the laws."*

On the other hand, Marcus Tullius Cicero explains that human law originates in things rooted in nature, approved by custom, and sanctioned by religion and by reverence for law itself.

This is a condensed paraphrase of a longer passage, in which Cicero explains, "Justice is a habit of the mind which attributes its proper dignity to everything, preserving a due regard to the general welfare. Its first principles proceed from nature. Subsequently some practices became established by universal custom, from a consideration of their utility; afterwards the fear of the laws, and religion, sanctioned proceedings which originated in nature, and had been approved of by custom."[12] What the *sed contra* takes from Cicero's argument is that although in a certain sense human enactments add to the natural law – a point explained in Question 94, Article 5 – even so they in some way begin with it.

[11] *Digest,* Book 1, Title 3, Section 20: *Non omnium, quae a maioribus constituta sunt, ratio reddi potest.*

[12] Marcus Tullius Cicero, *On Rhetorical Invention,* C.D. Yonge, trans., Book 2, Chapter 53 (public domain). I have added commas to separate "fear of the laws" from "religion" (Latin, *legum metus et religio*), so that Cicero does not seem to be saying that human institutions are sanctioned by fear of the laws and by *fear of* religion.

[1] *I answer that, As Augustine says (De Lib. Arb. i, 5) "that which is not just seems to be no law at all": wherefore the force of a law depends on the extent of its justice.* [2] *Now in human affairs a thing is said to be just, from being right, according to the rule of reason.* [3] *But the first rule of reason is the law of nature, as is clear from what has been stated above (91, 2, ad 2).* [4] *Consequently every human law has just so much of the nature of law, as it is derived from the law of nature.* [5] *But if in any point it deflects from the law of nature, it is no longer a law but a perversion of law.*

Here is my response. In his dialogue *On Free Choice of the Will,* St. Augustine denies that an unjust law is truly law. From this it follows that an ordinance is truly law only so far as it is just. In human life, we call something just when the rule of reason shows it to be right, but as we have already seen, the first such rule is the law of nature. From this in turn it follows that a human ordinance is truly law only so far as it is rooted in natural law. So whatever quarrels with natural law in any way is not true law, but a putrefied carcass of law.

[1]   A law is an ordinance of reason for the common good, made by public authority and promulgated. But an ordinance that is unjust lacks a reasonable relation to the common good. Therefore it is no law at all.

[2]   An act is said to be just (*iustum*) or right (*ius*) when is related to the acts of others by "some kind of equality." For example, a just wage is equal to what the laborer deserves for his service. Such equality is recognizable by the mind and expressed in law.[13]

[3]   The basic precepts of natural law are the starting points for reasoning about what to do.

[4]   The more it reflects the natural law, the more truly it is law; the less it reflects the natural law, the more it departs from law's authority.

[5]   Idiomatically, this translation is correct, but the word translated "perversion" is not *perversio*, twistedness, but *corruptio*, rottenness. Both terms express departure from how things should be, but in the former case how things should be is pictured by the straight and direct, while in the latter case it is pictured by the fresh and living.

[13] II-II, Q. 57, Art. 1, *respondeo* and ad 2.

[1] *But it must be noted that something may be derived from the natural law in two ways: first, as a conclusion from premises, secondly, by way of determination of certain generalities. [2] The first way is like to that by which, in sciences, demonstrated conclusions are drawn from the principles: [3] while the second mode is likened to that whereby, in the arts, general forms are particularized as to details: thus the craftsman needs to determine the general form of a house to some particular shape. [4] Some things are therefore derived from the general principles of the natural law, by way of conclusions; e.g. that "one must not kill" may be derived as a conclusion from the principle that "one should do harm to no man": [5] while some are derived therefrom by way of determination; e.g. the law of nature has it that the evil-doer should be punished; but that he be punished in this or that way, is a determination of the law of nature.*

But we must understand that something can be rooted in natural law in either of two ways. One way is that it follows from deeper considerations, as a conclusion. The other way is that it pins down something that these deeper considerations leave unspecified.

The first way is similar to the method of theoreticians, for they too draw conclusions from basic premises. The second way is similar to the method of craftsmen, for they too fill in details unspecified by general forms. For example, the carpenter does not originate the general form of a house, but to build a particular house he must specify many of the details. So too, some things are drawn from natural law by inference from premises, and others are drawn from natural law by settling details that the premises leave open.

We may call the first way "conclusion." In this way, from the premise of natural law that we must not harm anyone gratuitously, we conclude that we must not murder anyone. We may call the second way "determination" or "specification." In this way, from the premise of natural law that wrongdoers should be punished, we settle upon a particular punishment, which the premise does not require.

[1]   In both cases natural law gives us a principle or starting point, "something to go on," as we say in English. In one mode of derivation, the principle operates, so to speak, as an *axiom*; from it we can draw inferences about precisely what to do, just like theorems. In the other mode, it operates, so to speak, as a *consideration*; even though we must follow it, it does not prescribe every detail of our conduct.

[2]   The most obvious instance is geometry, but by "sciences" St. Thomas means all fields of knowledge that operate by strict inference rather than particular judgments.

[3]   As the example shows, by "arts" St. Thomas means the work of artisans – all crafts that make something, not just those that make objects of beauty. Carpentry, for example, is an art. He would call most of the "liberal arts" – if practiced in the right way – sciences rather than arts, although the writing of a history has elements of both science and art. The practitioner of an art works by particular judgments rather than by strict inference.

[4]   St. Thomas is writing in shorthand. His original readers recognized the fact; in his day everyone wrote that way. There was no need to explain in detail what he meant because the inference was so familiar. Since we don't write that way, we need the ellipses filled in.

First, although he says simply "one should do harm to no man," he does not mean all harm, for he does allow penal harm, or punishment.[14] Second, although he says simply "Do not kill," he does not mean all killing, but rather murder. It is not murder to kill termites that are eating the timbers of my house; it is not murder to have been involved in a fatal accident that I did everything possible to avoid; nor are just war, properly limited self-defense, or the properly reluctant administration of capital punishment murder, because the parties who are punished are not innocent.

So his abbreviated statement that the wrong of doing harm entails the wrong of killing actually means that the wrong of doing *gratuitous* harm entails the wrong of *murder,* or, more fully, that the wrong of doing harm *other than as just punishment* entails the wrong of *deliberately taking innocent human life.*

[5]   Although the judgment about what punishment is fitting is not arbitrary, it is not like a theorem; it cannot be worked out strictly, by conclusion from premises. Human legislators certainly rely on deeper considerations, which originate in the natural law, but to weigh or consider something is not the same as to draw a strict inference from it.

[1] *Accordingly both modes of derivation are found in the human law.* [2] *But those things which are derived in the first way, are contained in human law not as emanating therefrom exclusively, but have some force from the*	In human law, we meet with both modes of enactment. Ordinances of human law that are derived by conclusion are not "human law" in the sense that *everything about them* arises from human enactment, for they draw their power to obligate us partly from natural law too.

[14] I-II, Q. 73, Art. 8; II-II, Q. 19, Art. 6; II-II, Q. 108, Art. 1. Compare II-II, Q. 161, Art. 1, Obj. 1.

natural law also. [3] *But those things which are derived in the second way, have no other force than that of human law.*	On the other hand, various matters of human law are derived by determination, and these do draw their power to obligate solely from human enactment.

[1]   Although – provided that lawmakers are not foolish or corrupt – everything in human law is rooted in natural law, some aspects of human law are derived by conclusion, and others by determination.

[2]   The things human legislators derive by conclusion are certainly part of human law. But it would be mistaken to think "Since they are part of human law, they draw their authority entirely from human decisions," for they are derivations *from* natural law. In fact – though St. Thomas does not say so – they seem to be "additions" to natural law in the very sense spoken of in Question 94, Article 5.

[3]   This time St. Thomas is speaking of aspects of human law that result from determination, not from conclusion. The statement that these things are "derived" from natural law yet have no "force" from natural law at first seems a little odd. What St. Thomas means is that they really are rooted in natural law, but they are not rooted in it in such a way that they could not have been otherwise. For example, that human law punishes wrongdoing comes from natural law, but that it assigns *this* penalty and not *that* one comes from human enactment, guided by the exercise of prudence. Just because it has been enacted, this penalty is the right one to apply.

Reply to Objection 1. The Philosopher is speaking of those enactments which are by way of determination or specification of the precepts of the natural law.	Reply to Objection 1. Aristotle is right, but he is speaking only of the enactments drawn from the natural law by determination or specification.

This reply is highly elliptical. St. Thomas means that just insofar as judgments reached by determination pin down details that the precepts of natural law leave unspecified, they are not rooted in natural law. But insofar as the precepts themselves belong to natural law, such judgments are rooted in natural law.

Reply to Objection 2. This argument avails for those things that are derived from the natural law, by way of conclusions.	Reply to Objection 2. The *rational foundation* of those things derived from natural law by conclusion *does* belong to natural rather than human law.

In saying that the Objector's argument is valid for things derived from natural law by conclusion, St. Thomas seems to imply that it is *not* valid for things derived from natural law by determination. But it is a little obscure what, exactly, he thinks the Objector is right about, and what, exactly, he thinks that he is wrong about. His point may be put like this:

1. In saying that human laws reached by conclusion belong to natural law, the Objector is right.
2. But in suggesting that human laws reached by determination have nothing to do with natural law, the Objector is wrong. For they are determinations *of* natural law – they pin down the points that its general precepts leave unspecified.

These determinations may be viewed as "additions" to natural law in the sense of Question 94, Article 5. Yet just insofar as they are enacted by human authority, they belong to human law too.

[1] *Reply to Objection 3. The general principles of the natural law cannot be applied to all men in the same way on account of the great variety of human affairs:* [2] *and hence arises the diversity of positive laws among various people.*	Reply to Objection 3. Even though the basic principles of natural law are the same for everyone, they cannot be applied in the same way to everyone, just because human circumstances are so various. This is why diverse laws are established in different places.

[1]   In all cases, the general principles must be applied, so human laws cannot be completely diverse. Yet legislators do not apply the general principle that theft should be punished in exactly the same way to juvenile and adult perpetrators, to thefts of physical and intellectual property, or to untamed and civilized countries.

[2]   To say that the diversity arises *for this reason* is to say that there *is* a reason, though not the kind of reason that works like an axiom. The deliberations are rational, even though they are not, so to speak, geometrical. For if we ask the legislators of a particular country why they arrange a particular matter differently than the legislators of another country have arranged it, they are not struck dumb; they explain that they have found their arrangement more fitting in view of the conditions of their people.

Isn't this an overstatement? How could it have been more fitting for vehicles to drive on the right in some countries, but on the left in others?

Weren't these decisions made solely by chance? Suppose they were: That does not mean they were irrational. In some cases it may be perfectly reasonable to flip a coin – when it is imperative that either A or B must be done, but it really doesn't matter which one we settle on. Besides, even in cases like the side of the road on which we drive, lawmakers may be guided by other considerations, such as local custom. In fact, local custom itself may be guided by rational considerations.[15] For example, since most people are right-handed, people driving teams of horses on highly traveled roads will probably keep to the right, so that the right hand, which is the whip hand, faces away from other traffic – and that becomes the custom. On the other hand, people traveling on foot, especially through dangerous country, may prefer to keep to the left, so that the right hand, which is the sword hand, faces *toward* passersby – and that becomes the custom. Even in cases of pure determination, decisions by pure chance are probably rare.[16]

---

[1] *Reply to Objection 4. These words of the Jurist are to be understood as referring to decisions of rulers in determining particular points of the natural law: on which determinations the judgment of expert and prudent men is based as on its principles; in so far, to wit, as they see at once what is the best thing to decide.*

[2] *Hence the Philosopher says (Ethic. vi, 11) that in such matters, "we ought to pay as much attention to the undemonstrated sayings and opinions of persons who surpass us in experience, age and prudence, as to their demonstrations."*

Reply to Objection 4. The legal authority in question is speaking of the ways in which great men of the past settled matters that natural law did not specify. Experienced and prudent men of later times rightly take these ways of settling things as principles for their own judgments, in the sense that by following them as guides, they see at once, and with certainty, just how to resolve the particular matters that they in turn must decide.

This is why Aristotle says in his *Nicomachean Ethics* that we should attend no less closely to the judgments expressed in the unproven statements and opinions of men rich in practical wisdom, or experienced and seasoned in years, than to actual demonstrations.

---

[1] In many cases, the wise men of the past were forced to reach decisions by determination rather than by conclusion, because natural law only partly indicated what should be done. Just because they *were* using

---

[15] See the discussion of the rationality of custom in Question 97, Article 3.
[16] For further exploration, see the discussion of traffic rules in the discussion of Question 94, Article 5, in the online *Companion to the Commentary*.

this mode of derivation, they could not give the sort of reasons for their decisions that function like axioms. Yet the decisions they reach do function as guides for the decisions of those who come after them.

[2]   Aristotle adds, "for because experience has given them an eye, they see aright." The context of the quotation is an explanation of things which are grasped, not by argument, but by W.D. Ross translates as "intuitive reason." Judgments reached in this way can be recognized as wise, but cannot be proven to be wise. They are not confirmed by demonstrations, but presupposed by them. They are not completely analyzable, because they concern not universal principles but particular facts. Just because they do concern particulars, excellence in making them depends greatly on age and experience. However, it also owes something to natural endowment, for some people attain prudence more readily than others.[17] I return to these mysteries in the online *Companion to the Commentary*.

For further reflection on the preceding section of the *Treatise on Law*, the online *Companion to the Commentary*, accessible via the Resources link at the book's catalogue webpage, includes a discussion of the following topic:

DISCERNING THE REASONS FOR THE LAWS

Question 95, Article 3:
Whether Isidore's Description of the Quality of Positive Law Is Appropriate?

TEXT	PARAPHRASE
Whether Isidore's description of the quality of positive law is appropriate?	Is Isidore's list of the qualities to be sought in making laws correct and helpful? Do the nine qualities cover everything without duplication?

Do we really need to ask this question? Haven't we already answered it in Question 90, where we saw that to be truly law, an enactment must be an ordinance of reason, for the common good, made by public authority, and promulgated?

Yes, we do need to ask it; no, we haven't answered it already. In Question 90 we were inquiring into the *definition* of law. Here we are looking for a guide for public authority to follow in the *practice* of

---

[17] Aristotle, *Nicomachean Ethics*, trans. W.D. Ross, Book 6, chapter 11 (public domain).

lawmaking – a collection of suitable rules of thumb. Of course the two inquiries are related, for another way to describe the present one is to say we are looking for the qualities that help provide laws with their necessary foundation in reason and their necessary orientation to the common good. These are matters of degree. A law could be ineptly adapted to place and time, say, but although this would make it a poor and clumsy law, its would probably not deprive it of the very character of law. To do that, it clumsiness would have to be so severe as to incur actual injustice – to drive it beyond the bounds of reason and good.

Today, someone who wanted to know what these qualities are would probably not frame his question with reference to Isidore; he would simply ask, "What are they?" But this procedure is both unhelpful and somewhat arrogant – unhelpful because it sets us adrift on the seas of inquiry without even a compass heading, arrogant because it ignores centuries of previous reflection on the same problem. As always, then, St. Thomas frames the question against the background of the tradition, here represented by Isidore. Was the great encyclopedist right or wrong? The presumption is not that Isidore had to be right, but that we would be fools not to consider the possibility that he might be.

---

[1] *Objection 1. It would seem that Isidore's description of the quality of positive law is not appropriate, when he says (Etym. v, 21): "Law shall be virtuous [honesta], just, possible to nature, according to the custom of the country, suitable to place and time, necessary, useful; clearly expressed, lest by its obscurity it lead to misunderstanding; framed for no private benefit, but for the common good."* [2] *Because he had previously expressed the quality of law in three conditions,* [3] *saying that "law is anything founded on reason,* [4] *provided that it foster religion,* [5] *be helpful to discipline, and* [6] *further the common weal." Therefore it was needless to add any further conditions to these.*

Objection 1. Isidore's list of the qualities to be sought in making laws does not seem to be helpful. He lists nine of them, saying that law should be (a) honest and honorable [*honesta*], (b) just, (c) within the natural capacities of those subject to it, (d) compatible with the customs of the country, (e) fitting for the place and time, (f) necessary, (g) advantageous, (h) clearly expressed, and (i) framed with a view to the common good rather than accommodating private interests. But previously he had listed only three such qualities, saying that law is whatever is reasonable, provided that it (I) contains nothing incongruent with religion, (II) is helpful to discipline, and (III) promotes the common good. If his previous list of three qualities suffices, then we don't need his later list of nine.

[1]   The Dominican Fathers translation is a little misleading, because here it renders *honesta* by the word "virtuous," but a little later it renders *honestatis* by the word "honesty." *Honesta* and *honestatis* are different forms of the same Latin word, and refer to the same item in Isidore's list. Probably the translators were trying to deal with the fact that no single English word reflects all the shades of meaning of *honestum*. My own paraphrase uses a pair of words, "honest and honorable," taking the honest in the double sense of truthfulness and good faith, and taking the honorable in the double sense of receiving honor and being worthy to receive it.

[2]   Both lists are from Isidore's *Etymologies*. His previous list of three conditions is in Book 5, Chapter 3; his present list of nine qualities in the same book, Chapter 21.

[3]   As St. Thomas explains in Question 90, Article 1, the very first of law's essential properties is that it be an ordinance of reason.

[4]   In Latin, the wording is not that the law must "foster" religion, but that the law be *congruent* with religion, *religioni congruat*. In other words, the law must not violate, undermine, or hinder religion; it must be congenial and cooperative toward it. This is St. Thomas's view as well.

[5]   The law must promote rightly ordered peace, *tranquillitas ordinis*, as discussed later in Question 96, Article 3.

[6]   As St. Thomas establishes in Question 90, Article 2, promoting the common good is the very purpose of law.

Objection 2. Further, Justice is included in honesty [honestatis], *as Tully says (De Offic. vii). Therefore after saying "honest"* [honesta] *it was superfluous to add "just."*	Objection 2. Moreover, as Marcus Tullius Cicero declares, justice is an element in the honest and honorable [*honestatis*]. So if honesty is included on the list, there is no need to list justice too; it is already implied.

The Objector is probably thinking of the following passage from Marcus Tullius Cicero's *On Duties,* Book 1, Chapter 19, Section 62: *Nihil enim honestum esse potest, quod iustitia vacat,* roughly, "Without the honest and honorable there is no place for justice," or more idiomatically, "Nothing can be just without honesty and honor." The statement implies that justice is an *element* in the honest and honorable;

put differently, that the honest and honorable *includes* justice, as the Objector claims.

In citing a different place in *On Duties* as the source, Book 1, Chapter 7, the Dominican Fathers translators are probably thinking of Section 23, where Cicero remarks *Fundamentum autem est iustitiae fides, id est dictorum conventorumque constantia et veritas,* roughly, "But the foundation of justice (*iustitia*) is trustworthiness (*fides*), that is, truth (*veritas*) and firm adherence (*constantia*) to covenants (*conventorumque*)." However, this cannot be the statement that the Objector has in mind, because it connects justice not with *honestum*, but with *fides*. On the other hand, St. Thomas himself is probably thinking of this statement a little further on, as we will see.

Objection 3. Further, written law is condivided with custom, according to Isidore (Etym. ii, 10). Therefore it should not be stated in the definition of law that it is "according to the custom of the country."	Objection 3. Still further, Isidore contrasts written law from custom. If they are different things, then it is wrong to include compatibility with the custom in the definition of law.

"Division" is the old-fashioned term for classification, so when the Objector says that written law is "condivided against" custom, he means that it is distinguished from it. Apparently, he takes the fact that law and custom are not the same thing as implying that they should have nothing to do with each other: Law should be indifferent to custom, and custom, presumably, should be indifferent to law.

What does Isidore actually say? He expresses the distinction between law and custom in two passages. The first is in *Etymologies*, Book 2, Chapter 10, where he says that equity (*aequitas*) is made up of laws and customs; the second is in Book 5, Chapter 3, where he says that justice (*ius*) is made up of laws and customs. As he explains in both places, the difference is that law is written, but custom unwritten. Both passages argue that because both law and custom are grounded in reason, custom is viewed as law when written law is lacking. His list of the nine qualities of law, in Book 5, Chapter 21, does go a bit further, since it requires even written law to follow custom.

[1] *Objection 4. Further, a thing may be necessary in two ways. It may be necessary simply, because it cannot be otherwise: and that which is*	Objection 4. Besides, Isidore is wrong to include necessity on his list. Necessity may refer either to things that cannot be other than they are,

necessary in this way, is not subject to human judgment, wherefore human law is not concerned with necessity of this kind. [2] Again a thing may be necessary for an end: and this necessity is the same as usefulness. [3] Therefore it is superfluous to say both "necessary" and "useful."

or to things that are useful. Isidore cannot mean necessity in the former sense, because law has nothing to do with things that cannot be other than they are. But if he means necessity in the latter sense, then his list is redundant, because it includes usefulness already.

---

[1] We thoroughly examined the different senses of necessity when we were dealing with Question 93, Article 4. The root meaning of necessity, from which all its other meanings flow, is that which cannot be other than it is. All necessity is either intrinsic or extrinsic. Here the Objector is referring to intrinsic necessity, in which the cause of necessity lies in a thing's own nature.

[2] In the second kind of necessity, extrinsic, the cause of necessity lies in something other than the thing itself. One of the two types of extrinsic necessity is necessity of end, or usefulness, and that is the kind to which the Objector is referring here. Something can be useful either in the sense that without it, we cannot attain our end at all, or in the sense that without it, we cannot attain our end as well. (The Objector passes over the other kind of extrinsic necessity, necessity of coercion.)

[3] The Objector's point is that if, by necessity, Isidore means usefulness, then he is repeating himself, because usefulness is already on his list. Since he couldn't have been referring to the other kind of necessity, and any reference to this kind would be redundant, necessity should not have been on his list at all.

On the contrary, stands the authority of Isidore.

On the other hand, against these criticisms of Isidore's list lies the authority of Isidore himself.

The first, second, and fourth objection challenged Isidore's authority on grounds that in one way or another, his list is redundant. But the third objection tried to turn Isidore against himself, since it held that if Isidore is right about the difference between law and custom, he cannot be right to say law should follow custom.

[1] *I answer that,* Whenever a thing is for an end, its form must be determined proportionately to that end; as the form of a saw is such as to be suitable for cutting (Phys. ii, text. 88). [2] *Again, everything that is ruled and measured must have a form proportionate to its rule and measure.* [3a] *Now both these conditions are verified of human law: since it is both something ordained to an end;* [4] *and is a rule or measure ruled or measured by a higher measure. And this higher measure is twofold, viz. the Divine law and the natural law, as explained above (2; 93, 3).* [3b] *Now the end of human law is to be useful to man, as the jurist states [Pandect. Justin. lib. xxv, ff., tit. iii; De Leg. et Senat.].* [5] *Wherefore Isidore in determining the nature of law, lays down, at first, three conditions; viz. that it "foster religion," inasmuch as it is proportionate to the Divine law; that it be "helpful to discipline," inasmuch as it is proportionate to the natural law; and that it "further the common weal," inasmuch as it is proportionate to the utility of mankind.*

Here is my response. Two considerations guide our reasoning. First, anything made for a purpose must have a form appropriate to its purpose (for example, the form of a saw is appropriate to its purpose of cutting). Second, everything that is governed by a rule and measured by a standard must have a form appropriate to that rule and standard. Human law fulfills both of these considerations. In the first place, it is made for an end. In the second place, even though itself a rule and measure of human acts, it is subject to a still higher rule and measure. What then is this still higher rule and measure? As we have seen previously, a double one, Divine and natural law. And what is this purpose? As the great jurists of old taught, to be useful to man.

Taking all of this together, we obtain three great desiderata: (I) That human law be congruent with Divine law; (II) that it be congruent with natural law; and (III) that it be congruent with the welfare of mankind. Isidore has precisely these desiderata in mind, but expresses them differently: (I′) That human law contain nothing incongruent with religion; (II′) that it be helpful to discipline; and (III′) that it further the common good.

[1]   Aristotle says In *Physics,* Book 2, Chapter 9, that if a saw is for dividing things, then it must have teeth of the right kind, and it will not have the right kind unless they are made of iron. Purpose determines the necessary form, and form determines the necessary matter.

[2]   Question 90, Article 1, explained that law is both the governing ordinance and the measuring rod for distinctively human acts, because it makes us do the right thing (thus acting as a rule) in the right way (thus acting as a measure).

[3a,b] As we are reminded further on, however, the end of human law is not any human good, but the *common* good.

[4] The reason why the rule or measure is twofold is that God directs man not only to his natural happiness, but also to eternal happiness, which is beyond his natural power. Both are real ends in the sense that they are desirable for their own sake rather than as a means to something else. But eternal happiness is our *ultimate* end in the sense that it leaves nothing further to be desired.

Yet Divine law "measures" human law differently than natural law does. Human law is derived from the eternal law, which is the Wisdom in the mind of God, through the natural law, which is the reflection of that Wisdom in the created mind of man.[18] Although human law is illuminated by Divine law too, it is not derived from it *in the same sense*.[19] Recall St. Thomas's discussion of the four reasons why Divine law was needed. Regarding the first, man's supernatural end, the implications of Divine law for human law are purely negative, for the custodian of grace is the Church, not the state; though human law avoids infringing Divine law, it does not actually implement it. Regarding the second, the uncertainty of human judgment, the instruction of Divine law is not unrelated to natural law, but is more like a set of lenses to help human legislators see the remote implications of natural law more clearly. Regarding the third, the movements of the heart that human rulers cannot see, and the fourth, the inability of human law to punish every evil deed, it seems that human law is not informed by Divine law at all; Divine law is given because of what human law cannot do.[20]

[5] This is pretty clear, but some details may make it even clearer. To be "proportionate" to something means to correspond to it, to be fittingly related to it, to be congruent with it. As we saw above, St. Thomas does not actually speak of "fostering" religion, as the Dominican Fathers translation has it, but of containing nothing to hinder it, for to foster it is not the role of the state, guided by natural light alone, but the role of the Church, guided by the additional light of grace. To be "helpful to discipline" means to assist in bringing human acts under the discipline of reason, expressed in natural law; St. Thomas is about to elaborate. The word

---

[18] Q. 91, Art. 2; Q. 93, Art. 3; Q. 95, Art. 2.
[19] But see the commentary on Q. 97, Art. 3, Obj. 1, where the Objector does speak of derivation.
[20] Q. 91, Art. 4.

here translated as "common weal" is *saluti*, and the word here translated as "utility" is *utilitati*. They share the meaning of good health, which in context refers to the overall well-being of the community.

[1] *All the other conditions mentioned by him are reduced to these three. For it is called virtuous* [honesta] *because it fosters religion.* [2] *And when he goes on to say that it should be "just, possible to nature, according to the customs of the country, adapted to place and time," he implies that it should be helpful to discipline. For human discipline depends on first on the order of reason, to which he refers by saying "just":* [3] *secondly, it depends on the ability of the agent; because discipline should be adapted to each one according to his ability, taking also into account the ability of nature (for the same burdens should be not laid on children as adults);* [4] *and should be according to human customs; since man cannot live alone in society, paying no heed to others:* [5] *thirdly, it depends on certain circumstances, in respect of which he says, "adapted to place and time."* [6] *The remaining words, "necessary, useful," etc. mean that law should further the common weal: so that "necessity" refers to the removal of evils;* [7] *"usefulness" to the attainment of good;* [8] *"clearness of expression," to the need of preventing any harm ensuing from the law itself.* [9] *And since, as stated above (90, 2), law is ordained to the common good, this is expressed in the last part of the description.*

As we have seen, Isidore also lists nine more specific conditions. But the three great desiderata and the nine more specific conditions express the same ideas.

Desideratum I (or I′) corresponds to condition a, that law should be honest in the sense of good faith.

Desideratum II (or II′) corresponds to conditions b through e: To b, that law should be just, it corresponds because discipline depends primarily on the fact that the acts of different people are in right relationship according to the rule of reason, a relationship that Isidore rightly calls justice; to c, that law should be within the natural capacities of those subject to it (for example, the different natural capacities of children and adults), it corresponds because discipline depends next on the ability of persons under the law to do what is expected of them; to d, that law should be compatible with the customs of the country, it corresponds because man, living as he does in society, must pay attention to others; and to e, that law should be fitting for the place and time, it corresponds because which laws are appropriate depends on circumstances.

Desideratum III (or III′) corresponds to conditions f through i: It corresponds to f, that law should be necessary, taken in the sense of the removal of evils; it corresponds to g, that law should be advantageous, taken in the sense of the attaining of goods; it corresponds to h, that law should be clearly expressed, so that no harm results from the vagueness of the law itself; and it corresponds to i, that law should be for common rather than private benefit, because, as we have seen, this is the very end of law.

[1]   At first St. Thomas's claim seems to come out of nowhere; why should *honestum* mean the same thing as being congruous with religion? The connection of the two ideas seems odd to us only because we are speaking English, not Latin. We find a key in the two statements from Cicero's *On Duties* that we saw earlier, one linking justice with *honestum*, the other linking it with *fides*:

Nihil enim honestum esse potest, quod iustitia vacat: "Nothing can be honest and honorable (*honestum*) without justice."

Fundamentum autem est iustitiae fides, id est dictorum conventorumque constantia et veritas: "But the foundation of justice is trustworthiness (*fides*), that is, truth and firm adherence to covenant."

The similarity of the two passages shows that Cicero considers *honestum* and *fides* almost the same thing. But *fides* is also the very same word that the Latin version of the New Testament uses for "faith." Faith, in turn, is the foundation of religion. So it is not at all unreasonable for St. Thomas to infer that when Isidore says *honestum,* he has in mind the same kind of good faith that is involved in true religion.

[2]   As remarked in the previous Article, a person's acts are said to be just when they are in right relation to the acts of others, a relation recognizable by reason. St. Thomas takes the term "discipline" to mean the discipline of reason in exactly this sense.

[3]   It is obviously wrong to expect someone to do what he cannot do. Laying burdens on persons only in proportion to their capacities is an obvious corollary of the classical formula of justice, "Give each what is due to him."

[4]   Enacted law deals with many things. However, it does not follow that it may disturb and overturn them, arranging them in ways contrary to the settled wisdom of the community as expressed in long-standing habits. We return to the importance of custom for law in Question 97, Article 3.

[5]   As St. Thomas explained in the previous Article, "The general principles of the natural law cannot be applied to all men in the same way on account of the great variety of human affairs: and hence arises the diversity of positive laws among various people."

[6]   Removal of evils is the *negative* aspect of promoting public well-being. In medicine, this aspect of lawmaking is analogous to healing the

patient's injuries and diseases. Physicians are taught, "First, do no harm." As in medicine, so in lawmaking, for one can hardly do away with evils if the remedies themselves produce evils.

[7] Attaining the good is the *positive* aspect of promoting public well-being, analogous to keeping the patient fit and healthy.

[8] Just as doctors must clearly explain what is needed to both patients and pharmacists, so legislators must clearly explain what is needed to both citizens and administrators, for otherwise, ill might result.

[9] As we saw in Question 90, Article 2, a so-called law that makes the good of the community subservient to private interest is not a true law at all.

This suffices for the Replies to the Objections.	In view of the preceding explanation, a separate reply to each of the four Objections would be superfluous.

It suffices for the Reply to Objection 1, because it harmonizes the three great desiderata with the nine more specific conditions.

It suffices for the Reply to Objection 2, because it distinguishes the reason for listing the honest and honorable from the reason for listing justice, even though, of course, they are connected.

It suffices for the Reply to Objection 3, because it shows why written law should conform to unwritten custom, even though they are not the same thing.

And it suffices for the Reply to Objection 4, because it distinguishes (1) the attainment of good as such from (2) the restriction of law to looking after the *common* good, (3) the removal of evil that arises *independently* of the law, and (4) the prevention of evil that might arise because of the law itself. By usefulness, Isidore means only the first of these four conditions.

For further reflection on the preceding section of the *Treatise on Law*, the online *Companion to the Commentary*, accessible via the Resources link at the book's catalogue webpage, includes a discussion of the following topic:

RATIONALITY IS NOT THE SAME AS RATIONALISM

Question 95, Article 4:
Whether Isidore's Division of Human Laws Is
Appropriate?

TEXT	PARAPHRASE
Whether Isidore's division of human laws is appropriate?	Does Isidore's classification of human laws correspond to the real differences among them?

St. Thomas has previously distinguished among the varieties of law in general: Eternal, natural, Divine (both Old and New), and human, as well as the "law of sin," which is law only in an analogical sense. Now he inquires into the varieties of human law. Since the tradition already relies on Isidore's classification, the question becomes, "Did Isidore get it right?" Four aspects of the Isidorean classification are challenged: (1) The inclusion of the law of nations in human rather than natural law; (2) the distinction among laws that are the same in validity for the same group of people; (3) the distinction among laws according to the public offices they regulate; and (4) the distinction among laws according to who wrote them.

Isidore's classification is more like a list; for each kind of law, he provides only a terse description, as though they were entries in a dictionary. He makes his distinctions as he goes along. Plainly he is using more than one criterion for which kinds of laws to include, how to tell them apart, and in what order to list them. However, he never explains just what these criteria are, and part of St. Thomas's task is to tease them out. The result is much more systematic than what was passed down to us by Isidore himself.

| [1] **Objection 1.** *It would seem that Isidore wrongly divided human statutes or human law (Etym. v, 4, seqq.). For under this law he includes the "law of nations," so called, because, as he says, "nearly all nations use it." [2] But as he says, "natural law is that which is common to all nations." Therefore the law of nations is not contained under positive human law, but rather under natural law.* | Objection 1. Apparently, Isidore's classification of human law or justice is incorrect. For he counts the law of nations as a human law on grounds that almost all nations use it. Yet elsewhere, he defines *natural* law as the law common to all nations. So he should have included law of nations not in humanly enacted law, but in natural law. |

[1]   In our day the expression "law of nations" (*ius gentium*) is sometimes used for international law, for the customs and recognized agreements

that regulate relations among different countries. Originally, however, the term referred to a body of principles developed to provide for cases in Roman law in which not all of the parties were Roman citizens. It was based partly on good sense, and partly on customs shared among many nations. Isidore distinguishes it from civil law (*ius civile*), which is what each nation has enacted for itself.[21]

[2] We discussed Isidore's definition of natural law in Question 94, Article 4. The Objector is probably thinking of his statement that because natural law exists in all places by *instinctu naturae*, by the inspiration or instigation of nature, it is not in any way a *constitutione*, a work of man-made law. The argument works like this:

1. Whatever exists in in all places is natural law; but law of nations exists in (almost) all nations; therefore law of nations belongs to natural law.
2. But natural law arises by nature, not human enactment; therefore it is not human law.
3. Therefore law of nations is not human law.

This argument concerns only the origin of the law of nations. What it overlooks is the fact that although law of nations arises by nature, subsequently all nations recognize it and add the force of their own laws, whether written or unwritten.

---

[1] *Objection 2. Further, those laws which have the same force, seem to differ not formally but only materially.* [2] *But "statutes, decrees of the commonalty, senatorial decrees," and the like which he mentions (Etym. v, 9), all have the same force. Therefore they do not differ, except materially.* [3] *But art takes no notice of such a distinction: since it may go on to infinity. Therefore this division of human laws is not appropriate.*

Objection 2. Moreover, laws that have the same validity for the same people seem to be formally the same kind of law; if they differ, they differ only in their matter. But Isidore lists many laws that have the same validity for the same people – laws of the common people acting together with the senate, resolutions of the common people alone, decrees of the senate alone, and others of this kind. So they too differ only materially and not in form. Formal classification pays no attention to merely material differences, because they are endless. Yet Isidore does pay attention to them, so his distinctions are inappropriate.

---

[21] Isidore, *Etymologies*, Book 5, Chapters 5–6.

[1]   By the force of a law, the Objector means its validity for a particular group of people. He reasons that laws that have the same validity for the same group of people must be the same kind of law.

[2]   The Objector is referring to those laws that Isidore defines as "quirital" laws, *ius quiritum*, roughly "laws of citizens," because they regulate mutual relations among the Romans themselves. Inheritance laws, for example, are quirital laws. The Objector is not protesting the distinction between quirital and non-quirital laws; rather he is protesting Isidore's distinction among five different *kinds* of quirital laws.

In typically elliptical medieval fashion, the Objector mentions only three of these five kinds: (1) enactments of the great men and plain people together (which Isidore gives special distinction by calling them simply "laws"); (2) resolutions of the people alone (plebiscites, which the translator calls "decrees of the commonalty"); and (3) decisions of the senate alone (senatorial decrees). The other two, to which he breezily alludes with the phrase "and the like," are (4) edicts of kings and emperors, and (5) responses from legal authorities (*iurisconsults*) to questions set before them.[22]

Since laws from each of all of these different kinds are equal in "force" – equal in validity for the relations of Romans among themselves – the Objector argues that they are not formally diverse, but only materially diverse; the differences among them are not of such a nature as to make them fundamentally distinct kinds of thing.

[3]   If we waste our time on material distinctions, says the Objector, then there will be no end to them; the classification will go on and on.

---

[1] *Objection 3. Further, just as, in the state, there are princes, priests and soldiers, so are there other human offices.* [2] *Therefore it seems that, as this division includes "military law," and "public law," referring to priests and magistrates; so also it should include other laws pertaining to other offices of the state.*	Objection 3. Still further, just as the community includes great men, priests, and soldiers, so it includes men who provide human services of other kinds. Since Isidore's classification mentions public law, which applies to sacred matters and to priests insofar as they act as magistrates, and since it also mentions military law, which applies to soldiers, it should have listed laws that apply to these other kinds of service too. But it doesn't.

---

[22]   Isidore, *Etymologies*, Book 5, Chapter 9.

[1]   The word translated "state" is *civitate,* the community of citizens; the word translated "princes," *principes,* the foremost men; the word translated "offices," *officia,* services. The Objector is saying that the responsibilities attached to various publicly recognized services to the community, performed by various kinds of men, are formalized by various kinds of laws.

[2]   In military law, Isidore includes regulations for waging war, making peace, organizing the army, and distributing spoils. Concerning public law, the Objector refers simply to "priests and magistrates," *sacerdotibus et magistratibus.* Isidore himself had defined public law slightly differently, as that which concerns *sacris et sacerdotibus, in magistratibus,* meaning sacred matters and priests, *in a civic capacity.*[23]

Regarding priests as civic functionaries would not sit well with Christian theology, because it would subordinate the spiritual to the temporal, the Church to the state. But a priest can perform a civic service without being reduced to a civic functionary; the Church does not have to be turned into a department of state for the state to ask its blessing. For example, it is no offense to Christian principles – quite the opposite – if a priest is invited to offer a prayer for wisdom and justice at the opening of a session of the legislature. Suppose the legislators wish to regularize this practice. The obvious thing to do is pass a law: "Whenever a session of the legislature is opened, a priest shall be invited to offer prayer."

But let us not be distracted. More generally, the Objector is saying that to each form of recognized service to the community, there corresponds a different body of law. He complains that although Isidore has mentioned several such bodies of law, covering several kinds of service, he has ignored all the rest.

---

[1] *Objection 4. Further, those things that are accidental should be passed over.* [2] *But it is accidental to law that it be framed by this or that man.* [3] *Therefore it is unreasonable to divide laws according to the names of lawgivers, so that one be called the "Cornelian" law, another the "Falcidian" law, etc.*	Objection 4. Besides, formal classifications take account only of the "essential" or formal differences among things, not the "accidental" or incidental differences among them. But which person happened to write the law is merely incidental. So it is inappropriate to classify laws by their authors – the law of Cornelius, the law of Falcidius, and so forth.

---

[23] Isidore, *Etymologies,* Book 5, Chapters 7–8.

[1]   By an accident, St. Thomas does not mean something that happens by chance, but something that is distinct from the essence – something that does not pertain to what a thing is in itself. That Harry has a rational mind arises from the fact, and is contained in the idea, of being human. That he has green hair, however, is merely an accident; though green-haired humans are a subset of humans, they are not a basic *kind* of human. For this reason, a proper formal classification of the kinds of humans would pass over differences in hair color.

To be sure, a proper formal classification of the objects of the hairdresser's art would *not* pass over hair color, but there we are not classifying the same sorts of things; we are not considering humans in themselves; but as things that need help with their hair. Hopefully, the hairdresser is not silly enough to think that just because brunettes and redheads need their hair handled differently, they are different kinds of humans, fundamentally diverse in their modes of embodied rationality.

[2]   Who composed the law is irrelevant to what kind of law it is.

[3]   As Isidore explains, consular and tribunitial laws were customarily named after the consuls or tribunes who composed them. For example, the Law of Papius and Poppaeus was named after the two consuls who established rewards for fathering children, and the Law of Falcidius was named after the tribune who decreed that no one may bequeath more than three-quarters of his estate to persons outside his family.[24]

On the contrary,	**On the other hand,** we have the authority of Isidore
The authority of	himself, which is certainly enough to represent the
Isidore suffices.	tradition.

If Isidore's classification had not been so venerable, we would not be asking whether his classification is appropriate; it would not have served as the background for the *ultrum.*

[1] *I answer that, A thing can*	**Here is my response.** In themselves,
of itself be divided in respect of	things can be classified according
something contained in the notion	to the differences that are rationally
of that thing. [2] *Thus a soul either*	present in them – the distinctions that
rational or irrational is contained in	are included in their *ratio* or idea. For
the notion of animal: and therefore	example, the idea of an animal

---

[24] Isidore, *Etymologies,* Book 5, Chapter 15.

animal is divided properly and of
itself in respect of its being rational
or irrational; but not in the point of
its being white or black, which are
entirely beside the notion of animal.
[3] *Now, in the notion of human
law, many things are contained,
in respect of any of which human
law can be divided properly and of
itself. For in the first place it belongs
to the notion of human law, to be
derived from the law of nature,
as explained above (2). [4] In this
respect positive law is divided into
the "law of nations" and "civil
law," according to the two ways in
which something may be derived
from the law of nature, as stated
above (2). [5] Because, to the law of
nations belong those things which
are derived from the law of nature,
as conclusions from premises, e.g.
just buyings and sellings, and the
like, without which men cannot live
together, which is a point of the law
of nature, since man is by nature a
social animal, as is proved in Polit.
i, 2. [6] But those things which are
derived from the law of nature by
way of particular determination,
belong to the civil law, according as
each state decides on what is best
for itself.*

contains the idea of an *anima*, a
soul or life principle, and this soul
may be either rational or irrational.
In itself, then, "animal" is properly
distinguished according to whether the
animal is rational and irrational – not
according to whether it is, say, white
or black, for that would miss the point
of what an animal is. To apply the
point to our present topic: A number
of distinctions are rationally present
in human law, so in itself, human law
may be properly classified according to
any of them.

According to the first such distinction,
established laws may be classified into
law of nations and civil law, because
there is a real difference in the ways
in which they are derived from the
law of nature. Law of nations includes
things derived from natural law by
the method we have called *conclusion
from premises*. Because, as Aristotle
shows, man's natural potentialities
develop only in society, here we find
all the things necessary for people
to live together, for instance, rules
about justice in buying and selling.
By contrast, civil law includes things
derived from it by the method we have
called *particular determination*. Each
state practices this method in the way
it finds most appropriate for itself.

[1] The same view of classification was presupposed by Objection 4.
Formal classification considers only fundamental differences in things –
differences in essence, not in accident. Here St. Thomas calls these differences in their *ratio,* or idea.

[2] St. Thomas is treating us to a little play on words, because the Latin
words for "animal," *animal*, and "soul," *anima*, are so similar. But his
point is meant seriously. By the soul of a living thing, he means the form,
or pattern, of its embodied life. An animal is something with an animate
form of embodied life; this is the "idea" of an animal, what it *is*. So the

fundamental kinds of animal are "contained in" this idea – they correspond to the kinds of animate embodied life. For example, one kind is
rational (like us), and another kind is irrational (like birds and horses).

If this seems to us a cumbersome way of speaking, St. Thomas might
reply, "To be sure, we don't always have to speak that way. But if we are
calling to mind what is *fundamentally going on* in formal classification,
then we do."

[3]   To classify things according to their formal differences is *not* to suppose that there is only one right way to classify them, for they may have
more than one kind of formal difference. Each formal difference in things
of a certain kind arises from something about what that kind of thing *is*.

The first formal difference in human laws arises from the first element
in the definition of law, which we saw in Question 90, Article 1: Law is an
ordinance of reason. As we further learned in Question 94, Article 2, to
be an ordinance of reason a law must be derived from the starting points
of deliberation, which are found in the law of nature.

[4]   As we saw in Article 2, something may be derived from natural law
either by conclusion from premises or by determination of generalities.
To put this another way, we might derive it either as a strict inference, the
way a theorem is derived from axioms, or we might derive it by pinning
down one possibility among many, as when we "fill in the blanks" that a
general rule does not specify.

As St. Thomas points out in his commentary on Aristotle's *Nicomachean
Ethics*, the way in which the Roman jurists distinguished the law of
nations from civil law was somewhat misleading:

We must consider that that justice is natural to which nature inclines men. But
a twofold nature is observed in man. One, is that which is common to him and
other animals. The other nature belongs to man properly inasmuch as he is man,
as he distinguishes the disgraceful from the honorable by reason. However, jurists
call only that right natural which follows the inclination of nature common to
man and other animals, as the union of male and female, the education of offspring, and so forth. But the right which follows the inclination proper to the
nature of man, i.e., precisely as he is a rational animal, the jurists call the right
of the peoples (*jus gentium*) because all people are accustomed to follow it, for
example, that agreements are to be kept, legates are safe among enemies, and
so on.[25]

---

[25] Thomas Aquinas, *Commentary on Aristotle's Nicomachean Ethics*, Book 5, Lecture
12, trans. C.J. Litzinger, O.P., rev. ed. (Notre Dame, IN: Dumb Ox Books, 1993),
pp. 325–326.

Part of St. Thomas's intention, both there in his commentary and here and here in *Summa*, is to clear up the confusion.

[5] Here St. Thomas is referring to the first mode of derivation. For example, from the premises of justice, the conclusion follows strictly that if the customer pays the grocer a certain amount of money for lettuce, he should receive the amount of lettuce that he paid for.

[6] Here St. Thomas is referring to the second mode of derivation. For example, although the premises of justice require equality in exchanges, they leave many other things about exchanges unspecified, for example, how to validate contracts. In each country, the legislators settle just the matters they need settling, just to the degree they think necessary, and just in the way they deem appropriate for their own people. Consequently these things belong to civil law rather than law of nations.

[1] *Secondly, it belongs to the notion of human law, to be ordained to the common good of the state. In this respect human law may be divided according to the different kinds of men who work in a special way for the common good:* [2] *e.g. priests, by praying to God for the people; princes, by governing the people; soldiers, by fighting for the safety of the people. Wherefore certain special kinds of law are adapted to these men.*	A second distinction within human law arises from the fact that it is directed to the good of the whole community. But different kinds of law are adapted to different kinds of men, each of them responsible for the common good in a different way: Just as priests pray to God for everyone, so magistrates govern everyone and soldiers fight for the safety of everyone.

[1] The second formal difference in human laws arises from the second element in the definition of law, which we saw in Question 90, Article 2: Law is for the common good. For people who perform different services to the community, contributing to the common good in different ways, different kinds of law may be necessary.

[2] Again, we are not necessarily supposing that priests are functionaries of the government (though some were in pagan Rome). All the same, their services may be publicly recognized, just like the services of soldiers and members of the senatorial class. Consequently, law may take account of them, just as it takes account of these other kinds of service. Even in the United States, which distinguishes Church from State and forbids setting up an official national religion, written law requires that chaplains be made available to soldiers, and custom surrounds a new magistrate's

oath of office with reminders of the presence of God. Certain laws about ministers of religion, such as the law permitting the deduction of certain expenses of their calling from taxation, were enacted not in spite of the distinction between Church and State, but to protect it. So St. Thomas's examples seem entirely general; the fact that the law recognizes the service of ministers no more implies an official state church than the fact that the law recognizes the services of soldiers implies a military dictatorship.

---

[1] *Thirdly, it belongs to the notion of human law, to be framed by that one who governs the community of the state, as shown above (90, 3). In this respect, there are various human laws according to the various forms of government.* [2] *Of these, according to the Philosopher (Polit. iii, 10) one is "monarchy," i.e. when the state is governed by one; and then we have "Royal Ordinances."* [3] *Another form is "aristocracy," i.e. government by the best men or men of highest rank; and then we have the "Authoritative legal opinions" [Responsa Prudentum] and "Decrees of the Senate" [Senatus consulta].* [4] *Another form is "oligarchy," i.e. government by a few rich and powerful men; and then we have "Praetorian," also called "Honorary," law.* [5] *Another form of government is that of the people, which is called "democracy," and there we have "Decrees of the commonalty" [Plebiscita].* [6] *There is also tyrannical government, which is altogether corrupt, which, therefore, has no corresponding law.* [7] *Finally, there is a form of government made up of all these, and which is the best: and in this respect we have law sanctioned by the "Lords and Commons," as stated by Isidore (Etym. v, 4, seqq.).*

Yet another distinction within human law arises from the fact that it is instituted by the civic community's government; since there are various forms of government, there are various kinds of law. Suppose the government is monarchy, or the rule of one: Then we have what the Romans called *constitutiones principum*, the orders and decrees of the foremost man. But suppose it is aristocracy, or the rule of the best or highest. If taken in the former sense, rule by the best, then we have what the Romans called *responsa prudentum*, "responses of the wise," meaning the opinions of learned jurists. If taken in the latter sense, rule by the highest, then we have what they called *senatus consulta*, senatorial "consultations" or decrees. Another possibility is that the government is oligarchy, originally the rule of the rich and powerful few. Then we have what they called *praetorian* or honorary justice, the *praetors* being those who preside. Yet again, there might be rule of the people, or democracy. Then we have what they called *plebiscita*, resolutions of the assembly. Tyranny is a kind of rule, but since it is utterly rotten, it has no true law of its own, so our classification of law need not pay any attention to it. But last comes the best form of government, which blends all the other good kinds. Then, as Isidore says, we have law sanctioned by the great men acting together with the people.

---

[1]   The third formal difference in human laws arises from the third element in the definition of law, which we saw in Question 90, Article 3: Law is made by public authority. Despite the wording of the English translation, public authority need reside in a single man, for it may be placed in the hands of one, of a few, or of many – we have seen this before, and it is exactly the point that St. Thomas goes on to emphasize. Precisely because public authority can be organized in these different ways, different kinds of law result.

[2]   These include not only the enactments of pure monarchies, but any laws enacted by one man.

[3]   These include not only the enactments of pure aristocracies, but any laws enacted by the aristocratic class.

[4]   These include not only the enactments of pure oligarchies, but any laws enacted by the oligarchic class.

[5]   As by now one would expect, these include not only the enactments of pure democracies, but any laws enacted by the whole body of the people. St. Thomas is thinking of the popular assembly, where the people meet all together. He would consider the laws of our elected legislatures *partly* democratic, because the lawmakers are chosen by and from the people, but *partly* oligarchic, because the lawmakers are few. Just to the degree that eligibility to hold legislative office is restricted to the experienced and wise (for example, indirectly, by minimum age requirements), the arrangement is somewhat less democratic, somewhat less oligarchic, and somewhat more aristocratic.

[6]   The edicts of a tyrant are drawn by craftiness from his personal desires, rather than by reason from natural law; they serve his private interests and those of his cronies, rather than the common good; they are based on sheer power, rather than on rightful authority; and they may even be kept secret, like the official secrets "law" of the People's Republic of China, parts of which are themselves secret.[26] Therefore, as St. Augustine said, they are not true laws at all, but acts of violence.

[7]   "Made up of all these" means made up of all the lawful forms of rule; our purpose is to classify laws, and we have already seen that tyranny is lawless, so that form of rule may be passed over. Although Isidore does not explicitly state that mixed rule is the best, he strongly implies it

---

[26] For discussion, see Question 90, Article 4.

by giving the generic name "law" (*lex*) to a single kind of law, the kind made by great men and commoners acting together. The point of this metonymy is not that other kinds of laws are counterfeit, but that this is the kind that supremely deserves the name.[27] Later, in Question 105, discussed in the online *Companion to the Commentary*, St. Thomas explains why mixed government is the best; for now it suffices that it is.

Notice that in a mixed government, a law may arise in different ways, depending on the particular constitutional body that frames it. Thus, in the mixed government of Rome, certain laws were essentially monarchical, others aristocratic, others oligarchic, and others democratic. As St. Thomas and Isidore agree, however, the best kind of law – like the best kind of government – is by far the mixed.

[1] *Fourthly, it belongs to the notion of human law to direct human actions. In this respect, according to the various matters of which the law treats, there are various kinds of laws,* [2] *which are sometimes named after their authors: thus we have the "Lex Julia" about adultery, the "Lex Cornelia" concerning assassins, and so on, differentiated in this way, not on account of the authors, but on account of the matters to which they refer.*	The final distinction arises in human law arises from the fact that it guides human acts. Human acts must be guided with respect to various matters; therefore their guidance requires various laws. Sometimes laws about various matters are named after their various authors; for example, the law about adultery is named after Julius, and the law about assassins is named after Cornelius. Even so, the real basis of the distinction lies not in their authors but in their subject matter.

[1]   One might have expected that the fourth formal difference in human laws would arise from the fourth element in the definition of law, which we saw in Question 90, Article 4: Law is promulgated or made known. Instead, St. Thomas returns to the root idea from which *all* of the elements in the definition of law are derived: That law is a rule and measure of distinctively human acts. Why *not* classify laws according to the mode of promulgation? Presumably St. Thomas is reasoning that although it is essential to law *that* it be promulgated, it is unimportant *how* it is promulgated; laws of the same kind may be promulgated in different ways, and laws of different kinds may be promulgated in the same way. Isidore apparently agrees.

---

[27] Isidore gives the same definition two places: *Etymologies*, Book 2, Chapter 10, and Book 5, Chapter 10. Earlier in this *Treatise*, see also Question 90, Article 3.

[2] St. Thomas argues that the real basis for this classification is subject matter, that is, *which kinds* of human acts these laws direct. The names of the authors are merely labels. So the Law of Julius and the Law of Cornelius are formally different after all, not because one was framed by Julius and the other by Cornelius, but because one was about adultery and the other about assassins.

---

[1] *Reply to Objection 1. The law of nations is indeed, in some way, natural to man, in so far as he is a reasonable being, because it is derived from the natural law by way of a conclusion that is not very remote from its premises. Wherefore men easily agreed thereto.* [2] *Nevertheless it is distinct from the natural law, especially it is distinct from the natural law which is common to all animals.*	**Reply to Objection 1.** The law of nations certainly pertains to man's rational nature, for it follows from natural law as a conclusion. Because it is not a remote conclusion from its premises, but an immediate one, people agree to it easily. Yet even though derived from natural law, it is not the *same* as natural law, and it should especially be distinguished from those aspects of natural law to which Isidore was referring, the ones that we share with all animals.

---

[1] Some aspects of natural law are common to all nations because they are led to them by the distinctively rational nature with which humans are endowed; others are common to all nations because they are led to them by the aspects of nature that all humans share with the animals. Law of nations resembles the former because each of its precepts follows from the first principles of reason. Because it follows *closely* from them, even men of different nations can agree about how reasonable it is.

[2] It differs even from the aspects of natural law that arise purely from our rational nature, because it is not these things *per se,* but the *recognition* of these things in custom and formal enactments. It differs still more from the aspects of natural law that are connected with our animal nature, because these things do not acquire the nature of law until they are uplifted into rationality and transformed by it.

The remark about "the natural law which is common to all animals" is an allusion to the jurist Ulpian, who had written that natural law is "what nature has taught all animals."[28] Notice, though, that St. Thomas doesn't simply follow Ulpian's inadequate definition; he improves upon

---

[28] Ulpian is quoted in *Digest,* Book 1, Title 1, Section 3. Isidore begins with the same examples, union of male and female and the procreation and education of children.

it, making clear that what we share with animals is but one aspect of our nature.

The Replies to the other Objections are evident from what has been said.	No further explanation is needed; the answers to the remaining three objections are now plain.

What has already been said makes plain how to reply to Objection 2, because Isidore is distinguishing popular resolutions, senatorial decrees, and so forth, not according to their validity, but according to the constitutional body that enacts them. It also makes plain how to reply to Objection 4, because Isidore is not distinguishing the laws of Cornelius, of Falcidius, and so forth, according to their authors, but according to their subject matter.

Not so plain is how to reply to Objection 3. The Objector had made three points: (1) Different kinds of law are adapted to men performing different kinds of public service; (2) Isidore rightly includes the kinds of law adapted to magistrates, priests, and soldiers; but (3) Isidore wrongly omits the kinds of law adapted to men who perform other kinds of public service. The problem is that although St. Thomas agrees with points (1) and (2), he seems to ignore point (3), so the Objection is left standing.

Could it be that St. Thomas thinks ruling for all, praying for all, and fighting for the protection of all are the *only* fundamental services to the community, the only kinds included in its *ratio* or idea? No, because he prefaces them with the Latin word *sicut*, meaning "as," "like," or "for instance," indicating that they are merely examples. Thus, there could also be other kinds of laws, adapted to other kinds of men, performing other kinds of service to the people.

Then why then not list all of them? Because that would be impossible. If we did try to list every important kind of service to the community, the list would be endless. Laborers toil for all, carpenters build for all, professors profess for all, and so forth. On the other hand, not every important kind of service to the community requires equal attention *from law.* Consider carpentry: The fact that some men build houses certainly promotes the common good, but it does so because many houses are built for many families, not because all families live in a common dwelling. Perhaps what we should say is that that although there are many kinds of service to the public, there are not many kinds of service to the whole public *at once.* Of these few, perhaps the most prominent and most likely to need legal attention are ruling all, fighting for the protection of all, and praying for all *in magistratibus,* that is, in a public capacity. This may be what St. Thomas has in mind.

For further reflection on the preceding section of the *Treatise on Law,* the online *Companion to the Commentary,* accessible via the Resources link at the book's catalogue webpage, includes a discussion of the following topic:

WHY DOES CLASSIFICATION MATTER?

Before Reading Question 96

As explained in the Prologue to Question 90, four different causes make each kind of thing what it is. This applies to human law, just as to everything else. The form, or formal cause, of human law is an ordinance of reason; its end, or final cause, is the common good; its power, or efficient cause – that which brings it into being and maintains it in being – is public authority; and its matter, or material cause, consists of the particular enactments that are promulgated by such authority. So what St. Thomas means when he says that we are about to consider the power of human law is that we are going to investigate just how far public authority reaches, what kinds of enactments it *can* promulgate.

Though each of the six Articles that belong to this Question concerns the power or "reach" of human law, each concerns a different aspect of its reach. Why not just ask "How far does human law reach?" and look for a general answer? Or, if a "Yes" or "No" answer is desired, why not propose a general formula in advance, then simply ask, "Is this formula correct?" St. Thomas is certainly not averse to large-scale generalizations and first principles. Sometimes he proposes them himself; sometimes he draws them from the tradition, adding his own clarifications and refinements. Once a sufficiently general principle is achieved, detailed conclusions can be drawn from it by way of inference.

Yet reaching for Big Ideas too quickly can get us into trouble. My students often propose very general formulae for law's reach such as "Solving problems" or "Making the world better." These make the power of law all but unlimited; nothing is excluded but the attempt to do evil for its own sake. Starting from the opposite corner, the early modern thinker

346

John Locke proposed the formula that laws reach only so far as needed for the preservation of individual property against aggression and its regulation for the public good, taking "property" to mean meant life, liberty, and possessions.[1] Although this Big Idea had enormous influence on the early American republic, its meaning is far less clear than it might seem. Because of its glowing reference to such rights, it is commonly taken as authorizing a state highly protective of liberty, but the conclusion does not necessarily follow, for Locke nowhere explains just how far rightful liberty extends.[2] By itself his Big Idea does not answer a single one of St. Thomas's six questions about the power of law.

St. Thomas begins with the six questions because when the territory to be explored is slippery and uneven, it is more prudent to proceed in small steps, focusing on the places where the footing has proven treacherous in the past. By doing so, he makes the path safer, and holds open the possibility that later wayfarers may fare further.

---

[1] John Locke, *Second Treatise of Government*, Sections 3, 6 (public domain).

[2] For example, although Locke is widely regarded as a champion of religious liberty, the holes in his theory of toleration are large enough to criminalize the profession of Catholic faith. "That Church can have no right to be tolerated by the magistrate," he says, "which is constituted upon such a bottom that all those who enter into it do thereby, *ipso facto*, deliver themselves up to the protection and service of another prince." What he means is that Catholics are beyond the pale because they accept the authority of the Pope. John Locke, *Letter Concerning Toleration* (public domain).

St. Thomas's Prologue to Question 96: Of the Power of Human Law

TEXT	PARAPHRASE
[1] *We must now consider the power of human law. Under this head there are six points of inquiry:*	The second of the three broad inquiries in the investigation of human law is how far human law reaches. This involves us in six more detailed questions. Article 1 concerns whether every law must be a general rule. Article 2 considers whether laws should try to put down all vices, and Article 3 looks into whether they should try to command every different act of virtue. In Article 4, we investigate whether a person is conscientiously bound to obey a law even if it is unjust; in Article 5, whether law applies to all men, or only to certain categories of men; and in Article 6, whether someone who is subject to a law may ever set aside its precise instructions.
[2] *(1) Whether human law should be framed for the community?*	
[3] *(2) Whether human law should repress all vices?*	
[4] *(3) Whether human law is competent to direct all acts of virtue?*	
[5] *(4) Whether it binds man in conscience?*	
[6] *(5) Whether all men are subject to human law?*	
[7] *(6) Whether those who are under the law may act beside the letter of the law?*	

[1]   As explained in the Before Reading section, the "power" of human law means its reach – what kinds of enactments it may bring into being.

[2]   Do all laws deal with the whole community at once, or is there such a thing as a law for a particular individual or category of individuals?

[3]   It is nonsense to say law should be morally neutral; every law aims at the common good. Moreover, the good includes good character. But

does it follow that to bring about the good, law must take a utopian attitude to the extirpation of vice? We seem to land in difficulties whether we answer "Yes" or "No."

[4] As stated, the point to be investigated is whether law takes an interest in *each different virtue*. However, St. Thomas broadens the inquiry into whether it takes an interest in *every different exercise* of each virtue. For all we know before looking into the matter, it might require all acts of every virtue; certain acts of every virtue; all acts of certain virtues; or certain acts of certain virtues.

[5] One might suppose that we have the answer to this question already, because St. Thomas has stated previously that an unjust law is no law at all. But to ask whether an unjust law is a real law is not precisely the same as to ask whether one has a duty to obey it – or when, if ever, one may disobey.

[6] It is often said that laws are not made for good people but only for bad ones. How seriously is that maxim to be taken? And what about those who *make* the law – are they under the law too? How could they be "under" what they themselves command?

[7] Suppose the justice of the law is not in question. Even so, is it ever morally permissible to make an exception to what it literally requires?

For further reflection on the preceding section of the *Treatise on Law*, the online *Companion to the Commentary*, accessible via the Resources link at the book's catalogue webpage, includes a discussion of the following topic:
WHY JUST THESE QUESTIONS?

Question 96, Article 1:
Whether Human Law Should Be Framed
for the Community
Rather than for the Individual?

TEXT	PARAPHRASE
Whether human law should be framed for the community rather than for the individual?	To be true laws, must the enactments of human authority always be framed in general terms, rather than in application to particular persons or groups?

St. Thomas is not asking whether law must serve the common good rather than private interests; we have already seen that it must. Nor is he asking whether law may treat individual persons as mere tools of the common good; we have already seen that it must not. He is asking whether law must always be framed in general terms – "*No one* may murder," "*Everyone* must pay his taxes."

The question is more difficult than it may seem. Could there be a law, for instance, just about John Doe, or just about the Smith family? "Of course not!" Not so fast. Judicial verdicts concern individuals; don't they have the force of law? And aren't there special laws for such groups as physicians, soldiers, and air traffic controllers?

Objection 1. It would seem that human law should be framed not for the community, but rather for the individual. For the Philosopher says (Ethic. v, 7) that "the legal just ... includes all particular acts of legislation ... and all those matters which are the subject of decrees," which are also individual matters, since decrees are framed about individual actions. Therefore law is framed not only for the community, but also for the individual.	Objection 1. Apparently, human law may be framed not just in general terms, but even more about particular persons. Because, as we find in Aristotle, "legal" or conventional justice includes "particular" enactments, as well as "decrees," both of which concern particular individuals. So the view that laws must be framed in general terms is mistaken.

The Objector points out that legislators do make enactments for individual cases, which wise men, such as Aristotle, have not hesitated to view as having the force of law. Aristotle's example of a "particular" act of legislation is a decision of the lawmakers that a sacrifice shall be offered to honor Brasidas, who was a hero of the Peloponnesian wars.[3] A "decree" is a judgment rendered to settle a particular case.

The Dominican Fathers translation is misleading. If the first sentence of the Objection really said that human law should be framed *not at all* for the community, *but rather* for the individual," then it would be inconsistent with the third sentence, which says human law should be framed *not only* for the community, *but also* for the individual. But the Latin word *magis* should have been translated not "rather," but "more." So what the first sentence actually says is that human law should be framed *not [only]* for the community, but *even more* for the individual. This removes the inconsistency.

[3] A Spartan, not an Athenian: The example must have annoyed Aristotle's countrymen.

Objection 2. *Further, law is the director of human acts, as stated above (90, A1,2). But human acts are about individual matters. Therefore human laws should be framed, not for the community, but rather for the individual.*

Objection 2. Moreover, law governs human acts. But every human act is performed by *someone* about *something*. Since the acts that law governs are individual, the law must refer to individuals.

The Objector protests that human acts are much too different for general laws to govern them in all their particularity. His argument is similar to the argument in Question 95, Article 1, Objection 3: "[S]ince human actions are about singulars, which are infinite in number, matter pertaining to the direction of human actions cannot be taken into sufficient consideration except by a wise man, who looks into each one of them. Therefore it would have been better for human acts to be directed by the judgment of wise men, than by the framing of laws."

[1] **Objection 3.** *Further, law is a rule and measure of human acts, as stated above (90, A1,2). But a measure should be most certain, as stated in Metaph. x. [2] Since therefore in human acts no general proposition can be so certain as not to fail in some individual cases, it seems that laws should be framed not in general but for individual cases.*

Objection 3. Still further, we saw at the outset of our *Treatise* that law is a rule and measure of human acts. But as Aristotle points out, whatever we use as a measure must be exact. Now if the law had to be framed in general terms, it would lack exactness, because all generalizations have exceptions. Therefore, to be exact, laws must refer to individuals.

[1]   This time the Objector has loaded his gun with the same bullet from the *Metaphysics* that he used in Question 91, Article 3, Objection 3, from which he has already borrowed in another way. But just as he was overstating Aristotle's point there, so he is here. Aristotle is speaking of *quantitative* measurement, where we do seek an exact measure. But outside of quantitative measurement, he says, perfect exactness in measuring is impossible, and we can only "imitate" quantitative exactness.[4]

[2]   Suppose the lawmakers enact a general rule that for the safety of the people, no citizen may strike another. There may arise a few cases where the safety of the people requires striking, for example, to stop a criminal who is bent upon killing. The Objector argues that no general rule can be

[4] Aristotle, *Metaphysics*, Book 10, Chapter 1.

so perfectly drawn up that it has no exceptions. Since its very generality defeats its purpose, we should not require it to be general.

On the contrary, The jurist says (Pandect. Justin. lib. i, tit. iii, art. ii; De legibus, etc.) that "laws should be made to suit the majority of instances; and they are not framed according to what may possibly happen in an individual case."

On the other hand, as the great legal authority Julianus is quoted in the *Digest*, laws should be adapted to what *usually* happens – not to what *might* happen in the case of this or that person.

St. Thomas is paraphrasing Julianus's remark that "Neither statutes nor *senates consulta* [decrees of the senate] can be written in such a way that all cases which might at any time occur are covered; it is however sufficient that the things which very often happen are embraced." The *Digest* quotes statements to the same effect by the jurists Pomponius, Celsus, Paulus, and Ulpian.[5] These remarks imply that the sort of exactness that the Objector demands is inappropriate.

---

[1] *I answer that, Whatever is for an end should be proportionate to that end. Now the end of law is the common good; because, as Isidore says (Etym. v, 21) that "law should be framed, not for any private benefit, but for the common good of all the citizens." Hence human laws should be proportionate to the common good.* [2] *Now the common good comprises many things. Wherefore law should take account of many things, as to persons, as to matters, and as to times.* [3] *Because the community of the state is composed of many persons;* [4] *and its good is procured by*

Here is my response. Whenever something is directed to a purpose, it must be adapted to accomplish that purpose. Now the purpose of law is not the personal advantage of some, but the good of all in common – as confirmed by Isidore in his *Etymologies*. So far, it follows that human laws must be adapted to accomplish the common good.

But "the common good" corresponds to a multitude of things. Therefore law must also comprehend a multitude of things, not just in the ways they are similar, but even in the ways that they are different: Many persons, many affairs, many times. It takes in view many persons, because the civil community is made of a multitude of different sorts of citizen; many affairs, because a great variety of different sorts of acts contribute to the shared good; and

---

5 The citation in the Dominican Fathers translation is incorrect: Julianus is quoted in the *Digest*, Book 1, Title 3, Section 10, not Section 2. For the other statements mentioned, compare Sections 3–6 and 8. My quotation is from Alan Watson, ed., *The Digest of Justinian*, Vol. 1, rev. ed. (Philadelphia: University of Pennsylvania Press, 1998), p. 12. The translator of Book 1 in this edition is D.N. MacCormack.

many actions; [5] nor is it established to endure for only a short time, but to last for all time by the citizens succeeding one another, as Augustine says (De Civ. Dei ii, 21; xxii, 6).

many times, because, as St. Augustine says in the *City of God,* the commonwealth is set in place not to last for a little while, but to abide throughout diverse ages, each generation of citizens succeeding the one before.

---

[1]   To be proportionate to a purpose is to be a suitable means to its attainment, so for human law to be proportionate to its purpose, it must be a suitable means to the attainment of the common good. Isidore's statement that law should serve the common rather than the private good was discussed in Question 95, Article 3, but the point itself was established much earlier, in Question 90, Article 2.

[2]   This is the turning point in the argument, and it is easy to miss. Just because we share in the enjoyment of the common good, we slip into thinking that every person, every matter, and every time is related to it in the same way. St. Thomas points out that this is erroneous. The common good is not one-dimensional but many-dimensional, for all the many persons, matters, and times are related to it in different ways. Each person, and each act, contributes to it in a different manner; each age presents to it a different set of challenges. He goes on to explain in more detail.

[3]   "Many persons" should be taken as meaning many *kinds* of persons, which do not all require precisely the same attention from the law. Notice, by the way, that St. Thomas does not say "many," or "many men," or "many individuals," as he might have, but "many persons." This choice of term reminds us that although in a certain sense the citizens are parts of the community, they can never be *reduced* to being parts, because each of them possesses a kind of wholeness that the community itself never can: A person is a "substantial" unity, whereas the community has only the much weaker unity of order.

[4]   The point is that there is no such act as "procuring the common good." Rather a multitude of acts procure the common good in a multitude of ways; to list but a few: making laws, growing crops, raising families, practicing medicine, conducting worship, engaging in business, making discoveries, and passing on knowledge to the young.

[5]   Here St. Thomas means to stress that the common good may have somewhat different requirements in each age. Although the point is clear, his choice of authority, St. Augustine's *City of God,* is a bit surprising.

St. Thomas does not tell us what passage he has in mind,[6] but he may be thinking of St. Augustine's remark, in Book 22, Chapter 6, that "according to Cicero, a state should engage in war for the safety which preserves the state permanently in existence though its citizens change; as the foliage of an olive or laurel, or any tree of this kind, is perennial, the old leaves being replaced by fresh ones." What makes the reference odd, however, is that St. Augustine is not exactly endorsing Cicero's idea. St. Augustine would certainly agree that legislators should take the long view, and after all, that is St. Thomas's main point. But St. Augustine's own purpose is quite different: To show that the only commonwealth that really lasts "for all time" is the commonwealth of heaven, and that the succession of generations in the City of Man is but a pallid reflection of what is promised to the City of God. As he says in Chapter 1, the blessedness of the City of God is named "eternal,"

... not because it shall endure for many ages, though at last it shall come to an end, but because, according to the words of the gospel, of His kingdom there shall be no end. Neither shall it enjoy the mere appearance of perpetuity which is maintained by the rise of fresh generations to occupy the place of those that have died out, as in an evergreen the same freshness seems to continue permanently, and the same appearance of dense foliage is preserved by the growth of fresh leaves in the room of those that have withered and fallen; but in that city all the citizens shall be immortal, men now for the first time enjoying what the holy angels have never lost.

In another place, he says stingingly,

But since those Romans were in an earthly city, and had before them, as the end of all the offices undertaken in its behalf, its safety, and a kingdom, not in heaven, but in earth – not in the sphere of eternal life, but in the sphere of demise and succession, where the dead are succeeded by the dying – what else but glory should they love, by which they wished even after death to live in the mouths of their admirers?[7]

Although St. Thomas and St. Augustine are performing the same symphony, they are playing different movements of it. Both agree that earthly goods are real goods and ought to be sustained. Both agree that even so, they owe their entire being to the Creator, whose infinite goodness their finite goodness but reflects. And so both agree that to put these goods in the place of God, treating them as the Supreme Good, spells utter ruin.

---

[6] The two citations are provided by the translators.

[7] Augustine of Hippo, *City of God Against the Pagans*, trans. Marcus Dods, respectively Book 22, Chapter 6; Book 22, Chapter 1; and Book 5, Chapter 14 (public domain).

The difference is that St. Thomas is emphasizing that even though our earthly commonwealths are not eternal, we should build them to last; while St. Augustine is emphasizing that even though we should build our earthly commonwealths to last, they are not eternal.

---

[1] *Reply to Objection 1. The Philosopher (Ethic. v, 7) divides the legal just, i.e. positive law, into three parts.* [2] *For some things are laid down simply in a general way: and these are the general laws. Of these he says that "the legal [just] is that which originally was a matter of indifference, but which, when enacted, is so no longer": as the fixing of the ransom of a captive.* [3] *Some things affect the community in one respect, and individuals in another. These are called "privileges," i.e. "private laws," as it were, because they regard private persons, although their power extends to many matters; and in regard to these, he adds, "and further, all particular acts of legislation."* [4] *Other matters are legal, not through being laws, but through being applications of general laws to particular cases: such are decrees which have the force of law; and in regard to these, he adds "all matters subject to decrees."*

Reply to Objection 1. [Law must be general in the sense of serving the common good, but it does not follow that it must treat everything and everyone in the same way.[8]] We will see this more clearly if we consider all three kinds of "legal" justice.

(1) *General laws.* These are laws that are framed in general terms. Aristotle has general laws in mind when he remarks that the "legal just" is about things that apart from the intervention of human authority might as well be done one way as another, but that because of such intervention must be done in a particular way (for example, how much must be paid to ransom someone taken captive in war).

(2) *Privileges, or private laws.* These are laws that are general in one way but particular in another: For on the one hand, their power reaches many different kinds of affairs, but on the other hand, they address particular individuals. Aristotle has privileges in mind when he refers to "particular" enactments.

(3) *Judgments.* These are matters that belong to law not precisely because they are laws themselves, but because they *apply* general laws to particular deeds, and so have law's force. Aristotle has judgments in mind when he refers to decrees.

---

[1]   Only two of these three were mentioned in the Objections.

[2]   This is the first category of "legal" justice: Things that in themselves could be settled in more than one way, but that human authority settles in a particular way. We have discussed them more generally in Question 95, Article 2. The point St. Thomas makes here is that such enactments

---

[8] This is the tacit point of the reply; I have taken the liberty of making it explicit.

are framed in general terms: A particular amount is specified for the ransom of *any* captive.

[3] "Particular" enactments are the second category of "legal" justice. Calling them "private laws" may confuse many readers, because today we tend to think of "private law" as the law of contracts. For St. Thomas, the concept is much broader. As mentioned above, Aristotle's example is a legislative decision that a particular general be commemorated with a public sacrifice. Evidently St. Thomas views this commemoration as a special case of what Roman law and canon law call a "privilege": an enactment that gives a certain private or persons some power or distinction not given to others. For instance, it would be a privilege if the law specified that only qualified physicians may practice medicine, that only designated heirs may receive the property of deceased persons, or that only the signatories of contracts may sue for broken agreements.[9] In the *Etymologies,* Book 5, Chapter 18, Isidore says that privileges and so-called private laws are the same thing.

St. Thomas's point is that even though a privilege is framed in particular rather than general terms, it is framed with a view to the general good. If only qualified physicians may practice medicine, then everyone is better off, not just doctors.

[4] The third category of "legal" justice is decisions rendered by judges to settle particular cases. Because such a decree applies only to the case at hand, it may seem that it has no generality at all, but St. Thomas points out that it is the application of a general law *to* the case at hand; otherwise it could not have force of law.

A certain complication is presented by the fact that Aristotle uses similar language not only for judgments in cases of law, but also for judgments in cases of equity, where the letter of the general law is *not* applied because it would produce a result contrary to the intention of the legislators. "And this is the nature of the equitable," he says, "a correction of law where it is defective owing to its universality. In fact this is the reason why all things are not determined by law, that about some things it is impossible to lay down a law, so that a decree is needed."[10] We return to the question of equity in Question 97, Article 4. Here it is sufficient to say that even though judgment in a case of equity departs from the letter of

---

⁹ See also Book 5, Lecture 12 of St. Thomas's commentary on the *Nicomachean Ethics.*
¹⁰ Aristotle, *Nicomachean Ethics,* trans. W.D. Ross, Book 5, Chapters 7, 10 (public domain).

the law, it is not arbitrary. Though it does not apply the *letter of the law* to the case at hand, it does apply *general principles* to the case at hand.

As he sometimes does in his response to an Objection, St. Thomas buries the punchline. What he is trying to get us to see is that even though not all three kinds of enactment are framed in general terms, nevertheless all three are framed with a view to the general good. The first really is framed in general terms, the second does good generally even though *not* framed in general terms, and the third applies general principles to particular cases. This is enough.

---

[1] *Reply to Objection 2. A principle of direction should be applicable to many; wherefore (Metaph. x, text. 4) the Philosopher says that all things belonging to one genus, are measured by one, which is the principle in that genus.* [2] *For if there were as many rules or measures as there are things measured or ruled, they would cease to be of use, since their use consists in being applicable to many things. Hence law would be of no use, if it did not extend further than to one single act.* [3] *Because the decrees of prudent men are made for the purpose of directing individual actions; whereas law is a general precept,* [4] *as stated above (92, 2, Objection 2).*	Reply to Objection 2. Anything that directs, necessarily directs many things. For just this reason, Aristotle comments in his *Metaphysics* that in each general class of things, each element is measured by the same standard (which is the first such element, the point of origin of all the rest). What use would there be in having a different rule of governance, or a different measuring rod, for each thing to be governed or measured? None, for its whole point is to provide a common standard for a multitude of things. More particularly, what use would a law be if it governed only a single act of a single person? Again, none whatsoever. True, wise men do judge individual actions. But law, unlike their decrees, is a *general* precept. By the way, we have been over this ground once before in a different context [in Question 92, Article 2, Objection 2.]

---

[1] A fundamental rule for the direction of things of a particular sort needs to be applicable to all things of that sort. To say that all things belonging to one genus are measured by the "principle" of the genus is to say that their standard is the source from which they spring. As we saw in Question 90, Article 1, the same point is made in Aristotle, *Physics*, Book 2.

By quoting in this case from Aristotle's *Metaphysics*, Book 10, St. Thomas shows that the point just made is not only good sense, but sound ontology. Suppose we used a different scale of hardness for every mineral – say, the Mohs scale for pyrite, the Rockwell scale for hematite, the Leeb scale for gypsum, and so on. Without a common standard for these minerals, how could we say which was harder?[11]

Of course we do not use the same standard for all things whatsoever – only for things in the same genus. The same criterion is used for all poodles, and the same is used for all Great Danes, but a champion poodle is not judged by the same criterion as a champion Great Dane. True, in the final round of a dog show, the judges compare the best poodle with the best Great Dane, but to do this they must reduce the two criteria to a single common criterion. Hence they ask, "Which dog comes closer to perfection in its own breed – the poodle or the Great Dane?" Commensuration is not always helpful or meaningful. Only a joker would ask "Which was more intense – Martha's perfume, or Sidney's sneeze?" There may be some genus to which both sneezes and perfumes belong – and therefore some standard by which they could both be compared – but it would belong more to the realm of comedy than of philosophy.

[2] St. Thomas might have pointed out simply that if utterly different laws were applied to different acts, chaos would result, and the common good would be destroyed. But he wants us to see that this fact is an instance of an even more general truth: Law is a standard for acts, and as we have just seen above, *all* standards require generality.

[3] St. Thomas concedes that judgments that *apply* the law apply it to particular actions. What the Objector overlooks is that law *which the judgments apply* is general.

[4] Here St. Thomas refers to his previous refutation of the mistaken idea that laws include not only command, but also counsel.

| [1] *Reply to Objection 3.* "We must not seek the same degree of certainty in all things" (Ethic. i, 3). [2] Consequently in contingent matters, such as natural and human things, it is enough for a thing to be certain, as being true in the greater number of instances, though at times and less frequently it fail. | Reply to Objection 3. As Aristotle points out in his *Ethics*, we do not pursue the same precision in everything. This is why, in matters that can be other than they are, for instance natural occurrences and human affairs, it is sufficient that something is true in most cases, even though in a few cases it goes astray. |

[11] For those who are curious, these scales measure hardness not only in different ways but also in different senses: The Mohs scale, which is normally used for minerals, measures scratch hardness; the Rockwell scale, which is normally used for refined metals, measures indentation hardness; and the Leeb scale, which is also used for metals, measures rebound hardness.

[1]   Aristotle is referring to certainty primarily in the sense of clarity and exactness, rather than in the sense of subjective confidence, so I have used the term "precision." As Ross translates, "Our discussion will be adequate if it has as much clearness as the subject-matter admits of, for precision is not to be sought for alike in all discussions, any more than in all the products of the crafts .... for it is the mark of an educated man to look for precision in each class of things just so far as the nature of the subject admits; it is evidently equally foolish to accept probable reasoning from a mathematician and to demand from a rhetorician scientific proofs."[12]

[2]   We do not reject the proposition that milk is nutritious just because a few people are allergic to milk, or the proposition that deserts are arid just because every hundred years or so there may be rain. In the same way, we do not reject the law that quiet should be kept near hospitals just because an emergency may now and then require someone to shout. *What to do* when a general law is not suitable to a particular case is a good question, but St. Thomas puts off discussing it until Question 97, Article 4.

For further reflection on the preceding section of the *Treatise on Law*, the online *Companion to the Commentary*, accessible via the Resources link at the book's catalogue webpage, includes a discussion of the following topic:

LEGAL "PRIVILEGES"

Question 96, Article 2:
Whether It Belongs to the Human Law to Repress
All Vices?

TEXT	PARAPHRASE
Whether it belongs to the human law to repress all vices?	Should human law attempt to hold *every* vice in check?

Question 96 provides several of the few places in the *Summa* where the traditional answer to the *ultrum* is not "Yes," but "No," and this Article is one of them. The tradition does maintain that the law should aim at virtue. But it does *not* therefore conclude that legislators should

---

[12] Aristotle repeats the point later on: "We must also remember what has been said before, and not look for precision in all things alike, but in each class of things such precision as accords with the subject-matter, and so much as is appropriate to the inquiry." Aristotle, *Nicomachean Ethics*, trans. W.D. Ross, Book 1, Chapters 3, 7 (public domain).

declare all vices illegal, and neither does St. Thomas. This comes as a shock to most first-time readers, who tend to assume that the proponents of natural law want to "enforce morality."

But don't they? As we saw in Question 92, Article 1, in one sense all law enforces morality, whether lawmakers believe or disbelieve in natural law. For what else is there to enforce? The subject of morality is good and evil, and every law aims at promoting what lawmakers think good and restraining what they think evil. These legislators may be corrupt, ruling on the theory that the good is whatever serves themselves. They may be pragmatic, ruling on the theory that economic goods trump all other goods. They may be liberal, ruling on the theory that it is good to be neutral about the good (which in practice means pursuing ends without admitting that they are ends). Yet even a vicious, narrow, or disguised idea of the good is an idea of the good.

The notion that law promotes the enforcement of morality is true in a second sense too, for any reasonable view of the good includes good character. The idea of a good life in which no one has to be good is laughable. Where there is no virtue, everything else is insipid, and not even goods other than virtue can endure. Besides, it would be absurd for a legislator to care whether the citizens cut each other's throats, but not whether they are murderous. From what else do acts of vice arise, if not from vices?

But conceding all of this, does it follow that to encourage good character, lawmakers should be morality cops? Is it possible that not because of moral indifference, and not because of a "right" to do wrong, but *for the sake of morality itself*, there must be limits on the legal means of promoting morality? That is what St. Thomas is asking.

[1] *Objection 1. It would seem that it belongs to human law to repress all vices. For Isidore says (Etym. v, 20) that "laws were made in order that, in fear thereof, man's audacity might be held in check." [2] But it would not be held in check sufficiently, unless all evils were repressed by law. Therefore human laws should repress all evils.*	Objection 1. Apparently, human law should hold every vice in check. That is the very thing Isidore says law is for – restraining the insolent, meaning the vicious, by striking into them the fear of punishment. But the vicious would not be completely restrained unless *every* evil were held in check. It follows that law should hold in check every evil.

[1] A false impression might be taken from the fact that of all the possible ways to render the Latin term *cohibere,* the English translation has

chosen the harshest, "repress" – a verb that in our day makes one think of dungeons, inquisitors, and secret police. Another false impression might be taken from the fact that "audacity" (*audacia*) can refer to the virtue of valor, for here the term means impudence or defiance, a vice. To prevent these misunderstandings, I have tried to readjust the tone. Thus in the paraphrase, the Objector suggests not "repressing" all vices, but "keeping them in check," and Isidore does not say that laws were made to restrain "audacity," but that they were made to restrain "insolence."

[2] It may seem that the Objector has broadened the question and changed its meaning by replacing the term "vice" with the term "evil." Not really. Contemporary slang uses the term "vice" in the very narrow sense of habits that oppose temperance: Someone who says "my vice is chocolate cake" is confessing to gluttony, and the "vice squad" concerns itself with things like prostitution. However, both the Objector and St. Thomas use the term "vice" in its broad, classical sense, which includes all habits that pervert or oppose virtue. Vice, then, includes not only what is contrary to temperance, but also what is contrary to the other moral virtues. The Objector wants law to restrain *all* of these vices – not just, say, murder and robbery, but everything whatsoever that may grow from pride, envy, wrath, sloth, avarice, gluttony, and lust.[13]

Objection 2. Further, the intention of the lawgiver is to make the citizens virtuous. But a man cannot be virtuous unless he forbear from all kinds of vice. Therefore it belongs to human law to repress all vices.	Objection 2. Moreover, the aim of legislation is to foster good character in the citizens. But no one can have completely good character unless the practice of every vice is quenched. Plainly, then, human law must quench the practice of every vice.

If vice is what opposes virtue, as we saw above, then the complete development of virtue necessarily excludes all vice. This may seem too obvious to state, but as every teacher knows, it isn't. The doctrine that virtue lies in a mean between excess and deficiency is often mistakenly taken as meaning that one should aim at a mean *of vice* – as though, for

---

[13] These are the seven "capital" vices, so called not because they are the worst of them, but because they are roots from which all of them grow. As St. Thomas explains, "a capital vice is one from which other vices arise, chiefly by being their final cause .... Wherefore a capital vice is not only the principle of others, but is also their director and, in a way, their leader." I-II, Q. 84, Arts. 3, 4. This theme has been dramatized by Dante Alighieri, who pictures purgatory as a mountain with seven ledges, on each of which souls are cleansed of just one of the capital vices.

example, virtue meant having just the right amount of spite, or committing just the right amount of adultery – not too little and not too much. But as Aristotle explains (with St. Thomas's approval), "not every action nor every passion admits of a mean; for some have names that already imply badness, for example, spite, shamelessness, envy, and in the case of actions adultery, theft, murder; for all of these and suchlike things imply by their names that they are themselves bad, and not the excesses or deficiencies of them. It is not possible, then, ever to be right with regard to them; one must always be wrong." St. Thomas explains, "in such things a person cannot be virtuous no matter how he acts, but he always sins in doing them."[14]

The Objector jumps to the conclusion that because the law aims at a state of character that *excludes* all vice, it must therefore *forbid* all vice.

Objection 3. Further, human law is derived from the natural law, as stated above (95, 2). But all vices are contrary to the law of nature. Therefore human law should repress all vices.	Objection 3. Still further, human law is rooted in natural law, and natural law opposes every vice. It follows that human law must also oppose every vice.

St. Thomas has shown in Question 94, Article 3, that natural law points toward virtue; but if it points toward virtue, then it is opposed by every vice. For a clearer transition, the paraphrase replaces the idea that vice is contrary to natural law with the idea that natural law is contrary to vice. Since the relation of contrariness is reflexive, this does not change the argument.

[1] *On the contrary, We read in De Lib. Arb. i, 5: "It seems to me that the law which is written for the governing of the people rightly permits these things, and that Divine providence punishes them."* [2] *But Divine providence punishes nothing but vices.* [3] *Therefore human law rightly allows some vices, by not repressing them.*	On the other hand, one of the speakers in *On Freedom of the Will* says human law is *right* to permit certain things even though Divine Providence avenges itself upon them. He must be speaking of vices, for Divine providence punishes nothing else. What he means, then, is that human law is right to allow and leave unpunished certain *vices*, doing nothing to hold them in check.

[14] Aristotle, *Nicomachean Ethics*, Book 2, Chapter 6, trans. W.D. Ross (public domain); Thomas Aquinas, *Commentary on Aristotle's Nicomachean Ethics*, Book 2, Lecture 7, trans. C.J. Litzinger, O.P., rev. ed. (Notre Dame, IN: Dumb Ox Books, 1993), p. 109.

[1] Surprisingly, this statement from St. Augustine's *On Freedom of the Will* is made not by the saint himself, but by his friend and partner in dialogue, Evodius. What makes it an authoritative statement of the tradition is that St. Augustine agrees with him (as we see in the Reply to Objection 3).

[2] The term "vices" is used here both for acts and habitual dispositions. The term translated as "punishes," *vindicare*, is vivid and forceful; we might say that in the end God's claim against these acts is vindicated, or that His providence at last takes vengeance.

[3] In other words, for failing to punish everything that Divine providence punishes, human law should be not merely excused, but actually approved. Since the justice of Divine providence is not in question, we do not yet know the reason for such approval; that is what the *respondeo* must work out. All we know is that this is the tradition.

---

[1] *I answer that, As stated above (90, A1,2), law is framed as a rule or measure of human acts. Now a measure should be homogeneous with that which it measures, as stated in Metaph. x, text. 3,4, since different things are measured by different measures.* [2] *Wherefore laws imposed on men should also be in keeping with their condition, for, as Isidore says (Etym. v, 21), law should be "possible both according to nature, and according to the customs of the country."* [3] *Now possibility or faculty of action is due to an interior habit or disposition: since the same thing is not possible to one who has not a virtuous habit, as is possible to one who has.* [4] *Thus the same is not possible to a child as to a full-grown man: for which reason the law for children is not the same as for adults, since many things are permitted to children, which in an adult*

Here is my response. As we saw at the very beginning of this *Treatise*, law is set down as a directive for human acts, or as a standard to see whether they measure up. Observing that a variety of different measures are employed, Aristotle points out that any standard of measurement must partake of the same nature as the kind of thing that we use it to measure. Human laws, for example, must be based on a *human* standard [not, for example, a horsey standard]. But for the same reason, a measure used for human acts must correspond to the degree to which their natural capacities have developed. Isidore expresses the same idea when he says that law should be within the natural capacities of those subject to it, as well as compatible with the customs of the country.

Whether something is within a person's power or capacity depends not on an outward circumstance, but on the way he is habituated to make choices, on his disposition of character – since people who have not been habituated to virtue do not find it possible to act in the same way as people who have. This is why a child cannot act in the same way as a fully developed

are punished by law or at any rate are open to blame. [5] In like manner many things are permissible to men not perfect in virtue, which would be intolerable in a virtuous man.

man, and therefore why different laws are framed for children and adults – permitting to children much that in adults would be punished, or at least censured. In the same way, the law lets many things pass in the case of those who are not completely virtuous that would be insufferable in the case of the virtuous.

---

[1]   Law makes demands as well as providing a standard of measurement. Any measure must be appropriate to the kind of thing that it is measuring, and to be appropriate to it, it must belong to the same genus, or be the same kind of thing. The standard is the foremost member of the genus. Thus the standard for a horse is an ideal horse, the standard for a proof is a flawless and elegant proof, and the standard for a man is a perfect man. By the way, Aristotelian metaphysics and Christian revelation converge on the latter point like two locomotives meeting head on, but Christianity finds the perfect man in Jesus Christ.

In just the same way, the standard for acts is a perfect act. One might think this means human law should require men to act perfectly: Not so. To say that the law must *measure* men according to the ideal is to say not that it must *demand* the ideal, but that it must demand the closest feasible approach to the ideal.

[2]   In Question 90, Article 1, St. Thomas's point was that because man is essentially rational, any appropriate rule and measure for his acts must be based on reason. Here his point is that because men are unequally developed in rationality, they must be ruled and measured with different degrees of strictness. For this reason, Isidore says the laws should be within the natural capacities of those subject to it, and compatible with the customs of the country. By their "natural" capacities he means not only what is possible to them as human beings, but also what is possible to them in view of the stage of human development they have reached. We have discussed this passage from the *Etymologies* more fully in Question 95, Article 3.

[3]   St. Thomas is not speaking of the power to act in the sense of muscular strength, but in the sense of the ability to choose and follow through on the act. This depends on the disposition of one's character. For example, someone who has the virtue of fortitude or courage can stand his ground under circumstances in which someone who lacks it would be unable to do so.

[4]   The term translated as "full-grown man" is *viro perfecto*, "perfect man," meaning one whose potentialities are fully developed, especially his potentiality for virtue. The law rightly expects a greater development of virtue in adults than in children.

[5]   A temperate man is not praised for his sobriety; we expect it of him. If he does get drunk, we are disgusted, because he was perfectly capable of resisting the bottle, but chose not to. But we do not punish a habitual drunkard too severely for getting drunk, for he has a diminished ability to control himself. We lay on him only such demands as he can bear: Don't get drunk in public. Don't get drunk around the children. Don't get drunk and drive. About such things we are rightly severe.

In Question 97, Article 3, St. Thomas remarks that by the very fact that the rulers of the people tolerate a customary practice, they "seem" to approve it. Sometimes they really do approve it, and in any case they approve its toleration. In principle, however, toleration and approval are different things. We don't tolerate drunkenness because it is good for the drunkard to be drunk; but what is the use of telling him not to get drunk? The demand is impossible for him; it has no point.

On the other hand, the fact that toleration produces the appearance of approval does pose a certain danger to others, who may be led into bad practices they would otherwise have avoided. This reminds us that the question of tolerating vices is beginning to look rather complicated. Besides the evil of the vice itself, we must consider not only the possible evil result of attempting to suppress things that cannot be suppressed, but also the possible evil result of appearing to approve things that cannot be approved.

---

[1] *Now human law is framed for a number of human beings, the majority of whom are not perfect in virtue. Wherefore human laws do not forbid all vices, from which the virtuous abstain, but only the more grievous vices, from which it is possible for the majority to abstain;* [2] *and chiefly those that are to the hurt of others,* [3] *without the prohibition of which human society could not be maintained: thus human law prohibits murder, theft and such like.*

Bear in mind that human law is made for a multitude of human beings, most of them deficient in virtue to some degree. For this reason, human law does not prohibit all vices – those from which the fully virtuous abstain. It prohibits only the graver ones – those from which most people can abstain. Above all it prohibits the ones that cause trouble to others – the ones that, if left unchecked, would make human society impossible. Hence human law always prohibits such vices as murder and theft.

[1]   Law adapts itself not to the condition of the exceptional person, but to the condition of most people. Since most people are to some degree deficient in virtue, law adapts itself to people who are to some degree deficient in virtue, laying on them only such demands as they can obey.

[2]   Encountering this clause, contemporary readers are apt to think "Why, that is John Stuart Mill's harm principle!"[15] It is certainly a harm principle, but it is not the Millian harm principle. One difference is that unlike Mill, St. Thomas does not place tendentious restrictions on what counts as a hurt or harm; to these I return in the Discussion. Another difference is that St. Thomas's harm principle is not absolute: Rather than saying that human law forbids *only* those vices that cause trouble to others, it forbids *chiefly* such vices. Apparently, though preventing the citizens from hurting each other is the best reason for legal prohibition, it is not the only one.

What other reason might there be? Liberal political theorists accuse natural law thinkers of "paternalism," the idea that the law should prevent each citizen from hurting himself. Could paternalism then be the reason? Interestingly, no. As we will see more fully in Article 3, which follows, St. Thomas's principles exclude paternalism, because the fundamental purpose of law is to promote the *common* rather than the individual good; its interest is limited to what affects others. On the other hand, citizens can affect others either by commission or omission. Thus, law has a legitimate interest not only in how citizens hurt each other, but also in how they destroy their capacities to fulfill their *duties* to each other – a consideration that the Millian brand of harm principle ignores.

[3]   Just as some vices must probably always be tolerated, other vices, such as murder and theft, must always be forbidden, because they poison the very root of human society. For this reason, St. Thomas would not say that the taking of innocent human life might be permitted because the majority cannot abstain from it, or that theft need not be punished because the people are so attached to stealing that they cannot abide its prohibition. If property is not secure, nothing is secure; if life is not sacrosanct, nothing is sacrosanct.

But isn't it the case that some people are so deficient in virtue that they cannot bear even the demand not to murder or steal? Yes. So what about the consideration discussed previously – if murder and theft are forbidden them, isn't there a danger that they will burst out into yet graver

[15]   John Stuart Mill, *On Liberty.*

evils? Not in this case, because there are no greater evils; they are already behaving as wickedly as possible. If some can be deterred from murder and stealing by fear of punishment, then good. If others cannot be, then they should be taken out of circulation: by prison, or, in extreme cases in which nothing else suffices, by execution.

Reply to Objection 1. Audacity seems to refer to the assailing of others. Consequently it belongs to those sins chiefly whereby one's neighbor is injured: and these sins are forbidden by human law, as stated.	Reply to Objection 1. By "insolence," Isidore seems to mean the *invasion* of others [whether literal or figurative]. Invasion, then, pertains especially to those sins which trespass on others in such a way as to cause outrage. As I have explained, *these* sins are certainly forbidden by human law, so the argument I have presented is in no way at variance with Isidore.

St. Thomas is making the point that although the vices Isidore calls "audacious" or "insolent" are certainly forbidden by law, these are but a subset of vices in general.

But how small a subset? Perhaps not as small a subset as the translation of the Dominican Fathers might suggest. The term they render "assailing" is *invasionem,* invasion, which in Latin, as in English, includes not only the idea of physical attack, but also a great deal more. It suggests the idea of intrusion, irruption, or breaking in, of going into places one does not belong. Much the same is true of St. Thomas's term *iniuria,* which a far broader term than its English cognate, "injury." Hearing of injury, we tend to think only of things like wounds and broken bones, but in Roman law, *iniuria* means primarily outrage, including rape, insult, character defamation, and any grave and flagrant injustice. The breadth of the term's legal meaning strongly colors St. Thomas's remarks. Had St. Thomas understood Isidore's statement only in terms of physical violence, he certainly could not have listed *furtum,* theft, as one of the kinds of vice that law always forbids, because *furtum* means taking property not by violence but by stealth.

[1] *Reply to Objection 2. The purpose of human law is to lead men to virtue, not suddenly, but gradually.* [2] *Wherefore it does not lay upon the multitude of imperfect men the burdens of those who are already virtuous, viz. that they should abstain*	Reply to Objection 2. Human law does intend to lead men to virtue; but its intention is to lead them there not all at once, but step by step. And so it does not immediately impose on the multitude, who are imperfect, a demand to behave like people who are already virtuous, holding back from all evils. If the law did try to

from all evil. Otherwise these imperfect ones, being unable to bear such precepts, would break out into yet greater evils: [3] thus it is written (Proverbs[16] 30:33): "He that violently bloweth his nose, bringeth out blood"; [4] and (Matthew 9:17) that if "new wine," i.e. precepts of a perfect life, "is put into old bottles," i.e. into imperfect men, "the bottles break, and the wine runneth out," i.e. the precepts are despised, and those men, from contempt, break into evils worse still.

lay such precepts upon such unfinished persons, they would lack the strength to bear them. Consequently, they would burst out into even worse evils. One of the Proverbs expresses this point figuratively, saying that anyone who blows his nose too fiercely draws out blood. Another such figure is found in the Gospel of Matthew, where Christ reminds his listeners of what happens when new wine is poured into old wineskins: The skins break, and the wine spills out. He means that if the precepts of perfect life are poured right into the lives of imperfect men, these men despise them, and from their contempt, they burst out into evils even graver than before.

---

[1]   The idea of leading the citizens to virtue gradually may be taken in two different ways, depending on whether St. Thomas is thinking of the moral progress of the individual during his own life, or of the moral progress of the society through a span of generations.

If he is speaking only in the former sense, the meaning is simply that the law lays on citizens only such demands as most of them are able to obey. Yet from making such demands on them, it does have an educational effect on individuals. Consider, for example, young men who think getting roaring drunk with their friends is great fun. Lawmakers might find it prudent not to forbid getting drunk in public, but to severely punish, say, drunken assault on someone; in another passage St. Thomas borrows from Aristotle the example of an ancient Greek ordinance of this sort.[17] Now the young men of each generation may be much alike, but even so, as young men grow older, they may eventually comply with restraints that at first they resisted, and they may eventually comply not just for fear of punishment but because they see that they are right.

But if St. Thomas is also speaking in the latter sense, then although at any given point in a commonwealth's moral development a particular vice may have to be tolerated, perhaps, over time, the majority of citizens will be able to accept limitations. Thus, the law should discourage the vices it does tolerate with a view to the possibility of further restriction

---

[16]   Correcting the English translation, which gives the reference as Psalms 30:33.
[17]   I-II, Q. 75, Art. 4, ad 4.

later on. In one generation it may forbid only drunken knife fights; in the next, drunken fist fights; in the one after that, drunken driving. The same approach may be taken to other vices and evils. U.S. President Abraham Lincoln, for instance, adopted it for the abolition of slavery, although his strategy was interrupted by the Civil War.

Probably St. Thomas has in mind both senses, for he thinks that societies as well as individuals can advance and decline in moral virtue (we will see an example in Question 95, Article 1). Even in the long run, however, he would not promote a Puritan attitude toward law. The reason is that there are some vices from which the majority will probably never be able to abstain. To some degree, these must always be tolerated.

[2] The reason why a looser rule is applied to imperfect men is not that there is anything wrong with limiting vice in principle, but that if the limits are too strict, such men may do something worse. The *something worse* may be direct and obvious; for instance, drunkards who are no longer allowed to brawl in gin joints may seek an outlet for their pugnacity by looking for victims in the streets. But it might also be indirect, as it was in the U.S. Prohibition Era. In St. Thomas's view, the vice connected with alcohol is getting drunk.[18] By contrast, the Prohibitionists tried to put a complete end to drinking even short of getting drunk; they treated all use as abuse. Certainly the law had some success; mental health institutions treated fewer patients for alcoholic psychosis, police made fewer arrests for drunken and disorderly conduct, and welfare agencies reported less family violence due to alcohol abuse.[19] But the citizens "broke out" into buying from bootleggers, and the bootleggers in turn "broke out" into expanded criminal activities, using part of their swollen profits to corrupt the police with bribes.[20] All these things reduced public respect for law and its representatives.

[3] St. Thomas now surprises Puritans still further by showing that in expecting less of human law than of Divine providence, he has Scripture

---

[18] He classifies the vice of drunkenness as a species of the sin of gluttony. II-II, Q. 150, Art. 1.

[19] Joseph Califano, "Fictions and Facts About Drug Legalization," *America* 174:9 (March 16, 1996), p. 7.

[20] Califano, ibid., denies that Prohibition provoked men to break out into yet graver evils in the sense of generating a crime wave: "Homicide increased at a higher rate between 1900 and 1910 than during Prohibition, and organized crime was well established in the cities before 1920." But there are many offenses besides homicide, and the law seems to have catalyzed the gangs, even if it did not originate them.

on his side. Quoted in full, the Latin version of this startling proverb declares "he that strongly squeezeth the paps to bring out milk, straineth out butter: and he that violently bloweth his nose, bringeth out blood: and he that provoketh wrath bringeth forth strife."[21] The quotation is from the Old Law, but St. Thomas is about to round out the point by adding a quotation from the New.

[4]   Wineskins could be used only once, because they stretched and became brittle as their contents fermented. If new wine was introduced, they split open. This is one of several parables Jesus tells to convey the impossibility of taking in the new way of life that He preaches apart from divine grace.

[1] *Reply to Objection 3. The natural law is a participation in us of the eternal law: while human law falls short of the eternal law.* [2] *Now Augustine says (De Lib. Arb. i, 5): "The law which is framed for the government of states, allows and leaves unpunished many things that are punished by Divine providence. Nor, if this law does not attempt to do everything, is this a reason why it should be blamed for what it does."* [3] *Wherefore, too, human law does not prohibit everything that is forbidden by the natural law.*	Reply to Objection 3. Yes, human law is derived from natural law, and yes, natural law is our participation in the eternal law. We have written of these points earlier. Even so, human law falls short of eternal law. Augustine points out that God's providence avenges itself upon many deeds to which human law gives way without punishment – and yet that human law is *right* in giving way. It should not be condemned for what it does, he says, just because it does not try to do everything. We see then that human law does not forbid *everything* that natural law forbids.

[1]   As St. Thomas has explained in Question 91, Article 2, "among all others, the rational creature is subject to Divine providence in the most excellent way, in so far as it partakes of a share of providence, by being provident both for itself and for others. Wherefore it has a share of the Eternal Reason, whereby it has a natural inclination to its proper act and end: and this participation of the eternal law in the rational creature is called the natural law."

[2]   St. Thomas omits the beginning of the sentence, "It seems to you that"; St. Augustine is paraphrasing, extending, and approving the

---

[21] Proverbs 30:33 (DRA). The RSV-CE is only a little less vivid, but makes the parallelism clearer: "For pressing milk produces curds, pressing the nose produces blood, and pressing anger produces strife."

remark that Evodius has just made, which was quoted in the *sed contra*. His point is that even though human law cannot attain the full rigor of the Divine government, its work should be valued so far as it goes. The next section of the dialogue begins with St. Augustine's suggestion that he and Evodius investigate just how far human law *can* retribute evil, and what remains to be avenged – in a manner both more hidden and more sure – by God's providence.

[3] Which of the various naturally bad things will be forbidden by human law, and which ones not? We have just seen that the answer depends partly on which things can be forbidden without provoking even graver disturbances to public order. Where the line is best drawn must be determined by prudent judgment.

In this Article St. Thomas describes the line to be drawn in a slightly different way than in Question 91, Article 4. There the reason he gives as to why human law cannot do away with every evil is that by trying to do so, it would do away with many good things too. Here the reason he gives is that by trying to do so, it would provoke new evils. We need not choose between these two formulae; they are obviously complementary. For an example of how trying to regulate too much may do away with something good, consider how the attempt to do away with selfishness, by collectivizing farms, destroys diligence and innovation. For an example of how it may bring about a new evil, consider how the attempt to restrict exploitation, by excessively strict limits on credit, reduces the supply of credit and hurts those most in need of loans.

For further reflection on the preceding section of the *Treatise on Law*, the online *Companion to the Commentary*, accessible via the Resources link at the book's catalogue webpage, includes a discussion of the following topics:

WHAT COUNTS AS HARM TO OTHERS?
THE NEED AND THE BURDEN OF PRUDENCE

Question 96, Article 3:
Whether Human Law Prescribes Acts of All the Virtues?

TEXT	PARAPHRASE
Whether human law prescribes acts of all the virtues?	When properly framed, does human law command all virtuous acts?

In the previous Article, St. Thomas explored whether the nature of law might limit the *means* of attaining law's purpose: Could it be that some ways of discouraging bad character might backfire? In the present Article he looks more closely at the purpose itself: Could it be that some ways of encouraging even *good* character may exceed the scope of law? Proper treatment of the question requires a distinction between whether the law commands acts of every virtue, and whether it commands *all* acts of every virtue. As we go along, we see even more clearly than before that although St. Thomas's doctrine that law aims at making men good is certainly not libertine, it isn't Puritan either.

We must be careful to keep in mind that by "all the virtues," St. Thomas does not mean all virtues whatsoever, but all moral and intellectual virtues, epitomized by courage, temperance, justice, and prudence. These virtues pertain to our temporal good, and pursue objects that fall within the scope of unaided human reason. But the spiritual virtues, epitomized by faith, hope, and charity or love, pertain to our eternal good and surpass human reason's power.[22] Proper direction concerning them depends on the guidance of the Holy Spirit, which is given only to the Church, not the state.[23]

---

[1] *Objection 1. It would seem that human law does not prescribe acts of all the virtues. For vicious acts are contrary to acts of virtue.* [2] *But human law does not prohibit all vices, as stated above (2). Therefore neither does it prescribe all acts of virtue.*

Objection 1. Apparently, properly framed human law does not command all virtuous acts. Since acts of virtue and acts of vice are contraries, human law would command all virtuous acts only if it forbade all vices. But as we saw in the previous Article, it *doesn't* forbid all practice of the vices; so it doesn't command all virtuous acts.

---

[1] This is a very brief and intuitive way of saying something that takes a number of steps to work out fully. The crucial thing to understand is precisely what the Objector means by calling vicious and virtuous acts contraries. Each virtue has two contraries, not one, for as we learn from St. Thomas, and before him, Aristotle, moral virtue lies in a mean between two opposed vices. For example, in a dangerous situation I may act with too much caution, which is an act of the vice called cowardice; or with too little caution, which is an act of the vice called rashness; or with just the right amount of caution, which is an act of the virtue called courage.

[22] I-II, Q. 62, Art. 2.
[23] II-II, Q. 1, Art. 9; II-II, Q. 11, Art. 2, ad 3; II-II, Q. 177, Art. 1; III, Q. 8, Art. 6.

Now *provided* that the Objector confines himself to the acts themselves, setting aside the question of how they are performed (for that would introduce a different sense of the term "virtuous"), he reasons that the vicious and virtuous possibilities are mutually exclusive: To *not-do* a vicious act is to *do* the corresponding virtuous act, and vice versa. This might be questioned, because for some purposes we do distinguish acts of omission and commission. However, the present Article does not look into that distinction.

[2]   The Objector reasons as follows.

1. To forbid an act of vice is the same thing as to command not-doing it.
2. But as we saw just above, to *not-do* an act of vice is the same as to *do* the corresponding act of virtue.
3. Therefore to forbid an act of vice is the same thing as to command the corresponding act of virtue, and vice versa.
4. Therefore to forbid *all* acts of vice is the same thing as to command *all* acts of virtue.
5. But as we saw in the previous Article, law *doesn't* forbid all acts of vice.
6. Therefore law doesn't command every act of virtue.

---

[1] *Objection 2. Further, a virtuous act proceeds from a virtue.* [2] *But virtue is the end of law;* [3] *so that whatever is from a virtue, cannot come under a precept of law. Therefore human law does not prescribe all acts of virtue.*	Objection 2. Moreover, virtuous acts spring from virtuous character – the reason why a person performs a virtuous act is that he has virtue. But law commands what it commands *so that people will acquire* virtue. Commanding the exercise of virtue that they do not yet have is futile, so human law does not issue such commands.

---

[1]   Interestingly, Objection 2 takes the term "virtuous" in a different sense than Objection 1. When the first Objector calls an act virtuous, he means it is the right thing to do. But when the second Objector calls an act virtuous, he means it springs from the right motive.

Objector 1: "When the chips were down, the soldier stood his ground. I call that an act of courage."

Objector 2: "That soldier stood his ground only because his sergeant threatened him. The other soldier stood his ground because he had guts. Now *that's* an act of courage."

So you thought the same Objector was behind every Objection, did you?
Not always.

[2] This statement is elliptical. What the Objector means is that virtue
is the end of law *rather than the propositional content* of law. The law
doesn't say "Be virtuous!" It commands particular acts, and by doing
them the citizens become virtuous.

[3] If the citizens don't have virtue, then it is futile to command them
to act virtuously: What sense would it make to say "Exercise courage!" if
they have no courage to exercise? But if the citizens do have virtue, then
commanding them to exercise it is superfluous: That would be like commanding them to breathe. In neither case can law meaningfully command
that virtue be put into practice.

[1] *Objection 3. Further, law is ordained to the common good, as stated above (90, 2). [2] But some acts of virtue are ordained, not to the common good, but to private good. Therefore the law does not prescribe all acts of virtue.*	Objection 3. Still further, we established at the beginning of our inquiry that the purpose of law is the *common good*. But not all exercises of virtue are directed toward the common good; some are directed merely toward the private good. The latter sort are beyond the law's concern.

[1] As we saw in Question 90, law is an ordinance of reason, *for the
common good,* made by public authority and promulgated.

[2] Many acts of virtue, such as giving honest testimony in court, are
directed to the common good. But not all are. Limiting my consumption
of red meat is an act of temperance; defending myself against a burglar is
an act of courage. Although these too are acts of virtue, they are directed
to my private good.

On the contrary, The Philosopher says (Ethic. v, 1) that the law "prescribes the performance of the acts of a brave man ... and the acts of the temperate man ... and the acts of the meek man: and in like manner as regards the other virtues and vices, prescribing the former, forbidding the latter."	On the other hand, Aristotle says the law *does* command acts of each virtue (and forbid acts of vice); for example, it commands acts of courage, of temperance, and of gentleness.

Aristotle's examples of acts of courage are not deserting one's post
and not throwing down one's weapons (which signified surrender); his

examples of acts of temperance are not committing adultery and not gratifying lust; and his examples of gentleness are not striking another and not speaking evil. Each of these acts of virtue is an act of *not-doing* vice, showing that in this context he is calling acts virtuous in the sense that Objector 1 does so, rather than in the sense that Objector 2 does so.

What Aristotle says next anticipates the distinction St. Thomas makes in the *respondeo:* "This form of justice, then, is complete virtue, but not absolutely, but in relation to our neighbour." As St. Thomas explains elsewhere, it is "in agreement with every virtue prescribed by the law" and "a man who has this virtue can employ it in relation to another and not to himself only – something not characteristic of all virtuous people."[24]

---

[1] *I answer that, The species of virtues are distinguished by their objects, as explained above (54, 2; 60, 1; 62, 2).* [2] *Now all the objects of virtues can be referred either to the private good of an individual, or to the common good of the multitude: thus matters of fortitude may be achieved either for the safety of the state, or for upholding the rights of a friend, and in like manner with the other virtues.* [3] *But law, as stated above (90, 2) is ordained to the common good.* [4] *Wherefore there is no virtue whose acts cannot be prescribed by the law. Nevertheless human law does not prescribe concerning all the acts of every virtue: but only in regard to those that are ordainable to the common good–* [5] *either immediately, as when certain things are done directly for the common good–or mediately, as when a lawgiver prescribes certain*

Here is my response. The various kinds of virtue are distinguished according to the formal differences in the things toward which they are directed; this was established much earlier. Notice, though, that each virtue can be brought to bear on either the person's own good, or a good which he shares with many others. For example, I may exercise courage either to defend my friend's right, or to preserve the whole commonweath. With other virtues it is just the same.

Now since law is directed to the common good, and since every virtue can be directed to the common good, acts of every virtue can be commanded by law. Yet it is one thing to say that human law commands acts of each virtue, and quite another to say that it commands *every* act of each virtue. In fact, it commands only those acts of each virtue that *can* be directed to the common good.

We must not take this idea too narrowly, for some such acts are aimed at the common good directly, while others are aimed at it indirectly. For example, the legislator may command something immediately necessary to the preservation

---

[24] Aristotle, *Nicomachean Ethics*, W.D. Ross, trans., Book 5, Chapter 1 (public domain); Thomas Aquinas, *Commentary on Aristotle's Nicomachean Ethics*, Book 5, Lecture 2, trans. C.J. Litzinger, O.P., rev. ed. (Notre Dame, IN: Dumb Ox Books, 1993), p. 286.

things pertaining to good order, whereby the citizens are directed in the upholding of the common good of justice and peace.	of justice and peace, or he may command something in order to shape the habits of the citizens, so that later on they spontaneously do what is needed for the preservation of justice and peace.

[1] The object of fortitude is withstanding evils, and defending goods against them; the object of temperance is moderating the pleasures of sense, especially touch; the object of justice is the right, which is also called the just; and the object of prudence is things conducive to the end to be achieved.[25]

[2] I may avoid eating too much red meat, and I may abstain from drinking alcohol within eight hours of piloting an airliner. Although both of these are acts of temperance, and both have the object of regulating the pleasures of sense, nevertheless in the former case, the object is brought to bear on my health (a private good), while in the latter case, it is brought to bear on public safety (a common good).

St. Thomas's own example of an act referred to the private good, protecting the right of a friend, is more subtle. Interested readers may explore it in the online *Companion to the Commentary.*

[3] As Objection 3 has reminded us.

[4] Whether I eat too much red meat is left to my own decision, but abstinence from alcohol within eight hours of piloting an airliner is commanded by law.

[5] An example of law promoting the common good *directly* is commanding witnesses to tell the truth when called to give testimony in court. An example of law promoting it *indirectly* might be commanding teachers in public schools to expose students to virtuous examples, or to have them learn about the heroes of integrity.

St. Thomas's coupling of justice with peace reminds us of St. Augustine's teaching that the goal of the commonwealth is *tranquillitas ordinis* – not any peace, but rightly ordered peace, the tranquility of sound order itself:

The peace of body and soul is the well-ordered and harmonious life and health of the living creature. Peace between man and God is the well-ordered obedience

---

[25] For fortitude, see II-II, Q. 123, Art. 11, ad 2; temperance, I-II, Q. 35, Art. 6 and I-II, Q. 63, Art. 4; justice, II-II, Q. 57, Art. 1; and prudence, I-II, Q. 65, 1.

of faith to eternal law. Peace between man and man is well-ordered concord. Domestic peace is the well-ordered concord between those of the family who rule and those who obey. Civil peace is a similar concord among the citizens. The peace of the celestial city is the perfectly ordered and harmonious enjoyment of God, and of one another in God. The peace of all things is the tranquility of order.[26]

Right order is so necessary to true peace that according to St. Thomas, the seventh beatitude, "Blessed are the peacemakers," is not about those who say "Let's all just get along," but about the spiritual gift of wisdom, which enables true peacemakers to arrange things according to the right.[27]

[1] *Reply to Objection 1. Human law does not forbid all vicious acts, by the obligation of a precept, as neither does it prescribe all acts of virtue.* [2] *But it forbids certain acts of each vice, just as it prescribes some acts of each virtue.*	Reply to Objection 1. To this extent, the Objector is right: Just as human law does not forbid all vicious acts, so it does not command all virtuous acts. But he should have carried the parallel further: Just as it forbids *some* acts of each vice, so it commands *some* acts of each virtue.

[1]   Up to a point, the Objector is right: Human law commands only some virtuous acts.

[2]   Even though human law does not command every act of each virtue, it does command some acts of each virtue; there is no virtue that it completely overlooks. This claim may seem dubious: Surely, we think, the law takes no interest in, say, the virtue of wittiness. But we are mistaken. True, it doesn't command "Always remember the punchline when telling a funny story." But it does command "Never commit libel or slander, even to raise a laugh."

[1] *Reply to Objection 2. An act is said to be an act of virtue in two ways.* [2] *First, from the fact that a man does something virtuous; thus the act of justice is to do what is right, and an act of fortitude is to do brave things: and*	Reply to Objection 2. There are two senses in which an act may be called an act of virtue (or an act of a particular virtue), and the Objector is right about one of them but not the other. First, it may be given the name because of *what* is done. This is the sense in which we call doing a right deed an act of justice, and

---

[26] St. Augustine, *City of God*, trans. Marcus Dods, Book 19, Chapter 13 (public domain).
[27] II-II, Q. 45, Art. 6; compare I, Q. 103, Art. 2, Obj. 3 and ad 3, and II-II, Q. 29, Art. 1, Obj. 1 and ad 1.

in this way law prescribes certain acts of virtue. [3] *Secondly an act of virtue is when a man does a virtuous thing in a way in which a virtuous man does it. Such an act always proceeds from virtue:* [4] *and it does not come under a precept of law, but is the end at which every lawgiver aims.*

doing a brave deed an act of courage. The law does command certain virtuous deeds in this sense.

Second, an act may be given the name because of *how* it is done – because it is done in the way that a virtuous man would do it. A virtuous man would do it as an expression of a character trait that he actually possesses. The law does not – and cannot – command virtuous deeds in this sense. Concerning them, the Objector is quite right to say that virtue is what the law seeks to form, not what it commands.

[1]   Objector 1 had used the term "virtuous" in one sense, Objector 2 in another. Here St. Thomas brings the two senses together.

[2]   This is the sense in which Objector 1 used the term.

[3]   This in turn is the sense in which Objector 2 used the term. "The way a virtuous man does it" is at the prompting of his own virtue.

[4]   St. Thomas concedes that just as Objector 2 insisted, law does not command virtuous acts in sense 2. One can command someone to do something, but one cannot command him to do it *from the heart* unless he already has the heart for it. Rather, law intends that by having to do it, he may eventually *become* the kind of person who has the heart for it.

The point is left tacit: For although Objector 2 is right that law does not command virtuous acts in sense 2, nevertheless law does command virtuous acts in sense 1.

Reply to Objection 3. There is no virtue whose act is not ordainable to the common good, as stated above, either mediately or immediately.

Reply to Objection 3. True, not all acts of virtue aim at the common good. Even so, the exercise of every virtue *can* be aimed at the common good, whether directly or indirectly, as I said earlier. So law does command *some* acts of every virtue.

St. Thomas might almost have skipped composing the reply to Objection 3, instead writing "This suffices for the Reply to Objection 3." He has already explained in the *respondeo* that the objects of each virtue can be brought to bear on either the private or the common good; from this it follows immediately that there is no such thing as a virtue whose exercise *cannot* be directed to the common good; so he points this fact out. He is merely making the obvious more obvious still.

For further reflection on the preceding section of the *Treatise on Law*, the online *Companion to the Commentary*, accessible via the Resources link at the book's catalogue webpage, includes a discussion of the following topics:

SHARED PRIVATE GOODS
THE PROBLEM OF TOLERATION

Question 96, Article 4:
Whether Human Law Binds a Man in Conscience?

TEXT	PARAPHRASE
Whether human law binds a man in conscience?	Does the sheer fact that a human enactment commands "Do X" make it right to do X, so that if I fail to do X, a well-formed conscience will accuse me?

The question is *what kind of reason* the enactment of a law gives us to do what is commanded. Even anarchists, who deny the authority of law, might obey it just to avoid being punished; they regard avoidance of punishment as a reason for obeying it. But we are asking about a different kind of reason for obeying it. Does it *obligate* us? Taking the Latin, *obligandi*, literally, does it tie us up in bonds of duty?

The main issue is whether we may commit civil disobedience when the so-called law is unjust. Perhaps most contemporary discussion of civil disobedience concerns its use to exert pressure on the government to change unjust enactments, and I consider that matter in the online *Companion to the Commentary*. However, the focus of St. Thomas's discussion is different, and more fundamental: Confronted with unjust commands, how may we keep conscience unstained?

Objection 1. It would seem that human law does not bind man in conscience. For an inferior power has no jurisdiction in a court of higher power. But the power of man, which frames human law, is beneath the Divine power. Therefore human law cannot impose its precept in a Divine court, such as is the court of conscience.	Objection 1. Apparently, human law does not lay any moral necessity upon a man in the court of his conscience. For a lower authority cannot impose its law in a court of higher authority. But human law is brought in by human authority, which is lower than Divine authority. Therefore human law cannot impose its commands in the Divine court – and that is what the judgment of conscience is.

The Objector does not really speak of "binding" – that comes later on, in St. Thomas's response. Instead the Objector speaks of "imposing necessity." However, the meaning is the same. The important thing to keep in mind is that he is referring to moral rather than physical necessity, the kind of necessity that is imposed in the *foro conscientiae*, the court of conscience. Similarly, when he speaks of power, *potestas*, he is not referring to physical strength (in which case he would have used the term *potentia*) but to moral power, or authority. His argument is that even if the ruler has the physical strength to impose an unjust enactment, he does not have the authority to do so, because conscience is the court of a higher authority than his own. What higher authority? God's – because conscience is God's representative within us. St. Thomas entirely agrees with the Objector that this is what conscience is.

The image of conscience as a court has deep roots in Christian moral thought, and from it, in Western moral thought. As mentioned in the commentary on Question 94, Article 1, other metaphors for conscience have also been employed, especially *anamnesis*, a term from Plato's *Meno*, which means "remembering" Divine truth. In view of the fact that St. Thomas is discussing law, however, the courtroom image seems most fitting.

[1] *Objection 2. Further, the judgment of conscience depends chiefly on the commandments of God. [2] But sometimes God's commandments are made void[28] by human laws, according to Mt. 15:6: "You have made void[29] the commandment of God for your tradition." Therefore human law does not bind a man in conscience.*	Objection 2. Moreover, the judgment rendered in the court of conscience depends above all on the Divine commandments. Sometimes human laws trample the Divine commandments, as Christ complains in Matthew 15, when He tells the Pharisees, "For the sake of your national traditions, you have turned God's commandments into things of no importance." But obviously He is not *approving* what they did. Therefore human law does not in itself lay necessity upon conscience.

[1]   So far, St. Thomas agrees: "For conscience does not dictate something to be done or avoided, unless it believes that it is against or in accor-

[28] *Evacuantur.*
[29] *Irritum.*

dance with the law of God. For the law is applied to our actions only by means of our conscience."[30] We return to this point below.

[2] The Objector is arguing that just because human laws sometimes violate God's laws, they do not bind in conscience. When the Objector complains that sometimes human authorities make the Divine commandments void, he is not saying that their own so-called laws wipe out the authority of the Divine commandments, but that they violate them. His complaint takes in both written and customary human laws.

The context, recounted in the Gospel of Matthew, is that certain Pharisees and experts in the Law of Moses had criticized Jesus' disciples for failing to follow certain customs of the Jewish nation about the washing of hands before eating – practices that God had not commanded, but that had come to be treated as though He had. In the story, Christ replies by criticizing His questioners for another of their customary practices, one that allowed sons to evade their duty to give aid to needy parents by claiming that they had set apart their property for the service of God. "So, for the sake of your tradition, you have made void the word of God. You hypocrites! Well did Isaiah prophesy of you, when he said: 'This people honors me with their lips, but their heart is far from me; in vain do they worship me, teaching as doctrines the precepts of men.'"[31]

---

[1] *Objection 3. Further, human laws often bring loss of character and injury on man, according to Is. 10:1 et seqq.:* [2] *"Woe to them that make wicked laws, and when they write, write injustice; to oppress the poor in judgment, and do violence to the cause of the humble of My people."* [3] *But it is lawful for anyone to avoid oppression and violence. Therefore human laws do not bind man in conscience.*

Objection 3. Still further, human laws often load men down with slander and false accusations, as the prophet Isaiah warns when he says, "Woe to those who decree iniquitous decrees, and the writers who keep writing oppression, to turn aside the needy from justice and to rob the poor of my people of their right."[32] But it is morally permissible for anyone to stay clear of oppression and violence. Therefore human laws do not in themselves lay on anyone's conscience the necessity to obey.

---

[30] Thomas Aquinas, *Lectures on the Letter to the Romans*, trans. Fabian Larcher, ed. Jeremy Holmes (Naples, FL: Aquinas Center for Theological Renewal, Ave Maria University, 2008), Chapter 14, Lecture 2, Section 1120, available at http://nvjournal.net/files/Aquinas_on_Romans.pdf.

[31] Quoting the last three verses of the story, recounted in Matthew 15:1–9 (RSV-CE).

[32] Isaiah 10:1a, substituting RSV-CE for DRA.

[1]   The complaint is that rulers have often used laws as a pretext to heap *calumniam* and *iniuria* on the people – especially, as we are about to see, on the poor. These are Roman legal terms. *Calumniam* means bringing calumny or false charges; *inuria* means the specific injury of committing outrage, which could include a variety of things such as insult, defamation of character, and rape.

[2]   In the Latin text of the Bible, which St. Thomas is using, this terrifying warning to unjust lawmakers reads in full, "Woe to them that make wicked laws: and when they write, write injustice: To oppress the poor in judgment, and do violence to the cause of the humble of my people: that widows might be their prey, and that they might rob the fatherless. What will you do in the day of visitation, and of the calamity which cometh from afar? to whom will ye flee for help? and where will ye leave your glory?"[33]

[3]   The Objector reasons that human laws cannot generate moral duty, because no one has a moral duty to put up with oppression and violence. The translation obscures this point a bit, for the question on the table is whether human legal commands generate moral duty. So when the Objector says it is *licitum,* permitted, to avoid oppression and violence, he doesn't mean that it is *legally* permitted, but that it is *morally* permitted.

On the contrary, It is written (1 Peter 2:19): "This is thankworthy, if for conscience ... a man endure sorrows, suffering wrongfully."	On the other hand, St. Peter teaches that it is commendable to bear up under sorrow and submit to injustice for the sake of conscience.

In this context, submitting to injustice for the sake of conscience means patiently accepting unjust punishment from masters or authorities. The complete passage reads, "For one is approved if, mindful of God, he endures pain while suffering unjustly. For what credit is it, if when you do wrong and are beaten for it you take it patiently? But if when you do right and suffer for it you take it patiently, you have God's approval. For to this you have been called, because Christ also suffered for you, leaving you an example, that you should follow in his steps."[34]

[33] Isaiah 10:1–3 (DRA).
[34] 1 Peter 2:19–21 (RSV-CE).

[1] *I answer that, Laws framed by man are either just or unjust. If they be just, they have the power of binding in conscience, from the eternal law whence they are derived,* [2] *according to Prov. 8:15: "By Me kings reign, and lawgivers decree just things."* [3] *Now laws are said to be just, both from the end, when, to wit, they are ordained to the common good – and from their author, that is to say, when the law that is made does not exceed the power of the lawgiver – and from their form, when, to wit, burdens are laid on the subjects, according to an equality of proportion and with a view to the common good.* [4] *For, since one man is a part of the community, each man in all that he is and has, belongs to the community;* [5] *just as a part, in all that it is, belongs to the whole;* [6] *wherefore nature inflicts a loss on the part, in order to save the whole:* [7] *so that on this account, such laws as these, which impose proportionate burdens, are just and binding in conscience, and are legal laws.*

Here is my response. Laws that men lay down may be either just or unjust. When they are just, they derive from the eternal law the strength to tie a man up, like a bailiff in the court of his conscience. The book of Proverbs makes exactly this point in the verse where Divine Wisdom declares, "By me kings reign, and rulers decree what is just."[35]

Laws are called just when they fulfill three conditions. The first condition concerns their purpose, for they are directed to the common good. The second concerns their author, for what they command lies within the limits of the legislator's authority. The third concerns their form, for they apportion burdens among the people in just proportion to their ability to bear them, just as the common good requires.

Concerning the third condition, bear in mind that a single man is a part of the multitude, and his property is a part of its wealth. Just as when anything is a part of a whole, so also here, nature takes something away from the part in order to save the whole. It follows that laws of the sort I have been discussing – laws that do impose burdens proportionately – really are just, actually do bind us in the court of conscience, and truly do partake of law's nature.

[1]   My paraphrase takes a small liberty in inserting a reference to a bailiff. It we are to picture a defendant being bound in the court of conscience, then someone has to bind him. This is true to the experience of conscience as well, for it is one thing to know that something is wrong, and quite another to be inwardly seized by the fact.

[2]   These words are spoken by the personification of Divine Wisdom. The passage is one of St. Thomas's favorites. We have seen it in Question

---

[35] Proverbs 8:15 (RSV-CE).

91, Article 1, and in Question 93, Article 3, and we will return to it in the present Question, Article 6.

[3] St. Thomas lists three qualities that make laws just, each of them from Question 90. It is not enough for a law to satisfy one of them; it must satisfy all three. *Ordained to the common good:* This restates the conclusion of Question 90, Article 2. *Does not exceed the power of the lawmaker:* This is implicit in the argument of Question 90, Article 3, that law is made by those who have care of the community. *Lays burdens on the subjects according to an equality of proportion:* This is implicit in the argument of Question 90, Article 1, that law must be an ordinance of reason, for reason discerns what justice requires, and what justice requires is expressed in the classical formula of distributive justice, "Give each what is fitting or due to him," bearing in mind that one may "give" either a boon, such as an honor, or a burden, such as a tax. Even though the burden is not the same for every citizen, the proportion between what each citizen bears and what it is fitting for him to bear is the same for every citizen. In that sense, no one gets a special break. We return to the classical view of distributive justice in Question 96, Article 6.

And with a view to the common good: St. Thomas is not repeating himself. He had already said that the law must be directed to the common good, but now he invites us to consider how closely law's final cause, the common good, is related to its formal cause, equality of proportion. Anyone who thinks that the needs of the common good can justify a disproportionate law misunderstands the common good. Yet even if a law lays burdens among the subjects in proportion to their ability, it may yet do so for a wrong purpose, and that is not allowable either.

Since St. Thomas draws from Question 90, Articles 1, 2, and 3, why doesn't he draw from Article 4? Why doesn't he mention the fourth requirement of true law, that it be promulgated or made known? He hasn't dropped the fourth requirement; probably he thinks there is simply no need to mention it. After all, we do not debate whether law X obligates us unless we know about it.

[4] The English translation is gravely misleading at this point (though St. Thomas's terseness doesn't help). To say that an individual "in all that he is and has belongs to the community" is to suggest that the person is a less fundamental reality than the social group, and that he is merely its instrument. The first reason for thinking that this is not what St. Thomas means lies in his words: The term "all" is just not there in the Latin, and

the expression *est multitudinis* does not mean "belongs to the community" but simply "is of the multitude." But what clinches the case is what St. Thomas says elsewhere in his work, for he utterly and consistently repudiates collectivism. Persons, not groups, are made in the image of God. Persons, not groups, are substances. The person, not the group, is the more fundamental reality. Not only that, when the enactments of the community contradicts the enactments of God, the enactments of the community must give way.

Then what is St. Thomas telling us here? Simply that although the human person is always *more* than a member of the multitude, even so he is never *less* than a member of the multitude. Being a part *is a part* of what he is; as a social being, he cannot fully realize his human potentialities in isolation from others; nor may he ever forget his duties to them. This is what makes it right to impose proportionate burdens upon each person for the good of all. Just because I am a person, my private good is real, but it is not all there is to me; I also participate in a common good.[36]

[5] Again, there is no "all" or "belongs" in the Latin. St. Thomas is merely reminding us of what citizens have in common with other parts of wholes. To keep translators from going astray, one might wish St. Thomas had given equal emphasis to what *distinguishes* them from other parts of wholes. As he usually does, however, he speaks only of what is pertinent to the immediate point at hand.

[6] Just as we must avoid one extreme to understand St. Thomas, so we must avoid the other. The fact that I am not *only* a part does not mean that I am not in *any* way a part. Some things may not be done to me even for the sake of others (for example, the government may not shoot me so that others will eat better). Yet I may certainly be required to "carry my share," to make proportionate sacrifices for the sake of the community – and this is what St. Thomas emphasizes.

[7] As a translation of *en sunt leges legales,* the words "and are legal laws" are precisely and literally correct, but they may not convey what is meant. What St. Thomas is trying to say is that proportionate enactments *really are* laws, not just pretended laws, since they fulfill the essential conditions set forth in Question 90.

---

[36] See Q. 90, Art. 1; Q. 92, Arts. 1 and 2; Q. 93, Art. 2; and Q. 95, Art. 1.

[1] *On the other hand laws may be unjust in two ways: first, by being contrary to human good,* [2] *through being opposed to the things mentioned above – either in respect of the end, as when an authority imposes on his subjects burdensome laws, conducive, not to the common good, but rather to his own cupidity or vainglory –* [3] *or in respect of the author, as when a man makes a law that goes beyond the power committed to him–* [4] *or in respect of the form, as when burdens are imposed unequally on the community, although with a view to the common good.* [5] *The like are acts of violence rather than laws; because, as Augustine says (De Lib. Arb. i, 5), "a law that is not just, seems to be no law at all."* [6] *Wherefore such laws do not bind in conscience, except perhaps in order to avoid scandal or disturbance,* [7] *for which cause a man should even yield his right, according to Mt. 5:40,41: "If a man ... take away thy coat, let go thy cloak also unto him; and whosoever will force thee one mile, go with him other two."*

But laws may be unjust in either of two ways. The first way laws can be unjust is by undermining the *temporal* human good, which they do whenever they violate any of the three conditions we have just been discussing. (1) They are unjust with respect to their *purpose* when the presiding authority lays on the people onerous laws directed not to the common good but to his own grasping desires and lust for glory. (2) They are unjust with respect to their *author* when they exceed the commissioned authority of the lawmakers. (3) They are unjust with respect to their *form* when they apportion burdens upon the people disproportionately, even if the lawmakers do intend the common good.

Enactments of this sort should be viewed as acts of violence rather than laws, for as St. Augustine says, "An unjust thing seems not to be a law." Unlike just laws, unjust so-called laws do *not* tie us up in the court of conscience with bonds of duty – at least not generally, although there may be a duty to obey if disobedience would cause others to stumble morally, or if it would produce confusion or disorder. The reason for these possible exceptions is that for reasons like these, we should even be willing to go along with violations of our right. Christ speaks of this in the fifth chapter of the Gospel of Matthew, where he says that if anyone forces you to go a mile, you should go with him two miles, and if anyone [seeks legal judgment to] take your tunic, you should let him have your cloak too.

[1]   St. Thomas's wording here may be a little obscure, for the term "human good" which he uses here, and the term "Divine good" which he uses a little further on, are not meant to distinguish between what is good for man and what is good for God. Rather, "human good" refers to the *temporal* aspects of man's good, those that he can achieve by his natural power, and "Divine good" to the *eternal* aspects of man's good, those that he can achieve only with the assistance of God's grace. The context

for these terms is the distinction between man's natural and supernatural end, which St. Thomas explained in Question 91, Article 4.

[2] Officials may exploit government position to give themselves and their friends a comfortable or glamorous life at the expense of the people.

[3] Officials might exceed the authority committed to them in either of two ways. First, they may issue commands that exceed the authority committed to any government. For example, they may interject the state into the proper affairs of the family or the Church. Second, they may enact policies that might conceivably be properly set in place, but only if enacted by some other agency of government. For instance, in a system like that of the United States, federal officials might usurp the authority of the states (or vice versa), or the judiciary or the executive bureaucracy might encroach on the authority of Congress (or vice versa).

[4] Friends and political allies might be awarded special favors, such as subsidies, lower taxes, exemptions from burdensome laws, or exemptions from prosecution for violating proportionate laws. Or a policy might be enacted that awards and withholds civil service positions on grounds other than merit, such as race.

[5] Of course the government uses force to back up not only true laws but also counterfeits of law. Why not then say that the enforcement of a true law is an act of violence too? Because *violentiae* is not just force, but the *unreasoning* use of force, like the behavior of a wild beast. A true law is an ordinance of reason, but an unjust "law" is a sheer exercise of will.

[6] When I am confronted by an unjust and burdensome law, I am not obligated to obey *because it is a law,* for unjust laws are not true laws at all. Even so, it may be right to obey if disobedience would cause even greater harm to the common good than obedience would.

The two kinds of harm that St. Thomas mentions are *scandalum* and *turbationem,* scandal and disturbance. These terms are often misunderstood. In English, the word "scandal" has come to mean conduct that causes embarrassment – the sort of thing written up in gossip blogs and celebrity magazines. But in Latin, *scandalum* is anything that causes others to stumble, whether physically, like a banana peel, or morally, like a bad example. Of these two meanings, bad example is the pertinent one here. Suppose others see me disobeying an unjust law. If they are morally weak and undiscerning, they may not view my act as a protest against injustice; instead they may view it as getting away with something that they would like to get away with too. If I can evade laws that inconvenience me, why shouldn't they? In this case my example causes them to lose respect not just for counterfeit laws, but for law as such.

The term *turbationem* can refer to any sort of confusion, commotion, or disorder. Most obviously, the disobedience of one person might cause people to riot in the streets. But disturbance might take quieter forms too. Suppose the city council reduced the speed limit in my neighborhood from thirty miles per hour to five, just to punish the residents for their votes in the last election. Clearly the law would be unjust. Yet if all my neighbors complied with it, then my disobedience would probably endanger them. It could hardly be safe for one car to zip along at thirty while the others were creeping at five. This broader meaning of *turbationem* or disturbance is confirmed by St. Thomas's Reply to Objection 3, where he treats causing disturbance as equivalent to inflicting an even greater hurt.

[7] St. Thomas transposes Matthew 5, verses 40 and 41, and, as he often does, he provides only enough of the words of the passage to jog the memory. Unfortunately, the words he leaves out are precisely the ones that make the legal context of the Scriptural passage plain. The verse about being forced to go a mile is probably not about a bully who makes me walk with him, but about a military officer who abuses his legal power to demand that I engage in forced labor. The verse about taking my clothing is not about a thug who snatches my tunic, but about a lender who demands it from me as legal pledge on a loan – something the Law of Moses specifically forbids:

If you lend money to any of my people with you who is poor, you shall not be to him as a creditor, and you shall not exact interest from him. If ever you take your neighbor's garment in pledge, you shall restore it to him before the sun goes down; for that is his only covering, it is his mantle for his body; in what else shall he sleep? And if he cries to me, I will hear, for I m compassionate.[37]

These examples, from Christ's Sermon on the Mount, are intended hyperbolically; they make their point by deliberate exaggeration. A peasant who gave up not only his tunic but also his cloak would have been left all but naked, so it is as though Christ had said, "It would be better to go naked than to revenge yourself." Christ was teaching that for the sake

37 Exodus 22:25–27 (RSV-CE); compare Deuteronomy 24:10–13.

of love, we must forbear from retaliation; St. Thomas adapts the point to argue that for the same of the common good, we must avoid causing scandal or disturbance. The connection between love and common good is that love always intends the true good of others.

[1] *Secondly, laws may be unjust through being opposed to the Divine good: such are the laws of tyrants inducing to idolatry,* [2] *or to anything else contrary to the Divine law:*[3] *and laws of this kind must nowise be observed,* [4] *because, as stated in Acts 5:29, "we ought to obey God rather than man."*	The second way laws can be unjust is by leading us away from our *supernatural* good, which they do whenever they command us to commit violations of Divine law. As I mentioned above, there may sometimes arise cases in which it is right to obey laws that are unjust in the first way – but we must never in any way observe laws that are unjust in this second way. For as we are taught in the Acts of the Apostles, "We ought to listen to God, rather than man."

[1]   By the Divine good, St. Thomas means the eternal vision of God, enjoyed by the redeemed in heaven. Any law that induces us to rupture our relationship with God, steering us away from ultimate blessedness instead of toward it, is opposed to the Divine good. This includes every law that commands acts of disobedience to Divine law, since guiding us toward the Divine good is exactly what Divine law is for.

For an example of disobedience to a law commanding idolatry, see Daniel 3, which recounts the story of the Three Worthies, three noble young Hebrew captives who refused the law of their captors to worship a false god. The incident is also discussed by St. Augustine.[38]

[2]   These words are not just about written Divine law, for St. Thomas explains elsewhere that conscience binds "only in virtue of a divine command, either in written law *or in the law inherent in our nature.*"[39] Indeed, many precepts belong *both* to written Divine law and to natural law, such as the commandments of the Decalogue. Laws are unjust in this second way if they command violation of any of these commandments whatsoever.

[3]   Suppose the government commands that citizens turn over the aged to be euthanized, or that people of fertile age enroll in a forced breeding

---

[38] Augustine of Hippo, Letter 185, *To Boniface*, Section 8.
[39] Thomas Aquinas, *Disputed Questions on Truth*, Q. 17, Art. 5, trans. James V. McGlynn, S.J. (available at www.diafrica.org/kenny/CDtexts/QDdeVer.htm), emphasis added.

program, or that citizens assist in the confiscation of the property of the party that lost in the last election. The first command requires violation of both the precept to honor one's parents and the precept forbidding murder; the second, of both the general precept of sexual purity and the more specific commandment of faithfulness to spouses; and the third, of the precept forbidding stealing. Now the question arises: Are these laws unjust merely in the first way (because of their end, their author, or their form), so that I *might* disobey them, but only if disobedience would not cause scandal or disturbance? Or are they unjust in the second way (because they oppose the Divine good), so that I *must* disobey them? They are unjust in the second way. There is no need to weigh the respective effects of obedience and disobedience on the common good. I must disobey. Period. To obey would be mortal sin.

Compare St. Augustine: "Whosoever, therefore, refuses to obey the laws of the emperors which are enacted against the truth of God, wins for himself a great reward; but whosoever refuses to obey the laws of the emperors which are enacted in behalf of truth, wins for himself great condemnation." This quotation is also used by Gratian in the *Concordance of Discordant Canons*.[40]

[4] Here is the context of the statement. The Apostles have been teaching the Gospel and healing the sick. Outraged, the members of the Sadducee faction use their position in the Sanhedrin, or Council, to have them arrested. During the night, an angel of God releases the Apostles, commanding them to resume preaching. At daybreak, they obey the command. As soon as their activities become known, they are arrested again, brought in for questioning, and told "We gave you strict orders not to teach in this name," meaning the name of Christ. They reply, "We must obey God rather than men!" In the ensuing Council debate, the Sadducees seek to have the Apostles put to death, but Gamaliel, the great Pharisee and teacher of the Law, argues for their release. In the end, the Sanhedrin has the Apostles flogged, afterward releasing them with a warning to preach no more. The Apostles leave, rejoicing that God has considered them worthy to suffer for His sake. Needless to say, they continue to teach and preach.[41]

---

[40] Augustine of Hippo, Letter 185, *To Boniface*, trans. J.R. King (public domain), Section 8; Gratian, *Concordance of Discordant Canons*, Distinction 9, Chapter 1, Section 2.
[41] Acts 5:12–42.

[1] *Reply to Objection 1. As the Apostle says (Romans 13:1–2), all human power is from God ... "therefore he that resisteth the power," in matters that are within its scope, "resisteth the ordinance of God"; [2] so that he becomes guilty according to his conscience.*	Reply to Objection 1. As St. Paul says in his letter to the Romans, all human authority comes from God. He continues, "So whoever resists this authority" – in matters truly committed to it – "resists what God has ordained." This establishes his guilt before the seat of conscience.

[1]   The point of this Reply is that the Objector is quite right about unjust laws, but not about just laws. The beginning of Romans 13 reads, "Let every person be subject to the governing authorities. For there is no authority except from God, and those that exist have been instituted by God. Therefore he who resists the authorities resists what God has appointed."[42] St. Thomas's words, "in matters that are within its scope," are an interpolation, based on the following reasoning.

1. St. Paul says human rulers have authority from God.
2. For this reason, St. Paul says we should do as they command.
3. St. Thomas asks: Does St. Paul mean that we should obey *whatever* they command?
4. His answer: That could not be St. Paul's meaning, for if God is the source of their authority, then they have no authority to exceed what God has committed to them.
5. It follows that St. Paul's instructions to obey the authorities carries an implicit qualification, "in matters that are within their scope."

[2]   Right after saying "Therefore he who resists the authorities resists what God has appointed," St. Paul adds, "and those who resist will incur judgment."[43] The "judgment" to which he refers is a legal verdict of condemnation in the Divinely appointed court. Plainly, then, St. Thomas views the judgment as being rendered not only by God on the Day of Judgment, but also here and now in the court of conscience. For conscience is God's representative within us, and when it speaks with certainty, we cannot help but hear it as the judgment of God.

Suppose someone were to say, "But my conscience *doesn't* require me to obey the authorities God appoints, in the matters that God commits to them." In St. Thomas's view, this amounts to claiming "My conscience

---

[42] Romans 13:1–2a (RSV-CE).
[43] Ibid., verse 2b.

doesn't require me to obey God." That is impossible, for as we saw above, "conscience does not dictate something to be done or avoided, unless it believes that it is against or in accordance with the law of God. For the law is applied to our actions only by means of our conscience." He explains in another work,

[T]o compare the bond of conscience with the bond resulting from the command of a superior is nothing else than to compare the bond of a divine command with the bond of a superior's command. Consequently, since the bond of a divine command binds against a command of a superior, and is more binding than the command of a superior, the bond of conscience is also greater than that of the command of a superior. And conscience will bind even when there exists a command of a superior to the contrary.[44]

Does this teaching imply that conscience can never reach a false judgment? No; it can. Even so, when we enter the court of conscience and listen closely, the voice we are trying to hear is the voice of God – whether or not we fully realize that we are trying to do so.

This view of conscience also raises interesting questions about atheism. Atheist: "I hear the voice of conscience, but I deny the reality of God." St. Thomas: "That is like listening to someone speak, but denying that anyone is there." Atheist: "That's right; nobody is." St. Thomas: "Then you deny not only God but also conscience, because you consider it a hallucination." Atheist: "I misspoke. What I meant to say is that when I am listening to conscience, I am really listening to myself." St. Thomas: "Then you still deny conscience, because you deny its authority to judge you. Instead you claim to judge yourself, but no one can be judge in his own case."

Reply to Objection 2. This argument is true of laws that are contrary to the commandments of God, which is beyond the scope of (human) power. Wherefore in such matters human law should not be obeyed.	Reply to Objection 2. The Objector is not speaking of laws in general, but only of laws that command what is contrary to God's commandments. About these, he is correct: They should not be obeyed.

The problem with the Objector's argument is that he has failed to distinguish just laws from laws that are contrary to Divine law. Just as he thinks, laws of the latter kind must not be obeyed. What he overlooks is that just laws should be.

---

[44] Thomas Aquinas, *Disputed Questions on Truth*, Q. 17, Art. 5, cited above.

[1] *Reply to Objection 3. This argument is true of a law that inflicts unjust hurt on its subjects. The power that man holds from God does not extend to this:* [2] *wherefore neither in such matters is man bound to obey the law, provided he avoid giving scandal or inflicting a more grievous hurt.*	Reply to Objection 3. Here the Objector is speaking of laws that weigh down the citizens with unjust burdens. God has not committed to human rulers the authority to give such commands. It follows that citizens are not bound to obey them, provided that they can resist without causing others to stumble morally, and without causing an even greater hurt than the hurt of the unjust law itself.

[1]   What counts as an unjust hurt? The purpose of law is to uphold the common good. But even when the common good requires laying burdens on the citizens, say a tax to finance the strengthening of fortifications against an enemy, these burdens should be allocated among them in a manner that is proportionate to their ability to bear them. Burdens are unjust either when they are laid on the citizens for a purpose other than the common good, or when they are laid on them disproportionately.

[2]   The argument is that except to avoid hurting others even more, no one is morally required to give in to his own unjust treatment. Earlier St. Thomas had referred to avoiding scandal or disturbance; here he refers to avoiding scandal or "a more grievous hurt" (literally *maiori detrimento,* "a greater detriment or loss"). This shows how broadly the term "disturbance" is to be understood.

For further reflection on the preceding section of the *Treatise on Law,* the online *Companion to the Commentary,* accessible via the Resources link at the book's catalogue webpage, includes a discussion of the following topics:

CONSCIENCE, CONSCIENCE, AND CONSCIENCE, REVISITED
INVIOLABILITY OF CONSCIENCE
CONSCIENTIOUS DISOBEDIENCE TO UNJUST LAWS
CONSCIENTIOUS RESISTANCE TO UNJUST GOVERNMENTS

Question 96, Article 5: Whether All Are Subject to the Law?

TEXT	PARAPHRASE
Whether all are subject to the law?	Is everyone in the commonwealth under the authority of the law – and must everyone obey it?

Here St. Thomas is not asking whether every citizen must obey unjust so-called laws. Rather he is asking whether every citizen must obey his commonwealth's *true* laws. Are any citizens exempt from the duty of obedience? For example, must those who make the laws obey the laws, or are they above the laws?

As in so many cases throughout the *Treatise,* the Article is absorbing not just for its answer to the main question, but also for the light it sheds on side issues. The most important side issue is the freedom of the Church to govern itself in its own spiritual affairs, which is an aspect of what has come to be called "subsidiarity." Subsidiarity is the principle that each of the numerous forms of well-ordered association – not only the Church but also the marital association, the family, local neighborhoods, voluntary organizations, and so on – should be allowed to carry out its own natural or supernatural work on its own; the state should be no more than a *subsidium* or help. We deal with the independence of the Church in the commentary on Objection 3. For further remarks on subsidiarity in general, see the online *Companion to the Commentary.*

[1] *Objection 1. It would seem that not all are subject to the law. For those alone are subject to a law for whom a law is made.* [2] *But the Apostle says (1 Timothy 1:9): "The law is not made for the just man." Therefore the just are not subject to the law.*	Objection 1. Apparently, not everyone is under the authority of the law. Why? Because laws bind only those for whom they are laid down, and as St. Paul remarks in his first letter to Timothy, "the law is not laid down for the just." It follows that the just are not under the laws; only the unjust are.

[1] The law is "made" for John Smith if it is addressed to him with the object of directing his behavior. He is not obligated to obey it if that is not the case.

[2] Those who do what is right do not need to be told what to do; those who do what is wrong do need to be told what to do. The Objector uses St. Paul to argue that law is addressed only to the latter. In context, the passage from the Apostle's letter to Timothy reads as follows:

Now we know that the law is good, if any one uses it lawfully, understanding this, that the law is not laid down for the just but for the lawless and disobedient, for the ungodly and sinners, for the unholy and profane, for murderers of fathers and murderers of mothers, for manslayers, immoral persons, sodomites, kidnapers, liars, perjurers, and whatever else is contrary to sound doctrine, in accordance with the glorious gospel of the blessed God with which I have been entrusted.[45]

| [1] *Objection 2. Further, Pope Urban says [Decretals. caus. xix, qu. 2: "He that is guided by a private law need not for any reason be bound by the public law." [2] Now all spiritual men are led by the private law of the Holy Ghost, for they are the sons of God, of whom it is said (Romans 8:14): "Whosoever are led by the Spirit of God, they are the sons of God." Therefore not all men are subject to human law.* | Objection 2. Moreover, in a letter giving an authoritative decision on a point that had been raised in canon law, Pope Urban declared that the public law, laid down for everyone, does not apply to those who come under a legal "privilege" or exemption. Now even if the human rulers have not exempted anyone from their laws, God has, for He has adopted spiritual men as sons, placing them under the immediate direction of the Holy Spirit. We see this from St. Paul's letter to the Romans, in which he writes that everyone led by God's Spirit is one of God's sons. From this it follows that the spiritual are not bound by the commonwealth's laws; only the unspiritual are. |

---

[1]   By a private law, the Objector means a "privilege," in the sense discussed in Article 1, above. His point is that those to whom the privilege applies are exempt from what the law would otherwise have required. Doctors, for example, have the "privilege" of administering certain dangerous drugs, although others are forbidden to administer them. More to the present point, in all spiritual matters the Church governs itself, rather than being governed by the state. Gratian's *Concordance of Discordant Canons,* Distinction 10, Chapter 1, explains that "ecclesiastical laws may not be abrogated in any way by an imperial decree."[46]

[2]   To put his point more crassly, the Objector is saying "Since the Holy Spirit is my ruler, I am exempt from the commands of human rulers." Using the same quotation from St. Paul, much the same argument was offered in Question 93, Article 6, Objection 1. There the issue was whether all human affairs are under eternal law; here it is whether all

---

[45] 1 Timothy 1:8–11 (RSV-CE).
[46] Gratian, *The Treatise on Laws* [*Concordance of Discordant Canons*], trans. Augustine Thompson, *With the Ordinary Gloss*, trans. James Gordley (Washington, DC: Catholic University Press, 1993), p. 33.

citizens are under human law. Let us look into the Apostle's statement more closely:

> For all who are led by the Spirit of God are sons of God. For you did not receive the spirit of slavery to fall back into fear, but you have received the spirit of sonship. When we cry, "Abba! Father!" it is the Spirit himself bearing witness with our spirit that we are children of God, and if children, then heirs, heirs of God and fellow heirs with Christ, provided we suffer with him in order that we may also be glorified with him.[47]

The expression "son of" can be used to mean "of the nature of"; for example, Christ called James and John "sons of thunder" because of their thunderous qualities. In His Divine nature, Christ is the Son of God because He is of one substance with the Father. His followers are called "sons of God" in the lesser sense that God raises them to partake of His Spirit; they are sons "by adoption."[48] The sense in which the sons of God in the latter sense are exempted from human law is playfully illustrated by an incident in the gospel in which Christ puns on the double meanings of "sons" and "kings."

> When they came to Capernaum, the collectors of the half-shekel tax went up to Peter and said, "Does not your teacher pay the tax?" He said, "Yes." And when he came home, Jesus spoke to him first, saying, "What do you think, Simon? From whom do kings of the earth take toll or tribute? From their sons or from others?" And when he said, "From others," Jesus said to him, "Then the sons are free. However, not to give offense to them, go to the sea and cast a hook, and take the first fish that comes up, and when you open its mouth you will find a shekel; take that and give it to them for me and for yourself."[49]

Notice that even though the sons of God are under a higher authority than man's, Christ instructs them to submit to the tax voluntarily – a point the Objector overlooks.

---

[1] *Objection 3. Further, the jurist says [Pandect. Justin. i, ff., tit. 3, De Leg. et Senat.] that "the sovereign is exempt from the laws."* [2] *But he that is exempt from the law is not bound thereby. Therefore not all are subject to the law.*	Objection 3. Still further, the *Digests* quote the legal authority Ulpian as saying that the ruler is released from the laws. But if he is released from them, then he is not under their authority. It follows that *not* everyone is under their authority.

---

[47] Romans 8:14–17 (RSV-CE).
[48] "Sons of thunder," Mark 3:17; "partakers in the Holy Spirit," Hebrews 6:4; "partakers of the divine nature," 2 Peter 1:4; "adoption" as sons, Romans 8:23, Galatians 4:5; "sons," see also Matthew 5:9, 5:45, Luke 6:35; compare John 12:36.
[49] Matthew 17:24–27 (RSV-CE).

[1]   Ulpian's statement that the foremost man or ruler is absolved from the law is quoted in the *Digests,* Book 1, Title 3, Section 31. He adds the amusing observation that although the close female relatives of the ruler are *not* absolved, the Roman rulers have always given their close female relatives the same privileges that they enjoy themselves.[50] Compare Ulpian's statement that what pleases the foremost man has the force of law, discussed in Question 90, Article 1, Objection 3 and Reply.

[2]   The ruler is not exempt merely from this law or that; according to Ulpian, he is exempt from *all* law. The Objector reasons that in that case, he must not be under its authority.

On the contrary, The Apostle says (Romans 13:1): "Let every soul be subject to the higher powers." But subjection to a power seems to imply subjection to the laws framed by that power. Therefore all men should be subject to human law.	**On the other hand,** St. Paul writes to the Romans, "Let every person submit to the governing authorities."[51] But it would appear that a person does not submit to the authority unless he submits to the laws that it lays down. So everyone should be under the duty of submission to the laws.

We saw this verse in Article 4, where St. Thomas explained that the passage does not mean that souls are to be subject to the rulers even when the rulers command evil, but that they are to be subject to them when they command what lies within their authority for the common good. Here in Article 5, the question is not *what* must be obeyed, but *who* must obey, and the verse is quoted because it seems to give the answer, "Everyone." It may be helpful to see the verse in the context of the section:

Let every person be subject to the governing authorities. For there is no authority except from God, and those that exist have been instituted by God. Therefore he who resists the authorities resists what God has appointed, and those who resist will incur judgment. For rulers are not a terror to good conduct, but to bad. Would you have no fear of him who is in authority? Then do what is good, and you will receive his approval, for he is God's servant for your good. But if you do wrong, be afraid, for he does not bear the sword in vain; he is the servant of God to execute his wrath on the wrongdoer. Therefore one must be subject, not only to avoid God's wrath but also for the sake of conscience. For the same reason

[50]   *Princeps legibus solutus est: augusta autem licet legibus soluta non est, principes tamen eadem illi privilegia tribuunt, quae ipsi habent.* In Rome, the old republican term *princeps,* which means foremost man, was appropriated by the emperors for themselves. The term *augusta,* often translated "empress," means "august lady," and could refer not only to his wife but to his mother, daughter, or sister.
[51]   Substituting RSV-CE for DRA.

you also pay taxes, for the authorities are ministers of God, attending to this very thing. Pay all of them their dues, taxes to whom taxes are due, revenue to whom revenue is due, respect to whom respect is due, honor to whom honor is due. Owe no one anything, except to love one another; for he who loves his neighbor has fulfilled the law.[52]

---

[1] *I answer that, As stated above (90, A1,2; 3, ad 2), the notion of law contains two things: first, that it is a rule of human acts; secondly, that it has coercive power.* [2] *Wherefore a man may be subject to law in two ways. First, as the regulated is subject to the regulator: and, in this way, whoever is subject to a power, is subject to the law framed by that power.* [3] *But it may happen in two ways that one is not subject to a power. In one way, by being altogether free from its authority: hence the subjects of one city or kingdom are not bound by the laws of the sovereign of another city or kingdom, since they are not subject to his authority.* [4] *In another way, by being under a yet higher law; thus the subject of a proconsul should be ruled by his command, but not in those matters in which the subject receives his orders from the emperor: for in these matters, he is not bound by the mandate of the lower authority, since he is directed by that of a higher.* [5] *In this way, one who is simply subject to a law, may not be a subject thereto in certain matters, in respect of which he is ruled by a higher law.*

Here is my response. As I have explained previously, the idea of law has two elements. Not only is it a rule of human acts, but it is also enforceable – it has the strength to compel obedience. From these two elements follow two different ways in which someone may be said to be "under" a law.

The first way of being "under" a law is to be under it *because of the authority of a superior* – to be one of those whom he properly rules. In this way, *everyone* who is under a given authority is under the laws that it lays down. Suppose someone is *not* under the authority in question. This can happen in two ways. One is that a person is entirely exempt from it: This is why the citizens of one city or kingdom are not under the laws of the ruler of another city or kingdom; they are outside his dominion. The other is that the person is ruled by a higher law: For example, the citizen of a province should in general be ruled by the provincial governor's command – but not in those matters in which the emperor exempts him. In such matters, he is directed by the higher, imperial authority but is not under the command of the lower, provincial authority. Notice in this latter way, a person who is under a law may not be under it in *everything*, because in some matters he may be under a higher law.

---

[1]   In Question 90, St. Thomas took used four separate Articles to unpack the intuitive idea that "Law is a rule and measure of acts, whereby

---

[52] Romans 13:1–8 (RSV–CE).

man is induced to act or is restrained from acting." "First ... it is a rule" is shorthand the idea that it is a rule and measure of human acts," and "secondly ... it has coercive power" is shorthand for the idea that by it, man is induced to act or is restrained from acting. These two elements go together. Unless law is actually brought to bear on human acts, it cannot be their rule; that is to say, law, to be law, must among other things be enforceable.

St. Thomas invokes the requirement of enforceability at various points in the *Treatise on Law*. As he wrote at another point in Question 90, "A private person cannot lead another to virtue efficaciously: for he can only advise, and if his advice be not taken, it has no coercive power, such as the law should have, in order to prove an efficacious inducement to virtue." As he further explained in Question 95, "But since some are found to be depraved, and prone to vice, and not easily amenable to words, it was necessary for such to be restrained from evil by force and fear, in order that, at least, they might desist from evil-doing, and leave others in peace, and that they themselves, by being habituated in this way, might be brought to do willingly what hitherto they did from fear, and thus become virtuous. Now this kind of training, which compels through fear of punishment, is the discipline of laws."[53]

[2] In what sense is a regulated person subject to the regulator? In the sense of being under his authority. Both the just and the unjust are under his authority, although they obey the laws with very different motives, the former because of virtue, the latter because of fear.

[3] The citizens of Poland are not bound by the laws of Russia, nor the citizens of El Paso by the ordinances of New York City.

[4] A corporal should obey the commands of his sergeant, but not if the lieutenant overrides them. In the same way, the residents of Travis County should obey the Travis County ordinances, though not in cases where these ordinances have been overridden by the statutes of the State of Texas.

In the constitutional system of the United States, by the way, the latter example does not work. Although counties derive their authority from their states, states do not in turn derive their authority from the federal government.

---

[53] Q. 90, Art. 3, ad 2; Q. 95, Art. 1.

[5]   The corporal really is subject to he commands of his sergeant, yet this does not imply that he is subject to them in all cases whatsoever, for the commands of superior officers supersede them.

---

[1] *Secondly, a man is said to be subject to a law as the coerced is subject to the coercer. In this way the virtuous and righteous are not subject to the law, but only the wicked.* [2] *Because coercion and violence are contrary to the will: but the will of the good is in harmony with the law, whereas the will of the wicked is discordant from it. Wherefore in this sense the good are not subject to the law, but only the wicked.*	The second way of being "under" a law is to be under its *compulsion* – to obey it because one is forced to. In this way, virtuous and just persons are *not* under the law, but only bad persons. For to do something because of coercion and violence is to do it against one's will, and the will of good persons harmonizes with the law; only the will of bad persons clashes with it. Thus when we say that only the wicked and not the good are under the law, it is in this second sense that we are speaking.

---

[1]   In what way is a coerced person subject to the coercer? In the sense of doing what is needed to avoid punishment, even though he disdains the coercer's authority to command him.

[2]   When the wicked obey the law, they obey unwillingly because of the threat of punishment. Not so the virtuous and just, who recognize the authority of both lawmaker and law.

---

[1] *Reply to Objection 1. This argument is true of subjection by way of coercion: for, in this way, "the law is not made for the just men":* [2] *because "they are a law to themselves," since they "show the work of the law written in their hearts," as the Apostle says (Romans 2:14–15).* [3] *Consequently the law does not enforce itself upon them as it does on the wicked.*	Reply to Objection 1. If the Objector is speaking of subjection to law in the second sense – being coerced by it – then what he says is quite true. The reason why St. Paul writes to Timothy that "the law is not laid down for the just" is that the just do not need coercion, for as he writes to the Romans, "they show that what the law requires is written on their hearts." So the coercive force of law is not applied to them as it is to the unjust.

---

[1]   In other words, this law is *not* true of subjection in the other sense, for not only the unjust but also the just are included in the scope of the lawmaker's authority.

[2]   In full, "When Gentiles who have not the law do by nature what the law requires, they are a law to themselves, even though they do not

have the law. They show that what the law requires is written on their hearts, while their conscience also bears witness and their conflicting thoughts accuse or perhaps excuse them on that day when, according to my gospel, God judges the secrets of men by Christ Jesus."[54] We have already discussed these verses several times, especially in the commentary to Question 91, Article 2. St. Thomas most often brings them up in connection with natural law, but here he is using them to press a different point: Just men do not require *external* coercion, because their hearts are imprinted with an *internal* law.

[3] There is no need to threaten the just man with penalties for violation, because he is already doing the right thing. He recognizes both the justice of the just law, and the authority of the lawmaker who frames it.

---

[1] *Reply to Objection 2. The law of the Holy Ghost is above all law framed by man:* [2] *and therefore spiritual men, in so far as they are led by the law of the Holy Ghost, are not subject to the law in those matters that are inconsistent with the guidance of the Holy Ghost. Nevertheless the very fact that spiritual men are subject to law, is due to the leading of the Holy Ghost,* [3] *according to 1 Pt. 2:13: "Be ye subject ... to every human creature for God's sake."*	Reply to Objection 2. The Objector is right that the law of the Holy Spirit is above all human law. He is also right that because spiritual men are guided by the Holy Spirit, they are exempted from laws that command acts incompatible with this guidance. What he misses is that apart from these exceptions, spiritual men *are* under human law – and this too because of the Holy Spirit's instruction. For as St. Peter says in his first letter, under Divine inspiration, "Be subject *for God's sake* to everything that made or done by human authority."

---

[1] From time to time over the course of Christian history, sects have arisen that claim that persons who are obedient to God have no need to obey human law. As we are about to see, St. Thomas is careful not to give the impression of agreeing with them.

[2] In general, persons obedient to God *should* obey human law, although there are carefully defined exceptions. As explained in Article 4, one such exception is for *unjust* laws. As St. Thomas confirms here, the other is a legal *exemption* from a law that would otherwise be binding – in the language of Roman jurisprudence, a "privilege" or "private law." The implication of his argument is that even if the laws of the state did

54 Romans 2:14-16 (RSV-CE).

not recognize a privilege for the Church, guaranteeing its independence from state control, the higher law of God would overrule them.

[3]　In English, the exhortation to be subject to every "human creature" sounds a little strange. The phrase comes from the Greek, *anthropine ktisei,* meaning something made or done by man, in this context by human authority. Hence, the "human creature" is not the human *ruler,* but the laws and institutions that pertain to human *rule.* Commonly used translations render the phrase in a variety of ways, including "ordinance of man" (KJV, NKJV), "human institution" (RSV, RSV-CE, NAB, ESV), and "authority instituted among men" (NIV).

---

[1] *Reply to Objection 3. The sovereign is said to be "exempt from the law," as to its coercive power;* [2] *since, properly speaking, no man is coerced by himself, and law has no coercive power save from the authority of the sovereign.* [3] *Thus then is the sovereign said to be exempt from the law, because none is competent to pass sentence on him, if he acts against the law.* [4] *Wherefore on Ps. 50:6:*[55] *"To Thee only have I sinned," a gloss says that "there is no man who can judge the deeds of a king."* [5] *But as to the directive force of law, the sovereign is subject to the law by his own will, according to the statement (Extra, De Constit. cap. Cum omnes) that "whatever law a man makes for another, he should keep himself."* [6] *And a wise authority [Dionysius Cato, Dist. de Moribus] says: 'Obey the law that thou makest thyself.'"* [7] *Moreover the Lord reproaches those who "say and do not"; and who "bind heavy burdens and lay them on*

Reply to Objection 3. The ruler is "released" from the laws in the sense that they do not *coerce* him. For them to coerce him would be impossible, because it is only by the ruler's authority that laws do coerce, and no man can coerce himself. So we should take the statement "The ruler is exempt from the laws" to mean only that no one has the authority to bring sentence of condemnation upon him if he acts contrary to the law. This is why, in Psalm 51:4, where King David confesses to God, "Against Thee, Thee only, have I sinned," a well-known commentary takes David to be saying that the law provides no man who could pass judgment on David's deeds.

But with respect to law's force as a *rule,* matters stand otherwise, for as it is put in one of the section headings of *Digest,* if someone applies a rule of justice to another, he should follow the same rule himself.[56] To the same effect, a wise authority teaches, "Endure the same law that you yourself have made." Moreover, in Matthew 23 the Lord Himself rebukes those who "preach, but do not practice," and who "tie up heavy burdens and lay

---

[55]　In modern translations, this verse corresponds to Psalm 51:4.

[56]　St. Thomas paraphrases slightly (or perhaps he is quoting from memory): For the original, *quisque iuris in alterum statuerit, ut ipse eodem iure utatur,* he substitutes *quisque iuris in alterum statuit, ipse eodem iure uti debet.*

men's shoulders, but with a finger of their own they will not move them" (*Matthew* 23:3,4). [8] *Hence, in the judgment of God, the sovereign is not exempt from the law, as to its directive force;* [1] *but he should fulfil it to his own free-will and not of constraint.* [10] *Again the sovereign is above the law, in so far as, when it is expedient, he can change the law, and dispense in it according to time and place.*

them on men's shoulders, but will not lift a finger to move them."

So, because the ruler is under God as his judge, he is not released from the *authority* of the law. Even so, he should fulfill the law voluntarily, not by compulsion. In that sense, he is above the law, and he is also above it in the sense that he can change it and authorize exceptions to it – though only to the degree that doing so is suitable to the place and time.

---

[1]   St. Thomas is saying that we should take the motto that the ruler is released from the law to mean, not that he is not *directed* by it, but that he is not *coerced* by it. Once more we should remember that the word "sovereign" in the Dominican Fathers translation is a rendering of the term *princeps,* which means literally the "foremost man," and of course Ulpian was thinking of the emperor. However, we should not read monarchy into St. Thomas's argument, for as he said in Question 90, "coercive power is vested in *the whole people or* in some public personage, to whom it belongs to inflict penalties."[57] So the authority to coerce obedience to the law may belong to one person, or it may belong to a group of persons acting together, so long as they act in unity. Speaking of the ruler as a single man is merely a convenient shorthand.

[2]   *Why* can't the ruler be coerced by the law? Simply because he is the one who does the coercing; it is by his authority that the law is enforced. If there were someone else who could coerce him, then that someone else would be the ruler.

In making this argument, is St. Thomas ignorant of the constitutional device of checks and balances? No, he is well aware of it. Over the course of Roman constitutional history, checks had developed to a high art. Even after the fall of the republic and the institution of the imperium, the great check of the Tribunes of the People was a force to be reckoned with. St. Thomas certainly has checks in mind in *On Kingship*, when he urges that steps should be taken to prevent kings from falling into tyranny, and that tyrants be constitutionally removed from power. He may also have them in mind later on in the *Treatise on Law,* when he argues that the best government blends elements of kingship, aristocracy, and democracy. But

[57] Q. 90, Art. 3, ad 2, emphasis added.

although checks can *block* certain acts of governing, they cannot *govern*. St. Thomas would not take seriously the notion that the coercive power itself could be divided; at the point where the laws are actually carried into execution, there must be unity.

[3] St. Thomas is not saying that the ruler may not be removed from office; as we have seen above, he thinks the ruler can be. His point is that so long as the ruler *does* hold his office, there is no higher office to judge him. Sentence can certainly be passed on a deposed tyrant; but it cannot be passed upon a sitting tyrant.

[4] The Dominican Fathers translation of the words of the gloss mentions a king, but does not mention the law. In Latin, however, the words of the gloss mention the law, but do not precisely mention a king: *Lex non habet hominem qui sua facta diiudicet*, roughly "The law does not judge the actions of the one who judges." Why have the translators injected a king? Probably because Psalm 50:6 is a prayer of King David. David has sinned by plotting and bringing about the death of Uriah in order to take Uriah's wife, Bathsheba, as his own. After the prophet Nathan confronts him, he bitterly repents. Having done so, he confesses his sin directly to God, because no *human* judge has authority to judge him. "Against thee, thee only, have I sinned, and done that which is evil in thy sight, so that thou art justified in thy sentence and blameless in thy judgment."[58]

[5] The motto St. Thomas is paraphrasing,[59] so fragrant of the Golden Rule, "Do unto others as you would have them do unto you," provides the heading of an entire section of the *Digests*, containing extracts from Ulpian, Paulus, and Gaius. Ulpian, who is quoted first, writes:

This edict has the greatest equity without arousing the just indignation of anyone; for who will reject the application to himself of the same law which he has applied or caused to be applied to others? "If one who holds a magistracy or authority establishes a new law against anyone, he himself ought to employ the same law whenever his adversary demands it. If anyone should obtain a new law from a person holding a magistracy or authority, whenever his adversary subsequently demands it, let judgment be given against him in accordance with the same law." The reason, of course, is that what anyone believed to be fair, when applied to another, he should suffer to prevail in his own case.[60]

---

[58] Psalm 51:4 (RSV-CE), corresponding to Psalm 50:6 in the DRA.
[59] His *ipse eodem iure uti debet* paraphrases the original *ut ipse eodem iure utatur.*
[60] Alan Watson, ed., *The Digest of Justinian*, rev. ed., Vol. 1 (Philadelphia: University of Pennsylvania Press, 1998), p. 42. The translator of the passage I am quoting (in the system of the *Digest* itself, Book 2, Title 2) is Geoffrey MacCormack.

Compare the statement of Theodosius and Valentianus to Volusian, quoted in the *Codex,* Book 1, Title 14:

It is a statement worthy of the majesty of a reigning prince for him to profess to be subject to the laws; for our authority is dependent upon that of the law. And, indeed, it is the greatest attribute of imperial power for the sovereign to be subject to the laws; and we forbid to others what we do not suffer ourselves to do by the terms of the present edict.[61]

In the *Concordance of Discordant Canons,* Distinction 9, Chapter 2, Gratian comments as follows:

It is just that the prince be restrained by his own ordinances. For then, when he himself shows them respect, he shows that ordinances should be respected by all. That princes are to be bound by their own enactments in itself prohibits them from infringing the ordinances they have imposed on their own subjects. So, the authority of their pronouncements is just if they do now allow to themselves what they prohibit to their people.[62]

[6]   This epigram is attributed to an otherwise unknown Roman writer named Dionysus Cato. His *Monostichs,* a brief collection of one-line poems, and *Distichs,* a longer collection of couplets, were widely read for centuries, admired for good moral sense, and during the Middle Ages even used to teach Latin. To contemporary readers, the maxim may seem to have a Kantian ring, but Immanuel Kant would have taken it in a radically different sense. Whereas Kant thought finite human reason is the ultimate source of its own authority, St. Thomas thinks it reflects, and partakes in its finite way, of the infinite Reason of God.

[7]   The context of these quotations is Christ's rebuke of the teachers of the Law and the members of the sect of the Pharisees: "Then said Jesus to the crowds and to his disciples, 'The scribes and the Pharisees sit on Moses' seat; so practice and observe whatever they tell you, but not what they do; for they preach, but do not practice. They bind heavy burdens, hard to bear, and lay them on men's shoulders; but they themselves will not move them with their finger. They do all their deeds to be seen by men.'"[63]

---

[61] Samuel P. Scott, trans., *The Civil Law* (Cincinnati: Central Trust Company, 1932), Vol. 12, pp. 86–87. The *Codes,* like the *Digest,* is a part of the *Corpus Iuris Civilis* commissioned by the emperor Justinian; see Introduction.
[62] *Gratian, The Treatise on Laws,* trans. Augustine Thompson, With the Ordinary Gloss, trans. James Gordley (Washington, DC: Catholic University Press, 1993), p. 29.
[63] Matthew 23:1–5a (RSV-CE).

[8] To be subject to the law "as to its directive force" is to be subject to it "as the regulated is subject to the regulator" – to be under a ruler's authority. If we take this to mean that the regulator is under his *own* authority, this is impossible; he can no more be under himself than he can coerce himself. The paradox disappears when we recall that what he is really under is the still higher Divine authority. This is why St. Thomas begins with the words, "in the judgment of God."

[9] The ruler *is* under the law in the sense we have just been discussing. Now St. Thomas explains the two senses in which he is *not* under the law. The first of these senses is that he ought to fulfill it voluntarily. Indeed, as we have seen, there is no human being who *could* force the ruler to obey the law, because the ruler himself is the enforcer. Though God punishes tyrants, yet even God does not always stretch His hand out fully, for He desires human beings to *participate* in His providential care for the universe. This point is well put by Sirach 15:14 (DRA), "God left man in the hand of his own counsel," a passage St. Thomas quotes often.[64]

[10] Why "again" (*etiam*)? Because this is the *second* sense in which the ruler is above the law. His authority, by which law is made and enforced, can also amend or repeal it, and can even declare exceptions to it. The requirement that all this be done with due regard to time and place is one of the qualities of good law listed by Isidore, which St. Thomas has discussed at length in Question 95, Article 3.

For further reflection on the preceding section of the *Treatise on Law*, the online *Companion to the Commentary*, accessible via the Resources link at the book's catalogue webpage, includes a discussion of the following topic:

LEGAL "PRIVILEGES," REVISITED

Question 96, Article 6:
Whether He Who Is Under a Law May Act Beside the Letter of the Law?

TEXT	PARAPHRASE
Whether he who is under a law may act beside the letter of the law?	May those who are under the authority of a true law depart from its literal instructions?

[64] See the commentary on Q. 91, Art. 4, Obj. 2 and ad 2.

Again, the query concerns not unjust laws, as in Article 4, but just laws. St. Thomas is not asking whether someone may simply ignore a law; to that question, of course, the answer is "No." Rather he is asking whether someone may set aside the words of a law, following instead what he takes the intention of the lawgivers to have been – the purpose at which the legislators were aiming. What "someone"? Any citizen, for as we saw in Article 5, everyone is bound by the law. Insofar as rulers should follow the laws they make for others – a point stressed in Article 5 – the inquiry in the present Article is for them too.

Later on, in Question 97, Article 4, St. Thomas raises a similar query, but from a different perspective: Instead of asking whether citizens may act beside the letter of the law, he asks whether those who make the law may suspend it as need arises. Though in the present Article he *assumes* the "Yes" answer to that later question, he does not take it up directly.

---

[1] *Objection 1. It seems that he who is subject to a law may not act beside the letter of the law. For Augustine says (De Vera Relig. 31): "Although men judge about temporal laws when they make them, yet when once they are made they must pass judgment not on them, but according to them."* [2] *But if anyone disregard the letter of the law, saying that he observes the intention of the lawgiver, he seems to pass judgment on the law. Therefore it is not right for one who is under the law to disregard the letter of the law, in order to observe the intention of the lawgiver.*

Objection 1. Apparently, persons subject to a law may *not* act differently than its wording literally directs. As Augustine explains in *On True Religion,* men may judge temporal laws while they are making them, but they may not pass judgment on them once they are established and confirmed. After that point, they may no longer judge the laws; they may only judge *by* the laws. But if someone were to pass over the words of the law on the pretext of preserving the legislator's intention, it seems that he *would* be judging the law. It follows that to do so is wrong.

---

[1] St. Augustine does not mean that lawmakers may never have second thoughts and amend the laws; we return to that topic in Question 97. His point is this: When lawmakers are considering whether to enact a proposed law, they judge whether it would be fitting. But once the proposal has been judged fitting and enacted into law, the other public officials do not consider whether the law could be improved, or whether they themselves could have made a better one; rather they discern what the law requires in the cases that come up before them. The Objector agrees.

[2]   The Objector protests that when someone who claims to be following "the intention, not the letter" *is* deciding whether the law is good enough, he is pushing aside the legitimate legislators and making himself the legislator.

| [1] *Objection 2. Further, he alone is competent to interpret the law who can make the law. [2] But those who are subject to the law cannot make the law. [3] Therefore they have no right to interpret the intention of the lawgiver, but should always act according to the letter of the law.* | Objection 2. Moreover, the interpretation of the laws belongs solely to those who make them. But those who are directed by laws do not make them; so it is not up to them to interpret the intention of those who do make them. Instead, they should do as the words of the laws command. |

[1]   In the Objector's view, the authority to make law and the authority to expound law are not two different things; the latter is derived from the former. So only legislators (or those under their authority) can give binding interpretations of the meaning of the laws that they make. Objection 3, below, might be viewed as giving a reason for this premise, but here it stands on its own.

[2]   For two reasons, this is a rather surprising thing for the Objector to say. The first reason is that it implies that those who *do* make the law are *not* subject to it; otherwise they could not make it either. The previous Article took a very different line, maintaining that although in one way the lawmaker is not subject to the law, in another way he is: Although he who coerces cannot be coerced, even so he is under law's authority and ought to follow it.

The second reason why the statement is so surprising is that it seems to rule out republics, in which the citizens themselves meet in assembly to make the very laws that will govern them. But perhaps the Objector is distinguishing between the citizens in the assembly, who are acting as legislators, and the same citizens outside the assembly, who are acting as subjects.

[3]   The argument depends on the assumption that interpreting the law is the same as interpreting the intentions of the lawmakers. Only the lawmakers themselves are competent to do this; therefore non-lawmakers must not attempt to. Consequently, they must confine themselves to literal observance.

| [1] *Objection 3. Further, every wise man knows how to explain his intention by words.* [2] *But those who framed the laws should be reckoned wise: for Wisdom says (Proverbs 8:15): "By Me kings reign, and lawgivers decree just things."* [3] *Therefore we should not judge of the intention of the lawgiver otherwise than by the words of the law.* | Objection 3. Still further, wise men know how to translate their intentions into words. We should certainly count lawmakers as wise, for as Lady Wisdom declares in Proverbs 8:15, "By me kings reign, and rulers decree what is just." So legislative intention should be judged only by the wording of the law – not by anything else. |

[1]   The argument this time is not that non-lawmakers cannot interpret legislative intentions, but that that they can interpret them *only by legislative words.* The Objector suggests that we would hardly consider a man wise if he could not explain clearly what he intended. Is this true? Perhaps one can imagine someone who is wise yet inarticulate. One the other hand, wisdom and speech are so closely related that the first verse of the Gospel of John uses the same term for both: "In the beginning was the Word" (Latin *Verbum*; Greek *Logos*).

[2]   Here the Objector seems to suggest that lawmakers *are in fact wise.* This may be a bit of an overreach, because Lady Wisdom seems more intent on urging lawmakers to seek her than on asserting that they possess her: As she says two verses later, "I love them that love me: and they that in the morning early watch for me, shall find me." Only by seeking her can kings and lawgivers fulfill their offices.[65] But perhaps the Objector is not saying that lawmakers always have wisdom, but only that they should enjoy the presumption of having it, a presumption that can be overturned by experience.

[3]   If lawmakers do know how to say what they mean, the Objector asks, then who are we to go behind their words? What gives us the right to think we know what they mean better than their words tell what they mean? Isn't that what words are for? In the course of deliberation about what laws to enact, a lawmaker might ask another lawmaker what he means, but we should just do what the laws say.

---

[65] Proverbs 8:15–17 (DRA), previously cited in Q. 91, Art. 1; Q. 93, Art. 3; and Q. 96, Art. 4.

[1] *On the contrary, Hilary says*	On the other hand, St. Hilary of
(De Trin. iv): "The meaning of what	Poitiers in his work *On the Trinity*
is said is according to the motive	explains that the meaning of
for saying it: [2] *because things are*	someone's statement must be gathered
not subject to speech, but speech	from what caused him to make it. If
to things." [3] *Therefore we should*	so, then we should pay attention to
take account of the motive of the	the causes that move lawmakers to
lawgiver, rather than of his very	make laws, rather than to the words
words.	that they put in them.

[1]   The point of St. Hilary of Poitiers is that words are not always clear taken in isolation, so to discern their meaning, we must consider what moved the speaker to choose them. The Latin word rendered "motive" is actually "causes" (*causis*), which can have several meanings including motives, reasons, and even circumstances.

[2]   Hilary is saying that the lawmaker chooses his words, says what he says, in order to express his intention concerning real things, real states of affairs. A similar maxim was discussed in Question 91, Article 3, not about the relation between things and speech, but about the relation between things and reason. These two relations are parallel, because speech is the expression of reason.

[3]   So if what St. Hilary says is true, then sometimes, to understand what the lawmaker meant, we may have to look beyond his words to the "causes" of his words, to his intentions regarding the problem that he was facing.

A very Hilarian example comes up in a late nineteenth century case, *Church of the Holy Trinity v. United States.*[66] Congress had enacted a statute to "prohibit the importation and migration of foreigners and aliens under contract or agreement to perform labor in the United States, its Territories, and the District of Columbia." Certain categories of workers were explicitly exempted, including professional actors, singers, and lecturers, but ministers of religion did not happen to fall into one of these categories. When the Church of the Holy Trinity, a religious society duly incorporated under the laws of New York State, made a contract with an Englishman to come into the country in order to serve as its rector and pastor, the U.S. authorities took action against the church, and the church and rector sued.

Writing for the Court, Associate Justice Brewer begins by examining the words of the statute, arguing that "The common understanding of

[66]   143 U.S. 457 (1892).

the terms 'labor' and 'laborers' does not include preaching and preachers, and it is to be assumed that words and phrases are used in their ordinary meaning." But to further illuminate the meaning of the words, he points out that "another guide to the meaning of a statute is found in the evil which it is designed to remedy." The legislative history of the statute showed that the evil Congress had designed it to remedy was the influx of large numbers of unskilled manual contract laborers into the United States, which Congress deemed harmful to the domestic labor market. Because the importation of ministers of religion was not part of the evil that Congress was aiming to remedy, Justice Brewer concluded that ministers should receive the same exemption as other professionals.

---

[1] *I answer that, As stated above (4), every law is directed to the common weal of men, and derives the force and nature of law accordingly.* [2] *Hence the jurist says [Pandect. Justin. lib. i, ff., tit. 3, De Leg. et Senat.]: "By no reason of law, or favor of equity, is it allowable for us to interpret harshly, and render burdensome, those useful measures which have been enacted for the welfare of man."* [3] *Now it happens often that the observance of some point of law conduces to the common weal in the majority of instances, and yet, in some cases, is very hurtful.* [4] *Since then the lawgiver cannot have in view every single case, he shapes the law according to what happens most frequently, by directing his attention to the common good. Wherefore if a case arise wherein the observance of that law would be hurtful to the general welfare, it should not be observed.*

Here is my response. As discussed previously, law is framed with a view to the good of the community. Only to the degree that this is true does it have the nature and authority of law. Just for this reason, Modestinus declares in the *Digests* that "It is not allowable, under any principle of law or generous maxim of equity, that measures introduced favorably to men's interests should be extended by us through a sterner mode of interpretation, on the side of severity and against those very interests."[67]

Now we often encounter a provision of law that presents a certain dilemma: Although following the provision usually promotes the common good, in some cases following it causes great harm. Of course the lawgiver cannot look into every single case, so he only provides for things that typically happen, always aiming for well-being of the community. For this reason, when a case does turns up in which following a law would damage the common good, that law should not be followed.

---

[67] Alan Watson, ed., *The Digest of Justinian*, Vol. 1, rev. ed. (Philadelphia: University of Pennsylvania Press, 1998), p. 13. The translator of the passage I am quoting (in the system of the *Digest* itself, Book 1, Title 3, Section 25) is D.N. MacCormack. For clarity, I have added commas.

[5] *For instance, suppose that in a besieged city it be an established law that the gates of the city are to be kept closed, this is good for public welfare as a general rule: but, it were to happen that the enemy are in pursuit of certain citizens, who are defenders of the city, it would be a great loss to the city, if the gates were not opened to them: and so in that case the gates ought to be opened, contrary to the letter of the law, in order to maintain the common weal, which the lawgiver had in view.*	For example, a city might have a law directing that if the city is under siege, its gates must remain shut. Under most circumstances this rule promotes the common good, but does it always? Suppose the enemy is in hot pursuit of the city's own defenders. Wouldn't it greatly harm the city to obey the words of the law, deny the defenders entrance, and leave them at the mercy of the enemy? In such a case, even though the words of the law say "Keep the gates shut," the gates should be opened [just long enough to let the defenders back in]. Otherwise, the very intention of the legislators in making the law would be frustrated.

[1]   Laws do not merely happen to be directed to the common good; direction to the common good pertains to their very essence, a point that St. Thomas established in Question 90. If an enactment is not directed to the common good, it is not really a law, and it lacks law's authority.

[2]   The idea is that since rulers have the duty to serve the common good, and since their enactments have the reality and authority of law only if they do serve the common good, any interpretation that twists an enactment away from the common good also deprives it of the reality and authority of law, and no ruler has authority to do such a thing.

We might here illustrate with another of the arguments advanced by Justice Brewer in the *Holy Trinity* case: "[B]eyond all these matters, no purpose of action against religion can be imputed to any legislation, state or national, because this is a religious people .... Every constitution of every one of the 44 states contains language which, either directly or by clear implication, recognizes a profound reverence for religion, and an assumption that its influence in all human affairs is essential to the well-being of the community."

To paraphrase Justice Brewer's point in the language of Modestinus, the jurist whom St. Thomas is quoting: If the U.S. statute under examination were harshly construed as forbidding the importation of ministers of religion, it would be deflected from its purpose of serving the welfare of man and become burdensome. Such an interpretation would be defensible neither as an act of statutory construction ("by reason of law"), nor as a judgment of equity – equity being the correction of the law's application in cases where its literal instructions produce a result contrary to its intention. For interested readers, the matter of equity is further explored in the online *Companion to the Commentary*.

[3] The law that sets speed limits on highways, the law that requires quiet in hospital zones, the law that seals private medical information, all such measures may promote the common good. But the first would not do so if it were applied to emergency vehicles, the second would not do so if it silenced an air raid siren, and the third would not do so if it kept public health authorities from tracing the path of a contagious disease to prevent an epidemic.

[4] Because the lawmaker cannot anticipate each and every one of these exceptions, he does not try to; he simply commands, say, "Obey the speed limit." If he mentions any exceptions at all, he mentions only a few. Yet when an emergency arises that requires an exception, the exception should be presumed, even if it is not actually stated. Think again of the argument in the *Holy Trinity* case: Ministers were deemed to have been *tacitly* exempted from the statute for the same reason that actors and other professionals were exempted expressly.

[5] To let the city's defenders be cut to pieces would obviously violate the purpose of the law requiring shutting of the gates, so the gatekeeper may certainly keep it open – though presumably he may still be held responsible if he exercises bad judgment in doing so. St. Thomas might also have quoted the jurist Paulus, who says that doing what the law forbids is violation, but following its letter while circumventing its purpose is a fraud.[68]

The case of the gatekeeper is an easy one, since St. Thomas is merely illustrating a broad principle. In the online *Companion to the Commentary*, I explore several that are more difficult.

---

[68] *Contra legem facit, qui id facit quod lex prohibet, in fraudem vero, qui salvis verbis legis sententiam eius circumvenit. Digest*, Book 1, Chapter 2, Section 29.

[1] *Nevertheless it must be noted, that if the observance of the law according to the letter does not involve any sudden risk needing instant remedy, it is not competent for everyone to expound what is useful and what is not useful to the state: those alone can do this who are in authority, and who, on account of such like cases, have the power to dispense from the laws.* [2] *If, however, the peril be so sudden as not to allow of the delay involved by referring the matter to authority, the mere necessity brings with it a dispensation, since necessity knows no law.*	Yet we must remember that if literal obedience to the law does not pose an unexpected peril that must be met at once, not everyone may interpret what does and does not serve the well-being of the community. Only the foremost men may do this, who because of such cases have authority to make exceptions to the law. And yet if danger arises so suddenly as to forbid the delay that would result from consulting superiors, then necessity itself generates an exception to the law: For necessity is not subject to law.

[1]   St. Thomas does not want his principle to be used as a pretext for substituting one's own reasoning for that of the legislators. I may "take matters into my own hands" only to fulfill the law's intention, not to set it aside. Moreover, I may do so only in emergencies. In other cases, I must consult the authorities.

[2]   To ordinary civil law, St. Thomas is applying a maxim that originates in canon law: *Necessitas legem non habet*, literally "necessity has no law." The maxim is rather dangerously worded, and at some points in history has been twisted by people seeking pretexts for vile injustices, such as deliberately targeting non-combatants in time of war. But the classical canonists and natural law thinkers never intended the maxim to be taken to mean that one may commit evil for the sake of an end. They couldn't have, for their tradition also insisted, following St. Paul, that "Evil must not be done that good may come." St. Thomas heartily agrees.[69]

---

[69] St. Paul, commenting that some people have slanderously charged him with teaching that evil may be done so that good will ensue, says that they are justly condemned (Romans 3:8). St. Thomas cites the implied principle, that evil may *not* be done so that good will ensue, in a number of places, esp. I-II, Q. 79, Art. 4, ad 4, and II-II, Q. 64, Art. 5, ad 3. The term "evil" applies here to *moral* evil, to sin, to "evil of fault," such as injustice. One may of course do such things as vaccinating children against chickenpox, and punishing criminals as they deserve, but although the pain of the needle and the sorrow of imprisonment are evils of a sort, they are not evils of fault, for we are not violating the moral law by inflicting them.

The original intention of the maxim "necessity has no law" was not to cancel all rules, but to dispense individuals from subordinate regulations in cases where they work at cross-purposes with the greater ones that they are ordained to serve. Thus, St. Thomas explains that a dangerously ill person may receive the sacrament of communion even if he has not fasted, and a penitent at the point of death may seek absolution from a priest other than his own.[70] Much the same applies in civic affairs: If an emergency arises in which I must violate the letter of the law, say, to put out a fire, hold back the enemy, prevent an accident, or keep the city from flooding, I may set aside the letter of the law and follow its intention instead.

Reply to Objection 1. He who in a case of necessity acts beside the letter of the law, does not judge the law; but of a particular case in which he sees that the letter of the law is not to be observed.	Reply to Objection 1. Suppose a case of necessity arises, like the one we have just been discussing. Then someone who deviates from the literal direction of the law is judging not the law, but the case. He is not setting himself above the law and regarding it as bad; he is only judging only that in this particular circumstances it must not be followed.

He "does not judge the law": This means he does not stand in judgment on the law's intended purpose. He judges "of a particular case": He discerns that under the unusual circumstances that have arisen, literally following the law's instructions would produce a result *contrary* to its intended purpose, so one should not literally follow them.

[1] *Reply to Objection 2. He who follows the intention of the lawgiver, does not interpret the law simply;* [2] *but in a case in which it is evident, by reason of the manifest harm, that the lawgiver intended otherwise.* [3] *For if it be a matter of doubt, he must either act according to the letter of the law, or consult those in power.*	Reply to Objection 2. Just as a person acting in a case of necessity is *judging* not the law but the case, so he is *interpreting* not the law but the case. He realizes that the legislators would not have intended the literal meaning of the law to be followed in circumstances when doing so would cause obvious harm. If the harm is doubtful rather than obvious, however, then the person must either follow the literal meaning of the law, or consult his superiors.

---

[70] III, Q. 80, Art. 8; Supp., Q. 8, Art. 6.

[1]   The Objector took the view that whenever anyone claims to be following "the intention of the law, not its letter," he is imagining that he can understand its intention better than the legislators expressed it. St. Thomas flatly denies that this is true, and goes on to explain.

[2]   When, in an emergency, someone follows "the intention of the law, not the letter," he is not pretending that when the lawmakers said "Do X," they meant something different than doing X. He is merely recognizing that they would not have intended the citizens to do X in a case like this, when it would cause obvious harm to the community's well-being.

[3]   Suppose the man did carve himself an exemption from the law in a case where the necessity is not truly obvious. In that case, St. Thomas says, he really would be guilty of the Objector's accusation. He would be judging the law rather than the case; he would be shoving the legislator aside to make himself the legislator.

[1] *Reply to Objection 3. No man is so wise as to be able to take account of every single case;* [2] *wherefore he is not able sufficiently to express in words all those things that are suitable for the end he has in view.* [3] *And even if a lawgiver were able to take all the cases into consideration, he ought not to mention them all, in order to avoid confusion: but should frame the law according to that which is of most common occurrence.*	Reply to Objection 3. Nobody is wise enough to think of every single case. Consequently, no legislator can put into words *everything* appropriate to the purpose he intends. Even if he could consider every case, it would be unfitting to enact different instructions for each one of them, because this would be confusing. Instead, he should adapt the law to what happens in *most* cases.

[1]   As explained above, it would be impossible to anticipate every case in which, because of some unusual circumstance, a law might produce a result contrary to its intention.

[2]   Since the exceptional cases cannot all be anticipated, they cannot all be provided for in the law – not even if the law were hundreds of pages long (and many contemporary laws are).

[3]   What happens when the law does try to provide for every exception? It becomes extremely complex, therefore extremely confusing, and this is unreasonable because confusion itself is detrimental to the common good. In fact, insofar as a law is confusing, it has not been truly pro-

mulgated or made known, so it loses the nature and authority of law. This seems to be a difficult lesson for people of our day to learn.[71]

For further reflection on the preceding section of the *Treatise on Law*, the online *Companion to the Commentary*, accessible via the Resources link at the book's catalogue webpage, includes a discussion of the following topic:

HARDER EXAMPLES
EQUALITY OF JUSTICE

---

[71] See the discussion of Question 90, Article 4, in the online *Companion to the Commentary*.

Before Reading Question 97

The topic we are about to investigate is change in the laws. The only serious obstacle to be overcome is that in our day this topic is confused with at least four others. In raising the question of change of laws, St. Thomas is not asking about social revolution; he is not asking about utopian transformation in laws; he is not asking about evolution in the conception of law; and he is not asking about change for its own sake.

Indeed, all four topics would seem very strange to St. Thomas. Law is an instrument of justice and guardian of the common good, not an instrument of social revolution. Utopia is impossible, because fallen man has lost the gift of original justice, the harmony among ardor, desire, and reason that once was his. Having discerned the true nature of law – an ordinance for the common good, made and promulgated by public authority – we have no need to "evolve" another conception of it. And change is never for its own sake, but always for the sake of something else.

Yet each of these statements needs a bit of fine-tuning, lest it be misconstrued. As to the first: Though law is not an instrument of change per se, the sheer promotion of justice and guardianship of the common good may bring about certain changes. Again, although it would be wrong to resist the natural law itself, it does not follow that all our social arrangements fulfill the natural law, and to the extent that they depart from it, they are wrong.

As to the second: Though wise lawmakers are not utopian, they are not dystopian either. St. Thomas has no illusion that the lower foundation is firmer than the higher; to believe that a just social order can be maintained without any virtue is even more naïve than to think citizens will be perfectly virtuous.[1]

As to the third: Though the essence of law is unchanging, the circumstances to which law is applied may well change, and so may our understanding of what, under given circumstances, the common good requires. Precisely because we are *not* relativists, we may hope to learn more as we go along, discovering and overcoming our errors.

As to the fourth: Though law should not pursue change for its own sake, neither should it pursue changelessness for its own sake. Good customs and traditions are precious, but we should not be so deluded as to think that all existing customs and traditions are good.

---

[1] I allude to the remark of Leo Strauss concerning the modern belief that "By building civil society on the 'low but solid ground' of selfishness or of certain 'private vices,' one will achieve much greater 'public benefits' than by futilely appealing to virtue, which is by nature 'unendowed.'" Leo Strauss, *Natural Right and History* (Chicago: University of Chicago Press, 1953), p. 247. For discussion, see J. Budziszewski, "The Lower Is Not the More Solid," *Communio* 38 (Summer 2011), pp. 1–20.

St. Thomas's Prologue to Question 97:
Of Change in Laws

TEXT	PARAPHRASE
[1] *We must now consider change in laws: under which head there are four points of inquiry:*	We close our general inquiry into human law by looking into how it changes. Four queries present themselves for consideration. In
[2] *(1) Whether human law is changeable?*	Article 1, we ask whether human law can be changed at all, and in Article
[3] *(2) Whether it should be always changed, whenever anything better occurs?*	2, whether it should be changed whenever we discern an opportunity to improve it. Article 3 we investigate
[4] *(3) Whether it is abolished by custom, and whether custom obtains the force of law?*	whether custom can set written law aside and acquire its authority. Finally, in Article 4, we consider whether
[5] *(4) Whether the application of human law should be changed by dispensation of those in authority?*	the governing authorities may make exceptions to the law as need arises.

[1]   In Question 95 St. Thomas investigated what sort of thing human law is in itself, and in Question 96 he investigated how far its authority extends. How laws change is the third and last of the broad topics St. Thomas takes up under the rubric of human law.

[2]   This question is meant seriously, and until recent times was taken seriously. "Law is defined to be a rule of action," remarked James Madison, "but how can that be a rule, which is little known, and less fixed?" Madison was not proposing that laws never be changed at all, but that "a continual change even of good measures is inconsistent with every rule of prudence and every prospect of success."[2]

---

[2] *The Federalist*, No. 62 (James Madison).

[3]   St. Thomas recognizes compelling reasons for changing the laws, but he also recognizes compelling reasons for caution.

[4]   In Question 95, Article 3, we saw that law should conform to the custom of the country. But what if law doesn't conform to it? Does it still have the authority of law? Could custom itself have that authority? We are familiar with written laws that attempt to rescind custom, but can custom rescind the written laws? (I explore another twist in the *Companion to the Commentary*: Is custom a guide to the *meaning* of written laws?)

[5]   In Question 96, Article 3, St. Thomas considered the problem of making exceptions to the law from the perspective of the citizens: May we ever act other than as the law directs? Here he considers it from the perspective of the authorities: May they ever *authorize* citizens to act other than as the law directs?

For further reflection on the preceding section of the *Treatise on Law*, the online *Companion to the Commentary*, accessible via the Resources link at the book's catalogue webpage, includes a discussion of the following topic:
WHY NOT SKIP ARTICLE 1?

Question 97, Article 1:
Whether Human Laws Should Be Changed in Any Way?

TEXT	PARAPHRASE
Whether human law should be changed in any way?	Is it ever permissible to change human law, in any respect, by any means?

Is this question necessary? Who could think that change in laws is bad? Quite a few might think so. Although the impulse to limit change in laws has almost vanished at the present day, attempts to put at least some legal changes off limits are far from unknown even now. For readers who may wish to explore historical examples, I offer additional remarks in the online *Companion to the Commentary*.

| *Objection 1. It would seem that human law should not be changed in any way at all. Because human law is derived from the natural law, as stated above (95, 2). But the natural law endures unchangeably. Therefore human law should also remain without any change.* | Objection 1. Apparently, there should be no changes whatsoever in human law, because it is derived from an unchangeable source, the natural law. So the view that human may be changed should be rejected. |

The Objector reasons that the natural law is unchangeable because it reflects the eternal law, which is the Wisdom of God, the creator of our rational nature. He concludes that whatever is based on something fixed is also fixed; so human law is fixed.

Objection 2. Further, as the Philosopher says (Ethic. v, 5), a measure should be absolutely stable. But human law is the measure of human acts, as stated above (90, A1,2). Therefore it should remain without change.	Objection 2. Moreover, we have called human law a rule and measure of human acts, and as Aristotle argues, whatever we use as a measure should be fixed to the greatest degree. It follows that human law should be fixed unchangeably.[3]

The Objector is not quoting Aristotle directly; he is paraphrasing and generalizing an argument Aristotle makes in the context of justice in exchange. Without a stable measure, there is no way to determine equivalent values for the goods to be traded. Although the values of goods that are so different in themselves cannot be *directly* commensurated – how can I measure the goodness of a painting against the goodness of a meal at a café? – they can be *indirectly* commensurated through the demand for them. The medium employed for this purpose is money, the value of which is "fixed by agreement."

Objection 3. Further, it is of the essence of law to be just and right, as stated above (95, 2). But that which is right once is right always. Therefore that which is law once, should be always law.	Objection 3. Still further, it pertains to the very idea of law that it be just and right; this we have said before. But if something is right on one occasion, then it is right on all occasions. It follows that once something has been made law, it should always remain law.

We have seen that in many contexts St. Thomas uses the words *ius*, or right, and *lex*, or law, interchangeably. Question 96, Article 4, has also explained that a law that is not right is not a true law but an act of violence.

On the contrary, Augustine says (De Lib. Arb. i, 6): "A temporal law, however just, may be justly changed in course of time."	On the other hand, Augustine declares that no matter how just a temporal element of law may be, a time may come when it can be changed without injustice.

---

[3] St. Thomas says "immovably," *immobiliter*, but in his idiom the term "movement" refers to change of every sort, not just change in position, as in ours.

St. Augustine is using the expression "temporal law" for those aspects of human law the goodness of which depends on circumstances. Other elements in human law, by contrast, express the requirements of Supreme Reason. We saw in Question 91, Article 1, that St. Augustine holds that although these temporal elements in law change, the elements based on Supreme Reason are unchangeable and should always be obeyed. So when he says that even the most just temporal law can justly be changed in the course of time, he is not saying that a time will come when we may set aside even those elements that human lawmakers derive from Supreme Reason, such as the prohibition of theft and murder. The sorts of things that we might some day set aside would be rules human lawmakers did devise on their own, such as how each kind of crime is punished, or how those who have done conspicuous public good should be honored.

---

[1] *I answer that, As stated above (91, 3), human law is a dictate of reason, whereby human acts are directed.* [2] *Thus there may be two causes for the just change of human law: one on the part of reason; the other on the part of man whose acts are regulated by law.* [3] *The cause on the part of reason is that it seems natural to human reason to advance gradually from the imperfect to the perfect.* [4] *Hence, in speculative sciences, we see that the teaching of the early philosophers was imperfect, and that it was afterwards perfected by those who succeeded them.* [5] *So also in practical matters: for those who first endeavored to discover something useful for the human community, not being able by themselves to take everything into consideration, set up certain institutions which were deficient in many ways; and these were changed by subsequent lawgivers who made institutions that might prove less frequently deficient in respect of the common weal.*

Here is my response. We have already established that a human law is a *reasonable* rule for the direction of *human* acts. From this it follows that human laws may be changed justly for either of two different reasons. One has to do with reason, the director; the other has to do with man, the one directed. Let us consider these two reasons one at a time.

Concerning reason, the director: We see that when our rational powers are functioning well, we advance in small stages from a partial to a complete understanding of the matters we are trying to understand. So it is both in theoretical studies and in practical matters. What the early philosophers handed over was incomplete, and was completed by the later ones to whom they gave it. In works or deeds, it is just the same, for those who first investigated what institutions would be helpful to the commonwealth did not have the strength to consider everything themselves, and what they did establish had many deficiencies. Those who came afterward changed these institutions, so that they would fall short of the common good in fewer cases.

[1]   Question 90, Article 1: "Now the rule and measure of human acts is the reason, which is the first principle of human acts, ... since it belongs to the reason to direct to the end." Question 91, Article 3: "[F]rom the precepts of the natural law, as from general and indemonstrable principles, ... human reason needs to proceed to the more particular determination of certain matters. These particular determinations, devised by human reason, are called human laws."

[2]   One good reason for change in human law is a change in what is needed ("change on the part of man"); the other is an improved understanding of what is needed ("change on the part of reason").

[3]   St. Thomas's understanding of nature is teleological: The mode of functioning that is natural to something is the one that keeps it on the path to its fulfillment. So, just as it is natural for acorns to grow into oak trees, it is natural for human reason to advance from a partial to a complete understanding. Of course some acorns are blighted, and in the same way some minds wallow in confusion. The Angelic Doctor is not suggesting that this never happens, but that it is not what our natural powers are aimed at. When all goes well, the mind makes progress.

[4]   One example of such development might be the advance from the view of Thales that there is only one element, water, to the recognition by later philosophers that there must be a number of elements. Another example might be the advance from the hypothesis of Hipparchus that the sun and planets revolve around the earth, to the hypothesis of Copernicus, subsequent to St. Thomas himself, that the earth and planets revolve around the sun. In the First Part of the *Summa*, St. Thomas offers a more subtle example, concerning the gradual development of our understanding of how the intellect knows material bodies. In our own terminology, he is describing the advance from a materialist, to an idealist, to a moderate realist theory of knowledge.

The earliest philosophers, he explains, denied that the intellect could have any sure knowledge of bodies, because bodies always seem to be in flux. Plato made some progress by recognizing that along with material bodies, there also exist immaterial forms; for example, the body of a horse is just *that kind* of body because it shares in the form common to all horses, and the form is not itself a body. Yet Plato erred too, because he thought our minds could have sure knowledge only of the form itself, not of the thing that shares in the form – as though we could know horsiness, but could not know any actual horses. Later philosophers

(St. Thomas is thinking especially of Aristotle) corrected his theory in two ways. One correction was to realize that the way a form is present in a body is different from the way in which it is present in the intellect – for although the form of horse, present in the horse, is what makes it a horse, the form is present in some way my knowledge as well, and I am not a horse, nor is my intellect a horse. The other correction was to realize that forms may be present in different bodies in different ways, and our minds know these things too: For example, one horse may be a horsier one than another, one horse may be red but another brown, and one brown horse may be browner than another. This shows how we can attain sure knowledge of horses, which change, *through* the mind's grasp of forms, which do not change.[4]

[5]   St. Thomas would have been familiar with Aristotle's illustration of a law so deficient as to be almost farcical: "At Cumae there is a law about murder, to the effect that if the accuser produces a certain number of witnesses from among his own kinsmen, the accused shall be held guilty."[5] No great insight is necessary to see how unreliable such testimony would be.

By changes in institutions, however, St. Thomas is probably thinking especially of changes in what we call constitutional law. One great example would have been well known to him from the early history of Rome. The city began as a monarchy. After the overthrow of the first kings, a few monarchical elements were retained in the constitution, but now they were tempered by aristocracy. Still later, the constitution was further modified by the admixture of democratic elements. St. Thomas would certainly have considered this an advance, since he holds the best form of government to be neither pure monarchy, pure aristocracy, nor pure democracy, but a balance of all three.[6]

---

[1] *On the part of man, whose acts are regulated by law, the law can be rightly changed on account of the changed condition of man, to whom different things are expedient according to the difference of his condition.* [2] *An example is proposed by Augustine*	But concerning man, whose acts law directs: Law can be changed because man's condition changes, for differences in condition bring about differences in what is appropriate. St. Augustine offers an example: If the people are

[4] I, Q. 84, Art. 1.
[5] Aristotle, *Politics*, trans. W.D. Ross, Book 2, Chapter 8 (public domain).
[6] I-II, Q. 105, Art. 1.

| *(De Lib. Arb. i, 6): "If the people have a sense of moderation and responsibility, and are most careful guardians of the common weal, it is right to enact a law allowing such a people to choose their own magistrates for the government of the commonwealth. But if, as time goes on, the same people become so corrupt as to sell their votes, and entrust the government to scoundrels and criminals; then the right of appointing their public officials is rightly forfeit to such a people, and the choice devolves to a few good men."* | moderate and serious, if they are diligent custodians of the common good, then it is right to make a law permitting the people themselves to institute magistrates for the administration of the commonwealth. If later on, little by little, the same people fall into such depravity that they sell their votes, committing the administration of the commonwealth to flagrant criminals, then it is right to take away their authority to confer such honors, and give it to a few good men. |

[1]   The proposition that law can be changed on account of the changed condition of man follows from St. Thomas's argument in Question 95, Article 3, following Isidore, that law should be within the natural capacities of those subject to it, as well as suitable to the place and time. Changes in the "condition" of man may refer to changes in many things, including his character, status, development, circumstances, and way of life. Is he virtuous or vicious? Is he slave or free? What is his situation? How does he live?

[2]   St. Thomas's example is a change in the *moral* character of the community, drawn from St. Augustine's *On Free Choice of the Will*. Augustine and his friend Evodius, the participants in the dialogue, are probably thinking of the various forms of corruption endemic to the late Roman Republic, especially the buying and selling of votes in the elections of the Tribunes. St. Thomas turns St. Augustine's questions into statements, omits Evodius's murmurs of agreement, and condenses somewhat. For instance, he leaves out the interesting but inessential detail that before their corruption the people put public good before private, but after their corruption they put private good before public.

A much more intriguing and suggestive omission, however, is that while St. Augustine says that when the people become corrupt, choice devolves "to a few good men *or even one good man*," St. Thomas leaves it at "a few good men."[7] Since the word he uses for "few," *paucorum,* can

---

[7] St. Augustine writes *paucorum bonorum, vel etiam unius*; St. Thomas, *paucorum bonorum.* He also omits St. Augustine's remark that although at first the people cherish the common good, later they put private good first, which merely amplifies his predecessor's point.

mean "a small number," and since one is a small number, it might be said that this does not change the statement's literal meaning. But of course we usually take "few" to mean a small number *greater* than one, so it certainly changes its emphasis.

[1] *Reply to Objection 1. The natural law is a participation of the eternal law, as stated above (91, 2),* [2] *and therefore endures without change, owing to the unchangeableness and perfection of the Divine Reason, the Author of nature.* [3] *But the reason of man is changeable and imperfect: wherefore his law is subject to change.* [4] *Moreover the natural law contains certain universal precepts, which are everlasting: whereas human law contains certain particular precepts, according to various emergencies.*	Reply to Objection 1. As we saw earlier, the natural law is the way in which man's reason shares in the Divine Reason, which is eternal law. And yes, just as the Objector says, the natural law endures without change, because it is derived from the complete and unchangeable Divine Reason by which nature is established. But his conclusion does not follow. In itself, man's reason is changeable and incomplete; for this reason, human law is changeable too. Besides, natural law contains certain universal rules that endure forever. Human law, by contrast, contains rules men have laid down for the particulars of diverse cases that happened to arise.

[1] The eternal law is the Wisdom by which God created and governs nature. Although subrational creatures share in the eternal law just by being guided by it, the rational creature share in it by understanding it, even though in a limited way. Since law is something that proceeds from reason, the rational creature's mode of participation in eternal law is itself a kind of law. This law is called "natural" law because it flows from the natural power of reason, and because it takes up all the other natural inclinations into reason. We have already considered these points in Question 91, Article 2, and in all six Articles of Question 94.

[2] Just insofar as human reason shares in the eternal law, it does not change; this is why, despite our limitations, we grasp certain general and unchangeable truths – truths we do not invent, but discover, and that serve as the bedrock for all our subsequent reasoning.

It may at first seem that the Objector is overlooking the subtleties of "addition" and "subtraction" to natural law discussed in Question 94, Article 5. However, St. Thomas is speaking of the general principles of natural law, which these "additions" and "subtractions" do not alter.

[3] Our minds are limited. Thus, even though our intellects are able to grasp the unchanging foundational truths of natural law, our

understanding is incomplete and advances only by degrees. As our understanding advances, so may human law.

[4]   Even aside from the limitations of our understanding, those unchanging truths are very general, and may require different things of us in different circumstances. For example, in any society whatsoever, we should have concern for the safety of our neighbors, but it does not follow that the best traffic laws are the same at all times and everywhere. So, as circumstances change, the laws must change too.

The term "emergencies" in the Dominican Fathers translation is a misleading rendering of the Latin word *emergunt*, which simply means things that "emerge" or come to light, things that may happen to come up – not necessarily things of desperate urgency.

Reply to Objection 2. A measure should be as enduring as possible. But nothing can be absolutely unchangeable in things that are subject to change. And therefore human law cannot be altogether unchangeable.	Reply to Objection 2. Yes, a measure should be as lasting as possible. But in connection with changeable things, nothing can be utterly, immutably permanent. Therefore neither can human law be so.

St. Thomas is not saying that changeable things are changeable, which would be a mere tautology. He is saying that nothing that *can* change is capable of resisting change forever. This includes human law.

Reply to Objection 3. In corporal things, right is predicated absolutely: and therefore, as far as itself is concerned, always remains right. But right is predicated of law with reference to the common weal, to which one and the same thing is not always adapted, as stated above: wherefore rectitude of this kind is subject to change.	Reply to Objection 3. In connection with physical bodies, we apply the term "straight" or "right" in an absolute sense. So the "right," in this sense, is always right. What the Objector overlooks is that in law, we apply the term "right" not in an absolute but in a relative sense. The right is right *in relation to the good of the community* – which does not always correspond to the very same thing, as I have explained. This kind of rightness can change.

In St. Thomas's view, the Objector is treating laws like limbs. Suppose I break my leg, the bone is not set properly, and so the bone heals crookedly. Perhaps a surgeon could straighten it, but so long as it remains as it is, no change in other circumstances would justify calling it straight. With laws the matter stands differently, for a law that is rightly ordered to the common good in one era may not be rightly ordered to it in another. Allowing stagecoach passengers to carry firearms made sense on the

Western frontier; allowing the same liberty on our jetliners would be ill-advised.

For further reflection on the preceding section of the *Treatise on Law*, the online *Companion to the Commentary*, accessible via the Resources link at the book's catalogue webpage, includes a discussion of the following topic:

SHIELDING LAWS FROM CHANGE

Question 97, Article 2:
Whether Human Law Should Always Be Changed, Whenever Something Better Occurs?

TEXT	PARAPHRASE
Whether human law should always be changed, whenever something better occurs?	Should human laws be changed whenever we come across better ideas?

Today most people take for granted that law should be changed whenever someone has a Bright New Idea. Discussion among policymakers frequently focuses not on whether to change the law, but how to change it more quickly – if necessary, by chicanery. Cunning pretexts are occasionally proposed even in legal journals, and are admitted by all sides to be subterfuges.

One might think the only problem with all this is its deceitfulness. If we restricted ourselves to honest means of injecting our Bright New Ideas into law, then what could be wrong with injecting them as quickly as possible? After all, in the previous Article haven't we already established the mistakenness of the view that law should never be changed? But there is a difference between changing the law and changing it lightly. What *should* our attitude be when we hit upon a better idea?

Objection 1. It would seem that human law should be changed, whenever something better occurs. Because human laws are devised by human reason, like other arts. But in the other arts, the tenets of former times give place to others, if something better occurs. Therefore the same should apply to human laws.	Objection 1. Apparently, human law *should* be changed whenever we come up with something better. After all, just as other arts are devised by human reason, so the art of legislation is devised by reason. But in the other arts, when we come up with better ways of doing something, we leave the old ways behind. So it should be with the laws.

The underlying assumption of the argument is that the making of laws is like, say, medicine. Once upon a time it was believed that disease might be warded off by wearing charms; now we use vaccination and asepsis, and the new ways are better. The Objector reasons that in the same way, if the lawmaker comes up with a better way to govern society, then he ought to rescind the old laws and put in place new ones. As I discuss in the online *Companion to the Commentary,* this argument has been around for centuries; Aristotle dealt with it at some length.

Objection 2. Further, by taking note of the past we can provide for the future. Now unless human laws had been changed when it was found possible to improve them, considerable inconvenience would have ensued; because the laws of old were crude in many points. Therefore it seems that laws should be changed, whenever anything better occurs to be enacted.	Objection 2. Moreover, we provide for the future from considering what has already gone by. Many things in the old laws were still primitive. If we had not changed them when better ones were devised, we would have suffered numerous disadvantages. This shows that the laws should be changed just as often as we hit on something better.

The Objector thinks that the reason we should change the laws whenever we get a Bright New Idea is that we learn from our mistakes. If we don't put our Bright New Idea into practice, we will miss something good. Examples of crude old laws were offered in the commentary on the previous Article.

Objection 3. Further, human laws are enacted about single acts of man. But we cannot acquire perfect knowledge in singular matters, except by experience, which "requires time," as stated in Ethic. ii. Therefore it seems that as time goes on it is possible for something better to occur for legislation.	Objection 3. Still further, human laws are enacted about *particular* human acts, but the only way to reach complete knowledge of particulars is through experience. As Aristotle remarks in his *Nicomachean Ethics,* this takes time. We see then that as time goes on, we can devise better laws.

Objection 2 suggested merely that the early laws were crude. Objection 3 says they *had* to be crude; the lawmakers hadn't yet accumulated enough experience to legislate well. The Objector cites Book 2 of the *Nicomachean Ethics,* and is probably thinking of the place where Aristotle says that "intellectual virtue in the main owes both its birth and its growth to teaching (for which reason it requires experience and time), while moral virtue comes about as a result of habit, whence also its name, *ethike,* is one that is formed by a slight variation from the word *ethos,* habit."[8] More to the point, however, is the following passage in Book 6:

What has been said is confirmed by the fact that while young men become geo-metricians and mathematicians and wise in matters like these, it is thought that a young man of practical wisdom cannot be found. The cause is that such wisdom is concerned not only with universals but with particulars, which become familiar from experience, but a young man has no experience, for it is length of time that gives experience; indeed one might ask this question too, why a boy may become a mathematician, but not a philosopher or a physicist. It is because the objects of mathematics exist by abstraction, while the first principles of these other subjects come from experience, and because young men have no conviction about the lat-ter but merely use the proper language, while the essence of mathematical objects is plain enough to them.[9]

On the contrary, *It is stated in the Decretals (Dist. xii, 5): "It is absurd, and a detestable shame, that we should suffer those traditions to be changed which we have received from the fathers of old."*	**On the other hand,** Gratian quotes one of the popes as saying that it is a ridiculous and abominable shame to allow infringement of the traditions passed on to us from the Fathers of ancient times.

As he often does, St. Thomas is paraphrasing a slightly longer state-ment; the quotation marks are not present in the Latin. The passage is in Gratian's *Concordance of Discordant Canons,* Distinction 12, Chapter 5, where Gratian is quoting a letter of Pope Nicholas to Archbishop Hincmar:

It is a ridiculous and abominable disgrace that in our times we permit the holy Church of God to be slandered and that we suffer the traditions we have received from the fathers of ancient times to be infringed at will by those wandering from the truth.[10]

The *sed contra* treats habitual infringement of the laws as a mode of change – if the laws infringed are good laws, then the change is a bad

---

[8] Aristotle, *Nicomachean Ethics,* trans. W.D. Ross, Book 2, Chapter 2. A relation similar to that in Greek between *ethos* and *ethike* holds in Latin between *mos* and *mores,* as well as in English between "mores" and "morals."
[9] Aristotle, *Nicomachean Ethics,* trans. W.D. Ross, Book 6, Chapter 8. For clarity, I have slightly changed Ross's punctuation.
[10] Gratian, *The Treatise on Laws,* trans. Augustine Thompson, With the Ordinary Gloss, trans. James Gordley (Washington, DC: Catholic University Press, 1993), p. 44.

change. The general question of custom as a source of change in law is taken up in Article 3.

---

[1] *I answer that,* As stated above *(1),* human law is rightly changed, *in so far as such change is conducive to the common weal. But, to a certain extent, the mere change of law is of itself prejudicial to the common good:* [2] *because custom avails much for the observance of laws, seeing that what is done contrary to general custom, even in slight matters, is looked upon as grave. Consequently, when a law is changed, the binding power of the law is diminished, in so far as custom is abolished.* [3] *Wherefore human law should never be changed, unless, in some way or other, the common weal be compensated according to the extent of the harm done in this respect.* [4] *Such compensation may arise either from some very great and very evident benefit conferred by the new enactment; or from the extreme urgency of the case, due to the fact that either the existing law is clearly unjust, or its observance extremely harmful.* [5] *Wherefore the jurist says [Pandect. Justin. lib. i, ff., tit. 4, De Constit. Princip.] that "in establishing new laws, there should be evidence of the benefit to be derived, before departing from a law which has long been considered just."*

Here is my response. As I have explained in the previous Article, it is right to make a change in human law just to the degree that the change promotes the common good. In itself, however, change in laws has some tendency to undermine the common good, because the observance of law depends mostly on custom. Actions that violate custom are viewed seriously, even in things small in themselves. Consequently, when a law is changed, its authority is diminished to the same degree that custom is destroyed. For this reason, we should never change human law unless the common good is somehow compensated for the damage that it suffers.

One way the common good might be compensated is that some great and obvious good results from the new law itself. Another is the extreme necessity of change due to some great and obvious evil in the old law – either the old law is plainly unjust, or following it is very harmful. For this reason, the great legal authority Ulpian said that no new law should be set in place of an old one that has long been viewed as equitable, without evidence of the advantage of the new one.

---

[1] Even when the new law is really better than the old, the change brings about two results: the intended good resulting from the improvement and the unintended harm resulting from the sheer fact of change.

[2] The most universal unintended harm of change in laws is the weakening of custom, with its attendant weakening of the veneration in which citizens hold the law, and of their resulting readiness to follow them. There may of course be other unintended harms, which St. Thomas does

not mention, and keeping an eye out for them might be another good reason for making changes slowly. The harm of weakening custom, however, is not merely an occasional result of changing the law; it is in the nature of change to weaken custom. The harm occurs every time.

St. Thomas views custom and reason as allies, rather than, as we tend to view them, as enemies. Virtue itself is a kind of habituation, a settling of certain dispositions into the bones of deliberation and choice. Far from considering custom unreasonable, he argues in the next Article that custom has authority *just because* it is reasonable: It embodies the settled wisdom of the community. Yet even so, no matter how reasonable the common people may be, they are reasonable *slowly*. Consequently, for enacted laws to have the added strength of custom, they must not outpace the ability of the people to see that they are good.[11]

[3] So much of the disorder and existential discomfort of modern life is due to our poverty of habits and customs. What habits we have, we are often forced to change, and we try as hard as we can to get rid of those few that remain: Heaven forbid, we think, that we should become "creatures of habit"! Yet nothing that unsettles the habits of the people should be taken lightly; anything that protects the soil of custom from unnecessary disturbance is a good thing.

This passage is not the only place St. Thomas has proposed weighing intended goods against unintended harm. His frequent use of such tests might give the impression that every harm can be offset by a great enough good, but it is profoundly important to understand that this is not his view, for I may never commit an intrinsically evil act, no matter how great an advantage to the common good I think will result. It makes no difference whether I am one of the governing authorities or an ordinary citizen; the prohibition applies to everyone.

[4] One way to promote the common good is to bring about something good; the other way is to remove something evil. One kind of evil is formal injustice – allocating benefits and burdens unfairly. Another kind of evil is that even though a burden is allocated fairly, it is unnecessary or excessive. Yet another is that it was decreed without proper authority.

[11] For a similar argument, see James Madison, *The Federalist*, No. 49: "In a nation of philosophers ... reverence for the laws would be sufficiently inculcated by the voice of an enlightened reason. But a nation of philosophers is as little to be expected as the philosophical race of kings wished for by Plato. And in every other nation, the most rational government will not find it a superfluous advantage to have the prejudices of the community on its side."

[5]   A betting man would have guessed that if St. Thomas wanted to close the *respondeo* with a quotation from one of the jurists, he would have taken it from the part of the *Digest* that concerns law and custom (Book 1, Chapter 3). Surprisingly, the quotation actually comes from the next chapter of the *Digest,* on precedent-setting imperial enactments called "constitutions." What makes this choice of sources interesting is that an emperor, legislating by his sole authority, accustomed to having his decision regarded as law, would have been especially tempted to hold custom in contempt. So Ulpian's maxim stands as a warning: Not even such a person as the foremost man of Rome should lightly depart from what has long been viewed as fair and level ground.

| *Reply to Objection 1. Rules of art derive their force[12] from reason alone: and therefore whenever something better occurs, the rule followed hitherto should be changed. But "laws derive very great force[13] from custom," as the Philosopher states (Polit. ii, 5): consequently they should not be quickly changed.* | Reply to Objection 1. The principles of an art owe their effectiveness to reason alone; we follow them because doing so makes sense. This is why whenever practitioners of the arts hit upon an improvement, they change their ways. But as Aristotle reminds us, laws owe most of their vigor to custom. So the Objector's analogy is defective; laws should not be changed too readily. |

Up to a certain point, St. Thomas has no problem with the analogy between ruling and the crafts, or "arts." In fact, he has used it himself. As he wrote in Question 93:

Just as in every artificer there pre-exists a type of the things that are made by his art, so too in every governor there must pre-exist the type of the order of those things that are to be done by those who are subject to his government. And just as the type of the things yet to be made by an art is called the art or exemplar of the products of that art, so too the type in him who governs the acts of his subjects, bears the character of a law, provided the other conditions be present which we have mentioned above.[14]

In that place, St. Thomas was viewing law from the lawmaker's point of view; here, though, he is viewing it from the citizen's point of view, and he thinks the analogy breaks down. We use umbrellas when it is raining mostly because it is reasonable to do so. But we follow laws – perhaps

[12] Actually *efficaciam,* effectiveness.
[13] Actually *virtutem,* virtue or vigor. See notes 7 and 8.
[14] Q. 93, Art. 1.

we should say, we recognize why laws are reasonable – mostly because we are used to them. Since reason needs custom's help, whatever weakens custom should be avoided.

The Latin of the Reply refers simply to "the things that are of an art." In itself, this might refer either to the principles of the art (for example, what physicians do to cure disease), or to its products (for example, what shoemakers make). In this context St. Thomas seems to be thinking mainly of the principles. But it might be held that in a certain sense the products of an art also owe their effectiveness to reason alone; for example, we use shoes because we find them helpful for protecting our feet.

Reply to Objection 2. This argument proves that laws ought to be changed: not in view of any improvement, but for the sake of a great benefit or in a case of great urgency, as stated above.	Reply to Objection 2. What does the Objector's argument imply? Not that laws should be changed for the sake of *any* sort of improvement, but that they should be changed for the sake of a great gain or a great necessity. And that is exactly what I have shown.

The Objector thought it was sufficient to point out that often an old law can be improved. St. Thomas reminds us that even when the change gains us something, it loses us something too, just by the weakening of custom. To offset this loss, not any little gain is enough; the improvement must be great.

This answer applies also to the Third Objection.	The third objection may be answered in much the same way as the second.

As we recall, the third objection was but a variation on the second one. Whereas Objection 2 held merely that some old laws were crude, Objection 3 addresses the most common reason for their crudity, which is that the earliest lawmakers had insufficient experience to frame better ones. But St. Thomas does not question the fact that some laws could be improved. His point is that the benefit of any improvement must be great enough to offset the disadvantage of weakening custom. This point is sufficient to answer Objection 3.

For further reflection on the preceding section of the *Treatise on Law*, the online *Companion to the Commentary*, accessible via the Resources link at the book's catalogue webpage, includes a discussion of the following topic:

PROTOTYPE OF A RADICAL REFORMER

Question 97, Article 3:
Whether Custom Can Obtain Force of Law?

TEXT	PARAPHRASE
Whether custom can obtain force of law?	Can custom acquire the distinctive force of law, so that it sets enacted law aside?

Contemporary attitudes toward custom are profoundly inconsistent. We tend to scorn custom as an obstruction to the will of the people, as expressed through the majority of the legislature. But a more genuine offense against republican principles would seem to lie in *refusing* to accord custom the force of law. For which is more central to self-government: the sheer will of the people, or their reasonable will? And which is more expressive of their reasonable will: their transitory opinions and alignments, or their continuous and deeply rooted traditions and ways of life?

Could it be that custom *is* a kind of law? Could it be at least as fundamental to the life of a republic as the enacted kind of law? If this is true, then what follows?

[1] *Objection 1. It would seem that custom cannot obtain force of law, nor abolish a law. Because human law is derived from the natural law and from the Divine law, as stated above (93, 3; 95, 2).* [2] *But human custom cannot change either the law of nature or the Divine law. Therefore neither can it change human law.*	Objection 1. Apparently, custom *cannot* acquire the distinctive force of law or set law aside. For as we have already seen, human law is derived from the natural and Divine law. Because human custom cannot alter either of the sources of human law, it cannot alter human law itself.

[1]   One would have expected the Objector to say human law is derived from the *eternal* law *through* the natural law; instead he says it is derived from the *Divine* law *and* the natural law. Eternal and Divine law are not the same thing; the former is the Wisdom in the mind of God Himself, the latter is the reflection of that Wisdom in Scripture (as natural law is its reflection in nature). What then does he mean?

Possibly the Objector is using the expression "Divine law" in a broad sense, to mean the eternal law itself. This is unusual, but there is a precedent in Question 95, Article 3, where an Objector speaks of "that Divine law which is the eternal law." The other possibility is that he is using the term in its ordinary sense, to mean revealed law, but in this case we must bear in mind that human law is not "derived" from revealed law in the same sense that it is derived from natural law, because the state is not the custodian of the means of grace. We explored this difficulty in the Commentary on Question 95, Article 3, where St. Thomas spoke of natural and Divine law as the "twofold measure" of human law.

[2]   The Objector reasons that human custom could change human law only if it constituted a third source of authority, superior to the other two. He points out that this is not the case.

Objection 2. Further, many evils cannot make one good. But he who first acted against the law, did evil. Therefore by multiplying such acts, nothing good is the result. Now a law is something good; since it is a rule of human acts. Therefore law is not abolished by custom, so that the mere custom should obtain force of law.	Objection 2. Moreover, a multitude of evils cannot make a single good. So if the first violation of law is evil, the multiplication of violations cannot produce something good. But law *is* something good, because it rules human acts. It follows that custom *cannot make law* – it cannot acquire the distinctive force of law, setting enacted law aside.

The transitions and the order of ideas in this objection are a little hard to follow. Expanded, the argument runs like this:

1. Violating the law is evil.
2. But the multiplication of evils cannot make a good.
3. So the multiplication of violations cannot make a good.
4. But law *is* a good (because it guides human acts in a way that they need to be guided).
5. So the multiplication of violations cannot make the specific good *of law.*
6. But the multiplication of violations is all that a custom of violating the enacted law really is.
7. So the custom of violating an enacted law cannot make a new law, thereby setting the old one aside.

[1] *Objection 3. Further, the framing of laws belongs to those public men whose business it is to govern the community; wherefore private individuals cannot make laws.* [2] *But custom grows by the acts of private individuals.* [3] *Therefore custom cannot obtain force of law, so as to abolish the law.*	Objection 3. Still further, lawmaking pertains to the work of public persons, of the governors of the commonwealth. Thus laws cannot be made by private persons. Yet the force of custom *does* come from the acts of private persons. So however strong custom may be, it cannot acquire the distinctive force of law, and cannot set enacted law aside.

[1]   Of course a public person is not a *kind* of person but a person viewed with respect to a particular role; the term refers to public office. Senator Smith is viewed as a public person when he is acting as a senator, and as a private person when he is acting as Arnold Smith, husband of Petunia, father of Peter and Pam.

[2]   By private individuals, the Objector means people who do *not* hold public office. One might protest his argument on grounds that in a republic, citizenship itself confers public responsibilities; as we see later, this is precisely the ground of St. Thomas's reply.

[3]   If custom is made by private persons, but private persons cannot make law, then custom is not law. But if it is not law, it cannot affect that which is law.

---

[1] *On the contrary, Augustine says (Ep. ad Casulan. xxxvi): "The customs of God's people and the institutions of our ancestors are to be considered as laws.* [2] *And those who throw contempt on the customs of the Church ought to be punished as those who disobey the law of God."*	On the other hand, St. Augustine writes in Letter 36, *To Casulanus,* "The customs of God's people and the institutions of our Fathers are held as law." This is why those who scorn the customs of the Church are held back: By doing so, they prevaricate against divine law itself.

---

[1]   St. Augustine is responding to a query posed by his friend, Casulanus: Is it lawful to fast on the seventh day of the week, as some do? St. Augustine replies that it is not wholly unlawful, for Christ fasted for forty days. He goes on to say, however, that the idea of appointing the seventh day as a day of fasting is offensive, for it contradicts the custom of the Church. In matters concerning which Divine Scripture does not lay down a rule, such custom counts as law.[15]

[2]   The placement of quotation marks in the Dominican Fathers translation mistakenly treats this sentence as part of the quotation from St. Augustine. In the paraphrase, I have relocated the quotation marks to make clear that it isn't. St. Thomas has added the sentence to complete the *sed contra*'s argument about the relation between custom and law. Its point is that the ancestral customs of the people of God have the same force, in the law of the Church, as the laws given expressly by God. The

---

[15]   As usual, St. Thomas is quoting from memory, but the changes are trivial. *Vel* (or) becomes *et* (and), and *tenenda sunt* becomes *sunt tenenda*. In St. Augustine's letter, the passage occurs in Chapter 1, Section 2.

reason – not stated – is that they too came into being under the influence of the Holy Spirit.

It is easy to see why St. Thomas cannot rest with this point. One reason is that the question under investigation is human rather than Divine law, and the commonwealth does not enjoy the promise of Divine guidance that Christ gave to the Church. So, in the *respondeo*, St. Thomas must show how the customs of the civic people can have the force of law even apart from the supernatural help that God's people enjoy.

The other reason is that St. Augustine's expression "the people of God" refers not to the faithful *alone,* but to the people in communion with their bishops. Although the Holy Spirit guides the whole Church, the charism of authority was specifically committed by Christ to the Apostles and their successors;[16] thus the customs of the flock acquire legal force only insofar they are tacitly or explicitly approved by their shepherds. In the civil commonwealth, the parallel case arises when a popular custom has force of law not because the people themselves have legislative authority, but because those who do have such authority tolerate it. St. Thomas addresses this case not in the *respondeo,* but in the Reply to Objection 3.

---

[1] *I answer that, All law proceeds from the reason and will of the lawgiver; the Divine and natural laws from the reasonable will of God; the human law from the will of man, regulated by reason.* [2] *Now just as human reason and will, in practical matters, may be made manifest by speech, so may they be made known by deeds: since seemingly a man chooses as good that which he carries into execution.* [3] *But it is evident that by human speech, law can be both changed and expounded, in so far as it manifests the interior movement and thought of human reason.* [4] *Wherefore by actions also, especially if they be repeated, so as to make*

Here is my response. Law – *all* law – marches forth from the reason and will of the legislator. Divine and natural law come from the reason and will of God, human law from the reasonably regulated will of man.

Notice, though, that human reason and will display themselves in two different ways concerning things to be done. One way is by words, but another is by deeds, for we see what a man chooses as good from the acts he carries out. Plainly, just to the degree that law exhibits the interior movement of the lawmaker's will and the concept in his mind, it can be changed and explained by words. But a rational judgment is also declared by the fact that something is done

---

[16] Matthew 16:19, 18:18; Luke 10:16. See also 2 Corinthians 10:8, 1 Thessalonians 2:13, 2 Thessalonians 2:15, 2 Timothy 1:13–14, and 2 Peter 1:20–21.

a custom, law can be changed and expounded; and also something can be established which obtains force of law, in so far as by repeated external actions, the inward movement of the will, and concepts of reason are most effectually declared; for when a thing is done again and again, it seems to proceed from a deliberate judgment of reason. [5] Accordingly, custom has the force of a law, [6] abolishes law, [7] and is the interpreter of law.

many times. Indeed, the multiplication of exterior acts is the most effective way to place one's will and reason on display.

Therefore law can be changed and explained not only by words, but also by deeds, especially the many deeds that bring about a custom; and such acts can bring something into being that acquires the authority of law. From all this we conclude that custom has the distinctive force of law, rescinds enacted law, and tells what enacted law means.

[1]   In saying that the human law proceeds from the reasonable will of man, St. Thomas does not mean that it is independent of the reasonable will of God. It proceeds *proximately* from the reasonable will of man, but if his will really is reasonable, then it submits to the Divine will, which is inseparable from the Divine reason.

Before proceeding, I should add that for contemporary readers, the most difficult thing about the *respondeo* is the order in which the argument is presented. That is why the paraphrase takes such great liberties in rearranging it. Let no one suppose that I presume to better St. Thomas's logic. However, the same inferences can be expressed in many ways; for example, "If P, then Q" and "Q, since P" mean the same thing. In most cases, the most convenient phrasing depends largely on convention, which varies over time, over genres, and over nations.

[2]   One way to make manifest my choice of the good of eating dinner is to say "Let us eat." An even clearer way is to sit down and eat. By the way, when St. Thomas says that someone *seemingly* chooses as good that which he does, he is not expressing a doubt; it is as though he said that his choice *is seen* by that which he does.

[3]   The sort of practical matter we are presently considering is not whether to eat dinner, but whether to enact a particular law. Just as I express my intention to eat dinner by saying "Let us eat," so the legislator expresses his intention that all private automobiles stop at red lights by saying "Let all private automobiles stop at red lights." The difference is that in the right context, the latter utterance not only expresses an intention to do something, *but actually does it*. For my statement "Let us eat"

does not enact a dinner, but in the right context, the lawmaker's statement "Let all private automobiles stop at red lights" really does enact a law. Contemporary philosophers call the sort of utterance that brings something about a "performative" utterance.

A side issue: When St. Thomas speaks of "the interior movement and thought of human reason," it may at first seem that he is referring to the interior movement of *reason* and the concept of reason. As the rest of the paragraph shows, however, he means the interior movement of *will* and the concept of reason. The movement of the will is the inclination of the will to the end for which the person acts, as conceived by his reason.

[4] The argument is that since the people can express their reasonable will not only by words, but even more clearly by repeated deeds, it follows that if they have the authority to make law at all, then they have the authority to make law by custom. The argument is anticipated in a remark by Julianus, quoted in the *Digest:*

Age-encrusted custom is not undeservedly cherished as having almost statutory force, and this is the kind or law which is said to be established by use and wont. For given that statutes themselves are binding upon us for no other reason than that they have been accepted by the judgment or the populace, certainly it is fitting that what the populace has approved without any writing shall be binding upon everyone. What does it matter whether the people declares its will by voting or by the very substance or its actions?[17]

Except for Julianus's "almost," St. Thomas could have written the same words. Notice, though, that the argument is conditional: It depends on an "if" or a "given that." Thus it provokes the question, *do* the multitude have the authority to make law? In some countries yes, in others no. For this reason, St. Thomas concedes in the Reply to Objection 3 that the argument of the *respondeo* is restricted to peoples who do have such authority. Even among peoples who do not, custom still has force of law, but only in a qualified sense, which he there explains.

In effect, then, what St. Thomas is arguing here is that custom is to be viewed as law *when, and because,* it has the essential qualities of all true law, discussed in Question 90. It must be an ordinance of reason, for the common good, made by the public authority of the people themselves, and promulgated through repeated deeds.

---

[17] Alan Watson, ed., *The Digest of Justinian*, rev. ed., Vol. 1 (Philadelphia: University of Pennsylvania Press, 1998), p. 13, corresponding to Book 1, Title 3, Section 32. The translator of this passage, and of the next few that I quote, is D.N. MacCormick.

[5]   Now St. Thomas begins to draw the conclusions. Since custom has turned out to be a kind of law, the first such conclusion is that it has the distinctive force of law. Again he might have quoted from the *Digest*. Hermogenian says, "But we also keep to those rules which have been sanctioned by long custom and observed over very many years; we keep to them as being a tacit agreement of the citizens, no less than we keep to written rules of law." Paulus and Sabinus add, "This kind of law is held to be of particularly great authority, because approval of it has been so great that it has never been necessary to reduce it to writing." Callistratus remarks, "In fact, our reigning Emperor Severus has issued a rescript to the effect that in cases of ambiguity arising from statute law, statutory force ought to be ascribed to custom or to the authority of an unbroken line of similar judicial decisions." [18]

[6]   The second conclusion to follow from the fact that custom is a kind of law is that, just as law rescinds law, so custom rescinds law. Julianus again: "Accordingly, it is absolutely right to accept the point that statutes may be repealed not only by vote or the legislature but also by the silent agreement or everyone expressed through desuetude." [19]

Under indirect Roman influence, a doctrine of desuetude has also entered contemporary American jurisprudence. For example, the doctrine is applied in *Committee on Legal Ethics v. Printz,* 187 W.Va. 182 (1992), to hold that a provision of the West Virginia code of 1923 is invalid because it has not been enforced for many years. The court carefully qualifies the doctrine, holding among other things that if an act is prohibited by statute as *malum in se,* evil in itself, then it cannot be allowed just because of a long history of non-prosecution. This parallels the qualification St. Thomas adds to his own doctrine in the Reply to Objection 1: Custom cannot legitimize an act that violates Divine or natural law.

In one respect, though, St. Thomas's teaching that custom abolishes law is stronger than our own doctrine of desuetude. The West Virginia court conceded that a law can become void because of a custom of non-enforcement, but St. Thomas implies that it can even become void because of a custom of *violation,* quite apart from whether it has been enforced.

[7]   With his third conclusion, St. Thomas goes beyond the question posed in the *ultrum.* He now says that because custom is itself a kind

---

[18] Watson, p. 14, corresponding to *Digest,* Book 1, Title 3, Sections 35, 36, and 38.
[19] Watson, p. 13, corresponding to *Digest,* Book 1, Title 3, Section 32.

of law, it helps explain what other laws mean, for all laws interpret each other.

Paulus again: "If a question should arise about the interpretation of a statute, what ought to be looked into first is the law that the civitas had previously applied in cases of the same kind. For custom is the best interpreter of statutes."[20] It might be held that by custom, Paulus means only judicial history. But this seems unlikely in view of the maxim of Paulus previously quoted, not to mention the maxims of Julianus, Hermogenian, Paulus, Sabinus, and Callistratus. Besides, Paulus offers his remark, "custom is the best interpreter of statutes," as the *reason* for considering what has been done in previous cases; it is not a mere corollary to it.

Why doesn't St. Thomas himself use any of these convenient passages we have been quoting? He has certainly shown no reluctance to cite the *Digest* at other points in the *Treatise on Law*. In general, however, he uses quotations from secular authorities sparingly, either to call attention to possible objections, or as grace notes, showing the place of his argument in what has been said before. Their function is not to prove that he is right, for he realizes that his reasoning must stand on its own legs. Indeed, he sometimes considers the views of these authorities acceptable only with qualifications. For example, see what he makes of the juristic maxim that what pleases the ruler has the force of law, in Question 90, Article 1, ad 3: We may accept it only if it is taken as referring to the *reasonable* will of the ruler, "otherwise the sovereign's will would savor of lawlessness rather than of law."

For us, the value of what the Roman *iurisconsults* say about custom is that they explode the common notion that St. Thomas's high view of the legal force of custom is merely a relic of medieval times when there were so few enacted laws that the traditions of the people had to take their place. Whatever may have been the case in medieval times, the Rome of the jurists was not medieval, and it had plenty of enacted laws.

---

[1] *Reply to Objection 1. The natural and Divine laws proceed from the Divine will, as stated above.* [2] *Wherefore they cannot be changed by a custom proceeding from the will of man, but only by Divine authority.*

Reply to Objection 1. As we have previously explained, the natural and Divine laws issue from the will of God. For this reason, they cannot be altered by a custom that issues from the will of man. Only God's authority suffices for that. Consequently, the Objector's worry

[20] Watson, p. 14, corresponding to *Digest*, Book 1, Title 3, Section 37.

Hence it is that no custom can prevail over the Divine or natural laws: [3] for Isidore says (Synon. ii, 16): "Let custom yield to authority: evil customs should be eradicated by law and reason."	is needless, for no custom can acquire force against Divine or natural law. This is exactly what Isidore teaches in Book 2, Chapter 16, of his *Synonyms*, where he says "Custom submits to authority, and depraved customs are vanquished by law and reason."

[1]   This does not mean that the natural and Divine laws proceed from the will of God *apart* from His goodness or reason, because according to St. Thomas, God's attributes are inseparable from His personal nature and from each other. We speak of His reason, His goodness, His will, and His other attributes *as though* they were distinct, because this is the only way we can understand them. In us, such things are different, but in Him, they are one.[21]

[2]   St. Thomas agrees with the Objector that since the natural and Divine laws come from God, man's customs cannot change them. A custom of human sacrifice would not suspend the duty to honor and protect innocent human life; a custom of sexual promiscuity would not repeal the rightness of chastity; a custom of pickpocketry would not rescind the precept against stealing.

Does this contradict the ringing conclusion of the *respondeo* that "custom has the force of a law, abolishes law, and is the interpreter of law"? Not at all; it merely reminds us of its scope. For remember the premise of that argument: Custom counts as law *just because* it expresses the reasonable will of the people. So if their will is not reasonable, their custom does not count as law. To express the point another way, when St. Thomas says *custom* has the force of law and so on, he means *reasonable* custom, custom deserving of the name.

In Question 96, Article 4, he approvingly quoted St. Augustine's remark that an unjust law should be called not a law but an act of violence. Had he written a few centuries later, he might have quoted English jurist Edward Coke's remark that an unreasonable custom should be called not a custom but a usurpation.[22]

---

[21]   Concerning the simplicity and unity of God, see I, Q. 3 and 11; in relation to the three Persons of God, see also I, Q. 30 and 39.

[22]   *Consuetudo contra rationem introducta potius usurpatio quam consuetudo appellari debet.* Edward Coke, *The First Part of the Institutes of the Laws of England, or, a Commentary upon Littleton*, Section 113a (first published in 1628). "Littleton" is Thomas de Littleton, author of the fifteenth century *Treatise on Tenures*.

[3]   The second part of this statement explains and qualifies the first. Sound custom is reasonable, lawful, and authoritative, but evil custom is none of these things. Therefore, though law submits to sound custom, corrupt custom must submit to law.

Isidore's statement is quoted by Gratian, who in another place quotes Pope Nicholas to much the same effect: "An evil custom is no more to be tolerated than a dangerous infection because, unless the custom is quickly torn up by its roots, it will be adopted by wicked men as entitling them to a privilege."[23]

---

[1] *Reply to Objection 2. As stated above (96, 6), human laws fail in some cases: wherefore it is possible sometimes to act beside the law; namely, in a case where the law fails; yet the act will not be evil.* [2] *And when such cases are multiplied, by reason of some change in man, then custom shows that the law is no longer useful: just as it might be declared by the verbal promulgation of a law to the contrary.* [3] *If, however, the same reason remains, for which the law was useful hitherto, then it is not the custom that prevails against the law, but the law that overcomes the custom:* [4] *unless perhaps the sole reason for the law seeming useless, be that it is not "possible according to the custom of the country" [95, 3], which has been stated to be one of the conditions of law. For it is not easy to set aside the custom of a whole people.*

Reply to Objection 2. In a previous Article, we discussed whether one may act contrary to the letter of the law. As we showed there, human laws occasionally fall short of what is needed. The Objector is right that many evils do not add up to a good; but in such a plight, departing from the letter of the law is not evil.

Now suppose something changes, so that many such cases arise: People find it necessary to depart from the letter of the law so often that a custom arises of setting it aside. Such a custom serves to announce that the law is no longer useful, just as clearly as the enactment of a new law might have done.

There is an exception: Suppose the considerations that made the law helpful remain valid. Then what we said above must be reversed. Custom does not vanquish law; law vanquishes custom.

On the other hand, suppose that even though the original reasons for the law remain valid, custom is so strongly set against the law that the law is utterly useless – for it is difficult to set aside the custom of a multitude. In this case, [unfortunately,] our previous conclusion is reinstated, for custom vanquishes law after all. For as we showed in a previous Article, law should be compatible with the customs of the country.

---

[23] Gratian, *The Treatise on Laws [Concordance of Discordant Canons]*, trans. Augustine Thompson, With the Ordinary Gloss, trans. James Gordley (Washington, DC: Catholic University Press, 1993), pp. 37 and 28, respectively (corresponding to Distinction 11, Chapter 1, and Distinction 8, Chapter 3).

[1]   As St. Thomas has explained in Question 96, Article 6, the meaning of such "failure" is that a case arises in which following the letter of the law brings about a result contrary to what the legislators had intended. That at least some such cases will arise is inevitable, because, since laws are stated in general terms, they cannot anticipate every circumstance to which these terms will be applied.

[2]   The parenthetical remark "because of some change in man" seems to take in both of the two reasons for changing law that St. Thomas mentioned in Article 1, above. There might be a change in his understanding, so that what was formerly deemed fitting is now recognized as deficient, or there might be a change in his condition, so that what was formerly appropriate to him no longer is. A change in his condition may in turn be a change in various things including his character, status, development, circumstances, or way of life.

The change in the West Virginia case mentioned above was a change in his understanding. A provision of the 1923 law in question prohibited concealing a felony in return for money. Such a rule might be good in most cases, but taken literally, it would have prohibited a victim of a crime from privately seeking restitution instead of publicly bringing charges. For long, no victim in such a case had been prosecuted, and the court held that the legal provision was void through long disuse, just to the extent that it would have required prosecution even in circumstances like these.

[3]   So it was that the West Virginia court held several practices prohibited by the law were still prohibited, because the considerations that made them fitting were still valid. It would still not be allowed to seek payment *beyond* restitution in place of prosecution, and it would still be forbidden to seek payment in return for not giving testimony during a criminal trial. One surmises that St. Thomas would have approved.

[4]   The custom of the whole people is difficult to set aside *even if it is not the best,* for more harm might be done by fruitlessly attempting to suppress it than by putting up with it. St. Thomas may be thinking of a situation analogous to either the one he brought up in Question 96, Article 2, "whether it belongs to the human law to repress all vices?" or in Question 97, Article 2, "Whether human law should always be changed, whenever something better occurs?" If the former, the legislators are putting up with a custom that is actually bad; in the latter, they are putting up with one that is pretty good, but they can think of something better. In both cases, they are doing so just to avoid unnecessary disturbance.

[1] *Reply to Objection 3. The people among whom a custom is introduced may be of two conditions. For if they are free, and able to make their own laws, the consent of the whole people expressed by a custom counts far more in favor of a particular observance, that does the authority of the sovereign, [2] who has not the power to frame laws, except as representing the people. [3] Wherefore although each individual cannot make laws, yet the whole people can. [4] If however the people have not the free power to make their own laws, or to abolish a law made by a higher authority; nevertheless with such a people a prevailing custom obtains force of law, in so far as it is tolerated by those to whom it belongs to make laws for that people: [5] because by the very fact that they tolerate it they seem to approve of that which is introduced by custom.*

Reply to Objection 3. The multitude among whom a custom arises may be either free, able to make laws themselves, or not free, subject to laws made for them by someone else.

Suppose they are free. Then which of the following would give greater support to an observance: The authority of the foremost man, or the consent of the entire multitude, as declared by a custom? The latter, because the ability of the foremost man to compose laws comes solely from the fact that he stands in the multitude's place, that he represents them. So, although the Objector is right to say that an individual cannot make laws, the whole multitude *can* make laws.

Even if the people are *not* freely able to make their own laws, or to set aside a law made by superior authority, prevailing custom has the distinctive force of law just to the degree to which their legislators tolerate the custom. For then, even though the legislators could set the custom aside, they let it be; by tolerating it, they seem to approve of it.

[1] St. Thomas explains here that the strong conclusion of the *respondeo*, "custom has the force of law, abolishes law, and is the interpreter of law," holds only for a people with the authority to make its own laws. Not every people is free in this sense, nor, in his view, would that be right: For as he has explained in Article 1, agreeing with St. Augustine, a people so corrupt that they sell their votes should not have the power to choose magistrates.[24] However it is *better* for a people to be free, *better* to have both the moral capacity and the constitutional authority to make their own laws, and the argument seems to regard this as the normal case.

---

[24] He quotes St. Augustine to this effect in Q. 97, Art. 1. See also the Commentary on Q. 90, Art. 3, the Before Reading remarks on Q. 94, and for those who wish to explore further, the discussion of Q. 91, Art. 3 in the online *Companion to the Commentary.*

[2]   Literally, the foremost man has the authority to frame laws only insofar as he "bears the person" or "wears the character" of the people. Because they are free – we would say "because they are self-governing" or "because the commonwealth is a republic" – he can make laws only in their name, by their authority, and with their consent.

By making the expression for the governor singular, St. Thomas does not mean that there can only be one of him; see below, where he makes the term for the governors plural. In English, too, we sometimes use the singular to refer to a plurality: "*The* driver of *a* vehicle must stop at a stop light" means that *all* drivers of *all* vehicles must stop at stop lights.

[3]   St. Thomas's point is that when a free people make laws through the adoption of customs, they are not acting as private persons, as the Objector supposes, but as public persons. In effect, citizenship in a free community confers upon them a kind of public office.

[4]   In Question 92, Article 2, St. Thomas argued that the acts of law – those things in which law is actualized or completed, and by which it achieves its effect – are command, prohibition, permission and punishment. Here he says that even if the people do not have the authority to make their own laws, a custom that the legislators tolerate has the force of the third kind of act, a permission.

But there would seem to be two different ways in which a prevailing custom might be tolerated. One is that the legislators might decline to prohibit the behavior in question. The other is that even though a law prohibiting the behavior is on the books already, they might decline to insist on its enforcement (in effect depriving it of the character of law). For present purposes St. Thomas does not distinguish these cases.

[5]   As mentioned above, the term "seem" does not necessarily indicate hesitation; when St. Thomas says a man "seemingly" chooses as good that which he does, he means the man "is seen" to choose as good that which he does. Here, though, the term probably does indicate hesitation, for as we saw in Question 96, Article 2 – and as we were reminded in the reply to the previous objection – legislators tolerate certain things they do not approve, because they judge that the attempt to suppress them would be even more harmful than letting them be.

For further reflection on the preceding section of the *Treatise on Law*, the online *Companion to the Commentary*, accessible via the Resources link at the book's catalogue webpage, includes a discussion of the following topic:

THE CONTINUING VITALITY OF ST. THOMAS'S VIEW OF CUSTOM

Question 97, Article 4:
Whether the Rulers of the People Can Dispense from Human Laws?

TEXT	PARAPHRASE
Whether the rulers of the people can dispense from human laws?	Can those who govern the people set human laws aside, exempting certain persons from obedience in certain cases?

Sometimes St. Thomas considers similar questions from more than one point of view. The *ultrum* of this Article is closely related to the *ultra* of Question 96, Article 1, "Whether human law should be framed for the community rather than the individual?"; Question 96, Article 5, "Whether all are subject to the law?"; and Question 96, Article 6, "Whether he who is under a law may act beside the letter of the law?"

It may at first seem that dispensation has nothing to do with the topic of Question 97, change of law. But it changes the law by suspending its application to particular persons or circumstances, and such a change may become permanent by establishing a precedent.

[1] *Objection 1. It would seem that the rulers of the people cannot dispense from human laws. For the law is established for the "common weal," as Isidore says (Etym. v, 21).* [2] *But the common good should not be set aside for the private convenience of an individual: because, as the Philosopher says (Ethic. i, 2), "the good of the nation is more godlike than the good of one man."* [3] *Therefore it seems that a man should not be dispensed from acting in compliance with the general law.*	Objection 1. Apparently, the governors of the people are powerless to set aside human laws. These statutes are instituted for the good of all, and as Aristotle explains, to seek the good of the nation is more divine than to seek the good of a single individual. For this reason, it should not be suspended for anyone's private advantage. So it seems that from laws made for everyone, no one should be exempted.

[1] Aiming at the common good is one of the main Isidorean guidelines for law, discussed in Question 95, Article 3. According to St. Thomas, in Question 90, Article 2, it is more than a guideline; it is law's very purpose.

[2] St. Thomas takes Aristotle's statement to mean that to preserve the good of all rather than just one man is more like what God Himself does. As he explains the passage in his *Commentary on the Nicomachean Ethics:*

[I]t seems much better and more perfect to attain, that is, to procure and preserve the good of the whole state than the good of any one man. Certainly it is a part of that love which should exist among men that a man preserve the good even of a single human being. But it is much better and more divine that this be done for a whole people and for states. It is even sometimes desirable that this be done for one state only, but it is much more divine that it be done for a whole people that includes many states. This is said to be more divine because it shows greater likeness to God who is the ultimate cause of all good.[25]

[3]   The Objector reasons that if all that is truly lawful is directed to the common good, but dispensations are directed to private goods, then dispensations are not truly lawful.

| [1] *Objection 2. Further, those who are placed over others are commanded as follows (Deuteronomy 1:17): "You shall hear the little as well as the great; neither shall you respect any man's person, because it is the judgment of God." [2] But to allow one man to do that which is equally forbidden to all, seems to be respect of persons. Therefore the rulers of a community cannot grant such dispensations, since this is against a precept of the Divine law.* | Objection 2. Moreover, the biblical book of Deuteronomy warns those who are placed in authority to listen to the small as well as the great, preferring no person over another: This is the judgment of God. But to allow anyone what is denied to all alike would prefer one person over another. So for the governors of the people to make exceptions to the law would violate Divine law; this they must not do. |

[1]   Through Moses, God is reminding the Israelites of his instructions concerning the administration of justice. Quoted more fully, the passage reads as follows:

And I charged your judges at that time, "Hear the cases between your brethren, and judge righteously between a man and his brother or the alien that is with him. You shall not be partial in judgment; you shall hear the small and the great alike; you shall not be afraid of the face of man, for the judgment is God's; and the case that is too hard for you, you shall bring to me, and I will hear it."[26]

The English expression, "respect for persons," is archaic; students today commonly make the mistake of thinking "neither shall you respect any man's person" means "and you shall be haughty, contemptuous, and disrespectful toward everyone." This reverses the passage's meaning. In the

---

[25] Thomas Aquinas, *Commentary on Aristotle's Nicomachean Ethics*, Book 1, Lecture 2, trans. C.J. Litzinger, O.P., rev. ed. (Notre Dame, IN: Dumb Ox Books, 1993), p. 10.

[26] Deuteronomy 1:16–17 (RSV-CE).

Latin of the Vulgate, Deuteronomy warns judges that there is to be no "difference" of persons[27]; in St. Thomas's paraphrase, judges are not to "accept" them.[28] What this means is that no one is to be given special favors, that judges are not to give some persons special consideration or treatment just because of who they are or what rank they hold. In our own idiom, the point is not that judges should disrespect everyone, but that they should respect everyone equally.

[2] The Objector reasons that to exempt anyone from a law that everyone else must follow is to practice favoritism, thus to violate the Deuteronomic commandment.

---

[1] *Objection 3. Further, human law, in order to be just, should accord with the natural and Divine laws:* [2] *else it would not "foster religion," nor be "helpful to discipline," which is requisite to the nature of law, as laid down by Isidore (Etym. v, 3).* [3] *But no man can dispense from the Divine and natural laws. Neither, therefore, can he dispense from the human law.*

Objection 3. Still further, in order to be straight and not crooked, human law must be consonant with natural and Divine law. Otherwise it would violate two of the guidelines for law identified by Isidore – that it be congruent with true religion and that it be helpful to discipline. But can any man dispense from natural or Divine law? No. So no man can dispense from human law either.

---

[1] St. Thomas says *recta,* straight, rather than *ius,* just. Both terms mean "right," but I have preferred to retain the savor of the original.

[2] As in Question 95, Article 3, St. Thomas is not saying that human law must "foster" religion but that it should be congruent or congenial with it. By "religion," in turn, he does not mean any religion – Voodoo, New Age, what have you – but true religion, for in II-II, Question 81, Article 2, he defines religion as the virtue having to do with giving due honor to God, meaning the true God.

To be helpful to discipline does not mean to promote totalitarian regimentation, but to promote *tranquillitas ordinis,* rightly ordered peace, as discussed in Question 95, Article 3, and Question 96, Article 3.

[3] The Objector reasons that to exempt particular persons from Divine and natural law, a man would require authority superior to God's, which no man has.

---

[27] *Nulla erit distantia personarum.*
[28] *Nec accipietis cuiusquam personam.*

On the contrary, *The Apostle says (1 Corinthians 9:17): "A dispensation is committed to me."*	**On the other hand,** St. Paul says in 1 Corinthians 9:17 that a dispensation *has* been entrusted to him.

To understand what St. Paul is saying, one must recognize that the term "dispensation" is being used here in a broader sense than "exception" – a point St. Thomas himself will explain. To prepare for that explanation, let us explore the passage more closely. The Douay-Rheims translation, which closely follows the Latin Vulgate that St. Thomas was using, renders the passage's context as follows:

For if I preach the gospel, it is no glory to me, for a necessity lieth upon me: for woe is unto me if I preach not the gospel. For if I do this thing willingly, I have a reward: but if against my will, a dispensation is committed to me.[29]

The critical word, "dispensation" (*dispensatio*), is a translation of the New Testament Greek word *oikonomian,* an assignment or commission, as in the assignment of tasks in a household. For this reason a more contemporary translation renders the passage as follows:

For if I preach the gospel, that gives me no ground for boasting. For necessity is laid upon me. Woe to me if I do not preach the gospel! For if I do this of my own will, I have a reward; but if not of my own will, I am entrusted with a commission.[30]

Very clear. But what has a dispensation in the sense of an assignment or commission to do with a dispensation in the sense of setting aside the law? St. Thomas is about to explain.

[1] ***I answer that,*** *Dispensation, properly speaking, denotes a measuring out to individuals of some common goods: thus the head of a household is called a dispenser, because to each member of the household he distributes work and necessaries of life in due weight and measure.* [2] *Accordingly in every community a man is said to dispense, from the very fact that he*	**Here is my response.** In the strict sense to the term, "dispensation" means assigning to each individual his share of something common to all of them. For example, the head of the family "dispenses" in the sense that he allocates to each member of the family his proper share of tasks as well as necessities of life. Analogously, the governor of a people "dispenses" in the sense that though the directives of the

29 1 Corinthians 9:16–17 (DRA).
30 1 Corinthians 9:16–17 (RSV-CE).

directs how some general precept is to be fulfilled by each individual. [3a] Now it happens at times that a precept, which is conducive to the common weal as a general rule, is not good for a particular individual, [4] or in some particular case, [3b] either because it would hinder some greater good, or because it would be the occasion of some evil, as explained above (96, 6). [5] But it would be dangerous to leave this to the discretion of each individual, except perhaps by reason of an evident and sudden emergency, as stated above (96, 6). Consequently he who is placed over a community is empowered to dispense in a human law that rests upon his authority, so that, when the law fails in its application to persons or circumstances, he may allow the precept of the law not to be observed. [6] If however he grant this permission without any such reason, and of his mere will, he will be an unfaithful or an imprudent dispenser: unfaithful, if he has not the common good in view; [7] imprudent, if he ignores the reasons for granting dispensations. [8] Hence Our Lord says (Luke 12:42): "Who, thinkest thou, is the faithful and wise dispenser [Douay: steward], whom his lord setteth over his family?"

law apply to everyone in common, he directs the particular manner in which each individual is to fulfill them.

There is a difficulty. Sometimes a legal directive which promotes the good of all in most cases is not fitting for *this* person or in *this* case – either because it would prevent something still better, or because it would bring about something bad. When I discussed the problem previously, I pointed out the peril of allowing each individual to judge for himself whether this is the case, except perhaps cases of clear and sudden danger [in which there is no time to consult authority]. For this reason, the ruler of the community has the power to "dispense" or determine the individual application of any law that depends on his authority. Thus, when the law is unsuitable to particular persons under particular circumstances, he may release them from obeying it.

But suppose the ruler grants such license when no such case has arisen, simply by his own will. Then he is either an unfaithful steward or a foolish one: Unfaithful if he does not intend the common good, foolish if he is unaware of the reasons for granting dispensations. This is why, in the twelfth chapter of the gospel of Luke, after telling one of his parables, our Lord asks the question, "Who then is the faithful and wise steward, whom his master will set over his household?"

---

[1] St. Thomas begins not with the narrow meaning of dispensation, exempting someone from doing something, but the general meaning of dispensation, deciding who does what and who receives what. Dispensation takes place in any enterprise in which each of the various participants has his own part in what all of them have and do together. Those with the authority to direct the enterprise are the ones who decide on the assignments.

In the family, for example, the parents not only do their own work, but also apportion to each child distinct household responsibilities, as well as certain necessities from the common stock. Perpetua, the teenager, is allotted major chores and eats an adult portion at mealtime, but Felicity and Priscilla, who are much younger, are allotted minor chores and eat children's portions at mealtime.

[2]   Although each member participates in the common life of the family, each has a different place in the family. Similarly, although each citizen has a share in the common life of the nation, each has a different place in the nation. Of course not everything a family member does pertains to the family's shared life, and in the same way, not everything a citizen does pertains to the nation's shared life. Thus a well-ordered state does not assign marriage partners, abolish private property, or decide what each person will do for a living. Even so, it makes various arrangements concerning things that do pertain to the common good.

Thus in a well-ordered commonwealth, soldiers in the field are provided by the public with food and housing, but bricklayers at home are not. The law enforces the duty of absentee fathers to support their children, but it does not exact child-support payments from unrelated next-door neighbors. Entrepreneurs may develop businesses and pass them on to their children, but civil servants are paid a salary and do not have property rights in their offices. And so on.

[3a,b]   The good of the whole people is not somehow *distinct* from the good of each person; it *embraces* the good of each person. Yet there is no injury to the common good if certain individuals can be exempted from the operation of the law without harming the rest. For example, the law might command all young men to be ready to take up arms in defense of the country, but a dispensation might be granted to bishops and priests, because forcing them to fight would violate their calling.[31]

[4]   Neither does it undermine the common good if the law is suspended in circumstances in which obeying it would cause harm. St. Thomas gave an example in Question 96, Article 6: The law might command keeping the city gates closed during siege, but an emergency might require opening them to allow the city's defenders to escape from a pursuing enemy.

[31] See II-II, Q. 40, Art. 2, "Whether it is lawful for clerics and bishops to fight?"

[5] Notice that St. Thomas carefully limits the power to suspend the application of the law to the kinds of cases discussed in Question 96, Article 6, "Whether he who is under a law may act beside the letter of the law?" If exceptions are needed in more cases than that, then presumably the authorities should not be dispensing from the law, but making a new law!

[6] For example, he should not dispense his relatives, cronies, or political supporters from the law just because they are his relatives, cronies, or political supporters – as is all too common.

[7] The Dominican Fathers translation, "if he ignores," is misleading, for although the Latin verb *ignoret* can mean either ignoring something or being ignorant of it, in this context it means not the former but the latter. To be ignorant of something may be involuntary, but to ignore it is deliberate. A governor who knew the reasons for granting dispensations, yet ignored them, would be unfaithful, not imprudent – a scoundrel, not a mere fool.

[8] Along with a number of other parables, Jesus warns a crowd of people who have gathered to hear Him, "Blessed are those servants whom the master finds awake when he comes .... if the householder had known at what hour the thief was coming, he would have been awake and would not have left his house to be broken into. You also must be ready; for the Son of man is coming at an unexpected hour." Peter asks Jesus whether He is telling this parable for everyone, or just for them; Christ replies, in effect, "For all faithful stewards; who then do you suppose they are?"[32]

Reply to Objection 1. When a person is dispensed from observing the general law, this should not be done to the prejudice of, but with the intention of benefiting, the common good.	Reply to Objection 1. Had the Objector said that a law of general application must not be suspended *when doing so would injure the common good,* he would have been right; in such cases no dispensation should be granted.

St. Thomas fully agrees with the Objector that "the common good should not be set aside for the private convenience of an individual." But he points that this is not what is proposed. Not every dispensation to individuals does set aside the common good.

---

[32] For context, see Luke 12:37–48; my quotation is from verses 39–40 (RSV-CE).

---

[1] *Reply to Objection 2. It is not respect of persons if unequal measures are served out to those who are themselves unequal.* [2] *Wherefore when the condition of any person requires that he should reasonably receive special treatment, it is not respect of persons if he be the object of special favor.*

Reply to Objection 2. It is not favoritism to treat persons differently because they are really different. If there are good reasons for taking notice of someone's special condition, granting him a special privilege is not preferential treatment. Let it be.

---

[1] For example, it is not favoritism to punish only the guilty and not the innocent, or to allow only adults to vote and not children.

[2] The question should be not whether persons are treated differently, but whether the difference between them is germane to the difference in their treatment.

---

[1] *Reply to Objection 3. Natural law, so far as it contains general precepts, which never fail, does not allow of dispensations. In other precepts, however, which are as conclusions of the general precepts, man sometimes grants a dispensation: for instance, that a loan should not be paid back to the betrayer of his country, or something similar.* [2] *But to the Divine law each man stands as a private person to the public law to which he is subject.* [3] *Wherefore just as none can dispense from public human law, except the man from whom the law derives its authority, or his delegate; so, in the precepts of the Divine law, which are from God, none can dispense but God, or the man to whom He may give special power for that purpose.*

Reply to Objection 3. The general principles of the natural law are never mistaken. To these, no exceptions can be made. But man can sometimes grant a dispensation from one of the more detailed conclusions that follow from these general principles, for example that a loan should not be paid back to someone who is a traitor to his country, or something like that.

However, each man is subject to the Divine law in the same way that each private person is subject to the law of the commonwealth. So, just as there are only two who can grant dispensations from public human law, either the ruler on whose authority the law depends, or his representative – in the same way there are only two who can grant dispensations from the commandments of Divine law, either God, or someone He specially commissions.

---

[1] The Objector had argued that human rulers would be able to dispense from human law only if they were able to dispense from the natural and Divine laws on which its authority is based – which they say is

impossible. First, then, St. Thomas asks whether human rulers can dispense from natural law.

As St. Thomas has argued in Question 94, Articles 4 and 5, the general precepts of natural law are always binding, but the more detailed conclusions that follow from them are binding only in most cases; there are a few exceptions. May I ever steal? Never. May I ever refuse to return to someone an item of property he has entrusted to me? Usually, no, but in a few cases, yes; for example, if Joe asks me to return his rat poison because he wants to use it commit suicide, I should refuse. Now consider two human laws: One that enforces the root precept of natural law "Never steal," another that enforces the branch precept of natural law "Always return property held in trust when the owner demands it." No dispensation is possible from the former human law, but dispensation is possible from the latter human law. When? In exactly those cases in which the natural law precept on which it is based has lost its binding force.

[2]   Private persons are subject to the laws of the earthly commonwealth, but have no authority to frame them. St. Thomas points out that with respect to Divine law, we are all in that status; we are all private persons in the commonwealth of God. He alone is the legislator of Divine law; we are under its authority.

But why doesn't St. Thomas say the same thing about natural law? We do not make the Divine law, but we do not make the natural law either, do we? The answer is "Yes and no." Certainly we are not the enactors of the *general* precepts of natural law. Concerning these, yes, we are all private persons, just as we are with respect to Divine law. But even so, as St. Thomas has explained in Question 94, Article 5, there is a sense in which there can be both "additions to" and "subtractions from" the secondary precepts of natural law, and human reason and will are connected with both kinds of changes.

Addition to the secondary precepts of natural law occurs through what St. Thomas elsewhere calls "determination of generalities." For example, natural law tells us that we should take care for the safety of our neighbors, but human law adds that on certain roads we are to do so by driving only on the right, and this rule is binding in conscience.

Subtraction from the secondary precepts of natural law occurs when, because of some "obstacle," a precept that formerly belonged to the natural law ceases to belong to it. We dealt with an example just a few paragraphs above, for the precept "Always return property held in trust when the owner demands it" ceases to be binding because of Joe's suicidal intention. Did the human legislator subtract the precept from natural law? No, the obstacle subtracted it. But suppose the legislator had enacted a penalty for violating the precept, and when I refuse to return Joe's rat poison, he dispenses from the penalty. The penalty added to natural law, and the dispensation subtracts it again.

We see then that through legislative addition and subtraction, human law is a kind of extension of natural law for a particular community – a filling in of a picture, of which nature provides only the outlines. For though God is the ruler, He has made us in a small way partners in His providence, and though He is the legislator, He has made us little legislators under Him. Yes, human laws are derivative; their only possible starting points are the ones God has imprinted upon us, and we can neither add nor subtract from those. Yet for all that, they are real laws. So although all of us are private persons with respect to the general precepts of natural law, not all of us are *entirely* private persons with respect to its secondary precepts.

[3]   To recast the analogy offered here in the form of a syllogism: Only the legislator, or someone he commissions for the purpose, can dispense from a law based on His authority. But the sole legislator on whose authority Divine law rests is God. Therefore, only God, or someone He commissions for the purpose, can dispense from Divine law.

Two points need particular attention: Which precepts of Divine law are "dispensable" or suspendable in the first place, and what kind of commission this is. As to the first point: Since the passage does not distinguish among different kinds of Divine law precepts, it may at first seem that *all* precepts of Divine law are dispensable, but this is not so. As St. Thomas explains in Question 100, Article 8, dispensation is possible only in cases in which following a legal precept would frustrate the lawmaker's purpose. But certain precepts "contain the very intention" of the lawmaker rather than merely serving as means to its accomplishment, and such precepts are "indispensable," not subject to dispensation. In natural law, such are the general precepts; in Divine law, such are the precepts of the Decalogue or Ten Commandments. These can never be wrong, and not even God Himself could make it lawful to violate one of them. Yes, He is omnipotent, but omnipotence does not mean that He can do everything; He cannot change or contradict His own Being or Wisdom. A more complete discussion, with attention to the inevitable objections, is provided in the commentary on the Article itself, which is contained in the online *Companion.*

As to the second point: St. Thomas calls the commission to dispense from Divine law "special," but he does not call the commission to dispense from human public law "special." Why? Recall from Question 91, Article 2, that the natural law is the rational creature's mode of participation in eternal law; in other words we share in it just by having been created with rational natures. So in a certain sense, just by creating as with rational minds, God has already commissioned us as His delegates with respect to the natural law. Moreover this is a *general* commission – there is no need for God to say, "You, Edwin, I commission you." Indeed, this commission is so general that in certain respects it extends not only to human legislators, but even to the rest of us. Though I do not make laws for the whole community, I too can both "add" to the secondary precepts of natural law and recognize when something has been "subtracted" from them: By promising to meet you for dinner at six o'clock, I add a new duty to meet you for dinner at that time, and by withholding your car keys when you are falling-down drunk, I recognize that the duty to return entrusted property has ceased to be a duty in this case. With Divine law, matters stand differently. God has not commissioned human beings in general its custodians; only those whom He specifically appoints are its custodians. For example, in some cases, if someone has made a vow to God, he can be dispensed by his ecclesiastical superior, but only because Christ explicitly committed to the Apostles and their successors the power to "bind and loose."[33]

This concludes the *Commentary* proper. For further reflection on the preceding section of the *Treatise on Law*, the online *Companion to the Commentary*, accessible via the Resources link at the book's catalogue webpage, includes a discussion of the following topic:

THE USE AND ABUSE OF DISPENSATION

---

[33] Concerning dispensation from vows, see II-II, Q. 88, esp. Art. 12, with its internal reference to 2 Corinthians 2:10; concerning "binding and loosing" in general, see Matthew 16:19 and 18:18.

Index

The online *Companion to the Commentary* is not indexed because it is electronically searchable and its discussion topics are listed in the Table of Contents